Be Glad For The Song Has No Ending

Revised and Expanded Edition

An Incredible String Band Compendium
Edited by Adrian Whittaker

Be Glad For The Song Has No Ending: An Incredible String Band Compendium
Revised and expanded edition, published in 2023 by Strange Attractor Press

ISBN: 978-1-913689-506

Typesetting & interior design: Maïa Gaffney-Hyde
1968 ISB poster © Hapshash and the Coloured Coat /
Bridgeman Images. Thanks to V&A for the image file.
Family Tree: Mychael Gerstenberger

Strange Attractor Press
BM SAP, London, WC1N 3XX, UK
www.strangeattractor.co.uk

A CIP record for this book is available from the British Library.

Distributed by the MIT Press, Cambridge, Masschusetts.
And London, England
Printed and bound in Estonia by Tallinna Raamatutrükikoda

To Deena
'Stepping out of the grey day she came...'

'Dream The World Alive'

Special thanks for help with this new 2023 edition to
Raymond Greenoaken, Grahame Hood and Bill Allison

*Remembering Begladders past -
Bob Nutbein, George Boyter
and Kai Roberts*

Thanks to all the input from band members over the years: Robin Williamson, Mike Heron, Rose Simpson, Malcolm Le Maistre, Stan Schnier and Graham Forbes
In memoriam: Clive Palmer

Contents

Introduction to the second edition

Adrian Whittaker

The Incredible String Band were arguably the most multi-faceted group in British popular music, and this book attempts to mirror the complexity of their story. Yes, there is stuff about dates and albums and personnel changes, but you'll also find articles about their experiments with dance, film, theatre and lifestyles. Their music was always intertwined with the places they lived in, from Sixties Edinburgh to West Wales to the Scottish Borders, and these are all featured here.

Their songs ranged from early folk-club whimsy to the material on, say, *5000 Spirits* or *Wee Tam And The Big Huge* which, as Rowan Williams says, demanded an intimidating literacy to pick up all the allusions. The range of their musical palette was striking, too. In the first issue of the *BeGLAD* ISB fanzine, Paul Bryant summed up one aspect of the ISB appeal: 'At the heart of the music of this period were three extraordinary ideas. First was the idea that a song did not have to possess a stylistic unity, that it could wander through various genres, even within the span of a few lines or bars. What started as a hymn might transmogrify into a skipping rhyme and become eventually (after hitchhiking into Turkey and Iran) a jug band tune or a waltz. Then there was the idea of using exotic (non-Western) instrumentation for its own sake, as colouring. "We'd frequently play instruments we couldn't actually play," as Robin Williamson put it. Finally, all this was performed in the spirit of what Robin called "a kind of inspired amateurism...rather similar to naive art you see, with no technique".' The band later redefined their musical approach in their Seventies experiments with pop, jazz and rock genres and songs which were comedy vehicles for new member Malcolm Le Maistre. You'll find an attempt to reflect all this, ranging from erudite analyses to album reviews, reminiscence and cartoons – as well as arcane trivia! The idea is that you make your own selection, though my guess is that anyone with more than a passing interest in the ISB will find all of it interesting. And if you want a chronological overview, start with Raymond Greenoaken's Brief History, which follows this introduction.

Be Glad Issue 4 – cover design by Allan Frewin.

How did the book come about? As an ISB fan, you always had the sense of an strongly personal connection with the band and their music ('like joining an exclusive club', to quote Neil Tennant, now interviewed for this new edition). ISB concerts invariably defied categorisation, leaving the feeling you'd attended a unique event; and there was always an attempt at communicating with or actively involving their audience – in later years you could hang around after the gig and get to chat to them, and they were all industrious letter writers. There was a real feeling of a two-way relationship, a rarity between performers and fans; many of the articles in this book touch on this in some way. Writing in 1972, music journalist Michael Watts expanded on the ISB's relationship with their audience:

'The ISB are a total experience, urging from their audiences a complete and wholehearted absorption and identification with their activities. Perhaps that explains to an extent why their followers assume the mantle of votaries. It is very much a two-way response, a response based on camaraderie and a mutual tenderness. When they are gauche, which they frequently are, they become a subject not of derision but of endearment.'

All this bred an intense allegiance to the band rare outside the teeny-bop scene, an allegiance which still links people as diverse, say, as Robert Plant and the former Archbishop of Canterbury. This allegiance, with the advent of CDs and the re-release of the ISB albums, inspired a fanzine, *beGLAD*, which ran for a decade from 1992 to 2002 and supplied material for much of the first edition of the book, the result of years of research by about thirty different writers. I've always liked books with a multiplicity of voices (Jonathon Green's *Days In The Life* springs to mind), as well as books written from the fan's perspective, like Giles Smith's *Lost In Music* or Caroline Sullivan's *Bye Bye Baby*.

The *Be Glad Compendium* focuses on the period covering the life of the band, 1965-1974. I avoided pieces that struck me as too trainspotterly for mainstream consumption, made cuts here and there and added a bit of discreet updating where appropriate. It is arranged in a more or less sequential flow, and I've added links, written or commissioned new sections, obtained some previously unseen photos and memorabilia and solved a few little mysteries along the way.

For this new edition, I'm especially grateful to Mark Pilkington at Strange Attractor for the commission and to *BeGLAD* writers Raymond Greenoaken, Bill Allison and Grahame Hood for their contributions to all the new research, revisions and rewrites. Thanks too to Joe Boyd for continuing help with queries!

What's new?

The first edition often tended to focus on finished products such as albums, shows and films, but in revising the book I've tried to join this all up more coherently: the expansion in Internet usage since 2003 has led to a broader range of fan memories to draw on, and both Mike Heron and Rose Simpson have written ISB memoirs. For the 1966-1970 period, there are new pieces about the first US tour in summer 1968, an extended feature about the hidden history of ISB's short-lived but intense collaboration with classically-trained dancers Mimi and Mouse, and an updated piece on *U*, centred on the recently unearthed film of one of the 1970 Roundhouse performances. Rose Simpson has kindly written a couple of new pieces for us, about the Witchseason Productions experience ('it always felt like coming home') and recording with the ISB in the Sound Techniques studio.

Though the first edition did discuss the role of Scientology in the Seventies and the ending of the band, back then we tended to tiptoe around this side of things. I have added new pieces about the influence of Scientology on the ISB as an organisation in the Seventies, and the ill-fated late 1974 deal with Neighborhood Records which played a part in hastening the decision to break up. Scientology was an important influence; it was rare that it featured in a crass way lyrically, but it affected group dynamics and musical direction, possibly even encouraging the band to stay together when, as Robin has said, they should really have split up a couple of years earlier.

During a lockdown-enforced break for the Pet Shop Boys, I was lucky enough to get to interview Neil Tennant about his ISB fanboy days, and I also talked to more recent 'wyrd folk' artists Cobalt Chapel, Alasdair Roberts and Ossian Brown (Coil, Cyclobe) about their ISB influences. There are also long-overdue profiles of ISB associates John Gilston (their final, and best, drummer) and Stuart Gordon, the fiddle player who almost replaced Likky after *Earthspan*.

Be Glad 2003: readers' feedback answered...

Adrian Whittaker

At the back of the first edition of this book (2003), I invited readers to write in to Helter Skelter Publishing with their overall feedback, favourite articles, least favourite articles etc. While I was working on this edition, I dug out and re-read the responses. It was pre social media, so thanks to all those who sent me emails or, most often, actual letters!

20 years later, here is a sort of reply. The overall response was very positive, and we were delighted that *The Observer Music Magazine* made it their 'Book Of The Year'. Iain Taylor wanted more about Mimi and Mouse, with photos; as you will see, I rose to the challenge and tracked down Mouse in deepest California. He also pointed out there was no 'pre-ISB photo of Rose' and so she's kindly let me use one of her on the mountains from 1967. Can we hear more from Ivan Pawle, asked another correspondent. Well, you'll find various reminiscences from Ivan scattered through the book, especially in the Penwern sections. An index, requested by another reader, was well beyond the logistical capabilities of Helter Skelter back in 2003, but hopefully it's par for the course for Strange Attractor!

Opinions were divided about the late Bob Nutbein's lit-crit piece on Darling Belle. For a Danish reader, that and Raymond's Job's Tears piece were the articles he enjoyed most of all, while another reader found it 'arid and schoolmasterly.' I've kept it in. Gil Murray's *Hangman* on mushrooms' piece had the distinction of being singled out by one reader as the best article in the book, but by another as the worst. That stayed in too. Not everyone liked the more whimsical cartoons/graphic stories by Allan Frewin as much as I did ('The Incredible String Pistols' was singled out for especial opprobrium) and so I've pruned these down.

For the person who wanted more of a Witchseason history – over to Rose Simpson, who plans this as her next book but has also contributed a short Witchseason piece to this one. Finally, thanks to the Norwegian musician who put us right on the usual number of sympathetic strings on a Hardanger fiddle!

Rose, mountain climbing, 1967
(Rose Simpson Collection)

Foreword

Joe Boyd

I find it extremely unjust that The Incredible String Band are so often overlooked in histories of Sixties music. No other group from that era has such a wide gap between their popularity at the time and their relative obscurity today. Why do Sixties survivors find the Incredible String Band embarrassing? Is it the unashamed idealism of their music? Their flowery image? The crime of bringing acoustic instruments into rock venues?

It might astonish people to discover how famous and influential they were. The Rolling Stones tried to steal them away from Elektra as artists for their record label, Paul McCartney said *5000 Spirits Or The Layers Of The Onion* was 'his favourite record of 1967' (yes, 1967, the year of *Sgt. Pepper*!). Robin Williamson and Mike Heron were playing a kind of world music fusion two decades before anyone even heard the phrase.

When I first heard the original duo Robin and Clive in an Edinburgh pub in the Spring of 1965, I was astonished by their effortless drawing together of Scots folk music, Appalachian fiddle tunes, Middle Eastern and Balkan music and a twisted kind of psychedelic folk music. When Mike joined and encouraged Robin to start writing songs, the breadth and richness of their music completely enthralled me. I felt there was no limit to what they could accomplish. And during those wonderful years between 1966 and 1969, they did almost as much as I dreamed of and far more than anyone else imagined was possible.

They filled the Fillmore East four times in a year, transformed the Royal Albert Hall into an intimate hideaway in some mythical mountain kingdom. The originality of their songs and their arrangements dazzled me – and their audiences – for a glorious three years. No music I have been involved in before or since was as much fun to record as theirs. The ideas flew around the studio like mad bats at twilight. Having an unmixed ISB record awaiting me in the studio was like coming down the stairs on Christmas morning to find piles of gaily wrapped presents under the tree.

Purists might say that they were at their best as a duo. They might also point to the decline of their output in the 1970s. All artists have their high points – maintaining genius is pretty difficult. For me, watching Robin fiddling madly away on his gimbri while Mike sang 'the bent twig of darkness grows the petal of the morning' remains one of the high spots of my life as a passionate listener.

Joe Boyd
March 2003

Foreword

Rowan Williams

What is the job poetry is supposed to do? This may be a definition shaped by unfashionably archaic standards, but I think it's meant to do at least four things. It should take us into the realm of myth – that is, of the stories and symbols that lie so deep you can't work out who are the authors of them, the stories that give points of reference for plotting your way in the inner and outer world. It's meant to celebrate; to clothe ordinary experience with extraordinary words so that we see the radiance in the ordinary, whether it's in landscape or in love or whatever. It's meant to satirise – to give us a sideways glance on familiar ways of talking or of behaving or exercising power, so that we're not bewitched by what looks obvious and wants us to think it's obvious. It's meant to lament, to give us ways of looking at our losses and our failures that save us from despair and apathy.

If you listen to the ISB's songs, you realise rapidly that they correspond with astonishing completeness to the requirements of poetry. Plenty of songs of that period managed the celebration or the lament, few could do the myth or the satire. Perhaps for a lot of us growing up in the late Sixties and early Seventies, there was a gap in the heart where this very traditional bardic, even shamanic, sense of poetry was looking for expression; and the ISB did just that. Forget the cliches about psychedelic and hallucinogenic vagueness: this was work of extraordinary emotional clarity and metaphorical rigour – an unusual combination. Lyrics stick after decades – 'every cell in my body has it all writ down'; 'you know all the words and you sung all the notes, but you never quite learned the song'; 'the caves where sleep the stars by day'. And the literacy you might have needed to pick up all the allusions was and is intimidating – Sufism, Celtic myth, Biblical and Gnostic symbols. Combine this with a versatility in musical idiom worthy of Lennon and McCartney at their best, and you have a rare phenomenon: the contrapuntal intricacies of much of *Be Glad For The Song Has No Ending*, the Caribbean jog of the Hedgehog's Song, the sly parodies of Bob Dylan in more than one piece.

For those of us who fell in love with the ISB, there was a feeling of breathing the air of a very expansive imagination indeed. It was all right to be enchanted – but not bewitched (see above) by colossal and antique symbols; all right at the same time to be thinking about the experiences of 'ordinary' first loves and first betrayals; and all right to find the earnest nonsense of real hallucinogenic maunderings funny. There was no one quite like them; we liked to think it was a very grown-up taste, but that makes it sound too serious. If I go back to the start, I'd have to say again that it was simply a discovery of poetry; and as such – risking the embarrassment that so regularly goes with my particular vocation – I'd also have to say that it was a discovery of the holy; not the solemn, not the saintly, but the holy, which makes you silent and sometimes makes you laugh and which above all makes the landscape different once and for all.

Rowan Williams, Archbishop of Canterbury (2002-2012)
March 2003

...and a few more tributes:

'For me, the Incredible String Band was an inspiration and a sign...I suppose we started a kind of mutual admiration society...'—Robert Plant, Q *Magazine* 1993.

'A lot of British bands in the late Sixties would pretend to be American... but the ISB were very British and that was very attractive. They were one of the first groups [to mine] that whole British-stroke-Celtic-stroke-pre-Christian vibe...they seemed to be this complete thing that existed on its own terms outside of the mainstream, outside of any stream.'
—Bill Drummond, KLF, Q *Magazine.*

'It's uplifting to find that this strange assortment of Middle Eastern and Celtic folk-mystic stuff stands up remarkably well now. A summer-festival "must" in the 60s, myself and Marc Bolan both being huge fans.'
—David Bowie, speaking about the 5000 *Spirits* album to *Vanity Fair* magazine in 2003. It was one of his top 25 favourite LPs.

Incredible String Band – a brief history

Raymond Greenoaken

'Better than the Beatles!' That, in 1968, was the solemn verdict of *The Observer*'s music critic on the songwriting genius of two Scottish folkies rather grandly calling themselves The Incredible String Band. Such a pronouncement would have been dismissed as froth if it had been spotted in one of the excitable pop weeklies of the time, but this was a serious broadsheet dispensing the ultimate accolade. The word was out: here was something that was more than just fab 'n' groovy. Here was something that would disturb the counsels of the great, that would leave an indelible watermark on late 20th century popular music.

Robin Williamson and Mike Heron found themselves the critics' darlings with the release, in the Spring of 1968, of their third album, *The Hangman's Beautiful Daughter*. Their debut album a couple of years earlier on the US-based Elektra label (they were then a threesome, with banjoist Clive Palmer) had sent out a ripple or two through the contemporary music scene. It was brash and breezy and had been recorded around a single microphone in almost as little time as would be needed to play it back again. The follow-up, *The 5000 Spirits or The Layers Of The Onion*, sent the ripples spreading further: Mick and Marianne were studying it reverently with the *Tao Te Ching* and *The Secret Of The Golden Flower* at their elbows. But it was *Hangman* that really pushed the boat out.

Alternative and mainstream commentators alike vied to outshout each other, not always observing the canons of calm and lucid expression. 'A potpourri of Taoist tongues voiced in infantile innuendoes,' babbled *Rolling Stone*. A pot...*what*? Next, please... 'The nearest thing to godliness among the art-school set,' averred *The Financial Times*, that hip pinko hotbed of subversion. But the *FT* man duly noted their crossover potential: 'Judging by the Establishment figures scattered among the audience [at the album-launch concert at London's Royal Festival Hall], they are about to be taken up by a hard-bitten public.' The 'Establishment' in this context comprised the likes of Lennon and McCartney, Townshend, Jagger and Brian Jones. The *New York Magazine*'s London correspondent was equally enthused: 'Each song is a tone-poem etched in filigree, delicate yet sturdy. Each lyric is an utterly disarming cross between a hymn and a nursery rhyme.' Ah ha – the infantile innuendoes explained! In *The Sunday Times*,

Derek Jewell singled them out from the crowd. 'Quasi-poetry and phoney mysticism now cling to the skirts of popular music, but the Incredibles are not pseudo. Their work is convincing, beautiful, idiosyncratic, yielding more with each playing.'

More than fifty years down the long and winding road, the music of the Incredible String Band remains as beautiful, idiosyncratic and, yes, convincing as it was then. Though steeped in the preoccupations of the late Sixties, there's something strangely up-to-date about it. The reckless eclecticism and startling juxtapositions contain the seeds of post-modernist *bricolage*. The quick-witted assimilation of musics from all over the globe, both folk and popular, as Joe Boyd says, foreshadowed the World Music vogue by a couple of decades. And the sacramental, pantheistic tone of their lyrics offered a blueprint for the neo-Pagan and 'Green' movements that emerged from the cultural cauldron of the Sixties.

The Hangman's Beautiful Daughter sprinted up the charts on the back of this critical rodomontade, briefly making the ISB one of the hottest properties around. If your record collection has just one ISB album, it's likely to be *Hangman*. The Stones wooed Williamson and Heron with a view to signing them to their Mother Earth label; and though they enjoyed the experience of mingling with the Tarot readers, haruspicators and colourful charlatans of the Stones' entourage, they remained loyal to Elektra. A contract was a contract, after all.

That contract had been dangled in front of Williamson, Heron and Palmer in 1966 by Joe Boyd, then a producer and British label manager for Elektra Records. He'd seen Robin and Clive play as a duo the previous year, and travelled up to Edinburgh to sniff them out. By the time Boyd tracked them down they'd added Heron to the line-up, on the questionable basis that trios were more glamorous (Peter, Paul and Mary were in the charts at the time). The new trio, now calling themselves the Incredible String Band, went to London with Boyd to record their debut album. *The Incredible String Band* was, at first glance, an unprepossessing affair: a self-consciously folky group-shot on the front cover, and a rear cover devoted to Heron's jokey sleeve-notes. But the music spoke for itself – or, at least, some of it did. Heron's compositions were plainly those of a tyro songwriter, ranging from the fey to the merely workmanlike, though his way with a melody was already in evidence. Palmer contributed a single song, the lugubrious Empty Pocket Blues. Williamson, however, emerged fully-fledged as a writer of considerable power, eloquence and originality. His October Song, Womankind and Good As Gone bespeak a remarkable maturity. Indeed, October Song, his very first composition, is still reckoned by many to be his best.

An early 1966 publicity shot for Clive's Incredible Folk Club. From left: Mike Heron, Robin Williamson, Clive Palmer. (Ian Ferguson)

By the time the record hit the shops the ISB were seemingly no more. Williamson and Palmer had grabbed their Elektra advances and decamped to Morocco and Afghanistan respectively (it was the Sixties, after all), leaving Heron to work the Scottish club circuit as a soloist. But Williamson was back in Scotland three months later with a sackful of curious North African instruments and a head humming with Moorish modalities. He and Heron reformed the ISB in a country cottage in Balmore, north of Glasgow, and renewed their association with Joe Boyd. The second ISB album was a quantum jump over the first. *5000 Spirits* begins with the eerie whine of Williamson's bowed Moroccan gimbri and serves up fifty minutes of seriously strange and hauntingly beautiful songs. Williamson's contribution mixed the solemn and oracular (The Mad Hatter's Song, The Eyes Of Fate, My Name Is Death) with lysergic whimsy (No Sleep Blues, Way Back In The 1960s) and pensive romanticism (First Girl I Loved). Heron meanwhile had left his callow offerings of the first album far behind, discovering in the process a genius for matching melody and mood, crystallised in songs like Painting Box, Chinese White and Gently Tender. His celebrated Hedgehog's Song elegantly encapsulated a playful Zen wisdom.

5000 Spirits has been described as the alternative soundtrack to the Summer Of Love – a little misleadingly, perhaps, as it wasn't released until the autumn of 1967. Nevertheless, it certainly caught the attention of the movers and shakers of the emerging 'underground' culture. Jagger was grooving to it, as were Lennon, McCartney and Townshend. But Williamson and Heron were already moving on, into the spookier, weirder complexities that would find expression on *The Hangman's Beautiful Daughter*.

Hangman propelled the ISB into the higher reaches of the national album charts, where they rubbed shoulders with the likes of The Supremes, Scott Walker and Andy Williams. Their next release consolidated the artistic achievement of that record. A double album that hit the streets several months before the Beatles' White Album, *Wee Tam And The Big Huge* failed to trouble the charts on account of its half-baked marketing strategy. Released initially a double, it soon turned up in the racks as two separate single LPs, splitting the sales figures three ways. The songs, however, were extraordinary, running the gamut from ten-minute epics to Williamson's 16-second enigma The Son Of Noah's Brother. All the ingredients from *Hangman* were present, and then some. The album promptly sent the blood rushing back to the critics' brains, provoking the 'better than the Beatles' quote above.

With hindsight, *Wee Tam* can be seen as the high water mark in the band's fortunes, as well as the quality of their output. The following summer they flew the flag for Britain, along with Joe Cocker and The Who, at Woodstock. By this time Williamson and Heron had added their girlfriends Rose Simpson and Likky McKechnie to the line-up. Hitherto, Rose and Likky had occasionally stepped on stage to shake a tambourine, slap a drum or warble a bit of harmony; their presence was decorative rather than utilitarian. Nor had they any background as musicians (Rose had 'scraped a bit of fiddle in the school orchestra'). Under Mike and Robin's tutelage, however, they quickly proved their worth, winning the hearts of male fans and acting as unwitting role models for the female faction. How many other female rock instrumentalists can you remember from that time?

Woodstock was not their finest hour. An ill-advised change of programming sandwiched them between the Keef Hartley Band and Creedence Clearwater Revival. With three of them reeling from vertigo on the precipitous stage, they played one of their least-memorable sets. It was their last best chance to make a splash with that 'hard-bitten public'. Thereafter they chugged along as one of the cult bands whose names it was cool to drop, but were never to regain the loftier altitudes of the charts. Part of the problem was that they never had a hit single, preferring to confine themselves pure-mindedly to the album format. At the same time, they were studiously ignored by television, for which their music was reportedly too 'difficult'. BBC Television's *Omnibus* arts programme commissioned a documentary exploring their music and lifestyle (much of it was shot at Penwern, their communal farmhouse in West Wales), but after the band had 'taken it over' and turned it into a mythic panto, the TV execs booted it briskly into touch. Under the title *Be Glad For The Song Has No Ending* it lived an underground existence on the college and arts centre circuits for a year or two, and resurfaced in the1990s, garlanded with praises by pop historians for whom it opened a window onto strange and wondrous antique landscapes.

The ISB were a busy live act over the period 1968-74, customarily touring the UK once or twice a year and regularly visiting the US and the continent. Their concerts were not so much performances as tribal gatherings, in which band and audience melded into a single entity. Audience members were invited onto the stage to blow whistles and hit bells; Williamson and Heron would chat affably about their day to day affairs. They would invariably take the stage with a vast gallery of odd instruments, most of which proved resistant to their efforts to tune them. They broke all the rules of formal performance and invariably got away with it, such was the tender affection they inspired in their followers.

1969 marked a sea change in the ISB. All four members were inducted into L. Ron Hubbard's controversial Church of Scientology, variously described as a programme of self-discovery and a mind-control cult. Whether by chance or consequence their music began to lose some of its lucid magic at this time. *Changing Horses*, released in November of that year, lacked the lustre of its predecessors. The album hinged around two extremely lengthy songs, White Bird and Creation, which, while distinguished by passages of luminous, unearthly beauty, were marred by irksome digressions and careless execution. The next album, 1970's *I Looked Up*, was tighter and more focused, but seemed to be treading water. By this time the band were deep in preparations for an ambitious mixed-media harlequinade called *U*, a 'surreal parable in song and dance' that played for a week at London's Roundhouse before being toured around the United States. For this project, the ISB had drafted in a dance-troupe, Stone Monkey, which had recently congealed around two ex-members of David Medalla's experimental Exploding Galaxy. *U* was developed collectively by band and troupe in the wilds of the Scottish Border country near Innerleithen, where they'd recently relocated to Glen Row, a row of agricultural labourer's cottages on the estate of Lord Glenconner.

The shows were savaged by the critics for their allegedly amateurish, undisciplined presentation. As Williamson argues today, the pundits missed the point. 'The show was supposed to be the way we did it, we weren't failing to do it the way they thought it should have been done. It was, as meant to be, a raggle-taggle caravanserai keeping avant into garde with skipping-rope logic.' So there. Audiences, on the other hand, responded more favourably, but in nothing like the numbers needed to balance the budget on the American tour. The band withdrew to their rustic enclave to lick their wounds and take stock. Before returning to the UK, however, they'd pooled their shrunken resources and disappeared into a San Franciscan recording studio for a weekend, emerging with nearly two hours of recorded songs and music from the show. The album, also called simply *U*, was released in Autumn 1970. It suffered in places from the hectic pace of recording, but contained some of their most extraordinary songs. It was to be the last time, however, that the ISB played entirely by their own rulebook.

When the band moved from Elektra to Island in early 1971, change was everywhere in the air. The Sixties were blurring into the more hard-edged, less forgiving Seventies, and Williamson and Heron were sniffing the wind. Their growing interest in Scientology, with its stress on effective communication, was causing them to reconsider the content of their music and the way they were putting it across. And so the focus began to shift.

The dreamlike vistas and Zen parables they'd conjured so beguilingly in the high summer of hippiedom gave way by degrees to songs that were more rooted in the here and now, that addressed more sublunary concerns. Similarly, the exotic instrumentation they'd gathered together from all parts of the globe was largely replaced by the armamentarium of the rock band.

Nevertheless, to describe the ISB of the Island years as simply a mild form of Seventies rock would be to miss the target by a country mile. Always fond of weaving different stylistic strands into their musical skeins, Williamson and Heron became astonishingly adept at writing and performing in a dizzying range of genres, from trad-folk to ragtime, jugband, supper club jazz, reggae, Twenties pastiche, Berber street music and even a sort of primitive thrash metal. Each of their Island albums was a compendium of contrasting idioms.

Their first Island releases were a soundtrack album from the *Be Glad* film and *Smiling Men With Bad Reputations*, a solo album from Heron on which he jettisoned the ISB do-it-yourself ethic and brought in a roster of top-drawer sessioneers, including John Cale, Pete Townshend, Jimmy Page and Richard Thompson. It was heavier and rockier than anything the ISB had attempted hitherto. Williamson too released a solo album the following year, the quirky and resolutely folky *Myrrh*. In late 1971 the band put out the improbably-titled *Liquid Acrobat As Regards The Air*, a confident and diverse collection that edged purposefully towards a more mainstream soundworld. By this time Rose Simpson had left the band and been replaced by Stone Monkey main-man Malcolm Le Maistre, whose mime and dancing skills – and fondness for bizarre costumes – were promptly incorporated into the stage act; he also developed as an able if idiosyncratic songwriter. It was followed in late 1972 by *Earthspan*, if anything an even more stylistically diverse assemblage than *Acrobat*. It featured scores for strings and horns, and even a sleazy trumpet solo on Williamson's lounge-lizard jazz number Moon Hang Low. Critics – and even some fans – felt that the ISB were, by this time, replacing eclecticism with variety, that different genres were being explored as technical exercises rather than as a means of illuminating their unique personal vision. There was some truth in this, but it should be remembered that Williamson and Heron had never been over-troubled with artificial boundaries, and found it completely natural to allow their wide musical tastes to jostle creatively in their music making. What was new, however, was their concern to find a way of unifying the various stylistic elements at their disposal. This was made clear on their 1973 album *No Ruinous Feud*.

This album polarised the ISB's fan base like none before it. Unprecedentedly, every track was anchored to a conventional rock rhythm section of bass and drums, bringing the String sound as close as it would ever get to a standard soft-rock vibe. They'd also drafted in an eccentric jazzer, Gerard Dott, to replace Likky, who had reportedly gone off 'on holiday' and neglected to return (she eventually moved to Los Angeles and fell out of sight in the late Eighties). Though diehards decried such developments as a betrayal of the band's primal principles, Williamson and (especially) Heron were eager to make themselves more accessible to the casual ear. The songs, too, were pithier and more radio-friendly. Fifteen minute epics were now off the menu.

Or were they? The ISB's final album, *Hard Rope And Silken Twine*, released in early 1974, devoted an entire side to Ithkos, a Greek mythological fantasia assembled by Heron that counterpointed Williamson's oud and fiddle with histrionic Le Maistre vocals and blistering blues-tinged electric guitar from their latest recruit, Glaswegian rocker Graham Forbes. By this time, in concert the ISB were rocking as hard – though not perhaps as convincingly – as Taste or Black Sabbath. But not all the time. Their sets would be punctuated by gentler, folkier stuff, and they now seemed content to let these dual approaches run alongside each other rather than forcibly integrate them. Hard rope and silken twine...

It couldn't work, of course. The casual listener was merely bemused by such stark contrasts; nor did Williamson, a folkie at heart, feel comfortable with the high decibel bombast rumbling about him. His abrupt departure, on the verge of a world tour in September 1974, wrote the *finis* for the band. He relocated to Los Angeles to develop parallel careers as a writer and solo musician. Heron meantime rebranded the line-up as Mike Heron's Reputation and set about relaunching it on the club and college circuit.

The end had been inevitable, and probably long a-coming. As musicians and as personalities, Williamson and Heron were chalk and cheese. In the salad days of the ISB their different outlooks and approaches sparked each other off; but over time each man progressively 'reverted to type' (as Williamson later put it), and they found themselves tugged in ever more divergent directions. The end of the Incredible String Band was, as is the case with most bands, an anti-climax, a dying fall. It's true that even in their final phase they produced some remarkable, unforgettable music. But both men had their own rows to hoe, and their own roads to tread. Unexpectedly, at the turn of the Millennium, those roads converged again. But this is another story, and one that is only briefly covered in this book.

Let's go back, finally, to that 'better than the Beatles' rubric. Fact or hyperbole? Well, in one sense, there's no contest. The songs of Lennon and McCartney have a universality that the lucubrations of Williamson and Heron rarely pretended to. However much the Beatles pushed the envelope of acceptability, they still used the language of contemporary chart pop. The ISB, by contrast, were hermetic, literary, *otherly*. Accessibility was not their guiding gleam, for all that in their later career they fell somewhat under its spell. But in terms of sheer inventiveness, of risk-taking, of melodic finesse and lyrical élan, they were the equal of their more celebrated peers. Without stretching the point too far, it could be said that Williamson and Heron stood in similar relation to each other as Lennon and McCartney. Williamson, mercurial, muse-haunted, besotted with the sounds and meanings of words, relentlessly autobiographical in his songwriting – the Lennon figure, if you like; Heron, the more phlegmatic, earthy personality, more concerned with melody than lyric, and with more of a pop sensibility – the McCartney of the ISB. Whereas such comparisons are superficial and over-simple, they do help to illuminate why both sets of partners worked so well together. In both cases, the differences in personality created a fruitful rivalry, a necessary artistic tension. Each partner was the other's counterweight and restraining influence, ensuring that their joint achievement was greater than the sum of the parts.

Such partnerships, of course, tend to have a limited life span, as each person feels the increasing need to assert himself against the other. It was no surprise that, in the aftermath of the ISB's dissolution, Heron and Williamson quickly returned to their individual wellsprings of inspiration: in Williamson's case, to traditional folksong, in Heron's, the rockier end of pop. But in the eight years of the band's existence, these two men together created something that had never been heard before, and has rarely been heard since. It was a unique, unreproducible achievement, and it is the subject of this book.

Overleaf Wizz and Clive busking in St Germain Des Pres, Paris circa 1960 (Wizz Jones).

Chapter One

A brief ISB pre-history, Billy Connolly, Clive Palmer and Wizz Jones recall the early folk-club years, Jon Riley and Tony Corden take a critical look at the *First Album*, and we consider the transitional period leading to *5000 Spirits* in the light of the 'Balmore' rehearsal tapes.

Left 'There was an aeroplane stuck in it but I didn't notice at first...' Clive and Bert listen to Robin, Edinburgh 1963. (Rod Harbinson). *Right* Taking tea in an Edinburgh garret, 1963: Clive, Robin and Bert (Rod Harbinson)

A brief ISB pre-history

Adrian Whittaker

Edinburgh-born Robin Williamson left school and home 'rather precipitately' in 1958 and quickly became a part of the emergent folk/beatnik scene, playing acoustic and electric guitar in a couple of jazz bands as well as performing traditional songs in places like the Waverley Bar. In around 1961 he started sharing a flat with Bert Jansch, who remembers him as 'an absolute romantic who went round bestowing poems on young ladies' and as one of the best traditional singers in Scotland. Robin also became an accomplished fiddle player, touring Northern England at one point with bluegrass musician Tom Paley.

In January 1963 Bert and Robin got the overnight bus down to London to seek fame and fortune on the back of a gig Robin had acquired at the Troubador. The purist ethos of the London scene then, with a dour, Communist Party 'traditional material only' approach typified by Ewan MacColl, made it hard for them to find many other gigs. Back in Edinburgh, Archie Fisher had set up a Tuesday night folk club at the Crown Bar, where Robin and Bert became regulars. It was there Robin met Clive Palmer, a banjo-player from Edmonton who'd originally headed up to Edinburgh to visit some mates but also found a niche at the club. The three of them went on to share various insalubrious lodgings, including an infamous tenement called Society Buildings rented by Rod Harbinson, who supplied some of the early photos which illustrate this book. According to Barry Miles (in his book *In The Sixties*), when he visited Society Buildings in 1963 Clive had a sort of parallel career as a dealer in the smoky hazes of Edinburgh's emergent counter-culture, where he was known as 'Limpy'. At some point in 1963, Robin and Clive officially became a duo playing bluegrass and old-timey material, principally at the Crown Bar. By 1964 Bert Jansch had more or less departed from the Edinburgh scene; he was spending increasing amounts of time in London, where he had settled permanently by the end of that year.

Mike Heron, also from Edinburgh, had dropped out of university and was working out his indenture by day as a trainee cost accountant, playing electric guitar by night in R&B outfits such as Rock Bottom And The Deadbeats ('little furry waistcoats and maracas, you know the kind of thing') and pop bands like The Saracens and the Abstracts ('We make the Rolling Stones look respectable'). In 2017 Mike treated us to a fascinating account of his early music career up to 1966 in the book *You Know What You Could Be*, jointly written with Andrew Greig. Inspired by Dylan, he was starting to write his own songs; when he wasn't playing gigs, he'd often come and watch Robin and Clive at the Crown Bar. Folk clubs, he sensed, would offer a more receptive audience for the material he was starting to come up with. The Crown Bar was also where producer Joe Boyd first saw (and was impressed by) the Robin and Clive duo, on a fleeting visit to Edinburgh in April 1965.

Meanwhile, Robin and Clive were starting to get Scottish gigs outside the Crown Bar, and later in 1965 (no-one concerned is able to be very certain about dates) decided they needed 'a strummer' to fill out their sound. Mike got the gig, adding his own compositions to the eclectic mix. The Incredible String Band, as Clive dubbed them, was born.

Around March 1966, Ian Ferguson was starting up 'Clive's Incredible Folk Club' in Sauchiehall Street, Glasgow. Ian and his brother had run the venue as a dancehall, but after countless problems stemming from fire regulations and their lack of a licence for dancing, decided to start running folk 'all-nighters' there instead. Running from 10pm Saturday to 6am Sunday mornings, these rapidly acquired a very esoteric clientele indeed, as Billy Connolly recounts in the following interview. Ian's old friend Clive Palmer provided the connection with the folk network and fronted the club, which featured the Incredible String Band as residents. When Joe Boyd returned to Edinburgh that Spring in search of Robin and Clive in his new role as head of Elektra's UK office, he encountered a full-fledged three-piece group. Once he realised they were starting to write their own material, he persuaded them to record a five-song demo tape for Jac Holzman which was apparently approved. After a brief bidding war with Transatlantic Records, the three were signed up for an Elektra album with an advance of £100 each.

CLIVE'S INCREDIBLE FOLK CLUB

134 Sauchiehall Street,
Glasgow, C.3
(Next to Richards Shop)
Admit One

DATE

★ ★ ★ £1,000 ★ ★ ★

Our management will pay this sum to any group that are wilder, more primitive than the rhythm and blues group from Dalceny Woods, Scotland.

5/- THE ABSTRACTS 5/-

We make the Rolling Stones look respectable

Lock up your daughters, the Abstracts are in town

MARLBOROUGH HALL

7.45 to 11.45 THIS SATURDAY'S DANCE

★ ★ ★ ★ ★ ★ ★ ★ ★

December 1964

Clive and Robin (Ian Ferguson)

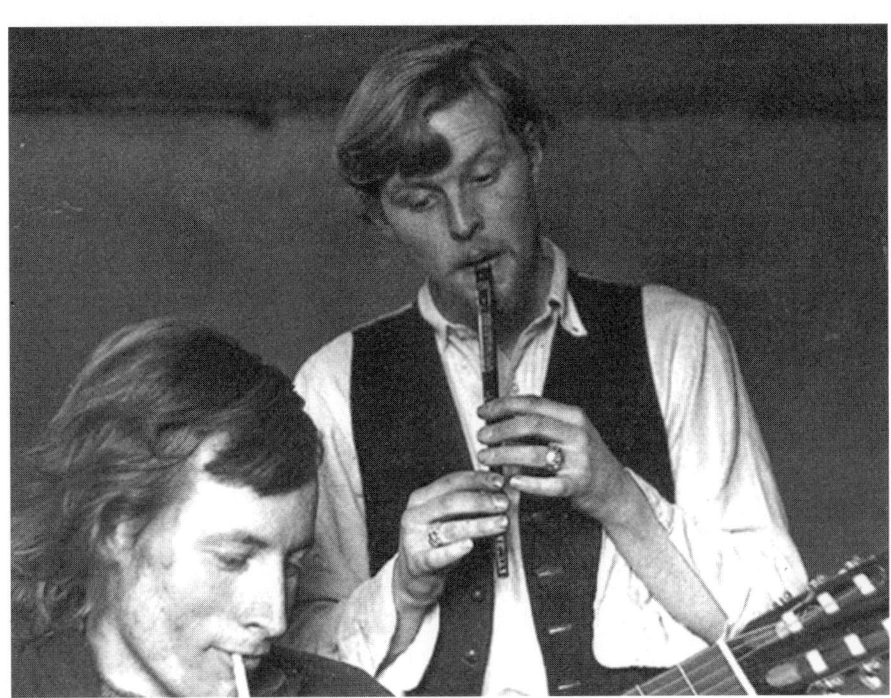

'They were brilliant, brilliant times'

Billy Connolly was part of the same Edinburgh/Glasgow folk scene as the early ISB, where he started his performing career playing autoharp and banjo and singing Carter Family songs. Alistair Fraser talked to him in 1997 about the early years.

Billy: I was very lucky because I was in right at the beginning of everything. I knew Robin Williamson and Clive Palmer from being solo performers and from performing together in Edinburgh. For some reason I liked going to Edinburgh to see them doing it; they seemed to fit better there, those old clubs like the Woolpack and all that. I liked them doing American stuff, you know, Uncle Dave Macon and all those hillbilly songs, 'cause I was a banjo player and that's what I really wanted to hear, but they did Scottish stuff unbelievably well, and Clive Palmer did great sort of music hall banjo, minstrel, classical banjo playing. He was just beyond belief, they all were.

At the Edinburgh Festival somebody gave me a handbill and it was for Clive's Incredible String Band, it wasn't the original show or anything remotely like it. And I thought I wonder if that's Clive Palmer, so I checked it out and it was – it was Clive and Robin and Mike Heron, and I'd never seen Mike Heron before. Apparently he came from a kind of rock background, bluesy background, but he had a lovely wee lady's Gibson, a wee sexy Gibson guitar which he played with big chunky chords; everybody who has that kind of guitar sort of tickles it you know, like it's precious, but he was giving it a serious doing, and I really loved it. They'd all got very hairy in the interim you know, long hair and earrings which, when I was a kid growing up there, I thought 'Oh my God, he's got two earrings, how exotic.' We'd be in Paisley up in a tenement, the Attic folk club, it was an old RAF Association room, and these extraordinary men...

Clive had polio or something, he had the most extraordinary limp, and every time he limped his hair would go 'woof' like that, and the people in the audience were going, 'What's this?' and rumour had it that he lived in a tent, in a house. He was living in a big Victorian room that he couldn't heat so he lived in a tent, with a heater and a banjo. I thought, 'Oh my God these are the people I've been looking for.' I was creeping around in cowboy boots – as I still do (*laughs*) – but I wanted to be hairy and exotic and interesting and there they were. But when they started to play, the three of them, I was nearly in tears, actually. Maybe you've loved the Rolling Stones, or The Who or Hendrix or somebody great and you've got all the albums and then you see them live, for the first time, and it's almost like tearful. But when those three started to play and had obviously rehearsed – folk music was all raggedy-arsed at that time, you started when you wanted and joined in – but they started at the right time and – bang – singing, oh I never heard anything like it in my life.

At that time they were still doing a lot of other songs, folk songs, hillbilly songs, different stuff from their various backgrounds, and as time went along the Smoke Shovelling Song and October Song and all those things began to creep in and they became that strange hippy court-jestery thing which I loved, but the beginning was the one for me. The power of it was breathtaking and then the album came out, it was just breathtakingly great.

Clive Palmer had an incredible voice. He could sound like the guy who sang with Bud Flanagan, Chesney Allen (*sings in deep voice*). He used to do a lovely version of After The Ball Was Over with this wonderful voice, then he would do Train On The Island or something with these high, long, long notes, and then he'd do a Frank Proffitt with a high lonesome sound; he could do anything. Clive Palmer was the most interesting person, and he had many harebrained schemes. Another thing he always did was having new necks made for his banjos: long necks made of cherry wood and all these weird things, and they always sounded crap to

me! His banjo was a Clifford Essex Concert Grand and it sounded lovely in the first place, but he had these ideas for necks away out here and oh, he thought they were wonderful. Clive never made any money. He made rolling pins at one point with designs on them and they were hugely admired, but he only sold two and then he said, 'Ach, I'm not doing this anymore.' He had about a million orders [*slight exaggeration here, we think – Ed.*] but ach, pooh to hell! Then he made one shoe for Diz Disley! I was speaking to Diz at Cambridge Folk Festival; he said 'I bought a shoe but he never made the left one, and he made a glove for someone else but he never made the other one.' Clive wasn't into finishing things. I remember going to see him at the McClelland Galleries and he turned up in a surgeon's outfit and wellington boots, playing the banjo. My father was there and he said, 'You like this?' That was Clive – everything he tried he would lose interest in after a couple of times, so around his club he wasn't too much in evidence.

'He was one of those irritating guys who had started good'

Robin always was away up there and in and around and decorative. He could sing like a woman, which always amazed me: he would sing like a man, but he would sing a song by Jeannie Robertson or Belle Stewart from

Robin, possibily singing Rothesay Bay, Edinburgh, 1963 (Rod Harbinson)

the north-east of Scotland and he would do it in a north-east of Scotland woman's style but still sound like a man, he still looked like a big sexy guy. He was the sort of heart-throb of the folk scene; we were an ugly bunch but he was handsome, so he stuck out a mile 'cause everybody else was trying to look dreadful. To this day when I meet him I always ask him to sing Rothesay Bay. He says it's the first song he ever learned, when he was on holiday in the Isle of Bute. It's a lovely old Scottish music hall song and he does it (*sings*) – I can't get up there, but he was by far the best singer in the folk scene, the most innovative guy in the folk scene. He was one of those irritating guys who had started good. Nobody ever remembers him learning – he turned up good when he was fourteen, that kind of guy you want to just slap or disfigure: he's handsome and he's good, it was just bloody great. He could draw and paint as well, these weird things, people with trees growing out of their groin and stuff – God how I loved him.

Mike Heron, long before Sting, had this laughing Caribbean tone in his voice, and with this bluesy hammering style on the guitar, it was so eclectic, but it came together with a crash and it was brilliant. The almost awful bit was just before Clive left; they were uncomfortable and it showed in the music – there are some jangly mixtures of when Clive's playing and they're joining in with flutes and stuff. I personally love it, but it's less harmonic than the stuff they were doing before that, but they were unhappy and it showed in the music 'cause they lived it and so if they were unhappy you could hear it. Well, I could anyway, maybe I'm just a bit of a hippy, but that's how I feel about it.

Alistair: Tell us about Clive's folk club.

Clive Palmer ran a club that was supposedly a folk club but not really, it was just a kind of happening place; it was next to the Odeon cinema in Sauchiehall Street. It's where the Savoy Market now is, but it was on the fourth or the fifth floor of this building. You got into a lift and there were no stairs up to it so it couldn't get fire brigade permission. It was one of those wee silly lifts you don't see anymore – there's only four people at a time, so it would take all night to get everybody up there. It was illegal, it was a real sweatbox and it was brilliant. Hamish Imlach was a resident and he made me resident: 'Right Billy, you'll be the resident autoharp player' – playing Carter Family songs. Hamish sort of organised everybody, Robin would always be talking to women and people, singers drifting by would come up and play. It was just the most outstanding club I was ever in. It was a failure inasmuch as, the way my memory has it, it lasted two or three months, maybe it was six weeks or so but it was an outstanding success – it would be jammed full. [*It ran March–May 1966 – Ed.*] It was like a shooting star – it flourished and if you were lucky you saw it, and then it was gone. It was a magical moment in music for me. I remember it with great joy. That's the first time I saw Wizz Jones and Pete Stanley. They were playing bluegrass – I couldn't believe it. The guests were fantastic, but the most wonderful thing about the club was that you had all the hairy people and the beautiful hippy people, but you also had the Glasgow people who had been to the dancing or been out for a drink, all the 'Heeey' mob, you know. They mixed brilliantly and nobody could ask you outside for a smack in the mouth, 'cause you couldn't get outside – you had to wait for the lift! If the place went on fire we'd all have been barbecued, but the thing that amazed me was, you would have Wizz Jones up there and all the Glasgow guys would be there with their suits and cufflinks and watches, 'cause Glasgow people used to be incredibly smart dressers, real clothes horses. Then the hippy crowd all lying around, the smell of marijuana drifting about, and you would have the Incredible String Band all there doing songs on their own and songs together, Wizz and Pete Stanley, but you'd also have old Davy Stewart the gypsy in the back room. He would get up and sing – I never knew what Davy was singing about. I always loved him but his teeth were missing and stuff, and he played this old accordion. It was like Zulu folk music to me – you know, you'd get a word every now and again that you recognised. I adored him. And then you'd have the bowed gimbri! They were brilliant, brilliant times.

It was a hugely successful club, and if memory serves me well the police closed it, but for safety – it wasn't because we were all weird! I think it was the fire hazard that nobody cared about. Of course in those days we were saying, 'But listen, it's me that's getting burned, what the hell's it to do with you, bugger off – I'm quite happy to be burned if I can be burned to that!' Well that's how we felt about Clive's club.

But the club itself was stunning. It was a brilliant idea whose life was very short but very very bright. Everybody who speaks about it speaks about it with great glowing memories. People fell in love there, or slept there or whatever; it was a perfect club, perfect, aye.

How did you feel about Clive's departure?

When Clive left I was the saddest guy on the planet – you could see Clive getting unhappy and you could see him doing less and less in the band as the other two were so excited about the new stuff, and you can imagine why: it must have been like striking gold. Clive was entrenched in the older stuff and he was magnificent at it, and he was getting less and less to do and you could see him leaving.

When Clive left, it became this other thing – it just took off. They moved to Milngavie just outside Glasgow, they lived up in Temple Cottage [*the cottage where Mike and Robin worked on the material for* 5000 Spirits, *see The Balmore Hoard article – Ed.*] with all these other strange weird and wonderful people all dressed in blankets. I remember I saw them at the Locarno – it's a dance hall on Sauchiehall Street – and I went to see them but then I was in capes and things, long hair, and they played the gig and I hung out at the back so as they would have to pass me and I could talk to them. And I went 'Hi!' and of course they remembered me,

Live at the Incredible Folk Club, 1966. (Ian Ferguson)

how you doing blah blah blah, but they smelt weird. I said, 'What's that?' It was a bit like marijuana, I thought, and it was patchouli or something.

They were always surrounded by the most exotic looking people. At a concert these people you've never seen in your life would come out of the woodwork. You'd think, 'Where do they live?' – people in velvet clothes, big lacy collars, people who looked like Charles the First. I thought Christ, what do they do during the day, are they under the bed waiting for the Incredible String Band or Grateful Dead concerts to come to town?... Crushed velvet people. There was a guy called Ricky who used to wear a big collar like he was at Eton or like Lord Snooty, long hair, came from Edinburgh, he was always around them. I was talking to Clive one day after all of this and he says Ricky was the coolest man on the planet. Clive had hitched to Afghanistan, the hippy trail, and he was in northern Greece or Turkey or some place and he was a bit fed up (*laughs*) sitting in the street, playing his banjo. And Ricky came round the corner and Clive says, 'Ricky!' and Ricky says, 'How you doing man?' and kept walking (*laughs*) – the coolest man on earth. So there were these guys, women with hair just closed at the front – there's a nose and eyes – with string and leather round their wrist; they all looked like those women who hung out with Charles Manson.

I was always dying to be closer to them, but I was more of a Glasgow teddy boy than a hippy. I kept trying to be a hippy but people could spot my origins. I tried so hard to be love and peace and Save the Whale and beads, but they could always say 'Watch him, he'll punch you in the jaw, he's a nasty bugger when he's got drink!'

You're a great champion of acoustic music.

My love of acoustic music has saved my life really, and has given my life a lovely sort of lacy edge because it has remained a kind of constant. Everything I love has lasted, everybody I liked made it and everybody I didn't like didn't make it. It's kind of weird, really. The second I saw the ISB I knew it was something amazing, something to behold, the same feeling you get when you first hear Bob Dylan.

The Incredible String Band have lasted the whole thing from my first attempts – even before I played, when I was going to folk clubs, Clive and Robin were big stars.

It was such an education. I didn't know what a sitar was; and there was a glockenspiel, a tubular bell with a piece of string at the end for hanging on, and you hit it and you dip it in a bucket of water and it goes 'plewwoo!' I learned later from the BBC that it used to be a radio signal during the war, which they would use as an introduction to programmes when there was a concealed message for the Free French or something! I thought, oh God I saw the Incredible String Band doing that to great effect, probably the place was full of Free French people in berets in the balcony going 'Ah ha!'

This was before Fairport Convention and all those other pseudo-rocky-folky outfits. I've always been wary of fusions, but the Incredible String Band weren't a fusion with rock – they were rock with poetry and folk, rock and folk, electric eclectic, poetic, they were everything, and they'd always been that; they were just letting different things come to the fore. 'Cause I remember when Robin and Clive were singing Glasgow songs that I'd never heard in my life. I remember when they wore uniforms – a dark blue shirt, grey slacks, black casual shoes and a black polo neck under the shirt. But then they were weird even though they were trying to look normal and get gigs.

'They were a profound influence on me'

It was a breathtaking time in Scottish acoustic music. Now that it's out on CD I'm living it all again. Funnily enough I just bought a [solo] album of Mike Heron's called *Where The Mystics Swim*, and there's a lovely tribute on it to the great blues player Robert Johnson and it's brilliant; he's still as good as he ever was.

They were a profound influence on me. Do you know why they influenced me most? That sort of 'be yourself' attitude, dress the way you think you should and get on with it, don't give a toss what they approve or disapprove of, get on with it. Although they were kind of hippy they were very very dynamic, they controlled from the front, they were the force. They've made an unbelievable contribution, as big as Bob Dylan, I would have thought.

The Roving Journeyman

Raymond Greenoaken talks to Clive Palmer

There's something changeless about Clive Palmer. He must have been young once (and there are photos that hint at it), but he somehow gives the impression of having been born middle aged. Throughout the Sixties, when to be young was everything, Clive seemed to carry the status of everyone's older brother; he'd been there, he'd done that... His early wanderings and range of journeyman skills set him apart from the whey-faced whippersnappers that made up Edinburgh's beatnik community in the early years of that decade. Despite cooking up a few hare-brained schemes, he seemed to have more savvy than his contemporaries. Gravitas, even. His passion for and deep knowledge of Edwardian banjo music and traditional balladry added to the impression of a man out of his time. When I first heard that gravelly, creaking voice singing Empty Pocket Blues, I took him to be fifty if he was a day; and fifty was old in 1966. There was always a sort of mystery surrounding his age. We knew Mike's and Robin's birthdates from the first ISB songbook. Nobody seemed to know Clive's.

Clive was gracious enough to submit to a prolonged grilling. He looks in pretty good shape, and still has a keen memory. At one point, I tried to describe a song I'd heard him and Robin perform on a recently-unearthed 1964 live tape, being unable to remember the title. 'You sang it, and Robin played whistle between the verses,' I said vaguely. 'The Working Chap!' he replied correctly, without a second's thought.

Improbable stories attach themselves to Clive like barnacles: the drug-smuggler with the hollowed-out wooden leg, the glove-maker who only ever made single gloves. There's more, much more. The truth may not be stranger than fiction, but it's been a lot harder to gather over the years.

Raymond: Did the ISB approach of having no barriers come out of the Edinburgh scene of the Sixties, or was it more to do with yourselves as individuals?

Clive: Well, when we first met, Robin was playing really beautiful stuff, very simple Scottish songs, but beautifully sung with nice guitar backings. They made an enormous impression. And when we played together we started to experiment more, changing things around a bit, adding a bit of this and a bit of that. What we did was very varied, yeah.

You certainly gained a reputation for pushing the envelope at that time. Presumably that was what got Joe Boyd on your trail?

Yeah, maybe... I don't know what Joe's memory's like – mine's pretty good! Not for dates, but my actual memory of events is good. What actually happened was, Robin and I used to work a lot around the clubs, and I was living in a cottage out near Glasgow – Mary Stewart's, at Balmore – and I woke up this morning and there was this guy at the door, who I'd never seen before, with a grey mac on. [*Mary Stewart, a vet at Glasgow University, played host to many Scottish folk musicians in the early Sixties – Ed.*] He said 'I've been getting a lot of reports about your playing, you and Robin, round the clubs and so on, and I'm over here representing Elektra, and we wondered if you'd be interested in a record.' And I said, well it depends on what the deal is, and by the way, there's three of us! Because Robin and I had been playing together for a few years, and we decided that we would add another person. We thought that we could do with a bit more sound, and we had two candidates. There was a guy who played at the Crown Bar, he was a resident, and there was Mike.

Can you put a name to the other one?

Billy... Billy something – Robin's not sure either. But we tried them both out. We went to Mike's house, and he played with us, tried out; and we went away again and discussed it. We were both pretty laid-back sort of guys, and I liked Mike's upfrontness; he was happy with the audience, talked to people, he was a good front man.

Anyway, all Joe's stuff about going down winding streets in search of us – that's embellishment, I think. Joe just turned up out of the blue, and we set the deal up.

How did you come to know Mike? Were you familiar with him as a performer at the time?

No. We put the word around that we were looking for a third member, and he approached us. We went round to see him at his father's house, just to see how we got on.

Is it true that there was some resistance around the local scene to his joining you?

It is true, yes. There was some clubs that used to book us that said specifically that it had to be just the two of us. But not that many. Some places, it really went well. They liked him, they liked him straight away. As soon as we added a third member, it started to work really very well – though it was working well already, of course.

Was Mike singing lead vocals from the outset, as well as 'strumming'?

Yeah, as far as I remember. At that time, we used to do that theme from Zorba; he did a big thing on that. People loved it!

Was it pressure from Joe that pushed you towards original material?

Joe did want original material, yes. You know, I was probably one of the first people to hear October Song, because Robin came to see me just after he'd written it, and he played it to us to ask us what we thought of it.

And what did you think of it, just then?

Oh, it was amazing. I always had enormous regard for their talents – both of them. Very much. But Robin's more my background, traditional, American influences...

Empty Pocket Blues was the only composition of yours on the first album. Was it the only song you'd written at that time?

I'd put together a few things. But I know Wizz Jones thinks I swiped it from him. What happened was, Wizz and I and a lot of others were staying in Barnes with a Mr and Mrs Reinay, whose son I knew. They were Jewish, they came from Austria and they had been timber merchants and had been quite wealthy. They lived in a nice house in Barnes and ran a laundry, a hand-press laundry in Mayfair. Very high class, it did MPs' shirts and stuff like that. And they were nice people. They put up all these beatniks and the like. And there was a guy there called Brian – I don't remember his second name. He used to play the piano, and was always playing bluesy stuff; and I remember he got into playing this thing which had this progression from C to A flat. And that stuck in my mind. What actually happened was, Wizz went off and started to knock something together around this chord sequence, and I was starting to knock something together with it too. But the guy who originally came up with that progression was Brian. He was a pretty spaced-out guy, and he came up with all these funny chord sequences. And they stick in your mind. That's where Empty Pocket Blues came from. Like most of my songs, I wrote it very quickly.

Have you always tended to work that way with other musicians?

Always. And with Robin, it's always been like that.

Back to the first ISB album. Is it true that it was recorded in a single day?

Yes, it was. Two sessions, with a break. All round one microphone, no overdubs, dead straight.

Given that you were on only five tracks out of the sixteen, did you feel out on the edge of things at all?

Well, no, I didn't particularly, because someone else is doing something and it's up to you if there's something in it you can add to. But I think they were moving already in a different direction. I had ideas of my own, but they weren't really the same – they still aren't! But I think Robin's moving back towards that old stuff again.

Then I went to India, and Robin went to Morocco. Robin left before I did, so Mike and I continued to work together for a while in Glasgow, did a few gigs together.

As the ISB?

No, just as the two of us. I'm not sure we actually played together; we just shared the gig. Just to keep things going. I think Mike was very much into keeping things going. We'd done the record, and we were sort of taking a rest. I don't think there were any plans to continue. I'd enjoyed playing with Robin, and as a three-piece, but I was feeling like having a break from it all. I don't think we really expected anything to come out of the first album, really.

I wasn't too much bothered, because we'd been working with each other for several years... I wanted to travel a bit, I was quite young.

You'd been staying at Mary Stewart's at Balmore around that time. How did you become acquainted with Mary?

I used to play in Glasgow a lot, and in those days I stayed in various places in Edinburgh. And at the time there used to be a lot of musicians round there – Hamish Imlach, Archie Fisher, Alex Campbell – who used to meet up at Mary's house. It was a sort of meeting place, and you could stay there any time you liked. It was a big house.

So you were fairly footloose at that time?

Yes, I stayed here and there, but I never had a place of my own. None of us did... We made money, but we spent it!

How did you and Robin come together as performers?

What happened was, I had an old friend that I'd known in the old beatnik days, and I'd been in Paris and I bumped into this guy, and we went down to Shoreham in Kent. Now, this guy was at Gordonstoun, and he had friends who'd left Gordonstoun at the same time. And I was down in Shoreham with them, 'cause in those days people did that, they hung around in groups, visiting and travelling. He said, I've got this friend who lives in a house in Edinburgh. I'm going to go and see him for the weekend, do you want to come? I'm going on ahead – you can catch me up.

So I arrived in Edinburgh with my banjo. I didn't actually have the address, but I knew someone up there – another of the Gordonstoun brigade – and I met him in the street. He knew where I wanted to be, and pointed me in the direction of Society Buildings. Rod Harbinson was there. It was just one enormous great room, and he rented it. His father was a whisky distiller, and he had a little cottage near Oban, on a little island called Kerrara. We used to go for weekends. Rod had a private income, and he lived in Edinburgh, and he rented this place, and we all stayed there. And as you do, being a musician, I found out there was a bar club at the Crown. I walked in one night and there was this red-faced guy with a white Arran sweater on. It was Robin. We just got talking.

Robin and I have a lot of affinities; it's very easy for us to play together, always has been. We're both very into the music. When we met, we just started playing, and we got on well, and the arrangements just fell into place. So we started working together, and ran a club at the Crown. We made quite good money. I don't know what the equivalent today would be, but we'd get about £35 a gig [*Ed's note – you could probably multiply that figure tenfold to get a current equivalent*].

Billy Connolly paints you as a magnificent eccentric at this time. Do you recognise yourself in his description at all?

I suppose you could call me eccentric in the sense that I'm perhaps a bit out of time. Most of my musical background is in music from the turn of the century. I grew up in that sort of environment. I went on stage when I was eight years old. I was a vocalist in a dance troupe, and I sang in a lot of shows, minstrel shows and stuff like that. My mother got me into the singing, and then I got banjo lessons when I was ten. My real introduction into music was playing in jazz bands.

When I was about fourteen I used to go to Soho and play in the jazz bands around the bars. Then I went off to Paris with Wizz, and we played in the streets there. I was there for a couple of years. That did me a lot of good. You're really on the spot when you're playing in the street, so your voice gets stronger and your playing gets stronger.

Clive Palmer, Edinburgh, 1963 (Rod Harbinson)

So that was your formative period as a musician?

Yes, I would say so.

How did you find your way into the Old Timey side of your repertoire?

That happened when I was in Edinburgh, really. I met a lot of American musicians there. Also the records were coming out of America, on Folkways, of these people; so we listened to a lot of this stuff, and British traditional singers too. We knew a lot of the old traditional singers personally, because we used to book them. Robin and I had a summer show that we did near the Castle. We had a little room, where we put on traditional music shows in the afternoon, the two of us. We'd take turns to hand out leaflets. That was originally Robin's idea, and like most of Robin's ideas, it was a damn good one: people rolled in. The place was always packed.

The impression I've always got from that period is that you were invariably the brains behind such schemes. But not in this case?

No, but I suppose I led a little at that time. But it's very hard to separate the threads of something like that. The main difference between Robin

Glasgow TV studio, 66 - Owen Hand, Robin, Lesley Hale and Clive.

and me is that I was a bit laid-back, whereas he was more serious. He was hard-working, and I was a bit lazy.

Was he more ambitious?

I don't know. You can be ambitious in different ways. Not really ambitious. He just wanted to do something with his music. I just knuckled down when I felt like it.

Do you remember much about recording Jazzbo's Holiday? [the only official recording by the first incarnation of Robin & Clive]

Yeah. I remember it completely. This guy called Nat Joseph, who ran Transatlantic Records, went round all the singers – Anne Briggs, Bert, Robin and I, various people – and he sent taxis round to bring us all down to the studio, which he'd booked on the outskirts of Edinburgh, and we all put a couple of tracks down each. They weren't live performances; they were all done in the studio. So he put out this record, called *Edinburgh Folk Festival*. There were Volume 1 and Volume 2, actually. We signed a contract, and got £5 each, a one-off payment – plus the taxi-ride!

Tell me about Clive's Incredible Folk Club.

It was a big room. Before that it was a dance hall. This guy rented the room, and he ran a disco there; a guy called Ian Ferguson. I stayed with him for a while, and he suggested we start a folk club there, 'cause I had all the contacts to get the artists, and we started running an all-night folk club. The first night, we turned away five hundred people! It only ran about three or four months.

Was the club named after the band then, rather than the other way around?

Neither. The band's name was my idea; I wasn't trading on it with the club.

It was almost like a brand name?

Sort of. What originally happened was that we had a brain-storming session, and we had the 'String Band' part of it, because we'd been playing quite a lot of American stuff, and we went through things like the Gaelic String Band and so on, and I came up with the idea of the Incredible

String Band. The club name just seemed like a good idea. It worked, I think. But it was a joint effort.

Let's spool forward again to the trip to India. Why India? Did it fit in with the temper of the times?

Yeah. I had a friend who I discussed it with, and we decided we'd do it. I was there for about a year. Just looning around, playing the banjo. I did two shows on Indian television. What happened was, we bumped into a couple of girls that we got talking to, 'cause they all speak English there. They said, 'So you play banjo? Well, we've got a little show, we sing together, and we're looking for someone to play music behind us.' They did English songs, English traditional songs. So I ended up backing them on the television. They lived in a girls' school, and I got a gig there as well. We were moving around, a couple of weeks here, a couple there, just working our way across the country.

When you got back to Britain, did you get back into playing straight away?

I stayed in London for a while and didn't do much musically. [*Ed: Clive has omitted the fact that in December 1966 he was the first person in Scotland to be arrested for possession of LSD, which had just been declared illegal in September that year. After a couple of uncomfortable weeks on remand in Barlinnie Prison, he escaped with a £100 fine.*]

Was banjo your first instrument?

Yeah. I had a guitar, but I swapped it, never played it at all. I got this old guitar, and my brother, who was a French polisher then, polished it up for me, and I swapped it in the end for a banjo.

What attracted you to the banjo?

The smell of the case! It had a lovely musty old smell. I loved it. It was a little five-string banjo, a zither banjo. They're the ones with the box on the back; the old Commayer banjos.

I believe you worked in schools in Cornwall?

I worked for the local council teaching woodwork and what you call 'life skills' – theoretical stuff. Pretty boring, but quite well paid, since there was no other work in Cornwall at all. I was quite heavily involved in trade unions then, and the Labour Party. I was a shop steward, and president of the local branch of the union.

But you're now a retired person...

Yes. I couldn't work any more because my back was playing me up. The County Council offered me a pension, so I retired. It's not much, of course. I still need to do things; but I do get some royalties.

You've now achieved the status of living legend. That might help things along...

That would be nice!

A final question. Your birthdate?

May the 13th, 1943...Edmonton, London.

Interview: 1999

For more on Clive's early life and his post-ISB career with The Famous Jug Band, Temple Creatures and COB, you are referred to Grahame Hood's excellent authorised biography, *Empty Pocket Blues: The Life and Music of Clive Palmer.*

'It was like Alice's Restaurant'

Raymond Greenoaken talks to Wizz Jones
about Balmore andClive's Incredible Folk Club

Around the time that Robin and Clive were playing as a 'gypsy bluegrass' duo, they were sharing – with several other people – a large room in a rotting Edinburgh tenement called Society Buildings, now demolished. Clive famously nailed a small tent to the floorboards in pursuit of a modicum of privacy. Eventually, he moved out to Mary Stewart's celebrated commune cum hostel cum madhouse at Temple Cottage in Balmore, a few miles to the north of Glasgow. Robin and Mike followed at intervals, and it was there that the songs on 5000 Spirits *and* The Hangman's Beautiful Daughter *were hatched and rehearsed. The Balmore Tapes (rehearsal tapes covered later in this chapter) show the very process of creation, as well as some of the social interaction between the Temple Cottage residents. Robin's dazzling CD,* Mirrorman's Sequences, *also sheds light on early ISB bohemian exploits in Edinburgh.*

The Dramatis Personae
Robin Williamson: musician, poet and 'prophet from the north'
Mike Heron: reluctant accountant, musician and fellow prophet
Clive Palmer: banjo wizard, professional catalyst and much else besides ('If he'd done half the things he claimed to have done, he'd need to have been Methuselah with turn for speed' – RW in *Mirrorman's Sequences*)
Mary Stewart: veterinary surgeon and mountaineer.
Wizz Jones: Numero Uno English blues guitarist

Supporting Cast
Bert Jansch: guitar hero and Pentangler
Archie Fisher: scion of Scottish folk dynasty
Davy Graham: cosmopolitan guitar hero
Robin Hall: Scottish folkie and *White Heather Club* icon
Jimmie McGregor: ditto
Long John Baldry: vertically-unchallenged 60s blueser and (briefly) pop balladeer
Hamish Imlach: Falstaffian Scottish folkie
Alex Campbell: gravel-voiced Scottish folkie

Wizz Jones is the blues guitarist's blues guitarist. There are good judges who reckon him the best of a generation that produced the likes of Graham, Jansch and Renbourn, though he's probably the least well-known to the music-listening public. He has however become somewhat better-known of late, as a result of Bruce Springsteen covering one of his compositions (When I Leave Berlin) in concert, and Keith Richards naming him as a formative influence in his fingerstyle guitar technique – according to Keith, he sat devotedly at Wizz's feet in the cloakrooms of Sidcup Art College in the early Sixties. Now into his seventh decade as a professional musician – and playing better than ever, by all accounts – Wizz flits in and out of the early chapters of the ISB story: he was a regular guest at Clive's Incredible Folk Club, and remembers (untrue) stories in the Glasgow papers of Clive scooting off to Afghanistan with the club's funds. Wizz also stayed at Mary Stewart's cottage on several occasions, and he and Pete Stanley can be heard on one of the Balmore Tapes. Raymond cornered him in 1997 at Bradford's Topic Folk Club, and grilled him for Balmore memories...

Wizz: I knew Clive Palmer from London originally, and then we stumbled across each other in Paris in 1959 and briefly worked together there, and then again in 60-61 with Clive and Mick Softly, busking there. And then I went solo, travelled round a bit and came back to England in about 63 or 64, had a kid, and started to play with Pete Stanley on the folk club circuit. I was with Pete till late 66, early 67. I didn't hear from Clive at all for ages – didn't know where he'd gone or what had happened to him – and then I got a letter from him in 1965 saying 'I've been living in Edinburgh in a flat with a guy called Robin Williamson' – he didn't mention Bert Jansch, but I subsequently found out that he was living there as well – 'and Robin and I have been working as a duo singing trad material and I've just opened a club called Clive's Incredible Folk Club, and I've formed a band called Clive's Incredible String Band which is doing Old Timey music. I hear you're working with Pete Stanley, why don't you come up and do a gig at the Incredible Folk Club and you can stay the night where I'm staying?'

So we went and that was an amazing gig, because he'd booked Davy Graham on the same bill. We arrived and there was Davy, dapper in a white suit with a blonde on his arm. The residents were Clive's Incredible String Band, Hamish Imlach and Archie Fisher, and, unknown to me at the time, Billy Connolly was in the audience, Rab Noakes and all these people.

We played the gig, which went fine, and, if I remember rightly, it was an all-night gig. We'd driven up the previous night, arrived in the morning and went straight up to Mary Stewart's, where Clive said he was living. It was difficult to find that first time because it was in the middle of a golf course and we had to drive down a muddy, rutted track. So we drove into this place, which was like Alice's Restaurant, because it was that kind of situation, there were kids and dogs running everywhere, and hundreds of people, and Clive came limping out to welcome us.

So we did the gig that night, and I remember going back at six or seven in the morning, and I went up to bed for a bit and my wife stayed up with the kids. [*Ed's note – Wizz travelled to gigs with his whole family, in a camper van.*] I remember waking up about mid-day and hearing a sitar outside – it was Archie Fisher sitting outside the cottage playing a sitar. It was one of those situations where amazing things happened.

The second time we were up there, which was 66, was when we got a tour of Scotland, and we stayed there for several days. That's the time that those tapes were made. [*See article on the Balmore Hoard – Ed.*] At that time Mike and Robin were living up in the loft, in the roof. We used to go to sleep in the room below and we'd hear them playing together. They were just a duo by then, and I think they'd probably made the first album. Of course, originally it was going to be an Old Timey album, but Joe Boyd heard that they wrote their own stuff, and the album was all original material. Clive hadn't written anything of his own, so he nicked a tune from me, Teapot Blues, and changed it to Empty Pocket Blues and copyrighted it! So I lost that song to Clive, but we're still friends!

Mary Stewart was an amazing woman – still is probably, I haven't seen her for a long time now. She was a vet and she was also involved in cancer research, so she had cages out at the back of the house with hundreds of cats in them. Temple Cottage was a mingling of the climbing fraternity and the folk fraternity in the way that in Cornwall there was a mingling of the surfing fraternity and the folk fraternity. These things don't happen

The three-piece outside Temple Cottage

anymore, they're kind of split, separate areas. But you always had famous climbers coming through – Chris Bonington, Tom Patey, people like that.

That muddy track was the only access to the cottage. We were always getting stuck on the way in or out, and having to be pulled out by the jeep, or a tractor. The cottage was a long, low kind of building; I've got a photograph somewhere of me and Clive sitting outside it. I think Mary's marriage had broken up, and she was there on her own with various students and other people. She had Alex Campbell's kids living there, 'cause Alex had gone off around the world touring and his wife was there with her kids. The house was always full to absolute overflowing. As you can hear on the tapes, you'd sit around at night playing and there'd be eight, nine, ten little kids in the room up 'til midnight just listening to the music. In those days it was unusual, that kind of attitude to everything, and it worked, it really did work. Okay, I'm sure there were problems

Outside Temple Cottage, trying out the new gimbri

there, as there are with any kind of community situation, but it was quite idyllic to come into it. And an amazing amount of good art must have come out of it, quite apart from the Incredibles, because it was such a conducive sort of atmosphere to be creative.

I remember Robin Williamson playing a Blind Boy Fuller blues and thinking, never knew how that one worked. I used to listen to Blind Boy Fuller records till my ears bled trying to work out how he did the guitar parts; and there was one particular song he did, and here was Robin playing it note for note and I thought, so that's how you do it! He'd worked out from the record what the chord shapes were. It was an unusual key that you wouldn't have thought it would be in. It was in G as opposed to A or E, which most Blind Boy Fuller things are in. I thought, bloody hell, what a talent – he can work out all the blues stuff as well as being a fantastic fiddle player!

He could do all that stuff. That's so often the case, isn't it? The Scottish singer Robin Hall, who used to sing with Jimmie McGregor, I remember seeing him one night with Long John Baldry singing gospel and blues, and he had a fantastic blues voice. It always amazes me how multi-talented people are. I've struggled away to play blues all my life, and Robin [Williamson] just did it all, effortlessly.

In later years I met the Incredibles only once. I was coming back from a folk club gig, just like what I'm doing tonight in exactly the same way thirty-odd years on. I stopped at the Blue Boar at Watford Gap, which in those days at two in the morning would be jumping. You'd see all the bands that had been playing at all the universities that night; any night of the week, it would be like that. You'd run into all kinds of people, and I remember bumping into Robin and Mike and Joe Boyd one night. They were obviously on the road touring, so we chatted for a bit. I've not seen Mike since then. I've seen Robin a few times – at a festival in Cornwall in the 80s, and then recently he and I were playing in Jersey at the same time. And we played together in Cornwall again a couple of summers ago, we did a concert together and he played harp on one of the songs I did.

But Temple Cottage, it'll go down in history... it *should* go down in history. It should have the blue plaque.

First Love

Joe Boyd brought the ISB down to London to record their first album around June 1966. Raymond Greenoaken sets it in context.

The First Album. Like the Beatles' so-called White Album, it doesn't have a proper title at all, so that's what it tends to be called. No doubt Joe Boyd concluded that the band's name was sufficiently arresting and memorable to ensnare the browsing eye. The cover design was a timid affair: a black background criss-crossed by thin laser-like red beams, and in the centre a snap of the lads looking earnestly folky and clutching strange instruments they'd clearly never played before in their lives. Flip the cover over and you're confronted by a lot of print: a whimsical and uncredited mini-biog of the band – evidently composed by Mike – introducing them in the guise of various animals, a track list and instrumental credits (no hint of anything more exotic than a kazoo or a mandolin), and pithy notes to each track again provided by Mike.

The message is clear enough: you have a folk album in your hands. And so it was... sort of.

But of course it was much, much more than just another slab of teak-voiced fol-de-rol with hearty choruses. The entry of Robin's fiddle like a demented wasp on Maybe Someday served notice to the listener that typical folk fare was not the speciality of the house. Although it sounds somewhat callow and unambitious set next to *5000 Spirits* or *Hangman*, the ISB's vinyl debut steered a thrilling course away from the mainstream of Sixties folkery. For those who heard it at the time of its release in mid-1966, it carried the force of revelation. This was a band to watch.

There were clues, if you cared to look. Robin's chemise was one such, with its girlish cut (Clive referred to it as 'his dress') and proto-psychedelic hues. Edinburgh contemporaries recall his sartorial extravagance even then. 'He looked like he'd beamed down from Venus,' says Edinburgh musician Barbara Dickson. 'I think he invented the hippy look.'

Clive and Mike, by contrast, look more recognisable as folk club denizens de jour. Mike wears a crisp bri-nylon shirt (accountant's issue), and Clive an ill-fitting lumberjack shirt surmounted by a vet's oilskin lab coat grabbed impulsively off his landlady's clothes-stand as he left Temple Cottage for the recording trip to London. After a weekend's wear in a metropolitan midsummer the smell of the coat, Mike recalls, was somewhere between a hamster cage and a burning tyre. A different, later, photo was used for the US version of the album cover, on which Mike daringly sports the pelt of some tundra-browsing ruminant, and a headband. Robin, by contrast, looks fairly restrained, and Clive, remarkably, is wearing a suit and tie, with matching cap. The cashmere suit had been made for him in India by 'Saville Roy.' It was obviously tough getting them all 'on message' at the same time.

The UK cover photo was taken in Moore's Classical and Early Music Record Store in Poland Street. Allegedly they just walked in, asked if they could take a few photographs, picked the instruments off the wall and posed. It's been suggested that the reason Clive's shirt looks a bit on the bulky side was that he'd secreted a selection of albums under it, though he put this down to the ill-fitting vet's clothes he'd borrowed from Mary Stewart ('I didn't have anything to go down to London in.'). Clive seemed to attract this kind of colourful speculation: another classic was his putative activities as a drug runner in Afghanistan, during which he evaded detection by hiding the contraband in a hollow part of his wooden leg! In fact, both legs were – and still are – flesh and bone; his pronounced limp, which clearly fuelled such rumours, and which Billy Connolly recalls, was the legacy of childhood polio.

Joe brought the trio down to London to record the album at Chelsea's Sound Techniques. Jac Holzman had been sufficiently impressed with October Song to trust Joe's judgement in the matter, and gave him a recording budget of around £150 – fairly miserly even by 1966 standards. According to Clive's account, the album was briskly polished off in a day and a half. The recording technology was somewhat less than state of the art. Clive remembers the three of them sat round a single microphone – but since the full ensemble is featured on only three tracks out of sixteen, this must have been a comparatively rare arrangement. Of course, one of the oddest aspects of the record is Clive's minimal input. This must be put down to Joe's insistence that they concentrate on original material. It's well known that Clive was unenamoured of the move away from their earlier traditional repertoire, and it's no accident that his trademark banjo playing is confined to two of the three traditional tracks. As hinted above, ensemble playing is pretty much at a premium throughout: more than half the tracks are solo pieces, mostly Robin or Mike on voice and guitar.

It will have surprised few observers, therefore, when Clive took his share of the recording advance and beat a path to the Himalayan foothills. Robin, for his part, headed Fez-wards with Licorice on the day he got back from the sessions, having 'not the faintest intention of ever returning to Britain', as he recalled in his chronicle of that era, *Mirrorman's Sequences*. In their absence, the album sailed to the top of the national folk charts and was garlanded by *Melody Maker* as its Folk Album Of The Year. There was unfinished business to be attended to, and when Robin returned to Scotland in the autumn, penniless but with an armful of Moroccan instruments, he and Mike re-forged a partnership that was – for a brief but astonishing couple of years – to shake the rock world to its foundations.

I was already intimate with everything from *5000 Spirits* to *Changing Horses* before I finally acquired a copy of the first album. For Jon Riley and Tony Corden, however, it was the skeleton key into the arcanum of the ISB...

The US sleeve (Elektra Records)

Weird as you could wish for

Jon Riley

Look at it this way. It's April 1967. I'm 17, been a guitar player for just over a year, and joined my first group, a sixth-form folk/skiffle/blues band, the previous summer as washtub bassist. I'm into Bob Dylan, Salvador Dali and Dylan Thomas. In other words, anything deep, weird and/or incomprehensible is automatically good, maaan. I'm also reading beat poetry (Ginsberg, Corso, Ferlinghetti) and absorbing the general experimental musical atmosphere that's abroad these days: these thrillingly fecund days between the Mothers Of Invention's debut *Freak Out!* and the Beatles' Strawberry Fields Forever, lingering in the recent past, and that zeitgeist-defining pair, *Sergeant Pepper* and the Floyd's debut *Piper At The Gates Of Dawn*, hovering in the imminent future.

Our musical self-education involves flipping through the record racks at local shops and swapping albums, seeking out the cool stuff. At that age, you can't define it, but – without any kind of instruction from the media – you know it when you see it. It jumps out at you. 'New' and 'unusual' are only the most obvious prerequisites. It's that naïve, adolescent hunger for the fresh, untrodden path, and our antennae are seeking out musicians who may be holding a light, further ahead on the track we're blindly groping our way down.

This month, I borrow an LP by the unknown 'incredible string band' (naffly named, but in fashionable lower case). Certainly the sleeve-notes don't augur well. The archness of the band's name is abetted by a twee false biog of the group in a kind of *Alice-In-Wonderland*-meets-*Wind-In-The-Willows* style. (Though I have to say this was also pretty fashionable then.) Mike Heron, one of the trio, has written track notes half cute and half quirkily humorous.

The cover photo, however, is enough to sell you the album unheard. (Remember the power of LP sleeves then, when pop 'magazines' were dull newspapers illustrated with poor quality, mostly tiny, black & white photos, and colour TV was still in its infancy?) On this one, three strange-looking guys seem to be standing in a museum basement (box files line the wall); the scruffy, long-haired one is holding what looks like a one-string fiddle made from an old chair leg; the short-haired, bearded beatnik (wearing what appears to be a stripy dress) is supporting a huge, triangular double bass; the one with the cropped Beatle cut and the crude, Red Indian bone structure has an extraordinary, giant guitar-zither thing, almost circular, with a Y-shaped carved head and serried ranks of piano tuning pegs around its edge. An awesomely foreign, unimaginably antique symphony in wood is being displayed. What the hell must those things sound like? Dig it – this band has to be Seriously Weird. The facts that the giant zither has no strings, and that the sleeve-notes mention only ordinary guitars and mandolins, are minor details: their pose is masterful enough; get out that slab of vinyl and shove it on the old Dansette!

Maybe Someday is an audaciously uncompromising opener, beginning with a spluttering fiddle straight out of an Eastern European gypsy camp [*the melody is possibly Moroccan – Ed.*] and an acoustic guitar played with an equally rough attack. I'd hoped for strangeness, but this was a little too strong to start with; like one's first taste of spicy food, I put this aside till later.

October Song is much more approachable. The acid-voiced Robin Williamson sings a sinewy, cleverly twisting melody to an open-tuned guitar. Gentle but sturdy; evocative and moving. 'Birds fly out behind the sun / And with them I'll be leaving'. (Feel that chill dusk breeze on your cheek?) Bob Dylan liked this track, and some lines are indeed worthy of the master:

First LP Cover

'Rulers like to lay down laws / And rebels like to break them / And the poor priests like to walk in chains / And God likes to forsake them' – expertly reducing politics and religion to irrelevant, even childish, little games. (In a reunion concert, Williamson sang the line 'There is no song before it' as 'I never wrote a song before it', implying this was his first composition. Extraordinary if so; he rarely succeeded so well.) Not my immediate favourite then, but eventually stood out as best track on the album.

When The Music Starts To Play: the subject of music itself crops up several times on this album (in Maybe Someday Heron sings of having 'my arms around my music'), especially its spiritual value as a kind of life force. Another common factor is the switches in time signature, the missing beats and lop-sided emphases that add to the music's trickiness. This is counteracted here by a slow, mournful tune of real warmth (in the verse at least, where Williamson adds an effective harmony), though the occasional pauses for whistle-and-guitar interludes break it up too much.

Schaeffer's Jig is a fiddle tune played by Williamson and doubled by third member Clive Palmer on banjo. The timbres mesh in boozy, raucous unison. Unlike the opening track, this harshness is immediately appealing, probably due to the familiarity of the form. This is followed by Womankind, where Williamson deftly mixes Eastern and North African influences with his Scots heritage. A Moroccan flavour was familiar on the fringes of the folk scene (thanks to Davy Graham and Bert Jansch and of course the beat writers before them), but this was more than tourist kasbah twiddly bits. The lyrics are a sensual ode to a lover (trans: it's about shagging), but Williamson has set it in a dark, minor key, and milks those depressive intervals to maximum effect. The vocal slides around the scale, slipping slyly out of it here and there, while the guitar (open-tuned again) pulls off strange chromatic swoops between the verses. Williamson sounds less like a young man in love than one of those unfortunate old ones muttering to themselves that you avoid on buses. 'My heart aches for her', he sings, and it sounds like it. I initially found this track one of the 'difficult' ones; it didn't come out to meet you half-way, was content and secure in itself; but I knew there was something there worth sticking with, a seductive dignity, a sense of authority.

Mike Heron used to talk to a tree when he was a kid. And The Tree is a song about it. [*Mike recently told Andrew Greig that it was an apple tree in his parents' Portobello back garden, and the 'green hills' in the song were Arthur's Seat – Ed.*] Another of those asymmetrical choruses, and hints of Indian influence in the guitar playing. (That Easter, BBC TV had shown Jonathan Miller's brilliant *Alice In Wonderland*, which used real locations and actors without animal costumes; its other masterstroke was to employ

Ravi Shankar for the incidental music. Henceforth, no sound would ever be more suggestive of a lazy, hot summer afternoon than the slow, buzzing twang of a sitar. This film, with its dream-like pace, Indian sounds and druggy overtones, really marked the beginning of the 'Summer of Love'.)

As Heron says in his notes, Williamson's Dandelion Blues is 'nothing to do with flowers and it isn't a blues', but it is one of the most immediately appealing tracks. A bouncy ragtime guitar duet plays a familiar descending chord line, illuminating a song about optimism. Life? 'I do believe it's easy / Don't even have to try'.

How Happy I Am features much the same philosophy, from Heron this time. No matter how badly your woman treats you (the lyrics owe much to old country blues), just tell her how happy you are. That'll really piss her off. It was also, Mike tells us in his memoir, his farewell to his old accountancy firm.

Empty Pocket Blues is Clive's one go in the vocal spotlight: an engagingly miserable dirge that was my second favourite track on first listen. It's not quite a blues, structurally, but is the closest they get, and is distinguished by a highly unusual chord change in the verse – D to B-flat and back, if you want to know. Williamson, on tin whistle, gets his teeth into that melodic droop from F# to F, the sound of true melancholy. (This is equivalent to the effect of changing from major to minor – 'how strange the change' – which Heron would go on to use on Chinese White and Williamson on many tunes, most effectively on Waltz Of The New Moon.)

Smoke Shovelling Song is Williamson solo again, but in robustly humorous mode. Musically resembling early Dylan, this is a tale of a poverty-stricken Edinburgh winter, when it was so cold the smoke from his fire froze solid; you can guess the rest. (Well, if you have the surreal, or dope-assisted, imagination of Williamson, you can.)

Can't Keep Me Here is one of those songs about escape beloved of adolescents, this is Heron at his simplest: a modest fragment of a tune.

Good As Gone has Williamson on the same theme but, typically, more introspective and tangential. An attractive, strong tune begins 'A strange thought just crossed my mind / Paid the rains back in kind / 'Twas the thought of sweet May coming on' – but there's an unsuccessful middle section. He's toying idly with the episodic structures he'd go on to develop at far greater length later.

Footsteps Of The Heron is a song – quite deliberately – about nothing at all: about being alone without being lonely, or inactive without being bored. Unfortunately, despite the song's optimism, this shows Heron at his worst: a 'cute' tune, archly sung, a verse about talking with a 'pussy cat', and other lyrics that sound like jokes but which aren't funny.

Even in 1967 Ni**ertown was a suspect title, but its brazenness was winning and anyway it's an old tune (no lyrics) played on banjo by Palmer. As Heron's notes say, 'this piece of music always seems to bring the smiles running from miles around'. It clanks along like a Heath Robinson machine, with precarious rationality, and is impossible to listen to without grinning.

Everything's Fine Right Now is one of only three tracks on which all three of the band are playing, this is possibly the straightest, simplest song on the album: 4/4 bars right through, every line four bars long, just one key change (in time-honoured fashion) between verse and chorus. Good heavens, they sound like an ordinary group! For me in 1967, the presence of a kazoo was the real imprimatur: these guys are hip to jug band music; they're OK!

I try to guess which of the trio in the photo is which. I get it wrong. I was saddened when the second album came out to see the band reduced to two, particularly because Clive Palmer was the one that had been dumped. How could they? He was the weirdest-looking!

BANJO MAN

Helmut Rheingans on Clive's banjo style

Clive was famed for his encyclopaedic knowledge of classical banjo tunes. 'Classical' in this sense refers to the style of playing rather than the repertoire: the term has replaced 'fingerstyle' as a way of distinguishing this style from the traditional 'clawhammer' playing associated with the south-eastern United States, and from the newer Bluegrass style that relies on finger picks. It was very popular between the 1890s and the 1940s, but declined in the Fifties, swept aside by the skiffle craze. The 'classical' repertoire was actually the popular music of the early 20th century, though it did include a smattering of light classical (in the conventional sense) pieces.

Clive began taking lessons in the early Fifties at the age of ten. By the time of the Incredible Folk Club he was something of a legend owing to his complete immersion in the genre. Joe Morley and Alfred Commayer were the leading composers for classical banjo, and it's to Morley that we must tip the cap for Ni**ertown, written in the 1920s.

Schaeffer's Jig, as the title suggests, was composed by a gent called Arling Schaeffer, a mandolin player active in the 1890s; it's still a favourite piece among classical banjo players both in the States and in the UK.

Dandelion days

Tony Corden finds mysticism, animism and early childhood memories on the First Album.

It's the early evening of a sunny April day and I've been sitting on Dartmoor listening to the sound of church bells from the valley below. All feels well in the world; the church bells are now silent and only myriad birdsong fills the air as I sit in contemplation of the first Incredible String Band album. Listening to it for the first time left me feeling awestruck and I realised that this was the music that I had been searching for all my life.

Mike Heron has said this is his favourite String Band album as the songs were very much played for the love of it, rather than fitting in with prevailing musical styles of the time. The songs are naïve in the positive sense of the word and completely uncool. Each song flutters like a leaf on a breeze and the lyrics and tunes are drenched with a sense of pantheism: the immanence of God in all things. 'My soul swims naked in her stream, and in her meadows lies to dream'.

As I was later to find out, this is the only album contributed to by Clive Palmer, that eccentric and highly original banjoist and writer of some of the most beautiful songs I have ever heard. Empty Pocket Blues is sung by Clive with plaintive whistle playing from Robin. Now maybe it's just me but the few recorded songs of Clive and Robin together seem to be possessed of a special magic. As well as Empty Pocket Blues, there's Schaeffer's Jig with Clive playing banjo accompanied by Robin on fiddle. It jumps and skips like a mad march hare and works for me as a potent anti-depressant. I always get the feeling that it was recorded in a mossy ferny cave below some wild moor.

October Song is a nugget of nature-mystic imagery: 'The fallen leaves that jewel the ground / They know the art of dying'. The miracle of being here at all on this planet shines forth in this song as it does in the others. Womankind is a hymn of reverence to the goddess. Radiant, garlanded faces drift across meadow and woodland.

The songs also seem to express the simplicity and lucidity of a child's vision. A small child tends to view all objects as alive, and this is known as animistic thinking. It is of note that we adults often encourage the child in this animistic viewpoint, finding it somehow attractive. For example, a mother might say when her child trips over a chair: 'bad chair to trip up my little boy'. Part of the charm of String Band lyrics might be the fairly frequent occurrence of animistic expressions. In The Tree we have 'and the light was fading dimly and the sky was crying'. In Empty Pocket Blues, 'even my old kettle is whistling the blues for you'. This album I suppose represents the early childhood of the Incredible String Band.

Smoke Shovelling Song is a delightful piece of whimsy very reminiscent of Lewis Carroll. The winter was so cold that the fire smoke froze in Robin's chimney, so on the possibly mischievous advice of the police Robin sets cheerfully to shovelling the smoke up the chimney with a spade and singing the smoke shovelling song. He goes out into the yard and sees 'just a thousand feet high way into the sky / Was a pillar of smoke full of song'.

On now to the village pub next to the church of the ringing bells to drink some whiskey. An appropriate place to consider How Happy I Am. This one's a playful bit of self-mockery on the subject of power dynamics in relationships. A jolly and completely inane song: 'I won't feel sad till the whiskey's gone'. Good As Gone evokes the carefree and joyous feeling of summer in a particularly lovely way. 'I'll take the southward road' I imagine refers to Robin journeying forth from his native Scotland. That politically incorrectly-titled tune, Ni**ertown, is a great classical banjo tune with lots of plickerty plonk. Mike's Everything's Fine Right Now is the last on this gossamer-bound collection of songs. It was also the first tune that Mike and Robin played at their Bloomsbury Theatre reunion gig in 1997.

October Song

John Quigley finds food for thought among the fallen leaves...

'Well there was one fellow singing those days and he was quite good, I mean to say that his name / Was Bob Dylan...'
– Robin Williamson, Way Back In The 1960s (1967)

John Cohen: Do you think [the Beatles] are more British or international?

Bob Dylan: They're British I suppose, but you can't say they've carried on with their poetic legacy, whereas the Incredible String Band who wrote this October Song... that was quite good.

As a finished thing – or did it reach you?

As a finished song it's quite good.

Bob Dylan, having lived quietly in Woodstock since his motorcycle accident of 1966, broke his silence in mid-1968 to give an interview to the US folk music magazine *Sing Out* – from which the above extract is taken. Talking with John Cohen of the New Lost City Ramblers (the revivalist string band who influenced the early ISB) and Happy Traum, guitarist, author of guitar instruction manuals and editor of the first Incredible String Band Songbook, he seems detached from his earlier career, emphasising his distance from the hurly-burly of contemporary events. It's 1968; the Vietnam war is tearing America apart, many of the younger generation are in open revolt against their parents, and the music industry is being transformed as a result of the changes set in motion by the Beatles, the Stones and himself.

Yet, judging by his comments in this interview, Bob seems to want little to do with all that – despite his interviewer's efforts to get him to 'take a stand'. It's as if, after his hectic mid-60s period of non-stop touring and recording, he just wants to be left alone to get on with his work... So he's reading poetry, he tells us, listening to 'the old songs' – and, presumably, to the ISB's first two albums...

Revival

It was Bob Dylan, of course, who made the poetic song-lyric acceptable in English language pop music (as distinct from Continental Europe, with its long tradition of chanson and cabaret song – Brecht, Brassens, Brel and other singers whose surnames don't begin with B); at the same time, he was responsible for much of the revival of interest in traditional folk music.

When I first heard him, in 1964 – With God On Our Side on Radio Caroline – I was immediately struck by the fact that he was using a traditional (Irish?) tune, and also by his voice, which bore more resemblance to a pub singer than a pop crooner. Within the following four years the folk revival, with Dylan as the dominant (if controversial) figure, bloomed in both the US and Britain and influenced a whole new generation of rock performers in the process.

In a 1967 *Melody Maker* interview, Mike Heron quoted from the lyric of Gates of Eden – a song which is one of Dylan's more ambitious poetic statements – to illustrate the ISB's (very) 1967 idea of personal freedom – 'Leaving men wholly, totally free to do anything they wish to do but die...' It's this kind of intensely word-laden, middle-period Dylan which seems to have had a strong influence on both Robin's and Mike's work on the first two ISB albums – and it's reflected in October Song in particular. So maybe it's no surprise that Dylan singles it out for special praise.

Audacious

And he wasn't alone; Karl Dallas, in a review of *5000 Spirits* in *Melody Maker*, remarks that none of the fine songs on that album are quite so perfect as October Song; and of course there is Mike Heron's tribute to it in the liner notes of the first ISB album:

'Most good songs are the reflection of the writer, upon some aspect of life, but sometimes a songwriter will attempt to throw his whole personality towards the entire area of life, and reflect his outlook fully. It seems to me that such an attempt has been made by Robin in this song, and the result is so beautiful that I can only ask you to listen to it with a mind as open as the one that wrote it.'

An audacious move indeed, and one which comes off. Yet, before I look at October Song in more detail, it's worth noticing how unusual it is in the context of what you might call their oeuvre. For one thing, unlike other early ISB classics – The Circle Is Unbroken, Log Cabin Home In The Sky, First Girl I Loved, Empty Pocket Blues, A Very Cellular Song – it was never revived in the second half of their career, at least not to my knowledge. Secondly, on record it's not, strictly speaking, a 'String Band' song at all but a solo performance by Robin. Thirdly, it hasn't attracted many cover versions – I know of one by The Corries, and another by Northumbrian music specialist Tom Gilfellon. A very singular song, you could say!

At my shiny new school, way back in the 1960s, I read Dylan Thomas's Poem in October. Robin has spoken of his admiration for this Dylan as well as the US one – and although Dylan Thomas wasn't among my own favourites, I enjoyed this poem. Here's how it begins:

It was my thirtieth year to heaven
Woke to my hearing from harbour and neighbour wood
And the mussel pooled and the heron
Priested shore
The morning beckon
With water praying and call of seagull and rook
And the knock of sailing boats on the net webbed wall
Myself to set foot
That second
In the still sleeping town and set forth.

It's a longish poem, but you get an impression of its atmosphere from this extract: a typically dense Dylan Thomas word-picture, a meditation on nature, the passing of time (it's the poet's birthday) and mortality (around 30 is when people traditionally start to think of such things). You'll also notice that the words are chosen for their sound as much as their sense – an indication of how Dylan Thomas influenced both Bob Dylan and Robin – and, if you're sensitive to British accents, a 'Welshness' in their musicality.

Challenging Tradition

This is, of course, another connection with Robin – he moved to Wales in the late Sixties during the Penwern commune era, and settled again there in the late Eighties. Surprisingly, you might think, given the 'Scottishness' of the ISB – which finds expression in the traditional-sounding tune of October Song. Perhaps he just got fed up with the Miserabilist Tendency which still looms large in the Scottish folk revival – inverted snobbery, crude, cliquish socialist-nationalist politics and an attitude of 'I've suffered for my music and now it's your turn' – in which case I don't blame him! However, you can't trace the tune directly back to a traditional ballad, and the words, too, are not exactly what you might expect from a revivalist folk singer:

The words and tune are none of my own
For my joys and sorrows bore it

'There is no song before it' – a statement that challenges, or even negates, the idea of tradition. The next lines express the idea found in much mystical or esoteric writing that the individual's essence, or real personality, is something quite separate from the secondary self which responds to the events and moods of the moment... and writes songs...

Birds fly out behind the sun
And with them I'll be leaving

Here, it's the idea of movement in nature, travel in the sense of a necessary journey towards... what exactly? Knowledge, wisdom, fulfilment? Traditional singers were usually compelled by economic circumstance to spend their whole lives in the same place; but now it's the 1960s and folk revivalists, particularly those brought up in financially-straitened post-World War Two Britain, where foreign travel was a luxury, are developing Wanderlust... Like writers, artists and bohemians before them, many are taking the traditional routes to the Mediterranean and the East... (Good As Gone on the same album also takes up this theme).

Mortality

Like Dylan Thomas's poem and the Tibetan and Egyptian Books of the Dead, usually on hippy reading lists in those days, the song talks of mortality: 'The fallen leaves...know the art of dying'. (Robin must have been in his early twenties when he wrote it). It also talks of longing – yet the singer's movements are still uncertain, 'other-directed'. Which isn't necessarily such a bad thing; indeed, a clearly defined goal and firm, decisive views might actually prevent an individual from gaining true insight into the nature of things:

But I've found a door behind my mind
And that's the greatest treasure
For rulers like to lay down laws
And rebels like to break them...

Note the detachment implied in those lines. Like Dylan in his Woodstock retreat, the singer sees events out in the 'real world' as less important than one might think: inevitable, repetitive, conforming to patterns of human behaviour which don't change, whatever era we (accidentally?) find ourselves living in. This contrasts with power relations; you can identify the 'rulers', 'rebels', and verse two's 'poor priests' and their idea of 'God' in every society. The real treasure, which enables us to break out of these patterns is within, or 'behind', one's mind. And how should one proceed with the relationship to this treasure? The final verse suggests that it's best not to be too pushy – if you're seeking truth you must stay cool, be patient and then truth might seek you in return: '...mostly I just stroll along / The path that [time] is taking.'

So this is a bold, young man's song in which Robin 'sets out his stall' as poet and singer/songwriter, preparing the listener for the path he would take in subsequent works – one which would be as surprising and as erratic as Mike's sleevenotes suggest.

But what about October Song's relationship to the rest of the ISB's work? In a contemporary interview with Robin and Mike, Rick Sanders confronted them with criticisms of their apparent detachment (that word again) during their 1968 London concerts. Fair enough, they responded: maybe that's how our performances struck some people, but we were doing it, not watching it... This was the time following the Beatles' encounter with the Maharishi, when meditation and the abandonment of worldly ambitions were fashionable in the entertainment industry; in summer 1968 *Melody Maker* could even run an article with the headline 'Two Zen monks called the Incredibles'.

Nevertheless that all began to change when the ISB incorporated Rose and Licorice into the band; the detachment was replaced by an exuberance which made their 1969/70 concerts highly enjoyable, until it spilled over into excess on *U*. The music on the *U* album demonstrates the change: the ecstatic gospel-style anthems (mostly Mike) are OK, but much of the remainder (mostly Robin) seems to lack depth. It's as if their reflective faculties are being overwhelmed by sheer enthusiasm, so that in seeking communion with the audience they actually lose a necessary detachment, the ability to step back and view their work from a different perspective...

But all that is water under the bridge now. Years on, Robin is still singing October Song and still pursuing his own path – for which you have to admire him.

After recording the first album, Robin and girlfriend Likky left for Morocco, intending never to return. Robin: 'I thought, having made a record, now's the time to retire.' Robin had arranged to rent out his Edinburgh flat and was intending to live on the proceeds whilst he studied North African flute in Fez and Essaouira. The finances didn't work out as intended, though, and he and Likky were repatriated in Autumn 1966.

Lovers of Evenings... Good Evening!

Raymond Greenoaken clues you in on the unearthing of the 'Balmore Hoard'.

> *In the period between Robin's return from Morocco in late 1966 and the move to Penwern in early 68, he and Licorice spent much of their time at Temple Cottage, Balmore, a few miles north of Glasgow on the A807. Mary Stewart, a veterinarian and intrepid mountain climber, lived there with her five children and kept open house to a constant cavalcade of mountaineers and itinerant musicians.*

During renovations at the farmhouse in the late Nineties, a number of unexpected items came to light, in particular a boxful of battered ¼ inch reel-to-reel tapes, consigned to a dark cupboard decades ago. Some were untitled; others bore the names of some of the wandering musos who had passed through the household. (For instance, there's an hour's worth of Pete Stanley and Wizz Jones running through their folk club set in the kitchen.) Excitingly, a few of the tapes were labelled with the names of 'Robin', 'Mike', and even 'Robin and Mike'. Were these dusty reels hitherto unknown ISB recordings? Mary eventually passed the whole cache on to a friend and ISB devotee, David Clark; with them came two additional items, also found in the same cupboard, which adjoined the room once occupied by Robin and Likky in the period late '66 to early '67. These were a home-made two-string fiddle of Robin's with a soundbox made from a large marine shell and an unfinished watercolour of his which seems to feature small faux primitif portraits of himself and Likky. Together, these articles form what we have come, with appropriate gravitas, to call the Balmore Hoard.

Since David, like Mary, had no access to reel-to-reel equipment, he kindly delivered the tapes into my keeping. And so it happened that in January 1997 your breathless scribe became the first person in thirty years to bend an ear to these extraordinary recordings. Readers, I felt like Howard Carter in the tomb of Tutankhamun...

Sadly, there's a catch: you may never hear any of it (apart from Relax Your Mind, see below)... but who knows?

For one thing, the recording quality is pretty rough. The recordings were evidently made on a lo-fi domestic tape recorder with a single microphone. The tape itself was in fairly fragile condition, and was then over thirty-five years old. Tape hiss and machine hum are frequently present to a distracting degree. In other words, these tapes make the average 70s bootleg sound like a miracle of acoustic technology.

Nothwithstanding all this, the Balmore ISB Tapes are of enormous interest. They fall roughly into three categories: rehearsal sessions, in which Robin and Mike, alone or together, give brand-new arrangements a tentative shake; casual music-making, in which they jam with other musicians passing through the cottage, or bang out selections from their individual repertoires just for the sport of it; and recordings where the tape is left running while they chat, play with the kids or act the goat.

The rehearsal tapes in particular are compulsive listening. We hear songs like The Mad Hatter's Song, The Eyes Of Fate and The Half-Remarkable Question in the very process of formation, often with different words, different chord progressions and different melodic turns. We hear songs we've never heard before. And we get an intimate sense of the personal dynamics between Robin and Mike (and also Likky) in the banter and discussion between the songs. If nothing else, it nails the old canard that they never practised!

Internal evidence suggests that the ISB-related recordings were made in the months between October 66 and February 67. They predate the Sound Techniques recordings [see *The Chelsea Sessions* article], and represent some of the earliest unreleased material that has yet come to light.

On one session, Mike and Robin are evidently assembling their set for the prestigious Albert Hall concert in November 66. They were low on the bill supporting Elektra label-mates Tom Paxton and Judy Collins; it was to be their first-ever appearance south of the Scottish border... followed by other shared appearances at concert halls in Manchester, Belfast and Birmingham. Apart from the songs, which include Chinese White (here referred to as 'Gimbri Song'), No Sleep Blues and Relax Your Mind (a Leadbelly song titivated lyrically by Robin), we hear them practising their introductions to each selection. Anyone who ever played in a band will find such earnestness amusingly familiar.

There are five sequences scattered around the tapes which feature Robin and Mike (occasionally abetted by Likky) performing original compositions of the period – including songs like First Girl I Loved and Blues For The Muse, which would find their way six months later onto the 5000 *Spirits* album. There are several others – including Alice Is A Long Time Gone and Lover Man – which remained unknown to the wider world

'UNLIKE ANYTHING MOST PEOPLE HAVE EVER HEARD BEFORE'

Joe Boyd's programme notes for the Albert Hall gig

'...Most of the songs are written by Mike and Robin, the 2/3 [*of the ISB*] you will hear tonight (Clive is visiting a dream in Kashmir at presstime). Their styles are quite different, but complementary. Their influences are many, and eager critics will enjoy finding a bit of Jansch here, a bit of Dylan there and an overall blues-cum-ragtime-cum Lennon-McCartney or whathaveyou. But 90% of it is all Williamson and Heron. Their songs are unlike anything most people have ever heard before, but as they begin to end their long Scottish exile and play the English clubs and concert halls, it won't be too long before their songs are familiar to the ears of all varieties of music-lovers.'

From the Albert Hall programme, 1966.

until the release of the *Chelsea Sessions* CD in 1996, and a handful that have never been heard again in any form. There are also traditional songs aplenty (mostly from Robin) and a couple of Tom Paxton numbers (one of which, Every Time I Hear The Sweet Birds Singing, Robin relearned from the original tapes to perform at the reunion concert in London in 1997). We also hear Robin extemporising on a Moroccan flute, and Likky reading from an apparently autobiographical story and making up a song around the names of colours. Perhaps the most significant of the Robin and Mike sessions are the following:

Albert Hall rehearsal reel:
Robin and Mike occasionally abetted by Likky
Songs: Gimbri Song (Chinese White)/intro and Gimbri Song/Alice Is A Long Time Gone/Everything's Fine Right Now/intro and When The Music Starts To Play/discussion /Lovers Of Evening.../Relax Your Mind/ discussion/No Sleep Blues/The Half-Remarkable Question

This is arguably the most interesting recording. There's lots of badinage and discussion between the songs, much of it hard to make out, but one can clearly hear Robin and Mike trying out their carefully-scripted introductions to individual songs.

These often take the form of little rhymes. Thus, Mike: 'No place for what the cautious say / When the music starts to play'. And prefixing Chinese White is this peculiar piece of doggerel, recited by Mike and Robin together: 'This magic mountain is going to grow a fountain with a *song* / This is the song he shortly will have sung...' (Imagine the italicised words rendered in singsong stage-Chinese accents.)

Robin, it transpires, had prepared an introduction to the entire set. 'Lovers of evenings – good evening. My name is Robin Williamson and this is Mike Heron. We're songwriters and players, and prophets from the North, and also Seers Extraordinary by appointment to the Wonder of the Universe.' Modest to a fault... In the course of repeated run-throughs, this changes briefly into 'lovers of good evening', amid cackles of mirth. There's also much deliberation over the running order, which Robin itemises as: Relax Your Mind, When The Music Starts To Play, October Song, Everything's Fine Right Now, No Sleep Blues, Gimbri Song and a cover, possibly called Any Kind Of Person. When Likky pipes up to query the order and the allocation of songs between the two prophets from the North, Robin patiently explains the complexities of playing 'in very awkward tunings'; and Mike, sounding a little defensive at having bagged one more song than Robin, bleats: '...but the last one is just as much his as

Backstage in 1966.

mine, and the Gimbri Song is very much a gimbri feature, so it's fairly well kind of balanced.' Robin concurs, and Likky appears mollified. 'Anyway,' says Robin brightly, 'we're sure to get an encore...' Reports suggest they didn't! (It seems that their set, for whatever reasons, was truncated to a mere three songs.)

The performances are utterly absorbing. When The Music and Everything's Fine are pretty close to the album versions, and Gimbri Song is Chinese White in all but name, but No Sleep Blues has a slightly different melody and chord sequence, and features two additional verses, of which the following is a tentative reconstruction:

'When you meet a dragon
Don't try to put him in a stew
Just speak to him politely
And he'll see what he will do
When the dragon answered
Well he didn't have too much to say
He just burned down a couple of towns
Said Follow me boys, that's the way'
(Likky chuckles off-mike)
'The lock mends the locksmith
Oh but there's a big lorry going by
Its dulcet intonations
Make a wild solilo-quy
Just then I had to leave for London
I felt like going right away
Travelled much faster than the speed of light
And even got there the previous day'

Metaphysical or what? The final item on this session may well have been recorded on a later occasion: certainly, it isn't mentioned as part of the running order referred to earlier. Unrecognisable from its instrumental intro, it turns out to be a very early version of The Half-Remarkable Question, with a different opening verse, a different riff, a different melody line, and a wholly dissimilar feel to the stately *Wee Tam* version a couple of years later.

This is a hectic, headlong, bluesy thrash with Mike's guitar sounding thoroughly un-sitarlike, and a wild, dishevelled vocal from Robin. It's plainly a long way from being well-rehearsed, and bumps to a halt on two occasions, but it absolutely roars with energy and passion. Intriguingly, it features the line 'I hear some kind of bird singing in my heart' to a fluttering, descending melody. At this stage, Robin hasn't mastered the tricky rhythm of the line, so Mike obligingly claps it out for him during a break in proceedings, adroitly adding a half-beat to tie it in more closely with the underlying pulse of the song. Here, distilled in a timeless, private moment, is that mysterious quality, that chemistry, that made Mike and Robin such a formidable and complementary team. Rivalry there may have been – jealousy, even, if Joe Boyd is to be believed – but here we can witness just how well they could work together and spark each other off.

'Tape hiss and machine hum' - the Balmore tapes. (Bryan Ledgard)

Mixed Reel: Robin and Mike/Robin solo/Robin and Mike/Robin and Likky

Songs: Relax Your Mind/Feet Off The Floor/ discussion and instrumental jam/Going To Leave This Country/Down On The Track/More Pretty Girls Than One/One Hundred Forty Three/Gypsy Girl/autoharp doodles/wordless song/How Sweet To Be A Cloud/two guitars (1)/two guitars (2)/The Half-Remarkable Question/The Eyes Of Fate/Anach Cuin/Ring-a-doo-a-daddy-o/ Month Of January/The Dreadful Wind And Rain/The Cruel Brother/George Collins/Sir Patrick Spens

This reel is probably a tessellation of several distinct sessions. The opening sequence finds Robin and Mike ambling through items from their joint repertoire, with Robin surprisingly strumming an autoharp throughout. Feet Off The Floor, evidently a Heron composition, sounds like a first cousin to Everything's Fine Right Now; the phrase I've used for the title is practically all I can make out of the lyric. It's followed by an impressively slovenly jam complete with occasional scat vocals. After a solo rendition of Lover Man, Mike drops out, leaving Robin to croon a selection of Carter Family and Uncle Dave Macon items to his own autoharp accompaniment. This medley concludes with avant-garde doodles on the autoharp, a wordless song of possibly Scottish provenance, and finally 'How Sweet To Be A Cloud' from the 50s radio adaptation of *Winnie The Pooh* – familiar in a slightly modified form as the prelude to 'Little Cloud' on *5000 Spirits*.

At this point the tape offers up a slice of clarinet-driven modern jazz, then the final chorus of Penny Lane on the radio ('I just love that trumpet!' chirps Alan Freeman), before returning us to the company of Robin and Mike. It's back to guitar for Robin as the two turn out a brace of short guitar duets. These sound largely improvised; the first includes a couple of phrases that eventually found their way into Gently Tender. Bert 'n' John it ain't, though it's tuneful enough – but at one point Robin declares 'It's a bit bland,' to which Mike shrugs, 'It is, yeah...'

Robin then runs through The Eyes Of Fate alone, and Mike rejoins him for another stab at The Half-Remarkable Question. By this time the words are as per the *Wee Tam* version, though without the third verse and with the bird still singing in the author's heart. Mike adds a vocal harmony to the chorus. It's fairly raucous, but rather more restrained than their earlier attempts on the Albert Hall rehearsal tape.

Robin returns to the autoharp for another medley of traditional songs, with Likky chipping in at intervals. This includes the Ulster song Anach Cuin, whose melody was later to do memorable service in The Circle Is Unbroken, and another Irish song, 'Twas In The Month Of January, which Robin and Likky reprised a capella in concert in 1971. Finally, reaching again for the guitar, he launches into a full-blown (almost 8 minutes) rendition of the briny old Scots ballad Sir Patrick Spens. This is a breathtaking performance, showing an extraordinarily mature grasp of traditional ballad idiom for a fluff-chinned whippersnapper just turned 23. Bert Jansch described the early 60s Williamson as one of the finest young traditional singers in Scotland. Here's the proof.

The Balmore Tapes offer an unparalleled insight into the everyday lives of Mike and Robin in those high and far-off times: a magic casement into a lost world of incense and nonsense, music-making, Mad Hatters and tea parties, and the forging of a musical partnership whose legacy still delights and engrosses more than half a century later. Lovers of evenings – good evening!

The Balmore recording of Relax Your Mind finally saw the light of day on the 2008 Hux Records ISB rarities compilation *Tricks Of The Senses*.

Overleaf 1967 promo pic. (Paul Hunter collection)

A variety of views on 5000 *Spirits Or The Layers Of The Onion* and *The Hangman's Beautiful Daughter*, the creative partnership with dancers Mimi and Mouse – and a look at ISB Edinburgh.

Chapter Two

In early 1967, the reformed two-piece ISB became regulars on the London music scene at such clubs as Les Cousins, Joe Boyd and Hoppy's UFO Club and The Speakeasy. They also made their first TV appearance, playing Chinese White on BBC2's Late Night Line-Up. *After some trial recordings featuring some of the Balmore material (see* The Chelsea Sessions *article), they released* 5000 Spirits *in July 1967. It was Number One in the folk charts for a couple of months, got them their first of many John Peel sessions, a slot on Julie Felix's TV show and a brief appearance at the Newport Folk Festival; it was compared by* Melody Maker *to* Sgt. Pepper. *Below, Raymond Greenoaken sets the album in stylistic context and Stuart Godfrey and Robert Pendleton provide their takes on it.*

Performing 'Little Cloud' on a 1967 Julie Felix show pilot.
(Raymond Greenoaken archive)

Songs from Planet Gimbri

Raymond Greenoaken

It was Summer 67, forever enshrined in the lexicon of journalistic clichés as The Summer Of Love. Ah yes, I remember it well: the Six Day War, the Nigerian invasion of Biafra, fighting on the streets of Hong Kong, 'negro riots' throughout the US, Peking and Canton devastated by Mao's Red Guards, the usual shenanigans in Vietnam... Peace, man!

But we had other things to occupy our idealistic young minds through those soft summer days. Flower Power was at the height of its pomp; we sang about going to San Francisco as though it were just a 37 bus ride away, and raided municipal flower beds to festoon our luxuriant locks. Change was in the air – everything seemed possible.

Events were soon to expose the fragility of our dreams, of course. But, during that summer which promised so much and delivered so little, a young man sat in a London recording studio, drew a double bass bow across the strings of a battered Moroccan lute, and sent me on a fifty-year journey of musical discovery.

Admit it: unless you were among the privileged few who had actually seen the Incredible String Band in concert around that time, you wouldn't have known a gimbri from a gladiolus. There must have been many of us who studied the rainbow-hued phantasmagoria that was the *5000 Spirits* sleeve and wondered what manner of creature a 'bowed gimbri' might be.

Ah yes – the sleeve. If ever an album sleeve said 'Buy me!' *5000 Spirits* was that sleeve; but I was 15, still at school, and my pocket money just about stretched to a few superhero comics and the *Football Monthly*. I only bought one album in the entire year – the Stones' *Satanic Majesties*. Better the devils you know, I thought, quite unaware of the ISB influence reputedly at work on that record. It wasn't until early 1968 that I finally got my hands on a copy of *Spirits*, and once the stylus landed on the groove, all was revealed.

Side one, track one: Chinese White. A bonny little Heron ditty about the pleasures of the contemplative life. Four introductory bars of staccato guitar, then out of the Dansette's tinny speaker it came – coiling and keening, an ancient, lonesome, unearthly, melancholic wail: the gimbri. I was electrified. It sounded like music from another planet, or conjured from one of those fantastical instruments described by Lord Dunsany in his tall tales of the kingdoms Beyond the Fields We Know – the ninninarb, or the zootibar. But this was the real thing: a small North African folk lute associated with the Berber people, and usually played with a plectrum made from a hard native reed. It looks as though Robin was the first person to play it with a bow. So we were hearing an entirely new voice, for all that it sounded like it had come from the morning of the world.

I wanted more of this. I could detect similarities with the Indian dilbuba (as featured on *Sgt. Pepper*) and the reedy trill of the Renaissance rebec. I later discovered that you could get a vaguely similar noise by bowing an Appalachian dulcimer. Nevertheless, the gimbri was in a class of one. It wasn't the only thing that attracted me to the band, but it stood as a sort of emblem for the unique, eerie, seductive music of the ISB.

Shortly thereafter, I saw the band in concert for the first time, and witnessed the gimbri in use. The spell was complete. But *5000 Spirits* was the door into the glittering dark, and Robin the smiling psychopomp that admitted me to a new realm of sonic experience.

There were other exotic sounds in there, of course: the sitar, the oud, the bamboo flute; and even the conventional instruments had an odd edge to them. Robin's guitar had been modified to produce a buzzy, sitar-like effect on the upper strings. His playing style, too, was extraordinary. During his sojourn in Fez he'd adapted the style of the Arabian oud to the guitar in a way that was quite unprecedented. Davy Graham had hinted at elements of oud-style in his playing a few years earlier, but Robin's guitar work on The Eyes Of Fate took it a lot further down the road; No Sleep Blues, Painting Box, The Mad Hatter's Song and First Girl I Loved also included oud-like passages, as do several songs on *The Chelsea Sessions*. In 2010 Robin told writer Jeanette Leech: 'I brought back a number of instruments, and with them the idea of trying to put a number of styles into one piece of music... I thought the idea was to make music without technique: try instruments you couldn't play and break down the barriers between performer and audience.'

The Joseph Spence Connection

Less well acknowledged is what Mike was doing on guitar at the time. Despite being originally recruited to the band as a 'strummer', he concentrated on finger-picking styles on the first album and *5000 Spirits*, broadly based on country-blues playing. Close scrutiny of tracks like Little Cloud and Gently Tender, however, shows something quite new creeping in. Here the picking patterns are syncopated in a way that seems to echo the playing of the Bahamian guitarist Joseph Spence.

Spence's style is, frankly, inimitable. At its most complex it often incorporates several distinct rhythms simultaneously, cunningly syncopated to mesh together indivisibly. Spence was a true original; few guitarists have attempted to follow the stylistic trail he blazed, and of those only Ry Cooder has made it round the first bend. Mike's project, if I'm right in my surmise, was less ambitious. On Cloud and Tender he plays the vocal line off against the picking pattern, syncopating each at different points in the bar to set up tense cross-rhythms. It's Spence, and yet it ain't... but whatever it is, it's thoroughly beguiling and shows he'd been listening closely to the Bahamian field recordings Elektra had put the band's way.

It's difficult in these days of World Music and hectic, rampant eclecticism to appreciate what a pioneering album *5000 Spirits* was, way back in the 1960s. Eastern influences were de rigeur at the time, but the ISB gave them a startling new spin. Sitars, in particular, were old hat – the Beatles, Stones, Yardbirds, Traffic and Donovan were all twanging away on them. On *Spirits*, however, the instrument was heard for the first time in the hands of an Indian master musician – the pseudonymous Soma – rather than a Western pop guitarist. Nazir Jairazbhoy was born in England of Indian parents, grew up in India and was appointed lecturer in Indian music in 1962 by the School of Oriental and African Studies in London. In 1967 he was giving sitar lessons, and taught Richard Thompson, Andy Summers and Mike, amongst others. The authority of his playing on The Mad Hatter's Song makes a stern contrast to the diffident efforts of Harrison, Mason et al.

The ISB also broke new ground by drawing inspiration from the musical idioms of North Africa and the Near East. Hitherto, musicians in search of exotic ingredients to spice up their homely fare had seldom looked further than the subcontinent. Robin's time in Morocco exposed him to the street music of the Rifs and Berbers and the ululations of the Muezzins, as well as the classical music of the oud and quanun. These influences clearly seeped into both his playing and composing during that period. On The Eyes Of Fate, we can hear the oud-like flurries of notes, the vocal arabesques, and a mournful modality that seems to hint of ancient lunar rites in the caves of the High Atlas. Another composition of the time, Born In Your Town [on *The Chelsea Sessions*], offers a similar mélange; probably its stylistic similarity to Eyes and My Name Is Death kept it off the LP.

From Delhi to the Mississippi Delta; from Balmore to the Bahamas; from Fez to Planet Gimbri – *5000 Spirits* was a ticket to ride for the flower children of 67. Once I'd heard that haunting 'animal voice' (as Gil Murray calls it) at the beginning of Chinese White, I knew there'd be no turning back. I'm still travelling...

Stuart Godfrey fell for the old 'hippy in a VW bus' routine...

Ah yes, I remember it all (from before...) *5000 Spirits*, the first album I loved. Incredible String Band, the first 'group' I loved. First Girl I Loved (you guessed it), the first song I loved. How old was I? Well, seventeen of course. Where was I? Not where I should have been – I was supposed to be taking part in the weekly cross-country run favoured by my sports-master for those boys not sufficiently motivated/skilled/fit (stupid?) to play rugby. I had however ended up (muddy plimsolls, shorts and all) in the wonderfully Bohemian-seeming flat of a good friend (Mick) who, a couple of years older than me, had already left school and parental home and was well into the hippy lifestyle...1968 and all that! There were a couple of other sports drop-outs with me; Mick was a kind soul who was happy to let us rest up in his flat for a while and then drop us off (battered VW microbus with 'psychedelic' stickers? – you bet!) near the end of the cross-country course. Mick was a real music aficionado and had a seemingly endless supply of albums and (by no means common in those days) a decent stereo to play them on.

'A knickerbocker glory of multicoloured delights'

Anyway, this particular day as I slumped in Mick's tatty but comfy armchair my senses were assailed by a disturbing yet beautiful sound... 'First girl I-I loved ... time is come I will sing this sad goodbye song...when I w-as seventeen-en...I used to kno-ow you...' I was, at the time, as desperately 'in love' as only a seventeen-year-old can be. The object of my desire was a nymph-like fledgling hippy chick with (inevitably) long red hair. By the time Robin had got to that line about 'me I remember your long red hair... falling in our faces as I kissed you...' I was GONE – I mean big-time. I also remember I cried (real tears!) at the end of that song: 'she is pretty... she's a true friend of mi-ine...' and the gut-wrenching interplay between Robin's guitar and Danny Thompson's bass...fortunately my companions were out of the room at the time. What else do I recall from that first hearing? Whimsical images of little clouds and funny hedgehogs...'hot' blues guitar licks...sitar and other strange whining or wailing instruments

I'd never heard of... 'I am the question that cannot be answered...' Who were these guys? I had little time to study the amazing cover for clues... but what a cover! A real knickerbocker glory of multi-coloured delights on the front and a mysterious shot on the back of two enigmatic faces peering out from some sort of undergrowth... strewth, just two of 'em? The flame-emblazoned names proclaimed 'Robin Williamson' and 'Mike Heron' – little did I realise that the names were transposed and so for a long while I believed that Robin was the dark-haired one... (I wonder how many others fell for that one?). All I knew, and this I cherished in my heart as Mick delivered us (each looking suitably exhausted from our 'run') near the finishing point, was I loved this album with a desperate passion and I had to possess it. I eventually bought a copy, even managing to get a loan from my bemused parents as I simply could not wait six weeks...

All other String Band albums eventually came my way, and all have a special place in my collection and in my affections, but *5000 Spirits* is so special that subjective consideration, even after so many years, is impossible. Sure, the next couple of albums were maybe stronger in terms of breadth, vision and cohesive creative input. *Wee Tam* in particular is a massive achievement, a sustained flight of creative fancy unequalled in popular music. *Hangman* is just breathtakingly beautiful... and yet, if for some bizarre reason I was forced to relinquish all my ISB albums save one, there would be no contest – *5000 Spirits* it would be. The first album is great, but it still had something believable, attainable about it. There are some wonderful songs, some fascinating images evoked, and a lot of it is plain good fun – but there was never any doubting that it was basically folk club stuff – the instruments, time signatures, vocals, the whole general approach was more or less familiar. That album could, with some justification, be filed under 'Folk... Contemporary'. And it remains a spot-on little indicator of what was happening at the sharper end of the progressive folk scene of the mid-Sixties.

But what are we to make of *5000 Spirits*? This did not seem to come directly from any one identifiable source. The cover alone gave so many apparent 'clues' to its meaning that it ended up a complete mystery. And unlike the muted, even severe, tones of the first album cover, this one fairly exploded upon your senses – as did the music! 'Psychedelic' was a much used (and abused) term at the time, but even that was so closely identified with the passing fashions of *Top Of The Pops* that it was clearly inadequate for music of such evident consequence as this. I came to the conclusion that, whatever its roots, the music on this album was pretty much beyond categorising. It is, after all, what it could be, why worry what it should be?

Simon & Marijke's flyer for the Painting Box single, early 1968 – still confused about who's who! (Elektra Records/Adrian Whittaker)

A revisit from Planet Gimbri

Chinese White ... the first time I guess that many of our sleeping ears were startled by the unique sawing, wailing sound of the bowed gimbri – definitely a sound from some strange, 'other' world, and prompting many a vague imagining as to what on earth it looked like – but it fits Mike's strangely beautiful song perfectly. Mike's vocal delivery is strong and controlled, the imagery suitably mysterious ('The bent twig of darkness grows the petals of the morning...' – think about it!) and Robin's stirring harmonies on the 'will your magic Christmas tree be sh-i-ning...(hold it!)...gently..all around' bit...brilliant. Mike's lovely little guitar figure (DEE dee dee DEE dee dee DEE dee dee DEE – with apologies to the musically literate) was one of the few snippets of music I mastered with my one-string guitar technique (along with 'Crossroads' on the bass string, natch!) but somehow it never sounded so good without the gimbri. Anyway, great song, not the 'breezy' opener of Bonzo Dog fame but a scene-setter and appetiser par excellence.

No Sleep Blues...aha, a blues song. But what's this, no 'woke up this mornin', my woman done gone left me'? Instead it's 'delerium nosleepum, in a cloud of nylon foam' [*Andy Roberts interjects: I couldn't help but comment on this bit. If No Sleep Blues isn't a song about trying to get to sleep whilst hallucinogens are coursing round the old bloodstream, I'll go buy a hat and eat it. Been there many times.*] and the dawn 'creeping up when it thinks I'm not looking...' and perhaps the most enchanting of Robin's observations in the song when he sings about mixing his feet with water 'just to see what could be seen, and the water it got dirty and the feet they got quite clean'. Superbly dextrous guitar from both Robin and Mike and (especially noticeable on the CD) the venerable Danny Thompson giving it some 'welly' on the double bass. A cracking little song which rips along in fine style; you can see the links with the first album but Robin's naively profound lyrics lift the song to another, higher level.

Back to Mike for Painting Box, one of the outstanding tracks on an outstanding album and our first meeting with Licorice and her finger cymbals. Danny Thompson is there in manful support again as Mike sings of a love so special it can only be described in the colours 'somewhere in my mind'. OK, it is very 1967, but no-one could deny the beauty of the piece with its delicate guitar/flute interplay and lovely harmonies from Robin, Mike and Likky. The less said about Julie Felix's version the better, eh folks! Mike was clearly on top song-writing form with this, followed as it is by the most remarkable Williamson composition to be heard so far.

Brilliant or barmy?

The Mad Hatter's Song is the longest piece on the album at five and a half minutes. Along with The Eyes Of Fate it is the most lyrically challenging and musically adventurous song of the collection and would not be out of place among the accomplished compositions found on *Wee Tam*. Sitar and tamboura duties were entrusted to Soma [*see above*], while John Hopkins plays some jazzy piano in the curious 'West-meets-East' honky-tonk section which is juxtaposed with the other-worldliness of 'Prometheus, the problem child, still juggling with his brains'...it's the kind of song that does juggle with your brains a bit...is it really as profound as it seems or is it just a bunch of very clever wordplay? Brilliant or barmy? Both, probably. While Robin's apparently profound musings on the meaning (or otherwise) of it all may not stand up to close scrutiny, the whole thing just sounds wonderful and helped establish the String Band (and Robin in particular) as dispensers of prime mythical/magical/wisdom. Sure, it was another time, and maybe we were all too willing to attribute profundity to anything which wasn't obvious, but still this song towers over most of the psychedelic pap which was being served up by all comers at this time.

Wherever the Mad Hatter takes you, it is still a surprise to encounter Mike's Little Cloud, the most twee song on the record and either a delight or an embarrassment depending, I guess, on your state of mind at the time. I know it features on many people's hate lists but me, I've never minded it. It certainly sounds like it was fun to do, Robin clearly had fun on the drums and rattles and all of my girlfriends liked it...it was meant to be a laugh and so it is, leave it alone why don't you! All together now: 'YAT-ta-ta-ta TA TA, Ta-ta-ta-ta BOW WOW'. Having bashed away happily on drums in Mike's song, Robin is very much more Williamsonesque (as well he might be) on Eyes Of Fate: a sort of 'if you thought Mad Hatter's Song was deep, just listen to this' song which again transports the listener to the mysterious recesses of the Williamson imagination. By this stage the album has become something of a roller-coaster ride between different musical styles, held together by the strength of the material and the quality of the production and recording, all well up on the first album.

Blues For The Muse is something of a return to the nimble fretwork and snappy lyrics of No Sleep Blues. Mike blows some trusty harmonica as Robin eulogises (I think) about his guitar, 'It's a low special, baby that's enough for me' – is this the lovely Levin? [*see Robin's instruments interview, Appendix*] Hedgehog's Song follows... ahh, what sweet memories this lovely little song brings forth. Lightweight it may be, but there's no denying its charm and accessibility. For many people I'm sure this was the first String Band song they actually liked and it was tremendously influential in winning the band a wider audience. Although it could be accused of plumbing the 'cute novelty song' depths (like Little Cloud) it is really far too accomplished and skilful a piece to be so lightly dismissed. And I'm not ashamed to say it is still one of my favourite ISB songs.

DESERT ISLAND HEDGEHOG

Rowan Williams, Archbishop of Canterbury, selected Hedgehog's Song as one of his Desert Island Discs: 'The chorus is a powerful summing-up of life and relationships'.

I can say little more about First Girl I Loved – an astonishingly mature and accomplished love song of jaw-sagging beauty and an immediate 'classic' by any standards. If Robin had never written or performed another song this alone would have ensured him a place among the greats. His guitar playing on this track is outstanding. I would put this song up there with Sandy Denny's Who Knows Where The Time Goes (interesting that Judy Collins covered them both). Just superb.

It Could Have Easily Been A Disaster

Robin gets the oud out for You Know What You Could Be, a sprightly Heron romp with up-beat lyrics and fluttering flute and also – never one to miss an opportunity – has another bash on the drums as well. Not a stand out track, it fills a perfectly happy space between First Girl and Robin's extraordinarily doomy My Name Is Death. A classic theme which brings to mind numerous medieval illustrations of Death and the Lady, this could easily have been a disaster; indeed in less capable hands the delivery could have sounded hopelessly melodramatic and contrived. Robin's sombre tones and sparse guitar, however, produce a haunting and starkly beautiful, if disturbing, piece.

Gently Tender is something of a second cousin to Chinese White in its overall feel – nice guitar licks from Mike, and Robin comes over all multi-instrumental again. Joe Boyd obviously enjoyed bunging on some echo and generally playing around with the protracted end sequence with nonsense jabberings and false endings – if it all seems a little contrived now it certainly didn't then; great stuff. The closer is Way Back In The 1960s, another slightly 'clubby' track with hot guitar and bass from the Heron/Williamson/Thompson trio (what must the grizzled jazz/folk stalwart have made of these two impossibly gifted, elfin hippy characters? We can but wonder...). The humour is of its time, of course: 'We made our own amusement then, going to the pictures' and 'We still used the wheel', but the song scored heavy credibility points with its mention of Bob Dylan. Probably did ol' Bob no harm at all, either.

It's difficult to imagine a more eclectic and yet completely satisfying collection of songs. *5000 Spirits* really is more than the sum of its parts. Although *Hangman* sold more copies and probably represents the supreme artistic achievement of the band, this album is such an encapsulation of a special moment, a breathtaking upswing which could never possibly be recaptured. The Beatles had progressed steadily to *Sgt. Pepper*, but the ISB's rise to familiar heights with only their second album was meteoric, to say the least. I am just glad I was around when it happened.

Kindred spirits

Robert Pendleton peels back the layers to examine the album's multiple themes and allusions.

Like myself, a lot of people probably first heard of The Incredible String Band in the summer of 1967, with this second album. My own earliest memory of the band is listening to The Hedgehog's Song early one Soho Sunday morning on a prototypical cassette recorder, huddled with some very stoned and sleepy people in the back of a Ford Anglia van after a night in Les Cousins' folk-blues cellar. I had never imagined that you could accompany 'folk' music with anything other than a guitar and harmonica, nor had I ever heard folk songs about hedgehogs, clouds and mice playing football! Although the full import may have escaped me that Sunday morning, I was hooked, and it must have been sometime later that year when I first saw Robin and Mike do a spot at Les Cousins' itself, a very cramped folk cellar in Greek Street which was only slightly bigger than the Anglia van. Although the only song I remember them playing is Way Back In The 1960s, I recall the tremendous energy they projected – both on their feet with two guitars and a harmonica on a tiny stage like an island in the crowded sea of bodies. And then, of course, I got the albums, and the rest is...

Well, it's not actually history at all. I can think of few other albums of the Sixties that I've played consistently and with such regularity through the years. *5000 Spirits*, together with those other four major ISB greats – the *First Album*, *The Hangman's Beautiful Daughter*, *Wee Tam And The Big Huge* – are impossible creations which open up completely fresh imaginative realities through the sheer inventiveness of their lyrical and musical achievements. And although we catch clear glimpses of this powerful innovatory quality on the first, more traditionally 'folky' album (The Tree especially comes to mind), it is *5000 Spirits* which fully succeeds in bringing the traditional genres of British and American folk music together with what we now call 'World Music'. More importantly, though, it merges different types of lyrics – those of love songs, children's songs, religious songs – to create the wonderful blend of whimsical fantasy, poetic rhapsody and mystical speculation that was to become the hallmark of the band.

The transcendent imagination

If the album possesses any single theme, it is that of the transcendent imagination, the mind's ability to generate and perceive alternative realities. Before we even place the record on the turntable, the cover gives us some strong pointers towards this. Both front and rear covers express an unfolding cosmic vision of the wonder and variety of natural forms perceived by the single, unified eye of mystical perception, which is surely also the eye of the artist creating and organising a balance of tensions between opposing forces. The expression or organisation of wonder and variety is a central concern of *5000 Spirits*, in which a range of genres and themes find expression in freshly imaginative imagery, while intricately-textured musical arrangements enact perceptions beyond the possibilities of verbal language. These are the 'layers of the onion' – but whether they correspond exactly to 'five thousand spirits', I couldn't really say.

This sense of wonder is especially clear on Mike's Chinese White, which introduces a dreamlike mood of heightened consciousness which is to be sustained throughout *5000 Spirits*. Robin's bowed gimbri and Mike's droning open E guitar tuning lead into a mantra-like chant which shifts unusually from major to minor, while the sense of estrangement is deepened by Robin's harmonies on the refrain, set in octave and second note intervals as well as more conventionally Western thirds. This sense of unfamiliarity is offset, however, by chord progressions more typically used in British and American folk music.

Just as the music shifts between the familiar and less accessible, so do the lyrics. The song appears to start with a dawn scene that encapsulates a kind of creation myth as a new day or world is (re)born: 'The bent twig of darkness / Grows the petals of the morning'. The ensuing invitation to 'Come dip into the cloud cream lapping' may be puzzling until we recall that Chinese White is a shade of paint. Together with the bent twig and petals, this seems to point towards a Chinese or Japanese print, perhaps in the book which the singer peruses in the second stanza.

[*The striking opening lines of Chinese White are reminiscent of a Basho haiku, though without the required syllable pattern. Rose, though, agrees they were inspired by 'a Japanese print – Hokusai or Hiroshige. I remember a picture of twig coming in from the foreground with a landscape in the background – but that may be something we painted, in imitation of the Japanese.' – Ed.*]

The song then moves to a more personal level with the singer's wish to transcend this material world, which in the process of creating itself is simultaneously headed towards entropy: 'I can't keep my hand on the plough because it's dying'. This plough – presumably in the painting –

turns up the earth and plunges the twigs and petals back into darkness, but the singer is not so much interested in these dying generations as in laying himself 'down to dream' with his 'arms round a rainbow'.

In the second stanza, the day grows brighter, as though we have now been magically drawn inside the world of the painting, where the singer is 'climbing up these figures with the 'sun tugging at [his] shoulder'. Creation is again balanced by death and decay: with every step the singer takes, he thinks his 'feet are getting older', and, although 'the crystal dreams' of physical existence may be 'unfolding', he 'can't keep [his] eyes on' the very medium through which these come to him, 'the book', which is 'mould'ring'. While the world evolves into light, it is his quest to transcend these material forms in favour of the 'rainbow' which he embraces in order to 'lay... down to dream'.

With this emphasis upon dream, Chinese White finds its setting in a twilight area between the darkness and the dawn where mystical insights may take place, perhaps those same 'twilight thoughts' that can 'melt the slush of what [we] have been taught' in Mike's You Know What You Could Be. Beginning impersonally, moving into conscious exhortation ('Come dip') and then into the first person ('I can't keep'), the forms of address

'Climbing up these figures...' painting by Steve Small.

seem to follow this emergence into a higher consciousness. Finally, the refrain shifts into the second person, with the singer including us listeners in his quest for transcendence: 'Oh will your magic Christmas tree be shining – gently all around?' That very special personal 'tree' from the first album has now become the mythological world tree, with roots in earth and water and branches in the air and the fire of the sun (of which the Christmas tree is a more recent manifestation). Here, it becomes a central core of our personal spiritual consciousness, an oddly familiar phenomenon, which we are invited to keep alight and glowing.

A zany romp through the unconscious

Hard on the heels of Chinese White, Robin's No Sleep Blues now switches the mood to one of bizarre humour, plunging us backwards, as it were, into 'delirium-no-sleepums' – a surreal, dreamlike state of consciousness somewhere between sleeping and waking – delivered in a more colloquial tone than Chinese White. This is surely the definitive ode to insomnia – which does seem to be a recurring motif in the blues (think of all those lyrics along the lines of 'I lay down last night turning from side to side'). Here, Robin takes the opportunity for a zany romp through the unconscious, accompanied by a jazzy flute and a sitar-sounding lead guitar – a musical texture considerably thickened by Danny Thompson's bass; who would want to get to sleep anyway?! Anyone who's experienced this kind of half-waking insomniac state will immediately recognise the phantasmagorical thought/image-association generated in the creaky old mansion where 'rains rot the rafters', 'mice play football', and 'the dawn comes sneaking up when it thinks [you're] not looking'. After the first and second stanzas, the imagery gets even more interesting, with language itself beginning to play the kinds of slippery tricks psychoanalysts of dream have often commented on. Here, though, Robin is concerned with seeing how far he can take the sheer artistic playfulness of the whole thing: putting a picture on a nail and then 'in a pail' is a delightful nonsense rhyme, leading with absurd logic to a flight of cartoonish fantasy around the pail itself, which 'got so rusty / I called it red, red, red for fun...' Robin moves effortlessly between this mode of freakish fancy and images that reverberate with a haunting sense of mystery: 'Aloof like a Sultan / In the autumn of your heart'. Not only this, but he can recapture the previous mood, taking off again through word association on wings of brilliant cartoon fantasy: 'But the heart got so hearty / That it pulled for the shore / And the sailors fired a big salute / And it made my ears quite sore'.

Beginnings of albums are always important for setting the tone of the whole: here, the eerily mystical Chinese White and the zanily

‘I know one of you two’s got my whistle and I’m staying here till I get it back!’ Up a tree, 1967. (Mary Stewart collection)

phantasmagorical No Sleep Blues offer us invitations to embark on a journey to alternative realities or different levels of consciousness. By continually modulating in this way between different kinds of songs, the album as a whole expresses a sense of transcendent wonder with the infinite variety of creation. Cutting across Robin's and Mike's contrasting styles of composition, we have the humorously bizarre romps of No Sleep Blues, Way Back In The 1960s and Blues For The Muse, which, together with the 'almost-children's songs' (Little Cloud and The Hedgehog's Song) complement the romantic love lyrics of Painting Box, Gently Tender and First Girl I Loved, and the mystical or philosophical speculations of You Know What You Could Be, My Name is Death, The Eyes Of Fate and The Mad Hatter's Song. These different genres are constantly played against each other – sometimes meeting and merging within the same song – to provide dazzling depictions of the infinite variety of existence.

A hymn to the transcendent power of music

We see humour and mystery coexisting again with perfect ease in the second of Robin's spoof blues songs on the album, Blues For The Muse, which sees the singer emerging from 'delirium-no-sleepums', drinking up his coffee 'to drive dreams away', and declaring 'most any morning, I like to be born into my guitar day'. While the song evokes the playfully erotic relationship which many guitar players have traditionally established with their instrument – She's a noted rider, / I just can't seem to let her be' – Blues For The Muse is also a hymn to the transcendent power of music, in which humour merges with and even intensifies the profoundly serious. In this way, the lyrics shift from the playful throwaway of 'They say it's all butterflies / Don't let your dreams get in your eyes' to the astounding pronouncement that 'Orpheus made the sun rise / 'Cause he knew how to play'. As if this is not enough, the refrain takes another sharp turn in musical and lyrical mood, when Robin cuts straight from this pæan to music into a kind of send-up version of My Name Is Death, the light tone of which comes across in a parody of a blues motif: 'Well it's all right / You're in the graveyard now'. Yet here the transition is as fitting as the musical progression from verse into refrain, for death is the other face of rebirth and creation – we're always in the graveyard, or what was later to become the 'dear old battlefield'. This suggestion of darkness balances the lightness of the verse, intimating that the bright Apollonian world of art and music is in part a wondrous dream which we erect as a bulwark against death and destruction: 'But lucky in life I swear sometimes / Surely going to have to meet your leaving day'.

Similarly, there is more than meets the eye in the last of Robin's spoof blues songs, Way Back In The 1960s. At first sight this seems (seemed?) no more than a humorous send-up of his/our generation growing into old age. Although it's a common human tendency, Sixties culture was so emphatically youth-oriented that even fewer of us may have been able to imagine that we would be like our granddads, saying things like 'Hey, you young people... I can't even understand you when you're trying to talk slow'. Developing this incongruity, the song has some great gags centred around the old man's long and rambling memories, which are deliberately compressed into shorter-than-appropriate lines to give the effect of him trying to get it all out: 'There was one fellow singing in those days and he was quite good, I mean to say that / His name was Bob Dylan'. But behind the romp, I now see hovering the grim reaper figure of My Name Is Death, which just happens to be pretty close (deliberately so?) to this last track. For we are getting older, as we thought we never would (you too, second-generation ISB fans, even though you were born in the 1980s!). This breezy little number has been ticking away all these years like a time-bomb, but the amazing thing is that the realisation by no means detracts from the humour: the song is still as funny as it ever was in spite of – perhaps because of – this sombre intertext. Thirty years on, we laugh even more heartily 'in the shadow of the gallows'.

Light Relief

There is also more depth beneath the surface of Mike's lighter contributions to the album – Little Cloud and The Hedgehog's Song. Although written loosely within the genre of the children's song, in which animals and natural phenomena assume characters and voices, these works also become parables for the theme of cosmic perception that *5000 Spirits* explores. With images like 'Happy rain come falling down / Red, green, blue and golden', and Robin's drums and rattles driving its delightful calypso rhythms, Little Cloud provides immediate light relief from the weighty philosophical considerations of The Mad Hatter's Song which has preceded it. In spite of this, Little Cloud also restates some of the themes of The Mad Hatter's Song – for example: the Chief Cloud, with his feeling that 'a cloud's supposed to be sad / To cry and weep and tear its hair and all', would be quite at home in the nightmare world of the 'ruined factory' with 'the normal soul insane / Who sets the sky beneath his heels / And learns away the pain'. And surely the spiritual guide – the 'archer' or 'the lover of laughter' – who appears at the end of The Mad Hatter's Song – finds a more youthfully innocent incarnation in the Little Cloud, who 'laugh[s] and dance[s] and sing[s] a song', inviting the insomniac narrator to 'Come float with me to distant lands wondrous and fair'.

When we come to The Hedgehog's Song, we find a somewhat similar soul guide, this time cast as a talking animal set in a parable which crosses the children's song with the type of love-lorn complaint found in Maybe Someday on the first album. The effect of this is to introduce a note of playful self-irony to the singer's over-fastidiousness: '...it isn't just me I got to please / There's this funny little hedgehog / Who's always around / And the only words he ever sings to me are these'.

[*From Mike's memoir,* You Know What You Could Be, *we now know that the original hedgehog was the logo on the label of his girlfriend Michelle's favourite French Burgundy, Le Hérisson – Ed.*]

While The Hedgehog's Song uses a children's fable to lament the tribulations of love, Painting Box takes a similarly playful tone to what at first sight seems a 'straight' or more conventional romantic love song. One of my all-time String Band favourites, this apparently simple ditty never becomes tarnished. It has a magical quality which can be traced to an especially rich vein of visual imagery as well as to its intricate musical texture. While Robin's flute and lead guitar, Licorice's backing vocals and Danny Thompson's bass together weave an enchanting pattern of arabesques around a fairly straightforward four-chord progression, there is a freshness of conception and playful innocence brought to this celebration of new love: 'When the morning of your eyes comes waking through my shadows...I whisper to the baby raindrops playing on my window / And tell them gently this is not the time that they should weep'. However, while the song does celebrate romantic love in some way, it does this in a cosmic rather than personal setting, drawing attention to how the experience can give a window onto a mysterious dimension of being. Although romantic love's transfiguration of the mundane world has been celebrated by poets throughout the ages, the emphasis of the refrain is more upon the depth and wonder of the mind's imaginative spectrum than any of the qualities supposedly possessed by the beloved: 'Somewhere in my mind there is a painting box... Just lately when I look inside my painting box / I seem to pick the colours of you'. The last line has rather the tone of an afterthought.

In the second stanza, the singer's new sense of transcendence carries his 'Friday evening's footsteps... far away' from the 'black town' that he's 'plodding dully through'. Although the playful images keep a sense of humorous distance from the singer's heightened state, the tone finally serves only to make it more mysterious: 'My eyes are listening to some sounds that I think just might be springtime...'. Throughout the song, this kind of whimsical humour combines with a poetic sense of estrangement to contextualise romantic love within its larger potential for allowing release of the ego. We see this most clearly in the final stanza, where this playfulness combines with a traditional image of the lover adrift upon a sea of turbulent emotions. As 'the purple sail above [him] catches all the strength of summer', passing fishes (aquatic agents of the hedgehog?) stop to inquire his destination: '...my little ship is sinking / But I kind of like the sea that I'm on and I don't mind if I do drown'. It would seem, though, that this is more an act of surrender to 'the song of life', as in You Know What You Could Be, than to the lover himself.

The personal and the eternal

Later on in the album, Mike's Gently Tender again takes up this theme of romantic love in a cosmic context, although now at the end of an affair [*Probably with French girlfriend Michelle – Ed.*] rather than the beginning. Just as Painting Box expresses equanimity in the blossoming of love, so here at the finale there is a sense of balance between the personal and the eternal: 'Sometimes I think I was true / But then I loved the stone beneath my feet as much – usually' (I've always greatly enjoyed the pregnant pause before that qualifying afterthought, which comes over as a wrenched cry of confessional anguish). The song begins as a mournful elegy: 'Gently tender falls the rain / Washing clean the slate again / But leave me please behind my brain / The slightest shadow on her'. Recurring as a repeated motif, this last line marks an interesting departure from what – if more conventionally-phrased – might instead have been 'shadow of her'. 'Shadow on her' seems a more detached expression, which focuses upon the acts of memory and perception themselves rather than their objects. Recalling themes and imagery from Painting Box, the mind, as the centre of all being, projects the objects of perception outward from itself as the rain falls and washes clean the slate of the emotions associated with the love affair.

However, some of these 'shadows' the singer does wish to retain, such as the ones 'dancing through the pink milk blankets / Where my mind lay dreaming gently..' and – reintroducing the playful tone – the 'shadows crawling through the green bush trees where my toes crept...'. In this way, Gently Tender oxymoronically fuses contrasting moods of elegy and celebration, setting memories of joy in the form of 'good good loving' against present pain: 'And now all my wine is water... / And my pearls are clay'.

The song maintains a delicate balance between regret for the passing of love and the possible destruction of that love itself though anger or jealousy: 'Slowly spitting crawls the snake...Venom that might easily shake the slightest shadow on her'. As if to emphasise this double perspective, the point of view shifts constantly from the third to first person, moving from the personal to the more detached and back again. This creative tension also comes over musically, in the joyful noise created by the richly textured harmonies of the refrain, which – together with Robin's spicy mix of bowed gimbri, drums and flute – qualifies the plangent tendency of the verse.

In a different way, Robin's First Girl I Loved also develops the conventional love song within a larger perspective. The tone of the lyrics seems immediately more personal, though, than Painting Box and Gently Tender, with such reminiscences as: 'We parted so hard / Me rushing round Britain with a guitar / Making love to people / That I didn't even like to see'. In spite of this, the primary appeal lies in the song's general relevance and application, for surely almost everyone has a first girl (or boy), now with a separate and independent life which contrasts poignantly with the original adolescent intimacy. This is surely the reason why First Girl I Loved is Robin's most covered song, with at least five versions to date. Delivered in a form hovering somewhere between a love lyric and an open letter, the initial declaration is one which many people could make and which many singers can identify with: 'First girl I loved / Time has come I will sing you this sad goodbye song...'. The mood of nostalgic elegy is enhanced by memories of love set in surroundings of romantic nature: 'But in the wide hills and beside many a long water / You have gathered flowers – and they do not smell for me'. In spite of such poignant musings, however, the singer is firmly grounded in the realities of the present, realising that this 'grown-up female stranger' is 'probably married now', with a 'house and car and all', and that if 'I was lying near you now / I wouldn't be here at all'.

In this way, First Girl I Loved retains the multiple perspective of the ISB love song, joining a mood of wistful romantic memory with a practical, down-to-earth approach which allows for some slightly humorous touches – such as his old flame having become a suburban mum who's joined the church of Jesus. It also offers a welcome critique of an over-used and inaccurate euphemism, in the form of the denial: 'I never slept with you / Though we must have made love a thousand times'. Again the double mood is reflected in the musical setting. Typically touching on as many as three or four different notes per single syllable, Robin's voice – higher and more plaintive than nowadays – embellishes the elegiac mood, while his beautiful flatpicking in the resonant open G tuning creates poignantly lyrical – almost harp-like – effects, especially on the sixth and major-seventh chords voiced high up on the guitar neck. By contrast, the refrain's straightforward bare chords and more conventional structure, rhythms and progressions have the effect of returning us temporarily to the real world of suburbs, kids, houses and cars, in which the singer is at pains to emphasise that he is not – and that if he were he wouldn't be here singing the song.

Clearly, all the songs discussed so far are 'philosophical' in the sense that they encourage us to see the world in a new way.

Life, death and fate

However, in contrast to the love songs and children's songs – in which philosophical speculation is somehow not the prime raison d'être – there is a final group of works that seems primarily concerned to interpret, or at least interrogate, the universe. In the first of these, You Know What You Could Be, Mike calls our attention to a transcendent reality existing beyond the illusions that make up our everyday mundane world and its assumptions: 'Read your book and lose yourself / In another's thoughts... His twilight words may melt the slush / Of what you have been taught'. These 'twilight words' of inspiration take up the theme of Chinese White again, with consciousness growing out of the 'dream' or 'night' world of spirit. Reinvoking the rainbow embraced by the spiritual quester in the earlier track, the chorus of You Know What You Could Be drives home this vision of the cosmic dimensions of consciousness: 'Listen to the song of life / Its rainbow's end won't hold you / Its crimson shapes and purple sounds / Softly will enfold you'. However, an element of threat or danger is added to the enticements of the 'crystal dream', for there is risk in engaging fully with 'the song of life', which as well as containing 'crimson shapes and purple sounds' also 'gurgles through the timeless glade / In quartertones of lightning'. The sombre note of the closing lines – 'No policy is up for sale / In case the truth be frightening' – creates a suggestive tension with the characteristically light and breezy texture of the song's accompaniment (comprising Robin on oud, mandolin, drums and flute, with Danny Thompson on bass). The song is not quite as innocent as it seems, then.

The end of You Know What You Could Be provides a fitting transition into Robin's monastic chant My Name Is Death – a reworking of a traditional ballad – which is as dark as You Know What You Could Be is light. The opening is couched in the form of a riddle – 'I am the question that cannot be answered / I am the lover that cannot be lost / Yet small are the gifts of my servant the soldier / For time is my offspring, pray what is my name?' Having captured our attention in this way, the song proceeds to draw us personally and insistently into its dark message: 'My name is

Death, cannot you see?... And you must come with me'. The fact is as bleak as it always is, and yet the song has a powerfully brooding sort of appeal, especially in the dramatic dialogue between the lady who wishes 'just one short year more' and the implacable dark figure that bids her: 'Lay your jewels aside / No more to glory in your pride... And you must come to clay'.

Different in tone and emotional texture as it is, though, My Name Is Death may in fact be the linchpin of the album, in that it throws into sudden relief the general celebratory tendency of the rest of the songs. Other tracks such as Blues For The Muse do this internally, but My Name Is Death sets up a vibration that reverberates darkly through *5000 Spirits*, even touching something as light as Way Back In The 1960s. Robin's best mystical songs are often imbued with a sense of tragedy, although this is usually combined with a compensatory tendency, a sense of the epic possibilities of rising above the contingencies of existence and taking flight upon the wings of spirit. Certainly this is the major focus of The Eyes Of Fate and The Mad Hatter's Song. Of these, The Eyes Of Fate is I feel the weaker of the two, a pale imitation of The Mad Hatter's Song – which for me is the album's tour-de-force. In The Eyes Of Fate, though, while Robin's voice creates a mantra-like chant around a bass drone and the chorus has some striking and resonant harmonies, the lyrics are the most abstract of all on the album – 'Oh who can see in the eyes of fate / All life alone in its chronic patterns'. This evokes none of the usual

My Name Is Death—painting by Steve Small.

vividly concrete mental pictures of the ISB's writing at its best, while even such initially promising lines as the invitation 'Oh swan, let me fly you to the land of no wind blowing' are not developed in any significant or consistent way. With its pronouncement that 'All is in the eye and in its blinks of seeing', the song creates a thinly abstract discussion of the Buddhist concept of 'Emptiness' or 'void', but in its denial of the world falls prey to a frequent misconception of Buddhist emptiness as nihilism.

In other ISB songs, nature embodies, reflects and expresses spirituality; here, however, by contrast, it becomes a series of conceptual assertions: 'All rivalry and opinion still cast their wild spells / Effort and contrariness change the directions of time'. There are some hints of Robin's usually brilliant flair for images, as in 'the lion [that] still growls in your hollowness,' but the final plea – 'Please let's be easy, please let's be friends / Watching and learning like small children' – seems weak and inconclusive, failing to provide any real clue as to how we can avoid being 'servant of fate or fate for a servant'. Again, in spite of resounding harmonies, the chorus promises musically what it does not deliver verbally. The 'wild and stormy rollers', although evidently intended to contrast a sense of cosmic wildness with our 'hollowness', break down when examined within the larger image pattern of the song. This is because there are two completely different and unresolved senses in which wildness is used: the cosmic sense of abandonment in 'wild and stormy rollers' contradicts the random wildness of the 'spells' cast by 'rivalry and opinion'; there is also a confusing contradiction between the lion's cosmic form of wildness and the stillness and apparent peace of 'the lands of no winds blowing', which is not resolved in the song.

A shamanic vision of a spiritually bereft world

Altogether, it seems to me that The Eyes Of Fate might well have been a rough draft for The Mad Hatter's Song, and therefore could have been omitted. The most positive thing I can say about it, I'm afraid, is that it serves to highlight the genius that shines through the rest of the album. Nowhere is this more apparent than in the magnificent Mad Hatter's Song. If there is a crowning achievement of Robin's writing on the first three albums, then this is it – a complex, shape-changing shamanic vision of a spiritually bereft world, which emerges finally as an inspiring message of beauty, hope and redemption.

The Mad Hatter's Song opens with Robin chanting a mantra-like Jeremiad on one minor chord against a sitar and occasional handclaps. The lines relentlessly build a stunning series of eloquent lamentations for a civilisation which, restlessly seeking happiness, ironically further loses touch with it in proportion to the desperation with which it attempts to grasp at it: 'Oh, seekers of spring, how could you not find contentment / In a time of riddling reason in this land of the blind?' However, this sternly judgmental first section soon modulates into a transition that takes a more compassionate stance towards the trials and tribulations of ordinary life, now bereft of the comforts of traditional religion: '...live till you die / My poor little man / For Jesus will stretch out his hand no more'.

The second section – a lyrical interlude, in which sitar and guitar pick out a double melody behind Robin's voice – develops this softer tone and affirms that there is still hope of redemption: 'But in the south there's many a wavy tree... In the warm south winds the lost flowers move again'. [*Musician Dick Paul wrote in to us to point out the autobiographical links here to Robin's mind-opening trip to Morocco and return to 'the land of the blind' – Ed.*] Taking up again the initial image 'seekers of spring', this sets in motion a complex vein of imagery which runs throughout the song, primarily setting in opposition winter and summer as figures for alienated discontent versus spiritual fulfilment, while also invoking associated oppositions such as city and country, north and south, industrial and pastoral.

In the third section, the song metamorphoses into a piano blues, a musical genre fittingly expressive of the rougher aspects of city life lived by the 'seekers of spring', where the voice of the stern prophet mingles

Probably the only time Mike & Robin spoke with one voice – first national press coverage in the *Observer*, July 1967. (*Observer*/Adrian Whittaker)

THE WATERSONS down home by the Hull docks (above). The Watersons – two sisters, Norma and Elaine, their brother Michael, and their cousin John Harrison – whose unaccompanied singing is the most exciting sound in the present traditional revival. Of gypsy descent, they were brought up by their tinker grandmother. They've recently retired from the highly profitable club scene to concentrate only on big concerts and recording. 'We sing because we enjoy it; club singing was just killing us so we stopped.' They wear mod clothes, and sing medieval ritual songs in a tough, earthy fashion, despite the complex harmonies. Now they are considering applying this technique to a pop song.

THE INCREDIBLE STRING BAND (left), tend to wear a strange assortment of clothes, play a strange assortment of instruments, litter their speech with metaphor and quote at length from Robert Graves' 'The White Goddess'. But that, they say, is the way they are. Mike Heron and Robin Williamson are in their mid-twenties, quiet, unassuming and intelligent. They've been playing in Scotland for some time, and were first launched on the London scene last autumn – and the London Folk world has never seen anything like them. 'Some people call it "silly music", but in a kind way,' they explain. 'It's just self-expression. People probably like it for the wrong reasons, but we try to sing about the things that really do matter . . .' Their unusual combination of Eastern and Western themes and rhymes are played on guitar, fiddle, gimbri, flute, whistle and mandolin.

with the gentler tone of the second section: 'And if you cried, you know you'd fill a lake with tears / Still wouldn't turn back the years since the city has took you'. This section concludes by invoking the title motif within a typical blues figure – 'Mad Hatter's on my mind' – to create the image of a raving urban lunatic, a denizen of the ruined Dickensian city in which the modern nightmare is seeded.

Changing tone again, the song briefly returns to the prophetic chant to warn us that we 'must have to see clear sometime'. The fourth section, which follows, is an astounding panoramic vision of the horrors of the industrial west, during the course of which Robin traces the roots of the post-Renaissance *Weltanschauung* to the pioneering attempts of Greek civilisation to master nature. The Titan Prometheus is cast as the villain of the piece, who by disobeying Zeus and giving man the gift of fire is arguably responsible for the entire development of technology. A personification of our Western tendency – ever on the increase – to place excessive faith in rational thought, the Titan is cast as a stunted subterranean computer nerd, a 'problem child still juggling with his brains', who, bereft of the wild and untamed visions of Dionysus and his leopardskin-clad followers, has only 'limping leopard visions' to make the miserly blood race in his veins. We then cut to 'the ruined factory', a haunting image of Western modernism, where 'the normal soul insane' perceives the world completely askew and, placing material and intellectual values over spiritual ones, 'sets the sky beneath his heel and learns away the pain'.

Conveyed in an impetuous rush of words and images, this nightmare vision of our so-called civilisation now dissolves into a lyrically fingerpicked transition in which the prophet shape-changes once again back into the more compassionate spiritual guide figure who can lead us out of 'the land of the blind' – he is, literally, the 'seer': 'I am the archer and my eyes yearn after the unsullied sight'. We then move into the inspiring affirmation of hope that comprises the fifth and final section, where this Sagittarian bowman shoots his spiritual arrow far beyond this dark illusion-filled world. Recalling the creation myth depicted on the album's cover, he tells us he was 'born of the dark waters of the daughters of night', and that paradoxically he dances 'without movement after the clear light'. Yet in spite of such metaphysical mind-twisters, finally the vision he presents is very simple and direct, couched in a plea for love and compassion towards our fellow beings: 'O prithee an fate be kind / In the rumbling and trundling rickshaw of time'. [*The songbook prints this line as 'Perithean fate' – Robin's since clarified that it's as above – using 'an' in its archaic form to mean 'if'. So now you know – Ed.*] The final message of the song – and perhaps of the entire album – is that behind the confusion, the links to a transcendent vision of the world remain in place, and we are still 'hooked by the heart to the kingfisher's line'. This image always recalls for me T.S. Eliot's poem sequence Four Quartets: 'After the kingfisher's wing / Has answered light to light, and is silent, the light is still / At the still point of the turning world'. While Eliot's image is more specifically Christian, The Mad Hatter's Song links the kingfisher with its own line of imagery expressive of nature, summer and the south, to signify the redemption that is ours for the asking. Finally, one last stunning sleight-of-hand manoeuvre shifts the song briefly back once again into the mantra-like mode of the opening. With the same multi-toned lingering on single syllables, the prophetic guide now declares his intention to return as a Bodhisattva to lead the fallen world towards the light: 'I will set my one eye for the shores of the blind'.

It is a happy thought that this is exactly what the Incredible String Band were themselves doing in creating works of art such as *5000 Spirits* which follow us untarnished down through the years, bringing us closer to the cosmic dimensions of consciousness through these ceremonies of musical and lyric magic. Perhaps I did dimly surmise this at the very beginning, slumped in the sleepy back of that Sunday morning Ford Anglia van.

The 5000 *Spirits* Cover

Raymond Greenoaken

Simon Posthuma and Marijke Koger, two Dutch artists known as The Fool, were invited by the band to design the *5000 Spirits* sleeve. The Beatles had commissioned a painting from them for the inside spread of the *Sgt. Pepper* gatefold which was never used, but their *Spirits* sleeve became an instant psychedelic classic. If *Pepper*, with its dayglo marching band and ironic juxtapositions, embodied a distinctly English sensibility, all surface glitter and brittle whimsy, *5000 Spirits* reached deep into the dark tarns of the mythopoeic mind to confect a dazzling heraldic assemblage of archetypal, pan-global motifs, all drenched in vibrant rainbow hues.

The composition is dominated by a winged, Janus-headed hermaphrodite, embodying the eternal polarities of dark and light, male and female, life and death. Around this figure surge the great cyclic forces of growth and decay; stars and planets whirl in their courses; and strung across this phantasmagoric scene like a line of psychedelic washing are the swirling letters of THE INCREDIBLE STRING BAND. Whatever else it was (pretentious, chaotic, deliriously daft?), it was certainly eye-catching. And, as importantly, it faithfully reflected the music it accompanied: songs that seemed to be coming from everywhere – from myth, dreams, nursery-rhymes, bedsits, haunted ruins, oriental souks and foggy Scottish backstreets. The rear cover carried the title *The 5000 Spirits Or The Layers Of the Onion*; below it Mike's and Robin's names are edged with flame. Framed by the lettering is a photo (actually a reverse image, trivia buffs) of the two minstrels looking mysterious among shrubbery, Robin resembling a furtive satyr, Mike as expressionless as a herm. You just knew these guys were interesting...

BRIEF ENCOUNTER – JOHN 'HOPPY' HOPKINS.

Interview by Adrian Whittaker.

The late John Hopkins, whose 16 short bars of recorded fame appear on The Mad Hatter's Song was a legendary Sixties mover and shaker. He was one of the founders of *International Times*, and set up the UFO Club with Joe Boyd. In 2001 I met him at his video training and production company, The Fantasy Factory.

It was Joe, apparently, who suggested a blues piano part on Mad Hatter and introduced him to the ISB. Hoppy had originally run into Joe in the States, where he was the *Melody Maker* photographer at one of the Newport Jazz festivals, and they'd been friends from the time Joe came to set up the London Elektra office. What did Hoppy remember of the session, I asked.

'Not much – I remember feeling nervous and a bit overawed, working with "real musicians". They played through the sequence and I rehearsed it a couple of times – in the key of G, I think. Joe would say – keep that bit in, leave that bit out. We recorded it in one take. The whole thing took less than an hour. One of them – Robin I think – had perfect pitch and I was impressed by the way he could sing these strange, North African scales perfectly – it was eerie.'

My own image of the *5000 Spirits* sessions is of a fog of dope and incense wafting through the studio. Not so, it seems:

> 'No. There was plenty of dope and incense *elsewhere* in that period... I was very unfamiliar with all the studio technology – in hindsight I wish I'd paid more attention to that side of it – but it felt more like being in a garage – a clutter of equipment, microphones and cables.'

Hoppy thinks he probably got a session fee ('Joe was always very honest and upfront about money') but, sadly, didn't hang around to watch any more of the recording. '*5000 Spirits* is one of the tapes I play in the car – it triggers strong memories of the time I was running around with Suzy [Creamcheese]. Joe was a great talent spotter, and his gift was to be able to take what musicians could do and turn that into a finished record. I think he should be in a hall of fame somewhere!'

'THE MOST INVENTIVE SOUNDS ON ANY SCENE BAR NONE'

A short but pretty comprehensive album review, possibly by Tony Palmer, in The Observer, *August 1967*

Mike Heron and Robin Williamson... are currently writing the most beautiful songs and making the most inventive sounds (with oud and bowed gimbri as well as conventional blown, fretted and struck things) on any scene bar none.

Traditional blues, free-form sounds, middle-eastern rhythms and harmonies, plainsong chant and madrigals are all effortlessly combined in the sounds whilst whimsy, fable, allegory, sly satire, science fiction and lofty metaphysical imagery conjoin in the lyrics. Emphatically not to be missed.

Joe Boyd's original try-out sessions for 5000 Spirits *surfaced on Pig's Whisker records about three decades later. David Kidman reviews the CD below.*

The Chelsea Sessions 1967

David Kidman

Why is this record so special? It can be seen as a kind of 'missing link' between the *First Album* and *5000 Spirits*. It comprises thirteen tracks recorded by Robin and Mike as demos of 'works in progress', for Joe Boyd at Sound Techniques Studios, Chelsea in early 1967, unearthed in the Island vaults in 1985. These thirteen tracks are of both musical and historical interest.

An important point is that of the 13 songs, only six – The Mad Hatter's Song, The Eyes Of Fate, Gently Tender, First Girl I Loved, Blues For The Muse and Little Cloud – actually ended up on the *5000 Spirits* album. As you'd expect, the arrangements are for the most part simpler, and there's a tentative air to the delivery at times; surprisingly, though, most of these demo versions sound close to being fully realised. They sound fresh and convincing, and could easily have formed a credible basis for the band's second album if the decision had been taken to produce it on similar lines to the first (i.e., keeping the arrangements fairly simple).

Comparing these demos with their final versions on *5000 Spirits* is fascinating: First Girl I Loved is less driven, more relaxed. Blues For The Muse comes over less obviously Dylanesque and, while not quite so tautly constructed (the demo version has a whole extra section and a repeat of the final verse), still almost manages to achieve overall coherence. Gently Tender gains by losing its concluding passage of chaotic babble, and has a wonderfully effective gimbri line accompanying the 'wine is water' section; I was also struck by how much You Get Brighter seems to owe to Gently Tender in terms of structure (e.g. Good good loving = Krishna colours on the wall...). The demo of The Eyes Of Fate is more compressed, spontaneous and urgent-sounding, with a more florid and undulating vocal line, the *5000 Spirits* version only superior in the 'Ory Ory' chant which generates a hypnotic momentum through its slower tempo.

The Mad Hatter's Song is perhaps the most interesting of the demo versions, with its impetuous rhythmic drive and improvisatory phrasing, particularly in the difficult opening section; Robin shows a command of a variety of different vocal styles, with the 'blues' section more believably shaded than on the final version. The demo's only real weakness is the unconvincing resolution of the 'Prometheus' section, which seems premature. Of the six demos of songs familiar from 5000 *Spirits*, Little Cloud is probably closest to its final version, but the demo sounds more fun, less prim and proper, as it really benefits from Robin's puckishly capricious harmonies, right from the more wayward unaccompanied introduction.

Of the other seven *Chelsea Sessions* songs, only three will be in any way familiar. The Iron Stone is a surprisingly early but successful 'first draft' of *Wee Tam*'s epic ballad, which, while missing all its instrumental embellishments, its final section of text and its delirious windblown instrumental 'cap and bells' apotheosis, includes some intriguing lines which surely would have been worthy of retention. There's Robin's simple and poignant God Dog (rendered just as unforgettably by Shirley & Dolly Collins on *Anthems In Eden*), which was presumably stockpiled because it just wouldn't have fitted right on 5000 *Spirits* (let alone *Hangman*). Mike's Lover Man (covered by Al Stewart on *Bed Sitter Images*) is full of period charm and whimsy. Despite an attractive pseudo-Caribbean lilt (reminiscent of Can't Keep Me Here), its melodic similarity to Painting Box may well have ruled against its inclusion on 5000 *Spirits*. [*Lover Man was actually recorded for the album and turned up decades later, labelled 'Song' on the tape box. We were researching material for* Tricks Of The Senses *and as soon as we heard the first notes of Danny Thompson's double-bass, we knew we'd got an outtake from* 5000 Spirits. *– Ed.*]

The remaining four songs comprise three of Robin's and one of Mike's. The latter, Frutch, is plain silly, somewhat Dylan-influenced, and would have undermined the integrity of 5000 *Spirits* if it had been included. Robin's hitherto-unreleased contributions, though, are emphatically not of a throwaway nature. Born In Your Town marries Robin's intense oud-style picking to brooding philosophical verse in a similar manner to The Eyes Of Fate (perhaps this explains its omission from the album), but more successfully and less obscurely. See Your Face And Know You is a little gem, a kind of minor-key Arabian hoe-down with a jaunty old-timey feel, embracing some acute and surreally humorous juxtapositions (pre-echoes of Lordly Nightshade and Maya here!). Finally, there's Alice Is A Long Time Gone, which, though lyrically enchanting, seems just a tad awkward melodically and stylistically in comparison with the other songs.

BORN IN YOUR TOWN

Robin explains the Edinburgh background to the song:

'I remember writing Born In Your Town, 'cos I used to like to walk by the Dean Village and along the Water of Leith to Stockbridge – it's a deep sort of gorge in the middle of Edinburgh, with a beautiful dark river, and in the autumn the yellow leaves fall onto this black water... you know, 'The autumn speaks leaves to the lost deeps forever / In the hands of the watchers a page is turned over / And the clouds echo on, on the face of the river'. You see the reflections in the water, giving the impression that the gods are watching from behind the clouds'.

‘Mike and Robin and some songs...’

Adrian Whittaker

When Al Stewart’s first LP, Bed Sitter Images, *came out in autumn 1967, String Band fans puzzled over these lines in his song ‘Beleeka Doodle Day’:*

‘I had a week once in Italy
With Mike and Robin and some songs...’

What was that all about, we wondered. The archives of *La Stampa* have turned up a brief Turin news item from April 1967:

‘The “Folk Club Italiano” opens tonight in the premises of the old horse-drawn tramway, in Corso Casale 90: it is the first club created in Italy with the precise aim of documenting the phenomena of popular culture and music. A large hall, with a capacity of 300 seats, will host shows, projections, lectures, debates, meetings and other events, focusing on a widespread vision of the new and traditional facts of “folk music”. The opening show will feature Al Stewart, one of Britain’s youngest and most famous folk singers, and “The Incredible String Band” consisting of two folk singers who play a variety of instruments and sing in an orchestra-like fashion.’ Hmm.

Roy Guest, Al Stewart’s producer at the time, was also the ISB’s agent, and it seems that he had arranged for the two acts to play a week of gigs commencing on the club’s opening night, from 29th April through to a final appearance on 3rd May.

Despite intensive queries by *Be Glad*’s Italian researcher, Federico Permutti, we have not been able to source any reviews of the events. But they were decidedly odd.

FOLK CLUB ITALIANO
Corso Casale, 90
AL STEWART
THE INCREDIBLE STRING BAND
Ultime due sere - Ore 21,30

Mike Heron had this to say: 'It was quite an extraordinary tour. It was in the town of Turin and we were given a cultural liaison officer and all we did, Robin, Al Stewart and I, was to be taken to this wonderful restaurant. But we had to listen to Al Stewart moaning all the time about some childhood love that he'd never got over, so that was the down side. We were there for a week and the funny thing was we had a residency in this cultural arena that they'd opened but they hadn't really publicised it and told people it wasn't the Communist Club any more and we had all these women with black shawls who were just sitting there. Waiting. And to top the humiliation there was this guy who got on stage and he would do a translation of the entire lyrics before we performed. He would read it out word for word and then we'd play.'

Mike, Robin, Mimi and Mouse...

Adrian Whittaker

An intense creative partnership that blossomed briefly – and then was precipitately abandoned.

After the success of *5000 Spirits*, in autumn 1967 Mike and Robin started working with two dancers, Mimi and Mouse. The two had studied and performed together in San Francisco and had come to London to study at the Royal Ballet School. Mimi Janislawski and Lesandre Ayrey ('My little mouse' had been Lesandre's Mum's pet name for her) roomed together and, says Mouse, 'developed a wonderful friendship that was to last us many years. After graduation we remained in London and were swept up in the counter-cultural revolution of the Sixties.'

Mouse: 'Our first foray into Eastern culture came in the form of Shiva's Children, consisting of a poet, a sitar player, and two dancers.'

The Shiva's Children ensemble, all four of them regulars at The Electric Garden/Middle Earth club (held in a basement in King Street, Covent Garden) was brought together in 1967 by Aberdonian poet Alan Reid.

Mouse: 'He was absolutely instrumental in furthering our newfound counterculture dance career. He wrote metaphysical poetry about things like the gardens of infinity which sound commonplace now, but at the time people were in awe of him.' Mimi and Mouse 'pantomimed his words interspersed with some probably absurd poses and Oriental hand positions gleaned from the local library.'

The fourth member was sitar-player Vytas Serelis, a visual artist and musician of Lithuanian origin who had studied sitar at the Akbar Khan School of Music in Calcutta. As well as performing regularly at Middle Earth, Shiva's Children played at the UFO

Mouse (L) and Mimi (R). Photobooth picture, 1967

club and at the 14-Hour Technicolour Dream, at which a brief clip of Mimi and Alan Reid blowing bubbles was filmed for a *Man Alive* TV documentary.

Mouse adds: 'Around this time we also choreographed a few of George Harrison's songs dealing with the nature of reality, such as Within You Without You.'

In a contemporary article in *Cosmopolitan* magazine, titled 'Yankee Takeover in London Town', they informed readers they performed 'celestial and mystical dancing, with bits of classical, Egyptian, Chinese, and Indian – sort of fairy tale and lovely.' They made their own costumes from odds and ends bought in antique markets or materials brought from the Far East by Mimi's father, a captain in the US Merchant Marine. As part of Shiva's Children, M&M danced every weekend at UFO in between sets played by the Pink Floyd and Tomorrow, among others.

Mouse: 'This was the cocoon stage of our development as dancers and as people... doing our darndest to go Orientale in response to Alan Reid's poetry and George Harrison's cosmic lyrics.'

Stone Monkey member Rakis, then part of The Exploding Galaxy, saw them a couple of times at UFO and a friend of Rakis, also a regular, knew them in this era: 'Scenes come back of smoking pipes together, having Mu

Mimi (L) and Mouse (R) blow bubbles at the 14-hour Technicolour Dream

tea after they came back in the early hours from a gig, watching them rehearsing in a small space dressed in flowing Indian clothes. The flower child description fitted them well. They were sweet people.'

Mouse: 'Joe Boyd had seen us dance many times at UFO and told us that the Incredibles were looking for dancers for their concerts. After a year of sharing tiny dressing rooms with Pink Floyd, Arthur Brown, Tomorrow, Social Deviants, etc we were ready to move on. We took a taxi to Joe's flat in Paddington to meet Robin and Mike, and spent a few hours in their company listening to the Rolling Stones LP *Between The Buttons* and drinking Chinese tea. We liked them immediately and they felt likewise, discussing their vision of how dancers could be incorporated into their presentations. It was like meeting old, dear friends again! We felt elated and confident about this new venture. Joe called a few days later to say that we were hired. We only found out some time later that Robin and Mike had consulted the *I Ching* after we left and their decision about whether or not to hire us depended entirely on the reading, which gratefully was a very positive one.'

It's interesting that the two very different dance groups which worked with the ISB during their career both came from the same era and same scene, even appearing together on some nights at UFO and on the same bill at the 14-hour Technicolour Dream event in Alexandra Palace. The Exploding Galaxy, though, 'had the idea that anybody could be an artist. Anybody could perform, anybody could get up there, be creative...' as Jill Drower says elsewhere in this book. Their movements, apart from Malcolm's, tended towards the approximate. In contrast there's some brief online footage of Shiva's Children, also at Alexandra Palace, where the precision of Mimi and Mouse's movements betrays their classical dance training. Unlike The Exploders (most of whom became Stone Monkey), they went for proper choreography.

'All the pieces were strictly choreographed'

Mouse: 'The ISB had two big concerts coming up in October [Saville Theatre and Queen Elizabeth Hall – Ed.]. We lived in South Kensington at the time, and Robin and Mike were there constantly, playing us their pieces and asking which ones we thought would be suitable for dance. New music from *Hangman* and dances to the same were in preparation. We were already familiar with their music as Mimi had bought their 5000 *Spirits* LP some months before, playing it constantly.'

It was Robin's (and perhaps also Joe's) idea to work with the duo. As their performances at that point were fairly lacking in projection, Robin felt that 'the audience should have something to look at to make the lyrics clearer.' As with all the ISB's dance/mime projects, Mike was not really convinced. In 2003 he recalled:

'One of the things Robin liked to do was multi-media stuff, involving the audience and so on. It left me completely cold, I didn't really like it, wasn't what I wanted to do. But being as how I was a fan of Robin's I liked to see him expand in that direction, he was fulfilling himself by doing that and it entertained the audience. So all the things with Malcolm and Mimi and Mouse were more condoned by me; Mimi and Mouse first joined to play the minotaur, they dressed in a minotaur's suit, one in the front and one at the back. I don't think they did any of my songs when I think about it! Joe Boyd might know where they are – he hated them!'

Memories differ here. Rose says: 'I remember them accompanying Mike's music and I saw nothing to suggest that Joe didn't like them – rather the opposite.' Joe agrees: 'I recall them as being quite sweet, and don't remember them getting on my nerves!' Mouse adds: 'Joe may have been irritated by our admittedly immature behaviour at times, but there was no ill-will between us.' In terms of the songs M&M performed on, Mike is to some extent correct about the choice of material – although Mouse remembers their regular dances to his Chinese White and Painting Box as big audience hits, the other songs were Robin's: Waltz Of The New Moon, The Water Song, October Song, Koeeoaddi There, and Three Is A Green Crown.

Mouse: 'Chinese White and Painting Box were pretty standard in their live performances. So very beautiful and also dance-able. Chinese White was one of the most popular numbers in the shows. Mimi had choreographed a complete solo Russian character dance to Maybe Someday before we had even met them but to her chagrin, Mike wouldn't sing it... he said he was tired of it and had done it too many times. We had studied mime at the Royal Ballet School in London, and used those skills to convey the words of the songs, and used dance steps in other parts of the songs. All the pieces were strictly choreographed, as either duos or solos – sometimes we danced in unison, sometimes the other one kept still in a pose. Robin and Mike had a large repertoire so we just waited backstage during the songs in which we were not participating. But oftentimes there was no backstage area! In that case we knelt quietly at the sides, as out of view as possible.

Double exposure: The end pose from Chinese White

The four-piece line-up

'Waltz Of The New Moon' costumes, with headdresses. *Below* There are no photos of the minotaur in action, so Steve Small has drawn us a sketch based round Mouse's description! *Opposite* M&M, Mike and Robin with the minotaur mask

'The short time with ISB started out wonderfully, with dinners at Baghdad House, whole nights of poetry recitation for the four of us, mostly done by Robin, taking taxis at first light to see the sunrise over London Bridge. It was pure enjoyment, and uncomplicated, as we had no romantic inclinations towards either of them, nor them to us. We had bonded as friends and revelled in each other's company. Mimi and I frequented Baghdad House very often, on Drayton Gardens, a couple of blocks down from Old Brompton Road. It was the place to go: Brian Jones and co trotted down the stairs one night, Nigel and Michael the Hapshash artists, Mickey Finn and so forth. Robin and Mike loved it. Live Middle Eastern music. Such a fun place and the food was to live for. We became friends of the owner, Abbass, who was from Iraq (his whole staff were as well), and were eventually invited to his home to meet his sweet British wife Mary, and his two children. There, one was treated like royalty, with pistachio and date sweetmeats, coffee as thick as potato soup, wonderful music. Ah, those Baghdad days!'

'One of our first appearances with the ISB was at the Saville Theatre in October 67. We had made new headdresses for Waltz Of The New Moon, constructed of hundreds of translucent glass beads. The lyrics for that song are particularly exquisite, and one could hear a pin drop. We had also choreographed The Minotaur's Song which was very cute. Robin and Mike had made a large cardboard bull's face. Mimi and I used a big army blanket, dark green, doubled it, stitched up at the ends. That was the Minotaur body. We were under the blanket, Mimi front, me back, and all one saw was our legs from the mid-calf down. The tail was a large Chinese tassel. Mimi held the mask by the sides, and I was behind her. We did the whole dance in pointe shoes, mostly in proper ballet style. It was difficult to do, as we had to stoop over and dance at the same time! That mask is immortalized in a photo with its lovely big curling horns. It was funny and a hit with audiences, but we may have only done it a few times.

'The Queen Elizabeth Hall concert was a few days later, and was more than ecstatic. We were all young and fairly carefree, and this new path that life had taken for us was exciting to say the least. Mimi and I had set a duo for October Song. For Water Song we were designated to be the accompaniment, by swishing water in containers (like buckets) that were set onstage next to microphones. Electra's President, Jac Holzman, was among the audience, and came backstage in his rose-coloured glasses, enthusiastically giving his approbation of the String Band's new merger of

> music and interpretive dance, giving Mimi and myself special attention. Jac became our friend too, and in fact, our friendship with him extended long after the ISB days were over. He shared with us that he felt he was the reincarnation of Pharaoh Thutmose III; as Mimi and I had deeply loved ancient Egypt since early childhood, we hit it off very well.'

Apart from the London gigs, the four-piece also played Middle Earth, some provincial university dates and short Scandinavian and Irish tours. M&M worked up routines mainly drawing on dance traditions from India, the Far and Middle East and Indonesia.

> Mouse: 'We did dance-pantomime to their songs while adding Eastern-type movements. Three Is A Green Crown ended with a long chanting of the Tibetan mantra Om Mani Padme Hum in which we did a series of difficult balletic spins encircling the stage, as we spun around, travelling in a big circle.'

Mike and Robin were still based in Scotland at this point, and so city-dwellers M&M may well have helped provide their entrée to some aspects of the emergent London scene.

> Mouse: 'Besides the rehearsals and venues, there was a lot of social exchange with Robin and Mike, often going out with them to Baghdad House, sometimes joined by Licorice. Licorice had a certain silent screen star quality to her and a winsome expression to match. She was a girl of few words though, and either she did not approve of us, or she was just very interior. Whatever the reason, there was not a lot of communication between us. That certainly could have been our fault too. Mimi and I were exceptionally close friends then, sometimes to the exclusion of most other people who were present.
>
> 'Looking back, Robin and Mike were like cherished brothers, who were fairly glowing with energy and creativity. Amazingly accomplished musicians, they had probably been the favourite court bards of many kings in centuries past, but it was more than that. They were both philosophers, in very different ways, and synergistically this worked very well for them. They were seekers who were beginning to dare enter the spiritual realm where only realized sages dwell. Robin was the poet of the two – a mystic without a monastery, although he was not altogether a serious person. His mind was deep and moved like quicksilver; his perspective on things and insight was amazing. I'm sure that the album title *Layers Of The Onion* came from him – a perfect metaphor for eternal souls in physical

bodies, trying to crack the mystery of God. Oftentimes Robin would just sit and recite from memory reams of poetry. He would ask if anyone else had any good poems, but of course no one did, so he would continue on, to our delight.

'Mike was another flavour altogether. He was consistently friendly and cheerful. Wonderfully, contagiously happy. He had a smile that lit up the room and he laughed often. I admired him so much. He possessed two rare qualities: humility and kindness. He was the more childlike of the two, and one only needs to hear his songs to know that. He sang of little clouds, baby raindrops, talking hedgehogs, and empathetic trees. A true Capricorn, he was a beautiful Earth child. He had a very connected relationship with Mother Nature, and even wore forest green trousers. Robin and Mike were both funny to the point of being hilarious, and the four of us were often in fits of laughter. They were very happy times indeed. We loved them both, but they were more like family.

'There was never any movement from them, nor from us, toward romantic feelings. For one thing, Robin already had a lady friend, and Mike seemed content just the way he was. His arms were wrapped around his music! At the time, anyway... There was much travelling. We performed to packed auditoriums and halls, always with a wonderful reception. There were many instruments and props to carry, but somehow always we made it on and off the trains each time. On one of these train journeys to Cambridge, I had my copy of *The Blue Fairy Book* with me. Robin thumbed through it, selected a story, and read aloud 'Prince Ahmed and the Fairy Paribanou'. It's quite long, but the train ride was too. As we all sat listening at attention, Robin revealed the trials of the Prince.

'In each place we stayed with a family who must have been selected in advance by Joe. We did one show in Manchester at the Free Trade Hall. We had a strange experience one of those nights there. About a dozen of us were sitting on the living room floor, in a circle, just talking after the show. All of a sudden, right in the centre of the room, there was an enormous crack of something like thunder, and then the sound of hundreds of hands clapping rapidly. It only lasted maybe 4-5 seconds. Everyone was totally shocked and silent. We were horrified and looked at Robin and Mike – they looked at each other, then Robin shook his head, shrugged his shoulders, laughed, and simply said, "Spirits!"

'We had some gigs in Scotland as well and were flown up there. We shot some numbers at the local TV station, and found that the cameramen wore kilts. Everyone was friendly there, but my goodness what a cold place. The concerts were in Glasgow and Edinburgh, which were conservative towns and the receptions were a bit mixed – some were fans, and some were hecklers. Robin, Mike, and Licorice were staying with a lady named Mary [Stewart] who had a lot of children. These were not ordinary children, but ones who saw pixies in the woods, and spoke about them with serious tones. We went into those woods with them, as they showed us the very spots where the "little people" lived, but were not so privileged to see anything more than lichen, trees, moss and mushrooms. Mary's house and the adjoining forest was the place where the photo for *Hangman* was taken. The children in this photo are hers. We were supposed to be in the picture as well, but had already booked tickets to go home to San Francisco for Christmas, so unfortunately had to miss the photo shoot, and being on their record cover. Could it have been an omen?

'One night in early December, Joe Boyd and we four took a taxi out to meet an artist who was quickly gaining attention and some notoriety in London – Yoko Ono. She and her American husband Tony Cox were housed in a modest flat, with a ladder placed right in the middle of the living room. She would later use the same ladder in her London exhibit which would catch John Lennon's interest. The men outnumbered the girls, so Yoko, Mimi, and myself sat apart and talked. She spoke English hesitantly and was very cordial. When we left, we three agreed that we must fly kites with her at the next Hamamatsu (Japanese Kite Festival). We were invited back for tea, but we never called to set a date, as we got caught up in the busy-ness of life.

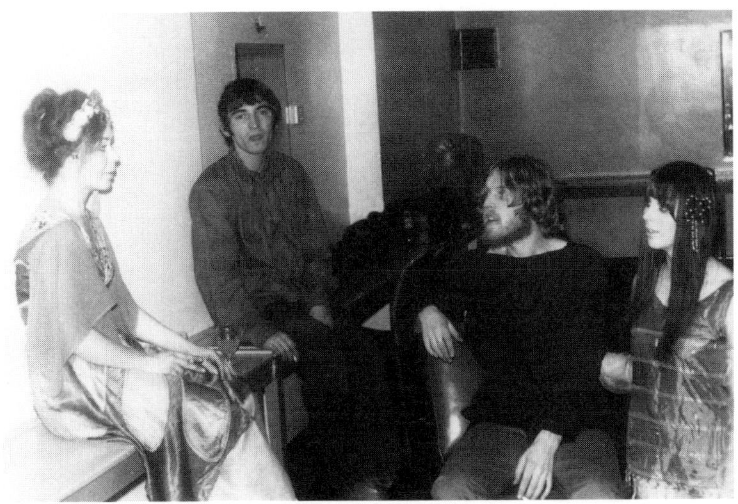

Late 1967 backstage shot

Scandinavian tour

'The tour of Scandinavia and Ireland was in early 1968 – winter everywhere, white landscapes with snow, and more snow. Robin was in a very downcast point of his life. He and Licorice had encountered major difficulties in their relationship, and there had been a split. Also he had somehow lost the notebook that contained all his notes, words, lyrics, poems, and inspired jottings for his old and future songs. In short, he was devastated on all levels. He was silent and moody on the flight over and for much of the tour. I didn't realize how much he was suffering and probably didn't offer anything in the way of concerned condolences or sympathetic counselling. But one is selfish when one is so young. Copenhagen was first stop. We were housed in a fancy hotel, and ate dinner in an enormous hall, empty except for us. It was at this point that Mike announced to us that he had fallen in love with a lady named Rose. This did not really go down well with us. Now, both of them were completely preoccupied with love issues, although at 180 degrees apart. Oh, the failings of the human heart! Next stop was Sweden, playing to rapt audiences, especially the University at Lund.'

On arrival at Kastrup airport, the band held a sort of press conference. One Danish paper informed its readers excitedly that 'the ISB that on Sunday will perform at Fjordvilla has, during the last three months, expanded their two-man-band with two lovely female dancers, Mimi and Mouse.' At the gig, the ISB were to be supported by 'Ebonies, a very musical and swinging band from Jamaica.' A far cry from Al Stewart.

Mike, Robin and Mouse, Copenhagen, 1968

Another newspaper piece expanded on the new-look ISB: '[M&M] are included in the duo's programme to illustrate the songs, among other things by using masks. "Because we mainly just perform our songs at concerts, we felt that the audience should have something to look at to make the lyrics clearer," Robin Williamson said when the troupe had a stopover at Kastrup this evening, on their way to Sweden before their weekend visit to Denmark on Saturday. However, he pointed out that there is a big difference between studio recording and stage performances. In each place one can utilise different means of expression.

'The two ladies... have studied, among other things, mime, theatre and Japanese dance. "We utilise everything now," Mimi and Mouse say. "We develop the choreography to the songs ourselves when they are presented to us. We prefer this form of dance compared to being in a dance troupe, because the form is looser than classical ballet and we decide ourselves what to dance."'

Brøndby Pop Club (in Copenhagen) had booked the ISB for a Saturday gig to celebrate their first anniversary. In a review headed 'ISB – new perspectives' reviewer Jørgen Kristiansen was dissatisfied: 'It was a great anniversary gift to the club members, but unfortunately the gift remained unwrapped. Problems with the PA caused ISB never to really get started – they only managed a couple of distorted samplings of their music. The only song that was more or less successful was the infinitely beautiful Painting Box, with the same theme as She's A Rainbow on the latest album by Rolling Stones.'

Mimi dances to Painting Box at the Pop Club. Photo © Steen Rasmussen

Kristiansen continued: 'The ISB has added new perspectives to folk music. They are not... rooted in the pub culture with the deadly songs and the frothy mugs of beer. There is a cheerfulness, a sensitivity in their songs that seems both surprising and pleasing. Instrumental-wise they are maybe closer to beat music than authentic folk music. Their time signature shifts and use of exotic instruments... make them one of the most exciting exponents of the newer English [sic] music. Not surprising that the duo has had several successes at home on London's hippy circuits. Emotionally they are a lot closer to Beatles, Stones, Donovan, Procol Harum and Cream than traditional folk groups...'

Finally, the dancers got a mention, but Kristiansen played it safe: 'The ISB's attempt to illustrate the contents of the songs with dancers in airy and colourful costumes was surprisingly new and because of that, hard to judge. In the moment, it seemed poetic and delightful.'

Mouse says it was an odd gig for that era: 'The performing area was adjacent to where people were dining – full on dinners, in a dim light. And hardly any space to dance in as well!'

After that came a visit to Malmö.
'Maharishi Mahesh Yogi, founder of the Transcendental Meditation movement, was also in Sweden at the time, and Robin, Mike, and myself (Mimi had a stomach bug) took a long, winding, snowy train ride out to meet him in Malmö. Snow and ice greeted us everywhere. This time, no hotels, but we were graciously housed by Anders Melander, the front man of a local pop group called Bread. Mike and Robin had some questions for the Maharishi, but as God did not hold any importance in my life at the time, the whole meeting was a bit lost on me. At the conclusion, the Maharishi handed me a small bunch of freesias – my absolute favourite flower, and I was moved to tears.

'On the ride back, Robin explained in detail his lyrics for Koeeoaddi There, and how they came about – he and Licorice were actually skating, and so on. The song had its debut on the Scandinavian tour. There was a lot of pantomime to the words with some Hungarian character dancing thrown in. On the flight from Sweden to Ireland, the Maharishi took the same plane as us and was at the airport surrounded by his devotees and retainers. He had at least a dozen flower garlands around his neck, and was smiling beneficently at everyone. We all felt safe on that plane ride. I am not a big fan of airplanes, but that day my heart was at ease! Next, arrival in Belfast. Foot and Mouth Disease had spread throughout Ireland. Everyone disembarking the plane was made to walk through disinfectant that was about two or three inches deep, and be sprayed with it as well. We had to carry all the instruments plus our luggage, and I believe that Robin and Mike had to make a few trips to get everything. They were not happy about this. It was very disconcerting and took a few hours.'

Tim Booth, of the embryonic Dr Strangely Strange, ran into the duo at this rather dispirited point: 'Anthea Joseph asked me if I would act as a sort of tour manager for the String Band on their Irish gigs. I was initially delighted to be working with the ISB as they were heroes of mine subsequent to the first two albums. The gigs started in Belfast, at Queens University, so I went up there and met the band at the airport and drove them to their accommodation and then on to the hall for a sound check and a bit of a run through. Mimi and Mouse had obviously undergone the Diva enhancement operation and needed a lot more care than Robin and Mike, who breezed along very nicely, all smiles and good vibes. The two girls were the polar opposite. Lots of frowns and moody hair tossing, even at the foot of the aircraft steps.' He quickly got on the wrong side of Mimi, who he remembers as particularly edgy. Apparently their star signs were ill-matched (they were both Virgos).

> Mouse: 'Ireland to me was a rather dreary-rainy unhappy-grey place. I recall one gig at a tiny Irish pub of all places, which was a near disaster, but then again it was not the right environment for philosophical, rather psychedelic songs. [*It was actually a Belfast hotel nightclub – Ed.*] We did a very short set and quickly got out of there! On to Dublin, and a nice concert at Liberty Hall that was standing room only.'

A reviewer of that January 1968 ISB gig in Dublin, with Dr Strangely Strange supporting, was sniffy: 'I found the two girls... rather unnecessary and slightly distracting, though they did perform to good effect as a bull during the Incredibles' anti-war song.' Though Tim was not at all taken by what he describes as 'wafting and sub-Isadora Duncan wallowing,' fellow Dr Strange member Ivan Pawle remembers 'they fitted in really well, especially on songs that incorporated Mike's sitar playing.'

> Mouse: 'Well, it looks like Ivan was our only ally, how nice of him. I never saw that review, nor any review. Just lot of smiling faces crowding around after the shows. Backstage, we were introduced to the heroine of Robin's First Girl I Loved and yes, she really did have that "long red hair." A tall, strong-looking lady. [*Someone was probably winding Mouse up here – Ivan thinks this was Johnny Moynihan's girlfriend Didi*

Delap – Ed.] We were put up by an Irish family, but there is not much to remember except that it was raining, it was cold, and there was nothing to eat. The next morning Joe arrived and took us out to do sightseeing and lunch. We probably got on his nerves that day as we were acting inordinately silly. Our imprudence was apparently stronger than our common sense. If we really and truly were little B's back at the airport, it was youthful, unconscious insolence, which needs letting go from all parties concerned. But we weren't feeling that happy about Robin and Mike either, as both of them had distanced themselves emotionally and artistically from us through their involvement in their own personal relationships, which dramatically affected the work we did with them.'

A major problem with researching this piece was that there are virtually no proper reviews, or even detailed memories, of how Mimi and Mouse went down with ISB audiences. A piece in *The Scotsman* is typical for this era: 'Presentation. Now there's a thing. Williamson and Heron show paintings to their concert audiences, recite poetry. And while they play, two girl dancers undulate with the music.' Malcolm Le Maistre saw the combination a few times in this era, but his memories are vague: 'They did Indian dance with them, kind of ethereal stuff.' In her memoir, Rose Simpson describes them as 'embodiments of the West Coast flower children' but she had her doubts. She says now: 'I've been thinking about the dancers and my then response to them. I guess that I saw them as theatrical performers and M&R were my friends who sang songs, not theatre. I wanted it to be like that, to hold onto the dream-life within the real one, not to see them as performers. Interesting how unpleasant we could all be underneath the love and peace banner. I suppose there was also a tinge of doubt and jealousy about girls who lived so close to them but I don't remember that. The dancers just seemed not to belong to the same world as M&R.'

A Mystical Pantomime with
The Incredible String Band
and
THEIR DANCERS!

'In short, we were no longer needed'

It was planned that M&M would feature heavily as part of the ISB's launch into the big time, the March *Hangman* tour of concert halls. The tour title, 'Mystical Pantomimes 1968' referenced their part in the shows and the advance flyers referred to 'A Mystical Pantomime with the Incredible String Band and THEIR DANCERS!' The two are even depicted, dancing bare-breasted, on the tour poster by Hapshash and The Coloured Coat, reproduced in the colour section of this book. Mouse: 'We were horrified when we saw this hanging up on the King's Road, depicted as dressed so skimpily; we were not happy about that at all, especially as we always had such wiggy costumes... Nigel Waymouth's and Michael English's rich imagination!' Nigel Waymouth says now: 'I remember Michael thinking it was quite cheeky to draw M&M fairly nude!'

There were some unspoken sexual tensions complicating the working relationship, though, which were never discussed, as was very common in that era (Rose's memoir has a lot to say about this). People who knew little about the band would have assumed that M&M were 'the girlfriends' and when Likky returned to Robin that February, she may well have laid down a few preconditions – we will never know!

Mouse says now: 'It was an interesting situation, because the four of us were young and fairly unattached. I knew that Robin liked me a whole lot, and he said some very sweet things to me a few times. We certainly admired each other. But with Mike and Mimi, only they know for sure. Something might have taken off but it didn't, and that was for the best.'

Mouse: 'Shortly after returning to the UK from the tour, Mike paid us a visit to introduce us to his new love, Rose. She was quiet and seemed to be a very organic, wholesome, nice girl. We were happy for him. She seemed a perfect match. He was ready for it. Mike was friendly to us as ever. Therefore, when Joe Boyd phoned us a few days later to tell us that Robin and Mike had decided to incorporate new, different acts into their sets, and in short that we were no longer needed, we were of course surprised and shocked. Robin and Lady Licorice would reunite, Mike's romance was in full swing. We wouldn't be returning to work with them, that was that. The times when we sat deep into the night utterly rapt in lively discussions covering just about everything, and then took taxis at sunrise to catch the sunrise over the Thames, were over. The gasoline in our karmic reunion had run out.' Mimi no longer talks about this part of her career, but has let it be known that 'it was one of the happiest times of my life.'

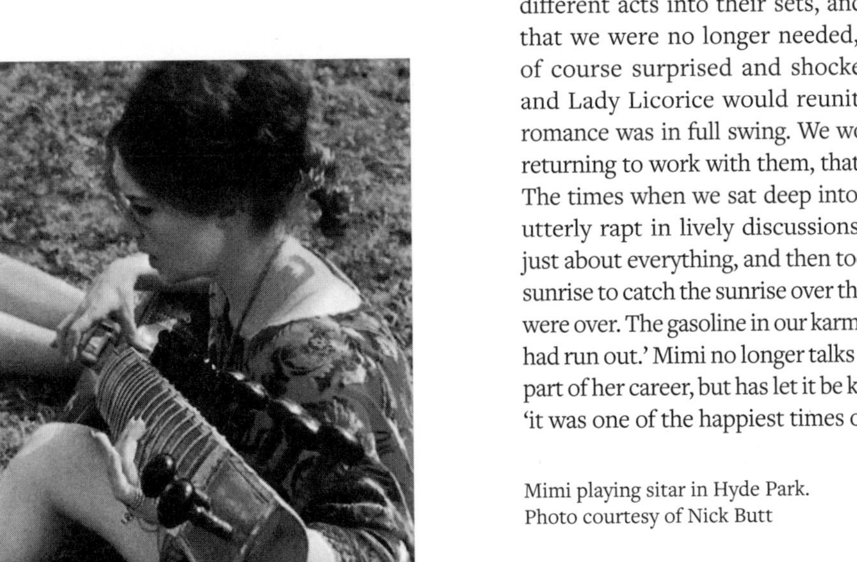

Mimi playing sitar in Hyde Park.
Photo courtesy of Nick Butt

Mouse: 'Mimi might recall that time as being happy, but realistically the balloon was popped abruptly and we were all thrown back onto Earth again.'

Looking back now, Lesandre Ayrey ('I'm not that Mouse anymore. I'm not even a new Mouse...') is philosophical about their precipitate departure from the first ever major ISB tour:

'The two girls were already in place to replace us, and that was really OK. Dance was our real passion in life, still is. Regarding our departure from ISB, we had our own internal life dramas to deal with and were acting immaturely. Joe Boyd was not that happy with us, probably because of those reasons. We did not give him the due recognition he may have deserved, attention that would have helped us to remain in his favour. I'm more aware of that now, of course, how to interact gracefully with others and to always honour their being. And if Tim Booth shared his sentiments with Joe, Mike and Robin, that may have put the finishing touches on our final days with the band. If he is responsible in that way, then I owe him a huge debt of gratitude. It was just what we needed!

'It all played out in the best way possible as we would not have been happy embracing a gypsy-like lifestyle in Glastonbury-type settings. It was basically the Universe taking care of us all, by moving us in separate directions, like chess pieces, so we could progress spiritually. That's how I think about it. By summer we were finally able to proceed with what we were meant to do – enlisting in formal studies of both Chinese and South Indian classical dance forms.'

On the five-date *Hangman* tour in March 68, Mike may well have regretted the decision to ditch the dancers, as Robin and he now had to provide the visual element themselves. Robin's theatre piece about Noah and The Dove saw Mike being made to read his lines from underneath a particularly inelegant bird mask made of baggy cloth with an orange-peel beak. It wasn't long though, till Robin picked up the multi-media thread again with Malcolm and Rakis. In June, M&M witnessed the UK ISB debut of this pairing.

Mouse: 'We decided, painful as it might be, to attend the ISB concert at the Royal Albert Hall, "On A Summer Evening." Predictably, we were not at all impressed with their songs nor any of the dancers, costumes, masks, etc. All the hullabaloo onstage detracted from the delicacy and beauty of the message in their songs. At the conclusion of the show, Robin announced that a prize would be given to the person who could solve this riddle: "White bird featherless flew from Paradise, Perched upon the castle wall; Along came Lord Landless, took it up handless, And rode away horseless to the King's white hall". We knew the answer, and wanted to yell out SNOW, as Robin had oft quoted it before. But it seemed best that we didn't answer to claim the prize. We saw them again a few months later, while standing in line to see Kurosawa's masterpiece, *The Seven Samurai*. Their whole troupe and entourage accompanied them. Our meeting was a little strained at best. Our lives were taking different directions...

'Meeting Robin and Mike, getting to know them so well, and dancing with them onstage was an extremely fortunate experience for us, but like so many other events in one's life, it lasted but a brief time. "Hitotoki" is a Japanese term which means "a moment in time", or "for one time only". Poetically translated:

For just one time,
Man is young,
Flowers bloom,
Love lasts. ...and so it was with the Incredible String Band!'

Researched and written for the new edition. Huge thanks to Lesandre Ayrey – and thanks also to Wolfgang Rostek for watching over the archive. Robin was asked if he'd like to contribute to this piece but decided to pass.

2021

In 1967 the ISB were still a bit of an inside tip for the cognoscenti (including most of the Stones and Paul McCartney), but 1968 was the year in which they started to reach a much wider public. The album which helped them make that transition had been recorded during the winter of 1967...

Andy Roberts introduces the ISB's most influential album, *The Hangman's Beautiful Daughter*

The *Hangman's Beautiful Daughter*: catalogue no EUK 258 to its matrix, but something vastly different to the people who know and love it for what it is, and what it has become over the years. Of all the String Band albums Hangman seems to give something the others don't, to touch places only hinted at elsewhere; if any album ever made you want to renounce temporal obligations and head for the wildwood this was the one. Maybe it was the times, maybe the chemicals. Maybe it was just the right people at the right time, tuned in and turned on, waiting to receive, to receive a transmission from *something*. The zeitgeist was never ensnared better than on *Hangman*. The Dave Barrett and Gil Murray articles which follow on from this piece exemplify the personal response to music which is just as interesting as the factual side. But that's for later – here's some surrounding 'facts' and, quite possibly, a few fictions...

Hangman was the album which finally catapulted the ISB from being quirky post-Dylan folkies to psychedelic stardom, in sales, live performances and critical appraisal. Prior to its release the String Band had played a few London clubs and smaller concert venues up and down the country; their biggest gigs to date had been as support to the Pink Floyd and Fairport Convention at the Saville Theatre in October 1967 and a double bill with Shirley & Dolly Collins at the Queen Elizabeth Hall later that month. Manager Joe Boyd had a masterplan which was to change all that, involving the band's first solo tour of big halls. Joe: 'I just knew it would be fine, the tour sold out and the second week the album was out it was at number three!'

The title? Karl Dallas interviewed the band just prior to the album's release and queried the title: 'It was an interview filled with sudden, reflective silences in which I sometimes felt that my questions were like rocks being thrown into a deep, clear pool, disturbing its calm.'

Double bill with Shirley and Dolly Collins, 1967, by Hapshash and the Coloured Coat.

Robin: 'In a way you could say the title thought of us. What does it mean? You can explain it at several levels.'

Mike: 'The hangman is death and his beautiful daughter is what comes after. Or you might say that the hangman is the past twenty years of our life and the beautiful daughter is now, what we are able to do after all these years. Or you can make up your own meaning. Your interpretation is probably just as good as ours.'

A biography of Dylan Thomas suggests another source. The young Thomas spent his childhood holidays at an aunt's house deep in the country. Local legend recounted how this house was once the dwelling place of the area's hangman. His daughter was so beautiful that he hid her away from the sight of any man lest she fall in love and leave him. She became depressed and whilst in this state took her own life – by hanging. But Robin, a big fan of Dylan Thomas, says he was unaware of this.

Robin once described *Hangman* as a 'winter album', and the original front cover finds Robin and Mike, suitably wrapped in stout winter garments, on a snowy moor near Balmore against a backdrop of icy blue sky. The rear cover photo catches them communing in a sheltered copse with Licorice, Robin's dog Leaf, two friends, Roger Marshall – with chain – and Nicky Walton, and a gaggle of perplexed-looking children (Mary Stewart's) in wacky hats. Mimi and Mouse were supposed to be part of the group photo too, but were over in the States for Christmas and so missed the shoot. Mike's future girlfriend Rose Simpson was also staying at Temple Cottage and was roped in, wearing a borrowed jacket of Likky's. Rose remembers: 'The first time I heard Mike and Robin playing was at Mary Stewart's – and that was it. That was when I was at York University, but I'd gone to Scotland to do this mountaineering. It was winter and the snow was bad so we didn't get out on the hill very much, and so I was stuck in this house where they were. This was when my life changed.'

The picture strongly evoked the communal ethic emerging in the Sixties counter-culture; hitherto it had been usual for musicians to be portrayed in splendid isolation from their social milieu. Another novel feature of the album's original sleeve design was the total absence of credits or even a track listing. These were included on an accompanying lyric sheet. Perhaps it was felt that the world wasn't quite ready for titles like *Koeeoaddi There* and *Three Is a Green Crown.*

Hangman was often regarded as the acid album, though Williamson claims to have given up psychedelics by then: '...by that time I'd probably stopped taking drugs, it was very much what was going on at the time but I'd pretty much lost interest in drugs by then.' However, Dolly Collins worked with Robin on some of the *Hangman* tracks, and told her sister Shirley that at that point Williamson was something of an acid evangelist, telling her: 'You've never seen a tree until you've taken LSD.'

It certainly was what was going on and, drugs or not, the ISB looked to be living the psychedelic lifestyle – the timeless life. In fact, whether *Hangman* was created with or without psychedelics is largely immaterial as once that viewpoint is attained it tends to manifest itself in your life and the drugs become, to a large extent, superfluous. However, their presence and influence cannot be ignored. Many musicians whose work was grounded in psychedelics try to play this side of things down somewhat, whether through embarrassed hindsight, to hide their pasts from their offspring, or whatever. Whether listener or artist is drawn into the labyrinth that psychedelics provide is a personal choice. Humour and awe were and are the key, I suspect.

A Very Cellular Song is a case in point here. Heron has often alluded to the fact that it had close connections with the LSD experience – as if we hadn't worked that one out – and told me: 'All it was, was a trip, and that was the music I was listening to, that and interspersed with Radio 4, bits of plays, people talking to each other, and I happened to be listening to the Pindar family before I started.' The Bahamian Pindar Family did the original version of We Bid You Goodnight from A Very Cellular Song – it was also, trivia delvers, done frequently by the Grateful Dead at the end of concerts. Although it was for some time erroneously claimed by a Kundalini Yoga group, the final 'long time sunshine' section owes no debt to anyone at all but Mike.

Contemporary reviews show the almost universal acclaim which met such a strange album – and also that critics could, when they wanted, write some pretty good descriptive stuff about music. *The Sunday Times*' Derek Jewell was well impressed, making *Hangman* Record Of The Month in March 68: 'Quasi-poetry and phoney mysticism now cling to the skirts of popular music, but the Incredibles are not pseudo. Their work is convincing, beautiful, idiosyncratic, yielding more with each playing.' *The Observer*'s Robin Denselow: 'Together with the Beatles' *Sgt Pepper* it seems...to be the most important disc to have been produced in Britain for several years.' *Melody Maker* ran a preview, opening with: 'When poet Pete Brown, lyric-writer for the Cream, heard...*Hangman*, he said: "That's what the Rolling Stones have been trying to do."' He was right, and on *Satanic Majesties Request* you can hear several *Hangman*-isms. But the Stones' media-hyped association with the dark forces (did you know Satan was originally known as just plain ol' 'Stan' until an extra 'a' was added by a mushroom-addled desert scribe?) was transparent when compared to the far deeper source that the ISB were tapping into on *Hangman*. Robin Denselow again: 'Taken as a whole, the songs are a plea for wonder at existence, a sometimes mystical, sometimes pantheistic involvement in a very live universe. In many ways it's a Wordsworthian romanticism, pro-nature, pro-imagination and anti-urban... The expression of awe at being alive and the sense of organic connecting between all things comes, at times, near to religious statement.'

Praise indeed from the establishment – and more followed in the reviews of the March 1968 concert at the Festival Hall. In the *Financial Times* Anthony Thorncroft penned a perceptive piece about the both concert and band: 'The ISB are the nearest thing to godliness among the art school set: judging by the Establishment figures scattered among the audience they are about to be taken up by a more hard-bitten public.' (You can just imagine Marc, Syd, Paul and the rest in the audience, furtively scribbling notes under their Afghans!) '...It is doubtful whether the delicate flavour of the Incredibles will make the transition. They

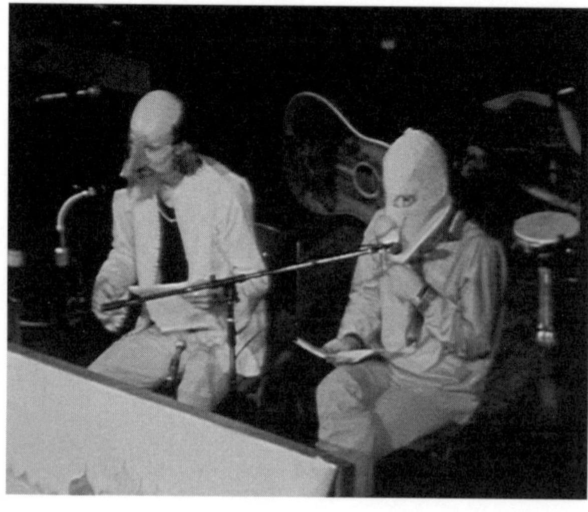

Noah and The Dove, Festival Hall, 1968. (Peter Neal)

compose their own mystical songs around melodies which ebb and flow with butterfly brittleness, and lyrics which link poetry and nonsense in an unholy marriage. The principal sources are Eastern and medieval music and, after a first hearing of disbelief, those prepared to accept the Incredibles' magical world can get on terms with the most unique talent to come out of the current song-writing revival.'

Americans were no less enthused; Richard Goldstein (*New York Magazine*) hit the nail on the head, describing Robin's voice as having a 'reedy whisper that sounds like water seeping out of ancient rocks', exhorting his readers to go out and buy *Hangman* so they could be the 'first (on your block) to worship at the universal church of magic'. Let's have some more Goldstein, it's nearly as good as the album! How about: 'Each song is a tone-poem etched in filigree; delicate yet sturdy. Each lyric is an utterly disarming cross between a hymn and a nursery rhyme.'

I couldn't find a bad review and the ones that weren't full of superlatives owed more to the reviewer's lack of imagination and skill with language rather than any dislike of the album. Everybody knew, to some degree or another that, in the words of Buffy St Marie, 'music is alive, magick is afoot'. Or something like that. And so it was. Switched-on people all over the country were rushing home and turning on to *Hangman*, their minds scarred and certainly scared by its austere, cold beauty to such an extent that we have to write pieces like this decades later. The power of music eh? Critical acclaim was such that *Hangman* was nominated for a Grammy award in the USA in 1969. *Cash Box* listed the Grammy nominees and there, in the 'Best Folk Performance' section along with Judy Collins' *Both Sides Now* and Dylan's *John Wesley Harding* is *The Hangman's Beautiful Daughter*. Strange days indeed.

Mike still classes it as his favourite ISB album, telling interviewer Chris Wade in 2013: 'I've always been drawn to songs. And when the songs on an album blend to make an experience bigger than themselves, that's a special bonus. For me, *Hangman* would be far and away the best example.'

Me? I love it, find it always challenging, always rewarding, always refreshing. If you haven't listened to it for a while I suggest you prime yourself by a long country walk, preferably in wild weather, slip it onto the turntable (or whatever) and connect with something. But remember: 'The opposite is also true'.

Updated 2021

Dave Barrett celebrates a 'true original'

This is quite simply the most important album in my collection, number one on my Desert Island list. So what is it about this album in particular that is so special to me?

Firstly, *The Hangman's Beautiful Daughter* was always more than just a collection of songs by Robin and Mike. The title, the cover, the enclosed lyric sheet, and the songs themselves were all good in their own right, but put together they became a wonderful example of one of life's riddles – the whole being greater than the sum of the parts. It was very much an album of its time, reflecting the philosophical and cultural melting pot that arose under the banner of the 'Alternative Society' in the latter half of the Sixties. The title echoed the Eastern philosophy of the lotus flower, where purity springs from base mud, but it did so in a way that fired the imagination of a Western youth preoccupied by thoughts of beautiful but unreachable women, thoughts heightened by reference to the fire king's daughter in The Waltz Of The New Moon. The influence of the East was further reinforced by the use of sitar, gimbri, pan pipes and other such instruments. The lyrics also reflected these influences, but more importantly they captured images of dreams and myths that resonated deep within me. Above all, they captured life itself – the microscopic world of the amoeba, the charming autobiographical world of young Robin and Licorice and the dangerous riches of young Mike's imagination, the world of the birds and the fishes, the choked and polluted world of the city, the world of magic and mythology, wizards and witches, angels and gods, and philosophical riddles – 'life, life, remembering', 'Put in a basket bound with skin'. With the elements that make up the album – the voice of Robin, which combined Celtic power and fluidity with the sensuousness and vocal dexterity of India, the strong and tender voice of Mike, the unconventional song structures, the inspired and imaginative musicianship, and the so-appropriate arrangements, the album is a masterpiece from start to finish.

Robin and Mike were, by the time they came to make this album, well-established artists in the vanguard of the Sixties Folk Revival. Whilst they could play other instruments (Robin spent some of his earlier days playing fiddle) they were both primarily guitarists as well as songwriters. It is with *Hangman* that they really started to expand their musical talents in many directions. The guitar still featured strongly on Robin's compositions, and his use of open tunings and unusual finger-picking helped to create his original style, but his use of other instruments was almost as important – the sound of gimbri and pan pipes has haunted me to this day. Not to be outdone, Mike took up keyboards and sitar to great effect (although purists may possibly disagree with me on the latter point). As with Robin's compositions, Mike's songs followed their own course, even into and out of someone else's song on one occasion, in blissful disregard of the established traditions of songwriting. And so to the songs. It all starts with three Robin Williamson compositions, each one totally different from the one before.

Koeeoaddi There begins in philosophical vein, setting the tone of the album with its opening line – 'the natural cards revolve, ever changing', and continuing the theme in the chorus. Interspersed with the philosophy are charming childhood memories ending with Robin and Licorice escaping 'across the mournful morning moor motoring away' – a typical example of Robin's playful use of language – leaving behind them the simple joys, fears and restrictions of childhood and moving into the wilder world, taking with them a child-like love of riddles and wonder.

The Minotaur's Song comes next, a nonsense song sung with pure theatricality, evidence of Robin's growing interest in the other performing arts. Each word is elaborated and emphasised to fullest effect, accompanied by a backdrop of guitar, piano, chorus and sound effects. Theatricality does not often move successfully from the stage and onto vinyl, but this song seems to work, largely because the melody is strong and sounds such fun.

Next comes Witches Hat, a song of two parents. It begins thoughtfully, with Robin singing mournfully about 'quiet places where the moss grows green', accompanied by some effective guitar picking. The lyrics are sad and wistful, and the music has a haunted, magical feel to it, never more so than when the words trail off into a vocal improvisation accompanied by echoey pan pipes and hammered dulcimer. The mood changes with the second part, originally a song for children. [*It was written for Mary*

Stewart's son Robbie – Ed.] The lyrics start up again, but this time with a collection of amusing images in the form of more nonsense rhymes.

The rest of the first side is taken up by A Very Cellular Song, a long composition by Mike. The song is of epic proportions, starting with images of childhood Christianity and opening out into a wonderful celebration of life, from the microscopic to the cosmic. The song is an anthem to the Hippy Movement, if such a thing ever existed. It is all there, the vibrations, the absurd and amusing imagery – the idea of riding backwards on a giraffe, stopping every so often to laugh, is quite exquisite – the joy, and the philosophy. It is interesting musically as well, stylistically eclectic, with the sound of organ, harpsichord, guitar, gimbri, Jew's harp and other assorted instruments blended imaginatively together. The first side ends of a positive, uplifting, devotional note with a chorus about letting the 'pure light within you guide you all the way on'.

Side two opens with Mercy I Cry City, a Mike Heron song which hits at the soulless, empty nature of the city with unerring accuracy and insight, a powerful ecological song well before it was fashionable to be Green. It works musically, too, with a strong melody and accompaniment, and the result is, I feel, Mike's best song.

After that, Robin launches into Waltz Of The New Moon. Up until I heard this song, I always associated waltzes with Strauss, and I had never enjoyed them. I still don't like Strauss, but the waltz has at least been liberated from its classical straightjacket. The lyrics are obscure, involving floating pan pipe victories, spinning castles, and Lord Krishna's ring, but the imagery is rich and the language eloquent. Somehow it all makes sense, even though I could never explain it. Once more, the melody is strong and original, and the music suitably accomplished, flowing beautifully into The Water Song, a short mystical hymn to the life-giving element. Robin's tin whistle accompaniment is as liquid as the 'dark or silvery mother of life' itself. Three Is A Green Crown follows, an example of Robin at his deepest; the title refers to the Tarot card which denotes nature. His guitar has the bottom E string dropped down to C, an unusual tuning which is used to good effect, providing a rhythmical droning that underpins his singing. The lyrics betray a literary background – with echoes of Blake – as well as the Eastern influences evident throughout the album, the latter being reinforced very effectively by Mike's sitar playing. The song is an inner exploration, sometimes painful (some think that it is drug related), sometimes profound, where Robin lays bare his psyche in a Faustian attempt to be granted 'the tongue that all the earth does sing'.

In Swift As The Wind, Mike tells us of the wild and wonderful imagination of his childhood, and the attempts of no doubt well meaning but misguided adults to curb his solitary passions and 'spend some time downstairs' with the other kids for his own good. Luckily for us, a compromise is reached which allows Mike to remain true to his inner self.

After all these emotional trials and tribulations, the album ends with Nightfall, a wonderfully serene lullaby. Robin's eloquent and elegant lyrics and soothing vocals are set to a perfect musical accompaniment, with Mike excelling himself on sitar, a fitting ending to a truly original album.

‘My god, those pills are good!’

Billy Connolly remembers a Hangman*-era gig in 1968:*

I went to see them in Glasgow. The worst thing about those days was that drugs were very new. Everybody knew about hash and grass, but there was a lot of other stuff flying around and it would be two or three pills – here try that, oh sure (*gulp!*), and it could have been those pills they give spies in case they get tortured too much. I remember I was in the bathroom in the Gaiety – it used to be the Gaiety cinema, it became the concert hall. This guy Kenny was bragging that he'd smoked dope with the Clancy Brothers, and I thought come on, surely they're into Guinness. I couldn't imagine these people in white pullovers smoking dope. And he says ‘Try these,’ and he gave me three pills. I remember a green one, a yellow one, I can't remember about the other one. I went sure, this is the trendiest thing on earth, I'm into this, and I went in to see the band. I don't know what it was I took, I was brainless, watching them running about, and I thought it was the drugs, but on reflection I think maybe nothing happened – maybe they were Smarties! The guys were doing that stuff about ‘the inscrutable buffalo man’, and they're running about with false faces and a bucket of water and a glockenspiel thing... I thought, my God these pills are good! (*laughs*) To this day I wonder how much of the concert was the dope and how much was the Incredibles. I had to go and see them again later to see how much! It sounded to me they were just making a song up as they went along.

You know they got to a period just after *The Hangman's Beautiful Daughter* where I was lost. I thought, what the hell is this now, I think you've let me behind – but I still loved it. I was still determined to be carried along by it because it was so wonderful compared to everything else I was listening to. There were still people singing about Scottish battles I've never heard of where the English run away. There was a great trend in Edinburgh then for big manly voices, and the guy in the Corries had started playing like he was chopping wood... and I thought Oh, Christ! And there was a lot of women then going, ‘Ooooh come back to meee...’, women with big polo necks who smelled a bit. Quite frankly, in those clubs it was like Laura Ashley meets the Clancy Brothers!

1997

The Hangman's Beautiful *Mother*

Gil Murray approaches the album in the spirit in which, quite possibly, it was conceived.

The walls of Dave's flat had long since receded into the twilight and were forgotten. Several resurrected Glasgow University students were glowing quietly, scattered around the room. Time had been well and truly opened by chemical agencies, but we had a musical movie to mark out the passing ages. A humble little cassette player projected great frames of sound and light onto the rafters of our minds.

And what music was it? Some time during the evening, a tape went on with *The Hangman's Beautiful Daughter* on one side and *Wee Tam* on the other. I looked on from my balcony and enjoyed. Straight, the String Band lyrics could seem difficult and incomprehensible – some of *5000 Spirits* was like this – but from this altitude, every line made sense. By the time of Waltz Of The New Moon I was shearing off into the timeless zone, big time. Living the timeless life. Certain lines still link me directly into the spiritual and emotional richness of those moments. How about these lofty lunar heights:

> *The new moon is shining, the angels are washing their windows*
> *above the years whose jumble sale goes spinning on below.*

Or these exultant Earth scenes of hazard-free spiritual abundance:

> *In the floating pan pipe victorie-ie-ies o-of the go-olden ha-a-arvest, safe in the care oooooof the deeeaar moooooooonnnnnnn*

I had read about *The Hangman's Beautiful Daughter* in *The Electric Muse* when I was sixteen. At that time my main interests were Bert Jansch and Fairport Convention. However, a chapter entitled 'Crazy British Individualists 2: The String Band' caught my eye, and I really liked the sound of what I read. Robin Denselow began by saying: 'Unlike Roy (Harper), they peaked after a couple of years, after a period in which I felt they could match even the Beatles in writing ability and sheer inventiveness...' He went on to describe the definitive first four albums. I found myself dwelling on the album titles. The *5000 Spirits Or The Layers Of The Onion* appealed to my sense of strangeness and humour, but there was something particularly beguiling about *The Hangman's Beautiful Daughter*. I chewed on it for a long time.

The four words brought Death and Life together – The Hangman and his Beautiful Daughter – but what exactly was the relationship?

1. Did the Beautiful Daughter *like* her father The Hangman? Could you run away with her? Or would the shadow of the Hangman stalk you, and hunt you down?

2. If you tried to make friends with The Hangman, would his Daughter despise you for it? Can you make friends with a Hangman? Would he hang you for your audacity? (Bummer.)

3. Do you have to die before you can achieve The Beautiful Daughter?

The Hangman's Beautiful Daughter. There were many possible meanings, and layers of meanings: The emergence of enlightenment after dull grey years of conformity and British schooling. Morning born of night, spring awakening out of winter, life after death, suffering begets creation...

It appeared that the Hangman and his Daughter were inextricably inter-locked. Perhaps if you could find the key, you could undo some of the chains and penetrate the Mystery. Perhaps we were looking at the very light and dark that are alloyed within us – the bitter-sweet Human Condition that is our greatest challenge. The theme is picked up in the opening song Koeeoaddi There:

Earth Water Fire and Air
Met together in a garden fair
Put in a basket bound with skin
If you answer this riddle, you'll never begin.

What sorcery is this? The arrival on Planet Earth (a garden fair) of ourselves in the form of spiritual beings? Our subsequent union with the physical humanoid life forms that had evolved on the planet (baskets bound with skin) and in which we are largely still trapped? The last line is the heaviest of all: 'If you answer this riddle, you'll never begin'. At first it seems like a heavy penalty designed to deter inquiring minds from penetrating the mystery – who wants to be totally undone, such that they have never begun? But you could look at it differently. Exactly *what* are we talking about undoing here? Perhaps this state of 'never beginning' is a desirable one – and doesn't imply non-existence at all! Perhaps we are talking about a native personal existence, so pure and essential that it transcends physical realities such as Time with its beginnings and endings. This highest quality of being would of course be entirely free from reliance on 'Baskets bound with skin', or physical bodies. An existence superior to all constraints, from which we have come, and into which we may pass again. Maybe we've forgotten that the *Hangman* also had a Beautiful Mother...

At this point, if there's anyone out there still reading, may I just say 'Koeėoaddi There!' and move on swiftly to the next bit – the second coming of *The Hangman's Beautiful Daughter*. It was on a hot autumn day in 1979 that the natural cards revolved again. By now I had actually bought my own copy of the record, because it was time to. The process had been explained to me by my friend Mike: '*Hangman* is my favourite. It's really trippy and mind-blowing, but you should get 5000 *Spirits* first, because it's easier to get into. *Then* get *Hangman*!'

I knew it was time, and had primed myself accordingly. Breakfast consisted of brown toast – overloaded with two hundred and twenty five Psilocybe semilanceata! An hour or so later I was doubled-up in pain, fighting my cramping gut like there was no tomorrow. Finally I gave in, put on *Hangman* and lit up the large (conical, Stars and Stripes) joint of Colombian that I'd prepared earlier. The result was miraculous. I stopped resisting the pain, the pain vanished, the one-dimensional black and white world dissolved and I found myself – or someone I seemed to recognise – dissolving into nursery garden embroideries of laughter and sorrow...

The natural cards revolve, ever changiiiinggggg...
seeded elsewheeere, planted in the garden fair
gro-ow trees, gro-ow tree-eeeees...

What was this wonderful seventh sense of wet and windy heath, mystical fertility and whispering of trees, gumboots and Christopher Robin? This sunny, damp and familiar magical folklore of trees, blossom, wind, the little people, the garden wall – sweet forgotten memories streaming from the past to meet me again. The tap of friendly dry bones from the bible black darkness, and the chanting of riddles. The wonderfully unexpected psychological theatre of The Minotaur's Song – an ancient Cretan, English opera. Spellbound I watched as the Chinese audience applauded.

Then back to the secret green depths of Nature, Her moss and quiet places. The reverence in Robin's voice as he channelled the Muse. The haunted hills that rose and fell and sang in childhood tongues... beaten out by light dwarfish hammers and strewn with coloured flowers.

Extraordinary and impossible wild shepherd note clusters trilled from Robin's whistle like totems in the sky above. I have never heard anyone else play whistle like that! And how the bowed gimbri at the beginning of A Very Cellular Song got inside me and surely everyone who heard it, like on Chinese White. Such a soulful, animal voice, rising and weaving like smoke.

Winter was cold and the clothing was thin

It was all too poor and too beautiful to bear, but comfort and warmth was in the wings as the organ ushered in salvation with soft friendly harmonies, hand-clapping and bells. Honest courage to help shore up the newly-bared core. I remember quite well, I remember quite well.

The cellular journey continued with memories of a simpler time flooding back from early childhood in all its wonderful diversity. Friends past and present paraded by. The games and pranks were invoked in all their gusto by earnest kazoo playing. You could feel the pain of remembered childhood innocence through the joyful jumble of living room chairs, dressing-up costumes and, of course, *crystallised ginger*.

Then, with another sudden Minotaur-like about-face, we were plunged down into the dimly-lit microscopic level of single-celled organisms, where the Amoeba told its timeless tale:

Oh ah ee oo, there's absolutely no strife.

And then Mike addressed our cells, beaming *energy projections* full of good intentions toward all fellow life forms, with Licorice a tiny whispered singing voice and Robin that deep core gimbri in accompaniment. With centuries of war and pain laid in, where do moments like this come from? Thank you, String Band, for letting the sunshine in. As heart, mind and cell unfolded, the last vestiges of resistance were laid down and washed away. Hammond organ and hand drums fired up to lay down a thumping, mighty, glorious plateau of good feeling. Angelic choruses rejoiced overhead. The little bowed gimbri sawed in exultation. Birds bobbed and weaved in garlands around the path and the sun shone fully upon the world.

The Hangman's Beautiful Flip Side

I was woken from this blissful reverie by a 'ssssss' and a 'clop' from the machine on the table. The black plastic thing with the blue-green butterfly in the middle slowed and stopped turning. Nerves quivering with the life energy coursing through them, I picked it up and turned it over. A rapid dulcimer cascade dropped me straight into Have Mercy I Cry City. The song resonated right down to my boots! There was a playful spirit of defiance. The city had been sussed:

You cover up your emptiness with brick and noise and rush
Oh I can see and touch you but you don't owe reality much

Mike's guitar picking was tantalisingly different and individual, while Robin was a one-man orchestra on harmonica, whistle, rattles, kazoo and backing vocals. That whistle! Tumbling, pealing cascades of wild and wilful notes, just as sublime as the playing on Witches Hat. Something about the next track just immediately hauled me up and out into the cool and the dark of space:

I hear tha-a-a-at the-e-e emp'ror of Chi-i-ina
used to wear i-ron shoes with eeeeeeease...

Things had become suddenly serious. It was like night moving in – cool, majestic and mystic. Angels with newly cleaned windows looked down upon the tilted Earth. A mysterious quest unravelled below:

Ask the snail beneath the stone
Ask the stone beneath the wall...

I turned to look through the window, over the gardens and streets of suburbia that nestled below. The cosmic, stately and enchanted strings of Waltz Of The New Moon gave way to the sound of silvery waters, flute organ and wooden whistle. Water swirled and gurgled to left and right, and silver coins rang in a perpetual jangling rain. A wizardly shepherd stepped forward and reverently sought the lesson of flowing.

There was another intensity change in the music, as a soft and earnest chorus of 'aaahs' ushered in the subterranean trance of Three Is A Green Crown with its sensual opening lines:

Not with the lips of skiiiiiiiiin
Nor ye-et with the li-i-ips o-of dark sno-o-o-ow

This turned swiftly into a driving, hypnotic tribute to the Celtic Triple Goddess – presumably the Three who is also a Green Crown. Hand drums propelled the trance along, dropping out periodically behind yawing gimbri, chirruping, zinging sitar, and masterfully attentive light rhythmic guitar:

Let the cracked crystal raindro-op be-e-e me-erged in the sea
Silent, shi-i-i-i-ning, thou-ought-le-ess, free

Swift As the Wind came next. On that High Morning it had a fresh magic all of its own. It was sincere and emotional and burrowed right down into the childhood world.

You must stop imagining all this
You must stop imagining all this for your own good

Slackening kettle-drums showed the way downstairs at the end of this piece. I thought that was the end, but amazingly, the best was still to come in the form of the wondrous Nightfall. How many true dreamers slowly sailed to the land of nod across that milky night lake? How many weary but wakeful visionaries tugged at the skirts of sleep, soft stars in the pools of their eyes:

Oh sleeeeeee-eep, o-o-o-o-oh come to me-e-e-e
you who are night's daughter

Nightfall, with her dark locks and her new dreams. She soothes the Beast at the Ending of the Wood, the Minotaur, the Fire King, and even the Hangman himself.

Perhaps she is the Hangman's Beautiful Daughter.

May the long time sun shine upon you All love surround you
And the pure light within you Guide you all the way on.

Hometown Thoughts

John Quigley examines Edinburgh's role in Mike and Robin's work

'We live in cities, and cities live in us,' proclaimed the director Wim Wenders somewhat portentously in his film *Notebook On Cities And Clothes*. This statement made me think a little. Maybe it's of relevance to the ISB. Both Robin and Mike were born and raised in Edinburgh. How much of Edinburgh 'lives' in their work? It's a question that's intrigued me ever since I first heard their music – and their Scottish accents. As an 'outsider' I'm conscious that my knowledge of Scotland's capital city is far from complete – but I hope that my perspective on the ISB's home-town 'roots' might be of interest for that very reason. So – here are some suggestions...

Edinburgh scarcely needs introduction nowadays; it's renowned worldwide as Britain's most beautiful city, as home of the world's biggest arts festival, as a centre for tourism, culture, education, finance, administration, etc. etc. In some ways, however, today's Edinburgh is a very different city from the quieter, more mysterious city which I first got to know around 25 years ago; I would suspect that this 'earlier' Edinburgh is the city in which Robin and Mike grew up, and which is reflected in many of their songs.

Like many incomers from the south, I came to Edinburgh in order to study; in the mid 1970s, after the ISB had broken up and Robin had headed west to Los Angeles, I took the train north. I found the 'city of grey spires and green parks' which Vivien Goldman talks about in the liner notes to the 1976 ISB compilation *Seasons They Change*, a city whose buildings 'are like very beautiful prisons', as Adrian Henri, Liverpool poet and Festival Fringe regular, put it. Having been raised in a middle England where 'New Town' meant places like Milton Keynes, Stevenage or Telford, I was knocked sideways by the beauty and dignity of Edinburgh's classical New Town. I remember spending hours walking around the city centre, the New and Old Towns and the solid, stone-built, 19th-century suburbs south of the Meadows, amazed that a city with so few ugly, functional modern buildings still existed. With its large student population and gentle 'alternative' scene, it often seemed a kind of Sleeping Beauty of a place. It only featured in the media during the Festival and when Five Nations rugby internationals were televised from Murrayfield, and thus didn't figure very prominently in Britain's national consciousness.

A mixture of dour Calvinism and a high-minded pursuit of knowledge... However, I did have problems with the prevailing mentality. It seemed very different from the down-to-earth, business-oriented and self-consciously 'modern' thinking I'd known in northern and middle England. The Edinburghers were quirky, irritable, occasionally aggressive, eccentric and slightly out of time; an odd mixture of dour, repressive Calvinism and a high-minded pursuit of knowledge and culture. The contradictions of this were most apparent during the Festival; sophisticated London critics frequently expressed their amazement that a city which could stage such high quality, cosmopolitan cultural fare closed down completely at 10.30 p.m. It's no accident that the key Edinburgh film of that period was *The Prime Of Miss Jean Brodie*, the film based on Muriel Spark's novel about an eccentric, artistic teacher at one of Edinburgh's selective schools – Maggie Smith won an Oscar for playing Miss Brodie, with an accent not unlike Robin's.

Scotland in general hadn't participated greatly in the increase of prosperity in 1950s and 60s Britain – but Edinburgh, for all its beauty,

Robin Williamson
Edinburgh 24 11 43
5'10 10½ fair
Family something else
Education school of life
Musician since leaving school at 17
Plans ambitions none
Favourite wild hills, sweet friend
licorice, dog leaf.
music is prayer everything else
is interesting in an infinite sort of wa
Addresses various

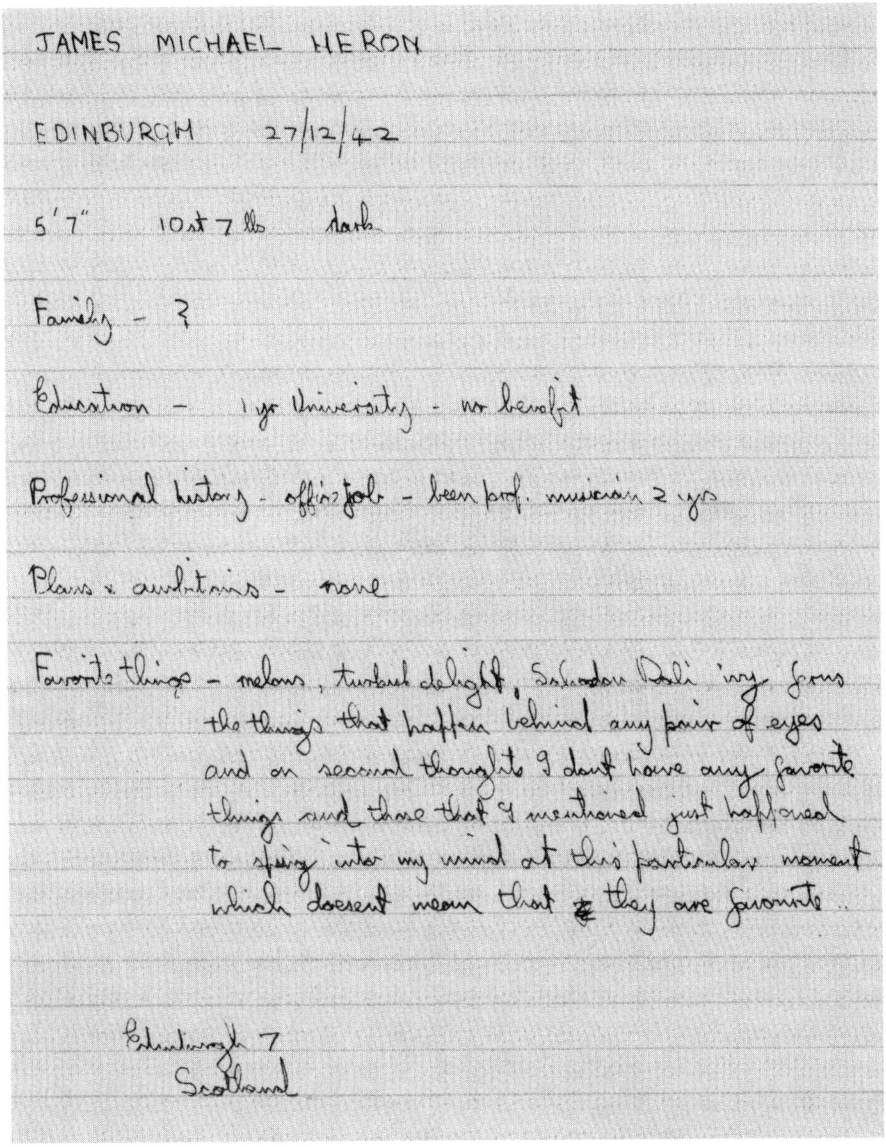

JAMES MICHAEL HERON

EDINBURGH 27/12/42

5'7" 10st 7 lbs dark

Family – ?

Education – 1 yr University – no benefit

Professional history – office job – been prof. musician 2 yrs

Plans & ambitions – none

Favorite things – melons, turkish delight, Salvador Dali, ivy, ferns
the things that happen behind any pair of eyes
and on second thoughts I dont have any favorite
things and those that I mentioned just happened
to spring into my mind at this particular moment
which doesent mean that they are favourite..

Edinburgh 7
Scotland

Those sketchy biogs from the first songbook.

hadn't developed much throughout the 20th century. Its lack of modern industry made it a very untypical British conurbation, both physically and socially. Class distinctions were drawn rather more sharply than elsewhere and snobbery was rife. 'Edinburgh has two classes – the ruling class and the servant class', proclaimed one Scottish actor sourly. The fast-growing, sceptical 'upper working class' to which my own family belonged (what advertising agencies and political pollsters now refer to as the C1s and C2s) was totally absent. Instead, an old-fashioned professional and administrative middle class – bankers, lawyers, civil servants, doctors, teachers, lecturers – dominated the city, sending its children to a network of public schools and private foundation schools whose conservative educational ethos ensured that 'Edinburgh values' were passed down from generation to generation. To me, it all seemed rather old-fashioned, if not without its own kind of wisdom – and even a certain quaint charm.

Among the pupils of these schools were Robin and Mike. It's interesting to look back to the hand-written biographical details they contributed to The Incredible String Band songbook. While Mike states that he spent a year at Edinburgh University ('no benefit'), Robin claims to have been educated at the 'school of life'. This was to be expected in the psychedelic 1960s, when a new, young world seemed to be emerging, making it more difficult than ever to identify with your family, old school tie or old boys' rugby team. Yet later they were both much less coy about their backgrounds. I don't know whether this is a result of simply growing older, or an example of Scientology's insistence that past experience shouldn't be denied, but anyway: in an interview with the *Edinburgh Evening News* Mike was described as a 'Herioter', i.e. a former pupil of George Heriot's School, and Robin was said to come from the coastal suburb of Portobello. A few years later the same paper reported that Robin was paying a visit to his old school, George Watson's College.

References to school in Robin's songs usually highlight the traumas and 'short, sharp shocks' of corporal punishment, for example in When You Find Out Who You Are – 'Remember, young man, the time before you first went to school / How did it feel, trying to live by the rule?' Whether he had indeed spent much time 'avoiding the rod of the cod-faced master' (Darling Belle) or experienced 'stormy weather...in the schoolhouse' (Weather The Storm) there, I have no idea, but one thing is certain – Scottish education in the 1950s, whether private or public, was a serious, sometimes painful business (miscreants were seldom spared the belt, cane or rod) and hardly a hotbed of progressive, child-centred ideas.

In Koeeoaddi There Robin goes back even further, to early childhood memories: 'Mrs Thomson gave me a bear / Bridget and some people lived upstairs', reflecting the tendency of Scots urban dwellers to live in flats rather than the modest two-up, two-down house of the typical English family. 'A busy main road where I wasn't to go' – a nicely ambiguous line, foretelling how he was destined not to take up a mainstream career and describing how his parents told him to keep away from the traffic... on Portobello High Street, perhaps? However, I have no idea where the 'skating on Happy Valley Pond' took place – does anyone? [*Yes! See Edinburgh map – Ed.*]

'Plodding dully through this black town'

Other ISB songs contain references to Edinburgh streets or well-known city sites. Hirem Pawnitof lived in Bread Street, which is near the entertainment district (Usher Hall, three theatres, Edinburgh's two best arthouse cinemas, numerous pubs and restaurants) of Lothian Road and Tollcross, and was formerly marked by a huge, sootblack Co-Op building, now cleaned up and converted into a hotel. [*Or was 'bread' just a 70s pun? – Ed.*]

Mike is usually less specific than Robin in his evocation of the past, but it's easy to see where his 'Friday evening's footsteps plodding dully through this black town' (Painting Box) come from – the tenement blocks and other 19th century buildings, blackened by decades of soot, grime and petrol fumes, a townscape which still exists in some Edinburgh districts. However, in many of the more affluent areas, the buildings have been restored to their original hue, which has lightened the gloom (and occasionally irritated the conservationists). And when Mike sings 'Climbing up these figures, the sun is tugging at my shoulder' (in Chinese White), it may be useful to know that he trained as an accountant, hence 'figures'. The feeling he expresses in those lines is familiar to everyone who's ever slaved over files in a stuffy office on a warm summer's day.

In one of the spoken passages of Waiting For You, Robin, in his most pukka voice, refers to a 'Mr. Jack McMarker, a bricklayer's labourer from Pilton'. Pilton has long been notorious as one of Edinburgh's most deprived and problem-ridden areas – one of the poor, outlying districts the tourists don't get to see, more 'Trainspotting country' than 'the Athens of the North'. I think the 'bronze horse by the clock tower', where the singer in Saturday Maybe will meet his lover, is the one at the east end of Princes Street, opposite the steps leading to Waverley Station.

Could this lead to a 'Heritage Trail' programme of walks conducted by the authors of this book ('assemble at Bronze Horse, Saturday 11 am prompt – maybe; bring stout shoes and a thermos')? Probably not. Here's a key to the sketch map:

1. Bronze horse and clock tower (Saturday Maybe): at the junction of Princes Street and North Bridge.
2. Greyfriars Bobby: The room in Society Buildings, now demolished, that played host to Clive, his tent, and a host of other oddballs.
3. Below the Castle: Likky and Robin lived in a tenement overlooking Princes Street gardens in the Sixties.
4. Craigentinny: Mike's childhood home.
5. Roman Camps: Near Broxburn. Where Mike and Rose lived and were filmed by Peter Neal in 1968 (off map).
6. Stockbridge/Water of Leith: Inspiration for Born In Your Town (see *Chelsea Sessions* article).
7. Glen Row: Near Innerleithen, in Borders.
8. The Howff: Early ISB venue. On the Royal Mile, opposite St. Giles' Cathedral, above what is now the International Newsagent!

9 & 10. Somewhere in the Old Town: According to Bruce Findlay, site of the Crown and possibly the Drummond Bar, Sixties Mike Heron 'harmonica rack' solo venues, mentioned in Mike's post-ISB song Trim Up Your Lovelight. The Crown Bar (very near Society Buildings, in Lothian Street and now demolished) was also home to the Robin and Clive duo in the early Sixties.

11. Not on map whatsoever: 'Music shop' from first album cover photo. That was in London.
12. Rosebury, near Murrayfield: Robin's childhood home.
13. Happy Valley Pond, where Robin skated with Likky, was Craiglockhart Pond, near Colinton Road in Happy Valley.
14. Northumberland Street: Robin lived here in his late teens, at the other end of the street from The Corries' Roy Williamson.
15. Castle Street: Lillian, Home and Cook, Mike's accountancy firm. Off Princes Street.
16. Jeanie McTavish's Plant Hire Yard: Probable location of woman with bulldozer.
17. Dumbiedykes: Another Sixties Robin haunt.
18. Usher Hall: Frequent ISB concert venue at the height of their success; also scene of Mike standing on the seat going crazy for Led Zeppelin!
19. Bruce's: Bruce Findlay's record shop, Rose Street. Unofficial fan club and ISB central pre-Scientology.
20. Waverley Studios: Bits of *U* recorded here – probably Overture and some of Rainbow.
21. St. Mary's Street: The shoe-shop site of *Dobson D. De Bray*, infamous 1970 Stone Monkey Edinburgh Festival show. Canongate.
22. Cramond Island, north-west of Edinburgh: where Robin found the actual Iron Stone.

Compiled by Adrian Whittaker and Norman Lamont. Map and icons by Deena Omar.

Weight of tradition

So much for specific Edinburgh references in the ISB's work. I think it might be possible to detect a more general influence running through their career, though probably deriving from the fact that Edinburgh was to some extent 'a place apart', with its own social and cultural world. As Ian MacDonald points out in his *Revolution In The Head*, much British culture in the 1960s – not just hippie culture – was intensely nostalgic for a lost childhood, or a lost Golden Age: concepts which are familiar to any ISB listener.

Edinburgh in the 50s and 60s, a city where the present moment seemed less important than the weight of tradition transmitted by architecture, education or religion, was perhaps an extreme example of this tendency – and this must surely have influenced Robin and Mike, even subconsciously.

Scottish, but middle-class ('Edinburgh people are imitation English', my grandfather used to say); conventional yet a haven for bohemians (Sandy Brown and other jazzmen educated at the Royal High School, the poets' pubs in Rose Street, the folk scene which nurtured the ISB, Better Books, the Traverse Theatre); insular yet cosmopolitan (the Festival bred numerous passionate Francophiles and stern devotees of German *Kultur*); so far behind the times as to be actually ahead of them (the city was run for a long time by a right-wing Conservative council – until Margaret Thatcher, who had learned to 'speak properly' by copying the accent of the Edinburgh-born headmistress of her school in Grantham, came along – and they were promptly thrown out)... the city revels in paradoxes ('and the opposite is also true').

However, if the ISB have changed with the years then so has their home town. Towards the end of the 1970s the Sleeping Beauty began to awaken. Graduates of the city's universities began to spread the word that here was a nice place to live. The Sunday colour supplements followed suit. New wealth began to flow in, thanks to the North Sea oil industry. The financial sector, too, boomed during the Thatcher years and Edinburgh was well placed to benefit. The dismal Tory councils of the 1970s were replaced by younger Labour administrators with more outward-looking, open-minded attitudes ('New Labour' before its time?). Suddenly, new houses and industrial sites grew on the periphery of the city; many of the notorious 'holes in the ground' in the city centre were at last filled in. Edinburgh nowadays is in many ways a much more lively, attractive and cosmopolitan place than it was 30 years ago. Of course, there are problems – traffic, drugs, general urban stress. But much of the worst aspects of 'old Edinburgh' – the prim snobbery, po-faced Calvinism and repressive ignorance – have disappeared, hopefully for ever. And it may well be that the ISB have contributed to this change for the better.

Overleaf One of the late George Boyter's Pan drawings, sent in to accompany the stories F&f sent to the Witchseason office.

Chapter Three

1968: *Wee Tam And The Big Huge*, US gigs, Sound Techniques, Witchseason and on to *Changing Horses*

1968 – the year the ISB really took off

Adrian Whittaker

'You played your strings like they led to the truth Sang your words like clear spring light' (from the lyrics to 1968 by Mike Heron, written in 1974)

1968 was a key year in the ISB's nine-year history. *Hangman* was released to great acclaim, and Rose and Likky joined Mike and Robin on live performances and in the studio, where they recorded the key double album, *Wee Tam And The Big Huge*. The creative partnership with dancers Mimi and Mouse came abruptly to an end, there was the first of many collaborations with dancers Rakis and future ISB member Malcolm Le Maistre, Peter Neal made his *Be Glad* film about and with them, they played two American tours and filled the Albert Hall – twice. It was the year the ISB really took off nationally, and internationally.

In January the band started playing abroad, with Swedish and Danish gigs and one at Liberty Hall, Dublin, still with Mimi and Mouse at this point. 'A glorious half-hour trance,' said one reviewer. The newly formed Dr Strangely Strange were on the same bill, oddly the only time the two outfits ever performed together, despite Robin and Likky's longstanding links with Ivan Pawle and the Mount Street Orphanage.

To coincide with the release of *Hangman* in March, Joe underwrote their first UK tour of major concert halls in London, Birmingham, Manchester, Liverpool and Glasgow. Before Mimi and Mouse were given their cards, a psychedelic poster by Hapshash and The Coloured Coat was commissioned to promote the tour, showing Mike and Robin spanning the globe, with M&M dancing attendance (see cover illustration). In later years the two semi-naked dancers on the poster were often taken to be Rose and Likky, though Rose at least was fairly philosophical about this. You can see the poster in the colour section.

2021

Mike and Robin at the Brøndby Pop Club, with Joe Boyd sitting patiently on the floor behind them. © Steen Rasmussen

Mystical Pantomimes 1968

Adrian Whittaker

In the Sixties, two key psychedelic ISB posters were designed by Hapshash and the Coloured Coat. Nigel Waymouth and Michael English had come together in late 1966 via Joe Boyd and Hoppy Hopkins, who were looking for a distinctive poster style to advertise their UFO Club. The two designers eventually chose the working name Hapshash and the Coloured Coat, which suggested both hashish and psychedelic patterning (Joseph's 'coat of many colours'). The posters were printed and distributed by Osiris Visions, originally owned by the *International Times*. Soon Osiris found a home in the Witchseason's Charlotte Street offices under the aegis of Danny Halperin, Joe's head of graphic design. Hapshash did a few posters for Witchseason artists, including an ISB poster for the 1967 October Songs concert with Shirley and Dolly Collins.

Nigel Waymouth: 'We worked on each poster together. Because always there were colour separations we would work on one separation each and often swap as the mood took us. Ideas were exchanged and mapped out beforehand, often on layout paper. Every poster was a collaboration and that's what gives Hapshash posters their distinct character.'

The 'Mystical Pantomimes' poster, produced in early 1968 for the first big ISB tour with Mimi and Mouse, was one of the later Hapshash works. Although it bears the Hapshash logo at the bottom right, it is undated. Nigel: 'The stamp marking is meaningless. It's something Michael wrote in the manner of a "spell", or so he said at the time. It just adds a bit of mystery to the overall design.'

It reflects the start of a move away from the classic psychedelia of the UFO posters. Nigel: 'What I remember was using the Ben-Day dots for the first time.' The dots, typically used in comics from the Fifties onwards, were used to create shading in images. You could get transparent overlay sheets from a stationery supplier, available in a wide variety of dot size and distribution, which gave the artist a range of tones to use in the work. The overlay material was cut in the shapes required, often as background, and rubbed onto the specific areas of the drawing with a burnisher.

'Wham!' artist Roy Lichtenstein foregrounded the use of the dots in his work, often using them in enlarged and exaggerated versions. Nigel did the same in the bottom half of the poster. There is also a transatlantic bridge, possibly suggested by Joe Boyd as part of his plan to break the ISB in the States later that year, although in some ways a bridge to North Africa might have been more appropriate! *The Beano*'s Biffo The Bear also makes an appearance, alongside some frankly phallic towers in the top section, which echoes work by Mucha and Beardsley. There's also a surprisingly small drawing of the Mike and Robin in 5000 *Spirits* mode. Rose: 'It always seemed a bit odd that M&R were such a small and pedestrian image but then it was all about cosmic whatsits and how do you draw a spirit-messenger?'

Mimi and Mouse are really the stars of the poster (and the transatlantic bridge could also be a nod to their San Francisco roots). In the lower section, they are prominently featured dancing, but without their amazing silk costumes. Nigel: 'I remember Michael thinking it was quite cheeky to draw M&M fairly nude.' It certainly came as a shock to the dancers when they finally saw the finished product. Rose: 'Because of the timing, inevitably, the images got shifted onto Lic and me, by implication if not by name. I don't think either of us were particularly unhappy about that. The phallic towers were very much the imagery of the time, the liberation from shame and the acknowledgement (again) of sex as something to be joyful about. Beardsley etc were the fashionable resources, outraging bourgeois sensibilities being part of the fun of it all.'

It's unclear whether, in the end, the poster was actually used for promotional purposes, especially as the dancers had been dropped from the tour at the last minute. Certainly there was a big pile of them on sale on the autumn 1969 ISB tour – which is where I bought mine for, I think, 7 shillings and sixpence. Nigel: 'I know nothing about the ISB tour or why M&M were dropped. I think we were paid £10 for the job!'

These days, the poster is archived at the V&A Museum, who describe it in their online catalogue as 'full of sexual and colourful symbolism. Fantastic multiple split colour passes of ink from gold to yellow and red and a dark to light blue over the top.'

The tour was a huge success and in May 1968 Joe decided to take Mike, Robin (and Likky, we think) to the States. At that point Mike and Robin had played only one gig there, the Newport Folk Festival the previous year. Their first major US gig was planned for the Fillmore East. In the past, Joe had done some shows for listener-funded New York radio station WBAI, and so a couple of weeks before the June concert date, he organised a late night studio session on Bob Fass' Radio Unnameable show. Bob (described as the 'father of freeform radio') favoured a rambling approach, often intercutting performances with a range of sound effects from his extensive collection. The ISB rose to the occasion by avoiding any songs that might be familiar to the audience from *Hangman* and playing an uncompromising set consisting entirely of unreleased material. The session was eventually released on *Tricks Of The Senses*.

After Bob's introductory fireworks ('to chase away the evil spirits'), Robin kicks off the session with an early version of his poem, The Head. Mike and Likky provide some suitably spacy background effects. The final version of The Head eventually surfaced on an insert in the *Wee Tam* And The *Big Huge* double, complete with a water-colour illustration by Robin. Then comes a leisurely version of Mike's Douglas Traherne Harding, a song he'd recorded for *Wee Tam* just a month before (the same session as All Too Much For Me). See All The People, which surfaced later on the *Be Glad For The Song Has No Ending* LP, here provides a vehicle for a contrapuntal jam, possibly with Likky on percussion. It's an odd little song, even by ISB standards, with a sense of Zen-like detachment from the world. The last song from this session is an intense rendering of Robin's Maya; this is a standout version, not long after it was recorded at the first *Wee Tam* session in February that year. On the WBAI session you get to hear the original ending, chopped off on the LP by Joe Boyd, (rather unwillingly!) to segue into Greatest Friend.

After that there was a New York University gig supporting the Grateful Dead, but the ISB 'didn't really hit it off' with them, says Mike. 'It was like an alien culture – they were running around playing American Football while we were into concepts like the barter economy.' John Sebastian and other Lovin' Spoonful members 'vied to entertain' them, showing Mike and Robin round the Greenwich Village clubs for a few days. Then, while waiting for more gigs to be set up, Joe took them off to Vermont to visit a friend of his, a classical pianist who lived in a cabin in the woods half-way up a mountain. 'It took us ages to get there,' remembers Mike. 'It was this very rustic setting, but in the middle of the cabin was this immaculate concert grand!' The friend's dog, Nina, had just had puppies, prompting Mike to come up with a new song in which Nina got a namecheck...

In 2012, when a Fillmore East live CD was released, Robin wrote a short piece about the tour for the booklet. This is an extract: 'They tell me I was there – these dates so long ago – I suppose I must have been. I remember bits and pieces. I remember coming through customs was always interesting. I remember I always had to explain that rosin was a violin accessory. 1968 New York, hot summer night, me and Mike sitting on the roof of the Chelsea Hotel listening to the city play its choir of car horns, sirens, shouts and occasional distant pistol shots. Automat food – quarters, nickels and dimes. Greyhound Station, voice off: "Clean up America, get a haircut!"

'Us opening for the Grateful Dead... Well all I can say is they were a hell of a lot louder than we were but we were far more entertainingly attired... full length red embroidered wizard style robe in my case, that or jester's outfit... I used to wear that stuff. There were log cabins in the woods upstate, beaver dams, porcupine quills as a dog hazard, June bugs...'

Some West Coast club gigs with Tim Buckley and Them, plus 3 nights supporting Country Joe And The Fish at the Fillmore West, were not always well received. 'They were much more of a rock audience,' says Mike. 'In some of the clubs they thought we were a comedy act!' They liked Country Joe and the Fish, who proved to be more on their wavelength, and got on well with Tim Buckley, who was then in his jazz/folk period, playing songs from *Happy/Sad*. 'It was only later that we got into his music, though,' says Mike. 'The jazzy stuff with vibes and so on was ahead of the culture we were aware of.'

After the Fillmore West gig, Joe and his brother took them off to Porvenir Canyon, a New Mexico nature reserve, where they rented cabins in the woods and did some hiking. Joe Boyd: 'After a while this got boring, so we decided to go to the nearest movie house. This was in Las Vegas and involved a two-hour walk each way to where the car was parked. It was a major undertaking, so we made a pact that whatever film was showing, we'd all go.' It turned out to be Otto Preminger's *Skidoo*, a bizarre film which they all loved. The plot climaxes with the hero, Jackie Gleason, in San Francisco Bay surrounded by a tribe of hippies in boats who save him from being killed by the Mafia. Back in LA, Joe had invited his friend Tom Law, at the time part of a hippie commune in New Mexico, to the gig with them at the Kaleidoscope Club. He came backstage afterwards with a group of friends. 'Amazingly, they were exactly the same tribe of hippies we'd just seen in the film,' says Joe. 'So of course there was a big party!'

After a short Hollywood recording session at Western Recorders on Sunset Boulevard (versions of Maya, Mountain Of God and Puppies, then titled His Own Bone) it was time to return to New York and probably the best gig the ISB ever did as a two-piece.

The Fillmore East concert, June 5th 1968

Adrian Whittaker

The Fillmore East was predominantly a weekend venue, characteristically with two or more shows a night on Fridays and Saturdays featuring two or three headliners. Jefferson Airplane and The Crazy World of Arthur Brown had been on a few weeks before the ISB show, and both Jimi Hendrix and Steppenwolf were on a few days later. On the quieter weekdays Bill Graham would let radical groups and Lower East Side community organisations use the hall, a former cinema, for benefit gigs.

On the night of the ISB concert, a Wednesday, Graham's staff were bemused to encounter a polite, reflective audience of laid-back hippies rather than the usual Hell's Angels, East Village 'Motherfuckers' and off-their-heads rock fans. *5000 Spirits* had already attracted a sizeable cult following in New York, and the listener-funded WBAI radio station had been playing *Hangman* (then in the *Billboard* Top 100) in heavy rotation; this, coupled with the appearance on Bob Fass' show a couple of weeks earlier and a few discreet ads in the underground press, meant the evening was probably sold out.

Bob Fass opened the show by explaining that it was a benefit for both WBAI and the audience, who would benefit from 'the art and the beauty of – the Incredible String Band.' There then followed an embarrassingly long pause, (born stoically by the audience) until Mike and Robin shuffled on: 'Two shaggy guys in pyjamas,' to quote one reviewer.

Of course they were magnificent. Joe Boyd feels this concert shows the ISB at their absolute apex, and I'm inclined to agree. Waltz Of the New Moon, preceded by an embryonic version of The Yellow Snake, was intense from the very start, Robin adeptly incorporating Dolly Collins' harpsichord lines into his guitar part. Mike's You Get Brighter (with Robin on organ) precedes a wonderful version of Cellular Song. Mike's in great voice and Robin supplies endlessly inventive harmonies. A very long October Song incorporates parts of Half-Remarkable Question, a work in progress since late 1966. The length clearly took Walter Gundy, the front-of-house sound engineer, by surprise as the tape ran out in the middle, leaving a few seconds gap in the recording. Mike's sitar-playing on this (and on Maya) is remarkable. 'Bells' is the famous audience participation section, where audience members, conducted by Robin, would play bells and whistles which had been taped up to play a specific note.

A long segue follows. The Pig Went Walking Over The Hill (Robin has no idea where the lyrics came from) is basically a two-guitar jam in the same vein as Mike's See All The People, the little Zen observation which follows it. Some rather scary wails (Mike in full voice again) introduce Swift As The Wind, another song on which Robin's harmonies go off into some deeply weird and dark territory, warbling and muttering like a man possessed. It ends perhaps a moment too soon, segueing into an accomplished Mercy I Cry City.

An intermission is followed by the 'Krishna Story' dance/mime piece which Mike and Robin had cooked up with Malcolm Le Maistre and Rakis (both later in the Stone Monkey dance group), whom they'd bumped into in the lobby of the Chelsea Hotel (see below). An early version of Ducks On A Pond follows – mainly Robin solo, but when Mike joins on harmonies towards the end the performance lifts to a whole other level. The ISB never believed in 'playing the new album' so another unreleased *Wee Tam* song follows; the audience doesn't seem remotely baffled by all this new material, though there's a huge roar of approval a bit later when they recognise Chinese White from *5000 Spirits*. This is probably the debut of Puppies, written just a couple of weeks earlier during a side trip to Vermont. After Chinese White comes what is probably the first ever concert performance of Maya; probably as a consequence of recording it in Hollywood the week before, Robin's finalised the lyrics, though oddly a few verses are missing at the end. Maybe they were up against a curfew? As on the WBAI studio recording it's a very intense performance, with strong vocal harmonies by Mike towards the end. The audience response at the end of the show is impressive; by this point they were up and dancing, according to one observer, and the cheers are deafening. Robin and Mike return to the stage to offer a heartfelt 'Thank you very much for coming'.

'Come on in, man, great vibes here!'

Mike and Robin met future ISB member Malcolm Le Maistre quite by chance, in the infamous New York hotel, the Chelsea. In her book *At The Chelsea*, Malcolm Le Maistre's mum Florence recounts how he and John Koumantarakis, a fellow ex- Exploding Galaxy member, landed at Kennedy Airport, 'deep-dyed enemies of the fuzz', and took up residence at the Chelsea where they spent a lot of time 'recording the sound of water, seated on the floor with a big bowl filled from the tap, splashing it melodiously'. As one did in those days. After unsuccessfully trying to persuade MGM Records to sign them they placed a notice in the hotel lobby which read:

Trans-Media Activators, Creators Sound/Light/Dance are
Needed to EXPLODE...
Exploiters of Mantric Sound structures, Chinese Ballet,
Quaki-Quali Akashic Records, Tantric Flesh-poems, Chakra
Actuations
And more and
All
Point Cosmic 0
NOW Contact
Come See Stone Monkey
Room 604
Transcend
Time/Space/Inertia/Inhibitions/Masturbation/New York hang-ups

Malcolm picks up the story:

> 'At 3am one morning we were listening to the hip station WBAI, and there were Mike and Robin in the studio doing Maya. I think Rakis said: 'Wow, maybe they're actually staying in this hotel,' and I told him not to be silly. He went off down to get breakfast and – outside the lobby – met Mike and Robin coming back from the studio. He told them we'd just been listening to them on the radio etc etc, and invited them to breakfast. I'd fallen asleep by this time, and was woken by a knock on the door – it was Mike Heron looking for breakfast! All I had was Sara Lee orange cakes! A bit later, Robin knocked too and Mike uttered the classic line 'Come on in, man, great vibes here.' I was delighted – I mean, these were my heroes – but there was nothing to offer them, and I was desperately hoping Rakis would get back with some food!
>
> 'We talked, and we got on very well, and they said, "We're off to the West Coast now, but we've got a gig at the Fillmore – would you like to come and do some dance with us when we get back?" And that's what we did. We didn't really rehearse. I think they said, come on during this number, and we had a vague story about Krishna and Arjuna. Of course, we'd been to the Fillmore lots of times, but there we were up on stage! It was amazing.' Rakis adds: 'The show at the Fillmore worked very well – we acted out a little story and they improvised. They asked us to do the same in Edinburgh and the Albert Hall later that year.'

The Fillmore East concert, June 5th 1968

Back in the UK, there was a triumphant concert on June 29th at the Royal Albert Hall, which the Beatles were half-expected to attend. In the end, though, biographer Mark Lewisohn tells us they didn't make it, knackered after a long week at Abbey Road recording for *The White Album*.

Rose made her first full appearance with the band; Likky had already started guesting on the occasional song, and as Rose says, 'my presence redressed the balance'. The concert was, as she writes in her memoir, 'more of a shared celebration than the performance of a new LP.... After the Albert Hall, we girls were part of the group'. The recording sessions for *Wee Tam* continued through the summer; the 'girls' contributed to the sound of what was increasingly becoming a four-piece, not just with added backing vocals and/or percussion on songs like Maya, but also fiddle (Rose on Log Cabin) and Irish harp (Likky on Iron Stone).

After their return from New York, Malcolm and Rakis had set up a sort of artistic commune with the other members of their new dance/mime project, Stone Monkey. Robin and Likky joined them in Penwern, an inhospitable Pembrokeshire farmhouse near Fishguard and together, they worked up a 'fable,' The Pirate And The Crystal Ball, filmed by Peter Neal for *Be Glad For The Song Has No Ending* (covered elsewhere in this book). In late 1968, Ivan Pawle left the embryonic Strangelies behind in Dublin and headed for Penwern. Ivan: 'When I arrived, I asked Farmer Luke how much rent I should pay him. He said I could pay him in kind, by cleaning out the pigsty. It was Big Ted's sty and so it took me a surprisingly long time!'

By the time Ivan turned up, Stone Monkey and the ISB had already completed work on the 'Pirate' film sequence but he was roped into the next joint project. *Wee Tam* was set for a November release, to be marked by a big concert at the Albert Hall the same month, where Stone Monkey were to join the ISB on stage for the finale. Ivan: 'When I arrived, Robin was writing Creation.' Robin had been reading a tract by Robert Graves titled *Adam's Rib*, which attempted a reconstruction of a pagan version of the seven days of creation. Using some of Graves' text as a centrepiece, Robin had woven in other arcane references and his own poetry, with enigmatic lines such as: 'the archetypal postman delivering your seed letters, whose eyes are black eggs really'. The result was a lengthy and ambitious spoken word and music concoction, which eventually appeared on *Changing Horses*. Ivan played piano and organ on the recorded version.

Ivan: 'The plan was that we would all play and dance when the ISB performed it. We were on a macrobiotic regime at the time, and had picked some Amanita Muscaria [Fly agaric or magic mushrooms] and fasted for a week. At one stage l went to Dublin and Linus [briefly a Dr Strangely Strange member] came back with me to Penwern, so she was part of it as well. At the gig I played a keyboard. It was a small electric organ, very basic, a kid's toy that Robin had picked up somewhere. The late Nicky Walton [the friend of Robin's who appears on the sleeve of *Hangman*] was Neptune.'

The Albert Hall audience appeared to like it and gave them all a five-minute ovation. The music press, however, was baffled. A journalist named only as 'Keef' reported: 'The finale was a poem (unintelligible unfortunately) set to music. During its performance, the company was swelled by assorted dance-mime characters including Neptune and several nebulous nymphs.' The ISB spurned encores in this era, seeing them as an artificial construct (they soon changed their minds), so Keef reported glumly that 'the only result was to have two more glimpses of the weirdy dancers. Rather a let-down after an original, overwhelming, incredible concert.'

Rose Simpson: 'I remember we were quite committed to Creation as a serious idea and that encouraged the refusal to do an encore because it shouldn't be regarded as a piece you could just treat like another set of miscellaneous songs. However, as usual, some of Robin's songs just rambled on too long. Because it did have an important theme, and it was early days for that multimedia venture, and because we were still quite idealistic and believed in it and each other, the performance was a bit hypnotic for us too.'

The year was rounded off by an American mini-tour, fuelled, according to Rose, by Dr Sam Hutt's prescription of a bright green 'ribbed glass bottle of tetrahydrocannabinol'; audiences at the Fillmore and the Lincoln Centre were treated to a selection of songs from *Hangman* and *Wee Tam* alongside the as-yet unrecorded epics White Bird and Creation. This was also the point where first Likky, then Robin, made a fateful visit to the New York Scientology centre...

/

11 AUG 1968

marquee artists

Artists representation & management

Marquee Artists Agency Limited
18 Carlisle Street, Soho Square,
London, W.1
Telephones: GERrard 6601/2/3

Directors:

D.C.Barber
H. Pendleton

Licensed annually by the Westminster City Council.

COMMISSION NOTE

Artiste's Name .... The Incredible String Band ....

Date .... 28th June 1968 ....

In consideration of your procuring for me the undermentioned engagement(s) which I hereby agree to accept through your Agency

with .... National Fazz Festival Limited ....

at .... Kempton Park, Sunbury on Thames. ....

on .... Sunday (afternoon) 11th August 1968. ....

at a Salary of .... £350.0.0. (Three hundred and fifty pounds). ....

I agree to pay MARQUEE ARTISTS AGENCY LTD. a·commission of .... ten* .... of the gross salary

* Equally divisable with Bryan Morrison Agency.

I also agree to pay a like commission on further engagements with the same Management when such re-engagement is made within twelve months of the expiration of the above mentioned engagement(s)

ARTISTE'S SIGNATURE .... J M Boyd ....

PERMANENT ADDRESS .... 83 Charlotte St .... W.1 ....

PLEASE SIGN AND RETURN ONE COPY TO MARQUEE ARTISTS AGENCY LTD AND RETAIN THE OTHER

Yours for £350—contract for the National Jazz Festival, 1968. (Witchseason archive)

In November 1968 Elektra released Wee Tam And The Big Huge, *the ISB's most ambitious album to date. It was conceived as a double; just to complicate matters it was also issued as two separate LPs* (Wee Tam *and* The Big Huge) *to allow poorer fans to get it on a sort of instalment basis. This of course played havoc with its chart listings; despite the success of* Hangman, *it didn't appear in a single Top Fifty. For the sake of brevity the whole thing is usually referred to in this book as* Wee Tam.

Wee Tam *reflected an even wider variety of influences than the previous two releases and was packed to overflowing with classic ISB songs; there was so much material from this very fertile period in 1968 that some of it spilled over onto later albums, notably* Be Glad For The Song Has No Ending *and* Changing Horses. *It was recorded as an ensemble, with fewer overdubs than before and much fuller use of* Rose *and* Licorice, *particularly in the way the vocal parts were arranged. Grahame Hood introduces the album; David Kidman picks up on the underlying allusions and motifs.*

Wee Tam And The Big Huge

Grahame Hood

The title struck me as particularly Scottish; 'huge big' is a common children's expression in the East of Scotland, e.g. 'I saw a man with a huge big dog'. Robin revealed in an interview: 'We knew somebody called Wee Tam, in Edinburgh. It seemed like it was a good idea in terms of like, one person looking up at the stars; *Wee Tam* and the *Big Huge*. Just like the vastness of the universe. Again, very light, not intended to be terribly heavy'.

Repeated listenings threw up puzzles to be investigated; who was the Son of Noah's Brother? And what in Mike's name was Douglas Traherne Harding all about? Heron didn't write songs like *that*... A friend suggested that Herman Hesse's *Siddhartha* held the key, so we read that and I enjoyed it (though I did feel sorry for Siddhartha's friend who joined the wrong cult) but didn't see the connection. I saw some relevance in the hiding of the sheep and goats to avoid the toll, but this made me think of a) the song The Rock Island Line (Mike's skiffle roots?) b) The *Odyssey*, where Odysseus leads his men out from the cave of the blinded Cyclops (my eye was single) under cover of the Cyclops' sheep. Of course I know what it's about *now*; the quotes from the poet Thomas Traherne used in Douglas Harding's book *On Having No Head*, and the references to the basement flat in York which Mike and Rose visited at the time.

I was also puzzled by the two (count 'em) references to Hitler. Had Robin's mum been frightened by a Heinkel perhaps? After all, the war was on when he was born...

Neither Mike nor Robin have ever denied their admiration for Dylan, and his influence is felt throughout the album. Mike's Greatest Friend may well be a tribute to the Carter Family in spirit, but the delivery dates right back to the tour Mike did of the Scottish folk clubs between the first and second albums with just his guitar 'and a harmonica on a wee rack' as he once put it. Robin's Lordly Nightshade is also, I think, an attempt to write a Dylan style stream-of-images song, though not entirely successfully ('Middle aged persons with dwarfish expressions and tinned conversations in Sunday blessed blue' – hint of the other Dylan there, too).

The boys had been to America for the first time at the 1967 Newport Folk Festival, and seemingly come back with the desire to tap earlier American influences. Puppies owes more than a nod to Leadbelly's Poor Howard ('Poor Howard's dead and gone / left me here to sing this song'), and Woody Guthrie's Ain't Got No Home plays a large part in the musical collage that is Ducks On A Pond. Ducks is also the title of a fiddle/banjo tune (the tune Robin flat-picks as the intro?).

Going back to Robin's lyrics, he succeeds nobly elsewhere on the album with many phrases that stick in the mind in a way that reminds me of the lovely phrase about poetry in *The White Goddess* where Graves writes: 'I am a wizard, who but I, sets the cool head aflame with smoke'. Consider 'Green-foot slow', 'Wandering beneath the empty skies' and the enigmatic thought of 'peacocks talking of the colour grey'.

The 1976 book *Electric Muse* goes so far as to say 'the entire double album possesses a lyric sensitivity that has yet to be found on any other modern music album – at least in English – and adds weight to the assertion that the best modern poetry is being written in the form of song. Of particular note is Maya, which develops a mystic, almost surrealistic vision couched in an imagery that has all the strength and beauty of the best of Dylan Thomas'. It does have to be said that it is Robin who carries off most of the lyrical accolades, though Mike's phrase 'fiddle head ferns' has a very pleasing ring to it. Musically, Mike cannot be criticised at all; You Get Brighter is a lovely song, with its unsubtle references to 'All things bright and beautiful'. The spectre of Scottish Sunday school crops up often throughout the album, especially on Job's Tears which is also notable for the girls' high harmonies; 'You could cut steel with those voices', as John Peel once quipped.

Robin's later solo CD *Mirrorman's Sequences* gives the clue that the Iron Stone was found on Cramond Island in the Forth in the Northwest part of Edinburgh. The island is connected at low tide to the mainland by a causeway and everyone in Edinburgh can tell an 'I know somebody who was stranded on Cramond Island' story. Robin certainly can! Iron Stone is a great song though, and it is a real thrill to see it performed in the *Be Glad* film.

In retrospective interviews, Joe Boyd has thrown a lot of light on the politics within the band at this time, Robin and Mike insisting on having a say in the arrangements of each other's songs, and in particular the introduction of Rose to balance Licorice. Both were really to the band's benefit musically: where would Maya or The Iron Stone be without the sitar? The added personnel made it easier to recreate the album material in live performance, and the arrangements on the album are much simpler than on *Hangman*, presumably with live work in mind.

The album closes with The Circle Is Unbroken. Using a traditional Irish melody called Lament For Anach Cuin, Robin hints at the Celtic direction he would later pursue in his solo career. With just whistle and harp over a simple organ backing, it provides a moving and apt end. It was the end of one cycle for the ISB; by *Changing Horses* their previous 'try and pinch anything from everywhere' attitude had become more focussed.

I'll finish there. I've just had the urge to light the candles and have a listen. 'Dust of the rivers...'

STUART GODFREY'S MOMENTOUS DECISION

It was a momentous decision for me: buy the double album and starve for the next month, or buy one of the single albums and starve for a fortnight? Having decided to go for one of the singles, a further dilemma now faced me: *Wee Tam* or the *Big Huge*? After much deliberation the seeds of my eventual career as a Civil Servant must have come to the fore and order prevailed – I got *Wee Tam* because it was the first bit.

A song-cycle

David Kidman sees Wee Tam And The Big Huge *as a song-cycle, an 'informal exploration of alternative beliefs'.*

There are problems in trying to convey the achievements of any important work of art, particularly a seminal one like *Wee Tam*. For seminal it is, undeniably. Popular critical opinion is invariably along the lines that *Wee Tam* is the pinnacle of the ISB's achievement.

For once, I won't disagree with the consensus: *Wee Tam* rates with Love's *Forever Changes* as one of the most important albums ever made, both albums at once of and ahead of their time. None of the 'big-league names' could ever come close to these in terms of spiritual awareness, commitment and sheer creativity. It is the way in which the various elements – music, lyrics, production, vision – combine that makes these albums so special and gives them their status.

Wee Tam, like other great albums, exudes a specific ambience – here, a pervasive sense of serenity, harmony and well-being. Unlike *Hangman's Beautiful Daughter*, where darker forces intrude, *Wee Tam* has a predominantly optimistic outlook on life, nature and the cosmos. Sure, there's mystery and magic, but this belongs more to benign powers or fantasy than to anything negative. Much of the album's atmosphere stems from its religious quality, but the term 'religious' is all too easy to misinterpret – perhaps a more accurate term would be 'pantheistic'. The dictionary definition of pantheistic is: 'belief that God is identifiable with the forces of nature and with natural substances', and/or 'worship that admits or tolerates all gods'. Both these aspects are relevant to *Wee Tam*'s world-view, concerned with the wonders of creation and faith in nature generally. There is a life-affirming outlook; its unifying ambience is of almost gospel fervour, though it is both a spiritual quest and a celebration. One important feature of *Wee Tam* which sets it apart from other 'progressive' albums of the period is that the instrumental passages are not unduly dominant, but function as interludes or for the purpose of scene-setting; even the sitar/guitar duet which closes The Iron Stone couldn't really be described as a 'jam'.

During the course of *Wee Tam*, an informal examination of alternative beliefs and philosophies is undertaken. The first side seems to comprise a kind of search for – or examination of – values, both material and spiritual. It begins in Job's Tears with the search for spiritual values, partly through conventional Biblical teachings. It goes on to seek – and perhaps, in Puppies, find – solace in nature, despite its apparent fickleness, concluding with Log Cabin in a celebration of traditional country comforts.

A call to attention

To begin at the beginning then – Job's Tears is rather an unexpected kind of song to choose to open an album with. Just as with Koeeoaddi There on *Hangman*, the listener is plunged in to the discourse without instrumental preamble, but the difference here is that it's a call to attention, and once our attention is grabbed the full impact of the unfolding images can be felt. Though the lyrics use standard Biblical imagery, their content and impact are subtly changed by being sensitively questioned. Raymond deals with Job's Tears in detail later in this book, so I'll confine the rest of my comments to the musical content. First, the stark, minimal instrumental setting – just Robin's guitar – allows for maximum concentration on the lyrics and the vocal delivery. Likky's ethereally pure vocal countermelody is truly delikkious (pardon the pun)! Second, although the song is tightly structured, there is a feeling of improvisation, almost storytelling, in the way the melodic lines develop along with – and in response to – the lyrics. Though the music differs for each individual section, it doe not come across as episodic; it could almost be described as 'durchkomponiert' – literally, 'through-composed'. Robin takes us with him on his quest and leads the song's final call-and-response section with the fervour of a gospel leader. Although the song is a free-associating attempt to make sense of an overload of sensations, surely the joyous concluding section conveys a temporary contentment with the experience that conventional religion has to offer? The range of Robin's voice is worth noting, encompassing high-register keening and resonant deep tones, as is the gamut of emotion conveyed by its expressive qualities. As a footnote, the musical figure for 'We're all still here, no-one has gone away' plays a similar role to the opening bars of Poulenc's *Gloria*, the rhythm of which it echoes.

Puppies neatly develops the exultant mood of the concluding section of Job's Tears. It has a fair bit in common with Mike's earlier 'nature' songs, but it lacks the twee quality that marred some of them. This time round there's a bittersweet feeling, a note of dissent, a sense that despite our attempts to live at one with nature, and to appease its creatures, it is in the end fickle. The puppies have gone, despite the singer's well-meaning efforts to play 'what [he] thought that new-born fur would like best'. Even the power of music cannot match the power and creativity of nature – 'music is so much less'. Musically, the structure of Puppies is satisfying in its symmetry: the 'Even the birds when they sing' section frames the main narrative, instigates both the experience with the puppies and rounds off the memory of it after lessons have been learnt, and leads finally to philosophical musings on the nature of music in relation to the music of nature. Some of the individual images in the song are delightful – I'd never come across anything like 'fiddle-head ferns' in real life until I started hill-walking and got to appreciate the endless varieties of fern. I'm still puzzled by the reference to Mother Nina though... [*Nina was the puppies' mother – 'a mongrel Alsatian' in Vermont – according to Mike – Ed.*] The instrumental interplay throughout Puppies is attractive and playful throughout, as befits the lyric.

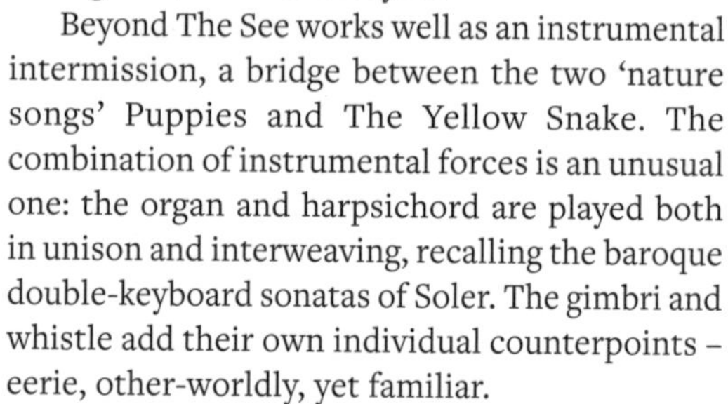

Beyond The See works well as an instrumental intermission, a bridge between the two 'nature songs' Puppies and The Yellow Snake. The combination of instrumental forces is an unusual one: the organ and harpsichord are played both in unison and interweaving, recalling the baroque double-keyboard sonatas of Soler. The gimbri and whistle add their own individual counterpoints – eerie, other-worldly, yet familiar.

The Yellow Snake is an exquisite miniature, yet ever so slightly understated, with a sense of unplumbed depths of wonder. The matching of the lyric 'refreshed' with the equally refreshing and unusual keening of the sarangi is the ideal choice for evoking the mystery and sinuousness of the snake's coils. The dreamy rhythm, the slow pulse of 'stretched sleeping on the sand' has an almost Twenties languorousness, helped along by the harmony and vocal delivery.

Log Cabin Home In The Sky is so different from everything else on the album, but stands out for the rich sound of its ensemble playing. The multiple fiddling gives the track an authentic 'string band' sound, to use the term in its true sense. Lyrically, the country clichés come thick and fast, but Mike's

Summer 1968. (From a Witchseason programme)

delivery transcends mere imitation, and the overall arrangement is an affectionate homage to the old-timey tradition.

'Pure Magic'

On to Side Two of the original vinyl with You Get Brighter, a hymn of praise which has that magical quality of simple intricacy characteristic of the best of the ISB's material. The musical settings have the formal perfection of the great classical song-cycles, yet each song remains self-contained. In You Get Brighter, the delicacy of the arrangement perfectly complements the lyrics, and there's a pre-echo of the neo-baroque harpsichord figurations on The Letter (from *I Looked Up*). Structurally, the song is impeccable; the 'Krishna colours' section is given just enough expansion and repetition, like a mantra, before the final chorus and then the ending with the coda of the opening phrase.

The Half-Remarkable Question is wholly remarkable: it typifies the band at their best, Robin and Mike working together to create pure magic. The song has a simple, logical musical structure (AABA) which, though tightly organised, retains the feel of a developing melody line. All is perfectly crafted, with not a note or phrase wasted. Yet this belies the complex, often obscure, content. On the page, the lyrics look somewhat impenetrable, yet you don't get that impression once Robin sings them. It all makes a kind of sense, a good example of the potential for responsive understanding. I spent years wondering who Gimmel and Daleth were, but though I now know they are characters from the Hebrew alphabet, I'm still no closer to unravelling the layers of meaning in the dark opening verse. The guitar/sitar interplay on this song is captivating; the percussion accompaniment is discreet yet important to the song's sense of movement, its questing purpose. Robin's guitar playing represents a development, in that the Arabic-influenced, oud-like strumming is now more integrated into his playing style, still expressive but more focussed, providing a perfect musical counterpoint to Mike's growing expertise on the sitar.

Air follows. Its hymn-like serenity has a kinship with A Very Cellular Song, but here the mood has been perfected and a sense of musical and spiritual harmony pervades the whole song. Mike's low-register vocal delivery enhances the ambience of hushed reverence created by the sustained chords and organ-flute combination ('breathing' through the pipes too). Air is another perfect miniature, depicting a state or mood rather than telling a story. Structurally, there is an element of recapitulation, more so than in The Yellow Snake as the whole melody is repeated, but this preserves the song's hymn-like character rather than detracting from its power.

Side Two's closing track, Ducks On A Pond, follows naturally from Air. Its episodic musical structure configures with the lyrics' stream of consciousness for a satisfying conclusion to the songs making up the first two sides, while pointing ahead to the delights and preoccupations to come. Robin's remarkable vocals and guitar-picking are underpinned by the ominous, resonant bass notes of the piano, whereas the delicacy and 'icy' fragility of the images is mirrored (as in a frozen pond) by Mike's glockenspiel traceries. The effect is magical. Robin's request to 'sing me something' is answered by whistling, which is an unusual timbre, yet another instrument or vocals wouldn't have sounded right. Lyrically Robin makes use of broadly religious imagery (as in Job's Tears), but here it is less pervasive, ensuring that maximum impact is reserved for the wailing 'Lovely Jesus nailed to a tree'. The song's stream of consciousness portrays a child's worldview, yet at the same time a knowing, adult one, and is a song of both innocence and experience. There is a parallel with William Blake – but here it is given an extra dimension by the weight of additional cultural heritage since Blake's time, and by the freedom of poetry to go beyond strict metrical parameters and represent an ever-expanding consciousness. Robin's writing has never been more inventive and evocative; there are so many memorable turns of phrase – 'inky scratches everywhere', indeed – and the constant juxtaposition of 'dark' and 'light' imagery is thought-provoking. Wonder and magic are never far away, despite our place in the scheme of things in the 'real' world.

So there we have it – complete in itself, but noteworthy when considered as the first half of a double bill.

Spiritual inconsistencies?

The second half begins and ends in real distinction, but in between something happens where it loses the level of internal consistency which was such a feature of the first half. Maya uses a similar opening gambit to Job's Tears to focus our attention – no instrumental prelude but unlike Job's Tears, the different sections of the lyric are punctuated by brief instrumental passages. The opening stanza is compelling – the almost tangible softness of the 'dust of the rivers' contrasts strongly with the 'hard and sharp laughter', just as 'murmur' contrasts with 'cut'. In both instances the allusions are unexpected. This technique recurs elsewhere in the song, where contradictory images – like Jesus and Hitler – become bedfellows in meaningful juxtaposition. Grahame Hood has already noted the two references to Hitler in Lordly Nightshade – does the character hold a personal significance for Robin, or is he simply used as shorthand for evil? All the diverse elements of humanity and nature are equal pieces in life's tapestry, which is 'soon to reach one glowing hue' by us working together to achieve. The theme of our spiritual quest is continued from *Wee Tam*, represented here by the 'troubled voyage in calm weather' on the 'ship of the world'. However, the philosophical content of Maya is more complex than it first appears. All is not what it seems; after all, 'maya' is the abstract Hindu concept of the material world of illusion – 'all this world is but a play' – but we are to enjoy it, by being the 'joyful players'. Perhaps even this is double-edged, since the goddess Maya herself died from joy just seven days after giving birth to Gautama, Prince Siddhartha. Furthermore, 'every face within your face does show' implies that we create our own kind of illusion in the face which we present to the world, hiding aspects of our personality, perhaps even ancestral presences; it is only by allowing these faces behind our face to show that the limitations of the illusion and the material world can be transcended. There are as many layers of meaning here as there are interpretations! Only recently I have become aware of the importance of the song's Irish connection, which grants an entirely new perspective. On a version of Maya from a May '68 American radio broadcast for WBAI, Robin's distinct enunciation of 'island' as 'Ireland' (in 'island I remember living here') may identify the female being 'whose hair grew long and swept the ground' – an allegorical representation of Ireland which is found in Irish literature. Furthermore, the influence of Celtic pre-Christian beliefs and legends provides a link forward to The Iron Stone and The Circle Is Unbroken (on Side 4) and also continues the pantheistic theme of *Wee Tam* by presenting the dichotomy between Hinduism's ascetic worldview and that of Celtic pre-Christianity.

In the main, Maya's instrumental arrangement perfectly complements the lyrics. There are moments where the lyrics are almost too much for the music, the cleverness of the wordplay and imagery working against the song's effectiveness by calling attention to itself too much. One such moment of awkwardness is 'Twelve yellow willows shall fellow the shallows' – maybe the effect of excessive assonance was not intended, but the verb 'to fellow' is obscure. The other problem is disconcerting shifts in viewpoint during the course of the song – from second person to third person and back in such lines as 'Ah, but every face within your face does show / Going gladly now to give himself his own', and 'her hair grew long... be thou the joyful player'. If the singer was indeed evoking and addressing Maya the goddess, why suddenly shift to the impersonal third person? Such inconsistencies jar, and serve to undermine the song's power. Aside from such logistical considerations though, Maya contains plenty of unforgettable images, like 'the hawk of truth is swift and flies with a still cry'. And there's another minor riddle to ponder – the recurrence of the number 12 in 'twelve yellow willows' and 'Ye twelve that will enter the seasons'. I find the abrupt ending a bit contrived, especially as it cuts straight to recorded birdsong, inviting the listener to make a conceptual connection.

Greatest Friend is a fine song, simple and sincere, but musically derivative. I feel that its folk-club/early-Dylan delivery, even down to the use of harmonica, takes away something of the uniqueness that characterise most other songs of Mike's. Was the song actually written earlier than the rest of *Wee Tam*, perhaps?

We then come to the riddle of riddles, the gnomic The Son Of Noah's Brother. I've never been able to get anywhere with this one. Musically, it promises much – an ominous descending chord sequence which you think is going to be a prelude to one of Robin's semi-epic journey songs. But instead the final note is unexpectedly sustained, indicating the song is over almost before it's begun. No sooner have we set out on our journey than we've arrived – but we know not where, which is disconcerting. We suddenly find ourselves in the fantasy world of Lordly Nightshade, which somehow doesn't fit.

Lordly Nightshade is a curiosity – dreamlike and surreal, yet conveying very concrete images with clarity. With the exception of The Son Of Noah's Brother, this song took the longest to get through to me; at first, I didn't respond to its peculiar combination of childlike and adult fantasy and real world. Some of the wordplay is over-the-top, and the whole song doesn't work as it's more of a stream of images than a stream of consciousness, lacking the sense of an evolving narrative. However, this ain't necessarily such a bad thing, and the song's structure is satisfying. The combination of simultaneous repose and unease is well caught in the match of music to lyrics and in the juxtaposition of folk-myth, half-memory, dream, Gothic fantasy and circus entertainment. Note the almost waltz-time snare drum rhythm, a close cousin of the later Circus Girl, but here used with real imagination! I hear more than a hint of the showman in the florid delivery and alliterations. Truly, 'all we can do is smile' – despite the presence of dark forces we sometimes glimpse on the rim of our existence. We can access all kinds of images through the process of storytelling, but they can easily be relegated to the status of a mere dream, 'all on a summer's day'. It's only a story, we 'just can't die'. There are certainly hints of other master storytellers – both Dylans, yes, but shades of Mervyn Peake too ('gallons of glandular corridors of the dark castle…'), and there's also a nice line in story-teller's self-mockery ('hippies in chains'). As in all our dreams, familiar and not-quite-so-familiar stories, memories and shadows are almost thrown together at random, but somehow end up making a peculiar kind of linear sense. Charles Dickens and wartime newsreels are just as much a part of Alice's topsy-turvy looking-glass world as Red Riding Hood. Like Alice, if we want to escape, all we can do is grow – or smile – or fly!

When the dreamy jingling of Lordly Nightshade's fairy chimes has finally dissipated, leaving a lingering aftertaste rather like coming out of sleep or an altered state, we are brought back to earth (or heaven?) by The Mountain Of God. This is a free-association of snatches of half-remembered childhood worship rituals, continuing the theme of a child's perspective. Its final section is delivered in a kind of quasi-parental exhortation, bringing the spiritual inconsistencies of Side Three to a close with a resounding 'Amen', temporarily resolving the album's religious quest.

'A startling triptych'

A natural continuation for Side Four would be to explore pre-Christian beliefs and legends. The Iron Stone would be perfect here, but what do we get? – Cousin Caterpillar! I'm sorry, but when I consider the thoughtfulness with which *Wee Tam* seems to have been put together, I just can't place Cousin Caterpillar within the scheme of things. The song seems to be a throwback to *5000 Spirits* in its slightly precious cuteness. It's a fun song, but that's really all, and it suffers in comparison with the deeper resonances of the rest of *Wee Tam*, so let's pass on.

On to the startling triptych of The Iron Stone, Douglas Traherne Harding and The Circle Is Unbroken, which travels from myth and legend to abstract philosophy, and concludes with a powerful realisation of the primitive forces that control our destinies yet convey real hope for the future. The Iron Stone first, then. Again, we launch straight into the tale, Robin's voice accompanied simply by sitar and guitar and punctuated by the Celtic timbre of Irish harp. This imparts a distinctive sound-world, primitive yet exotic, and is another instance of a combination of instrumental colours to define a mood. This song has characteristics of Robin's 'through-composed' style, yet departs from his usual approach in that it ends with a fairly lengthy improvisatory instrumental passage. This is a wonderful duet for sitar and guitar reminiscent of the classical Indian 'jugalbandi' manner, with both imitative and interactive counterpoint, enhanced by a lively percussion accompaniment. The lyrics themselves convey a strong sense of wonder, an almost tangible presence of genius loci, where the past and legend impact on the commonplace. It recalls those Alan Garner stories where objets trouvés are a gateway into another world. By harnessing the power of the stone, the singer is able to access memories of his former existence; thus ‘reunited’, he rounds the tale off with an ecstatic dance of jubilation. The way the mood of the opening slow section is sustained, then transformed into the exultant closing dance is real magic. The Iron Stone has always cast a special spell for me; figuring large in this is Robin’s arresting delivery, with its distinctive inflections – I’d never heard anyone else pronounce the ‘r’ in ‘iron’ this way!

Douglas Traherne Harding continues the theme of the triptych in its preoccupation with the effect of things ancient on our present existence. Even though it’s a Heron song, it has an unusual slant on everyday experiences which is absorbing right from the start. I wonder what effect it would have had if Robin had used bowed gimbri instead of violin on this track: did he retain the violin in order to keep the sound closer to home and to a kind of folkish sensibility? Either way, the violin sounds suitably ‘rustic’, and the peasant-like pathos is conveyed well in the ‘detuned’ passages. Throughout, the hypnotic, nagging drone of the accompaniment perfectly complements the insistent drone of Mike’s vocal narrative, which exhibits characteristics of both Eastern and medieval melismatic vocal styles. Perhaps this is responsible for the polarisation of reactions to the song. I wish Mike had written more in this mystic, musically rich vein – like Swift As The Wind, it’s compellingly enigmatic, with layers of meaning. The singer’s exposition appears natural, and we are buoyed by the simple, straightforward imagery in the episode of the river crossing – a resonance with folk-memory (fable, parable, Noh drama even) to which we can relate. This is another example of a song where it all paradoxically sounds right and makes a kind of unspoken sense, even though the overall meaning of the song may be almost wilfully obscured. Back to the music – I can’t let the final a cappella refrain (‘You’ll never enjoy the world aright’) go unremarked – it really does close the song neatly and sets a harmonious seal on the proceedings.

The Circle Is Unbroken closes the album with a feeling of optimism, a faith in mankind’s ability to learn from its predecessors and their ‘ancient patterns’. The instrumental setting is stark but effective, the organ imparting an almost religious feel to the song. It’s a skilful re-creation of a traditional, almost primitive folk idiom which never degenerates into pastiche. The instrumental arrangement and Robin’s vocal intonation/invocation combine into a riveting experience. The lyrics are carefully considered, each word, syllable and nuance having its due significance within the song’s overall structure. Unlike some of Robin’s songs, The Circle Is Unbroken exhibits no clumsiness or awkward phrasing. Nothing is overstated, and the setting is one of his most terse and economical. The sparse Irish harp arpeggios perform a similar function to those in The Iron Stone, but the effect is unique due to the different instrumentation. The use of a whistle – its glissandi mirroring the vocal slides – is a masterstroke, sounding eerie, chilly even. It's emotionless and plaintive, almost voice-like, craving yet also containing human companionship. There was nothing else remotely like it at the time or since, not even within the ISB canon – at least until Cold Days Of February, five years later.

I should mention that the original double album included a printed insert giving the illustrated text of Robin's epic poem The Head. The final phrase, 'Be glad for the song has no ending', was the source of the title of the subsequent ISB film and album. Taken purely as a work of literature, it's a fine poem, full of Robin's memorable and inventive turns of phrase.

'True fusion music'

I'll now sum up. First, I think it's noteworthy that, despite its relative lack of what might be termed 'up-tempo material', the whole of *Wee Tam* manages to maintain a sense of momentum and progress. By the end of Side Four, you feel you've arrived somewhere, yet you want to begin again, to relive the journey and its pleasures. Second, although there's some necessary structural repetition in the individual songs, at no time does *Wee Tam* become boring. Third, *Wee Tam* is true fusion music. It presents an eclectic mix of styles and influences but, unusually for polystylistic music, each shift never seems forced and is always used to enhance the lyrical settings. On later albums, I don't think the band was as successful at integrating musical styles, and stylistic juxtapositions often seemed contrived or clumsy. Fourth, *Wee Tam* is so multi-faceted; the music can provoke such different reactions in listeners, but the sheer breadth and quality of writing is remarkable by any standards. In the final analysis, *Wee Tam* is so damned fine an album because it has so much to offer, on so many different counts and at so many different levels. Not only does it contain many of Robin's and Mike's finest songs, arrangements and collaborations ('creative tension' and all), but it also marks a stage in the band's development where their major influences were being integrated in such a manner that they transcended mere borrowing or imitation. The ISB were never ashamed to admit to their influences, and, unlike many bands of the era, never tried to pass off their work as something it wasn't.

The resurgence of interest in world and roots music has provided a more receptive musical climate where cross-fertilisation of musical styles is again acceptable, making it easier for the pioneering work of the ISB in this field to be re-evaluated. *Wee Tam* holds the key to this re-evaluation.

BILLY CONNOLLY ON *WEE TAM*:

1997

I was in the Humblebums with Gerry Rafferty and we ran out – well *I* ran out – and bought *Wee Tam And The Big Huge*. It was at a great time for me, it was around the time Bob Dylan had *John Wesley Harding*, it was an exhilarating time. Gerry didn't like the music much and I just went to my room and shut my eyes and listened to the double album again and again and again. There's something extraordinary when you're from my background about listening to these extraordinary lyrics about people being stabbed with a sword of willow, and Robin's singing then was just to die for, from incredible depths to incredible heights. He always had a lovely, lovely sense of comedy you know – 'I hear my mother calling and I must be on my way'. In the middle of it all he would become music hall and wouldn't take it seriously. And then staggering musicianship, but just as a throwaway. God I love them, I still I love them to this day.

Hey, man, the words are *important*!

Raymond Greenoaken

The *Wee Tam* sleeve design was a masterstroke. *Sgt. Pepper* had established the fashion of including the song lyrics on the sleeve, but this broke the mould by blazoning the lyrics across the *front* cover. The message was unmistakable: hey, man, the words are *important*. Against a chaste white background resembling the page of a book the various lyrics were set down in four elegant columns, each commencing with a large, intricately decorative capital borrowed from an Art Nouveau alphabet of 1889 (used on the cover of the first edition of this book).

The back cover of each (the inside spread on the double album) is given over to a photo portrait of Mike and Robin, by then in the full bloom of shimmering androgyny: Mike dons a swirly high-collared blouse, beads and cummerbund to deflect attention from his five o'clock shadow; Robin, now beardless, looks impossibly angelic and appears to be turning by degrees into Brigitte Bardot. The feminist movement in the late Sixties was just beginning its project of deconstructing masculinity, and here were the ISB seeming to offer a new model of manhood, shorn of macho swagger, that helped to shape the mood of the times. (I recall a friend of mine studying the sleeve closely and confidently asserting that Robin and Mike must be a gay couple...)

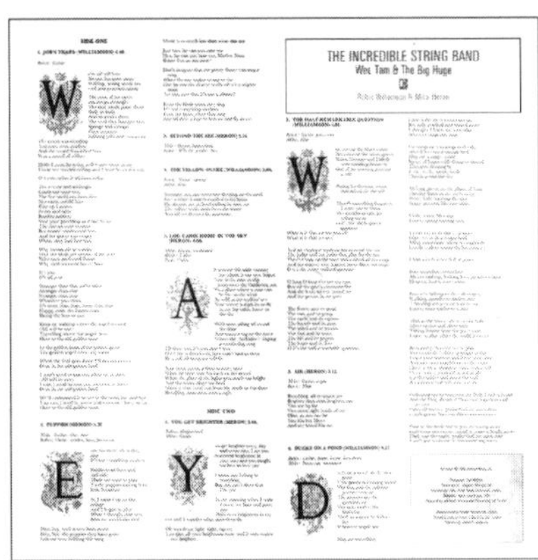

Log cabin home in the sky

Andy Roberts remembers a conversation with Mike Heron and looks in his record collection.

Log Cabin Home In The Sky is one of a number of String Band songs which take their inspiration from other sources. In this case Mike first heard the tune on a cassette of Woody Guthrie songs which he obtained by mail order from the States in the mid-Sixties. You made your own amusement then, you know!

Anyway, thinking it was a Guthrie-penned song Mike subsequently attempted to ensure that Woody received royalties for the ISB version and was surprised to learn that the song was just one of many re-workings of a traditional American folk tune. [*Woody's was a fiddle instrumental titled Cowboy Waltz on* The Asch Recordings Vol. 4 (1944) – *Ed.*] Mike wrote a set of lyrics and it subsequently became one of the best-known ISB songs. Log Cabin was also featured in the mid-Nineties TV drama series *Roughnecks*, where Mike and his Incredible Acoustic Band did a cameo spot in a wedding scene. My ailing memory also tells me that it is one of only two Heron songs which Robin has performed live in his post-ISB career.

After quizzing Mike as to the song's provenance, I asked him if he knew that his version of both the song and its content followed in a long line of songs in the North American Old Timey genre. Mike claims he had no knowledge of this, but Log Cabin songs are a staple of the Old Timey tradition. One version has the distinction of being the first 'hillbilly' tune ever to be recorded, and was originally composed by Will Shakespeare Hays in 1871 (though in all probability nicked from an earlier tune).

By far the best of these versions of Log Cabin is that performed by the stunningly named Ernest V. Stoneman And The Blue Ridge Corn Shuckers, in the 1920s or 30s (I listen to nothing else y'know!). The tune is pretty similar to Heron's and the lyrics also echo its yearning:

Oh, the hinges they are rusty and the door is tumbled in
The leak lets in the sunshine and the rain
And the only friend I've got now is that good old dog of mine
And the little old log cabin in the lane

Many of the other Old Timey versions of Log Cabin express a rather different sentiment: rather than being a place to return to, it is just a fond childhood memory lost to the exigencies of the real world. Another possible source is the Carter Family song, Mountains Of Tennessee – 'take me back to my old log cabin home.' Mike's version, though, could be read as a paean to the end of the flower power era and hippies in general, the back to the country/commune movement when people did, indeed head off to log cabins – usually as near to the sky as they could find them!

In 1956 bluegrass pickers Lester Flatts and Earl Scruggs also recorded a Log Cabin song, Blue Ridge Cabin Home which, like Mike's version, harks back to a better time in a rural idyll, with the final chorus:

> *I'll return to that old cabin home with a sigh / I've a longing for days gone by / When I die won't you bury me on that old mountainside / Make my resting place upon the hill so high.*

There are several cover versions of Heron's Log Cabin, though unfortunately most should have a public health warning on them. For instance American bluegrass band Corn Bred (eeuch, that name) covered the tune on their album *It's Hot*. Their version, far from hot, was like tepid dishwater. One more thing I can tell you is that, as opposed to what has been written in various articles about the ISB, Log Cabin was most definitely not written for Rose to learn the fiddle to! Or that's what Mike and Rose say anyway, and that's as near to any truth as we are going to get!

Here are two charming little tales from the Wee Tam *era which appeared in a 1969 tour programme, credited to 'Fate and ferret from Pittenweem.'*

THE INCREDIBLE STRING BAND

love to Jill from Robin Licorice Rose Mike

WEE TAM
EKS 74036 EKL 4036
THE BIG HUGE
EKS 74037 EKL 4037

DOUBLE ALBUM: WEE TAM & THE BIG HUGE
EKS 74036/37 EKL 4036/37

Edited & Designed by Diogenic Attempts Ltd. for Witchseason Productions Ltd. Setting by James C. Joyce Ltd. Printed by Cross Keys.

1969 Witchseason programme autographed by all four members. (Gillian Symonds collection)

Concerning Fuzz and Pan

It was a warm still summer evening all over the quiet countryside which humped and wrinkled under the light of Venus, the pale evening star. There was a new moon and Pan was on the loose. He was stampeding across the fields, taking running jumps at anyone he might meet. He was feeling even more sharp and mischievous than usual, that goat-footed scatterer of nymphs. But where the Increds, who were as close to him as the curls on his shaggy loins? Where were they, who should be chasing across the peppermint fields, searching for flowers in the long light? He sat down in a small grotto to think and soon his eyes twinkled with merry mischief and his great laugh woke the birds in the forest, where they sang as though it was still day...

Truth to tell (and it shames me to say so) Robin and Mike and Rose and Licorice were all at the flat practising. This is to say, with the two girls holding Mike down, they were just about to start when...

In burst Fate and ferret, all hard frenzy, and before Robin could say, "Almighty Pan!" they burst out: "It's the fuzz! The fuzz! The fuzz are coming! They've got a fudge-making in public charge!"

Was it bluff? The company froze, listening for the sound of those heavy footfalls. Mike was the first to break. With a cry of "Aargh! They won't take me alive!" he dived for the window and shinned down with the speed of long practice.

Clutching her broomstick, Licorice followed. Trying to cool it, Robin stepped over the window-sill and glided to the street below as does thistledown waft in the summer winds when that season comes upon us. Rose slipped out of the room after Robin, but not before winding up all the clocks, dusting the furniture ("I hadn't expected visitors") and leaving a note for Joe which read:

Dear Joe,

There are four steaks under the grill. Do try to eat at least three so they will not be wasted and I think you need a little fattening. Tell Angie I'll see her whenever possible. Feed the cat. Dust the furniture. Keep the guitars in tune. While Mike and Robin are still away please put up the nice curtains Licorice and I wanted. We may be some while.

Love, Rose.

Concerning Mike

Course when Mike has a pain or illness of any sort he makes sure Robin and Licorice and Rose know all about it. But of course Robin was ill much more often than Mike because of his habit of walking about in most inclement weather in most unsuitable clothes, despite all of Rose's efforts.

"Mind ye wrap up well, Robin," was the cry that would ring in Robin's ears as, like a dignified stork, he sailed out of the flat.

So when he came back one day with a shocking cold no one was very surprised, least of all Robin who was secretly quite pleased, for the boys like having Rose fussing round them. Rose gave him a good scolding as he stood there dripping and sneezing. "Serves ye right. Going out on a day like this. At your age, Robin."

Uttering small cries of agreement and consolation, Licorice was trying to dry Robin off, using sponges and cloths. She puzzled him in front of the fire. Clouds of steam rose and the edges of his cloak caught fire. At the sight of all this blundering Rose clapped her hands to her eyes and for the 400th time wondered how she had ever got herself in charge of three such idiot children.

However, she got Robin to bed where she and Licorice brought him relays of hot food, hot water-bottles and hot toddies. "Hey, that's ma whisky!" howled Mike as he dived for the bottle.

"Aak phooey," said Licorice as she neatly tripped him up.

All that day the two girls fussed around Robin, lending him most every want. "What about me?" Mike protested. "O, go and write a song, Michael," said Rose, as is usual on such occasions. Mike rushed screaming round the room, beat the walls and writhed on the floor. "I'm dying, I'm dying! My head's falling off!" "Take two aspirin," said Licorice helpfully.

"Aw, c'mon, Rose," whined wee Mike, "look at all those songs I wrote you. Look at Log Cabin and how about Puppies? Yes, sir, an' then You Get Brighter! What more do you want? An' Air; how about that for a song?"

"Very nice, dear," said Rose as she brought Robin another bowl of nectar. Mike swore a dreadful oath and, with a great cry, threw himself on her. Her squeaks for help became more smothered and, we suspect, turned to laughter as Robin and Licorice slipped out of the room, out into the rain of that one gentle night.

Fate & ferret unmasked

Andrew Greig

In the heady and for us provincials oddly innocent days of 68-70, as 'Fate & ferret' my school pal George Boyter and I would catch the scampi lorry from East Fife to London, with our latest recordings, and guitars in plastic bags just in case. Smelling strongly of fish we would present ourselves at Joe Boyd's office.

We were one of a thousand other raggle-taggle wannabees; our meticulously mocked-up albums were made on our 2-track in George's bedroom (on one track his mother is heard calling 'George, your tea's ready' at a particularly intense and meaningful moment). But we did spend time with Joe Boyd and the ISB and opened for John Martyn, who as Ian MacGeachy was the nephew of our gym-teacher at school, and offered us a slot at Les Cousins when we bumped into each other in Soho. He and others were very kind, which was as well because we were very trusting. When we met the Strangelies in Joe's they were young and scruffy and hopeful like us. The only difference was they got recorded.

When we were faint with hunger – we lived off onions – Ivan Pawle took us to the Golden Egg and bought me beans on toast with fried egg on top. Never forgot that.

Anyway, I saw sense and became a writer rather than musician (you can look me up at www.andrew-greig.weebly.com), and that has been my life. [*George, on the other hand, went on to some success with power-pop band The Headboys, appearing on TOTP in 1977 with the single The Shape Of Things To Come – Ed.*] My book *At The Loch Of The Green Corrie* contained a memoir of that period in London, mentioning 'Fate & ferret of Pittenweem'. Adrian Whittaker got in touch, very excited: the secret was out! We never committed ourselves when someone asked 'So who is Fate and who is ferret?' That was the point: we were jointly *Fate & ferret.*

In what we felt was the true ISB spirit, our stories were a kazoo rasped from the sidelines. Mike was being impulsive, horny and bouncy, while Robin floated ethereally and Likky was a sighing princess. Rose was practical, exasperated, coping with these idiot children. Our guesses, as always, were based on very little evidence – though now they seem not entirely inappropriate.

[*There's much more about F&f in* You Know What You Could Be, *an extended memoir of this period which Andrew later co-wrote with Mike – Ed.*]

2021

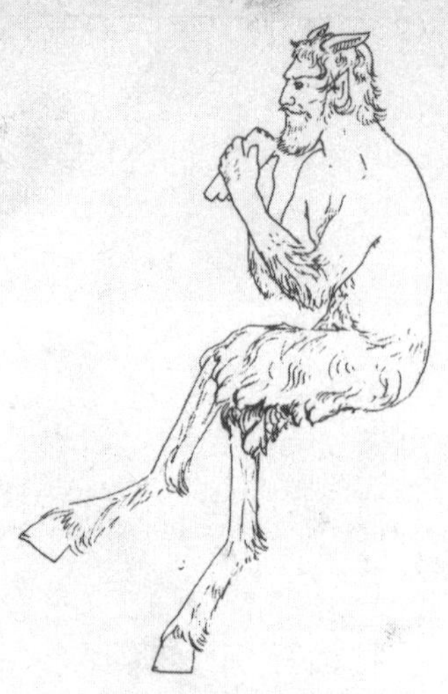

IN CONCERT

THE INCREDIBLE STRING BAND

PRESENTED BY ROY GUEST AND
NEMS ENTERPRISES LTD.

Programme cover
illustration by George Boyter

Job's Tears

Raymond Greenoaken quarries for nuggets of nuance and seams of meaning in one of Robin's strangest songs.

Bob Dylan has a lot to answer for. In the balmy pre-Bob days of teen angst and how much is that doggy in the window, the popular song lyric was an unchallenging thing. You could be pretty sure that a song meant exactly what it said, no more and no less. Bob Dylan changed all that. The words of a song no longer had to make literal, linear sense; a lyric could unfold in an allusive, disconnected sequence following the logic of dream. The language of myth and symbol replaced that of the concrete and everyday.

In Dylan's own case, this quickly led to the establishment of an industry devoted to the interpretation of his increasingly runic utterances. Who exactly is Mr Jones? What are the ceremonies of the horsemen? Why an *Arabian* drum? The guiding principle was that even the most baffling tropes must mean *something* – even if Dylan himself didn't realise it at the time. The density and ambiguity of his more ambitious lyrics, in other words, invited the same sort of attention that we try to bring to poetry. Songsmiths on both sides of the Atlantic were quick to follow his example. In most cases, the result was no more than the whimsical obfuscations of psychedelia. But there were some that stretched the idiom to its fullest extent, and by 1968 the leaders of the pack, in the UK at least, were the Incredible String Band.

For Robin Williamson in particular this approach came as naturally as breathing. His deep interest in poetry and esoteric branches of knowledge made him one of the most gifted apprentices of His Bobness, the grand magus of the mystifying lyric. As an example of the concentration of meaning Robin could instil into a song, Job's Tears is worth close and extended scrutiny.

The first song on any album inevitably acquires a certain significance in the listener's mind, and to no small degree helps to define his or her response to the entire album. The choice of an opening song is, therefore, rarely a casual affair, and it's clear that Robin, Mike Heron and Joe Boyd were on the case when the album's running order was finalised, for Job's Tears might almost have been specifically designed as an introduction to the delights of *Wee Tam*.

JT's Biblical allusions and hymnal cadences find answering echoes in many of the other songs; its ebb and flow of tension and resolution, its cyclic patterns, its idiomatic lurches from the hieratic to the demotic and back again, its frankly religious sense of communion – these are all devices that are used with almost reckless élan throughout the album. And there's no instrumental preamble: the lyric unfolds from the opening bar, as though to emphasise that words carry more than their usual weight of significance in this collection of songs. JT sets the tone for *Wee Tam* as well as you could wish; and yet it has a dark enchantment all its own, and an unsettling ambiguity that intrigues and perplexes, and draws one back to it again and again.

In any analysis of the song, it must be remembered that words and music are not discrete entities but elements in the same discourse, whereby each illumines and enlarges the other. The performance, too, is (or can be) a crucial ingredient in the weaving of meaning; so the following discussion will consider all three aspects as they act upon each other.

Can we expect a simple answer to the question: what does Job's Tears mean? Ostensibly, the business of the song seems to be the evocation of the Passion of Christ in raw detail and its resolution by means of rosy anticipation of heavenly bliss. It addresses itself, then, to the core message of Christianity. On this reading one may be tempted to call it a religious song, a song that concerns itself with the expression of religious faith and certitude. But JT is no orthodox exposition of the Christian credo. Contradictions are carefully threaded into the narrative, through which the nature of the Passion is pointedly questioned.

The language and imagery of the song are plainly 'Biblical', but in many key instances they are mediated through traditional song rather than drawn directly from canonical texts. This mediation is not merely adventitious, but turns the key to our understanding of the song. It's worth, therefore, exploring Robin's immediate sources, and I'd suggest the most fruitful place on which to train our searchlight is the legendary Nonesuch field recording of Bahamian spirituals, *The Real Bahamas, Volume One*, source of the Pindar Family's sublime funeral chant Bid You Goodnight. The opening song on *TRB* bears the title We Will Understand It Better By And By, of which JT's 'We'll understand it better in the sweet by and by' is a fairly faithful approximation. The following song Sheep Know When Thy Shepherd Calling offers some further nuggets: 'John saw a golden angel...with a crown... with a book in his hand'. It's hard to resist the conclusion that the latter part of JT, with its 'In the golden book of the golden game / The golden angel wrote my name' refrain, was assembled around these lines. In this mysterious sermon, John is John the Revelator, who saw the future – 'the sweet by and by' – through a telescope! Looking further, we find in Won't That Be A Happy Time the line 'Over yonder in that fair and sunny clime'; I don't think it's fanciful to hear a paraphrase of this in 'Over in the old golden land'. Nor is there any essential difference between 'There will be no more of sorrow when we reach that lovely place' and Robin's 'You won't need to worry and you won't have to cry'. And in a spooky, fragmentary song called Come For Your Dinner, the repeated phrase 'Let me go home' functions in much the same way as 'Let me go through' does in JT.

It's no exaggeration to call *The Real Bahamas* a veritable mother-lode for Robin and Mike, both musically and lyrically. Phrases from these Bahamian folksongs unerringly find their way into ISB compositions over the period 1968-72; and the nature of their performance – random scriptural phrases linked together in a free-associating, improvisatory way, often incorporating unexpected elements – has strong echoes in the ISB's own practice: The Mountain Of God and *Changing Horses*' Creation leap readily to mind.

So let's take it from the top. The title of the song immediately confronts us with a riddle: how did Job find his way from the Old Testament into the narrative of Christ's Passion? The answer must begin with another question: What exactly are Job's Tears? There's both a botanical and a scriptural answer. Job's Tears is the name of an Asiatic grass whose grains are said to resemble tears; it's also a popular name given to the fleabane, a plant of the daisy family (day's eye = the sun), and Solomon's Seal, a plant with pale, dependent tear-like flowers. (Solomon's Seal is another name for the six-pointed star, representing the six wounds of Christ.) In the Old Testament, Job is a type of patient, innocent suffering and uncorrodable certitude. God, we read, exposed Job to persistent torments as a test of his faith. Through the long years of his trial the phlegmatic Job never wavered; for him, the tears shed in his suffering were an earnest of his faith: 'My friends scorn me, but mine eye poureth out tears unto God' (Job 16:20). It's not hard to tie these associations together in the figure of Jesus. On the cross he suffered, like Job, without God's intercession, but in the ultimate fulfilment of God's purpose. It's probably not possible to know whether Robin was aware of this concatenation of meaning when he chose the title of the song. But, at the risk of sounding mystical, that's the way real poetry often works – not only at a conscious, ratiocinative level, but also at a deeper, oracular level of symbol and association, sometimes even without the poet's full understanding.

It's time to look at other possible sources. Robin knows his Psalms well, as his 2000-onwards *Carmina* project confirms. He would probably, therefore, have been familiar with the maxim in Psalm 126:5 – 'That sown in tears shall reap in joy'. This could stand as a rubric to the song – 'the old golden land' irresistibly conjures up swaying acres of golden grain. But a more crucial source, I think, is Robert Graves' study of the religious and mythical foundations of poetry, *The White Goddess*. Robin says that he first encountered the book at the age of 19, but didn't read it thoroughly until years later. Nevertheless, it's likely he will have been familiar with Graves' interpretation, in *The White Goddess*, of the character of the historical Jesus, and the 'myth' of Christ. Briefly, Graves suggests that Jesus was an apocalyptic Prophet who was secretly crowned the King-Messiah Son Of David, and who attempted to bring forward the 'Pangs of the Messiah' (a series of natural convulsions that would prefigure the coming of the Kingdom of Heaven) by acting out the chiliastic prophecy of the Worthless Shepherd. It was also Graves' view that Jesus was the agent of a patriarchal religious revolution determined to overthrow the old matriarchal order, but by a grim irony met his end in the same way as the matriarchal sacred kings, who were sacrificed at the end of a cycle, often by crucifixion, to appease the Mother Goddess. This scenario was dramatised by Graves in his novel *King Jesus*, in some ways a companion work to *The White Goddess* and one which Robin knows well. I'd suggest, therefore, that it's helpful here to consider the figure of Jesus as a type of sacred king conforming to Graves' 'matriarchal' thesis, but one who attempted to reinvent himself as a self-styled prophet of the patriarchal Father God Yahweh. 'I am come', he is reported in the Apocryphal Gospel Of Thomas as saying, 'to overthrow the works of the Female.' Contradictory? Superficially, perhaps, but contradiction can be a potent weapon in the poet's armoury – 'Speaking truth in contradiction'.

It's clear from the opening line that JT is not a straightforward expression of Christian theology. 'We're all still here / No-one has gone away...' There's no hint here of the Judeao-Christian afterlife; rather, Robin seems to say, we're part of the cyclic flow of life, returning after our natural span into new bodies for another turn of the wheel. The world is but a play, he avers in Maya, and we're 'acting much too well' – being 'joyful players' – to break away from the cycles of time; 'procrastinating' – because there will always be a tomorrow. It should be pointed out that there is little scriptural authority for the notion of reincarnation. Admittedly, Jesus himself identified John The Baptist as the embodiment of the Prophet Elijah, who had been carried off in a celestial chariot (2 Kings 2:11) and who, according to Malachi 4:5, would reappear on earth just before the coming of the Messiah. But this can be seen as a political ploy to invest John with the necessary divine authority to declare Jesus the Messiah: there's no other reference to reincarnation in either Testament. The concept is Indo-European rather than Semitic (it was shared by, inter alia, the Hindus, the Pythagorean Greeks, and the Celts). We know that Robin was interested in the concept at the time, as songs like Maya and Veshengro (and later Pictures In A Mirror and Dear Old Battlefield) confirm. And, it's worth adding, reincarnation is a central tenet of Scientology.

After this meditative opening, the song kicks into a harrowing tableau of the Crucifixion. Robin's thin, eerie vocal is positively Sibylline, his brusque strumming imparting a tremendous forward motion, with Licorice wailing through the gaps in the lyric like a gaoled spirit. (The call-and-response form of this passage owes much, I think, to the Bahamian spiritual.) The 'cross of the earth' – the material world – becomes, by an adroit poetic conceit, the Cross of Christ, rooting him to the earth, to the physical cycles of birth, death, and rebirth. In Gnostic thought – which has been shown to have been carefully quarried by St Paul in his own highly personalised formulation of Christianity – the world is the work of the Cosmocrator, the Devil, and therefore inherently evil. Gnosticism drew on the Hindu concept of *maya*, of the physical world as sensual and illusory, to be transcended on the path to enlightenment. Carnality, in this reading, is vile and animalistic, a notion that poisoned Christian thought for millennia, provoking the sacerdotal horror of humans coupling 'body to body... seas to anoint them'. Why seas? In the Prophetic tradition, the sea was often an symbol of femaleness, and therefore of sensuality. In Revelations (21:1), true believers are promised there will be 'no sea' in the Kingdom of Heaven. (Interestingly, Solomon's Seal – the six-pointed star – is a pre-Pauline emblem of sexual desire: the two triangles, representing male and female, lying one on top of the other.)

The combination of Robin's vocal delivery and accompaniment, and the hallucinatory imagery, makes this section astonishingly vivid and compelling. Onlookers taunt Jesus with a sponge dunked in sour wine, serpents spit gold and cinnamon – ironic attributes of royalty for the sacrificial king. The Moon itself bleeds, which may be implying that the whole of physical creation shares in Jesus' death agonies, even the very luminaries. But there's a Gravesian slant to this, I think. Graves makes much of lunar symbolism in his version of matriarchal religion. The Moon's three phases represent the lunar Triple Goddess in her trinity of maiden, mother and crone. The Moon, indeed, is the female symbol par excellence, for 'moon' and 'menses' share the same etymological root. The Moon may bleed in agonies of grief, yet her menstrual effusion promises the continuation of the cycle: from the spilt blood of death springs new life.

In *The White Goddess*, Graves explores the mythic and religious significance of various trees and plants, to the extent of constructing – or reconstructing – a 'tree calendar' from surviving elements of Druidic tradition. In this arboreal calendar, the willow represents the fourth (or, in a variant, the fifth) month of the sacral year. It is therefore identified with the time of year of Christ's death, and this may be why Robin insists that 'the sword that killed him / Was a sword of willow'. Moreover, throughout Europe and the Near East, the willow is intimately associated with the Moon: in the words of the Elizabethan herbalist Nicholas Culpepper, 'The Moon owns it'. This makes sound mythic sense in our context: the Moon Goddess takes her Son, who dies for her sake, back into her womb to be reborn: 'I hear my mother calling and I must be on my way'.

Whether or not one accepts this reading, it must be acknowledged that the 'willow' reference has some significance for Robin. He's sufficiently keen to have it in to yoke it to an uncharacteristically lame image – 'the stars were shallow' – for the sake of a serviceable rhyme. It's as though, having decided that 'willow' has to be there, and wanting the stars to amplify the celestial imagery, he groped for a suitable rhyme, didn't find one, then remembered he'd joined 'willow' and 'shallow' together in Maya. Whatever his thinking, it's hard to see how stars can be shallow, unless perhaps they're reflections on the surface of a body of water, and this is the only example of slapdash prosody in the entire song: every other line, every image, seems to pull its full weight.

At this point Robin pulls off a dazzling feat of musical and lyrical impudence. He yanks the tune out of its dark, wailing modality and into a cheerful, affirmative major key, capsizes the rhythm into a jaunty 2/4, and pitches Groucho Marx into the middle of this ancient ritual tableau! 'Hello I must be going...' is of course one of Groucho's catch phrases, first leaping from his lips in *Animal Crackers*. This cavalier interpolation could easily have shattered the mood of the song; in fact, it's breathtakingly effective – the sort of thing only the ISB could pull off. It punctures the almost unbearable tension built up by the Crucifixion section just long enough for the listener to draw breath before plunging back again into the maelstrom of mythic event.

'O, I remember it all from before...' The cycle of death and rebirth recapitulates itself endlessly, and we're back into the Biblical drama with Lazarus, the gambling soldiers, the crucified thieves and the empty tomb. As the solar king, the Son of the Moon Goddess, Jesus is reborn out of the frozen dark – 'The winter and midnight / Could not hold him'. Nor can the fire of pure reason burn away the ties that bind him to the natural cycle, and the funereal earth must release him again into the light of waking life. 'Rise up Lazarus...' – That injunction finds an answering chime in midwinter folk dramas: 'Rise up St George/Old 'Oss...' and so on, as the slain warrior or animal is restored to rude health to fight or dance again. (The interpretation of the slain figure in these dramas as the defeated solar hero of Indo-European myth, though dismissed by modern scholars, is still popular in non-academic circles.) But Jesus rejects the apparent randomness of the old cyclic world view – he rebukes the soldiers for their gambling, their trust in blind fate rather than in a moral system of reward and punishment founded on 'reason'. In Graves' view, Reason – arid rationality – is the attribute of the patriarchal male God, in contrast to the intuitive, watery, lunar nature of the Goddess. If Jesus forswore the intuitive for the rational in the name of Yahweh, a bitter irony awaited him. 'Reason', in the form of Roman law, condemned him to the Cross, and in so doing bound him anew to the earthly cycle, for Yahweh's own curse denied a crucified man admittance to Heaven. 'The grave was empty' – but the Son had returned to his mother's watery clasp, where he remembers it all from before: for in Graves' memorable phrase, 'There is one story and one story only'. It is the story that tells 'why heroes die at sunrise' (usually midwinter sunrise, as the builders of Newgrange and Stonehenge knew), 'why birds are arrows of the wise' (because migratory birds make arrow-shapes as they fly together, which resemble the wedge-shaped cuneiform characters in which early religious texts were set down), 'why each perfumed flower' (why certain flowers are emblematic of attributes of the Goddess or her Son – fleabane and Solomon's Seal, to take two pertinent examples), and 'why each moment has its hour' (why nothing is purely adventitious, but is an essential functioning part of a larger scheme).

Robin sings these four lines to a tense, ascending melody which culminates in a hair-raising ululation: 'It's you / It's all true'. The Yahwist rebel, reborn, becomes Everyman again. 'You' and 'true' plunge in a dive-bombing descent down the octave, in which Robin's voice rips through the crack between falsetto and his normal register as though penetrating the boundaries between the timeless womb-world and the temporal world – for me the most magical moments on the entire magical album. It sounds like nothing so much as a birth-cry, a wild infant howl of ecstasy and anguish... and, sure enough, 'we're alive' again, alive for always, bound to the natural world by grief and by joy: the circle is unbroken. And – this is pure Williamson – explain it any way you like, it's altogether 'stranger that that' and more wonderful. 'Whatever you think, it's more than that'. Beyond reason, beyond dogma, we simply *are* – doing the best we can.

If Job's Tears had ended there, it would be an impressively complex and challenging statement, as well as a song (and performance) of extraordinary visceral force. But there's more... and here we bump into another apparent contradiction. Having asserted that eternal bliss is better sought in the here and now than in the 'sweet by and by', Robin promptly leads the congregation into a buoyant Salvation Army singalong extolling the anticipated delights of the 'old golden land'. Perverse, or what? Well, only if you're expecting a logical, linear narrative progression. Talk of ironic juxtaposition may sound pretty glib in these post-modernist times, but the relationship between the earlier section and the old golden land singalong is, in my view, exquisitely ironic. The 'golden' imagery is, I think, deliberately ambiguous, for in the Bible gold is often emblematic of vanity and cupidity, qualities we'd hardly expect to find in the Judeao-Christian afterlife. Heaven, Robin may be hinting, is no more than the world we inhabit, transmuted by spiritual insight but within the reach of us all. The final section of JT is a respectful tip of the cap to the exuberant Bahamian rhymers, as well as a wistful contrast to the intense mythic theatre of the rest of the song. You may take a dim view (as many do) of Pauline Christianity as an accumulation of ancient superstition and political chicanery, but it's harder to dismiss the sheer life-affirming jouissance of the music on *The Real Bahamas* as irrelevant to the human condition. After all, part of the beauty and mystery of life is that all metaphysical belief systems are ultimately untestable: the dangers of manacling oneself to a single rigid dogma should be only too clear. Having said all that, however, I'm left with the feeling that Robin – at that time, at least – finds the tidy moral universe posited by Christianity to be insufficient in its denial of the 'sheer unspeakable strangeness of being here at all'. The inexplicableness of life is central to its wonder, and our proper response to it is awe and delight, paradoxically tempered by fear. As Job's Tears seems to suggest, we sometimes need to drink at a colder and more ancient spring.

In the complexity and ambiguity of its text, as well as in its performance as a piece of music, Job's Tears is, as I suggested earlier, far closer to the stuff of poetry than to 'popular' song. This is an attitude Robin has remained faithful to throughout his subsequent career – which may help to explain why, despite his prodigious gifts, he remains very much a coterie taste. Of course, such an exegesis as I've attempted here runs the risk of being essentially a projection of the writer's own presumptions and preconceptions. In a sense, however, it matters little if I've got it wrong: that's what Job's Tears means to me, it possesses an internal coherence and seems to dramatise an important insight, and it thereby enlarges my understanding of the human condition. These layers of meaning, intended or not, are nevertheless present, and they work their enchantments on me. A cop-out, you may say... I don't see it that way. The truest art can often work in ways its creator never, or only vaguely, intended (think of Blake's Tyger). In this way it becomes independent of the artist, an autonomous magical force at work in the world. When quizzed about the meaning of their songs, Robin and Mike were fond of raquetting the question back. 'What', they'd quip, 'does it mean to *you*?' 'Isn't there a danger', an interviewer asked Robin and Mike early in 1970, 'of people reading meanings into the songs that did not exist in the first place?' 'But that's no danger,' Robin replies. 'That's everyone's private right, to form their own interpretation of the music.' And Mike adds: 'It's the listener's privilege to relate whatever he wants to [a] particular song'. Is this mere Celtic mischief, or a denial of artistic responsibility? Or are they saying that the song belongs as much to the hearer as to the writer or the singer? That's how I see it myself, and it's this sense of communion between performers and audience, that feeling of interchange and the blurring of boundaries, that was the unique gift of the ISB.

Mike, Robin and dog Leaf: also from a Witchseason programme, this shot ended up on the sleeve of the *Relics* Elektra compilation.

Douglas who?

Prydwyn Piper introduces two unwitting ISB collaborators...

As with most things Incredible, *Wee Tam And The Big Huge* (or, for purposes of this article, at least the latter half of it, in its single album form) is indelibly imprinted in my mind with the time of my life when I first acquired it. I was living in Brooklyn at the time and working in Manhattan, and I spent many months commuting be-Walkmanned, with a 90-minute tape that had *The Big Huge* on the one side and Robin's solo *Journey's Edge* on the other. Maya always seemed to be drawing to a close as the bus pulled up to the subway station, and Lordly Nightshade invariably saw me on the train and on my way to another day's drudgery. Arrival at my destination saw me grappling with a singularly strange beast – 'that song with the delectably detuned fiddle solo', as I seem to remember remembering it – bearing the name of some no-doubt mysterious individual, a Douglas somebody or other.

It was not until many years later that I learned something more about the man – or men – behind the myth. I read in *beGLAD* that 'Mike dug out books to try and explain, including... Douglas Harding's books on comparative religion, Thomas Traherne's Christian mysticism...' Hmmm... I was living in Edinburgh at the time, and ran out to the library and got me a copy of that old-time Christian mysticism, quite backwardsly, as it would turn out, leaving Mr. Harding for future perusals. I was not long into *Thomas Traherne – Centuries, Poems, And Thanksgivings* (published by Oxford in 1958) – before I struck quotational pay dirt.

But first, a little background on the man himself would be appropriate. Thomas Traherne was born in 1637 to a poor Hereford shoemaker, but, his parents having died when he was quite young, was raised as a son by the 'rich and important innkeeper' Philip Traherne. He took his BA from Brasenose in 1656, and received an MA from Oxford in 1661. On 20 October 1660 he was episcopally ordained as deacon and priest. In 1669 he took his Divinity degree from Oxford, and from then until his death in 1674 he served as chaplain to Sir Orlando Bridgeman, being based for the most part in London and Teddington. Most of his literary output seems to date from these last five years of his life, much of it being dedicated to one Susanna Hopton, a friend of his from Herefordshire who headed an informal religious circle there.

Looking at Mike's song, the work by Traherne which most concerns us is his Centuries. There are five of these, and the title refers to the fact that each is made up of one hundred 'paragraphs' (this is a prose work, for the most part – although Traherne's prose is always very 'poetic'), linked together into larger groups by various common themes.

Paragraph number 29 from The First Century reads:

> 'You never Enjoy the World aright, till the Sea it self floweth in your Veins, till you are Clothed with the Heavens, and Crowned with the Stars: and Perceive your self to be the Sole Heir of the whole World: and more then so, because Men are in it who are every one Sole Heirs, as well as you. Till you can Sing and Rejoyce and Delight in GOD, as Misers do in Gold, and Kings in Scepters, you never Enjoy the World.'

It was clear to me from this point that Douglas Traherne Harding employed a liberal dose 'inspired borrowing' (nothing wrong with that, of course – it's a truly ancient practice). This passage is one of a number which share that common theme, and phrase.

One of Traherne's major themes in both his poetry and prose, and the one which would seem most obviously to endear him to the 'psychedelic' mindset, is that of the 'Infant Ey' – the ecstatic, unclouded perception which he recalls having had as a child, which was driven out of him in the course of his early education and experience, but which he finally recovered and is able to enjoy a second time in adulthood. Sort of the 'turn-on', as it were. The beginning of Traherne's Third Century (the first twenty-eight paragraphs, in fact) is devoted to the subject of this infant perception and its loss, and it is here that we find yet more of the raw material from which Douglas Traherne Harding was forged:

'The Corn was Orient and Immortal Wheat, which never should be reaped, nor was ever sown...The Dust and Stones of the Street were as Precious as GOLD. The Gates were at first the End of the World, The Green Trees when I saw them first through one of the Gates Transported and Ravished me; their Sweetnes and unusual Beauty made my Heart to leap, and almost mad with Exstasie...The Citie seemed to stand in Eden or to be Built in Heaven – The Streets were mine, the Temple was mine, the People were mine, their Clothes of Gold and Silver was mine, as much as their Sparkling Eys Fair Skins and ruddy

Douglas Harding

faces. The Skies were mine, and so were the Sun and Moon and Stars, and all the World was mine, and I the only Spectator and Enjoyer of it.' (III, 3)

For the ultimate source of 'My eye was single', however, as of much else which goes to make up the substance of our song (including the central concept of the 'headless man'), it is necessary to turn to the work of Douglas Harding. Douglas Edison Harding was born in 1909 and died in 2007. At first glance would seem a strange individual to be cast in the role of religious guru. As the blurb to one of his books states: 'D.E. Harding is no blinkered specialist. While a partner in a flourishing architectural practice, he taught comparative religion for Cambridge University. While a wartime major, he developed a unique means to spiritual enlightenment. He describes his field as the meeting-place of psychology, physical science, philosophy and religion. His published works include a whodunnit, a philosophical treatise that took eight years to write, books on religion and the arts of living and dying and articles in the *Transactional Analysis Journal*, *Architectural Review*, *Middle Way*, and *The Saturday Evening Post*... Anne Bancroft's *20th Century Mystics and Sages* has a chapter on Harding as 'the man without a head' – a reputation which the Incredible String Band helped to establish with their Douglas Harding Song [you'd think they could get these things right...]. At the age of eighty he still conducts workshops around the world. Attendances – and "decapitations" – have ranged from a handful to thousands.'

Among Harding's publications is a relatively small book titled *On Having No Head* which was first published in 1961. The core of the book is laid out in its first three pages, which describe the following astonishing revelation, visited upon the author during a wartime stroll in the Himalayas:

'The best day of my life – my rebirthday, so to speak – was when I found I had no head...What actually happened was something absurdly simple and unspectacular: just for the moment I stopped thinking... It was as if I had been born that instant, brand new, mindless, innocent of all memories. There existed only the Now, that present moment and what was clearly given in it. To look was enough. And what I found was khaki trouserlegs terminating downwards in a pair of brown shoes, khaki sleeves terminating sideways in a pair of pink hands, and a khaki shirtfront terminating upwards in – absolutely nothing whatever!

'It took me no time at all to notice that this nothing...was no ordinary vacancy, no mere nothing. On the contrary...it was a vast emptiness vastly filled, a nothing that found room for everything – room for grass, trees, shadowy distant hills, and far above them snow-peaks like a row of angular clouds riding the blue sky. I had lost a head and gained a world.'

The remainder of Harding's book is in large part an exploration and explanation of this basic revelation, culminating with his happy discovery of Zen some years after his original 'experience of headlessness'.

I enjoyed reading all the Traherne – I did always have a soft spot for old Christian mystics (like Mother Julian of Norwich), but once I had read *On Having No Head* I realised that however much Traherne Mike may or may not have read circa 1968, all of the quotes which he used in Douglas Traherne Harding appear in *On Having No Head*. Another relevant passage:

> 'Nor is Christianity...unaware of the fact that genuine illumination must dispel the dark opacity of our bodies no less than of our souls. "When thy eye is single," said Jesus mysteriously, "thy whole body also is full of light." This single eye is surely identical with the precious Third Eye of Indian mysticism, which enables the seer simultaneously to look in at his Emptiness and out at what's filling it.'

The lyrics of Douglas Traherne Harding are a wonderful synthesis of spiritual teachings drawn from a variety of sources – the words of Jesus, Thomas Traherne's 17th-century ecstatic worldliness, D. E. Harding's 20th-century headlessness – all ultimately traceable to their appearances in Harding's *On Having No Head*. I hope that this brief overview of those sources will have whetted your appetites to explore them further as they're all well worth the read. And how about that delectably detuned fiddle solo!!

[*Ed: The wheel turned full circle: in Douglas Harding's* Religions Of The World, *the 'Suggested Reading' appendix listed Mike's song, complete with* Wee Tam *Elektra catalogue number! Harding commented: 'A pop song can be more enlightening than some of the books listed above.'*]

OUT-TAKES AND ALTERNATES

One track from the *Wee Tam* sessions was omitted from the album. A 'rough mix' of Robin's All Too Much For Me had surfaced in the past, probably bootlegged from a 1985 tape library listening session, but for *Tricks Of The Senses* we worked from the original four-track tape, recorded at Sound Techniques on April 30, 1968 alongside Douglas Traherne Harding. Though it's tempting to read it as a farewell to the psychedelic era, Robin regards the song as none too serious. He's fond, though, of the two gospel tunes which follow as a segue, both learnt from Blind Willie Johnson. Mike adds organ to the first section, harmonies and handclaps to the gospel tunes. Also on *Tricks Of The Senses*, from a later *Wee Tam* session, is a fascinating alternate master take of The Iron Stone and ensuing jam (Robin on guitar and Mike on sitar). It's one of the first recording of the 'four-piece' ISB; Likky McKechnie had a few cameos on the previous two albums, but started recording with the band in earnest on these sessions; here she plays harp (you can hear Robin checking the tuning with her at the start of the take). Rose makes an early recorded appearance on tablas.

1969

Adrian Whittaker

The band had a month off at the start of 1969 before making a third appearance on Julie Felix's TV show and recording a BBC *Nightride* session. On both, the four-piece line-up performed Fine Fingered Hands, a remarkable Williamson composition: described by one commentator as 'a song that would grace any album,' it remained unreleased until Robin re-recorded it many years later for his solo CD, *Ring Dance*. Like the later Darling Belle, it's a song which is based on a dream of Robin's: one 'small door' leads to the next and so on, in an endless cycle of different planes.

John Peel's *Nightride* radio programme, broadcast in March 1969, has been preserved in its entirety. The ISB songs were played alongside a graphologist analysing Peel's handwriting, a session from Mississippi Fred McDowell and some live readings from poet Adrian Mitchell. Peel became so involved in his chats with Mitchell that he ran out of time, meaning that Fine Fingered Hands had to be shunted into the following programme, after the one am news bulletin. Consequently, the original tape of this was lost and we owe the excellent off-air recording included on the Hux BBC sessions compilation *Across The Airwaves* to Richard Bartram, an ISB fan who kept his reel-to-reel running. On the show, the ISB previewed Dust Be Diamonds (from *Changing Horses*) alongside Theta, an instrumental later released on the *Be Glad For The Song Has No Ending* soundtrack, as was Mike's All Writ Down, on which Robin added some sinuous wah-wah guitar. Fine Fingered Hands was the standout.

Sound Techniques: 'You immediately felt at home'

Rose Simpson

From mid 1968 through to 1970, the band spent increasing amounts of time in John Wood's Sound Techniques studio in Old Church Street, Chelsea, with Joe producing. For The Parts You Can't Hear, *his forthcoming documentary about the studio, film-maker Nick Turner interviewed Rose in 2018 about her time there. This is an extract, used with permission.*

Nick: Do you remember the first time going to Sound Techniques?

Rose: What was so great about Sound Techniques was you immediately felt at home because it was just so open. It was everything that you thought work ought to be, it was just an extension of what you played in the living room. You played there, and with the same feeling about it. This was work going on and it seemed so easy, watching them move the sliders up and down on the desk, and listening to them saying, 'Well, we should bring that up and bring that down?' and putting the spools back on the machines and all that.

I knew the people around them as musicians who were always around – they were part of the Sound Techniques scenery really, for me. No one ever seemed to be wanting to be a star. Whatever they did outside, in that studio, I was never aware of anyone pulling rank or pulling star status. It was always really that everyone was trying to do their best for everyone else. It was a very cooperative atmosphere and it was very egalitarian. I felt as good playing my bass with Dave Mattacks, I was just as valid as Richard Thompson, this wonderful guitarist who was musical to the core. You just felt you were as much there as they were. I just think that's an amazing tribute to them really. I find it quite moving really because it sort of validates what we were all about. Maybe you can only do it for a bit and maybe you can only do it in these enclosed spaces. But the world did go like that for me in Sound Techniques and it worked! It made it possible for them to be things that they couldn't be in other places, because the minute you have an audience in front of you, you have to perform and there they didn't have to perform because everyone knew each other. I saw it there, because it was like your front room, but this was making it available big time, you know? Wonderful to see them. What a privilege!'

What was your first impression of John Wood?

John Wood was from a much more serious world, he was like a working person. I got the impression from Joe that he kind of almost lived in that studio... I often wondered if he had a home or a family or was there a room somewhere, because I couldn't quite figure how someone who seemed to me, compared to everyone else, conventional... there must be a structure behind this. But the structure was never obvious.

He was super tolerant. When I think how fey someone like me was, playing instruments very badly and then trying to get the most out of it, that you could actually make this thing sound okay, the tolerance level must have been phenomenal when you think of all that that he had to contend with, and how wearing that must have been. This was someone who was working with fantastic musicians and yet I felt as valid there as anybody. He was just welcoming and treating me with the same respect as Pete Townshend and with the same care. I just took that for granted, but it's only looking back, I think, my goodness, he must have been something else, on that personal level, never mind the skill and all that. He was doing the job so well that there was no ego. No, "I am the great engineer, I am the person that's made all this possible". You did get that in other places, but [at ST] they were making it possible for Mike and Robin (and us of course) to do this music and to make it work as well as it could possibly work.'

When there was a break in recording, the band members could visit musician friends down the road. In summer 1969, the Brazilian songwriters Gilberto Gil and Caetano Veloso were sent into exile by the Brazilian military government as they were seen as 'bad influences' on the youth. The two initially lived in in Redesdale Street, Chelsea, a couple of blocks away from the studio. In 2008, Gilberto Gil remembered: 'London was a very big scene then. I was there from '69 to '72. I arrived in London the day the Rolling Stones gave the concert at Hyde Park, and I was able to mingle with different people, from the Moody Blues and from Pink Floyd. Terry Reid became a very close friend. The Incredible String Band members used to come to our place three days a week and play and talk and discuss.'

'Three days a week' is probably pushing it; another friend remembers more accurately that 'Caetano and Gil became friendly with, and played with, the Incredibles, who visited the Chelsea house several times.' Rose has an even more down-to-earth take: 'It was very pleasant – I just used to drop in and have a cup of tea.'

Alongside Sound Techniques, the Witchseason office at 83 Charlotte Street W1 was another regular London haunt. Rose says it was 'the anchor for our wanderings and the hub of our contacts of the wider world of friends and other musicians.' This is a new piece, written by Rose in 2021 for this edition.

WITCHSEASON

PRODUCTIONS LTD 83 CHARLOTTE ST W1 DIRECTORS JOE BOYD, TOD LLOYD 01-636 9436

Turning into the comparative quiet and emptiness of Charlotte Street was always a relief, after the noise, traffic and crowds of Tottenham Court Road. The whole street looked a bit shabby as if it belonged to a good family fallen on hard times, who were doing their best to keep up a tidy front while the back roof leaked. Number 83, the home of Witchseason Productions, was no different, with its flaking paint and cracked cornices.

There was no sign to mark its presence on the street and, as we walked up the well-known path to the front door, it always felt like coming home. We pushed open the door, which was unlocked in daytime, and stepped into a dingy hallway, never really dirty but always looking as if the cleaner hadn't been in lately. There must have been a cleaner, whose invisible presence kept the old cord carpets hoovered and desks dusted, but it was a thankless task when musicians and roadies traipsed through the rooms daily. After the long drive from the last gig and oppressed by worries about the next one, Witchseason became the Left-luggage Office, Waiting-Room and Information Desk for all comers. Coats were thrown in corners, guitars parked on the floor while their owners sorted out the day ahead and cans, bottles and paper cups abandoned on the nearest flat surface.

She, and almost inevitably it was a woman who did the cleaning, must have been there in the early morning, before the working day started for those staff who aimed to keep office-hours. There seemed to be someone around the office at most times of the day and night and cleaning round their feet was irritating. Very few Witchseason employees had any sense of regular working patterns but someone had to be there to answer the phone and propose frameworks for the chaotic lives which orbited around the small office-rooms. Those duties too fell on women, nearly always young, pretty, or downright beautiful but also, if they lasted more than a few days, highly competent at whatever job they were called upon to undertake. If shorthand, typing and a good telephone manner were the basic qualifications for the job, discretion, patience, good-humour and, above all, flexibility were equally essential. 'The girls' were called upon to cover all the emergencies generated by any number of musicians. Cool cat African jazz players, fey English folk-singers and hip American guitarists all depended on 'the girls' to sort out schedules, accommodation and subsistence, as well as their immediate personal demands.

When someone came in wrecked after a bad LSD trip but still required to be in the studio that morning, one of the girls would be a sympathetic ear and nursemaid, keeping the coffee flowing from the old percolator in the corner. At the last possible moment, the sufferer was packed into a taxi and delivered to Sound Techniques in Chelsea in a better frame of mind. Taking delicate stage clothes to specialist dry-cleaners which only they knew about, tracking down lost luggage from airports and train stations, booking travel tickets for a new boy- or girl-friend and never looking surprised or shocked were all part of the job. All the things that a roadie arranged when the bands were on tour, the Witchseason office girls picked up when the musicians were staying in London.

I never asked who was supposed to do what, just asked the nearest girl and she dealt with the problem, whether it was an urgent dental appointment for a severe toothache or some immediate cash to get me through the day.

Anthea Joseph was the exception. She wasn't one of 'the girls' but a woman to be approached with care and some hesitation. In extremis I would have asked for her help but there was never a problem serious enough to warrant disturbing Anthea herself. Others, I noticed, had no such qualms and she sorted out their dilemmas with apparent goodwill but she had a cool sharp look that repelled further intrusions on her time. Some musician might think himself a star but Anthea was the boss offstage. Joe Boyd's easy self-assurance ebbed slightly when faced with Anthea's impenetrable certainty. She knew the music business through and through, with all its vagaries, extreme personalities and potential for immense successes and catastrophic failures. But despite all her professional skills and knowledge, I was always certain that, if it were really important, she could be relied upon to help in times of trouble.

I never did the grand tour of the rooms in 83 and my direct recollection centres on the reception area, with Joe's office opening off it at the Charlotte Street side of the building. His room was the lightest, brightest and most open to the world outside, as people walked along the street beneath his window. In that large reception area were, I think, two or three desks – the girl on reception, someone else who was in charge of immediate finances and (probably) Marion Bain who was Joe's assistant and secretary. Moving towards the back of the building, the spaces seemed to get darker, with Huw Price and Anthea emerging from their lairs into the light of Joe's (and everyone else's) presence. I guess they tried to keep those spaces free from the intrusion of tiresome musicians.

I know there was a back office, up a couple of steps, in which Danny Halperin and Todd Lloyd worked but I don't think I ever went in there at all. Sitting around in reception, waiting for things to happen, I saw people coming and going into that office but generally not the music-people I recognised. There was often a more hectic air about them, as if they were calling in on some business that was urgent and, maybe, clandestine. Since Todd was vaguely known as the money-man and Danny as the art and design person, their days were even more indeterminate than those of musicians bound by the times and dates of their gigs, so what they got up to in their room I never knew.

The street outside was all part of the Witchseason experience, with the shop opposite supplying it, more or less on a daily basis, with cigarettes, cans of coke, Rizla cigarette papers and straws. The shopkeeper seemed to know the habits of his customers well enough. The restaurants were our canteens, catering for all tastes.

There were spring tours of the UK and the US, and then a US festival tour in August where the band were lined up for 'a little upstate folk festival' in Woodstock. More about that later. Before the autumn UK tour, the entire band moved into a row of small cottages on the Glen Estate, near Innerleithen, then slotted in an Amsterdam concert with Fairport Convention before a further UK tour and then another US tour which took them right up to 31st December, with a New Year's Eve concert in Berkeley. 1969 was a particularly busy year as Mike and, more sceptically, Rose had by now also become Scientologists, and the whole band had to fit in a growing number of Scientology courses and commitments in between gigs.

MIKE IN MIC SHOCK

Mike's fear of on-stage electrocution (see Woodstock chapter) was validated when he appeared in the Dutch press after getting a shock from a live radio mic at the Amsterdam gig: 'Shortly after the beginning of the performance of the British pop-folk-group Incredible String Band... guitarist / vocalist and sitar player Mike Heron was hit by an electric shock and fell down screaming on stage. After a pause the British group Fairport Convention played, then the entire String Band continued its performance. The shock had no adverse effects left over for singer Mike Heron.'

The newspaper photo shows Rose 'bending carefully over him', but credit must also go to Joe Boyd for quickly dragging Mike off the electrics.

Britse gitarist Mike Heron stond onder spanning

GEVLOERD DOOR VOLTTREFFER

Van onze verslaggever

AMSTERDAM, 20 okt. — Het optreden van de *Incredible Stringband* zaterdagnacht in het concertgebouw in Amsterdam, ontaardde in een letterlijk en figuurlijk schokkende gebeurtenis toen één van de leden, Mike Heron, onder stroom kwam te staan tijdens het verzetten van een microfoon. Hij had ook een gitaar in zijn hand en tussen deze attributen bleek 220 Volt te staan. Na enige ogenblikken van verwarring wist één van de zangeressen, Rose, hem de gitaar uit zijn hand te slaan en werd ook de aansluiting van de microfoon verbroken.

Volgens de technische assistenten van de groep was hun hele circuit een afgesloten en geaard systeem. Zij weten het incident aan de opnamemicrofoons van de VPRO, die eveneens op het podium stonden, voor radio-opnamen van de daarna optredende *Fairport Convention*. De opnameploeg verzekerde echter, dat ook hun apparatuur geaard was, hetgeen ook bleek bij het door de politie ingestelde onderzoek.

Omdat na het gebeurde beide installaties direct afgesloten werden, was het verder zeer moeilijk om alsnog de ware oorzaak van het met een sisser afgelopen ongeluk op te sporen.

Mike Heron van de Incredible Stringband ligt getroffen door 220 Volt op het podium van het Concertgebouw. Zangeres Rose buigt zich zorgzaam over hem heen.

„INCREDIBLE STRINGBAND"

Gestroomd popconcert onder hoogspanning

Thanks to Koninklijke Bibliotheek, The Hague

Changing Horses *was released in November. The band had spent much of 1969 on the road, both in the UK and the States. By now an established four-piece with Rose and Licorice, the ISB was becoming less consciously esoteric and also better at communicating with their audiences – both changes due, in some part at least, to their involvement with Scientology. The album reflected these developments; it came as a bit of a shock to people expecting something along the lines of* Wee Tam.

Changing Horses – a time of transition

Adrian Whittaker

In potted histories of the ISB, *Changing Horses* is often represented as the first 'Scientology album'. The title lends itself so easily, after all. But that's not really true, as Rose Simpson says: 'I think the "changing horses" was more about ceasing to be a folky duo, and becoming a group. It was a time of transition.'

In fact, the two (long) key songs on the album, Creation and White Bird, were already complete and being performed at the November 1968 US gigs, predating Likky's fateful encounter with The Church. As we've seen, Creation, like Veshengro, had its origins in a damp splurge of creativity in West Wales, and White Bird stems from a 'glory morning' after a 'night of tortured travelling' at Rose and Mike's cottage in Roman Camps, near Glasgow. Rose: 'I was never clear whether it was a specific incident remembered or a composite half-dreamed, half seen, definitely drug-hazed.' Scientology is reflected, though, in at least two of the lesser songs. As Andy Roberts has said, 'the lyrical focus on a dysfunctional family in Robin's Mr & Mrs has identified it to some as a by-product of Scientology auditing'. And quite apart from the cryptic references to indexes and a 'secret crime' in Dust Be Diamonds, it was written to order after a Scientology instruction that Mike and Robin should address some of their creative rivalry by writing a song together. Mike dutifully wrote the music and Robin the words, making it the only fully-formed joint composition in band history.

Where the Scientology influence is more evident is in the selection of the newer material. Sleepers Awake could have easily fitted into earlier sets, and showcases the four-piece vocal harmonies of the new 'group.' However, the other three songs on the LP are, as several reviewers have noted, not that great, but they are direct, accessible and poppy, in line with Scientology's emphasis on clear communication. Raymond Greenoaken points out in his piece below how much other excellent material there was that could have been used but which was disregarded. Big Ted and Dust Be Diamonds could be fun live, but why use them on an album instead of, say, Robin's Fine Fingered Hands? In November 1969, my friend Keith and I, heads awash with Job's Tears and Douglas Traherne Harding, crammed into a Woolworth's listening booth during school lunchbreak to check out the long awaited new offering. I can still remember the disappointment when we clocked the tone set by the first song, a naff country-and-western ditty about a dead pig who 'ate all the rice and...forgot to pay.' Contrast that as an opening statement with 'We're all still here, no-one has gone away – acting much too well and procrastinating...'

Rose's point about 'becoming a group' is on the nail. All four members got equal billing in the LP cover photo, and from the credits it was clear that Rose was 'the bass-player' and Likky 'the keyboard player'. Both of them sang on all the tracks, too, a promotion from their sporadic appearances on *Wee Tam*. Andy Roberts again: '*Changing Horses* was the album where the best ISB line-up, that of Robin, Mike, Rose and Likky, came together and gelled, both Likky and Rose playing a far more active part than before (if not actually writing any songs).'

The group also took control of the album artwork for the first time. Inside the gatefold, a painting by Robin is on the left; the temptation is to interpret it as an illustration of Creation but it is, to quote Raymond Greenoaken, 'mainly decorative and resolutely un-symbolic'. Mike's handwritten lyrics for White Bird are on the right, illustrated with five paintings, four by an uncredited Rose: 'Mike did the blond head looking down at the little man on the bottom left. The others I did but I thought then, as I think now, that they are no great shakes as paintings...'

The photoshoot for the cover was in New York, at The Met Cloisters art gallery in Upper Manhattan, situated on a hill overlooking the Hudson. Rose writes in her memoir: 'Mike is cheerfully proprietorial... casually patting my face as I sit adoringly at his feet. He still wears the androgynous clothes of hippiedom... Robin is carefully posed above us in meditative profile, his more conventional jeans and t-shirt swathed in a floating scarf. A flower-crowned Licorice is arranged at the highest point, gazing determinedly at the camera, unsmiling and fixed.' The woman behind that camera was Janet Shankman, a newcomer to the ISB scene and Robin's eventual wife, so Likky may have been expressing a touch of rivalry – who knows?

2021

Below, Andy Roberts and Raymond Greenoaken provide their takes on the album.

Andy Roberts saddles up

Completed by the summer of 1969 – Big Ted at least was recorded in New York – *Changing Horses* received mixed reviews on release and reached a very respectable number 30 in the UK album charts. But things had changed somewhere in the minds of its creators. Scientology had arrived, Heron commenting that 'the album which marked our conversion, if you will, was *Changing Horses*'. And so it does, producing a clear, confident, and palpably different album to its predecessors.

As Gil Murray writes in his Scientology article [q.v.], '*Changing Horses* was just what the title suggests. The then-tired chemical horses were being exchanged for cleaner, healthier beasts... aiming to be happy all the time time time.'

Some reviewers at the time took issue with this 'new' ISB and even now retrospectives are strangely harsh on the *Horses* period: 'By 1969 the rot had set in...the loss of plot was well under way' (Mark Ellen in Q). Strange. These allegations that following *Wee Tam* the ISB fell from grace in some way really need more analysis, but reflect on this – it was mainly men who were saying it – then and now – and what had changed exactly? Well, the girls had become a major feature in the band, one step on from mere hippy chick girlfriends, and – dare we say it – breaking up the perceived hippy chappishness that Robin and Mike as a duo had. Were the male fans jealous? I think so. And worse – for some – Scientology had arrived – unpalatable evidence, perhaps, to the druggies amongst the fans that acid wasn't 'The Way' after all, that communication was far more useful than introspection if you actually wanted to get anything done in the world. The general impression that the ISB were coming more out of their shells was backed by statements such as this from Robin: 'Our earlier albums were looking inside rather than out – now I'm more interested in looking at other people and looking out.' Times and people change.

Big Ted lures you into the album in a jolly mood and is one of the songs people always seem to make fun of – String Band fans included – but that's because it's silly, makes you feel happy and because it's about a pig who might be reincarnated. The real pig-hero of the song is duly chased across the screen by a knife-wielding human in the *Be Glad For The Song Has No Ending* film. A single was drawn from the album featuring an edited version of Big Ted backed with All Writ Down, later to appear on the *Be Glad* soundtrack. The mysterious Walter Gundy, who adds harmonica on Big Ted? Well, courtesy of Joe Boyd we now know that he was no less than Maria 'Midnight At The Oasis' Muldaur's first hubby and later the US road manager for the String Band.

White Bird was originally called Reflection (in a *Wee Tam* tour programme and also in Mike's sleeve representation of its lyrics). Peter Cole of the *London Evening News* singled it out: '*Changing Horses* is more encouraging than their Royal Festival Hall concert – not as good as their last, but worth buying for one superb track, White Bird.'

Rose tells us the song was written after a night of 'storming tormented thoughts.... when dawn is a relief from darkness, and a new beginning... Mike's voice with its bending, yearning tones accompanied by Robin's flute was always exquisite and, as it flies over the quiet peace of our accompaniment, it captures the beautiful image of the morning swan. I never thought the guitar solo was too long, although Robin sometimes got impatient. As the melodies resolved themselves back into the White Bird theme it was a rebirth after the cold death, returning us to life and warmth and being together.'

Dust Be Diamonds is a paean to seeing 'good' things in the most ostensibly plain ones – a 'heaven in a grain of sand' sort of way. It is followed by Sleepers Awake, a beautiful a cappella song, credited to Heron but actually drawing heavily on – if not actually originating in – the Sacred Harp tradition of America (from which Bright Morning Star on the later *In Concert* CD is also drawn). The String Band were at their vocal best here, one reviewer claiming: 'the group transcends spiritual propaganda in songs that have the spacious simplicity of folk hymns.' Wow. Mr & Mrs is dodgier territory, seems out of context lyrically and musically and suffers from a lumbering arrangement. Pass.

All this is merely the entree to the main course of Creation, a staggering masterpiece which descends immediately into mythic territory via Robin's measured, certain tones, and by the time we are at 'open your rooms' the hairs are standing up and we're off on another exploration of interpretation. What's it about? Buggered if I know. Everything. Creation and the aftermath. It is invocatory in its delivery, subtle in its musical componentry and with just that final touch of ragtime lunacy with which to send us on our starry way, delighted. Dr Strangely Strange's Ivan Pawle, a firm friend of Robin's from the Penwern commune days and before, had been roped in on an April recording session to add distinctive organ and piano: 'It all passed off very smoothly in a couple of takes... it was done in a day and a half with very little overdubbing. I remember a feeling of freedom and improvisation.'

Creation is also a distant harbinger of Robin's later storytelling predilection, to be followed by similar excursions on *I Looked Up* and *Liquid Acrobat*. And even if you were one of those people who thought that *Changing Horses* was but a pale reflection of what had gone before, Creation took you back there, with mystery bells on, leaving you feeling high, elated and happy with the world.

Following an initial Elektra CD release of *Changing Horses* in the UK, the album was remastered by Joe Boyd's Rykodisc, and by golly gumdrops if it doesn't sound even better. The voices are clearer and more defined, the instrumentation crisper and the percussion, especially on White Bird and Creation, is sat on the sofa at your side tapping a tabla. Highly recommended.

Changing Horses – the masterpiece that might have been

Raymond Greenoaken

The ISB's career graph has been well documented: a brief but brilliant efflorescence producing four classic albums, a gradual loss of direction (or inspiration) and years of slow but ineluctable decline. There is a half-hearted counter-argument to this, which says that novelty should not be the prime or sole measure of artistic progress. On *5000 Spirits*, *Hangman* and *Wee Tam* the ISB had astonished the pundits with the originality and diversity of their music. Each successive album had some dazzling surprise for the listener. But *Changing Horses* was simply *more of the same* – or less of the same. The only surprise was the lightweight quality of some of the songs. Originality and diversity were promptly redefined as obscurity, self-indulgence, diffuseness. The virtues were suddenly vices.

It's hard to demur from the view that *Changing Horses* was not of the quality of its predecessors. But was this the first evidence of decline in the ISB's artistry? Or was it more to do with an uncharacteristic and needless caution in assembling the album? With a main course consisting of two tracks – White Bird and Creation – that between them ran to over half an hour of playing time, a decision seems to have been to serve them up alongside a selection of much lighter and more digestible fare. In the ISB songbook, the likes of Big Ted, Dust Be Diamonds and Mr and Mrs are not regarded as compositions of great substance, whatever their other virtues. They are frothy, amiable ditties, but were never designed to transport the listener to the lunar extremes of imagination, to unlock the gate of the soft mystery. Moreover, all were sung by Robin, but none really offered him the opportunity to cut loose vocally – and few will dispute that Robin in full spate, swooping, wailing, ululating, pushing his voice to its vertiginous limits, is one of the core experiences of the faith. Now, consider what other songs were theoretically available for inclusion on *Changing Horses* – Veshengro, Won't You Come See Me, Fine Fingered Hands, All Writ Down to name but four. Copper-bottomed classics every one. And though Veshengro and All Writ Down eventually surfaced on the *Be Glad* sound track album, the other two bafflingly never made the transition from concert hall and radio session to cold vinyl.

Perversely, then, I'm tempted to assess *Changing Horses* more on the basis of what it could (and arguably should) have been, than what it actually is. And what it could have been is a great album, at least the equal of *Wee Tam* and *5000 Spirits*, rather than merely a very good one, on a par with, say, *I Looked Up* or *Liquid Acrobat*.

What can't be gainsaid, however, is that, in White Bird and Creation at least, *Changing Horses* offered first class tickets to those places only the String Band could take you. You've grinned along to Big Ted: Boodgie-boodgie-boodgie...sham-sham-shadoo! There's Robin's final note hanging in the air, high and strange, hinting that there's more than just country corn on the menu. A gently descending figure on the guitar, a flute floats like a moth over darkening reed beds, and here's Mike at his most tenderly confidential: 'Who among you...?' The journey begins...

Music's a very subjective thing, obviously. You may disagree forcefully with me when I say that only a listener with a breast of solid obsidian would not be moved by the heart-stopping minor seventh cadences, the lambent vocal harmonies and Mike's keening counterpoint in that magical opening section of White Bird. And just when you think that no music could be more nakedly emotional than this, Robin's sarangi comes sawing and soaring in. 'Warm in his ecstasy' indeed – this is better than sex! But it's not a serene, oceanic beauty. An intense poignancy throbs within it like a wound, and it's almost a relief when the tension breaks and, after a second chorus, the song wanders off into a cool,

ISB, 1969. (Rose Simpson collection)

meandering guitar meditation, punctuated by a brief wintry vocal. 'Seeing not water but ice / Death not life'. The suspicion begins to form that the rest of the band have nipped off down the road for a curry, leaving only Mike plunking abstractedly in an empty studio. But wait... a hymnal feel begins to develop, and suddenly the organ and sarangi are back, and the congregation kicks into a final jubilant chorus to a backdrop of skittering hand drums and finger cymbals. The title phase is repeated like a mantra until an emphatic slap on the drum brings the track to a close.

White Bird demands to be taken on its own terms. There's little profit in arguing that that long, rickety guitar break should have been ruthlessly pruned, leaving a ten-minute song of heartbreaking loveliness and emotional force. When the ISB take you on a journey you have to go wherever they lead you and trust to their sense of direction, however wayward it may sometimes appear. That guitar break might be hesitant, might seem directionless – it might break all the rules the academic critic holds inviolable – but it's as crucial to the song, and to the journey, as any other element. It's part of the deal.

Creation is a journey of quite a different sort. Where White Bird carries you lightly on swanback over twilight landscapes as a small symbolic drama unfolds below, Creation bears you across perilous seas to faery lands forlorn, on an amethyst galleon laden with scriptures, amulets, fabulous beasts, spices and sweetmeats, crewed by godlings recruited from assorted mythologies... and at the tiller, chanting wild rhapsodic stanzas into the salty wind, Robin himself. This is Robin at his most voluminous, most encyclopaedic, and most abstruse. He has always veered away from offering precise interpretations of his more esoteric utterances, preferring to let the listener interpret them in the light of his or her own experiences and perceptions. In an interview in the late Seventies he said: 'There's a chap in America who did a PhD thesis on Creation... a whole thesis he'd written in terms of Freudian and Jungian analysis and as far as I was concerned it was total bullshit, but it was very sweet of him to do it.' It's fair to say that the piece is thunderous with unshed meaning, and that anyone attempting a line-by-line exposition of the text is doomed to inevitable disappointment. It's 'based around the seven days of Creation with a whole bunch of other ideas thrown in there,' says Robin helpfully.

In truth, it hardly matters whether this is correct or not; what Creation does reflect vividly is Robin's own artistic project of making meaningful connections between bodies of tradition and belief throughout the world and throughout time. Little wonder, then, that this piece seemed to draw so much of its terms of reference from Robert Graves' *The White Goddess*.

1969 flyer. (Witchseason archive)

In particular, the 'seven days of creation' sequence is deeply indebted to Graves' examination (in chapter 15, The Seven Pillars) of the Genesis account, and his development of the theme in the companion work *Adam's Rib*, where he supplies a King James Bible-style 'restoration' that is evidently the model for Robin's version. (Graves traces the account back to an early Babylonian creation myth, in which a planetary power is assigned to each day; in Graves' scheme, as in Robin's, the Creator is female.) As a poem – and it's included as such in Robin's book of verse, *Home Thoughts From Abroad* – it is just too opaque and disconnected to satisfy. But of course it is much more than a poem: it's 16 minutes and four seconds of the Incredible String Band at their most Williamsonian – an experience to be cherished. There is not a single supererogatory second in Creation, from Robin's eerie wordless invocation at the beginning to the preposterous vaudevillian lullaby a quarter of an hour later. It would be easy enough in these cynical times to snigger at the hieratic solemnity of Robin's recitative – the ragged harmonies and all that 'verily, verily' stuff. Personally I love it from first to last, and I've made that journey many a time over the following decades. It never fails to delight, exhilarate and amuse.

Creation and White Bird guarantee *Changing Horses* an honourable place in the ISB canon. The critics, as I've hinted, were not comfortable with such ambitious exercises. Wide-screen epics of this sort required too much sustained attention of a listening public weaned on the three-minute pop single. Put simply, they were just too *demanding*. Not even the inclusion of Sleepers Awake, a piece of Heronesque hymnody that distilled the essence of the band's world-view into two verses and a chorus, served to mitigate the charge. The critics, of course, were missing the point. To the fans, 'demanding' material was food and drink. We *wanted* to be stretched, to be challenged.

Not quite a neglected masterpiece, then: to my mind, *Changing Horses* is the masterpiece that Might Have Been. Give Dust Be Diamonds and Mr And Mrs the old heave-ho, replace with Fine Fingered Hands and Won't You Come See Me (or All Writ Down, to give Mike a fair crack of the whip), and you've got an album that would stand with the very best of the ISB catalogue. After all, what's the value of history if you can't rewrite it now and again?

Overleaf 'Remember to keep your mouth shut, Likky!'
1969 ISB line-up. (Rose Simpson collection)

The ISB's supper party, scones with Robin, some backstage stories – and a mug.

Interlude

One of the joys of the fanzine was being able to print individual one-off pieces you'd never find in a straight biography. Here are four of them.

You're bringing *who* home for supper?

John Taylor shares his cocoa with the Increds

On the first of March 1969, the Incredible String Band were due to appear at Bristol's Colston Hall. I had introduced a couple of friends – the local curate Terry and his wife Rosemary – to the joys of ISB listening. Naturally we were going to the gig, but I was a bit surprised to learn that Rosemary had had the cheek to write to them inviting them to a supper party afterward. I was even more surprised when they accepted!

After a concert that finished with a stunning performance of Creation, the ISB, with Joe Boyd in tow, found their way to a crowded living-room in the suburbs. Their slight reserve soon melted away amid candlelight and herb cookery smells and their smiles and accents grew broader. A collection of ethnic music was playing, to which Robin paid particular attention and asked questions from time to time.

Joe Boyd settled his tall frame onto the floor, endeavouring not to look like an important man with a lot on his mind. He remained politely taciturn until the Jersey-born Rosemary managed to draw out the New Jersey-ite Boyd with some gentle banter about which was the 'real' Jersey. When someone asked him exactly what a manager's function was, he informed us that a manager's job was to make sure things did not go wrong. His voice might have belonged to Sisyphus.

During the concert I had noticed Licorice's habit of fixing a stare on various members of the audience. I was intrigued by her Mona Lisa expression, but soon found out the reason for the tight-lipped smile when somebody made her laugh. One of her front teeth was missing. A dentist present offered to fill the gap for her but she declined, apparently having an aversion to anything artificial.

Rose was the most garrulous of them all and chatted away energetically when she was not attempting to eat Mike. When I showed her The Fool's LP, she waved it excitedly at the others announcing that Simon and Marijke had made a record. (That should remove any remaining rumours that the ISB had a hand in it.)

My main impression of that evening is that of sitting in a swarm of anecdotes. For example, we learned that Big Ted was a bona fide creature of enormous proportions, who had a habit of raiding their kitchen for rice and other food. According to Mike, he had even swallowed a bottle of tamale sauce, which might well have caused his demise. Their answers to questions ranged from the disarmingly direct to the deliberately obscure:

'Why are you called Licorice?' 'Because I eat it.' 'What does "wearing black cherries for rings" mean?' 'Well, what does it mean to you?'

They were quite candid about personal feelings, making no secret of the fact that Licorice and Rose did not get on at all. Scientology was credited with their ability to tolerate each other.

Cheerfully they admitted their ignorance of any chords. 'Happy Traum will work them out,' smiled Mike – a remark clear to anyone who owned the songbooks. An example of their ability to instinctively make music came when Licorice picked up an ocarina and asked what it was. On being told that it was a musical instrument, she experimented and within minutes was picking out a tune on it.

Eventually they decided to entertain us with a few songs. Mike's quarry-blasting vocals at close quarters have to be experienced to be believed. After The Minotaur's Song we were treated to an old spiritual, This Little Light Of Mine. They then managed a rendition of Creation. This was followed by a medley consisting of Take Your Burden To The Lord and two Dylan numbers – I Dreamed I Saw St Augustine and I Shall Be Released.

Eartha Kitt could never have dreamed that Old Fashioned Girl could be rendered in ISB style, but that is exactly what followed. Air came next, based on an old Tahitian melody, according to Mike. This impromptu gig was rounded off with Big Ted.

All too soon they were off again, leaving several people glad that they had picked our particular bend of the road to stop at for a while.

Close encounters of the string kind

The Incredible diary of Raymond Greenoaken aged 17¾

It's well known that the band were easier to approach after gigs than almost any other act on the scene. If you nipped round to the stage door you'd rarely find any beetle-browed, bow-tied ruffians barring your way. The first occasion on which I penetrated the sanctum sanctorum of String was after a concert at the Exhibition Hall in Newcastle-upon-Tyne. The date: sometime in February 1970. It was the first time I'd attended a String Band concert on my own, but I quickly fell in with a couple of fellow Stringheads who assured me that it was a piece of cake to get into the dressing room afterwards. 'Just walk in,' they said. 'They're cool!' A-quiver with fear and anticipation, I followed my new pals round the side of the stage as the multitudes were shuffling out of the hall. Sure enough, the door was open. In we sauntered...

What do I remember? A lot of people milling about in state-of-the-emporium attire, acting cool as fuck but probably as awestruck as I was. Rose chatting to a couple of shaggy admirers. Likky puffing a ciggy quietly in a corner. And Mike and Robin each holding court and fielding daft questions with patience and great goodwill. 'You dig the Dead, man?' 'What's the chords to Ducks On A Pond?' 'When's the Revolution starting?' I had my copy of *Wee Tam*'s illustrated insert of The Head with me, and a pen handy. Diligently I sought the autographs of all four, arriving finally at Robin. He signed with a grin, and pointed to the winged sprite on the insert. 'Have you seen one of those?' he asked. 'Not just lately,' I quipped urbanely, which appeared to amuse him. Feeling I'd got his attention, I cudgelled my brains for some elegant aperçu. After an eternity lasting approximately one and a half seconds, I blurted out: 'You're much shorter than you look on stage!' 'Yeah, right,' he said with a thin smile. It was time to leave...

Readers, I was distraught. I drifted out into the corridor, downcast, to wait for my chums. After a few minutes, the dressing room emptied, and Robin came wafting down the corridor, no doubt making for a stretch limo parked outside. As he approached me, he took out a packet of Wrigley's Spearmint Gum (the rock aristocracy's drug of choice) and offered me a stick of it. I accepted with pitiable gratitude. Forgiven! I kept the wrapper until it finally disintegrated some years later. (And I've still got the autographs...)

Close Encounter Two was not long delayed. The ISB returned to Newcastle later that year for their annual City Hall concert, and I made for the stage door almost before the strains of Long Time Sunshine had melted into the Autumn night. Again, no problem getting in: a couple of amused City Hall lackeys just waved me through. I quickly joined a knot of Stringheads awkwardly chatting with Mike, who was sitting cross-legged on the floor (hangers-on had commandeered all the chairs), and lobbed in the odd trainspotterly question. Close up, I was completely riveted by the Heron grin. I was irresistibly reminded of the horror flick *Dr Sardonicus*, and its protagonist's permanent, mirthless rictus – the risus sardonicus from which he took his name, and which supplied the leitmotif for the film. Nothing mirthless about Mike's sunny smile, however; but it was big, it was wide, and it was pretty much permanent, even in the face of a volley of asinine questions from us doting devotees.

Eventually I sidled over to Robin, besieged as ever by doe-eyed girls and earnest young men [*One of them was Neil Tennant, we now reckon – Ed.*] seeking answers to the mysteries of the cosmos. I'd just addressed a penetrating enquiry about how he achieved the buzzy fiddle sound in the middle section of Rainbow ('I put the fiddle through a fuzz box,' – So now you know), when a young female fan, fortified by illicit substances, began to suffer the initial effects of a Bad Trip and became hysterical. Nowadays this would be the cue for the appearance of several bullet-headed bouncers, but these were gentler times. Robin clasped her twitching hands, polished her fingernails with a scrap of tissue and tenderly talked her down.

The following Spring, the ISB inexplicably omitted Newcastle from their concert itinerary, so my pal Terry and I made the trek down to Leeds, where he had friends at whose 'pad' we could 'crash', as we termed it in the patois of the times. This was the tour on which Malcolm made his full String debut. A cracking gig, and Malcolm certainly shone. His Runaway Train routine, extemporised to cover tuning problems with Mike's and Likky's guitars, brought the house down. Sadly, and shamefully, when we strolled imperiously into the dressing room afterwards, we noticed Malcolm standing entirely alone, leaning introspectively against the

1970ish photo (Rose Simpson collection)

wall. More shamefully still, we ignored him completely and made a beeline for Robin, resplendent in a magnificent moss-coloured crushed velvet tunic. By this time a veteran of backstage Close Encounters, I manoeuvred myself to the front of the admiring throng and effortlessly monopolised the conversation. Pal Terry, like myself a lapsed Marc Bolan aficionado – the recently truncated T. Rex were currently heading the British charts with Hot Love – sought Robin's opinion on the, ahem, T. Rextasy phenomenon. Our man chuckled ruefully. 'He seems to be having a great time,' was his diplomatic reply. Did he like T. Rex? 'Don't really listen to the charts much.' Moving swiftly on... My enquiry about the genesis of Darling Belle elicited a detailed disquisition on the circumstances surrounding his various 'given' songs – those like Belle, Veshengro and Pictures In A Mirror that had been visited on him in dreams or reveries. After basking in his attention for several golden minutes I gallantly allowed other eager questioners to squeeze a word in edgeways. I glanced round the room and was gratified to see that somebody had finally engaged Malcolm in conversation. At that moment I felt a hand seeking out my jacket pocket and discreetly removing from it the copy of Joseph Jacobs' classic *Celtic Fairy Tales* that I habitually carried about with me. Indignantly I spun round, only to find RW himself leafing through its pages with keen interest. 'Looks nice,' he murmured. 'It's great,' I beamed, instantly mollified. 'Available at all good bookshops!' I've often wondered in latter years whether he followed my recommendation and sought out a copy. Several of the tales therein have since featured in his storytelling repertoire. You never know...

The ISB were back at Newcastle City Hall in the autumn of 1971, but things seemed to have changed in the interim. We made for the stage door as usual but found the way barred by apologetic stewards. Whether this was now the venue's general policy, or whether they were acting at the band's request we never found out. We learned, however, that a couple of minutes earlier Robin had made a brief appearance to say hello and sign a few autographs. It looked like the end of an era.

I managed to get to only two String Band concerts after that, and they were once again distant, godlike figures 'shining on a wire-tripped stage', as a reviewer in IT famously put it. Of course, through *beGLAD* I've met Robin, Mike, Malcolm and Rose on various occasions; but nothing quite matches the frisson when you're starstruck and seventeen.

Fate & ferret eat scones with Robin

George Boyter

Memories of our trip to London, (courtesy of the local fish lorry) to deliver our tape of self-composed and recorded songs to Joe Boyd, are like a series of snapshots. I think it was after we had our meeting, when he graciously accepted our tape (recorded at 1 7/8ths speed), that we walked on air from Witchseason Productions and round the corner into Tottenham Court Road.

There was the Scientology 'shop' front. We looked at each other and fell in the door.

Everyone was smiling and staring into our eyes as we sat down to be initiated with the E-Meter malarkey. To our utter amazement Robin Williamson walked in. Having played finger cymbals on stage with our god at a String Band concert in Edinburgh, we had the means to make ourselves known and open a conversation.

We babbled about our tape and the meeting with Joe. Robin astounded us by inviting us back to his flat in a nearby street. This development was beyond our wildest dreams.

I remember going up a flight of stairs and then we were in a spacious, dimly lit apartment smelling of sandalwood – I think this is the 'service flat' Rose mentions at one point in her memoir.

Robin was very chatty and asked if we were hungry as he was baking some kind of macrobiotic scones. In the kitchen we ate a magical burnt scone each, wondering if they were in any way hallucinogenic. We then followed him through to a bedroom. Licorice was there, smiling. We asked him about a song of his that we'd learned from a John Peel radio show – Won't You Come See Me. Licorice left the room. The song had bad vibes, he said, as it was written about a period when Likky and he were 'not together'. He'd done his best to forget it. We ploughed on regardless showing Robin Williamson the chord progression to his own song. Andrew remembers: 'There was some kind of keyboard there, a harmonium or electric piano, and I remember clumsily and excitedly following the chords on it while George and I think Robin played guitars. We were astounded he'd forgotten some of the words to his own song – we of course had them inscribed on our hearts, along with most of Mike and Robin's songs.'

Far out – that really did blow our minds! The whole experience was quite extraordinary for two boys still at school. Another song we had learned from the Peel session was entitled All Too Much For Me, so we played that. Robin seemed disarmingly human in comparison to the fantasy figure we had conjured up in our teenage imaginations.

A pause. Our olfactory presence seemed to rise above the sweet incense. Time to go.

2021

‘We’ve built a plinth for your mug...’

Robin Bynoe on souvenirs and second chances.

> *I have a friend who is a curator of art shows. Some time ago she told me she was doing one in Winchester. It was rather conceptual. It was going to be about memory and obsession and it was going to feature things collected by fans.*
>
> *I said, ‘You’d better borrow my Incredible String Band mug,’ and explained about it. I got an unexpected reaction. ‘Amazing,’ she said. ‘Have you got any records to go with it?’ So I delivered them, and a few weeks later she rang up again. ‘We’ve built a plinth for the mug,’ she said, ‘and it’s under a sort of perspex dome. It looks great, but we need a text to go with it.’*
>
> *So I said I would do a text to go with the mug. And here it is.*

In 1967 the world was young, our forefathers had yet to inherit the earth, and commemorative mugs were confined to royalty; I never thought to own one.

My first String Band record was their second, The *5000 Spirits Or The Layers Of The Onion*. It was 1967, in Colletts’ Folk Record Shop in New Oxford Street. I remember being faintly embarrassed having to produce the garish cover art for inspection by the Stalinist folkies hanging round the counter. Stalinist folkies were the norm in Collets’ Folk Record Shop in 1967, but were not to be, to some degree because of the String Band, for much longer. Not having ever heard of the group, I bought the record partly for the garish cover and partly because one of them was called Robin.

They became an obsession. I caught up on the first album and bought the next as soon as it came out, followed shortly by a smock like Mike’s on the cover. I went to see them whenever I could and bored my friends and family on the subject. A girlfriend told me that I was welcome in her house only on condition I didn’t mention them or her brother would hit me, and he was at Sandhurst.

At one concert they played You Get Brighter, which hadn't yet been released on record. Such was the almost religious concentration we brought to their music that my friend Kevin and I learnt the song, tune and words, from that single hearing, and played it in the folk clubs; and when it finally came out on record it turned out we'd got it pretty much right.

The high point was *Wee Tam And The Big Huge*. A succession of release dates was announced in the *New Musical Express*, but for some reason it was delayed. Each day I walked to Robert Maxwell's music shop in Oxford (Stalinist record shops becoming unconsciously a theme) and I got it at last. I thought it was breathtaking, and I still do, although these days I feel able to express more openly my reservations about Puppies.

It is hard to explain how what they did was fantastic, particularly since you have to distinguish them from the mass of fey hippy bands around at the time. It is, I suppose, the outrageously strange musical combinations: the bowed gimbri, banjo and sitar together, the Moroccan arabesques on guitar; then the lyrics: Celtic mythology and an allusiveness worthy of, but not as self-satisfied as, Eliot; vertiginous wordplay; overall an absurd optimism, 'waiting for the world to begin'.

Anyway, it didn't last. The next record was *Changing Horses*. It came out on the same day that I received my first ever hurt letter from a bank manager. The bank manager suggested that further expenditure was out of the question, but I bought it anyway. It was horrible. I felt betrayed. Everything was graceless, curdled, wrong. In the unforgiving way of youth I fell immediately out of love and crossed them off my list. It was my loss. *Changing Horses* is still unlistenable, just as *Wee Tam* grows in stature with the years, but there was other stuff which was good, as I discovered twenty years later.

Since this is art and not nature, I got a second chance. In the 1980s I was in the Highlands of Scotland; I saw Robin Williamson doing one of his solo concerts and fell in love all over again. He was in his forties, tubbier and wearing corduroy, but as hieratic as ever. All sorts of new directions for me, musical and otherwise, started with that gig.

Since by this time the earth has long since been inherited (by entirely the wrong people, incidentally), I was older and wiser and knew the score. I became a fan. I grubbed around for the records I had scorned at the time. I met men with bootlegs to sell, who said, 'How many have you got? I've got thirty-five.' And in 1994 I went against my better judgement to Leeds for a weekend for String Band fans, where I bought a commemorative mug. It reminds me of an impossible golden age and it annoys the hell out of other people, which is more than you can say for most mugs.

Overleaf Be Glad (LP) Cover

music by
The Incredible
String Band

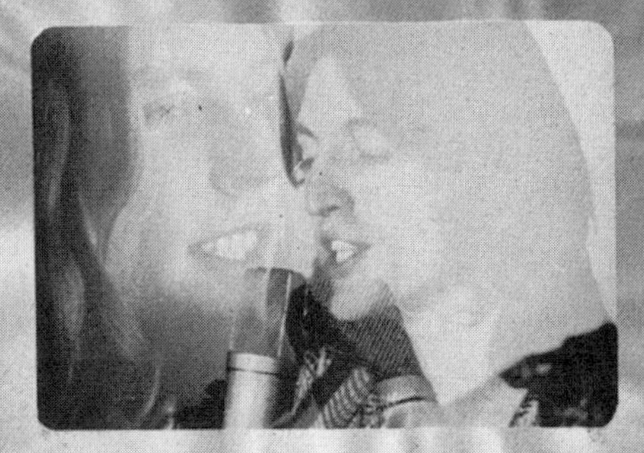

Chapter Four

Life in the ISB communal farmhouse in Pembrokeshire, Peter Neal's *Be Glad* film and the *Be Glad* 'soundtrack' album.

Incredible String Land

Raymond Greenoaken

On a wooded hillside overlooking Newport Bay on the Pembrokeshire coast stands a strikingly beautiful cromlech called Pentre Ifan. String Band fans would recognise the elegant megalithic structure from its starring role in the fantasy sequence from the film *Be Glad For The Song Has No Ending*. The view from Pentre Ifan is a fine one: if you rotate slowly on your axis in a clockwise direction you take in Carn Ingli (The Hill of Angels), the ruined cone of an ancient volcano that dominates this stretch of coast; Newport Bay and the fishing village of Newport itself; and the nearby hamlets of Nevern and Velindre. Halfway down the hill as you gaze towards Velindre, you can descry the whitewashed chimneys of a large farmhouse. This is Penwern, where Robin, Licorice, assorted Stone Monkeys, the odd Strangely and various camp followers sampled the delights of the communal lifestyle in the second half of 1968.

The area around Penwern is a timeless, dreamlike place of winding, high-hedged lanes, shady copses and little rivers. Quintessential String Band country, you might think; Robin has remarked: 'It's fantastic, probably the most inspirited place I've ever lived, an enchanted place... just the most beautiful part of Wales.'

There does, in truth, seem to be a sort of spell lying over the area. It seems to belong as much to the wildlife as to the human population. Foxes 'just waltz across the road', in the words of one local, unheeding of vehicles or passers-by. As we drove round the lanes during a visit, a sparrowhawk glided sedately alongside the car, swooping up to a nearby treetop as we pulled up on the roadside.

On the other side of the hill from Pentre Ifan, beyond the tiny village of Brynberian, the landscape changes abruptly, the rolling meadows and woods giving way to the bare, rather forbidding heights of the Preseli Hills, where the bluestones that make up the inner circle of Stonehenge are known to have been quarried. The nearest sizeable towns are Fishguard to the west, where the ferry departs for Rosslare in the Irish Republic, and Cardigan to the north east.

Pentre Ifan cromlech. (Raymond Greenoaken)

The road that joins them, the A487, is pretty busy, and tourist traffic is fairly heavy in the summer months. Despite this, the little land in the Newport-Velindre-Brynberian triangle has a hushed and secret charm. Bleak hills, gentle pastureland and rugged seacliffs, all within a few square miles. For about eighteen months in the late Sixties, this was Incredible String Land.

The chronology is roughly thus: Malcolm and Rakis, late of the Exploding Galaxy and briefly based in New York, met Robin and Mike at the Chelsea Hotel in May 1968 and plans were hatched for future mixed-media collaborations. The idea of living together seemed to flow naturally from this, so, upon their return to Britain, Malcolm and Rakis tracked down a dilapidated farmhouse – unoccupied since the Thirties – that was spacious enough for serious communal living. This was Penwern. Over to Rakis.

> Rakis: 'A vague "Let's look for a house together" idea hatched with Robin in New York materialised when I came back from travelling in Nigeria with some money and we rented a car to look "somewhere in Wales." John, Malcolm, Mike Chapman, a six foot seven sound poet from the Exploding Galaxy, and myself squashed into a Ford Escort. We slept in the car and next day stumbled on the Pentre Ifan dolmen – at the foot of which stood that dreadful house. The farmer had a long-cherished dream of turning it into a country club, but without too much persuasion took our two quid a week.
>
> 'We divvied up the rooms. I think Malcolm and Mal were together, John and Ishy too by now. I took a small room. No hot water, cooking on camping gas... living on a sack of brown rice the pig famously ate and mackerel tossed over the fence by a patronising neighbour – a retired doctor who was amused by us and later rented us two of his houses for the winter.'

Robin and Likky moved in on their return from the ISB's American tour, as did a few of Malcolm's and Rakis' erstwhile Galaxy cohorts. Mike and Rose, somewhat wary of the communal lifestyle, restricted their involvement to the occasional visit. On one such occasion, in late summer, the Pirate And The Crystal Ball fable was filmed for inclusion in the *Be Glad* film.

Throughout the Penwern occupation, the composition of the household was in constant flux. According to Roy Luke, the son of the farmhouse's owner, 'There might be three of them there one week, and the next week there'd be six, and the week after there'd be ten of 'em there. Some would be leaving, others coming in...'

Peter O'Connor arrived at Penwern towards the end of the year, and remained part of the String Band extended family until the end of the Glen Row period (he's on the *Myrrh* sleeve). Here he tells it like it was...

Penwern during preparations for filming *The Pirate And The Crystal Ball* – Peter Neal on far right. (Peter Sanders)

Houses of the Indigent and Half-Remarkable: Penwern, Trehaid and Gelli

Peter O'Connor

In November or early December 1968, I turned up at Penwern, near Newport, Pembrokeshire. I came at the invitation of Rakis (John Koumantarakis, now the Oliphant of Rossie) and Malcolm Le Maistre, both old schoolfriends from Frensham Heights, a coeducational boarding school in Surrey with an undeserved reputation for progressivism.

Since leaving Frensham prematurely in 1965, I had been watching Rakis and Malcolm's metamorphosis from effete adolescence to unbridled creative licence in London and New York. While I ground away at A levels in dowdy Tottenham, Rakis was dropping his loin-cloth and Malcolm was displaying his Y-fronts in Exploding Galaxy performances at UFO in the Tottenham Court Road. While I was just getting into lager and limes in tatty Crouch End, these two supped daily on forbidden fruit in the Galaxy's commune in Ball's Pond Road. To cap it all, they had both decamped to the Chelsea Hotel in New York, met the String Band and danced with them at the Fillmore East. Their world seemed impeccably avant-garde, and I longed to be part of it.

In July 1968, Rakis and Malcolm, John Schofield and Ishy, the poet Mike Chapman, and other members of the Exploding Galaxy had gone to Penwern farmhouse with Robin and Licorice. Around the same time, I had left London and gone to live and study history at the Catholic Chaplaincy in St. Aldate's, Oxford. Throughout that summer and into the autumn, Rakis sent me astonishing letters describing high times at Penwern: making a film in which he played a pirate, shenanigans with Mr. Luke's prize pig Big Ted, uncanny experiences with the dolmen above the house, plus useful tips for the novice, viz. 'Astrology's where it's really at' and 'Remember, bread is money'. In late November or early December, I met up with Malcolm, Rakis and possibly Mal on the train at Oxford and we travelled up to Fishguard together.

Penwern was a big old house with plenty of space, but it was bitterly cold. We all spent a lot of time in front of a log fire in the large room downstairs, with breaks for fuel gathering and hurried visits to the WC, located in a romantic ivy-hung shed a little way from the main house. I remember a sort of cupboard off this room, and inside a collection of animals huddled together for warmth. Robin's elegant whippet, Leaf, had already moved with him to Trehaid, but there was a Persian cat called Ching, mother of the three-legged Chamomile, later adopted by Robin and Janet, Lucy, a Welsh Border Collie puppy, a young cat of stunted growth called Luan, and Tashy, a selfish, matronly, flatulent Jack Russell belonging to friends of Malcolm's father Ian.

Penwern was freezing. At night, it was so cold that Rakis and I tossed coins to see who would have Tashy in his bed. Food was in short supply, and I, used to the groaning tables of the Catholic Chaplaincy, soon began to wonder whether I was really cut out for this life of rural spontaneity. Both Malcolm and Rakis were adepts of George Ohsawa's 10-day brown rice diet, but I soon joined Rakis on covert visits to Velindre to binge on Jaffa cakes, ginger snaps and ice cream. On one occasion, Rakis indulged so heavily that he was unable to leap a two-foot stream on our way home through the woods, and just sort of sank into it.

When I arrived, the atmosphere was a little strained, as everybody had received notice to quit from Mr Luke, the farmer who owned Penwern. Robin's friend Nicky Walton and Ivan Pawle (of Dr Strangely Strange) had already moved to Trehaid, a warmer, more commodious house nearby, and Robin and Likky had joined them there. John, Ishy, Malcolm, Rakis, and John's first wife, Mal, and their baby daughter, Sarah, tried to work out where to go next. Eventually, these returned to Sheffield and London, with plans to regroup in another house in the New Year. Meanwhile, Rakis and I and the cats and dogs were offered a house called Gelli, belonging to a Mr Conran, who also owned Trehaid.

Gelli was smaller and uglier than Penwern, but it was a lot warmer as it had a Rayburn range. Rakis had invested in a movie camera, so to pass the time, we made an arty horror film. The film opened with the undersized black cat Luan yowling as it slid significantly down the snow covered slates of Gelli. I remember hurling it up to the eaves again and again, as Rakis called 'Action!' in the approved neo-Realist manner.

Trehaid was near Brynberian village, just a short walk away from Gelli, and I started going over there to commune with Ivan and Nicky Walton. I remember Ivan leaning against the stove there and playing me a thirty-second setting of the words 'Mares' tails in the sky' to music.

Just before Christmas, Robin and Likky returned from touring America, and I met them for the first time at Trehaid. They had just discovered Scientology in New York, and their excitement showed. What seemed to intrigue them most were just those elements that seemed least likely to appeal: its modernity, its American brashness and lack of mystery, and its technological vocabulary. But maybe Scientology's hard edges really suited the String Band better than the older, more romantically satisfying systems that seemed to inform the first few albums. So much of their music celebrated nature, mystery, and myth, but the String Band were really children of the post-war city – like all of us at Penwern and many of the people who bought their records. Before Scientology, these differences between what Robin and Mike were and had known and what they sang about provided their music with powerful, unresolved tensions. There is no contradiction in saying that these differences and tensions helped make their music the Real Thing. Maybe the music they made together grew weaker when these tensions were ironed out – hence the split.

In any case, these were early days, and even while they talked excitedly in the downstairs room at Trehaid about their findings in New York, Robin rolled long, elegant joints (on the sleeve of a String Band album). Even now, I have a sense of ships passing in the night, because I had my first (terrifying) taste of dope at Trehaid, thanks to Nicky Walton's home-made eight-hole hubble bubble, just as Robin and Likky were getting out of that world, more or less for good.

For all our macrobiotic principles, Christmas was Christmas, and Rakis had ordered a seventeen-pound turkey for the 25th. We fired up the Rayburn early on Christmas morning, lopped off the turkey's head and pulled out the giblets for Tashy and the cats, stuffed it to bursting

Ishy settles into Penwern: 'You mean these two Jaffa cakes are all we have left to eat?' (Schofield archive)

with sage and onions, added all the trimmings and waited. Sometime in the late afternoon, Ivan, Robin and Likky, and Nicky Walton showed up, and we laid a table on the floor in front of the window and set to. Ivan and Nicky were unhappy about breaking their vegetarian diet, but Robin suggested that by eating it we were helping the turkey onto a higher path of evolution. I think Ivan was the only one to abstain (but this may have been because he had gone to Dublin). After dinner, Robin produced a jarful of a seasonal tipple he had mixed up, called Hangman's Blood, and this produced a philosophical ambience.

One question that stays with me, regarding Penwern, Kilmanoyadd, and especially the Glen, was why Robin and Mike chose to associate so closely with us. In 1968 and 1969, they were highly regarded, not just in the rock world but by people with a real eye for quality. They could have swum more significant seas – set themselves up as musical avatars in London or New York, for instance. Instead (though this was probably Robin's more than Mike's decision), they chose to associate with a group of unknowns, of whom Malcolm and Ivan were the only ones who were at all serious about their work. We were all young and friendly enough, with some outstanding personalities like Rakis, but we weren't musicians, and not many would have called us dancers.

Part of the explanation for this affinity may have lain in a common quality of naïveté among Malcolm, Rakis, John and Ishy, Mal, Robin and Licorice. They all had at least one completely impractical idea or obsession, about which they would talk as if it was all as plain as the nose on your face. Mal's visits to Venus, Rakis' business and film making plans, John and Ishy's general otherworldliness and disproportionate tolerance, Malcolm's cherished three-day ballet based on Waley's translation of the Chinese classic *Monkey*, for which he had done piles of multicoloured drawings, Licorice's theories and lives, and Robin's strange, defiant, vicarly innocence. This naïveté may have been the glue that bound them together at Penwern and later, and it did achieve staggeringly beautiful expression in the pantomime *U*, and for most of them it outlasted youth itself.

And me? I was innocent enough at 18, but my inner life was too awkward and difficult for me to belong properly in such a community of idealists. It wasn't so much a case of running before I could walk, as of flying before I could crawl. It took me years to realise that I had to learn to walk ordinarily before I could run or fly with anyone, let alone people like these. I dare say there are some people reading this who know what I mean.

Gone – but not forgotten

Raymond Greenoaken trawls through neighbourly recollections.
Interviews by Colin Thomas.

Years have now elapsed since the communards decamped from the Newport area. Physically, nothing remains of their occupation but local residents have long memories. Tommy and Ruby Llewellyn lived in Trehaid shortly before Robin et al moved in; the couple later lived next door, in a house they built themselves. 'They were a good bunch altogether,' Tommy recalls. 'I used to go and listen to them, but I finished with them for a while because they had this incense stuff. There was a hell of a stink and I couldn't cope with that flipping lot.

'They had all kinds of flipping instruments, big boxes of different things, and all kinds of beautiful tape recorders, and they would be singing away, and oh it used to be really beautiful. I used to enjoy myself sitting down and listening to them.'

Pete Bury was less enamoured of the sounds of String. 'I was in the Army at the time, and being a squaddie I was into Jim Reeves more than anything, but I was just getting into Cream and stuff like that. A mate of mine was very keen on the String Band, and he came down over Christmas and brought this [String Band] tape. It was really weird, warbly sort of music.

'Well, he went back home, and the same night we got a call from a farmer, out of the blue, saying there's a party, come and see these people, and it was the String Band doing a sort of Christmas pantomime involving music. So my mate missed the very people he'd most have liked to hear! About ten of us went up to Ty Canol, and there was a sort of scratch concert going on in the barn there. Really weird sort of music. It was probably pretty good, thinking back, but I was freaked out because I was a squaddie at the time.'

Tommy Llewellyn remembers Robin communing with the Muse. 'The biggest laugh I had... He used to go round with a sort of leopardskin cloak on him, marvellous blooming thing, and he had these clapper things and a load of bells, and he was going along the road and he passed the house and said "How are you getting on? I'm composing a song." And there he was jigging away, and off he went. And just around the corner these two horses came: the owner of Trehaid at the time and her friend, on horseback. And of course he didn't look where he was going, he was in a sort of trance, you know, and the horses bolted at the sight of him! There was hell to pay...'

Tommy, it turns out, had a special name for Robin. 'The Sugar Boy', I called him! They didn't have much money at that time, and they were always on the bum, especially the Sugar Boy there – he used to call by practically every day, knocking on the door: "Could you spare me a cup of sugar, we've run out of sugar." They had very little money.'

The commune's dress code certainly left an indelible impression on their neighbours. 'You'd hardly recognise some of them,' says Tommy, 'the way they were dolled up. And when Sugar Boy came round, crikey you'd look twice, with his leopardskin cloak and the clappers and the bells going...' Licorice's fondness for déshabillé was also a popular subject for local gossip. 'Oh yes, she used to walk around starkers,' grins Pete Bury. 'The postman was terrified of her. He used to go down the lane and just chuck the letters down the hallway and bugger off!'

Tommy Llewellyn had a closer encounter. 'I was going fishing one day and came past [Penwern] – there's a little brook running down there, you see – and I walked past the house and she said "Where are you going, Tom?"... "Fishing"... "Can I come with you?"... "Not bloody likely! Christ, I'd be shot if anybody saw me with you in the state you're in!" She had nowt on! So I said you can put something on, and she put a pair of shorts on – she might as well have been without – and a bit of a bra. She came down fishing with me then. I didn't catch anything... She didn't care two hoots. None of them did!'

Sugarboy summons the muse – Penwern, 1968. (Peter Sanders)

Interestingly, the communards weren't the only eccentrics resident in the locality. Pete Bury remembers Trehaid's landlord, Mr Conran, as an unpredictable sort of cove. 'I always wondered if Ivan Pawle named Dr Strangely Strange after this bloke, 'cause he was a doctor and a right funny bugger besides. When I worked for him he sometimes wouldn't talk in the mornings, he'd just totally ignore me... By dinner time he was as right as rain.'

And then there was Bachelor Sam. Sam kept pigs, and pace Peter O'Connor, may have been the owner of the celebrated Big Ted. Tommy Llewellyn: 'Sam used to live in a run-down old place like a flipping hermit. He bought up second-hand clothes and things. I've never seen so much junk...' Ruby: 'He had old Army clothes and that. In latter years he had a second hand shop.' Tommy: 'I love a bargain, and with Sam you could get a pair of boots for ten bob. Oh, he was a character...'

An opinion that the Sugar Boy himself endorses. 'Bachelor Sam was a complete character, he was,' says Robin. 'I once went to visit him, and he had a fox under a bucket. And he used to speak polite Welsh, very politely and quietly, and speak English very loudly and profanely, because he learned it in the Army.'

Robin remembers an unexpected encounter in Los Angeles with one of his former neighbours. 'Mrs Francis, who ran the baker's shop at Brynberian... her son became quite a famous actor and I bumped into him in Los Angeles when I was living there in Hollywood, and he was working for Steven Berkoff. I was invited to a New Year's party, and he was there with his mum, who'd flown out, and she'd never been out of Wales before.' He clearly has fond memories of the local community. 'One of the nice things about that time was that the local people were very tolerant of us. We must have been quite exotic 'cause we wore very colourful clothes and lived on rice, but they were frightfully nice to us, very very kind, the Lukes and the other people – very very nice people.'

'All the locals were scared of them,' says Tommy Llewellyn, 'because nobody around here then knew what they were – they'd never heard of hippies! But I thought they were wonderful, really wonderful'.

Be Glad For The Song Has No Ending

Adrian Whittaker

After completing the first ever Hendrix film (*Experience*), Peter Neal and Austin John Marshall were looking for a new music/film project. For them, the Sixties fusion of music and ideas and the energy that came from it could fuel an approach to film-making which used images to illustrate, comment on or underline the age-old theme of artists as society's licensed dreamers, reflecting back to us our own shared mythology. The Incredible String Band had to be the next subject.

The connection was made through Marshall, who Peter had first met when doing a BBC folk programme on Shirley Collins (married to Marshall at the time). Her sister, Dolly, had of course played on *Hangman*.

Be Glad For The Song Has No Ending (a title taken from Robin's poem The Head, which he reads in one sequence) evolved much like the Hendrix film had done; rather than a conscious overall plan, the subject dictated the next steps. Funding came in dribs and drabs, and filming was carried out over a year-long period beginning with the success of *Hangman* and ending at the turning point where the ISB became Scientologists and started a more consciously direct, less allusive and elliptical approach to songwriting and performing.

The earliest sequences in the film are a Festival Hall concert from March 1968; BBC's *Omnibus* put up some money for what they fondly imagined would be a straightforward, balanced concert/documentary programme. There were only two cameras and a limited amount of film available so Peter pre-selected some material, including Mercy I Cry City, See All The People, a playlet about Noah (Robin) and The Dove (Mike) and A Very Cellular Song. He remembers the BBC showing brief clips of the concert at the time, probably in a folk music documentary. Frustratingly, the initial cut of the film which featured most of the Cellular Song performance has been lost.

The interview segments were next. Dick Steele, a *Newsweek* staffer, had been despatched to Mike's home at Roman Camps, between Edinburgh and Glasgow, for a feature to coincide with the ISB's May visit to the States. He was rapidly cast in a straight man role for the interview, with a rather stoned Mike trying to suppress giggles. The communication problems are underlined by an image which sets them side by side as Air, the space between them, plays in the background. Also filmed at this point was a sequence where Mike and Rose wander down a country lane, hand in hand (as Peter's tribute to the old Start-Rite ad).

Peter Neal saw Robin as a magician/wizard figure, and so his cameo bits are set in leafy forest glades (in reality, a London municipal park!) with Licorice and his dog, Leaf. A visit to guitar-maker John Bailey was also shot in the same period.

The second half of the film is taken up with a fable, Pirate And The Crystal Ball, which was devised by the ISB. Joe Boyd referred to it at the time as pretty much Robin's idea, and certainly it was Robin who was expressing interest in film-making in interviews at the time. Whilst on tour in the States the ISB had met Malcolm Le Maistre and Rakis, and then outlined the story and made all the costumes in Penwern. Peter Neal and Joe Boyd drove down from London for the filming, carried out over one hectic summer weekend in 1968. Time was tight, as Peter had to be back at work in London on Monday morning, and much of the detail was improvised on the spot. Mike and Robin wanted an intimate atmosphere for the fable, without the presence of a large film crew, and Peter's earlier film apprenticeship aided him in being a one-man crew. He'd rented a camera with an enormous lens, meaning that shots could be filmed from up to half a mile away, enhancing the fairy-tale quality of the images.

The basic story-line, set around the Pentre Ifan cromlech, was that of a Pirate (Rakis), who attempts to control destiny by stealing a crystal ball from the three fates (Rose, Licorice and 'Uiscebo' – aka Ishy Schofield). They enlist Herne the Hunter (Malcolm Le Maistre) to set matters aright – and the Pirate is duly judged by the Gods (who else but Mike and Robin), found lacking and, to the accompaniment of much arm-waving, sentenced to return to the reincarnation cycle. This scene was shot at night and the 'lighting' comes courtesy of a large amount of Bacofoil and a lot of candles! There's a brief sequence as 'memories of his past life' flash before him, which features a guest appearance from the pig Big Ted, pursued by a knife and fork wielding roadie. Peter Sanders, a friend of Peter Neal's and stills photographer for the project, is seen trying to suck up the earth through a straw. Joe Boyd's cameo, standing on a roof in a leopardskin loincloth, was edited out, but see colour section for a still. Much of the visual material in this section came from a collection of old photos and prints amassed by Robin. Finally, a baby's cry is heard and the Pirate starts all over again as the Miller's son. Mr & Mrs Miller are played by Big Ted's real-life owners, the local farmer Mr Luke and his wife.

The Pirate And the Crystal Ball sequence was, as Rakis remembers, 'cobbled together.' Writing in her memoir *Muse, Odalisque, Handmaiden*, Rose Simpson recalls Malcolm's costume: 'Wrapping himself in a sheet to become Herne the Hunter, he glared furiously through eye makeup out of Victorian melodrama. The antlers he attached to his head drooped irregularly and hilariously, failing to look awesome or mysterious.'

Rakis differs: 'I thought Malcolm's costume as Herne the Hunter worked well. His movements betrayed a bit of dance training – something to be kept quiet about in those days. I saw the pirate as comedic – sometimes I have the delusional idea Johnny Depp copied aspects of it – on the LA music scene he is a pal of Devendra Banhart, who is a big String Band fan, and I know he saw it.

'For the pirate we had a sword painted silver, a parrot made of crepe paper and silver foil and a beard glued on – when I pointed out this was a bit school play Robin loved the idea. It was shot in two days if I remember rightly, or perhaps even one. I do remember Claude and his sister Paloma Picasso coming down, he to take photographs. He had a huge number of candles lit as a backdrop. I don't know what happened to his pictures.... I also remember Rose and Mike arriving, less than enthusiastic.'

There was a considerable food shortage at the farmhouse (apart from the inevitable bags of brown rice, which no-one could be bothered to cook) and at one point the entire 'cast' decided to go out for a meal – in costume! Unsurprisingly, Pembrokeshire restaurants in 1968 weren't too receptive to this sort of thing, and they ended up eating fish and chips in the back of the communal van.

Filming finished late on Sunday night and the journey was fraught. The car broke down and Peter, Joe, Mike and Rose were forced to knock up the nearest farmer and cadge a lift to the station, finally arriving in London at six o'clock in the morning.

The ISB produced a tape of instrumental music to accompany the mime (most of which is on the soundtrack album); a further track, Penwern, is on *Tricks Of The Senses*. Some time was spent editing these together before the final element of *Be Glad* was shot, a studio session at Sound Techniques in Chelsea when the photos on the cover of this book were taken. This was probably in early 1969; the ISB were already changing horses, and the atmosphere was somewhat tense. Apparently there'd just been a fairly major row, so Peter had to wait for things to settle down before filming could get going. A couple of straightforward song performances were needed to round off the film, one each. Robin chose The Iron Stone, and Mike All Writ Down. Peter Neal also filmed a studio version of A Very Cellular Song, which he later intercut with the

Festival Hall footage. Mike chose to stick with All Writ Down for the final cut, presumably as more representative of new directions. The ISB eclectic approach was wittily mirrored at the editing stage by intercutting various visual references to world cultures (folk dances, lantern slides etc), and the film was completed in late 1969.

Omnibus cried off – 'too advanced' for their audience – and the film was eventually released in the summer of 1970. After an unprepossessing debut at a tiny cinema it moved on to the Paris Pullman and then an extended run at the ICA (the promoter disappeared with the proceeds from this), and was bought by TV companies in Holland, Sweden, Germany and by America's NET Educational Network. Sadly it never took off in the way that the distributors had hoped; Cineindependent's David Speechly decided it didn't warrant the expense of producing the enlarged 35mm print needed for more extensive distribution.

Be Glad played at various British university cinemas in the early Seventies, but never did much more than cover its distributor's costs – certainly none of the participants ever saw a penny back from it. It disappeared without trace in the mid-Seventies (followed shortly by its distributors, Cineindependent).

Critical reaction to *Be Glad* was muted. *The Guardian* sniffily called it, 'a busy little film which persists in highlighting the whimsical and serio-comic aspects of the group's style'. *Melody Maker* gave it a brief, favourable mention and *Sight and Sound* called it 'loving and unexploitative... brings out the ISB's disconcerting combination of music, myth and magic'. Below are two of the more interesting reviews.

From the BFI's monthly film bulletin:

Lovingly and respectfully made (its producer has described the group as 'apostles of acid enlightenment'), the film's first thirty minutes are of somewhat humorously presented documentary material: footage from their Royal Festival Hall concert in March 1968, including an amazing Noah's Ark inventory of their numerous stringed and other instruments; *Newsweek* reporter Dick Steele interviewing Mike Heron ('If I could describe my songs I wouldn't sing them'); and a visit from Robin and Licorice to Edinburgh guitar-maker John Bailey, with the camerawork momentarily turning the rows of polished instruments hanging on his walls into a Spanish oil-painting. At their best, Robin Williamson's lyrics evoke a fairy-tale Camelot country, so that for once the shots of couples walking through sunlit forests seem entirely relevant. Similarly, since the band's performances are an amalgam of music, magic and pantomime, the transition to the final fable – of a pirate who attempts to alter destiny by stealing a crystal ball from three Grecian-looking fates – seems utterly natural. The fable itself, shot on location in Wales and accompanied by the Incredibles' first, haunting excursion into electronic [*sic*] music, is enchanting: ornately costumed, simply mimed, beautifully capturing that combination of child-like innocence and philosophical seriousness that makes the group unique.

The *Evening Standard*'s Alexander Walker was impressed:
...It is an unearthly blend of myth and magic set in a Celtic Camelot where animals abound in the tree-tops, a gila monster swivels its ball-bearing eyes, faces look like lichen, and the feel of wind, rain and sunlight mingles with music, masque and witchcraft rites. Film-makers are seldom as much in sympathy with their subjects: it's a genuinely original movie.

Updated 2021

SO WHAT KIND OF ARTICLE DID DICK STEELE MANAGE TO WRITE?

Peter says that Dick Steele was encouraged to play up his straight man role just a little bit. Certainly he wrote quite a sensible article for Newsweek *which, for reasons best known to them, remained unpublished. Here's a bit of it.*

Robin: 'My songs reflect my insights into the relationships between people and nature. They're just thoughts really. They reflect the various roles I assume, like a gypsy etc.'

Mike: 'Songs mix music and thoughts – they're a register of feelings beyond definition'.

Steele wrote of the ISB's spontaneity – as Mike and Robin lived and wrote separately and didn't always rehearse fully, sometimes concerts were the first time they played together. Mike said songs were 'never the same each time – they were affected by the time and the environment.' Steele described them as part-time workers, not overly keen on piling up lists of things to be done. Robin told him he didn't see himself as a musician, just as 'living'. Music involved dying because you had to give so much to it. He liked creating, but not being a figurehead, and was interested in developing his pottery and poetry, and in films. He was interested to see how the year would develop, without trusting too much about the future.

Finally, Steele stressed their kinship with people everywhere – Mike saw them as 'world citizens' – and said both were eager for their first US tour that summer. Mike was expecting to be influenced, 'especially by the West Coast'. He rounded off the article by saying that they'd return with nothing planned, and nothing radically changed – that they wouldn't alter their basic lifestyles. He was wrong!

Looking for *Be Glad*

Adrian Whittaker

In the early Nineties, I decided to put on a double bill of ISB films – which involved finding them first. *Rehearsal* [q.v.] was easy, but when I eventually located Peter Neal, he told me that the one remaining print of *Be Glad* was too badly damaged to be shown. I decided to track down the original distributors (long since defunct). After searches at Companies House, obscure queries to the British Film Institute, and getting someone to search through hundreds of film canisters in a lock up garage in St John's Wood, it was fairly clear that no other prints had survived. In addition, Universal Film Labs had gone bankrupt, meaning the negatives had also gone missing!

By now I'd got the local Rio cinema, Dalston, interested in the retrospective. The Rio boasts a particularly 'tolerant' 16mm projector, so Peter warily agreed to let the projectionist check out his print – which is how I ended up in an audience of one watching *Be Glad* again, twenty-two years after I'd last seen it. It was in good enough condition to be watchable and so the retrospective went ahead – attended by most of the co-authors of this book, I now realise!

By this point Peter, Mike and Robin had agreed to put out the film as a video – for which they needed the negatives to produce a 'clean' print – so, by now seriously into my archivist bit, I offered to help find them. After the collapse of Universal it turned out their films had been stored, uncatalogued, on pallets in a barn in Cambridgeshire. Thousands of canisters had sat there rusting until the owners of this cinematic cemetery decided to sell up and go to India. The negatives had then passed in turn to a film archive near Heathrow Airport, which is where I finally found them; the *Be Glad* reels had only just been identified and catalogued. There was one extra tin marked 'Prologue', which raised hopes that we'd found the long-rumoured out-take of A Very Cellular Song; when we ran through it at Peter's Screen Ventures, it turned out to be nothing more exciting than a couple of minutes of John Peel 'explaining' the ISB appeal!

The film was released on video and then DVD and is now available on YouTube as a Director's Cut.

Peter Neal talks to Raymond Greenoaken

Peter starts the interview by talking about the origins of the film.

I was never interested in making a documentary about the String Band, or an explanation of who they were, piecing together their backgrounds or where they were born. That didn't really interest me. I think what *Be Glad* started out to be was a parallel universe, trying to put over in a visual sense what the String Band where trying to do musically. The film is very much *their* film, I'll say that to start with, but if you're making a film, then part of you is going to be reflected in it, because at the end of the day you're the one that has the control, however much of a co-operative effort it is. So, in a sense, it's like trying to reflect what they were doing musically, and what touched me musically about them in terms of a film. I wouldn't call the film a documentary in that sense.

> *Raymond: Had you been aware of them very long before you approached them with the idea of doing a film?*

Peter Neal, 2001. (Room Full Of Mirrors archive)

I guess it was a year or so before I started cottoning on to their music, and I'd not heard anything like it. It was extraordinary. I had been working in film to try to work within the mythological structure of this country, you know, *The Mabinogion* and so forth. I'd been working on scripts for films of Alan Garner's books, and got very interested in that whole background. I'd been doing that for a long time, but it came together at that point. So, when I saw the String Band, I could see that musically they were doing a similar thing. In fact, when I got to know Mike and Robin and could see how well versed they were in all the literature of this country and the background of common mythology, the folklore... but also the way their music really seemed to me to bring alive the landscape and the vibrations – to use a much over-used word – of this country, which had always fascinated me.

Did you get to know them with the intention of filming them, or did it just come together?

It just happened, in that way. I'd only just finished working on the Hendrix film [*Experience*], and once you'd done Jimi Hendrix, you really had to say, what can one do next, because he was extraordinary. And it seemed to me that the only other people on the scene who were as extraordinary were the String Band, because what they were doing was inimitable. What they were doing was uniquely their own, and the way they brought in all these instruments and sounds, influences from all over the world, just worked so well with what one felt to be quite traditional material.

The filmic possibilities of those instruments come out in the sequence where the instruments are enumerated...

The Noah's Ark of instruments!

...and you pan across the stage and there they all are, gleaming in the spotlights... It's a very evocative sight, isn't it?

I think so, yes. It was quite an inspirational way to start the film. It was John Marshall's idea. He was very much involved in the concepts and things behind the scenes, and the idea of using the Noah's Ark playlet interlinked with the roadies' list of instruments going through customs... as it took shape, with filming the Festival Hall and filming all the instruments being unloaded and laid out. It just happened to come together in rather a nice way. And that sets up the whole idea of what a

String Band concert was like: When does the concert start? Has it already started? And so on...

Did the ISB themselves need much persuading to co-operate with the filming?

They were very easy people to film. They were reticent about certain things... They were very particular about what they were doing, and had an integrity about it, and therefore anyone who was going to come in from the outside and work with them on something as personal as a film, they were obviously going to be somewhat wary of. I understood that, and of course part of the process of working with any band, I think, is politicking – saying 'I'm on your side, I'm not going to expose you to anything you don't want to see'. I never felt at any time during the making of the film, in either the shooting or the editing afterwards, that there was any problem. They were welcome to come and see what was being done and make comments on it, change things... It was a very free exchange.

So they were involved in the editing stage?

Well, they weren't too interested in the editing stage, actually. I think they had a pretty busy schedule. The major input as far as they were concerned was the fable, which really was something they desperately wanted to do. And that was really a process of me discovering what was going on. It wasn't like they were going to tell me! [*laughs*] So it was in the process of actually doing it that I was discovering what was happening, which was quite a nice way of working.

Did you feel at any time that they'd taken over the film from you?

Not at all. It was a very good working relationship – from my point of view, at least; I don't know what they might say about it... I think that in retrospect they both feel that the film is quite reflective of what the String Band were, which is something that is very hard to capture. If you set out specifically to capture what the String Band were in the Sixties, I think you'd fail. If you try to examine it or take it apart or piece it together in kind of orthodox way I think you'd fail. It was because the film happened organically in this very Sixties way that I think it worked. If we'd tried to make it in a much more formal way, we might have ended up with a film that would not be being seen now, rather than as a real piece of history. It still stands up as a piece – rather quaint in places, but it has a quality about it which still works, I think.

The BBC dithered over it for quite a long time, I seem to remember. Reports would appear periodically in the music press saying 'It's going to be shown at last – next Friday!', and you'd dutifully tune in and get some obscure Bulgarian novelist being profiled...

...who was much more avant-garde! [*laughs*] I guess if we'd done some straight interviews in the traditional documentary way and intercut the footage with that, they may well have accepted it, but we never entered that realm at all in the film – every interview in there is a throwaway, used like a piece of music... Robin's words, Mike's words, all used as part of the composition of the film. There's some lovely little asides in there. I remember Robin saying, 'Some people say we're somewhere between Manitas de Plata and Jimi Hendrix...' And there's a pause. '...Just thought you'd like to know what you're hearing!' It was just put in like a pause in the music, in the same way that the music is edited together in different ways. It's a mosaic of their music as well; there's quite a lot of bits of music cut up and juxtaposed, as with their words, as with the interviews. The only real interview there is the Dick Steele, the *Newsweek* reporter interview, which we took as a kind of surreal incident – which it really was. The only way Mike could cope with being interviewed was to go outside and... *prepare himself*. And he came back in with this beatific smile on his face and eyes like sheets of glass... 'If I could tell you what it meant, I wouldn't sing about it...' and all these wonderful answers he gave. It was a very nice relationship, actually. It wasn't taking the mickey out of Dick Steele at all; it's not meant to do that, it's very gentle. But that was this kind of cultural confrontation going on. I like Mike's answers; I think they say an awful lot about Mike's approach to music, because he's always talked about his songs as being thoughts and dreams, and how can they possibly be explained? Just like talking about *Be Glad*, really: I can't really explain *Be Glad* just as a film... It was like a creation, the way it happened, and people either enter it or they can't enter it. I remember showing the film to some neighbours down in Kent a year or two after we finished it, and there was this stunned silence at the end and people saying, 'What were you on?' and I said, 'Nothing, actually!' We were all having fun: you don't have to be on anything to have fun! But I realised at the time that there would be a lot of people who just would not get it. But that's always been, for me, part of the String Band's magic: you either get it or you don't. And if you get it, you can't explain it: you just get lost in the explanation...

Being around them must have been quite interesting...

Malcolm as Herne The Hunter. (Peter Sanders)

Ace reporter Dick Steele attempts to get some sense out of Mike and Rose. (Peter Neal)

Yes. I was knocking around with various odd groups of people, communes and so on, at that time anyway. Though I was a bit old to be a hippy – more of a beatnik. But the hippy movement interested me because it came out of that Kerouac-type thing in some ways. It was very familiar on that level. I remember when the String Band were in London – I think when we were doing the music for the fable – and going round to their hotel somewhere near Ladbroke Grove, and going in and seeing how they'd pushed all the beds aside and were living on the floor in this hotel room. Which was very familiar to me, because we all did that wherever we went: we would dismantle the beds and sleep on the floor, and make a kind of encampment. So there was a way of socialising that was very familiar to me, sitting around and smoking dope, talking and falling over each other and ignoring each other... It was very simple and very open. They were very easy to get on with. Yes, they had their artistic protectiveness, but they were young and they weren't very experienced in fending off that kind of interest... It's very difficult for a band like the String Band not to become scooped up with the business of being icons. But I never had any problem with them. The only tension ever during the making of the film was when we were shooting at Sound Techniques. That was them: they'd just had some kind of big family row, and we had to wait while they went outside and sorted it out. But it's understandable that if you're living like a family you're going to have family rows. There wasn't a problem with the filming itself, ever; they were totally co-operative. No tantrums or preciousness about them at all. Which surprised me, in a way, because you kind of almost expect them to be aloof or what have you, but I think that's a kind of misconception that people have. They're just good guys, very friendly. They're very absorbed in what they're doing, which might make people feel that they're aloof at times. But I've worked with a lot of musicians, and quite honestly, they come in two styles: there's the ordinary guys, and there's the guys who feel terribly threatened and who are therefore awful to work with. There are plenty of the second sort! Very prima donna-ish...

I see films as being much closer to being music than theatre or TV; they're something that works in movement and tones and colours, so to me there's much more similarity between a film and a piece of music than there is between a film and anything else. I get on with musicians for that reason: I sort of bond with them, I suppose, on the basis of how we work. It's very hard to say how you work as a film-maker, because it's not necessarily an intellectual process. You can intellectualise afterwards, but at the time you just go by what feels right. I think film, like music – well, first of all it hits you here [*points to heart*] and it's an emotional, subconscious response, and the intellectual part comes later. In that way I find it's very easy to get on with musicians. There are some musicians who are so screwed up; it's very hard to maintain your sense of just being another human being. But certainly Mike and Robin were never like that. I think they were just too interested in what they were doing to bother with any of that. The amount of stuff they turned out, they didn't have time to get precious about it! And their approach to music was very different to a lot of other people's. It wasn't planned in the way that a lot of people plan their music, and that means you have to be on your toes all the time; you've got to give a lot in every performance. Audiences appreciate that, which is why you get so many faithful fans, because they get such a lot from the String Band and they want to give it back. You get a lot of people whose lives are changed by it to some extent, as music can do, and as films, for me, can do too. There are certain films and certain pieces of music that I can remember as vividly now as the moment I experienced them, and I know that they effected a shift in terms of my consciousness, in the way that doors opened for me that may not have opened so soon, or at all. And of course the String Band's music was catching a part of the atmosphere of the times that nobody else was touching. It was pulling together certain threads of things that were happening in the Sixties, the opening up of knowledge... Certain kinds of knowledge that up to that time had been quite hidden suddenly became available to people at all kinds of levels. You could do things that had not been possible to do en masse before, but had been confined to little secret societies and such. And I think that they caught that, and also the power residing in the landscape of this country: the stories and the heritage we've got here, which is very rich. If you'd been brought up in the Forties, as I was, all you might read in this area would be the Greek myths, and then we suddenly discovered that we've got these incredible stories and myths of our own. Because they come from our landscape and embody the qualities of our land, they have a very different kind of power for someone born here. And making [people] value their own soil, their own country, is a very great achievement, I think.

Did you feel any sense of the power inherent in the landscape when you were down at Penwern?

Oh absolutely. I'm Welsh anyway, so my heart is always in Wales. That landscape is very much in my make-up. It's this whole idea with shamanic practice that it's strongest where the shaman is born, because the shaman has been brought up in the particular vibrations of that area: the idea that the earth has a tone, but the landscape plays a melody, and so if you were born in a certain area you might have the same bass tone that everybody has, the drone of the earth, if you like, but your particular tune relates to your native landscape; I feel that very strongly, and I suspect that, instinctively, most people do. And to be able to conjure that up through music is great, and that's what musicians in this country should be doing – certainly some of them! And even though the String Band's music pulled in all these exotic instruments from all over the world, it was still very much from our landscape. Sitar? – It doesn't matter; it fits in perfectly with the old Celtic poems. But forgetting the words for the moment, just the sound they made is for me the key thing. It's like you can listen to the words and understand them, but anybody can say the words, and if they study enough can write the words, or write something saying a similar thing, because it becomes a body of knowledge that can be passed down in words; but to pull out the sounds of it is magic. That takes artistry. So what always affected me about their music, more so than the words, was the sound they made together. Not just the sound of the instruments, but the sound of the voices. And hearing them again recently, at Cropredy, I was wandering around the field and I suddenly heard this sound – and it suddenly took me straight back. This very strange quality they managed to evoke through sounds. That's the magic of the String Band.

2003

Be Glad For The Song Has No Ending (soundtrack)

Adrian Whittaker

The 'soundtrack' album from the film wasn't released till several years later, by which point the ISB had moved to Island Records and embarked on the new course signalled by Liquid Acrobat. *Not surprisingly, it wasn't a big seller.*

It was hard to work out how *Be Glad* fitted into the ISB's scheme of things when it was released in March 1971. The brash dayglo sleeve design hinted at a new, more pop-oriented direction; Malcolm Le Maistre had just joined the band as a replacement for Rose Simpson, and the new line-up was on a major Spring tour featuring lots of new songs. Contemporary material, however, wouldn't be released (on *Liquid Acrobat*) until that October.

Instead, record-buyers got, in Joe Boyd's words, 'a kind of clear out the cupboard thing'. Joe had just sold his Witchseason company to Island Records and put the *Be Glad* running order together virtually as he was packing to leave for a new job in the States. The tracks stemmed from 1968 and 1969, and were largely connected with the much-delayed film, which had eventually been released in July 1970, triggering the album.

Adding to the confusion, *Be Glad* was released within a week of *Relics*, an Elektra-era compilation, and the two records were often reviewed together. Critics were hard put to assess the album: 'Not among the band's most distinctive works,' complained *Melody Maker*; *Sounds* noted a 'warm, pleasant feeling' and told readers: 'Approach it on its own terms and you won't be disappointed.' Sales, correspondingly, were limited, though it did briefly reach number eleven in the Virgin Records Chart (oddly enough, the official charts were on strike when it came out).

The music spans a transitional era between *Wee Tam* and *I Looked Up*, where Rose and Licorice were increasingly playing a fuller part in the band's recordings and gigs. At the same time, the songwriting was moving from eclectic, sometimes obscure dreams and incantations to a more consciously direct approach – a by-product of the band's involvement in Scientology, with its emphasis on effective communication.

See All The People is a live cut from the Festival Hall concert shown in the film. Zen lyrics aside, it's more of an excuse for Mike and Robin to have a kind of contrapuntal jam. Mike reckons one of the melody lines was taken from a classical piece he'd been listening to at the time.

All Writ Down is another Heron song. Mike thinks this was probably part of the *Changing Horses* sessions; certainly a longer, alternate take was released as the B-side of the Big Ted single from this album in October 1969. The song, about the trials of young love, might also have a Scientology sub-text, according to Joe Boyd: 'That's about engrams – cellular memories.' Mike disagrees: 'No, I didn't set out to write a Scientology song – certainly not at that point in my career, it was still early days as far as Scientology was concerned.' It has an unusual structure – short verses and a very long chorus – and features some strong, snaky wah-wah guitar lines – by Robin! The long version is now on *Tricks Of The Senses* – here's the extra verse:

I though those women were so cruel
And were so low
But they just moved by Nature's law
Didn't feel right to stay
Thought that they'd just go

In Elvis Costello's 2015 autobiography, *Unfaithful Music*, he singled out All Writ Down as an ISB favourite: '...as true and heartbreaking to me today as it was at the age of fifteen.'

The Song Has No Ending, Side B's collection of nine instrumental pieces, formed the soundtrack to the Pirate And The Crystal Ball fable. The music was probably recorded some time after the last *Wee Tam* sessions (though Beyond The See is common to both records. Otherwise, no titles are known apart from Theta (this really is a Scientology reference) which turned up in March 1969 as a session track on John Peel's *Nightride* programme. It's a pleasant enough collection but, Beyond The See apart, lacks focus without the accompanying visuals. An out-take, Penwern, was included on *Tricks Of The Senses*. Robin plays some shimmering Spanish guitar lines and Mike adds bass, with either Joe Boyd or Mike on organ.

After the film's eventual release, more songs were needed to make up a full LP and three more Williamson tracks were added from the Witchseason vaults. Veshengro, an outstanding composition, was written at Penwern and dates back to July 1968 and the final *Wee Tam* sessions. Robin: 'Veshengro – the title and the song – was a dream I had. I wrote it out and a few days later I stumbled across a dictionary of Romany cant in the library! Vesh means wood, engro means man, thus Veshengro is woodsman.' The song relates to the King of the Gypsies, Abraham Wood: the Wood family moved to Wales in the 17th century and became cut off from other gypsy clans, evolving their own unique language mixture of Romany and Welsh. Other characters threading their way through the song are Finn McCool, the legendary Irish chieftain and Jalal Uddin Rumi, the Sufi poet and mystic who founded the whirling dervish order at Konya in Turkey. The song is the equal of anything on *Wee Tam* – perhaps it was seen as too much of a solo piece to be included on that album.

The other two songs are very much ensemble pieces, both, according to Robin, with their origins in Penwern days: 'We had a lot of fun there that summer – the winter afterwards was awful, though.' Come With Me is, like Job's Tears, somewhat of a call and response number, with Rose and Licorice much to the fore on vocals and recorders. Was the song's protagonist based on a mythological figure, I asked Robin: 'Well I usually did do that wherever possible, but in this case, no! I was trying out a song based on a variety of folk motifs.' Waiting For You, like Evolution Rag, is one of his 'musical acting' specials – a vaudeville number based around a series of lists, which includes little cameos for all the band. It became a good live vehicle for the four-piece ISB, and offered some light relief after, say, Pictures In A Mirror on their autumn 69 tour. My guess is the actual recording dates from that year. Some of the characters, Robin notes, took on a life of their own in the fanzine – and anyone who spent time in Reading in the early Seventies will know 'the man they call Shine' sold loon pants, T-shirts and other, more nefarious, products on his stall in the Reading Emporium!

Waiting For You

John Quigley

I've had a soft spot for Robin's Waiting For You ever since hearing him and Mike and Rose and Likky perform it in autumn 1969 at Brum Town Hall. I was puzzled when it didn't appear on *I Looked Up* in Spring 70 – like Come With Me and Queen Juanita, also performed that night, it must have been recorded during those sessions. I suppose one could argue that it's a bit self-indulgent at nearly seven minutes – maybe Joe Boyd did, at the time – but it does give off that joie de vivre typical of the ISB then. Robin sounds as though he is, in the words of another song, 'getting some fun out of life' and contributes some ingenious and cheeky lyrics. These seem to reflect the song's cod-1920s feel; trivia hunters may note that this is the only String Band song to contain no less than three references to Louis Armstrong classics, in the lines 'I'm waiting for Willie the Weeper to wake', referring to a famous Hot 7 track from 1927 [*a 'cocaine blues', Grahame Hood tells us – Ed.*], and 'I'm waiting for the man they call Shine', Shine being the vaudeville song recorded by Louis in 1930; and in the exclamation 'Hold that tiger!', from, of course, Tiger Rag. No doubt this also reflects Robin's early musical career in the 'Mound City Jazz Band' with Gerard Dott, as well as the fact that in Robin's youth Edinburgh was a trad jazz town, producing Alex Welsh, Sandy Brown, etc. As British films of the Fifties and Sixties demonstrate, trad was an important part of what passed for the bohemian lifestyle in Great Britain back then. But, watching an old Bing Crosby film, *Pennies From Heaven* (1936), I was surprised to hear Bing sing a song with the refrain 'I'm waiting for you', sounding as though it might have inspired Robin's similar, but hardly identical song. The exuberance didn't last, though; compare it with Evolution Rag on *Liquid Acrobat*, written in more or less the same style and recorded around eighteen months later. That may have worked well as a live number, but its jollity seems forced and its lyrics a mixture of the sloppy and downright daft – reflecting, for me, the ISB in decline. Ah, well, seasons they change...

Overleaf Music press ad for the *U* album. (Elektra Records)

Chapter Five

The ISB at Woodstock, *I Looked Up* and the *U* show

In May 1969 the ISB were made an offer they couldn't refuse...

‘A Little Upstate Folk Festival’ – Woodstock & The ISB

Ever thought you were the dust of stars? Or perhaps you perceived yourself to be the colour of gold? Or maybe you’ve simply experienced a strong desire to ‘get back to the garden’. If so then you’re part of the Woodstock generation. The Incredible String Band, however, were more that that, they were the only Scottish group to play the festival. Andy Roberts roots about a bit... Updated by Adrian Whittaker, 2021

By the time *I* got to Woodstock, well, it was twenty five years too late for a start and the nearest I ever did get was interviewing Rose Simpson of the ISB Woodstock line-up in the study of her Welsh home on the 25th anniversary of the event. But more of that elsewhere in this book. In retrospect Woodstock has become everything the idea (rather than the reality) of the Sixties counter-culture stood for, and consequently is frequently derided and ridiculed. You had to be there, I suppose. ‘Yeah, yeah’, you might say, ‘so what’, before flipping on another Maximum Throb Japanese import, ‘what’s all that got to do with anything in these parlous times?’ Not much really, but the fact remains that the event happened, is now a touchstone for some, a millstone for others and a benchmark for everyone when it comes to the archaeology of rock festivals. And of course the Incredible String Band played there.

So, what do we know? Well various bits from various sources...

If *Barefoot In Babylon* by Robert Spitz is to be believed, on May 28th 1969 Michael Lang, the Executive Producer of the festival, phoned Artie Kornfeld, the guy dealing with Publicity and Subsidiary Rights, to tell him that he had obtained the services of the String Band for the sum of $4500. No small amount and in fact the same sum they paid for Ravi Shankar. Artie was apparently impressed by the acquisition of both and commented in the argot of those far off days, ‘Far out! They’ll be dynamite to open the evening’s shows, soft, moody.’ Little did he know what was to actually happen! Described to the String Band as a ‘little upstate folk festival’, they had no idea what to expect as they flew in. Robin: ‘It was a military helicopter with only one side. As we flew over the site, all you could see was millions of tiny dots, spreading right up to the heavens. I realised then it was the biggest thing I had been at.’

Heron's memory of the Woodstock gig: 'That was through people who knew Joe [Boyd]; we'd done this show in New York the night before [*Carnegie Hall on 13th August – Ed.*] and the organisers were keen to have us on. A helicopter took us to the site, and I recall all these people looking like ants trapped in a sea of mud. I don't know what we were doing then but we played and left again. I think the girls were with us then.' They certainly were, Mike!

The String Band flew into Woodstock from New York's White Lake heliport where, incidentally, Robin met the Grateful Dead's Tom Constanten, leading to him later doing the arrangements on Queen Of Love from the *U* album. They travelled with Ravi Shankar and John Sebastian, who wasn't booked to appear, but happened to be on the chopper because he was very 'close' to Licorice at the time. The ISB were due to appear late on the Friday evening, after Ravi Shankar, but the festival was running late. As their revised performance time of 1.00 am drew close they were confronted with every festival performer and organiser's worst nightmare – torrential rain.

The Woodstock 50th Anniversary boxed set recordings captured the on-stage deliberations and revealed a slightly different narrative from the one that had been rehearsed so many times over the years. Headed up by Mike, the most concerned of the four, the band understandably refused to go on with electric instruments due to the lack of proper overhead cover and threat of electrocution. Joe: 'They didn't have a proper stage roof, just very flimsy tarpaulin, which was the most elementary cover you can imagine.' Festival organiser John Morris suggested that Mike and Robin could play an acoustic set as a duo and do some of their older numbers. Joe wasn't too sure about this, as the repertoire had changed so much – and if Rose and Likky had tried to join in, Rose says 'the outcome would have been unpredictable and possibly disastrous, as Joe well knew.'

'What about the girls?' Joe asks the boys. Robin says he is willing to play the acoustic set but Mike says nothing. So, as Rose says, 'Joe stood up for us... recognising that we girls were by then central to the ISB performance.' He re-arranged the set for the following afternoon and they were replaced by Melanie, who also had not even been booked to appear and was hanging around backstage to see if she could be fitted in. The effect and imagined consequences of this rearranging seems to have grown out of all proportion over the years and is the most written-about aspect of the String Band at Woodstock. Mark Ellen, writing in Q magazine (June 93) noted that despite the ISB having cancelled, the helicopters had now stopped flying (cock-up on the cash front) and the String Band, not being able to hotel it for the night, spent a gloomy nocturnal sojourn 'damp and muddy, packed like sardines, intensely uncomfortable and wearing our stage gear', be-tented together with John Sebastian, Joe Boyd and Melanie. A no sleep blues situation ensued and the percussion drums got somewhat moistened.

Joe Boyd's view of these events is now tempered by the passage of time but still tinged with a hint of the 'what ifs'. This from Adrian Whittaker's interview with him:

'We were booked to go on on Friday night. We had a perfect slot... and it started to rain. At that time the ISB had started very actively with amps, so they had a pick-up on the sitar, pick-up on the gimbri etc and the electric bass. Of course you couldn't play in the rain with all these electric instruments – so we were stuck. I said: "Just go on with your acoustic instruments and play," and they said: "We can't, wait till it's stopped raining".

'What happened then was I said: "You don't know what's going to happen – you may never get on stage" – but they wanted to wait for the rain to stop and so someone else went on – Melanie – who triumphed in that slot and wrote Candles In The Rain about that exact moment! We talked to John Morris, who was a friend of mine, about the logistics of where we could pick up on the following day... and it sort of haunted me, that moment, because I should've pushed – just *dragged* them bodily to the stage and said 'Forget the amps, just play acoustically'. It might have been wonderful. We ended up going on the following afternoon after [*The Keef Hartley Band*] in the baking sun. People were ready for something heavy and loud and they came on and just – died!'

Mmmmm – it might equally have been terrible. Sounds like Joe is being a bit 'wise after the event' on his involvement. But there was obviously tension about the event and perhaps confusion about just what Boyd's role was and exactly what power he could exercise over the band. Looking back in 2020, Rose Simpson has mixed feelings: 'We had no sense of being called upon to respond to a challenge... No one had the positive energy to get up on that wet stage with dodgy electrics and instruments that wouldn't stay in tune.'

Boyd again, finally: 'It was Joe Boyd's Greatest Mistake. If I could do it all over again I would have put them on in the rain. They would have triumphed like Melanie. They would have been in the movie, and everyone who was in the movie had a huge break. Who knows what would have happened?' Who knows?

The ISB's moment of glory at Woodstock finally came, rather dissonantly, after The Keef Hartley Band and before Canned Heat at 6.00 on the Saturday afternoon when the crowd were high, hot and rocking.

Not a good place to be and as a result they were apparently the only band at the festival not to be called back for an encore. 'Not appealing,' noted 17-year-old audience member Kevin Marvelle in his festival diary.

Heron: 'It was incredibly high, right up on this scaffolding, and three out of four of us had vertigo. Little flimsy dresses on the girls, acoustic guitars out of tune, the drums still damp, up this bloody tower, like playing off the Forth Bridge to these seas of people cooking beans in the mud. Oh it was impossible. We were terrible.'

Heron again: 'It was terrible for us. We got helicoptered out, we had a gig that night [*at Flushing Meadows*], so we didn't have to stay there. Canned Heat was the best for me, kind of latrine digging music, really brilliant, you could thrust the spade in time with the music! But some of the stuff seemed not really suitable. Certainly not us, we were terrible for it.'

Williamson: 'Our performance at Woodstock was not great. But we did enjoy being there.'

As part of the 25th anniversary of Woodstock celebrations the ISB footage turned up and some was used in the new film of the event. Not all the set was filmed, apparently due to the high price of film stock, but it all exists on audio and was eventually released in full on the Woodstock boxed set (see below). The song used in the film is When You Find Out Who You Are. The ISB performance appears not to be as bad as either Mike and Robin's memories suggest, considering the problems which surrounded it. The musicianship is fine, Robin's vocals are strong and clear and Likky adds excellent backing vocals while Rose grins and plunks bass and Mike delivers trademark piano. [*Editor's note: Since this was written, more of the Woodstock set has turned up on the Net. Contrary to the collective band memory, the performances of* The Letter, This Moment *and* When You Find Out Who You Are *are confident, in tune, and rather good actually.*] Sartorially, Rose has some form of diaphanous garb draped about her person, Mike sticks to a simple T-shirt and trouser arrangement, Robin, in seriously striped trousers and attempted moustache, looks very 1969 and Likky deports herself wonderfully in dress with ring of flowers head accessory.

Rose now says that, by this point in the festival, 'the audience needed strong stimuli to take their minds off their other problems. We were too quiet, too self-absorbed and we lost our chance. But we had also seen it all with our own eyes and been part of it.' Out of all the festival acts, only seven female musicians actually played at Woodstock and of course Rose and Likky were two of them.

The final viewpoint here, from Robin, takes a step back from the performance aspect and concentrates on his views on the festival as a whole – views which were shared by many that attended the festival. 'I thought it was the beginning of a new era and I think that people at that time thought everything would change at that point, that money would break down, that we'd go back to a barter economy, that the world was forever going to go back to a more idyllic state. Everyone was very optimistic about it, and it was very disheartening to find that this did not occur. A lot of people got cynical and then you had the cynical and self-seeking Seventies.'

And that, really, is the true spirit of Woodstock. Ah well, looks like the sun's coming out. Time to get back to the garden I guess...

Fifty years on, Adrian Whittaker finally got to listen to the entire Woodstock set...

So, it's about 6.00 on the Saturday evening and The Keef Harley Band has just finished. While Chip Monck runs through a list of announcements about the dangers of brown acid and missing children – you know the drill – Mike and Rose run gamely through The Letter riff in rehearsal mode.

The Woodstock set was entirely composed of unreleased and unrecorded material destined largely for *I Looked Up* (at a point when *Changing Horses* wasn't even out) so it was a challenging experience for the audience. The ISB struggled with tuning problems, too, as many of the instruments had got wet the evening before. They begin with an early version of Robin's Invocation (the *U* version was longer and re-shaped). A bold move to start the set with a poem but it works! Then comes The Letter – Andy Zax, who worked on the sound for the boxed set, was clearly not a fan of Robin's fairly random piano playing, which he has mixed right down compared with the sound on the video version, as he has also done with Likky's wibbly percussion. It's a good opener and a strong performance from Rose and Mike. After the customary exhortations from Chip to get off the scaffolding it's Gather Round – Mike on steel guitar, I think, Likky (and Rose?) on backing vocals – and there are whistling solos! I've never really liked this song, which appears to be about some kind of seer. About Robin himself? Robin, sounding awed, chooses this moment to tell everyone he's 'never been to anything like this before and the thing that surprises me is how many of us there are. It makes me fantastically happy, I'd just like to say that.'

This Moment works well. Robin changes the backing vocals to 'grass at your feet' instead of 'walls of this room' – very appropriate. Unusually, Mike doesn't extemporise much on the 'Oh no' bits – probably he wasn't relaxed enough, as it was near bedlam on stage with roadies scurrying everywhere. Come With Me is a creditable performance, and at one point Robin turns a forgotten line ('if you will flee away with me') into a weird quasi-operatic effect. The backing vocalists appear to have dozed off at the start of this song (or maybe are watching the helicopters) but gradually regain presence.

Fifty years on, Adrian Whittaker finally got to liksten...

Mike has clearly picked up on some dissatisfaction in the audience, who had been asking for old songs, and apologises for the brand-new nature of the set – 'We hope you don't mind that.' In later days, it was Mike who would usually dig up a couple of reworked old songs as crowd-pleasers. The set ends with When You Find Out Who You Are, prefaced by an apology from Robin for all the tuning delays because 'all the instruments got wet last night'. The song is a bit long for this audience and this point in the programme perhaps, but there's an anthemic vibe to it which kinda works well. At least it wasn't Pictures In A Mirror! There's an oddly brisk announcement from Robin: 'We have to leave now, I'd like to say goodbye to you' – and the band are helicoptered off to their evening gig in Flushing Meadows, New York.

2021

But what if things had gone differently at Woodstock? Allan Frewin and Raymond Greenoaken present an Alternative History of the ISB over the page.

HAMMER OF THE FAERIE-FOLK
WOODSTOCK - 1969
A little lick of moisture never hurt anybody. Get out and PLAY!
But we're artistes!
Och, man! we'll get drookit!
whit aboot ma new perm?
WHITE BOYD
Ey oop! Bugger this for a game of darts!
WARBLE
Swear we're gonna weather the Storm...
ISB WOW WOODSTOCK
"Best set of the event..." — HENDRIX
"Zo, so good!" — Jimmy PAGE
The Incredible String Band played a blinding set despite adverse weather conditions.
Hey Joe
Let's go acoustic and play the folk clubs for a few years...
It's real music, man!
Let me manage you and you'll go right to the top!
Not now Jimi!
Let's take a little walk...
Wow!
Help ma boab!
THUGS R US
First you gotta ditch the broads. Then you need a good, solid rhythm section and some catchy tunes for USA FM radio. Then you'll need a snappy new name. Hey! I got it...
Yeah—magick!
INCRED-ZEPPELIN
SKREEEEE
Hey girls — wanna join a folk band?
You're the first girl ahhhh lur-r-rved, woh, yeah, bay-bee, woooh-hooh, yeah...
words: Raymond Greenoaken. Pictures: Allan Frewin
NEXT ISSUE: WORLD DOMINATION...

JOE BOYD REMEMBERS!
NOW IN HIS 95TH YEAR VETERAN ROCK MANAGER JOE RECALLS HIS MOST CELEBRATED ACT - THE INCREDIBLE STRING BAND
DRUGS!
DEBAUCHERY!
DESTRUCTION!
HOLIDAY INN
Well, once they went electric and changed their name to Incred-Zeppelin, they lived the Rock'n'Roll lifestyle to the hilt...
At the height of their fame, however, their private airship sprung a leak over Tottenham Court Road and plunged to its doom through the roof of the Church of Sciurentology. After that, they were never the same...
SCIURIENTOLOGY
Hmm, looks interesting...
THEY ENTHUSIASTICALLY EMBRACED SCIURENTOLOGY...
Ever had the feeling you're being watched?
Help ma boab! It's freezing!
THE PHILOSOPHY DEVELOPED BY ECCENTRIC NATURALIST L. ROY HUBCAP AFTER A LIFETIME'S STUDY OF SQUIRRELS (Lat. sciurus). HUBCAP MAINTAINED THAT THE KEY TO FULFILMENT LAY IN RENOUNCING SENSUAL PLEASURES AND EATING LARGE QUANTITIES OF NUTS.
THEY ABANDONED ROCK'N'ROLL EXCESS...
NUTZ
...AND CAME TO ME TO RELAUNCH THEIR CAREERS
How about this one?
this chestnut is different from any before it...
Sorry guys - it won't sell. What the public wants is glamour and glitz. Look at ABBA!
ABBA
Here's my plan...
SO WE GOT THE GIRLS BACK, RENAMED THE BAND MЯRL (pronounced "mrrl") AND PUSHED THEM AS THE SCOTTISH ABBA! IT WAS A MASTERSTROKE...
MЯRL
NME
INC-ZEP COME CLEAN
"No more Sex'n'Drugs 'n' cruelty to fish..." - WILLIAMSON
I used to be randy - now I'm a new man. M.H.
Melody Maker
1 (1) The Waterloo Song..... MRRL
1 (6) Mama Maya
1. (3) Dancing Queen of Love... MRRL

WELL, AFTER YEARS AT THE TOP, THEY SPLIT TO PURSUE THEIR OWN INTERESTS...
Robin got a gig presenting Jackanory...
It wasn't in your time, and it wasn't in my time...
While Mike retired to Glen Row to write songs for Bonnie Langford and other ass-kickin' rock chicks...
Baby Goodnight...
ROSE AND LIKKY WENT INTO POLITICS, AND WHEN, IN THE WOODSTOCK ANNIVERSARY YEAR, ROSE WAS ELECTED LORD MAYOR OF LONDON...
... AND LIKKY BECAME GOVERNOR OF CALIFORNIA...
VOTE LIKKY
SUDDENLY EVERYONE WANTED TO HEAR ABOUT THE I.S.B AGAIN...
Tell me again, Grandad — what was it really like in the Sixties?
Well, you made your own amusement then...
Deep in the hollo-o-o-www jail...
SO I GOT IN TOUCH WITH ROBIN AND MIKE...
RRRRIIIINNNG RRRIIIINNNG
Er, Mr. Heron?
Too much!! got a letter!
... LINED THEM UP A MEGA-BUCK RECORDING DEAL WITH PIG'S WHISKER/SONY, AND GOT THEM BACK ON STAGE FOR THE FIRST TIME IN 20 YEARS! YUP, THE CIRCLE TRULY IS UNBROKEN!
?
Now, where did I leave my hearing aid?
A Greenoaken/Frewin Production

Maria, Chicago Illinois

Several decades later, Maria Sosa came out on the ISB Facebook page as the subject of The Letter:

> 'It was a very simple story. I was 18 years old in my first year of college. I don't remember exactly what I said except that it was a long letter, combination fan letter and soul baring. As you may remember, those were turbulent times. I was a very innocent girl, away from home for the first time, missing my loving but sheltering family and longing for the courage to make myself in the image that I felt was really me. Of course the music of ISB was both a refuge and a guidepost. I was surrounded in college by people who were much more sophisticated than me, or so I thought, and I felt intimidated and even slightly ashamed to express my inner doubts and feelings. So basically one day I just sat down and poured it all out to Mike Heron in a letter that I honestly never believed would reach him. I had planned to go to Woodstock so I would have heard the song there, but my parents found out and sent me to Puerto Rico to my grandmother's house (I forgave them!). News then didn't travel the way it does now so I literally didn't hear the song until *I Looked Up* came out! By that time, I had indeed "worked out" a lot of my "problems" and it was like a sweet, warm embrace of understanding coming to me from far away, although I did meet the band twice backstage after concerts - once in Oxford when I was studying abroad and another time in Chicago, also after a concert. And now many, many years later I am, I suppose, who I was meant to be!'

In November 1969, the ISB established a secure and permanent base at Glen Row [q.v.], together with a motley crew of musicians, dancers and footsoldiers. By this point, Robin's relationship with Licorice had ended and he moved in with Janet Shankman, a Californian artist whom he'd met in May that year and eventually married in December 1970. Mike's relationship with Rose was already in a state of flux.

In between the touring – by now a much more constant part of their lives – they were working on an ambitious multi-media stage show, U. *But first there was the material they had toured in late 1969, released in April 1970 on* I Looked Up*...*

I Looked Up – a study in transition

Wot – no sitar? Raymond Greenoaken remembers it well.

King's Road, Chelsea... a sunny Saturday afternoon in April. Even strutting through the crowds in billowing black cape and matching floppy-brimmed hat, I attracted disappointingly little attention. For this was 1970, and the King's Road was a conflagration of sartorial extravagance. I was in London for the final performance of *U* at the Roundhouse, having travelled down on the overnight train from Newcastle. I had a whole day to kill, and was scurrying around the capital, taking in as many of its attractions as time allowed while trying to cut as striking a figure as I could.

It was in King's Road that afternoon that I first clapped eyes on a copy of *I Looked Up*. Naturally, I bought it on the spot. Later, in an Indian café off Trafalgar Square, I minutely scrutinised the cover for clues as to the nature of the music therein. A sitar droned dreamily on the cafe Tannoy, but there was no mention of that instrument to be found among the album's instrumental credits. Bad sign. An ISB album without sitar was surely akin to a curry without curry powder. And what's this? – Dave Mattacks on drums!? It was all beginning to sound suspiciously like that mongrel newcomer Folk Rock... Had the ISB abandoned their effortless eclecticism for the dubious delights of drums 'n' bass? Were they now merely running with the pack?

When I finally got to hear the album, on my friend Sue's stereo in Newcastle the following day, my apprehensions largely evaporated. Yes, the band were certainly using a smaller palette of instrumental shades and tints than hitherto; and yes, the use of a Proper Drummer on The Letter gave that track an uncharacteristic solidity. ('Who's Dave, and what are Mattacks drums?' asked Sue, bemused by the lack of punctuation on the album credits.) But it was still recognisably the ISB. There wasn't another band on the planet who could have made that album.

'It was,' says Robin now, 'very much a transitional album. It was all a bit up in the air; really it was just a quickie on the way to *U*. We were trying a few things that came off better on *Liquid Acrobat*.' Certainly, it is more pared down and sharply focused than the dazzling sprawl of *U*, and shows the band toying with the tighter structures that were to define *Liquid Acrobat*. And there's another development, little remarked on at the time: the emphasis on linear narrative.

Although the ISB had always drawn upon folksong for stylistic and melodic inspiration, they had largely eschewed folk's narrative conventions in favour of fractured, impressionistic storytelling. Yet the first side of *I Looked Up* is pretty much devoted to straightforward linear narrative. The opening song Black Jack Davy, indeed, is a fairly faithful retelling of the traditional ballad of the same title; The Letter is a simple narrative about getting out of bed to check the post; and the extraordinary Pictures In A Mirror, for all its cinematic shifts of scene and perspective, has an irresistible linear pull, and even though it drops us in halfway through the tale – we never learn the circumstances of Lord Randal's incarceration – it moves relentlessly to climax, catharsis, and a new beginning.

With future manager Susi Watson-Taylor (centre), 1970. (Rose Simpson collection)

Robin confirms this thesis. 'Yes, both me and Mike were trying to write story songs at the time of *I Looked Up*, and you can see that on the album and on other songs we were doing at the time, which were essentially tales – like Come With Me [on *Be Glad*], which is a sort of Restoration pastorale.' And, of course, Queen Juanita And Her Fisherman Lover, also a prominent feature in the Autumn 69 concerts.

Side Two, by contrast, is breezily unconfined by any narrative framework. This Moment is precisely that: a celebration of a golden momentariness. When You Find Out Who You Are also aims for a stillness, a timelessness to be found in the midst of a 'strange and furious time'. And Fair As You is a simple – though delightful – pastoral tableau, in, according to Mike, 'Juliet on the Balcony' mode.

The spare, live feel of *I Looked Up* seems to confirm that the album was, as Robin suggests, 'a quickie'. Come With Me and Waiting For You were evidently recorded at much the same time, and have a similar 'live in the studio' feel to them. But what are we to make of Queen Juanita? Robin hints that it was written essentially as a concert piece; others in the String Band camp have implied that it was never intended for release; and yet it bristles with overdubs, and they'd even hired an Ondes Martenot and a wave machine for the occasion, so it must have taken a fair time to sort out and lay down. Robin confesses to being fairly foggy on this point. 'I really can't remember,' he shrugs, adding with a grin: 'I guess it must have seemed like a good idea at the time!' [*The track was released on a 1976 Best Of,* Seasons They Change, *and a remastered version was on* Tricks Of The Senses.]

I Looked Up is one of the ISB's 'difficult' albums, in the sense that Stringfandom has never really made up its mind about it. It's not a towering achievement, but nor is it a dog's breakfast. Commentators have largely passed it over, except to compare it unfavourably to *Hangman* or *Wee Tam*. Reviewers at the time were non-committal. *Disc* awarded it three stars, signifying cautious approval, but 'pleasant' was as enthusiastic as the unnamed reviewer could manage. 'Heavy going,' averred the *Melody Maker*, 'although some of the lyrics are entertaining.' 'This is a weirdo album,' pouted the *NME*.

Well, I'm ready to stand up and be counted. I love it. Sure, it's no *Hangman*, no *Wee Tam*, but it does the business for me every time. Just hearing that fiddle intro to Black Jack Davy, with its sly nod to Kenneth McKellar's perennial Road To The Isles, instantly pastes a grin onto my face.

Black Jack Davy is an exemplary opener. Robin's burst of solo fiddle is the knock at the door, and at the seventh bar the whole band charge in with a gleeful swagger, knocking over the ashtrays, trampling mud into the carpet and sending the cats racing for cover. The boys – and girls – are back in town...

The Letter catches you a bit off-guard with its precision and discipline. Mike's multiple guitar parts and iridescent harpsichord lines mesh tightly together, underpinned by Rose's crisp bass and that man Mattacks kicking things along nicely on the kit. The arrangement has a tidy, almost mathematical quality about it, foreshadowing developments on *Liquid Acrobat* some eighteen months down the road. If it all sounds a bit over-deliberate after Davy, Mike's flighty, exuberant vocal injects the necessary freshness: by golly, he really is pleased to get that letter from Maria in Chicago, Illinois. Who is this woman whom he's never met, but who 'sounds sweet'? Mike Heron: 'The song's subject was an actual fan-letter that I got, detailing such a long series of personal tragedies that you could just imagine the words trailing off to be replaced by random blood-drips...' It's worth mentioning in passing that the ISB were unusually conscientious in communicating with their followers, judging by the number of fans who own handwritten letters from members of the band.

Following this brace of frisky, upbeat Heron ditties, Pictures In A Mirror is as violent a contrast as you could imagine. The reviewers in the pop papers couldn't deal with it at all. 'Rather frightening,' bleated *NME*, reaching for the valium. There's no escaping the fact that this is

1970 promo shot. (Elektra Records, courtesy of Philip Newby)

The Incredible String Band

EXCLUSIVELY ON ELEKTRA RECORDS

the most extreme piece of music the ISB ever committed to vinyl. Dark, tense and dissonant, it gives the lie to the enduring caricature of the band as whimsical, warbling folk beside whom Donovan came across as a testosterone-fuelled beserker. Robin's tale of a medieval feud culminating in execution and rebirth (reincarnation being a favoured theme of his at the time) has an almost brutal vividness, and an intensity that rarely flags throughout its 11-minute length. It's fair to say that Pictures is not the ideal song with which to introduce a friend to the music of the ISB – unless your friend is already a devotee of Death Metal and Diamanda Galas.

Personally, I think Pictures In A Mirror is a magnificent thing, a glittering Smaug-like monster of musical and theatrical excess, carried by a performance of sustained intensity and vehemence. (For those of you interested in such things, it looks like Robin derived the atmosphere, setting and much of the detail from Algernon Charles Swinburne's border ballad pastiche Lord Scales: 'Lord Randal lay in low prison / He looked against the wa'...') Yes, you could say it was, ahem, 'rather frightening', but who said that art should be dainty and reassuring? Not the *NME*, for sure. Play it again, Sam...

After the turmoil and nightmarish wailings of Pictures, This Moment chimes in to restore the feel-good factor. One of Mike's classic, lapidary love songs, This Moment deservedly remained in the band's repertoire until the parting of the ways. The version released as a single was faded out halfway through, but this hardly mattered since nobody bought it. The mighty edifice that is When You Find Out Who You Are was, according to Robin, assembled around an apothegm from the Upanishads. 'Yes, Tat Tvam Asi – it means You Are That,' he says. 'The notion is that everyone's looking for God and Truth and Infinity and Spirituality and what-not, and basically they already have all that. But that doesn't mean to say that you don't have to journey to arrive – the journey's part of the arriving. Which seems to make perfect sense to me now, but that was the first time I really clocked on to it, and the song just sprang from that.'

In the absence of a lyric sheet, listeners unfamiliar with classical Sanskrit have over the years made ingenious attempts to decode the phrase Tat Tvam Asi as Robin sings it. My own guess was 'Tide upon my sea', which seemed to fit the oceanic mood. Some, I've heard, favoured 'Tighter Pharmacy' – though without, I'd imagine, much confidence. When You Find Out Who You Are walks a thin line between ponderous didacticism and drifting, oceanic serenity. The gently unrolling repetition of the title phrase and 'You are the way' beautifully evokes the timelessness of the eternal Now, with Robin improvising rhapsodically in whoops and glissandos over Rose's and Likky's angelic chorale. But the lyric is, for Robin, a touch on the stodgy side, and not altogether convincing. The performance, similarly, veers between the deft and the turgid. Some elements just aren't right: at least one string on Rose's bass is out of tune, Likky sounds like she's drumming on a stack of suitcases, and Mike's lovely high-register piano lines are punctuated by mystifying excursions into unrelated keys. Robin just about holds it together with solid guitar and another bravura vocal performance.

Fair As You is arguably one of the most neglected songs in the ISB canon. Puzzling, really, because it's a perfectly bewitching composition, a thing of gossamer and sunlight. It's very much of its time – no-one today could warble 'Songs to give our hearts some wings /And soar like pretty birds that sing' without inviting cascades of scorn – and yet it captures exquisitely a feeling of timeless joy. 'It's a trusting, naïve love song in Juliet on the balcony mode,' says Mike. Rose and Likky share the lead vocal, with Mike nipping in to take the chorus. His intricate guitar work is expertly counterpointed by Robin's breathy flute and gracefully swooping gimbri. Although the song is longer than Bohemian Rhapsody, you never notice the minutes passing; you're lost in a drowsy, bee-humming summer afternoon without a worry in the world. Like Nightfall at the end of *Hangman*, it just leaves you feeling better than you have any right to be.

The album cover consisted of one of Janet Shankman's otherworldly El Wool paintings. [*See* U *feature for more about these.*] At its best Janet's work could be inventive, charming and graceful. But this one was a stinker: messily organised, rudely executed and tooth-rottingly twee. Four elfin dancers, winged and spiny-haired, caper earnestly on a sand dune. Above

them a mermaid and a hippogriff hold out a string, about three inches in length, from which dangle the letters of THE INCREDIBLE STRING BAND over which an orange-skinned acrobat vaults while puffing at a globular musical instrument. At the dancers' feet the words *I Looked Up*, on another readable string, are suspended between a toadstool and a plant-creature. This, unhappily, was the kind of composition that gave hippies a bad name, and ensured that only fanatical Stringheads would risk being seen in public with a copy.

A note on the album title. Like most ISB titles, it's suggestive without being too specific. For me it conjures up a similar image to that evoked by *Wee Tam And The Big Huge*: of someone gazing upward with solemn awe at a star-filled sky. The *Melody Maker* writer Michael Watts saw it differently, however. In a brief, whimsical effusion on the subject of 'naughty' album titles in February 1971, he cited both *Wee Tam And The Big Huge* and *I Looked Up* as examples of lewd humour. What, one wonders, would he have made of *Hard Rope And Silken Twine*...?

Queen Juanita

Adrian Whittaker

Mike's Queen Juanita (And Her Fisherman Lover), an out-take from *I Looked Up*, was recorded in February 1970. It's one of the ISB's story songs, written as a vehicle for all four members, and was probably left off the released album because it already contained two very long tracks in Pictures In A Mirror and When You Find Out Who You Are. Juanita is an inventive piece, though, and the energy on this version is contagious. Critical opinions about Juanita vary, but it was a live favourite. ISB fan Jeff Rockwell saw an 'incomparable' ISB gig in Philadelphia around this time. After the show, he remembers, 'five hundred people [were] walking down Arch Street holding hands with friends and strangers, singing the chorus from Queen Juanita.'

For *Tricks Of The Senses*, we remastered the mix Joe Boyd produced in 1976 when the track was first released on long-deleted compilation *Seasons They Change*. On the sessions for Juanita, Mike recalls that the band got hold of a catalogue of obscure instruments to rent in. One was an Ondes Martenot, a quirky electronic instrument using oscillating frequencies. In the Thirties, it was popular with composers such as Messiaen and Varèse, and in recent years with musicians like Jonny Greenwood of Radiohead. It's a complicated instrument and Mike says no-one could really work out how to play it, though I think you can hear a few Ondes at 2.20 and 4.40. More successful was the 'sea machine'; the band expected some sort of small box but, remembers Mike, 'it was the size of the room!' It turned out to be a huge wooden trough filled with pebbles; to use it you added water and then held one end up. Rose: 'It got in the way of cables and mics, threatening a deluge and soaking any roadie called on to tip it or shake it around to vary the effect.' It's there in the mix if you listen carefully, and you can also hear Robin stifling a laugh in the middle of his declamatory 'demon of the deep' section. I think the band had fun recording this track.

Overleaf Allan Frewin's treatment of Pictures In A Mirror

Pictures in a MIRROR
Deep in the hollow jail Sleeps Lord Randall
The mixed voices speak of bread ~
~ and of sheets that were scarlet and blue are at his head
His heart like a cat
drowns in a well
He thinks of all the girls ~
~ he will not love
He thinks not of the future ~
~ or of the past
Blue lightning spikes the hills above the sea
Where Kasa's ship sets sail for Otherwhere

There stands the Chief with gold on his hair ~
~ two fingers thick each link of coiled ore
Speaks to his white-skinned wife ~
~ she answers not
He hurls his question angry to the gulls
His wife strikes her mouth with a skull-like sound
The bleeding image of her loss revolves above her mind
With every line in its design an accusing eye that pierces Kasa's soul
The slaves row on beneath the dragon flag
His heart recoils recall his red-haired son ~
~ beneath the burning walls that he razed down
His wife and he speak not ~
~ as wine is brought
A cup that seethes ~
~ like the black blood of wolves
His wife's dagger is hidden in her dress ~
~ he drinks joyless to a dark sleep

The gaoler bangs the iron door
Lord Randall wakes in pain
He shakes his shackles in the beaten gloom
The blood of his wounds is hard as coal
The gaoler leads him out ~
~ upon the blinding bright stair
He feels uneven turf beneath his feet
The priest intones
The sword falls on his neck ~
~ the pain is boiling cold
They lay him in the tomb at break of day
They close the earthen door upon his clay
The birds are plucking worms from the ground
Their feathers grey as mist on a cloudy morn
The white sun turns to stone

My mother lies in her labour nine days long
She called on St Bridget in her time
I looked out on the room of my birth
With hangings rich of many strange designs
Nobles stand with their wine cups in the room
Saluting me and she the King's Queen
My mother lifts me to her huge soft breast
Her nipple like a berry both hard and brown
Her eyes look on me like waves of the sea
Already I am forgetting ~
~ who I am
Already I've forgotten ~
~who I've been
And with small lips~
~the yellow milk I draw.

The *U* show and album

U was the most controversial project the ISB ever did. Joe Boyd disliked it, the critics, by and large, panned it... but it was in many ways a both ambitious and groundbreaking mixed-media production. Andy Roberts probes the paradox. Updated by Adrian Whittaker 2021

'...and it ended up in *U* which was the ultimate mixed-media, and I was pretty much outside, thinking well it's nice to see this develop but it's not that much to do with me.'

That's Mike Heron on what is probably the Incredible String Band's most paradoxical work – *U*. Both album and shows are often given poor treatment in any articles about the ISB. Was it really 'A surreal parable in song and dance' as the show's subtitle proclaimed, or just a mish-mash of bad dancing and interminable tunes?

Following my introduction to the music of the String Band in 1974 (better late than never!), I idled around *Relics* and toyed with *Liquid Acrobat* and *5000 Spirits* but the biggy was always *U*. Neither of my two ISB gurus hit me with *U* straight away. Keep the hard stuff till later eh?

Stranger still was the fact that odd rumours abounded concerning *U*. It was widely held that the only way to hear it was with the aid of powerful psychedelics... Obviously none of these hoary hippies had read the music press when *U* came out or they would have known what it was supposed to be about. But you know how hippy mythology worked and of course I swallowed it whole, in all senses of the word – and for years I don't think I ever listened to *U* in a 'straight' frame of mind. When I eventually did it sounded exactly the same! Maybe there's a moral in there somewhere.

First intimations of *U* came in the music press of 1969, with Robin saying 'It's just a psychological extension of what we're already doing', and although the String Band had used Mimi and Mouse on stage in their early days, *U* was to be different, very different. Robin again: 'We'll include dancing, and write the whole thing on a romantic theme.'

The dancing was to be supplied by Stone Monkey, a dance troupe formed from the ashes of David Medalla's 'Exploding Galaxy' – (in) famous for their house in Hackney's Balls Pond Road where all manner of what-have-you apparently took place. [*Out now is a fascinating book on the Exploding Galaxy by Jill Drower, details in Appendix – Ed.*]

After their 1968 Fillmore East concert spot, Malcolm and Rakis were brought into the ISB's enclave, immediately altering and expanding the whole venture, enabling Robin to realise more easily his multi-media visions. The next of these was the *Be Glad* film, which also featured Malcolm and Rakis and was a direct precursor to *U*. As this is featured elsewhere in this book we shall move swiftly on to November 1969 when the ISB plus members of Stone Monkey took up residence in a row of cottages on a country estate near Peebles in south Scotland. This was Glen Row, to be featured in many an ISB photo-opportunity over the next few years. Previously to this the ISB had lived in a variety of situations [*see Penwern article*]. Mike apparently wasn't too keen on communal living and so a row of simple cottages where each member could have their own space, yet be very close, seemed to satisfy the need for community without communality.

The Guardian's Robin Denselow visited Glen Row during rehearsals for *U* and found it all a little strange, 'If it is to be the success in London it deserves it won't be because it is intelligible, or because of the dancing, but because it is funny and frightening and the music by Williamson and Mike Heron is among their finest yet.' Denselow expressed some doubts, full of insight in retrospect, about the validity of a multi-coloured, multi-media pantomime in the early 1970s, when the underground was beginning to fracture, but concluded: 'Williamson knows what he believes and pop fashion has no place in his work'. Robin revealed to him that the early ISB albums 'explained what a state of awareness is' and that *U* 'would be about that original awareness lost and found'. With a portent of things to come, Denselow concluded: 'In America there should be no problems, in spite of the plot and dancers. Reaction in Chalk Farm should, at least, be interesting.' It was, in both places.

Rose on tablas, Robin on gimbri, Mike on sitar: a *U* rehearsal. (Witchseason)

The show opened at London's Roundhouse on April 8th and ran for ten days, alternating evening shows only with days of matinee and evening performances. The cost? A mere 20 shillings for the most expensive days. The Roundhouse, a converted locomotive turning shed in Chalk Farm, had been the venue for a number of other well-known underground extravaganzas, so the London audiences were primed for an event of this nature. Excellent advertising preceded the event and attendances were generally good, with several of the rock pantheon at the time (such as Marc Bolan) showing up to see and be seen – and no doubt to pinch some ideas. A young Elvis Costello was there too, remembering in his 2015 autobiography that 'they had papier-mâché masks, a sitar and a girl called Licorice, which wasn't the kind of thing you admitted liking in 1977.' Sadly I was too young and geographically challenged to attend myself but in the interests of accuracy Adrian Whittaker remembers it like this:

'Trying to work out the "U-shaped story" was a bit like trying to find a consistent narrative thread in *Sgt. Pepper*. The musical performances were great, though. Hearing songs like Queen Of Love live was breathtaking. Songs which don't come across so well on the record (Glad To See You, Rainbow) fed on the energy a live performance generated. I was also impressed by the pace of the show. The need to have quick change-overs between the songs meant that, for the first time, the band had a collection of guitars in different tunings in easy reach. Previously there had been interminable re-tuning breaks between songs.

'The dancing, however, was predominantly a foot-thumping mishmash of obscure multicultural references. The ISB were capable of representing eclecticism at its best and Stone Monkey (with the exceptions of Malcolm and Rakis) were the flip-side of the coin. Now I've watched the whole thing again on film, though, I can see that some of Malcolm's pieces, in particular, were pretty good.'

The reviewers, through whose eyes most people at the time saw the performances, were generally not over-keen on the whole event. 'Incredible Panto But Much Too Long', was one headline. 'Minority Pop' another. Tony Palmer, writing in *The Observer*, was nothing less than cruel, commenting that 'Heron and Williamson have peddled their dirge-like wailings on disc and in the concert hall for some while now. They specialise in synthetic Orientalism and hope that the obscurity of their vision will be mistaken for wisdom.' Palmer finished his piece by saying that Heron and Williamson rarely give press interviews (not true anyway) because 'they have nothing left to say and have left all to the fairies.' Tony Palmer had fallen into the generation gap with only his pipe and slippers for company.

But even that bastion of the English underground, *IT*, had some harsh things to say about the stage show. Miles, whilst considering the music 'masterful', was less complimentary about the dancing. Stone Monkey were, he suggested, 'an appalling group of amateurs... nowhere as good as Pan's People'. Harsh words indeed but it did seem to accentuate the point that London might have been a bad choice for *U*; provincial audiences and reviewers may have been more appreciative.

Actually not all the critics were totally against *U*. *Rolling Stone*'s man in London for the event, Jan Holdenfield, checking the show out prior to its American debut, was (reservedly) impressed with Stone Monkey but strangely referred to the String Band's music as being 'Fifties folk diluted by time, expanded by dope, and derivative'. In another attempt to find out what the whole thing was about he queried the PR rep for the show, only to be told:

'To me it started on another planet and everyone was very innocent and just loved and played with each other and there was no evil, nothing bad. Then for one reason or another, they were all stranded on another planet, going through time and space and everything, and they appeared on the planet we're on and became aware of it and showed, to me, and brought to the surface, how ridiculous and synthetic the things in our life are.'

So, not much help there then. Robin, in the same interview, was more concise; 'It's about love across time and space. It's in a U-shaped direction, going from a high level of awareness in the beginning to a low level of awareness and then up to a high level of awareness and communication.' Aware by that time that audience and reviewer reactions were quite critical, he added: 'It requires imagination. It's got a do-it-yourself message. We keep getting different flashes on it. I like incredibly vague, rambling structures. Of course they don't seem vague to me.' The dissonance was beginning to emerge between the imaginative, creative vision of the String Band and the inability of audiences and critics alike to keep up with it, a problem that was to dog every album and venture post-*Wee Tam*, leading to the sort of thinking which has that it was the girls/Malcolm/Gerard Dott/Scientology which 'ruined' them. In your dreams.

The overall message seemed to be that while the music was good, if not fantastic, it was the dancing and stage show which failed miserably; in fact I could only locate one reviewer who actually liked Stone

Monkey's contribution to the show, Gary Von Tersch of *Rolling Stone*, who suggested people 'catch the full show with the presence of the ensnaring Stone Monkey...'

Perhaps because Heron was the most distanced of the band from the multi-media idea, he was able to see the flaws in the show and (in retrospect) to be quite frank about them. 'The show was not presented as a TV show would have been. There was no leader. Every one of us, 12 in number, was a producer and director. This gave the impression of disorder. The Incredibles have a certain magic on stage, and the Stone Monkey tried very hard to blend in with it, but I suppose it didn't work as well as it should have done.' Mike went on to suggest that if anyone in the audience disliked anything about the performance it was because they weren't in a happy mood, and their feelings were reflected back at them. Malcolm says that 'those who understood the kind of innocence of it kind of got it.'

This apparent dislike of the performance side of *U* is quite ironic really, considering the ISB were merely mirroring the artistic aspirations of the underground. If *U* was run on the basis that all concerned were writers and directors, then surely that was the anarchism the underground demanded in action. Yet the flaws inherent in any venture involving low budgets and joint decisions (surely the acme of hippiedom) were seized upon and vilified for the next twenty years by both audience members and music writers alike.

What did audiences and critics want? Slick professionalism in Carnaby Street-tailored outfits? Dance routines choreographed by Lindsay Kemp? Lionel Blair and Una Stubbs cockneesing it up as Bad Sadie Lee and the Queen Of Love? Surely the audiences got exactly what they asked for and should have expected. As for critics, they rarely like anything bright and colourful as a matter of course, in case it means people are having good old-fashioned FUN. Perhaps London, jaded by the UFO parties and other events of the late Sixties, always wanting to move on even if it didn't know what to, was just too sophisticated now for events of this nature, too self-conscious to have fun and be part of someone else's fun. *The Times* certainly thought so, Michael Wale reservedly commenting: 'A worthy enough experiment but with the often tenuous eastern music and mumbo jumbo fixed firmly in the drug period of 18 months or so ago it all seemed rather dated.' The split was now obviously beginning to show between those who lived their culture and those who merely commented on it, any 'generation gap' that existed now being magnified. The show ran its intended number of nights at the Roundhouse, then costumes, backdrop and instruments were packed away; *U* was probably the last real 'happening' London ever saw.

U moved to the US where the String Band had to finance it themselves, needing a series of sold-out nights at the Fillmore East to make it financially viable on the rest of the tour. Sadly it wasn't to be. Perhaps the fact that they were on the week before *Tommy* opened had something to do with it, or perhaps it was simply because the imagination had gone out of New York, just as it had in London, scattered by the events at, and repercussions of, Woodstock and Altamont. These festivals, together with the Isle Of Wight in the UK (and to a lesser and later extent *U*), marked the end of the media love/hate involvement with 'hippies'. The hardcore hippies, those who had chosen it as a way of life, were moving out of the big cities to 'get it together in the country', or re-locating to smaller towns.

Whatever the case, the broadsheet reviews, written by the staffers who would normally review Broadway musicals and the like, were mostly terrible. The audiences didn't turn out in enough numbers to make the event a viable proposition, and Stone Monkey returned to the UK, leaving the String Band to continue the *U* tour on a music-only basis. Stone Monkey went east, the ISB went west, to Boston, Cincinnati and San Francisco. Malcolm: 'Joe Boyd said it was losing money, we've got to recoup the money we've lost and we were given £40 each to get home! That was a very summary dismissal really.'

In the final analysis the stage show of *U* was just too late. The Sixties had drawn to a close and nostalgia for those times was not yet with us – or usefully marketable. But the explosion of imagination which psychedelia had engendered was still expanding with ever-increasing energy, and a bright counterpoint to the heavy 'progressive' music was slowly gaining ground. And whether you like to discuss these things or not, the drugs had changed, from good acid to green microdot, mind expanders to downers, and belief systems were slipping slowly but surely from amazement at the universe to anguish at how to pay the mortgage or to refuge in some bizarre, spartan religious sect. The *U* generation was losing out inexorably to the 'me' decade and in those terms alone the *U* performances were a fitting epitaph to the Sixties.

But it was a grand adventure, proving beyond a shadow of doubt that not all those brightly coloured people with their strange ideas about life, the universe and anything vanished on the stroke of midnight, December 31st 1969.

ROUNDHOUSE LONDON NW1 (OPPOSITE CHALK FARM TUBE) TEL: 485 807

THE INCREDIBLE STRING

STONE MONKEY in "U"

MUSIC.........INCREDIBLE STRING BAND

CHOREOGRAPHY.........STONE MONKEY

SETTINGS.........JANET SHANKMAN

COSTUMES..JANE MOCK of "SKIN" LOS ANGELES

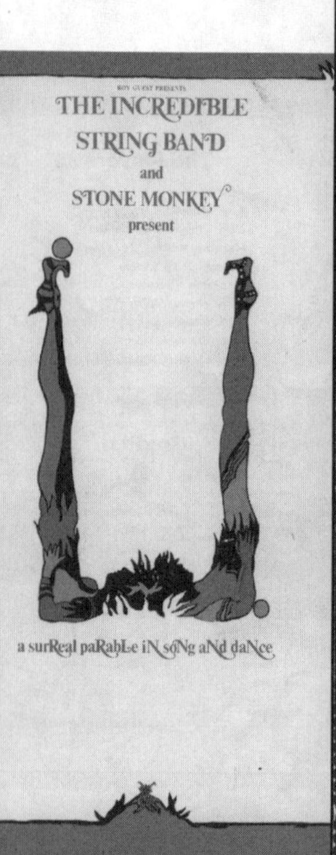

13th March 1970.

Dear Adrian,

Thank you for your letter enquiring about publicity hand-outs for the Incredible String Band. Sorry Adrian, but I am afraid we do not have any hand-outs or pictures etc that we could let you have. The best I can do is to let you have this old programme.

I hope you will be able to make the String Band Pantomime which is running for ten days in April at the Roundhouse from the 8th till the 18th. Tickets can be obtained from the Roundhouse, Chalk Farm.

All the best,

Ginny Purton

U memorabilia.
(Adrian Whittaker)

UEST PRESENTS...
AND &
EAL PARRABLE
AND DANCE
,15,16 AT 8·30P.M.
18 AT 5P.M & 9P.M.
SDAY EVENINGS ... 15/-
RDAY EVENINGS ... 20/-
RDAY MATINEES ... 10/-
nems

2
ROUNDHOUSE
at 8.30 p.m.
Thursday 9/4/70
'U'
15/-
ISB
23
TO BE RETAINED

ROUNDHOUSE N.W.1
Roy Guest presents the
INCREDIBLE STRING BAND and STONE MONKEY
in
U
A SURREAL PARABLE IN SONG & DANCE
MUSIC: INCREDIBLE STRING BAND CHOREOGRAPHY: STONE MONKEY
SETTINGS: JANET SHANKMAN COSTUMES: JANE MOCK' LOS ANGELES
A NEMS PRESENTATION
PERFORMANCES: APRIL 8 9 10 11 13 14 15 16 17 18 at 8.30PM MATS. April 10 11 17 18 Sat 5.30PM

Here's looking at *U*

Raymond Greenoaken was there...

The band and dancers had set themselves a challenging schedule with the live show: fourteen two-hours-plus performances at the Roundhouse in ten days, before flying out to tour the show at prestige venues on the east and west coasts of America. Hopes were high, but the critics turned surly. The pop periodicals were not so much hostile as bamboozled: good music, amateurish dancing, too long ('Bring a cushion,' counselled *Disc*'s Caroline Boucher sensibly) and – what's it all about? But the 'serious' critics went for the jugular. 'The dead-weight of boredom is too much,' groaned Derek Jewell in the *Sunday Times*. From the lofty battlements of *The Observer*, Tony Palmer excoriated everything from the music and dancing to the lighting and the collapsing scenery, even tutting about the 'clutter of instruments'. And in the house journal of the counter-culture, *IT*, Barry Miles (then sans first name) famously inveighed against 'sad groping and vacuous hand-waving'.

The ISB, who had enjoyed an extended critical honeymoon since the release of *5000 Spirits* two and a half years earlier, were forced onto the defensive. Robin, Mike and even Rose rushed into print to explain that the critics had missed the point. It wasn't devised as a slick West End entertainment, but as a kind of naïve art. Audiences were invited to bring a degree of creative engagement to the experience, to interpret it in their own ways and to identify with the homespun ethos of the whole thing. 'If anyone saw anything bad in the performance,' said Mike with the ghost of a sulk, 'it was because they weren't in a happy mood. I thought it was like a mirror, showing you what you were.' But their protests lacked conviction. It looked like they'd fatally misread the temper of the times – or at least of the *International Times*. When the *U* film was shown at The Rio, Dalston in 2019, Rose set out the underlying ethos: 'The critics took it so seriously, but really, for us it was like our end-of-term play.'

Worse was to follow. The show had been booked into the Fillmore East for four consecutive nights at the band's own expense. A combination of bad initial notices and the word from across the water ensured that House Full notices stayed in storage. Robin: 'We were there for too many days, though the first few days were quite good. There was no way we could manage to finance it after that.'

The financial fallout was such that the dancers had to be packed off home, with the ISB playing the rest of the tour in a straight concert format. In an attempt to recoup some of the losses, Joe Boyd booked the band into a San Francisco studio for a weekend to cut the entire soundtrack for vinyl release. Working through the nights in shifts, they emerged with nearly two hours worth of extensively overdubbed recordings, which duly hit the shops the following autumn. The sessions were fraught. In her memoir, Rose explains that the studio atmosphere, in contrast to Sound Techniques, was oppressive: 'There was no feeling of sympathy for the music or sense of personal interaction.' The band did not perform well under pressure, and at one point, frustrated by Likky's protracted attempts to get a drum track right, Joe Boyd even walked out for a while ('but thought better of it and came back.')

The ISB returned to Britain to find that, for them at least, the world had changed. The dream is over, a crop-headed John Lennon was proclaiming. The sun was setting on the hippy idyll of love, peace and lysergic voyaging. The ISB had always been a step ahead. Now they were simply out of step. Things were never going to be quite the same.

To put matters in some sort of historical context, just over a year earlier, The Who had unleashed their 'rock opera' *Tommy* to unanimous critical acclaim. The similarities between *Tommy* and *U* are obvious enough, vastly different though the two works are in terms of content and attitude. The 'concept album' was still in its mewling infancy as the Seventies dawned. Following the example of *Sgt. Pepper*, assorted popsters had toyed with the thematic song-sequence as a framework for articulating a major statement on life, the universe and everything. These tended to the earnest and portentous, with the Moody Blues (*Days Of Future Passed*, *In Search Of The Lost Chord*, etc.) emerging as brand leaders. The Small Faces, by contrast, devoted the second side of their *Ogden's Nut Gone Flake* album to a whimsical song-cycle similar in tone to *U*. But it was The Who that took a hob-nailed boot to the genre and, in so doing, redefined it.

Tommy was defiantly downmarket, aggressively streetwise. There was no place on Pete Townshend's storyboard for the wispy beatitudes of the flower generation. His magnum opus was a sort of phantasmagoric take on social realism, mixing sexual depravity, mental illness, gangland menace and *Carry On*-style vulgarity with The Who's thunderous riffs and dry-ice histrionics. It was brash, it was simple-minded – and it was enormous. A pivotal moment in the metamorphosis of pop into rock.

Although *Tommy* was eventually filmed, like its antecedents in the 'concept' field it was initially presented to live audiences simply as a high-intensity rock concert with a storyline. The ISB were therefore breaking new ground with their plans for *U*, which was conceived at the outset as a mixed-media spectacle. A tricky notion, perhaps, to put across to the public. With ill-advised self-effacement, therefore, they flagged it to the press as a 'pantomime'.

'Pantomime is a logical progression for the group,' Robin declared to David Franklin of *Disc*, making it sound like some rarefied classical form. To the British, at least, pantomime has quite different connotations: a couple of hours of jolly, spangly, low-brow post-Christmas slapstick and cross-dressing for boisterous kids and their bored parents. *U*, by contrast, was intended to be mime- and dance-driven with minimal dialogue, and the music a continuous presence. Nearer the time, they began to describe it more accurately, if less concisely, as 'a surreal parable in song and dance'. But the tag had stuck: 'Incredible panto' was a not-untypical headline.

Now, it's an old canard that music fans in those high and far-off times were an intractably 'either-or' breed. If you were into heavy rock, you couldn't be into the String Band. Well, if you were around at the time, you'll know that it ain't necessarily so. Your record collection probably featured Deep Purple as well as Donovan, and quite possibly Joni nestling next to Judas Priest. The ISB's constituency was never a separate race of winsome, woodland-dwelling flower children; they appealed to the idealistic, poetry-scribbling, ecologically-aware side of many young people of the time who were equally happy to pull out the air guitars whenever Zepp or Sabbath hit town.

The Media, however, prefer grand simplicities and delight in

Versatile Incredible String Band (left to right) Likky, Rose, Mike, Robin

'INCREDIBLE' PANTO, BUT MUCH TOO LONG!

Rose's thonged sandals: one of the *U* rehearsal photos. (Witchseason)

portraying conflict where none exists. *Tommy* and *U* were merely two sides of the same coin, but this was evidently too complex a concept for most critics, who gleefully proclaimed that the ISB were last year's thing and *U* a twee self-indulgence by a band that had lost touch with market realities. You had to read between the lines of the reviews to descry the awkward fact that the Roundhouse shows were, on the whole, very well attended and that audience response was highly enthusiastic. It might be argued that the poor view posterity has taken of *U* is more a creation of those who wrote about it than those who shelled out their 15 shillings to see it.

So – was it any good? Well, I was present at the final night of the Roundhouse run. Let me set the scene for you. My trip to London was the first occasion on which I'd travelled further south than Sunderland on my own. I'd taken the overnight train from Newcastle in order to sample the fleshpots of the metropolis at my leisure before reporting to the Roundhouse. My perambulations that day had taken me to the hippest parts of the capital: King's Road, Ladbroke Grove and World's End (where I saw the boarded-up shopfront of Granny Takes A Trip, and inhaled several lungfuls of incense in Gandalf's Garden). The posters advertising *U* were indeed U-biquitous (see what I did there?). In that high summer of psychedelic poster art you might see any number of designs that were more intricate and finely-turned, but Janet Shankman's eye-luring green and butter-yellow confection burned your eyeballs from the billboards.

And so, at last, to the Roundhouse. It's a circular building – some of you may have guessed this already – with the stage area nestling in the south-eastern curve. There was no visible seating. But we were young, don't y'know, and adept at holding the lotus position for long and agonising periods of time. Of course, in the absence of numbered seats you could park yourself wherever you wanted. I made a beeline for the front, and (typically with String Band gigs) soon befriended a gaggle of fellow fans seated nearby as the 'Overture', a medley of themes from the show stitched rudely together, played over the PA. At the appointed hour (untypically with String Band gigs), the show commenced.

On the left of the performing space, in a sort of alcove, assorted guitars and stringed things were arranged. A grand piano, a couple of drumkits and the String Band's trusty Hammond organ were all parked at the rear. Slightly uncertain applause filled the auditorium as Mike and Rose appeared and made their way to sitar and tabla positions. No Robin? No Likky? Explanations forthcoming, no doubt... We settled into the woozy opening movement of El Wool Suite as gauzily robed dancers drifted out of the wings – and look! There were Robin and Lik, giving it

ROYAL ALBERT HALL

TUESDAY, OCTOBER 20th, at 7.30

the INCREDIBLE STRING BAND

Tickets: 25/- 20/- 15/- 10/- 5/- from R.A.H., London, S.W.7
and all ticket agencies
Telephone: 01-589 8212

When applying for tickets by post, please enclose a stamped self-addressed envelope and cheque or postal order for the correct money. Thanks!

the old knees-up alongside assorted mermaids, centaurs and plant beings on the dancefloor. Such versatility! Two of the male dancers – John and Rakis, presumably – assumed the static poses depicted in Janet's poster design. Above and behind this saltatory spectacle a hand-painted back projection depicted birds, hooded nymphs and half-human trees root-stepping across a Japanese watercolour landscape. The lovely planet El Wool, ladies and gentlemen. After a couple of minutes in dance mode, Robin made for the minstrel's gallery and switched adroitly between clay drums, gimbri and flute as the El Wool Suite progressed through its several sections.

El Wool, we were led to understand, was a sort of prelapsarian dream world, somewhere between the Garden of Eden and Teletubby Land. This paradisal realm, it appears, was the creation of Janet Shankman, who later described it in a letter to a fan as 'an imaginary planet that I like to draw. It had many lovely people on it and the favourite game was creating – they created water where they liked, unicycles, things to juggle, music, strange shapes for themselves, disguises for fun, etc.' It's worth pointing out that Janet's description anticipates with uncanny fidelity the world later imagined by Michael Moorcock in his *Dancers At The End Of Time* trilogy. We know that the likes of Bolan and Townshend turned up to the show to look and learn; could it be that Moorcock, already lionised for his Jerry Cornelius tales, was also present, sniffing around for ideas?

Into this Edenic world, then, wafted the dancers of Stone Monkey in suitably exotic guise. The programme identifies them as: Resell, a lady; a fluttery-eyed bird; Laoo, a mermaid; Thlamar, a centaur; two planet (*sic* – a misprint in the programme, presumably for plant) beings; a jester; and a harper. The dancers loped, pranced and insinuated their way around the stage while the music buzzed beguilingly. As a spectacle, it was a dazzling whirl of bizarre costumes and flying tresses. But could they actually dance? This question, of course, lies at the heart of the critical froideur the show inspired.

At the time, I was deeply involved in 'experimental' youth theatre, and therefore had a keen interest in the type of free-form modern dance ('movement', we called it) that Stone Monkey were aiming at. In those days there was little in the way of a critical framework for this form of artistic expression. Basically, you did what felt good, felt spontaneous, and if you were sufficiently adept you would communicate your feelings to the onlooker. There was minimal emphasis on conventional choreography and group discipline. This lack of identifiable reference points may have nonplussed the critics – though perhaps not as much as the general impression of a lack of choreography and discipline.

Left A 1970 Janet Shankman flyer. (Adrian Whittaker archive)

Mal as Laoo the levitating mermaid. (Witchseason)

Rakis and John Schofield caught in the spotlights. (Paul Hunter collection)

Stone Monkey, as far as I recall, were not especially polished practitioners of their chosen form. They writhed, they gambolled, they waved their hands; but ultimately, with the exception of Malcolm, they lacked clarity of expression and native grace. They left you feeling – if you were interested in modern dance – that you could do quite as well yourself. Now, that's not necessarily a bad thing. The ISB, in their own way, cultivated the same approach – a sort of democratic levelling, in which the audience could feel they inhabited the same plane of being as the performers. You always felt that you could play those three guitar chords as well as Likky, or whack a drum more or less on the beat: in other words, you could be up there too! You never got that feeling at a Santana concert... It's no exaggeration to say that this inspired a generation of aspiring musicians, many of whom have since risen to positions of some eminence in their various fields.

Whether Stone Monkey had the same effect on a generation of dancers is harder to say. I certainly felt I could do as well as they could, and found this liberating – empowering, we'd say today. But would an audience even as forgiving as the ISB's be happy to part with 15/- to watch a bunch of hippies demonstrating they can't dance? Empowering may not be the word that leaps to mind...

Scene Two: Time Travel. According to a précis of the story, the Edenic bliss of El Wool is shattered by the arrival of Time. In a sort of creation rite, one of the El Woolites – presumably the Jester from Scene One – is juggling with a set of coloured balls representing Substance, Space, Power...and Time, as Robin and Likky perform The Juggler's Song. The juggler, however, can't manage four balls at once, and has to jettison that orange and blue ball. (This may not have been enacted in literal detail, however. Malcolm le Maistre – and he should know – has revealed that the Juggler, John Schofield, did not possess the requisite juggling skills for this sequence, and merely flipped a single ball from one hand to the other. If so, I confess I didn't notice...). Time, accordingly, enters the material universe. A plant being slips offstage and returns in a purple leotard and with a clock on his head. Robin reaches for the twelve-string and delivers a spine-tingling performance of Time, the song.

The El Wool backdrop dissolves into darkness, and one of the dancers – Malcolm, naked apart from (let's be blunt here) a sort of nappy – emerges as a character called in the programme The Mournful Page for reasons that never become clear. He finds himself alone in the lightless gulfs of the cosmos, and embarks upon a Bunyanesque pilgrimage towards Enlightenment – as you do. He decides it might be found somewhere Stage Right, but somehow fetches up on Earth in Renaissance Spain (or

Malcolm as the Seeker. (Paul Hunter collection)

Hirem Pawnitof: L-R: Robin, Ishy as the milkmaid,
Rakis and Janet as highwaypersons. (Schofield archive)

Italy – it's never entirely clear) where he assumes the role of El Rato ('the Aristocrato"), complete with unflattering tights and surprisingly bulky Y-fronts. The scene then shifts to the Wild West, where we meet feisty cowgirl Bad Sadie Lee. These scenes, perhaps unsurprisingly, lead nowhere particularly and seem designed purely for light relief.

El Rato never made it onto the *U* album. [*A live recording is now on* Tricks Of The Senses – *Ed.*] Perhaps it was too dependent on the terpsichorean element, or perhaps there just wasn't room. Either way, it was an amusing confection of Robin's with a strong and impressively executed undertow of Flamenco. El Rato and his rival El Cato engage in a duel for the hand of their mutual paramour. Rose joins the action at this point, stepping up to hand El Rato his rapier. Our hero decides, however, that *prudencia* is the better part of *valor*, and contemplates an extended career in the Foreign Legion.

Moving swiftly on to the Wild West, a quick costume change finds Robin bare-chested and in braces and Janet tricked out as a saloon-bar floozy for a love-it-or-hate-it rendering of Bad Sadie Lee, the leading contender, along with Circus Girl, for the dubious accolade of Least Favourite ISB Song. Hey, loosen up out there! As a piece of harmless whimsy, it's perfectly enjoyable. Mal unwisely dons a Sixties-style kiddy-cowgirl outfit to portray the sassy Sadie, which unfortunately is prominently featured on the album's inner gatefold.

Scene Three: The Egg. A sort of rebirth tableau, in which the Mournful Page is resurrected as the Newborn Seeker. He's evidently had enough of temporality and desires to reconnect with his primal state. This scene is enacted to the accompaniment of Mike's solo piece Long Long Road, another song that was left off the soundtrack album. Here it has a single verse, though he added a further two when the song was worked up in concert later in 1970.

Scene Four is subtitled The Demons. Our Seeker isn't far along the Road For Sorrow (as Robin describes it at this point) before he falls into a demonic ambuscade fronted by Ravana, Lord Of Tears, and the Mad Horseman (and his Horse). Ravana is played by Rakis in one of the more memorable *U* costumes, featuring gigantic pendulous breasts and a male member the size of Little Jimmy Osmond. He and Malcolm enact the encounter somewhat in the style of Indian classical dance. They had a certain facility in this idiom, but the sequence is stretched out far beyond its natural length. Unusually, the musical accompaniment, a thunderous mixture of percussion and electronic noise, is pre-recorded and played over the PA. The encounter, happily, seems to end well for our hero, and he meets up with a beautiful girl (helpfully identified as Beautiful Girl in the programme, played by Mal), and they sensibly decide to continue the journey together. Mike's plangent Light In Time Of Darkness provides the soundtrack to this tender scene.

As we wait in antsy anticipation for the second half, this is probably the place to flag up one of the enigmas of *U*: Robin's song Queen Of Love. It was listed in the programme as falling between El Rato and Long Long Road, and some attendees claim to have heard it (including our esteemed Editor), but it seems to have fallen through a trapdoor early(-ish) in the Roundhouse run. I didn't witness it, nor is it captured on Hoppy Hopkins' recently unearthed video of the penultimate Roundhouse performance. An audience bootleg of one of the Fillmore East shows is similarly Queenless. What can explain this? Well, it was quite long and occurred at a point where nothing much was happening on the dancefloor, so maybe it was dropped to keep the pace up. Or maybe it didn't go down well... Which would be remarkable, as it's generally acknowledged as one of Robin's lyrical and melodic masterworks, a thing of awesome grace and profundity that exudes eloquence like honey from a comb. It was clearly always in the frame for the soundtrack album, as Tom Constanten of the Grateful Dead had been commissioned to confect a luscious baroque arrangement for strings and woodwind to wrap around Robin's voice and guitar. So, a bit of a mystery, all in all – but we like our mysteries here.

The second half of the show begins with Rose stepping foxily up to the mike in a ballgown the colour of dried blood and emoting Mike's charming Walking Along With You like a Thirties vamp. Why not, you reasonably ask? She periodically sashays away from the mic to cut a rug with Rakis and John Schofield, tricked out as an improbable and rather camp pair of young flâneurs. What does it all mean? Naturally, we never find out. In Scene Two the stage is invaded by a sorry rabble of would-be highwaymen captained by the less-then-legendary Hirem Pawnitoff (Rakis in a frock-coat and what may be the same false beard he wore in The Pirate And The Crystal Ball). The ISB go trad-folk with strutting Williamson fiddle and Likky on spoons. The scene ends with an extemporised knockabout sequence spotlighting Robin's range of farmyard animal impressions.

Scene Three brings the travellers to The Bridge. You don't have to be a rocket scientist to descry in the *U* plotline references of greater or lesser subtlety to the teachings of L. Ron Hubbard. The early scenes, for instance, recall L. Ron's notion of the arrival on Earth of Thetans in corporeal form, and their subsequent striving to reattain spiritual awareness. One of Scientology's central tenets is the Bridge to Total Freedom, over which the practising Scientologist aspires to cross. In *U*, likewise, the travellers must cross the Bridge to reach the celestial city. It transpires that the Beautiful Girl has collected the required number of spiritual Brownie points to make the crossing. The Seeker, by contrast, is still too entangled with materiality. Hence they part – temporarily, they hope, while the Seeker continues his search for enlightenment. Trite though that may sound in précis, Mike's Bridge Song bathed the scene in a luminous, ghostly beauty, with Likky's ethereal sopranino wail sending bats' navigational systems haywire throughout NW1.

Either side of Bridge Song, the instrumental pieces Bridge Theme and Astral Plane Theme will have been played. I remember the latter vividly, an energetic Williamson solo thrash on the Levin. At this point, the Seeker must ascend to the Astral Plane to accomplish the final stage of his spiritual journey. Robin, by this time clad in cape and cowl, clasps a small tinkling bell in either hand and ghosts to the mic to perform Invocation, the finest piece of poetry in the ISB canon. In the gaps between stanzas he spins Dervish-like on his axis and tinkles his bells with Delphic solemnity. No 'voice sitar' as featured on the album version, but still a brilliantly effective piece of ritual theatre.

Then, in typical String style, we were swept along from the sublime to the sublimely ridiculous, from Robin's incantatory sortilege to the humming and bleeping purlieus of Robot City to witness a small domestic drama in the lives of three of its automatonic citizens. Robin moved to the piano, assuming the persona of 'Robot Johnson, blues singer'. This was the best joke in the show: Robot Blues is a pastiche of Robert Johnson's Terraplane Blues, in which carnal impulses are expressed in the imagery of the internal combustion engine. 'When I see that Number Three, my piston fills with oil...' drawls Robot J. We get the picture, I think. Quite what the significance of this episode was to the larger narrative remains unclear, other than as an excuse for some bravura blues piano, all crunching basslines and chromatic trills.

And that, dear reader, was the last of *U* for me. A glance at my watch alerted me to the fact that my last train back to Newcastle departed in half an hour. I shuffled to the exit as Puppet Song unfolded. According to the programme there were only two more songs to follow – I Know You and Rainbow, with everything drawn together in El Grande Finale. But, as I was to learn when the soundtrack album hit the shops in the autumn, there was another Robin song in the final segment – Cutting The Strings, at this stage a single-verse fragment stitched onto the end of Puppet Song. By the time the soundtrack was recorded, the song had acquired a further two sections and stood alone. It's safe to suppose from these songs that the Seeker and his inamorata are reunited, the 'U-shaped story of love across time and space' concluding with the two of them attaining a mutual state of grace and heightened awareness. 'Winged we were before Time was / How we've flown,' as Likky tremulously expresses it in I Know You.

Rainbow, of course, was the climax, a classic Heron love song of melting, lingering beauty, playing out with a communal chant (à la Long Time Sunshine) of 'I will see you there', which was given a distinct Township flavour on the album. Live, this was Mike and Robin on keyboards and percussion respectively. Rose and Lik provided the 'I will see you there' vocal interjections in best Sue and Sunny stylee as the dancers once again abandoned all pretence of choreography and did what came naturally. Doubtless the audience were singing along in scarf-waving abandon as the Tube was shuttling me off to St Pancras. At least there was the album to look forward to...

In retrospect, it wasn't at all clear to the average fan what a chastening experience *U* had been for the ISB. The band put a brave face on it all in the press. The critical mauling was merely brushed aside, and audience response presented as a fairer measure. 'Funny that the only people who didn't like it were the critics,' Mike mused. Like many bands of the time, the ISB had reached a point at which audiences would have cheered them to the echo if they'd stood on stage and recited *The Daily Telegraph* Financial Section in Serbo-Croat. Had artistic hubris robbed them of the capacity for self-criticism?

Many years later, Joe Boyd suggested that this had indeed been the case. Joe acknowledged that '...it was a process I went through with all the artists I've worked with.' A healthy measure of arrogance is often necessary to propel the artist into that leap into the dark that all great innovations represent. By the same token, it can also pull down the blinds on the tedious practicalities of getting one's work out to the public. Joe's opposition to the *U* project was both artistic and financial. He'd consistently viewed the addition of personnel to the working unit as 'a dilution of what the fundamental thing was'. For this reason, *U* filled him with apprehension: another six people of dubious ability added to the mix. At the same time, he cannily anticipated that the financial outlay would be ruinous without packed houses both here and in the States. 'I just had no confidence in it whatever,' he sighed.

Today, Robin cheerfully admits that they had little close interest in or understanding of the financial underpinning of the String Band. Asked whether he thought at the time that *U* had undermined the band's viability, he chuckled, 'I'm not sure that the String Band was ever that viable...!'

Witchseason paid each band member a weekly wage; in addition, there were record royalties for Robin and Mike. It seems they lived a fairly frugal lifestyle. 'Between tours', says Robin, 'I made sure I was living the life of a Buddhist monk'. It may be, therefore, that Joe had been too successful in insulating them from financial realities.

U was also fuelled by the same communistic idealism that led to Penwern and later to Glen Row: a case of 'let's get our friends in on this!' To the cynical, this might sound like a case of small men consorting with pygmies in order to make themselves appear taller. However, Peter O'Connor probably puts his finger on it when he reflects that there was '...a common quality of naïveté among us,' which '...may have been the glue that bound us together.' Significantly, he adds, '...it did achieve staggeringly beautiful expression in *U*, and for most of us it outlasted youth itself.'

Naïveté and idealism, particularly in the late Sixties, were essentially indistinguishable. The financial basis of *U* could certainly be described as naïve, as could the band's – or at least Robin's – belief that technique was simply not an issue, no more in dance than in music. Nevertheless, it would be harsh not to view the enterprise as motivated essentially by idealism of a generous-spirited and even tender sort. The music of the ISB was an extension of their lifestyle, not merely an expression of it, and therein lies much of its power to charm and move the listener.

The pundits' battering of *U* can, with the benefit of hindsight, be recognised as the first stirrings of a sea-change in popular culture at the very end of the Sixties. The dream was over... For the String Band, laureates of the hippy dream, there were some hard choices to be made. Living the timeless life would not be an option for much longer. They still had a faithful audience. They still had things to say. But it was clear they were going to have to trim their sails somewhat to stay afloat in the choppy currents of the Seventies. It looked, at the least, to be the end of the beginning; perhaps it was also the beginning of the end...

Revised, 2021

What they said...

Robin

It's called *U* because it's U in shape. It starts off with somebody in some ancient period of the Golden Age in the past, who survives successive lifetimes coming down through lesser and lesser awarenesses and finally gets back to a good state of mind again. *March 1970*

An interesting thing that came out of the project for Mike and myself was that for the first time we had to change our method of writing. Up till now we have always written what came out, what we were feeling. But for the pantomime we had to write something specific to suit the mood of a dance, or convey the atmosphere of a scene. I think that was very good for us both. *May 1970*

Mike

It was a complete inter-relationship. Some of the dances inspired songs, some of the songs gave the dancers ideas. The saddest thing about the Roundhouse shows was that against everyone's will it became a practice for America. We really didn't want that to happen, but there was that feeling. *April 1970*

It was a flow, very like our music. *Dec 1972*

I'm not very fond of *U*. I've never been a 'mixed media' sort of person. I've always been more interested in writing songs and delivering them. So the mixed media approach of *U* was not something I was creatively excited about, although I thought it was probably a good thing to do at the time. I was fairly aloof from the plot. I just wrote songs for various situations in the plot. So my involvement was purely as a songwriter, and not with the theatrics of it. *May 1991*

Rose

The ordinary kid who came to see it dug it fairly much. Some of the critics were fairly nice. But the general reaction was that the music is nice but what are those people doing hopping about? *June 1970*

I wasn't into [the multi-media approach] – not because I didn't like it, but I didn't feel we were the people to do it. I felt that other people could do it better, and that once we started doing that we were stepping into fields where none of us had any expertise. Mike and Robin were good musicians, but that didn't make them good actors, directors, artists or any of these other things, and I felt that once you go into that you either get people who are good at it or you don't do it at all. *August 1994*

Joe Boyd
I told them it would be a disaster. No-one would guarantee it and they had to do it on a percentage. I just had no confidence in it whatsoever and I told them that – I was prepared to help them, but against my better judgement. *May 1995*

I felt that *U* was where the Scientology rot had set in, and the material wasn't too hot – it had some good moments, but I haven't dared listen to it for years, because it was such a disaster of an event. *1996*

I have plenty of aesthetic objections to the horrible dancing and twee costumes and plot of *U*. The group committed a mammoth slice of its resources to the US tour when I thought it was obvious that it would not be well received and would cripple them financially. Two years before, they had filled Fillmore East for days at a time, but within that short span of time they started losing money on their US tours. Was that because the audiences had changed? I don't think so. *November 1995*

Billy Connolly
I saw *U* at the Roundhouse and it was mercilessly hammered by everybody: by the folk press, the hippy press, the regular press. I loved every second of it! They were dancing and...being little goblins and running about and gambolling, but the music was just...(*sighs*). You knew they were about to break up because they had done Woodstock and all that stuff, it was over really; but they were still creating, it was still on the move. *1997*

Tom Constanten
When Peter Grant [*session banjo player on* U, *session pedal steel player on the Grateful Dead's* Aoxomoxoa] suggested to Robin Williamson that I was available for a recording session, things naturally fell together. I have nothing but pleasant memories of working with Robin and Mike, Licorice, Rose and Janet and Joe Boyd. I'm not saying this to be polite or anything, because I have a couple of choice opinions about people; I'm sure anyone my age does.

Robin has an elfin, patrician quality about him that gives extra momentum to his delivery of a song that makes it almost irresistible... It makes it believable when he sings a ballad, that he was actually there when the legendary events happened, as if he fell into this world from a different age perhaps; and Mike Heron has a smile that has to be broader than a human face can bear. But he pulls it off in some miraculous way and is able to infectiously bring it across also. Their recording sessions were as placid as the Dead's were chaotic, although the results might or might not display that. *1981*

What the critics said:

Alan Smith (*NME*)
A weirdly attractive blend of ballet fantasy and the undisputably-excellent music of the Incredible String Band... plenty of colour; a certain magic; and enough unusuality to make it worth seeing... Full marks for imagination to all concerned.

Caroline Boucher (*Disc*)
Visually it was very exciting at times... but alas, after three hours sitting on the Roundhouse floor [the masks and costumes] ceased to appeal. And though Stone Monkey were fun to watch at first, they tended to annoy with their low standard (except for one man) of dancing... For the most part, the music was nice – very varied, from medieval to Eastern.

Jerry Gilbert (*Melody Maker*)
Some of the scenes were quite brilliant, and the Incredible String Band maintained a high standard of musicianship throughout... But from Stone Monkey's mime, it was totally impossible to follow the story, despite their exuberant cavorting around the stage, which frequently tended to end in the same stance... Only Malcolm Le Maistre seemed able to divert the mass of fixed eyes from the stage to the dance floor... It seemed that the audience's acclaim came in acknowledgement of the all-round endurance of performers and spectators rather than in recognition of a good evening's entertainment.

Eddie Woods (*Evening News*)
Some of the music, particularly in the second half, is inventive and quite beautiful, at other times, with strange atonal harmonies and massive amplification, rather frightening.

Derek Jewell (*The Sunday Times*)
...that cosy impromptu feel which marks many pop happenings, as well as a less expected quality of worthy banality in the continual dance and mime show. The Stone Monkey troupe were, indeed, touchingly reminiscent of those busty ladies who were once so strong on classic Greek dance. There were a few good ideas floating around. But a

smattering of undeveloped ideas do not make a performance. Jokes slowly deflate if they're stretched too long. And earnest derivations from exotic cultures, chiefly Eastern folk theatre and dance, are merely embarrassing when done so mundanely.

Miles (*International Times*)
After the first five minutes of vacuous hand-waving they began to appear as an animated underwater weed, or a stomped upon octopus, occupying space rather than describing it, revealing their lack of ability rather than expressing their roles. Untrained dancers move too much, have too little control of their bodies and resort to vaguely descriptive hand-gestures (similar to go-go dancers at your local psychedelic dungeon) to justify their presence on stage. A master choreographer would have at least controlled their sad gropings.
...The music of Mike and Robin was masterful. Sometimes their handling of the more exotic instruments (sitar and shahanai) was not as technically perfect as some might like but the sensual and seductive sounds of those instruments made up for it, particularly as they were being used primarily for reasons of colour and texture.

Maurice Rosenbaum (*Daily Telegraph*)
The musical skill and inventiveness of the Incredibles seem to be limitless. They play and sing together as if music has just been discovered and its possibilities are being explored for the first time.
This is their unique contribution to the folk-based popular music of our time and a recording of the musical sequences, images and combinations they create in this philosophical pantomime would repay close – and delighted – study. All the colour and movement needed to bring their conceptions to life are in the music itself...there are memorable moments and superb costumes. But there are, too, passages of uninspired dancing and mime and reminders that mixed media sometimes means little more than a dissipation of impact...

Tony Palmer (*The Observer*)
Last Wednesday there was this fairy, poncing about the Roundhouse stage like Isadora Duncan on roller skates. 'God's eyebrows,' shouted a voice off as the fairy mounted a plastic toadstool...it replied, 'It's all right, dearie; it's just something to blow your mind away.' Meanwhile, Kabuki beasties of no fixed abode trolled with a fairy who was disguised as the Hunchback of King's Road and became deeply mystical. A girl looking amazingly like Mary Hopkin with a twitch toyed with El Rato,

a Spanish aristocrato, who also looked like Mary Hopkin with a twitch. The hero, a lad called Malcolm Le Maistre, had 'ideas' (according to the programme) for the dancing. These were not particularly evident until he impersonated Charlie Chaplin and Ram Gopal – simultaneously...

The Incredibles...nest on one side of the stage beneath a canopy which shelters a clutter of instruments...These they bang from time to time in a purposeful, almost spiritual way, whilst on the other side of the stage Stone Monkey, a team of Medieval Leapers, leap and grunt and attempt to perform the ancient parable of love and truth called *U*.

Indeed, it is so ancient that its meaning has been lost to the leapers... As they push out with their hands, they succeed only in pushing out their bottoms. The scenery falls down, the lighting has that special distinction of always missing the action...The back projections have a curious originality about them. When El Rato, the Spanish aristocrato, is having his leap, the back projection shows a picture labelled 'Venetian Balcony Scene', the subtlety of which has so far escaped me....

Of course it might all have been satirical. There was a version of *Annie Get Your Gun*. Pyramus and Thisbe turned up, too. But it's more likely that these musical doodlings are intended to enlighten our complex lives with their naive simplicity. Heron and Williamson rarely give press interviews. Maybe that's because they have nothing to say and have left it to the fairies.

Janet, Rakis and Robin pose for a U publicity shot. (Witchseason)

'It was more like communal fireside entertainment...'

Raymond Greenoaken asked Robin to describe how the project took form.

Robin: Well, fairly haphazardly is the honest answer to that. By the time *U* started to evolve, Mike and me and all the members of Stone Monkey and a lot of other people had moved to Glen Row, and being there together was how it was possible to make it. 'Cause there was space to hop around...!

> *Raymond: Was it a continuation of the* Be Glad *film, in particular of the ideas you were kicking around with The Pirate And The Crystal Ball?*

It was a natural continuation of many things that Stone Monkey had been doing really, because all their ideas about how to move and so on were things that went right back to their earlier connections with other dance and theatre groups... David Medalla and Exploding Galaxy – that was kind of a street dance theatre. It was from that background that the whole thing loosely grew.

> *You were interested in mixed-media performance well before the film, weren't you?*

Yes, I was. I always liked mixed-media, in terms of mixing up music and trying to do a bit of this and a bit of that. I had seen a few things that Geoff Moore had done early on. The first quotes unquotes mixed-media show I ever saw was one of his, *Alice In Wonderland*, that had dance, film, acting and music in it all hodgepodged together, and was also using the notion of quite a lot of borrowed texts... things that we never got into with the String Band.

> *You felt that mixed-media could be incorporated into the String Band's modus operandi?*

Well, I like every kind of storytelling, and I've always had a tendency to go for the most lavish and least financially feasible...ha ha ha!

Legend has it that Mike wasn't so enthusiastic about that side of things. Did you sense any resistance from him towards U *in particular?*

There didn't seem to be any resistance especially, but I don't think it was so much his bag as mine... But he really dived wholeheartedly in there and produced the best songs, I'd say.

Were you surprised by the press hostility to the show?

Well, it ran into the usual trap that, if you've got anything that involves dance, people tend to review it as dance and the fact of the matter is that it really wasn't a dance piece as such at all. None of those guys were professionally trained as dancers or actors any more than me and Mike were professionally trained as musicians, but we'd got a niche in the inspired amateur class, you know... So you just run into people's expectations.

Did it hurt? Or were you able to brush it off?

Well, I'd be lying if I said you could just brush it off. But on the other hand, I didn't take it that seriously either. I didn't sit there and languish for more than about...three days, ha ha ha!

The serious press in particular seemed to have the knives out...

I think we got some good press, if I remember. Obviously there was the famous Tony Palmer thing in *The Observer*, which was a piece of vitriol. But, you know, I've met him a few times since and he's hinted that, with hindsight, he kind of liked it.

What did Joe make of it all? He's suggested he had serious misgivings...

He may have done. Certainly he could see that it was going to run into financial hazards. But everyone seemed to be quite enthusiastic at the outset, Joe included. The Roundhouse went quite well, I think, in terms of attendances. It was New York that was the problem – we were too long in the Fillmore. We were there for too many days, though the first few days were quite good. We were there for six days [*probably four – Ed.*]. There was no way we could manage to finance it after that.

'It was morelike communal fireside entertainment...'

Queen Of Love was a sort of free-floating song, not tightly tethered lyrically to the narrative...

Well, let's face it, the concept was fairly all encompassing. You could get away with anything in there! If someone had brought a song about... frying eggs, we could have fitted it in there.

History records that the audience reaction was pretty favourable.

Oh yeah, it went down extremely well with the audiences, 'cause it had a good sort of feel – if you liked that sort of thing! It was more like communal fireside entertainment than high art. It would have worked very well in later years outdoors at Glastonbury. It was more like... you know, something you might do down on the rocks of West Wales, it was that sort of vibe; or in the woods of Mendocino. But I don't think it should be judged as either theatre or dance.

How did the Fillmore audiences react to it?

They loved it, actually. You see, we got very specific audiences at the Fillmore, the sort who would show up with loaves of bread and sackfuls of peyote buttons...

Was it as much of a financial disaster as Joe suggests?

I'm sure it was a total disaster!

Did it threaten the viability of the ISB as a result?

Well, I wouldn't be very well qualified to judge that because my head was firmly in the clouds, so I didn't pay much attention. I'm not sure that the String Band was ever that viable, actually, and whatever money there was, was something we never paid any attention to. We were getting paid a weekly wage.

There was no crisis meeting with Joe saying 'We're doomed!'?

No. If there was, he was saying it to his own office staff, not us! I think all the bands that were in Witchseason were contributing to the survival of Witchseason, and I think the String Band was just one of the irons that Joe had in the fire; so I don't think his entire operation was doomed.

Basically, he was getting tired of the music business at that point. He wanted to get into films. He moved to LA shortly after that, but I don't think it was because of *U* particularly.

Would it be accurate to say that Joe protected you from some of the grosser realities of the music business?

Hmmm... I don't know. I think we did a pretty good job of protecting ourselves, by diving off into the country in between tours. I know I made sure I was living the life of a Buddhist monk. While other bands were hitting the cocaine I was hitting the brown rice! That's the reason I'm so healthy and vigorous now, ha ha! Prior to Glen Row, Mike would go back to Roman Camps in between tours and I would go back to West Wales. Joe was great in a lot of ways, and he didn't intrude in the production end of things; he let us just get on with it to a large extent. But I know he doesn't like the record *U*.

What are your own feelings about it?

It's not one of my favourite ones. It's got a few nice things on it. The thing is, I very rarely listen to records from the past. I find it hard to view them without viewing them as tied up with the times. It's hard to be objective. There are some things on it that I like, but it's not my favourite String Band record of all time.

Is it true that the whole double album was recorded over a weekend?

Yes, two days and two nights.

Not only are there nearly two hours of music on there, it's also stiff with overdubs – mainly yours. Were they just cooked up in the studio, on the spot?

Yes, just cooked up, yeah. I quite enjoyed it, really. I remember sleeping during the day and coming in at night, while Mike did the opposite. We were doing it in shifts. The studio was outside of San Francisco, in a suburb to the south. It was one of those places where there was nowhere you could go except the studio. There was a liquor store and that was about it. The recording was almost like an afterthought, because the tour had been such an intense sort of thing. Mike put down his bits, I put down mine, and I came in and did some overdubs on whatever I could, and that was about the end of that.

Right Robin on chenai. (Paul Hunter collection)

How quickly was the orchestral arrangement to Queen Of Love *thrown together?*

Very quickly, a couple of days before. Tom Constanten certainly knows how to write music, and he pulled out all the stops. There's a bit of everything on there! It's a bit busy...

But you knew when you left the studio what it was going to sound like?

Oh yes. I mean, there wasn't any time to make any adjustments – on anything, not just on that song. It was just one take of this, one take of that...

Was there any sense, in the aftermath of U, *that you and Mike were pulling in somewhat different directions?*

Well, I think he was getting ready to do a few things on his own at that time. Shortly after *U* he went for a holiday down in Russian River and vanished into the redwoods, and a lot of the things on *Smiling Men* came out of that. So I think he was getting ready to go and do his West Coast thing, and I think that I was getting ready to come back to Wales.

You were feeling the call of the Cymric hills?

Well, the Preseli Mountains to be precise, but yes. I've always loved Wales.

The *U* double album

The double album of the U *soundtrack was released in October 1970 to mixed critical opinion. Allan Frewin and Andy Roberts rise to its defence.*

Allan Frewin was 'sucked in, body and soul'

I've always been a sucker for double albums. You name it, I got it. *The White Album. Electric Ladyland. Wheels Of Fire. Uncle Meat. Wee Tam. Trout Mask Replica. HMS Donovan. The Lamb Lies Down On Broadway. Tales From Topographic*...yeah, well, let's not get carried away. And then there's *U*. The thing with me is this: when I buy an album, I'm affected by the whole package, if you know what I mean. It's a boy thing, my wife tells me, this obsession with album covers. Maybe so. Now, had the front cover of *U* been a photo of Williamson conducting the audience in his mystic robes, I'd probably have snapped it up. But it wasn't. It was another Shankman picture. (I digress to confess: the Shankman cover put me off buying *I Looked Up* for almost six months. I nearly screamed when first I picked it out of the rack in my local record shop (deceased). How could they relegate such a great band picture to the back cover, and then... Well, maybe it's a boy thing, you know?)

The whole *U* cover looked as if it had been thrown together by a committee during a coffee break. Bitty. Scrappy. Bear in mind that this was some years before *No Ruinous Feud* and the faux-photo-booth pics. My pal Rob bought *U* almost before the glue had set on the cover. He always was a bigger ISB fan than me, really. I remember him playing it to me in his bedroom in that flat over the shop somewhere between Herne Hill and Brixton, about twenty million years ago, if my memory isn't playing tricks. (Memory: Hey, you! How many years am I holding up? Me: Er...twenty one? Memory: Ha! Wrong! Forty-six! Me: Noooooooooooo!)

I didn't dislike it. But I didn't like it much, either. I felt kind of indifferent, to be honest. Maybe it was too much information to take in at once. Well, of course it was too much information to take in at once. Are you mad? It was nearly two hours long. There's a very irritating little phrase that's cruising the corridors of the publishing industry right now: 'The Ronseal Effect', they say smugly. 'This doesn't have the Ronseal Effect.' The Ronseal Effect is code for a kind of facile simplicity. It does what it says on the can: what you see is what you get. The wonderful and enduring joy of the ISB is that you get a whole lot more than what you see. Now isn't that the point with all music that slowly insinuates itself into your mind, wraps itself around your brain-stem and refuses to go away? You have to listen to it! Nothing comes of nothing. Listen to *U* once and maybe nothing happens. Listen to it twice and, lo! small threads of melody come floating off the turntable (sorry, kids – a 'turntable' was a thing on which you used to play things called 'records'. Go and ask Grandad). Listen to it three times and the great glad glittering eye starts to open and to hold you with its mystic stare. Play it a few more times and you're sucked in, body and soul.

I can't quite understand why Joe Boyd dislikes it so much. I suspect it's not the music that pisses him off – I think it's the whole package: the galumphing floor show and the Scientology and the anaconda length and weight of it. I recall a comment that greeted the release of the original movie of *The Wizard Of Oz*: 'the fantasy weighs as heavy as five pounds of sodden fruit cake'. Maybe the fantasy of *U* weighed on Joe like that?

Speaking of loving music by paying it attention, Matt [*Simpsons*] Groening said he hated *Trout Mask Replica* until he'd listened to it seven times – and now he thinks it's the most wonderful album in the world, ever. ISB albums can be like that: I thought *Hangman* was a muddy mess for the first few listens. The point is that I persevered. The idea of persevering with music that doesn't 'get you' immediately is a nonsense to a huge number of people. When I suggested to my wife that she might get to like *Trout Mask Replica* if she heard it more than once, she pointed out – quite sternly, I thought – that life was too short for listening to that thing seven times. Heigh ho.

I was confronted by another problem when I finally bought *U*, a few months after Rob had insisted on playing it over and over to me until I got the point. My copy didn't have a lyric sheet, dammit. So, what did your intrepid reporter do? He went out and bought a large sheet of cartridge paper. Then he bought a fine-point Rotring pen and a bottle of red ink. Then he borrowed Rob's lyric sheet. Then he cut the cartridge paper to the correct size and very carefully pencilled in guide lines so that he could sit for a few hours with his pen and his bottle of red ink, listening to *U* over and over again and making an exact duplicate of Rob's lyric sheet, that's what he did.

This lunatic endeavour was brought about because I had finally listened to the album carefully enough to love it. I'm not going to dissect it or natter about this track and that track. I'm not even going to raise a quizzical eyebrow in the general direction of Bad Sadie Lee. Nor shall I recall for you now the way I would faint in coils at the sound of Likky's voice on I Know You. I shan't enthuse over the unearthly keening of her voice on Bridge Song, nor comment on the fabulous intimacy of Queen Of Love, nor... nor...

All I will say is that, if *U* were surgically removed from my life, I would be diminished by the loss. Many years on, and I wouldn't change a single note, even if I could. So there you go. Me and *U* and *U* and me and both of us together. And do you know what I really like about writing this? It's that it makes me want to rush off and listen to the album again. Right now. Which is exactly what I'm going to do.

Perseverance pays off for Andy Roberts

One writer called *U* 'perhaps the most difficult to approach of all String Band albums'. That is certainly the case but as with most things 'difficult' perseverance invariably pays off, though I make no claims whatsoever to be able to match the songs to the story or even understand any of the songs themselves.

By the way, Heron's comments which open this *U* section are by far too modest. Out of the eighteen tracks, seven are actually Heron compositions, with two major ones, El Wool Suite and Rainbow opening and closing both album and performance; his is an integral part of the whole *U* phenomenon, whether intentional or not.

Straight into El Wool Suite, a stunning piece of atmospheric music. Like a morning raga it picks, plucks and thrums at first, warming and welcoming the listener, then the clay drums kick in and off we go with the musical landscape opening before you. Robin's wife-to-be, Janet Shankman, painted and drew scenes from this mythical realm between 1968 and 1971. The drawing here comes from the El Wool series and as you can see is very String Band.

The Juggler's Song: a metaphysical juggler tosses his cosmic balls to a jolly sing-along tune, time in the U-niverse is created for us and we're into an exploration of the problems of temporality, courtesy of Robin's Time. A slow and mournful meditation, just Robin's voice and guitar setting time free to do its thing.

Bad Sadie Lee: God knows. It's just a bizarre cowboy song, yodel a yodelipi, yodeli don't you know.

Queen of Love: what can you say? One of Williamson's finest compositions (and one of his own personal favourites), a fantastic, rich song. I always get an image of it being sung at a medieval court somewhere, don't know why, that's just how it strikes me! Voice and instruments eventually melt it to an end leaving you sighing and swooning with happiness and sadness in equal parts.

Flip the record to Side Two for another opening Heron instrumental, Partial Belated Overture. We always used to call this 'the rubber band song' and it does have a boingy sort of feel but with the chenai squeaking away on top of it. Into Heron's first biggie, Light In Time Of Darkness/ Glad To See You. Hymn-like, simple but plaintive piano and bass accompany Mike's bell-clear voice, leading to a rousing end chorus of Glad To See You, with Mike leaving you in no doubt that he is pretty damn 'glad to see you'.

Walking Along With You I don't really like, Rose's vocal is a bit thin and the tune isn't up to much either, piano's too plinky-plonky and so on. File under Cosmic Boy. [*one of the weaker songs on* Liquid Acrobat – *Ed.*]

Hirem Pawnitof: a jiggy-type thing, all motley sidekicks and Zen enlightenment from a tray. Nothing special but a great crowd-pleaser with Fairies' Hornpipe tagged on at the end somewhat turgidly. Bridge Theme closes Side Two and Bridge Song opens Side Three. Piercing vocals from Likky and excellent lead guitar work from Robin make this track a perennial favourite. The almost religious wail-athon of considerable proportions brings us nicely to...

Invocation, something very special indeed, is one of my all-time favourite String Band songs. I say song using the term loosely, as Invocation is really just what it says – an invocation which invokes the power which moves and is everything, 'I make reverence to you, round wakefulness

Above An El Wool resident communes with the local flora.
(Janet Shankman, courtesy of Chris Taylor)

we call the earth'. In an age when now numerous 'new-agers' and self-styled pagans talk about ecology and pantheism etc we would do well to remember this song. Musically it's just Robin's best incantatory voice shimmering above Greg Heet's voice sitar [*see appendix*], which drones in the background. Eerie. Invocation, debuted at Woodstock, is another of Robin's favourite songs which makes two on the *U* album out of five or six favourites he once listed. Proof enough for me anyway that *U* is of far more significance in the ISB's musical canon than it is given credit for.

What can you say about Robot Blues – from the same stable as Bad Sadie Lee out of Big Ted, it's fun, fun, fun till daddy takes the oil can away. [*Matt (Simpsons) Groening has been reported as saying that Robot Blues was the original inspiration for his Futurama series – Ed.*]

Puppet Song – simple. Man gets confused – asks wife – tackles politics – takes on money and hot-foots it to meet God, who of course is dead cool about it all and lays it on the line: You're in charge, have fun and for God's sake get on with it. It's a dirty job being an infinite mind but we've got it to do... There's nothing more I can say.

Side Four, the home straight now and Cutting The Strings. One writer described the lyrics as being about, here we go again, 'the therapeutic and liberating effects of Scientology' – and that was written by a Scientologist so he should know. 'Free to make my own tomorrow, Free to be me, Free to be free'. Robin and Likky's voices soar, and the musical backing is distinctly Indian until just near the end when a sort of circusy feel enters the proceedings.

I Know You is one of the few Likky compositions and it makes me wish she'd done more. It's just downright strange: achingly beautiful voice and even a whistling solo! The 'wing' motif occurs in both songs; the girl obviously just had a thing about winged beings!

And now the grand finale, Heron's Rainbow. 'Golden threads of autumn streak the purple sky', and so forth, giving Mal and Malcolm of Stone Monkey a turn at the lead vocals. These days it's easy to dismiss it as being hippy shit of the nature the punk wars were fought for but even thirty years later it has integrity and sounds as if it were actually meant. Everybody gets to sing their little hearts out and it builds slowly to a rousing crescendo and you just know, even without having seen the stage show, that the story is resolved and that they all lived happily ever after. Rainbow is a glowing suffusion of the String Band at their very best and by the time the last 'I have seen you there', has faded into the distance you're sated but perhaps just a little sad and alone in the world because it's finished. Taking *U* off the turntable is like an old friend or lover leaving, inevitable. But you know he/she'll be back so it's OK.

The whole idea of *U* seems as though it is intended to create a mood or atmosphere, like a raga or a good classical work, and I find it best to listen to it in the morning or at dusk. It just has that effect on me. Try it over the period that the light just begins to fade – you'll see what I mean. Hey, sorry about that momentary weird interlude there, back to the *facts*.

The String Band's following was still such that the album could reach number 25 in the *Melody Maker* chart in October 1970 before vanishing a couple of weeks later. *Tommy* it was not!

Elements of *U* found their way into future String Band performances by way of the small plays and skits which often accompanied songs. The actual songs from the album were rarely done again live and gradually *U* became just another rare record in the catalogues. So there we almost have it. It's not catchy and it's not immediate, requiring attention and concentration – best listened to as a whole piece if possible and ideal for having a good contemplate to, but it is much under-rated.

I think Robin may think so too. He certainly did in December 1970 following the album's release, sticking to his guns about the entire concept in an interview with Michael Watts. 'It had a lot of hard reviews,' he said, 'but a lot of critics were unwilling to give something of themselves. By watching *U* they were required to think for themselves.'

Just as *Liquid Acrobat* marked the transition between acoustic and electric String Band, *U* hinted at the end of the 'hippy dream' period, the reaction to it indicating that critics and audiences alike wanted something more focused and clearly defined. Imagination within the String Band was never at a higher level, but it couldn't be matched by the concert-going public or the reviewers. Like Frank Zappa said, 'You can't do that on stage anymore.' Hello 1970s.

The last word goes to Mike Heron: 'We do not try to tell people what to think – to give them an entity to accept or reject. We want to give them a seed on which they can imagine'.

U was that seed and that's why we're still listening to it.

Music press ad for the *U* album. (Elektra Records)

U out-takes (on *Tricks Of The Senses*)

Adrian Whittaker

Two songs from the show were omitted from the studio recording for space reasons, but we located them on a very crackly live mono recording taped from the Roundhouse PA. El Rato suffers slightly when detached from Malcolm Le Maistre's accompanying mime of the cowardly Spanish grandee, but we found a *U* rehearsal photo which will give you an idea. Robin's in top form though. Mike delivers a bravura performance of Long Long Road, managing to play and tune his guitar at the same time. Long Long Road comes at a point in the show where the Newborn Seeker (Malcolm) takes 'the road for sorrow' on his search for enlightenment, but is ambushed by demons en route. We left on a bit of the Demons section to give you more of the *U* flavour.

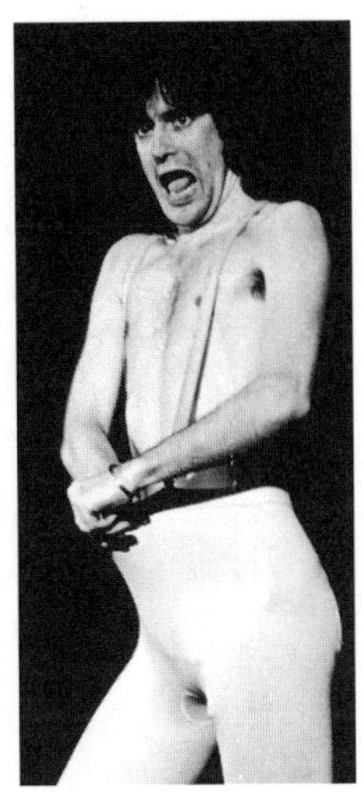

Malcolm in a moving scene from El Rato. (Thomas Stout)

U – the video

Adrian Whittaker

An almost complete Roundhouse video tape of *U* has now turned up and a restored version was shown at The Rio Cinema, Dalston in 2018, when Rose, Malcolm and John Schofield were guests of honour. Commissioned by Joe Boyd for his Witchseason company, the black-and-white footage was filmed by Hoppy Hopkins on four cameras, edited and mixed, and then stored in the Witchseason archive, where it was discovered a few years back, misfiled as an audio tape. There was a lot of work to do on it: at least one of the cameras was out of sync, producing scrolling lines which had been cemented into the mix. The audio recording, too, was problematic and occasionally distorted. It had been set to the levels of the quiet acoustic El Wool Suite and then just left running, with no subsequent monitoring of levels during the rockier sections. A group of fans funded a painstaking digital clean-up, getting rid of blotches, improving the overall sound quality and removing audio glitches and crackles, but occasional picture slippage remains. Although those interested in the ISB would find it very watchable indeed, both Mike and Robin are reluctant to commit to an official DVD or YouTube release. Two otherwise unreleased tracks, transferred from the audio, are on *Tricks Of The Senses*.

U – by the dancers

In 2015 Malcolm and Rakis sat down to watch themselves perform in U *for the first time, to record a commentary for the sadly unreleased* U *DVD. Here are some extracts.*

> Malcolm: The costumes were always quite a thing – by Jane Mock. That poor woman had about two weeks to make the whole thing – they flew her over from California, locked her up with a sewing machine and she literally worked day and night...

Mary Pawle adds: Both Linus and I helped out with a lot of the finishing off of the costumes; Jane was the real seamstress but I had been making a lot of clothes for sale back in Dublin, embroidered shirts / blouses and skirts mainly. Never trained as a dressmaker, just something that I had been doing since my early teens. It was our early days at The Row and I think that the costume deadline was looming. The costumes were really exotic and it was fun to be involved in a small way.

> Malcolm: There was a lot of silver and satin... the bird costume, that one really works – it's Ishy. Those legs in the *U* are John Scofield. And there's Mal in sort of silvery scalloped trousers. In many ways, the costumes were rather extraordinary. I mean, if the dancing had been up to the costumes....

Reflecting on this as someone who's now got experience doing directing, the very first thing I would have done was to shorten the opening scene. It's sort of sluggish. It's challenging for a dancer to be up on stage that long. Even a proper dancer! I suppose the directing would have been, Robin's going to do this guitar solo, Ishy, go on stage and dance. In any of the pieces, was there a director of any kind? At the time there was no constructive criticism. I'm sure that Joe was probably walking around in the background with his head in his hands thinking, I want to say something... It would have been very helpful, in fact, to have had somebody to at least give us a bit of guidance. It's nothing like anything that had been around. There is a kind of Stone Monkey Exploding Galaxy line here. I mean, the very fact that it wasn't classical ballet or modern dance is in a way what marks it out: it's a bunch of guys doing their best. I think in a way there's nothing wrong with that. That kind of pantomime spirit, which Tony Palmer completely failed to observe...

Rakis: There were far too many bodies milling around the stage most of the time.

Malcolm: In The Demons section, the dance moves are very Kathakali and a little bit Kabuki. Rakis' huge breasts and the dildo are quite impressive. It could be a shock to some to see that the whole thing, Rakis dressed like that, me looking stick-thin. Not as bad as I remember it. I think these sequences are actually quite arresting because Rakis is doing that kind of actor dancer thing and I'm trying to be a very poor version of a latter-day Nijinsky. It's unfortunate that my loincloth seems to have come around to the point where it looks like I've also got a dildo... Certainly there was nothing like it on the stage in London.

Rakis: Clive Barnes reviewed it – he murdered us in the New York Times, he was the most vicious critic... He made or broke every show on Broadway and he broke us. He was totally the wrong critic to come and view this, he just wouldn't have got this at all.

Malcolm: He wouldn't have understood its kind of innocence. It is very naive. There's nothing very knowing about it. I mean for God's sake, we were 20! But I think that is also part of its charm, so it's a mixed blessing. But it certainly lacked a director who would have stepped in and cut this way back by now.

If you take all the dance out and you listen to all the songs, is there a narrative that makes sense through all the songs? No, nothing is really connected. That's another aspect where it would have been helpful to have had a director, because there is obviously a strong idea there – it's just not being not being developed into something that makes some coherent sense.

Lindsay Kemp told us: 'Oh you two have very expressive faces, but you've got to do a lot more work with your hands,' which actually I took on board because when I dance now, 45 years later, I can't really dance like this [in *U*] any more, so I have to use my hands to make it look like I'm dancing. Lindsay Kemp got that hand thing from Marcel Marceau, who told him his hands were like sausages when he saw him performing and took him away and showed him how to use his hands.

It's very touching, seeing Mal again. Mal developed a really good line as an actress, years later with the Mandarin Theatre company stuff. She had a really sort of Northern sense of timing. I think she could have done very well if she hadn't sadly gone. When she died she was 31 – really strange. I feel quite sad watching this, and I was very close to Mal. I felt sad also because she didn't fulfil that desire to be an actress, she never got there because she never had the chance. Mal had one dance movement, it didn't change really... That's very UFO acid-type dancing, she's obviously celebrating... glad to see you – How many times can you say that ?

Rakis: That's the thing, it's very hard to dance to repeated bits.

Malcolm: I'm thinking that since I came on I've barely been off the stage – I'm just dancing all the bloody time. How did I stay upright?

Is there a gay subtext in the routine to Walking Along With You? At the beginning, that is the impression you get, isn't it? Two men walking along together, not anything to do with her. I suppose you can do anything you like with a song title like that. It's even that stance, the hand on the hip... Do you think we just didn't spot the subtext or do you think we did it on purpose?

Rakis: I don't know whether we really knew about that kind of thing...

Malcolm: Hirem Pawnitof is more folk String Band. It's sort of a different energy. The rest of the music has been very idiosyncratic String Band...

In Bridge Song, there's a kind of repetitiveness about the music which doesn't assist the repetitiveness of the dancing. So you got two repetitive elements, where if one of them had been a bit more varied, I think it may have taken the attention off the other a bit. What an actual choreographer would have done is sorted out our arms. There's too much arm waving a in a sort of rather pointless, random way.

Adrian: That was the 'vacuous hand-waving' quote.

Malcolm: I think he's right. And he's probably particularly talking about me. I could leap around and move quite well, but I was definitely waving my hands.

Every so often you do get some proper little bits of theatre, that have been obviously thought out a bit and they work. This is being discovered and is getting an airing – again, like the Galaxy, there's a similar thing, you know, it got written out and *U* got sort of dismissed by the so-called art intelligentsia. And yet every so often it has a real arresting quality to it, even just the idea of some of the costumes and visual ideas. This could have been developed, but I don't know we had an outside eye with any common sense. I'd love to take this now and redo it as organized bit of theatre... I think you could do something interesting with it. I remember this was good in London, but it fell absolutely flat at the Fillmore. I can't recall what Joe's reaction was when this idea was first mooted. If we'd stopped it at London, it would not have ended in tears...

It absolutely has to be on record that this was very much the first time anyone had done this. I think people genuinely enjoyed it. And those who understood the kind of innocence of it kind of got it.

Rakis: I mean, it wasn't something to be watched with a critical eye.

Malcolm: Not like watching blinking Ballet Russe or something....

Jill Drower adds a Galactic perspective

Exploding Galaxy member (and biographer) Jill Drower missed the U *shows, but recorded a commentary for the film 45 years later.*

> *Adrian: So Jill, you were away when* U *was on – how did it feel watching it now?*

Jill: Well, I have to say it was very good fun because it took me back to the time, in a way that a documentary wouldn't. I think it's because it conveys the joyful innocence of the flower children. And it is so anti-slick. Now at that time, a big important part of the flower child culture, which is parallel to the Fluxus art movement, was this idea that anybody could be an artist. Anybody could perform anybody could get up, there be creative...

> *That was Robin Williamson's big thing as well at the time.*

Well, that was very Galactic, very Exploding Galaxy thinking, and you get a sense of that, cause it's very unpolished and, some of it might make you cringe, but the point is there was a principle here. I think actually the Incredible String Band were unusual because to see a line-up with women in it, and a woman playing drums, was certainly unusual. So that was a very much an Incredible String Band thing, not a main counterculture feature. The ISB were a Marmite band in the sense that people loved them or hated them. And it was generally the psychedelic bluesy types that were a bit disparaging.

Now I was very much involved with folk music and I performed in folk clubs, so I adored them from the word go. I thought they were utterly brilliant and I hung on their every word. So I suppose I'm biased, but it was quite interesting seeing the film because it conveyed something of what is not conveyed with documentaries now and books about the time. I have to say that being in something like that was probably much more fun if you were in it than if you were watching it. And that is very similar to the Galaxy. The individual turns that people did were accompanied by improvised music and they were what I call unbounded. In other words, they'd go on as long as they went on and that would probably be slightly too long.

That was very much a feature of the Bird Ballet, which was in October 67. So that was a legacy definitely from the Bird Ballet and this idea that the Galaxy had, which you can see here as well, of children staring into a rock pool and getting absolutely fascinated by the time they're spending doing it – there was that feeling about it.

I think from what you've told me, the Galaxy stuff was much more interactive with the audience. The audience in U *was very passive. You just sat there.*

There are several differences. First of all, there were several ex-Galaxy members in *U*, but only two, Malcolm and Rakis, were consistently dancing in the Galaxy. I never, ever saw Ishy or Mal on stage. Whereas John Scofield, he was our music. I mean, he had a background in a rock band and he played an inner tube of a carpet, which was about 10 foot long and it had a nice echo in it and he was the percussionist for that. And he did perform in Orange And Blue, one of our artworks, but generally, there were only two Galaxy members, maybe three, that moved from the Galaxy to *U*.

Did you notice routines that were really recycled Galaxy routines?

Yes, with Malcolm and Rakis. The Kathakali dance that came for the first time to London in 67 through Brian Epstein's Saville Theatre absolutely blew away the Exploding Galaxy and we used to copy and mimic little bits of it. I remember seeing the bits of it that we saw in the *U* film being performed by the Galaxy at Parliament Hill fields.

There's something in *U* that was absolutely not Galactic and makes it very, very different from the Exploding Galaxy. We were a sort of living artwork and our costumes were found objects from the street. Now those costumes in *U* are very nice, but they are not what we did in the Galaxy. We'd find things in skips and we'd turn them into sculptures or Mike Chapman would drag a chair round as part of his costume. So it, the costumes were very different – that was the thing that stood out more.

Overleaf Glen Row, 1969. (Rose Simpson collection)

Life at Glen Row

Chapter Six

Village Of The Band

Raymond Greenoaken

When the ISB left the picturesque squalor of Wales and installed themselves in eight small terraced houses snuggled among the Peeblesshire hills, we began to learn something of their home life. Prior to the move, Robin and Mike had invariably conducted the obligatory press interviews in London. Readers learned almost nothing of their various rural hideaways. But now, reporters were actively encouraged to visit and we began to build up a picture of life at Glen Row.

The picture that emerged was fabulously romantic: a sort of Coleridgean artistic community living a pure and contemplative life in a remote, magical landscape.

One of the earliest pilgrims was *The Guardian*'s Robin Denselow, seeking enlightenment on the final preparations for *U* in early April of 1970: 'Four in the afternoon on an estate built by a Victorian soap baron in the desolate heart of the Scottish border country. A mock-Gothic Dracula castle in the valley, snow on the hills, and from a row of semi-detached artisan houses the plaintive sound of flute and the banging of Indian drums. In a setting worthy of a Polanski take-off, a wispy girl dressed scantily as a mermaid sits eating oatcakes; a farmer rounding up his sheep ignores her...' Denselow was made privy to a rehearsal 'in a freezing back room behind a barnyard,' and, impressed as he was by the music and the colourful costumes, he confessed that his 'main concern was the biting cold'. The article was accompanied by a photo of the cast striking artistic postures in front of the Row against a backdrop of mist-hackled hills. Smoke from one of the chimneys streaks out horizontally and hair is whipped across faces. And is that an icicle hanging from Malcolm's papier-mâché headpiece?

Melody Maker's Michael Watts got the summons round about the same time. His piece was dramatically titled 'In Search Of The Incredibles'. Watts was driven to the Row by one of those nervous taxi-drivers you get in Hammer horror flicks. 'They're the people who live up on the estate with strange clothes and long hair...' he croaks in tones of superstitious dread.

On arrival, Watts is taken by Rose on a tour of the eight cottages and introduced to their tenants. He's clearly impressed by their 'totally surreal and romantic' lifestyle, but has little to say about their taste in decor. Just like a man, eh?

Glen Estate (Raymond Greenoaken collection)

By contrast, when *Disc*'s Rosalind Russell blew in a year or so later, she gave her readers a fusillade of domestic detail. Robin 'stalking over the hills like a youthful laird, in velvet jacket and puffing his pipe' and 'vainly attempting to mend a sewing machine'; Licorice drying her hair for the photo-shoot; she and Malcolm practising archery – 'Oh can you find ma arrow, Robin?'; Malcolm cutting the grass with a huge scythe. The decor of the band members' cottages is also described in satisfying detail. Licorice, we learned, 'has a spotless sitting room, with brown carpet and sofa, old-fashioned lace curtains and shining hearth.' Mike's cottage 'has a definite Eastern atmosphere... Indian posters on the walls, and everything is painted in bright colours – yellow walls, white floor, blue hall and purple door.' The colours in Malcolm's cottage 'are more muted than the others, and he has a large collection of books', including *The Monkey King*, *The Golden Bough* and *Celtic Fairy Tales*. Robin's cottage 'houses old curios collected over many years'. (Rose, by this time, had taken her leave of both band and Row.) Russell's report featured a memorable photo of Likky and Malcolm at the archery butts with Mike and Robin looking tolerantly on.

So much for the outsider's take on life at the Row. In the following pages, two of the many residents of the Incredible Village offer accounts of what it was like on the inside. Peter O'Connor had been a part of the ISB entourage since the Penwern days and moved in at the same time as the band:

Sex, Drugs and Interior Decorating: Glen Row Remembered

Peter O'Connor

Glen Row was built in the 1890s by the Tennant family to house farm workers on their newly acquired estate, Glen, a few miles and a pleasant walk from the small town of Innerleithen in Peeblesshire, birthplace of Irn Bru and still not a bad place for a haggis supper, with salt or sauce. The Tennants had made their fortune in chemical dyeing, with huge works whose chimneys dominated the skyline around Glasgow and belched out fumes so noxious as to force their owners south-west to the Borders and the acquisition of a country seat, Glen, to go with the title, Glenconner, and a town house in Tite Street, S.W.

In a tremendous burst of arriviste energy, the Tennants drove a line to power with the marriage of Margot Tennant to Henry Asquith, and established formidable base camps among the upper class intelligentsia and in the City. However, in the process of ennoblement, the Lowland thrift and ruthlessness which had carried the Tennant genes to such comfort and elevation was diluted by various effete strains imported by marriage among the despairing English upper classes, not least among them the ineffable Wyndhams.

All this, plus the odd Gainsborough, completed the Tennants' set of what passed and still passes for bona fides in Albion, and leads naturally to the charms and contradictions of the present Lord Glenconner, the Hon. Colin Tennant, a man so confused by early promise and imminent tragedy as to be forced, during a motorway journey, to stop his car for fear he was turning to gold dust.

It seems more or less appropriate that some time in the late summer of 1969 The Hon. Colin Tennant should advertise for artistic tenants for his cottages at Glen Row, and that Mike Heron should see the advertisement, view the property and arrange tenancies for the Incredible String Band and the Stone Monkey dance troupe. The decision to move to the Glen was easily made: in the late Sixties the estate had yet to give way to hard-headed management, and it contained, in many thousands of acres, wonderful stretches of open country, mature woodland, rilling streams and a wonderful isolated loch with a boathouse, all connected by neat little roads and lanes just wide enough for the Laird's Bentley, driven by the soft-spoken Mr. Thomas Neilands, and the dashing Land Rover of Doug, the gamekeeper.

Into this sylvan paradise came Mike Heron and Rose Simpson, John Koumantarakis (Rakis), Malcolm Le Maistre, Mal (Schofield of Stone Monkey) and Sarah, Robin Williamson, John Schofield and Ishy (Stone Monkey), Licorice, and later Ivan Pawle (Dr Strangely Strange) and Mary MacSweeney, settling more or less in that order into houses number 1 to 8, from October 1969. The purpose of the move was to create and rehearse the pantomime *U*, due to open at the Fillmore East, New York, the following year.

The Glen was a distinct social phenomenon, maybe more social than musical. Very British too, with its squirearchy, and below that a meritocracy of sorts, with the truly gifted lording it over the truly lost – among whose number you could almost certainly count yours truly. As usual, my part in all this was uncertain. I was desperate to belong at the centre of events, but I also had a university course to follow down south, and I could only get up to the Glen in the holidays.

I can remember, sometime during the Christmas holiday in 1969, sitting on the freezing ground on the low hill overlooking the Row while the others held a late night meeting at number 5 to discuss whether to include me in the cast of *U*. As I could neither dance even the simplest steps nor play an instrument in tune or rhythm and I had no theatrical

Malcolm in winter sports mode at The Glen. (from second ISB Songbook)

experience, the decision to exclude me, delivered near midnight by Mal, came as a great shock to the system.

In this Pete Best-ish sort of position, I returned to university. The following spring I travelled around Eastern Europe making recordings for a book about Romanian music. *U* opened at the Roundhouse on the day I returned to England. I arrived half-way through and was pulled on stage by Rose to join a sort of dance of the proles at the climax.

Household economies

I lived at the Row on and off between 1969 and 1973, with periods in the Yorkshire Dales and Jedburgh. At the beginning I shared No.2 with Rakis, but late in 1970 or 1971 John and Ishy moved up from number 6 to Feathery Castle, the hen-wife's house on a hill to the side of the Row, and I moved into the pheasant sheds behind them, with ex-Exploding Galaxy member Edward Pope in a shed on the other side. My rent for three pheasant sheds knocked into one, with no plumbing or sanitation, and heat provided by a Bonnybridge Dover stove, was something like 10 shillings a month. Edward must have paid the same. Feathery Castle had a kitchen, bedroom and living room, but there was no bathroom. They paid more than I or Edward, but less than they had paid for No. 6, Glen Row, where I think the rent was £2 a week.

We lived very cheaply. My chief extravagances were bacon and tomatoes and Golden Virginia tobacco. John Schofield's costs were higher, as his first son Rufus was born at Feathery Castle, and he had his Ford Utility van to run. Firewood came courtesy of the Glen forests, and the occasional salmon found its way onto our table but hard cash was not easily come by, so it became necessary, from time to time, for us to work.

At one stage, John Schofield and I sold off-cuts from the Innerleithen saw-mill, delivered to householders in Innerleithen and Walkerburn in used coal sacks, calling ourselves ScofLog, maybe. Another source of income lay in beating work for the grouse shoots in late summer, and the pheasant shoots over the winter. This was arduous, only occasionally exciting work involving a great deal of hard walking up and down hills and over moorland on the Glen, and through forests banging the pine trees and calling out to frighten the birds forward onto the guns of the noisy Pools winners and mustard magnates waiting in comfort in the hides beyond. Our chief excitement and pleasure came when one of the guns shot another man or his dog, our greatest boredom when a dog failed to find a bird which had been brought down, because then everybody had to root around in the bracken until the bird was found. We were paid around £2.10 shillings for a day of this work, plus a bottle of beer at lunchtime.

Interior decorator to the stars

Another source of income came from repairs and painting and decorating work in the houses on the Row. As the wealthiest members of the community, the String Band were naturally our best customers. John Schofield tended to get the better joinery work, while I took a lot of the decorating work. Rooting in the archives has turned up an undated squib from Licorice herself, post haste from the Hotel Lundia, in Lund, to John Schofield:

Dear John,
If you wish to do a little work for me for bread in the next two days I would be glad. If not pass this on to Peter if he would like to. It is this.
1. buy enough white gloss paint (+ a brush) for A/ to paint inside of cupboard in my front room
2. first take the door off the cupboard i.e. I don't want it there anymore. Then clean up the shelves and paint it beautifully white the tops + underneath + every part of the shelves and wall inside the cupboard. I imagine 2 coats will be essential at least.
3. Schedule it so it will be all finished by when I arrive on Wednesday night!
4. If neither of you wish to do it then of course don't!
5. State fee when I return. I shall pay on return.
6. [more detailed instructions]
7. If you get some done it's better than none but the 1st 3 days I have to work on my songs for the record so I wanted to do just that, more or less.
X much love X to you X X Libby P.S. hallo Peter if you are reading this. X

Likky was a stickler for detail, but Robin and Janet were fairly easy customers. Robin's downstairs back room had to be painted midnight blue or black at one stage, with care to be taken not to splash over the legend 'The thousand mile journey begins with one step' painted over the architrave of the door leading into the back room. Mike did his own paintwork, orange and yellow mostly (orange ceilings). Malcolm's front room ceiling had to be painted entirely in Humbrol model aeroplane gold paint, the stuff you might occasionally use for the RAF insignia on an Airfix WW2 fighter, but not an entire ceiling.

Mashed toes

There was a great deal of coming and going at the Glen. The String Band's arrivals and departures for tours and recordings; the Tennants' arrivals at Glen, the Big House, to which we would all be invited for the annual New Year party; the occasional visit by Princess Margaret, whom Sir Colin Once Very Nearly Married (Rakis gallantly took the floor with 'Ma'am' for a Gay Gordons and mashed her toes with his brogues); and various blow-ins such as Jel-Al who walked cross-country from Harrogate, never spoke, simply arrived and sat there picking his verucas and sucking his cavities; towards the end a dire procession of bores and hustlers, mostly from Bournemouth; and the very occasional groupie.

Below The Glen Row 'mummers' from the *Myrrh* sleeve L–R: Isaac, John Gilston, Likky, John Schofield, Chucho Le Barron, Sarah Schofield, Edward Pope (sans hat), Lucienne, Paolo Lionni, dog Simon, Kiki Obermeier, Malcolm, Mrs Hudson, Peter O'Connor, Unknown, Mrs Hudson's daughter, Stan Schnier, Janet Shankman, Chris Hudson, dog Magic Sam, RW.

Sex

In an age of tremendous hedonism, the String Band must have been the least sexually adventurous band in the country. Robin had a strong following among middle-class university men and public school gypsies, with the occasional female aristocrat, but he was no Russ Conway. In full crushed velvet Cuban-heeled album-sleeve signing mode, Mike held considerable appeal for swinging housewives and mature students, but was he a Heinz? Malcolm did attract a very beautiful girl from California named Earthstar, who sat around his house in diaphanous silks waiting for the right moment to oil his back with Chinese unguents, but he was forever going upstairs to his study, quill in hand, to write his book about Wooks, so she gave up in disgust and returned to the Home of the Free via a visit to Tim Goulding (of Dr Strangely Strange) in Allihies in West Cork, where she interested the locals by going around naked.

[*Tim Booth, also a Glen Rower in 1971-2, tells us that one of Malcolm's literary heroes was fantasy novelist Lord Dunsany, whose work was penned with quill pens which he made himself. – Ed.*]

Drugs

After the adoption of Scientological practices, the Row was divided, effectively between those who did drugs and those who didn't, or said they didn't. Needless to say, I managed to belong to all three camps. Because the non-druggies tended to be Scientologists, the String Band avoided unusual cigarettes and soggy sugar cubes, but there was no hard and fast line until sometime in 1972/3 when a Rule Book was compiled, which all parties were happy to sign.

Looking back, Feathery Castle seems to have become the home of high times at the Row, with Webster's Dictionary and Malted Milk for those of a more solemn bent down on the Row. However, with incarnations of Dick Turpin, Beethoven, a German infantryman from the Great War, Shelley, Pico della Mirandola, a lower deck seaman from Nelson's flagship, a lesser god, Byron himself (according to Percy Bysshe) and Antoine de Saint-Exupéry all resident and more or less up to date with the rent on the Row and up in the Castle, who is to say whose times were really the highest?

Clement Weather And The Wiggers

Adrian Whittaker

Not many people know that, apart from the ISB, there was another band based at Glen Row – and they even released a single!

Stan Schnier: 'The ISB was on the road quite a lot, playing all around the UK and the continent and once-yearly trips to the US. Scotland was the quiet retreat but truthfully, we were not there all that much. When not rehearsing, recording and touring, the band often travelled to the Scientology headquarters in East Grinstead. In those days, a lot of fans and friends were either hanging around or living in the Glen Row area. Everyone was involved in their own thing, writers, musicians, artists of all sorts. Musically, the guys who were around at the time were Peter O'Connor, Malcolm's oldest friend, a fine fiddler and vocalist. Around the corner was John Schofield from Stone Monkey who was a wood turner/carpenter and also an excellent bass player. Frank Usher had arrived from Gateshead and was a top notch guitarist. At some point in the early 70s, drummer John Gilston arrived, and there you have it. A band.'

The outfit was christened Clement Weather And The Wiggers by Tim Booth, before he departed Glen Row for London. Malcolm says they 'had great potential as a pastoral punk band. Peter had real star quality.'

Their shot at fame came with a single deal with the infamous Jonathan King. Stan: 'In Edinburgh there was a charming pre-war cafe at the end of Leith Walk, which felt like a movie set even then. The owners had a son who was a songwriter, named Angelo Di Placido, and we would stop by for a coffee when we could. Charming place. In 1973 Angelo wrote a couple of songs, demoed them with The Wiggers and submitted them to Jonathan King's UK Records. Angelo: 'I was being managed by Roy Guest at the time, and we thought a one-off single deal might be a way on to greater success!'

King liked Angelo's Good Time Girl but also the treatment that the Wiggers gave it, especially the rather strange gypsy violin part. He arranged for the band to come down to London to record the A and B sides of a single with Angelo on vocals. Good Time Girl was the A side and King's song Mainline Lady was the flip. As Peter described it, they arrived exhausted in London after a van ride down the A1 and went directly into the studio where they were given something like three hours to set up and record both tunes. The date didn't go all that well. The record was released (credited to 'Angelo') whereupon Emperor Rosko famously "smashed it."'

John Schofield: 'That was the only time we worked with Angelo. He opened his own deli on the Royal Mile shortly after... which was more successful.'

Stan: 'They put together some shows around Innerleithen. I vaguely recall that Mike was understandably upset that the Wiggers had been generously borrowing the ISB backline and sound system while they were away.'

John: 'The Wiggers went on to do a few more local gigs as well as New Year's parties in the Glen Village Hall, culminating in a very ambitious self-promotion in the Memorial Hall in Innerleithen, which also featured various ISB members doing individual turns. Posters were printed and a lot of tickets sold. The tickets were printed locally by Robert Smail's Printing Works (now a museum in the care of the National Trust for Scotland). Unfortunately it was in the early spring of 1974, in the middle of the three-day week and electricity rationing. We went on stage about 8pm and Clement had just rocked into the first line of "Just give me some of that rock'n'roll music" when there was a government power cut! I think that was the last Wiggers gig.'

2021

MYSTICAL
PANTOMIMES
1968.....

Previous page Hapshash tour poster with Mimi and Mouse, 1968. © Hapshash and the Coloured Coat / Bridgeman Images. *This page* Mike, Robin, Mimi and Mouse backstage with the Minotaur head, late 1967. Pictorial Press/Alamy

Left Cover still on the CD of *Chelsea Sessions*, an out-take from the *5000 Spirits* photo session. *Below right* Robin and Mike at Sound Techniques 1968/69. Peter Neal. *Below left* 4-piece playing The Iron Stone at Sound Techniques 1968/69. Peter Neal

Below Joe Boyd as Mr Universe, on a Penwern roof. *Be Glad* film out-take. Peter Neal/Peter Sanders 1968/9. *Right* Likky still from *Be Glad* film. Peter Neal/Peter Sanders 1968/9.

Top right Mike and Robin as Gods from *Be Glad* film. Peter Neal/Peter Sanders 1968/9. *Left* 4-piece, Robin's cottage at Glen Row. Rose Simpson collection. *Bottom right* Original poster for the *Be Glad* film by Austin John Marshall.

DAVIS & SONS

Overleaf left 4-piece get a cab outside Scientology HQ, Tottenham Court Road, 1970. Rose Simpson collection. *Overleaf right* 4-piece outside Scientology HQ, Tottenham Court Road, 1970. Rose Simpson collection. *Left* Outside a US airport, 1970 – Mike, roadie, Robin, Janet, Likky. Pic by Rose. *Right Tricks Of The Senses* cover (an out-take from the *I Looked Up* cover shoot)

Archery with Malcolm and Likky at Glen Row, 1971

Lighting The Path

Lizzie McDougall

I was first aware of the String Band long before the move to the Glen, in Edinburgh before they were famous, when Edinburgh was old and dirty, crumbling with the history of Scotland: the Grassmarket, Canongate, Candlemakers' Row echoing with the sounds and songs of hundreds of years.

The Beat Scene had opened up strange possibilities, people drawn together to talk and talk about freedom, politics, the Bomb, the soul. Empty tenements became Pads, the walls hung with wonderful old paisley shawls and real lace curtains found in rag stores for pennies, the air hung with incense. Legendary characters like Frank de Bear and Gary Field keeping roomfuls of people spellbound with extraordinary tales.

In the daytime people would hang out in a cafe called the Stockpot in Hanover Street. Folk like Bert Jansch, Tom and Bill Smith and Paddy Bell, the whole room singing songs old and new, harmonies creating strange effects of joy and light-headedness... Out into the streets and the dawn of an awareness that we are part of something much bigger. The String Band went on to cast their magic on the world of the time, awakening deep Celtic energies, freeing the imagination.

So when I think about the Glen it is such a big thing; living there with so many interesting and creative souls was wonderful. I don't know if we managed to fulfil our ideals; we nearly and mostly did – which is remarkable. I still feel a deep love for all who lived there (even the one I'm not talking to at the moment!).

It is impossible to pick out one story: it's not like that. The Glen was part of a big story, but at least I can give bits of colour. I first stayed at the Glen in 71 (I think), after becoming very disillusioned with the big-time music scene. I had been working for a while as John and Yoko's cook – not that there was anything wrong with them: they were lovely. It was the industry of greed that had surrounded them, closing in on their creativity, attempting to steal their fame and glory – it was horrid. The Glen was so different. Of course there were human weaknesses, but the strength of true companionship was so strong and so much more fun.

My friend Lindsey and I had agreed to take Robert and Vashti (Bunyan)'s black horse Bess to Ireland, as they were moving there. So we moved into Number 2, where they had lived, made giant saddlebags and gathered the equipment – tent, kettle, drawing pad and paints etc. – for our journey, helped Robert and Vashti pack their worldly goods into their old Beetle, including the cat Grimbly Feendish, who had been found as an abandoned kitten and lived in the top oven. (The top ovens of Glen fireplaces were not hot. Neither were the bottom ones – except Frank Usher's in number 8; Frank, as well as being one of the world's finest guitarists and guitar makers, had got his oven to work so well he roasted the Christmas turkey in it.) So off went the Beetle and off went Lindsey and I up the hill to catch Bess. Now Bess had been living on the hill for a year and didn't want to be caught. Eventually, with the help of the farm workers, we got her into a stable in the courtyard where we calmed her down and got to know her, taking her for walks around Glen Estate, down past the castle to the loch and boat house. Later we led her up behind the walled garden, to Rusty Mountain through the beech trees where years later we took a note to the fairies. Annabel had by mistake thrown away the tissue in which my daughter Rosie had put her tooth. Disaster – no tooth to put under the pillow! So instead of going to bed we put wellies and coats over the children's 'jamas, wrote a note in tiny writing on a tiny piece of paper, made a jam jar lantern, went across the bridge up into the beech wood and found a fairy castle tree! The hard part was remembering which tree, as it was a dark and windy night. First thing in the morning Rosie and Leonie excitedly dragged us back to the woods, we found the tree, and there was a 50p piece. After that, of course, all sorts of presents had to be given to the fairies and Annabel or I would have to go out at night and swap little drawings for specially beautiful shiny pebbles.

But that was years later! After delivering Bess, we hitch-hiked to Ireland, where we travelled across the country in two barrel tops. Rakis and Peter O'Connor came too. And after my own life had been struck a massive blow – my love, with whom I had left Edinburgh to discover the world, suddenly died. I had a broken heart, a beautiful baby daughter and not a clue. The Glen gave us safety, and Mike in particular put me back together. It was during that time that he played me his favourite music: music from Bulgaria, Romania, North Africa and Kashmir.

The Glen was a hive of activity. Robin and Mike were very influential in keeping the energy flowing along positive lines. Lots of work, lots of fun, with the occasional invitation to the Big House. Colin Tennant had a flair for throwing parties. I remember one in particular when the house guests, who included Princess Margaret, put on an entertainment. It was very funny. PM, as she was known, also sang, very beautifully. [*Ed: Robin remembers her giving a deathless rendition of I've Got A Ferret Sticking Up My Nose.*] She had the most extraordinarily green eyes I have ever seen.

Christmas was of course very special. We would always have a party in the hall, sometimes with a play, always with music. I remember one year Robin singing Amazing Grace and Honky Tonk Women. Another favourite party song was Goodnight Irene, sung by all for Ishy, in gratitude for all the kindness, laughter and tea she made. Out of one of the Christmas shows Malcolm evolved the Mandarin Theatre Co., which toured two wonderful shows around the Scottish borders.

In amongst all the joy and beauty there was also pain and sadness. Mally [*Mal Schofield*]'s cancer and eventual death were very hard. And yet, knowing Mal, her beliefs and her dreams, to die surrounded by the love of those you love during the height of that flowering is OK – as long as one believes, as she did, in the survival of the spirit. To me Mally's spirit lives on forever in her favourite blue silk velvet dress, up among the wise.

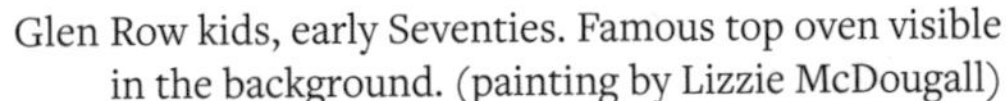

Glen Row kids, early Seventies. Famous top oven visible in the background. (painting by Lizzie McDougall)

Maybe the Row never quite recovered. The world claimed us and we began to commit ourselves to projects that might bring some of the brightness to the wider community. Some of us joined the committee of the Traquair Fair, which blossomed into a wondrous event. I work now as a storyteller and artist, travelling around the Highlands and Islands gathering, telling and sharing Highland stories. Stories, art and music are a magic way of connecting people beyond time and place, and in that space all dear Glen Row neighbours are still my dear neighbours.

Overleaf Rose and Mike onstage, 1970. (Rose Simpson collection)

Chapter Seven

Individual views – Joe Boyd, Rose Simpson and Bruce Findlay give their take on the ISB

As manager and producer of the ISB from 1966-1970, Joe Boyd has an interesting and important angle on their history. He grew up in Boston, surrounded by a very broad range of music – his grandmother was a concert pianist, and his school years were dominated by Fifties pop, old jazz, Woody Guthrie and blues artists from Robert Johnson to Leadbelly. At Harvard he went on to promote folk and blues concerts, and first arrived in Britain managing a blues and gospel tour in 1964.

Robin and Clive, Crown Bar, 1965

Joe Boyd talks to Adrian Whittaker

The interview dates largely from 1994.

Joe was determined to set a few things up when he returned in early 1965 with Jack Elliott and Reverend Gary Davies: 'I went with Bill Leader up to Newcastle to help him record the Fisher Family LP for Topic; I was his assistant and took the photos used on the cover. Then I wanted to hitchhike up into Scotland and Bill gave me the number of George Brown and Dolina MacLennan. I went up to Edinburgh and rang up Dolina [*a respected traditional singer of the day*], who said, "Come right over and stay with us" – she and her husband George Brown. And that night was amazing, because they used my arrival as an excuse for a gigantic party. I met Hamish Henderson, the last man in the world who spoke Pictish, and a whole group of amazing Scots people, and went and had the last round at Sandy Bell's Bar [*premier watering hole for the Edinburgh folk fraternity*] before they shut, and got completely drunk. The next night George said, "There's an interesting pair of guys you'd better see, they're playing tonight at a pub not far from here". We walked through the back streets of Edinburgh to a little pub [*the Crown Bar – Ed.*], and there was Robin Williamson and Clive Palmer, and I thought they were wonderful. It struck me that they were sort of taking Scots songs that hadn't necessarily made the trip over to the Appalachians and playing them as if they had, in a kind of oblique way. They really stuck in my mind, I remember them very vividly'.

After an unenviable task as onstage sound mixer at Newport in 1965 when Dylan went electric, Joe came back in November 1965 to run Elektra's London office. Determined to sign up this Scottish bluegrass duo, there then follows the well-worn story of his arrival, early in 1966, in Sauchiehall Street, Glasgow, to see a gig by the newly expanded ISB (Mike Heron having joined as a 'strummer'), only to find the Incredible Folk Club closed for licensing reasons (some say being raided by the police) and the musicians fled to Mary Stewart's cottage.

Recording the *First Album*, in Spring 1966, was pretty straightforward – just two days in the studio! October Song stands out as one of his favourites. After Robin's return from Morocco, the ISB reconvened without Clive to play a short November 66 tour supporting Tom Paxton and Judy Collins; Joe had been lobbying Elektra furiously to get them on the bill. He can't remember whether there was the still a chance of Clive rejoining, but certainly his programme notes bill Mike and Robin as 'two thirds of the ISB'. I asked him if the *Chelsea Sessions* were partly to see how recording worked as a two-piece:

'You're probably right – it's funny cos just the other day for some reason the melody of Alice Is A Long Time Gone came into my head'.

In spring 1967 work started on *5000 Spirits* proper – the most exciting record Joe worked on with them, he says.

'Joyful Experimentation'

Joe: I knew at the first sessions it was going to be as great as I'd hoped. Recording the *First Album* had made them aware of the potential of the studio in terms of overdubbing, and recording it was a lot of fun – smoking a bit of dope in the studio, experimenting with recording technology – though it was limited to 4-track then, whereas *Hangman* was on 8-track. Work was incredibly fast-moving and productive – there wasn't a lot of dithering, there was general agreement as to how we would proceed – they were such fertile musicians. The fact that it was acoustic instruments meant we didn't have to get a rhythm track, or a drum sound, or make sure the timing didn't waver – the kind of problems you have with a band – it was just a question of doing takes and selecting the best one.

We just had a ball, we just discovered this great new world, putting down a track with vocal and guitar, and then adding sitar and gimbri and flute and jew's harp and harmony singing and organ and harpsichord and you name it – we'd just grab an instrument and they'd go down and overdub something. And for me it was a fantastic exercise, learning about working in the studio, because nobody had done this kind of thing with folk instruments before – we were in uncharted territory. John Wood, the engineer, was classically trained – he'd never confronted this sort of stuff before. He's a fantastic engineer, so we were all learning together. Particularly with *5000 Spirits* and *Hangman*, there was a tremendous feeling of joyful experimentation – listening to something back and one of them saying – 'let's try this!' Occasionally someone would say 'I don't think that worked', but as I recall they were pretty smooth, action-packed sessions. A lot of producers talk about how they end up restructuring songs, telling writers to write another middle eight and so on. My contribution is much more listening to two ways of doing it and saying 'I like this one better'. I'm not the person who says 'What you should think is this'.

Adrian: You've said you saw them pretty early on as a psychedelic band?

I thought they had an audience wider than the folk audience – they transcended the folk scene. It was a combination of factors – including hallucinogens – and they were part of the spirit of the time. For me there was no difference between Syd Barrett and Robin Williamson. They were both talented guys who wrote original stuff – I even booked the Incredible String Band to open for the Pink Floyd a number of times, and I saw their audience as being potentially the same as the Pink Floyd's audience. The 5000 *Spirits* cover painting was a signal to the audience of what they'd grown from. [*During the sessions, Joe had taken Robin and Mike to a basement flat in St Stephens Gardens to meet the cover artists, Simon and Marijke, and they sat around listening to studio takes and jamming with them, David Crosby and Graham Nash.*]

Was the Painting Box single aimed at being an underground hit?

It was pretty much like today – those things were released as single mainly to get airplay. It didn't really work! What really worked was John Peel's *Perfumed Garden* show on Radio London – he played the LP all the time!

It was around this time that Joe became their manager:

I left Elektra in November 1966 and at that point I was faced with a choice – going back to America or staying in Britain – so I had to figure out whether I could earn a living, whether I could get a visa to stay. I got a visa and the UFO Club which I ran with John Hopkins provided me with the weekly cash to pay my rent [it also subsidised *International Times* and, later, Release]. I got a production deal for them with Elektra and started managing them through Witchseason – but the management was never a very lucrative proposition!

Witchseason, in its famous headquarters at 83 Charlotte Street, was Joe's management and production company for a whole extended family of 'folk-rockers' including the Fairports, Strangely Strange and Nick Drake. Wearing his manager's hat, he got the ISB 'a very brief slot' at the Newport Folk Festival in 1967. He also recalls the Big Sur Festival (September 1969) where Rose met David Crosby et al and sang Swing Low Sweet Chariot in a hot spring with them!

'Everything fell into place' – *Hangman* and beyond

The next recordings, in winter 1967, were for Hangman. *Again, there were a lot of overdubs:*

A lot of time and care was taken recording *Hangman* – it was my most satisfying record with them, and they were sessions where you couldn't get bored. I felt at the time it was a great record – we put it out and it went straight into the Top 5 in the pop charts. It didn't *last* there very long – it sank! – but it did very well for that era. It sold twice as fast as anything had done before in America or Britain.

Were Shirley and Dolly Collins [Dolly guested on the sessions] friends of the band?

Yes. Shirley was married to John Marshall, who was the editor of *The Observer* Colour Supplement – and he did a big feature on the ISB.

The band hadn't gigged very much in 1967 but touring moved up a gear with the release of Hangman *in March 1968. Mike told Jeanette Leech (2010):'Joe was very conscious of not promoting us as a folk band... [and] took us out of that folk circuit, which I think was probably a good move.'*

The two and a half years of their career from 1968-70 were just about what I'd hoped for as a manager when I set out – that sort of thing, that sort of audience. I guess the big turning point for me was when I went to Roy Guest [*folk music promoter*] and suggested a solo tour of big halls. These gigs were supposed to have been the month after the album was released but because of production delays the album was released the same week as the tour. Roy thought I was completely mad and refused to promote the concerts, so I agreed to take the risk, to hire him for a fee to make the arrangements. They were all sold out.

The same thing happened in America – Jay Hoffman, who'd seen them in London at the Festival Hall, put them on at the Lincoln Centre, New York. I just flew to San Francisco to meet Bill Graham and arranged a concert at the San Francisco Fillmore, he saw them, saw the way the audience responded and said fine. From then on, every time we came to the States we did two or three solo concerts at the Fillmore East and in San Francisco. It was one of those things that seemed effortless, everything fell into place.

After one Lincoln Centre gig in late 1968 came the conversion to Scientology, unwittingly engineered by Joe. The band met up after a gig with an old Boston mate of his, David Simmons, who was a recent Scientology convert. Robin and Licorice were impressed enough by his new-found togetherness to demand their portion of the Lincoln Centre fee in cash and to enrol in the Church of Scientology the following morning. Mike and Rose followed suit later on, back in London. Joe talks about Scientology later, but we're now in the middle of recording Wee Tam. *Sessions were held in April, June and July 1968.*

'My only regret is allowing Mike to talk me into cutting off Maya'

Some of that was done in the States; we did some sessions at Elektra studios in Los Angeles including Puppies, I think. The cover shots were taken in Frank Zappa's garden...

My only regret is allowing Mike to talk me into cutting off Maya at the last chorus. Originally it was recorded the way they performed it, with a final chorus at the end. But one day – I think when we were putting the running order together – Mike came in with the idea, instead of having Maya finish just as it gets to the big climax, to take a razor blade and cut it off and go straight into the birdsong (and Greatest Friend). I tried to persuade them otherwise, but in the end I succumbed. Listening to it now, I still regret it!

I've always admired the running order on Wee Tam, *which was decided jointly by Mike, Robin and Joe; it was on those sessions he evolved the patented Boyd system of juggling track sequences using columns of paper cut in proportional length to the timings!*

Adrian: There were some incredible collage songs – like Job's Tears, Ducks On A Pond – lots of different musical parts.

All those were products of the way they worked, in which Robin would write long epic songs and Mike would kinda roll his eyes a bit...

Didn't Mike start doing that too – Douglas Traherne Harding is quite an episodic song?

Yeah, but it's not as stylistically varied. Robin would go from rhythm to rhythm and mode to mode, so Mike would say – 'OK, on this bit I'm gonna put *this* instrument, on this bit I'm going to play that instrument, I'm gonna sing harmonies on this bit – and, in a way, accentuate the differences between the two sections, make them more stylistically varied – and it worked!'

We went on to talk about the creative tension between Mike and Robin, whereby they'd only agree to use each other's song if they could play a role in it, adding the instrumental colouring and virtually doing the arrangement, leading to intensive input on each other's compositions. Mike tended to be slightly more disciplined about his contributions, apparently. I asked at which point this had started – 5000 Spirits, *maybe?*

I think I was aware at a fairly early point that Clive had been the connection. They were both friends of Clive's – they weren't friends of each other, so when he disappeared it left these two people who weren't quite sure about each other, locked in this group which they'd each joined really because of Clive – and so there was a bit of wariness or uncertainty. Over a period of time, as they became more successful and had to spend more and more time together and work together, I guess the rivalry and antipathy, whatever, grew rather than dissipated.

Joe feels this didn't really affect their studio work – in fact it made for much more intensive collaboration. With the incorporation of Rose and Licorice, Wee Tam *was recorded with less overdubs and much more as an ensemble, with each of the four playing what they might play in concert. Although he felt Rose and Licorice added an extra dimension live, their studio work was a different matter:*

They ended up spending a long time getting their parts right and we disagreed on the extent of their involvement – the need for endless takes led to some tensions. But Licorice was quite a powerful personality in her own quiet way and I don't think Robin was prepared at that point to risk her wrath.

How did the two girls get involved?

Well, it began with Licorice's participation on *Hangman*. Robin encouraged her to add her voice to harmonies and neither Mike nor I had any real objection – she had a very weird voice but it sort of worked and added to the atmosphere and the success of the album. Licorice went everywhere with Robin, and he said if they were going on a concert tour doing these songs she might as well come on stage and sing the bits she sings or play tambourine or whatever... and Rose later told me that the day Robin released that notion was the day Mike bought her a bass and said 'here – learn this!' – because he saw it as becoming outnumbered, suddenly Licorice was part of the band and it was going to be two against one. That was my depression about that – the whole logic of it didn't seem to be musical. I think if you're charting their career you chart a meteoric rise to a pinnacle of *Hangman*, holding for *Wee Tam*, then a slow decline and a falling-off at the end...

'Clear out the cupboard'

On now to the *Be Glad* soundtrack. The album's release was delayed to coincide with the film premiere, by which time Joe, who'd been getting disillusioned with Elektra, had set up the Island deal. 'It was a kind of clear out the cupboard thing,' says Joe, and as the running order was put together when he was about to relocate to the States, it's a blur in his memory. He makes his only recorded appearance on Side 2, playing harmonium. As for the film itself – 'a little special' – he hadn't got round to watching the video release but had vague memories of some of the 1968 Festival Hall footage being shown on TV at the time. As for the inclusion of All Writ Down instead of Cellular Song: 'That's a very Scientology song – engrams – about cellular memories.'

The ISB's final Julie Felix show TV appearance was around this point (February 1969), and I asked him about his views on the virtual TV 'ban' some writers have perceived – nothing of the kind in his view. The link with Julie originated via Jo Lustig, her manager at the time. Still on management, Joe remembers the Stones sending round a limousine to pick up the band for a meeting about signing to Mother Records, but of course proposals were thwarted at an early stage by the existing Elektra contract.

Rose practices her scales.
(Rose Simpson collection)

'Less drugs, for a start...'

Adrian: The sessions for Changing Horses *seemed to represent the whole changeover of the conversion to Scientology, and born of that was this desire to consciously communicate very directly and clearly. It also seemed to influence the song content and their structures; the arrangements became less esoteric.*

Joe: Well, less drugs for a start, so that obviously had a role. There were obviously a lot of changes, and initially some of the effects of Scientology were positive in a superficial way, but it always alarmed and depressed me. I think there's an inevitable... it's very hard to sustain an unselfconscious originality, but certainly Scientology is full of 'self awareness'. Dealing with them was in some ways more straightforward because they were prepared to confront and deal with issues – they'd also become very good friends, the rivalry was put aside. I think, because they were conscious about a lot of people's misgivings about Scientology – it was them against the scepticism of the world – there was a bond between them.

Joe feels that, whilst Scientology helped them to communicate more openly and honestly with each other and with the outside world, it didn't benefit their music. Interestingly, he tried out Scientology himself after moving to the States (60 hours of Auditing in LA) but, though acknowledging its insights into the human mind, he didn't like the feel of the organisation. On now to I Looked Up, *recorded in early 1970.*

'They were very conscious not to invalidate anything...'

Adrian: I Looked Up *seemed to me to fall very flat as a record – two extremely rambling Williamson songs and four short Heron songs of uneven quality – it didn't have much unity.*

Joe: As it progressed it became more and more difficult in a way. In retrospect, that's one of the upshots of this bonding between Mike and Robin – whereas earlier they would have been critical of each other's contributions and very adamant about shortening *this* or leaving *that* out, now they were very conscious not to *invalidate* anything. So if someone wanted to write a song that didn't really fit the record no one would say – 'that doesn't work!' I still like This Moment though!

Did you try to intervene?

I did, to no real success – it was the nadir with, of course, *U*. It was during a whole period of erosion of my ability to influence them. In the past they had been much more prepared to listen to what I was saying – they'd play me songs, ask my opinion, and were very responsive to that kind of thing. It was a process I went through with all the artists I've worked with in a way. With the first record the process was mysterious, I was the producer and they looked to me to guide them through it. But as the process became less mysterious they were less prepared to ask me what I thought – the whole thing was no longer such an inspiration or challenge.

So by the time you left to work for Warners in the States you'd slowly become less a part of that creative partnership?

I think that was part of the reason I accepted the job in America – with every artist I was involved with I was less satisfied – and to a certain degree with the ISB I'd kind of thrown up my hands at a certain point – certainly by *U*. The other thing, as a manager, was the Woodstock business. It's something I don't blame them for at all really, it was symptomatic of the same thing, but I think if I'd been more alert I could have done something about it.

'I haven't dared to listen to it since...'

So the culmination of this for you was U. *I gather you weren't too keen on the mixed media...*

I thought Robin and Mike were great musicians – but one way or another there were a lot more people added to the band. They'd had those two dancers in the past, Mimi and Mouse, but to me that was a dilution of what the fundamental thing was. U was a disaster in the States – I told them it'd be a disaster. No one would guarantee it and they had to do it on a percentage. I just had no confidence in it whatsoever and I told them that – I was prepared to help them, but against my better judgement.

The LP feels like it was done really quickly.

They'd realised the show was a financial disaster and we needed to cut down on recording costs. They were talking about going back to London to record, but I said let's do it right at the end of the tour, whilst it's still fresh. There were time constraints – we had three or four days between

> tours – and I got a weekend deal in a San Mateo [*San Francisco*] studio. It was recorded in 48 hours – we all checked into the Gaylord Hotel, piled into two station wagons each morning and off to the studio. I think it was mixed back in London. I have to say that I hate it – I haven't dared listen to the record since. But at the same time I was doing Mike's solo – which I really enjoyed!

Joe clearly hadn't lost faith totally, though. Around this time he was holding forth to Frank Kermode for a 1970 Radio Three programme called Pop Audience, Pop Elite. Here's a snippet:

> The most interesting thing about the ISB and their music is their incredible eclecticism. Just after I first met them I had a very humbling experience in discussing oriental philosophy which they were very interested in and concerned with at that time, and I discovered that not only had they read the entire works of Krishnamurti but also *The Lotus and the Robot*, and this is their approach. They will immerse themselves in the primitive music of a certain area for its melody and directness, and also in the techniques and the intellectual approaches of a Cage or a Stockhausen and listen as avidly to both and in certain ways use both influences in their music.

'Pete Townshend would go right back to the beginning and start again...'

Smiling Men With Bad Reputations *was Joe's last ISB-ish production (recorded Summer and December 1970). The sessions were great fun, apparently, with Mike and Joe wheeling in virtually every musician they knew between them. He was particularly impressed with Pete Townshend's approach to rehearsals:*

> He sat there in a corner and learned Warm Heart Pastry with Mike – perfectly – and then took the group through it. Every time someone made a mistake they'd go back to the beginning and start again. It was so different from the ISB approach, which was not to worry about odd mistakes and choose the take with the best feel!

Smiling Men *was a great critical success, and Joe agreed it might have paved the way for Mike's later 'rhythm section' approach to ISB recordings. Lady Wonder, originally released only as a single B-side, was left off 'cos it wasn't good enough.'*

Joe has no recollection of involvement with Relics, *the Elektra compilation released in early 1971. By this time he was feeling that all the Witchseason artists had outgrown the need for his creative input and it was time for someone else to take over and maybe move things in a new direction – 'I'm always more interested in getting things started.' As part of the changeover before selling Witchseason, he'd brought in Susie Watson-Taylor (an ex-girlfriend) to look after ISB affairs. Having sold the company to Island, he moved back to the States in early 1971 for a job at Warner Brothers, co-ordinating film sound tracks and producing a Hendrix film biography. It wasn't quite the end though:*

Susie Watson-Taylor called and said they were putting together a compilation LP (*Seasons They Change*, 1976) and did I have any suggestions – so I said let's put out Queen Juanita And Her Fisherman Lover at last! I'd always liked it, and it's one of those things we'd never actually got on a record [*it was recorded at the time of* I Looked Up] – and so we got hold of the tapes and mixed them. In retrospect I can see that it was a bit unfair to do it without consulting Robin [*who reportedly dislikes the song!*].

In the Nineties Joe was involved with the American ISB re-releases; the early CD masters had in some cases been taken from second or third generation copies, and so he and John Wood supervised remastering direct from the original two-track master tapes. The resulting CDs (on Rykodisc) are much superior to the British Elektra versions. [*Joe also did an even better set of ISB remasters in 2010 for Fledg'ling Records – Ed.*]

Joe kept up a loose contact with Mike and Robin over the years, and in 1987 *Musin' Music* asked them both to assess his producer role:

Mike: 'I think if the songs had been more commercial in production and they had been the same songs, no-one would have bought them at all – the whole point was that they were just something different.'

Robin: 'Joe Boyd did an excellent job on some of those productions; John Wood and he had a lot to do with the sound of those central few [*Sixties*] records.'

A WORD FROM THE ENGINEER:

As the ISB recordings became more complex, the mixing sessions became a method of highlighting particular instruments or voices, or, sometimes, 'losing' them in the mix if they were out of tune or time. You can hear quite a lot of this on *Wee Tam*, for example, where the bass seems to wander in and out of the mix. Sound Techniques engineer John Wood: 'The interesting thing about their recordings is they never ever came to the mixes. One would tend to censor their arrangement or their performance by what one did with the mix. You'd make things sound more in tune by putting them on top of one another, or if they were out of time you'd move them as wide as possible to the edge of the stereo image. Quite a lot of that went on with the ISB...'

'An incredible girl called Rose'

From rock-climber to rock-chick to pillar of the community – the strange ride of Rose Simpson.

For most of her career as Incredible Stringperson, Rose Simpson was simply Rose: one of the two semi-anonymous 'beautiful girls' (to quote Karl Dallas in *Melody Maker*) who seemed to act as musical handmaidens to Robin and Mike. Initially, she and Licorice found their way into the act as girlfriends who were occasionally summoned on stage to bang a drum, shake a tambourine or warble a quavery vocal line while the lads did all the difficult stuff. Their promotion to full band membership was, in the view of some commentators – Joe Boyd in particular – more a matter of internal politics than musical necessity. Whatever the truth of this, however, most fans would contend that they made a significant contribution to the band. And it shouldn't be forgotten that, way back in the 1960s, female musicians were as rare as frog's whiskers in the world of popular music. In their largely unacknowledged way, Rose and Likky blazed a trail that many women would follow in the 70s and 80s.

After 20-odd years of decent obscurity, raising a family and 'pottering around thinking about my pension', Rose was suddenly catapulted back into prominence in the summer of 1994. 'Lady Mayoress played at Woodstock' was the story that quickened the hearts of news-editors throughout the land. By a cosmic coincidence, the 25th anniversary of history's largest mudbath fell around the time that Rose's then partner, Lib Dem councillor Bob Griffin, was appointed Lord Mayor of Aberystwyth, with Rose as the Mayoral consort. The media descended on the sleepy Welsh resort like locusts, and for a few weeks Rose, revealed as primly attired and looking younger than her years, was everywhere – in the *Radio Times*, in the *Guardian*, on Radio Four. It was one of the hottest stories of the so-called 'silly season'. There's a much more interesting story lying behind it: how a student rock-climber who'd scraped a bit of fiddle at school found herself playing the world's most prestigious rock venues – all because of a chance meeting on a Scottish farm.

Andy Roberts took tea with Rose in her kitchen at the height of the media hoo-ha in 1994 – as it happened, on the very day of the Woodstock anniversary – and got the full story. Additional interviewing by Alistair Fraser.

Andy: Let's take it from the top – where do you hail from originally?

I come from Yorkshire – I was born in Otley.

And how did you fall in with the ISB?

I met them in Yorkshire because I think they must have been playing there, but what happened in between that and me going to Scotland I'm not quite so clear about. The time I properly met them was when I went up to Scotland to do some snow climbing; I was President of the student mountaineering club. It was just after Christmas 1967, and I went up there armed with my ice axe and crampons and all the gear, and it was really bad weather and the snow was avalanching so I didn't get to do any climbing. The cottage I stayed in was Mary Stewart's – she was a vet and also a good mountaineer. She knew a lot of the climbing fraternity, but she also knew lots of folky people, so that's when I met them. Robin was living there at the time. I was about nine and a half stone of fighting fury when I arrived and about three months later I was about seven and a half stone of wet rag.

Were you, so to speak, part of the hippy scene?

Oh no – I was part of the mountaineering scene.

Did you have musical leanings?

I played violin and stuff at school. I always enjoyed it, but I didn't have a particularly musical background. The first album I remember being involved with is *Hangman*. I don't think I actually played anything, but I was on the cover. I have a vague idea that I was on a chorus somewhere. The first one I really did anything on was *Wee Tam*.

Ah yes – is it true that Log Cabin Home In The Sky *was written for you?*

Not that I'm aware of. I don't think it was anything to do with me. You Get Brighter was – that definitely was me.

How did you come to join the band?

Well I didn't do anything quite so positive as joining it, but the thing that actually sprung it, was I was supposed to be doing a final year at York University, and one spring day – and it was Yorkshire, it's not exactly the forefront of culture – and suddenly this vision appeared in the refectory. I think it was breakfast time and this walked in and everyone went 'Ahhh', and it was Robin in full flower power panoply, floating through the refectory, incense smells and things dangling and floating, and I must say my main thought at the time was 'I've got to get him off the premises'. It was too bizarre for words really, 'cos I mean I had been President of the Mountaineering Club. I mean I had a certain position to keep up here, so I thought the easiest thing was to go as well. So I said, 'Why don't we go to London or something?' It was quite funny 'cos there was also this pressure to dress up for the situation and I didn't really have anything that I could possibly dress up in to go along with what he looked like. The only thing I had was a dressing gown which I got in a jumble sale in Harrogate, which was actually very handy because it was one of those Indian print things, so I actually did go down to London on the train in my dressing gown; it was the only thing I could think of. It looked quite normal for the time really, and it was quite strange 'cos also on the train was my year tutor, and I think he was legging it to London with someone he shouldn't have been with, so it was a kind of mutual OK, best if we don't recognise each other! So that's how I joined the String Band, because after that it was a bit irrevocable really – after that it all got so complicated it was easier just not to fight it but to go with the flow. Licorice and I were integrated into the band just because we were there. Mike and Robin wanted to use lots of different instruments, not necessarily played well but more for sounds, you know – so you obviously need more hands. I think we were convenient insofar as we were willing hands who could make sounds from things. Neither of us had any intention particularly to compete with Mike and Robin as musicians.

How did it feel to be part of the counter-culture?

Oh, it just seemed quite normal at the time! It was so alien to anything I'd known about that I just accepted it as an entirely different set of rules. I distinctly remember being in London and it crossing my mind as to where my next meal was coming from, because it was like being landed on Mars. I didn't know any of the people, I had never met people like this, I didn't know what on earth anything was about it, and so you just bumble along, just smile and say hello and do whatever comes to hand and if someone gives you something you ring it or hit it or whatever seems the right thing to do with it and just go along with it all really. It was fun and it was just fascinating to find out how it all hung together, because these were the people that I'd seen in – well I hadn't really even seen them in magazines – and suddenly to find how these people lived and the houses they lived in and the restaurants they went to and what they ate and what they did was so unusual to me. I didn't even know how you cooked a green pepper, I'd never had anything to do with a green pepper... It was just all totally new, a total culture shift, but it was fun.

How did you feel about performing?

Well the same thing was true, because if you've got no idea of it, you also have no fear of it, so I think the first time I was actually on a stage was at the Royal Albert Hall, but to me it was no different from being in the local bus station, it was just where I happened to be at the time. I knew the people I was sitting on the stage with and we could chat, and there were a lot of people out there and they seemed to be happy too, so that was fine. There was no question of stage fright, it was like it would be if they'd put you on a desert island and told you to get on with the natives – you'd do your best and try and enjoy it. Recording studios – again, it was all totally exciting, I'd never seen anything like it. Someone told me that when we played the Royal Albert Hall, apparently the wattage of our amplifier was only twenty-five watts, but that sounded deafening, you know.

It was totally interesting, all novelty, like being a child in a sweetshop, like walking into a film set or a magazine or something. Lik and I were both born performers; we were absolutely delighted to be sitting on a stage doing anything. We would have played anything, danced, sung, stood on our heads, juggled... We were happy doing that, and I think our happiness came across. We just really loved doing it.

Were you worried about the audience's reactions?

No, they seemed to be enjoying themselves and we were quite enjoying ourselves as well, and if we weren't enjoying ourselves, well, we didn't make an awful lot of effort to hide it. I mean, sometimes Licorice and I were in tears, we had a row or something and we just snivelled away and got on with it and people were either sympathetic or not. But we never really saw it as a band performing to an audience, it was just that we were the ones who were sitting up there with the instruments and they were the ones down there, who were not really friends but potentially friends, it was just like being at home really.

Was it a pressure on you, playing larger venues?

No, it never was, and I think probably the credit for that goes to Mike and Robin because I think they accepted that so easily that everyone around them accepted it also. It didn't change the way that they thought about their work, or it didn't seem to. They approached their concerts in the same degree of 'amateurism' – I don't mean amateur in a bad sense, but amateur in the sense that they didn't make a fuss, they wore whatever they felt like wearing, it was not produced in any way, we just went along to every gig, whatever it was, regardless. I think it wouldn't have made much difference if it had been the local pub or the Festival Hall, we just did it. Maybe that's Joe Boyd, maybe he was just so protective that we never noticed, but we never really felt that much pressure about it.

Rose and Mike onstage, 1970. (Rose Simpson collection)

Did you get on with Licorice? There are rumours that you were not best pals...

Well, we didn't really have much to do with each other, quite honestly. We didn't not get on, so far as I can recall, but we didn't have much in common. I don't think we really understood very much about each other, and we never really found a need to talk about it. We never clashed as such, but then we were never pals either – it was just someone else who was there. She was not the sort of personality I would have made a close friend of. [*Rose writes at much more length about Likky in her 2020 memoir,* Muse, Odalisque, Handmaiden – *Ed.*]

How did Mike and Robin work together?

They seemed to work terribly well. I can't really be very specific because I wasn't really involved in it – we knew our place – and our place definitely wasn't being involved in the production or the dealings between Mike and Robin and the record producer. I never saw them fight or anything like that and they seemed to compromise very well on the way things were done. I think we never gave Joe any particular credit for what he was actually doing. We never thought how much he stood between the band and critics, and the band and fans or the band itself. I never noticed it and I guess the others didn't because we would have talked about it, and I think he probably nurtured it far more than we were aware of, looking back. It seems too much to believe that it did just happen – you feel that it must have been more guided. We were just jolly lucky that we had good people that seemed to get along so well with Mike and Robin, seemed to adapt so well to their creative mode, but managed to also keep it on that level where you did feel it was all friends together playing in your front room.

Some people have suggested that they made the music they did because of the tensions between them...

I think that might be true. There was a lot of tension, but very rarely did any tension surface between any of us. It's strange – I can't imagine living like that now, but then... it was the climate of the time: you didn't find any need to bring out your differences and discuss them and resolve them. We weren't really into encounter groups: if we had problems we'd just deal with them somewhere else.

The Be Glad *film – what part did you play in that?*

I just sort of floated around! Wales was not the greatest. I was not a sybaritic person (*laughs*) – you don't go climbing up mountains because you like an easy life, but I'm not one for persisting in misery. Wales was a persistence in a totally uncomfortable, joyless, miserable way of living. I can't see that it was good for anyone's creative spirit, but maybe it was – people do create out of misery! Everyone seemed to be uncomfortable, not just me, but everybody seemed to be trying to evade the issue – maybe that's a fairly jaundiced view but it certainly wasn't a high point in the career as I saw it. But maybe it's a good thing to strip off all the extraneous things and get back to grovelling around an open fire and trying to cook a bit of brown rice now and again and wade through the farmyard, but I found it choking and dreadful. It was like tunnelling in a jungle to get there somehow, those overhanging green lanes and it was all damp. My prime impression was it was just so wet, and doing that film too, again it was tipping it down most of the time. I had these blessed false eyelashes on that were getting in my eyes. I'd got conjunctivitis. It was just a nightmare, I can't describe it any other way (*laughs*). Yes, it was fun seeing Joe being a film director, he looked jolly good. He did it very well actually, had a very nice jacket on – it was a Liberty print – and he looked so impressive, floating around the landscape, waving his arms about and they all looked very nice in their outfits...I mean it's fun, but it would also be nice to have the discretion to say nah, we'll forget it because you can have too much of these things – the charm is in the editing rather than letting it run.

Mike has said that he wasn't into the multimedia side of things...

I wasn't either – not because I didn't like it, but I felt that other people could do it better, and that once we started to do that we were stepping into fields where none of us had any expertise. I mean, Lik and I had no expertise in anything in particular; Mike and Robin were good musicians, but that didn't make either of them good actors, directors, artists or any of these other things, and I felt that once you go into that you either get people who are good at it or you don't do it at all.

Rose in the *Be Glad* film. (Peter Neal)

The impetus for that came mainly from Robin...

Yeah, pretty much. I think we were all interested in it and sort of enthusiastic about it on certain levels. It was very nice to do it, but I don't think it should have become part of the mainstream of the band.

At what point did Scientology enter the picture?

Can't remember – 69 or something, wasn't it?

Were you involved yourself?

Yes, I was, but it wasn't quite as simple as that. I always wanted to know about things, and the best way of finding out about something is to do it – and so to that extent I was willing to go along with it, but I don't think I had any great belief or commitment.

Do you think it affected things in the band?

Yes, definitely – I think it was pretty disastrous. I don't think it contributed anything to Mike and Robin's musicianship or their poetic abilities. It didn't look like it gave them anything, and I think that it reinforced the less positive side of their personalities, which inevitably creates an imbalance. I don't think it added to their way of looking at the world. I think it contracted it: before, they were willing to take on anything and everything. That became part of their poetic vision of the universe – a mixture of religions and a mixture of literatures and all that. Suddenly there was this one, and that closed all the other doors.

Why do you think it appealed so much to Mike and Robin?

I really can't imagine... You see, I can only see it in negative terms – I can't be a proper judge of that.

Changing Horses *was the first Scientology album...*

I'd have thought that was pre-Scientology. I think the 'changing horses' was more about ceasing to be a folky duo, and becoming a group. It was a time of transition.

To Woodstock, then: how much do you remember about the event?

As far as we knew, it was just another gig. It was fairly disastrous really but I was glad I did it! We should have played on the Friday night – but that was a typical String Band self-indulgence, and we were self-indulgent in lots of ways. It was a disaster, one of our big mistakes really, but I can see why we refused to play. We were a bit miffed, really – it was just unpleasant being wet and cold and hungry and not knowing how we were going to go anywhere. It was really uncomfortable, and the only thing you could get to eat at that point was strawberries and cream and champagne. I mean, we were lucky, we were the band, at least we had that. We stayed the night in this tent and it was soaking wet and a bit chilly and it was just so unpleasant and... It was the failure of our expectations: it was the first night and it seemed to be going wrong. But also there were the moments even then, like John Sebastian playing and everyone pulling together, and this feeling of pulling together did actually generate itself somehow over that night. The next day I think we very clearly had that feeling of 'We're all in this together, we're going to really have to make the best of this, we owe it to all those people out there who are an awful lot wetter than we are – we're going to be flown out tonight, we'll be all right'. And also we didn't have to be responsible for ourselves; that's always a let-out with a band, you can blame the people who got you there, it's someone else's problem and that makes it an awful lot easier to cope with things. That is the privilege of a successful band I suppose, you are protected because of your art and it's very easy then to convey this atmosphere of peace, light and beauty, because that's all you need to see – well, not quite, but more or less.

Joe Boyd always erred on the side of letting Mike and Robin do whatever they wanted in the hope that something good would come out of it, rather than taking a more editorial and managerial role, and I certainly think that on that Friday night – and I know he thinks this too – he should just have said 'You just get on that blessed stage and play, and shut up moaning about getting wet and getting shocked.' He regrets it, I know. The String Band would have had a different history if we had. In a way, I wouldn't want it to be different, because you can't change one thing without changing a whole lot of other things. If Joe had taken a strong line he might have squashed a lot of really lovely things too... I think it was, on the whole, a question of no-one defining what they wanted to do, and to that extent Scientology did provide definitions, and maybe there was that degree of insecurity where it would have been better to just sit down and say 'Where exactly do you want to go? – Do you actually want to be pop stars, or what? Do you want however many millions of people to buy your records? Do you want to do gigs all over the world and all that stuff? If this is what you want, you should do this, this and this.'

But I think Mike and Robin would probably have had quite specific ideas about what they wanted to do, and that's the sort of occasion where it could have been worked out and where they could have avoided lots of problems, by just sitting down and working on a larger scale. Obviously, if you write something you want lots of people to hear it – although I'm sure they were never motivated by money; it was never a priority for any of us. There was never any question of selling out. In that way they were very pure. There's no blame attached to anybody – we were all part of that time; we enjoyed it, but I somehow feel it could have been done better.

Do you remember much about U*?*

Yes (*laughs*). It's not something that I personally adapted to very well, it's not my forte – even then I liked a much clearer structure to things and I was always put out by the lack of that. Also the feeling that they had tremendous strengths and incredible abilities and this wasn't it, for me. It could have been so well done and I think it wasn't and I'm disappointed by that, because they had the ability. They could have done it so much better. They maybe could have done the big show or the good film – they could maybe have expanded into other media much better. Maybe that's the flip side of the 'playing in the front room' syndrome, which is lovely as long as you're still working in that format, even if your front room happens to be extremely large. But the minute you start to bring other things into it then you've got to abandon that and go in for a different way of working. I am really sorry that I can't be more positive about it. I'm not saying something in retrospect. I'm saying what I thought at the time, because I was aware of it, but that wasn't what they wanted. I think possibly what they were looking for may well have been what they produced.

The move to Glen Row?

I think that was a thoroughly good idea because you could have this protective environment which did lift a lot of the burden from everybody. You could pursue your whims and fancies without causing too much damage to yourself or anybody else. You had the closeness to work together and to practise and have a group social life without it being oppressive. It was a very beautiful place to live as well. I don't quite know how we got there, there seemed to be an awful lot of upheavals on the way; I guess someone else organised everything and that's what I mean about being a very sheltered existence. Scotland was very good.

Glen Row brought lots of other people in and some of that must have been good for Mike and Robin, I suppose. They did what they thought was right for them and they were the creative artists, that was their right, it's all very well for me to sit and criticise it now but I do it with a smile, I do it with a laugh because I'm looking back thirty years and from that position things are totally different; hindsight is wonderful. I wish they'd been kept within a more specific framework, but again that's not for me to argue with really.

What made you decide to leave the ISB?

We have to take responsibility for the way one's own life is going. The band didn't make my life go a particular way; I chose the way my life was going, but when that clashed with the way they saw their life going, then there comes a point you can't accept it. There weren't overt clashes; we didn't have rows. We had very different lifestyles and it was healthier for me and for everybody just to say no thank you, best do something different. So I suppose that's the summary of it; and the specific incident, as far as I remember it, we were doing a tour in the States, and we did a radio interview about the Vietnam war. I had some views on it which I expressed and they decided that it was best to edit the tape at that point, and I decided if I couldn't say what I wanted to say – which was very little, and I was always desperately trying to be tactful – there comes a point when you can no longer sit there and smile politely all the time. It's not really my line (*laughs*). I just needed to feel my feet on what I saw as firm ground and have back again the control of my life that I'd cheerfully given up; I thought let's face it and get down to the nitty gritty. [*Rose writes at much more length about this in* Muse, Odalisque, Handmaiden – *Ed.*]

Did you leave on amicable terms?

Yeah, well... We were never what you'd call close friends. That didn't mean we didn't have quite strong ties to each other, but we were all very different and separate people. I think they must have known, like I did, that I'd reached the end of the road. I don't think I was ever really a musician, because musicians can't live without it. I can, but I couldn't live without books and reading. That's my art thing, not music. But when I listen to String Band albums – though I very rarely do – it moves me to tears, it's really just so beautiful. Mind you, some of the songs I also found incredibly boring – you know, sitting on stage thinking: God, not another ten minutes!

It was reported that you were planning to take up sound engineering...

That's what I intended to do, but I was pregnant at the time and I thought, well what do you do? – Do you park the baby under the amplifier? – and I suppose the more pregnant you get the more you feel like sitting in one place and nest-building. Leaving was really hard because it's very difficult to come down from that pinnacle to cleaning Global Tours at four o'clock in the morning, which is one of the more entertaining jobs I had straight after leaving the band. Also I think it was really a fight to leave it; in a sense you've got to reconstruct your life and that's the fight that Robin and Mike had also when they had to make their lives.

The obvious question – 20-odd years on, how does being Lady Mayoress of Aberystwyth compare with being in a high-profile Sixties pop band?

Well actually I see it in the same way, and I get the same sort of high out of opening a local fête as I did playing the Albert Hall – a lesser high, obviously, but I get the same satisfaction from doing it. It's just doing something I know I can do.

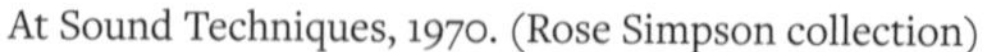

At Sound Techniques, 1970. (Rose Simpson collection)

What did you think of the ISB's later development?

I didn't like that – I felt they were dissipating their energy by involving a lot of people over whom they didn't have the same creative control. They had a very instinctive talent then, whatever they've developed since. At that time their whole musicianship was fairly instinctive and that was so impressive, the fact that Robin could pick up some instrument he'd never seen before in his life and he could make music out of it. I found that so exciting and the same with Mike – I mean, Mike's skill with words was a skill of simplicity. When his lyrics were very simple they had such a strength and such a charm, and the minute this became bigger scale those strengths got lost in a welter of other things that I don't think were so good, and I think their strengths were subsumed in all that. I didn't have any right to criticise it anyway, I wasn't the creator, they were the creators; all you could do was execute as well you could what they wanted you to do and leave them to make the creative decisions and they made them; I personally don't think they were the best ones.

Did you see them after you'd left?

I found it impossible to keep up the contacts really. I was leading a very different life and it was uncomfortable because if I saw them I always wanted to be on stage because I liked being with them on the stage too. When I criticise the band it's a partial criticism and what doesn't come over is just how good it was when it was good; they were wonderful artists and the shows were just delightful to be part of. On a good day when they were doing a concert and the place was full and the people were kind people – and they nearly always were – Mike and Robin walked on and... I knew them really well but I still admired the way they took over the audience, and it was so low key, so unassuming. They didn't bounce on waving their arms about, there were no big fanfares, they just picked up the audience straight away and they glowed at the audience and it was wonderful to be part of that. I was high as a kite from the warmth of the theatre, which they generated. It's so difficult to tell you what that was and the power they had; I mean I would weep because of how lovely it was. It still gets me now – what it was like to sit there watching them sing and be part of it and say 'I'm with them'. I was knocked out, I was proud as punch to be there. They were splendid people to be with, they were exciting and entertaining and fun and they were constantly challenging my life, they were constantly challenging my ideas. They were digging into you all the time for what you yourself could produce, and that's what they demanded of everybody who worked with them. They brought out a tremendous amount in lots of people, and they changed people's lives. People still come up and say you changed my life, and I didn't change anyone's life, I was window dressing or background – I was part of it, yes, but it was Mike and Robin that did the life changing – and they did: you read all the books about how they influenced so many bands and that's all very true. But what people don't always get a clear picture of is the really good things.

They were enormous personalities, they were beautiful looking men and they were such a visually exciting thing to look at: obviously the blond one, the dark one, the clothes they wore and the way the lights all used to glint off all the instruments and all the rugs and everything. It used to just look gorgeous. It was lovely, it was rich and exciting and then they sang and they just held the audience in their hands – they didn't manipulate the audience, they welcomed it to them. Children would come on stage and they would be happy for the children to be there because they were so at ease, we were all having such a wonderful time that you just wanted everyone to share it. Licorice and I added to it, but all of that hung on Mike and Robin, their personalities, their creative ability, also their looks and their manner and their voices... And they were incredibly powerful.

They were great for making people believe in themselves, and it was almost their willingness to believe in the strength of other people that I think to some extent was part of their downfall. You shouldn't criticise someone for that; you maybe should say there should be limits but you should also admire that they were prepared to take those risks. I mean, they were prepared to put their music, their lives, their careers on the line for people they didn't know because they believed in their inner spirit, and that's a hell of a risk to take. They took it willingly and they took it every day, and they took it happily, joyfully. It was a privilege to be on the stage with them, it was probably the best thing I'll ever know; I'll never forget being on the stage with those men and that music.

2003

Rose's memoir of her time with ISB, *Muse, Odalisque, Handmaiden*, was published by Strange Attractor Press in 2021.

‘As far as I am concerned, Robin came from Mars...’ – Bruce Findlay

Norman Lamont

If you were au fait with anything in Scotland in the late Sixties to early Seventies, you bought your records from Bruce’s in Rose Street, Edinburgh. There you’d get the String Band gossip, previews and get your records in a shop staffed by music fans – probably the first of the rock generation, in Scotland at least. You’d go home with your String Band album in a red ‘I found it at Bruce’s’ bag. Bruce Findlay went on to manage Simple Minds and the Silencers, among other adventures, but he never misses a chance to evangelise about his biggest heroes, the Incredible String Band, Bob Dylan and John Lennon. We talked for a few hours, ranging from the Sixties to Oasis. His grasshopper mind makes a Williamson song look as logical as a computer program, so this is very much my sifted version of what he said. We started by talking about the ISB’s first demo.

Bruce: Mike played with a rock group, and in his spare time during the Festival would sing Ode To Bob Dylan. He would do his own acoustic, folky stuff at Hendersons [*an Edinburgh vegetarian restaurant*]. We became friends and used to hang out together at the Place, a sort of beat club. I never saw Mike as a folknik – Robin and Clive, of course were, and were very young. The interesting thing about folk in that period is that it was extraordinarily hip. It was as hip to be into Woody Guthrie in 1963-4 as to be into Pearl Jam or Oasis in 94. And so lots of young people were into the folk revival – OK, fingers in the ear stuff, but good. Young people would respect the older musicians and older tunes. Just before that, in the Fifties, was like now, where they didn’t give a shit. But when things become hip, people take notice. So you had the beat boom – the first Britpop scene in the early Sixties – coinciding with a folk revival.

Mike Heron was in a pretty cool rock group – he was the lead singer. I had a record stall in a mod coffee bar in Lothian Road called Mr Smith’s. This was 1965, and I was selling soul imports, but I also loved blues and folk music – I preferred the lyrics of folk singers but the music of pop or soul people, so I liked it when people like Bob Dylan began to blend the two and become hip.

And Robin and Mike too – to me the ISB were the hippest band of all time – the perfect combination: young and beautiful, hip and like street kids as well. Neither of them were poverty-stricken youngsters, but they weren't rich either – they were just Edinburgh kids, but they hung around in Bohemia, you know, lots of artists, and Edinburgh being that kind of city, it was a great place for that sort of thing to emerge. I don't think that's often recognised, because Edinburgh's a place you bring the arts to – it doesn't usually produce art. That's wrong. Clive's Incredible Folk Club was in Glasgow, and it wasn't obvious they came from Edinburgh. As far as I was concerned Robin came from Mars – he was a space cadet, with this weird, lovely accent – so it didn't matter where they came from, but they came from Edinburgh and I knew them, so I loved it. It pleases Glaswegians to take credit – the String Band *did* start in Glasgow, but they're an Edinburgh band – there's no argument about it!

They also made their first demo in Edinburgh in Alan Coventry's house. Alan Coventry was a schoolmate of Mike's and he played bass with the Boston Dexters. Mike invited me up – I knew him and Alan because of selling records and generally knowing people in groups. Alan was a very funny guy who had a Revox tape recorder, so they went in there and made their first set of demos. A few weeks later Mike came back to the stall and I asked how it was going. He said great, they had serious interest from two record companies – Transatlantic and Elektra. I said it had to be Elektra – they were cutting edge – but I was teaching them to suck eggs. They already knew. To be absolutely honest, I can't remember what was on that demo, I was probably out of my face! I just remember being excited at being there. I think maybe Maybe Someday was on it. I don't know what happened to the tape – of course they didn't have a cassette machine to do copies on!

Norman: How do you think Mike viewed Robin in those days? Did he see him as extraordinary too?

I really don't know, because to me they're like the Gallagher brothers in Oasis, or Lennon and McCartney. Who'll ever really know? It's a good question, because only Lennon and McCartney have that richness of talent, and quite diverse. They were both space cadets, in fact – what about Mike's fixed grin – unbelievable. It's funny that Robin looks now like he looked then, with the little goatee beard. He'd cultivated the kind of folkie 'old man' look. I think Mike did wonders for Robin. It wasn't till the String Band that he discarded the beard and put on the robes, and then he looked beautiful, he looked like God. He looked as beautiful as

David Bowie was in Ziggy, without the obvious artifice. He looked natural, like he came from the hills, like he came from Tibet. He'd walk on stage and people just went AAAH! It was contrived as anything else, the way we all looked, but there was an attempt to look uncontrived.

It's hard to imagine there would have been a String Band without Robin, but would there have been a String Band without Mike?

Well again it's like Lennon and McCartney, only the String Band were better than the Beatles. Comparisons are not fair. So I'd say Lennon is a bit like Robin and McCartney is a bit like Mike, but Mike still has a bit of Lennon in him as well, that McCartney doesn't have. He's much sweeter than Mike. Mike could write quite nice, commercial, focused songs, more acceptable to more people, but he could rock out too. He has some pair of lungs in him. But one of my favourite Mike songs is Air, which is very short, gentle and sexy, and it could have been written by Robin, except Robin wouldn't have made it so commercial – he'd have wandered off for ten minutes. So it's like Lennon and McCartney – Yin and Yang – you couldn't have had it without one or the other. Just Robin and Mike – you could still have the String Band without Malcolm or Likky or any of the rest of them.

It was a magic time, when we had Wilson and Benn and the promise of the future, with the String Band and the folk revival and all the wonder of the past. Until it all went wrong.

What did you think about Joe Boyd's comments on the creative rivalry between Robin and Mike?

Maybe it was only people like Joe that saw that – I never really did, and I was close to them for a long time. They were always very friendly to each other, and they gave each other space. They seemed to have a much more grown-up attitude than some...

What went wrong?

I don't know. I think Scientology had an effect on them, but I wouldn't blame Scientology as one thing. It could have been anything – it could have been a heavyweight lawyer, it could have been a friend – but ultimately outside influences affected them. The String Band were part of a messy kind of family – the band, Joe Boyd, Elektra, the fans, the record shops that sold their records, the promoters – and when the corporate thing came in and they switched labels, some of the fun seemed to... I think they stopped believing in their own magic in a way. I lost touch around that time. Scientology didn't interest me at all. I was a camp follower, always down at Innerleithen, but the atmosphere had changed. I wouldn't knock them for it. Also the authorities were against it, which added to its allure. Robin and Mike to me were always positive anyway, they didn't need Scientology to tell them that...

Is there one concert that sticks in your mind?

It must be in 1968, when they came back in triumph to Edinburgh after *Hangman*. After playing pub gigs they were suddenly in the Usher Hall, the biggest venue in the city, with all their mums and dads cheering. It was like the whole city saying Yeah!

1996

Overleaf Smiling Men With Bad Reputations LP.

Chapter Eight

Mike and Robin Go Solo

Smiling Men With Bad Reputations: 'One of the all-time great session LPs'

Adrian Whittaker sets the album in context.

It's my guess that, in summer 1970, Mike Heron was doing some thinking about the limitations imposed on him by being in the ISB. The *U* project, probably his least favourite collaboration with Robin, had foundered in the States and he'd taken off after the tour for an extended holiday.

'I kind of got off the track. I wound up going to various places like Vermont and Mendocino. Arlo Guthrie took me to a few places, I think.' Joe Boyd had been pushing him for some time to do an album where he could get in touch with his 'rocky roots', and Mike had already come up with a few songs Joe felt wouldn't work in the ISB format. When the idea first came up, Mike 'didn't have the material. I wanted the stuff to be separate from the band's but at the same time I wanted to keep contributing to the band so I wasn't starving them. So when I had enough material, I started recording. I began in the summer for about a week, then went on holiday to San Francisco. I was really excited by the project, it was like a breath of fresh air.'

Many of *Smiling Men*'s songs were written during Mike's stay with macrobiotic friends, an old-style hippy couple, in Russian River, about 100 miles north of San Francisco, where he 'spent a week drinking homebrewed coffee. I was speeding on it after a while. Call Me Diamond came out of a surfeit of coffee. I just wrote and wrote and drank a lot of coffee. It was very rural hippy, very laid back. A couple of songs I'd had from before, but the bulk of the album comes from that holiday. My friends split up shortly afterwards – maybe all that coffee was to blame!'

It's the more StringBandy songs which predate Mike's caffeine-fuelled songwriting spree: Beautiful Stranger, Spirit Beautiful, Flowers Of The Forest and, more surprisingly, a strumalong version of Lady Wonder had all been played live by the ISB in July of that year.

Back in London, Joe Boyd (who'd 'kind of thrown up his hands' with the ISB after *U*) got behind the project. He'd already had a shot at trying to get Mike's songs covered by other artists, producing mainstream-friendly publishing demos of You Get Brighter and This Moment featuring a rock rhythm section, Elton John on piano and Linda Thompson on vocals – which didn't succeed. Joe started lining up the stellar guests at Sound Techniques: 'They weren't all String Band fans,' said Mike, 'but they were interested enough in it as an odd kind of music that they were happy to play on. And they all liked Joe – he was very street-cred at that time. He really set up those partnerships very well.'

The album was completed in a flurry of activity in December, Mike pronouncing himself 'delighted' with the whole experience, particularly the collaboration with other musicians. 'It was never a question of me holding on tightly to what the songs were, and they went in the direction of the people [guesting on them]. It was one of the first albums of its type, one with great artists on each track. That aspect of it was very much Joe's idea.' What Mike learnt about production (and the importance of a solid rhythm track) from Boyd and Cale influenced the clean, clear approach of the next ISB album, *Liquid Acrobat As Regards The Air*. 'John Cale said to me that a lot of our material was being wasted because there was no way to relate to it, because of how it was recorded.' Mike became, at least temporarily, a revisionist: 'I think if some of the Beatles' tunes had been done in the same way as the early ISB albums they would have immediately excluded a huge audience.' A decade or so later, he was less sure, telling an interviewer, 'If the (same) songs had been more commercial in production no-one would have bought them at all.'

The LP package and Island publicity materials were intended to demonstrate very clearly that this was nothing like an ISB album. Photos of Mike as studio whizzkid featured in the music press ads and the Call Me Diamond single sleeve. The gatefold sleeve, according to Mike, 'was a deliberate attempt to do a complete turnaround from the tasteful, countrified, kind of beautiful covers in the String Band. It was an attempt to do a gross magazine-style cover in glaring, brassy colours. I thought, let's make it clear that this music has got very little to do with the String Band.' The people on the cover weren't, as some thought, Mike's dealers – they came from an agency! And the title comes from a section in Timothy Leary's *Psychedelic Prayers* about where 'the lesson of the Tao is more likely to be found...'.

Smiling Men was released on April 30th, 1971, following (confusingly) on the heels of the 'old-style' *Relics* and *Be Glad* albums. Reviews were glowing: 'The best rock album from any source since *Stage Fright*,' raved Dave Pirie in *Time Out*, and *Sounds* deemed it 'a revelation'. Mike's vocals were consistently singled out for praise, with many a Van Morrison comparison. There were criticisms too – *Melody Maker* felt that it could be seen as self-indulgent, and several reviewers agreed that the arrangement on Beautiful Stranger overpowered the song.

The album's success was what probably gave Mike the impetus and confidence to come forward more as the ISB's eventual producer, as well as his growing insistence on a more structured approach to recording and a new willingness to be the group spokesman in music press interviews. That's all speculation. Here's some detail on the individual songs, starting with the more String Bandish tracks.

Flowers Of The Forest, a straightforward love song, features Rose's last (and best) bass line on record. She officially left the ISB in January 71, just after the album sessions finished. Apart from Richard Thompson's lead guitar part, it hasn't changed very much from the ISB version recorded for *Top Gear* in July 1970. Audrey, another love song, stems from the Russian River holiday. John Cale was over to work on Nico's *Desertshore* album and was roped in by Joe. He plays harmonium and bass on this, and may have influenced the arrangement too – it's reminiscent of his work on Nico's *Chelsea Girl*. On Brindaban, Gerard Dott [q.v.] first appears on the ISB scene, credited for helping Mike to score his string arrangement for this. Brindaban was also 'adopted' by the ISB, turning up on live gigs around October. The 'peacocks' and 'kokilas' (nightingales) mentioned in the lyrics are mnemonics for notes in the classical Indian sol-fa scale, in which each note corresponds to the cry of an animal or bird. Brindaban is Krishna's home village and Malati and Madhava are medieval Indian poets. But under all these trappings it's another love song.

Spirit Beautiful plays with a theme of spiritual growth – seeds becoming forests, pebbles becoming mountains – and is not a radical departure from the ISB's live version. The Indian musicians used on this track came from the local Indian community; Heather Wood, an erstwhile member of a cappella folkies the Young Tradition, joined Dr Strangely Strange on backing vocals. Their new drummer Neil Hopwood recalled: 'With a voice like mine, I volunteered to make the coffee, whilst the valiant trio laid down their part.'

The other songs explore musical settings rather further away from paths the ISB had trodden till then. Call Me Diamond has a distinct township feel to it. The late Dudu Pukwana (of South African expats Brotherhood of Breath – produced by Joe Boyd) did the brass arrangement, using the Brotherhood horn section with Osibisa's Teddy Osei on tenor and flute. No relation to the later solo song Diamond Of Dreams, said Mike, and 'totally incomprehensible. It's a good song, but I don't know why. A lot of people really feel those lyrics. I think a lot of my best songs are written that way.' One critic was reminded of Van's Brown-Eyed Girl. Mike Kowalski (drums) also worked with Joe Boyd on Nick Drake's *Bryter Layter*, which shares several of its sessioneers with *Smiling Men*. Beautiful Stranger is a radical departure from the live ISB version, full of synthesiser washes and a rather overpowering brass section, arranged by John Cale. Tony Cox (who had produced and played with Trees) plays a VCS3 – an early synth, as used on Roxy Music's first album. Mike worked with Cox again in the mid-Eighties.

On Feast Of Stephen John Cale 'took over the studio', even asking for production credits (no, said Joe). 'He told me I put too many chords in the song,' said Mike, 'and made me play it through as far as I could go without changing chord. I went along with it because I had the feeling something great was going to happen.' Cale ended up with credits for piano, 12-string guitar, bass, viola, backing vocals and vocal arrangement. In his autobiography *What's Welsh For Zen?* he remembers *Smiling Men* as 'one of the all-time great session LPs ever made.' Mike's since said that, of all the people he'd worked with on the album, Cale was the most interesting. He repaid the favour by guesting (on acoustic lead guitar and backing vocals) at a January 71 Cale gig at the Roundhouse. There's a muffled tape in circulation of Mike 'n' John doing Child's Christmas In Wales, Gideon's Bible, Please and Bring It On Up.

Warm Heart Pastry was the last song to be recorded for the LP, in a rather boozy session with Pete Townshend and Keith Moon, plus Ronnie Lane (Faces) on bass, masquerading as 'Tommy And The Bijoux', just before Mike went back to the Glen for Christmas. John Cale's viola must be an overdub as he never made it out of the pub across the road that evening! Townshend took charge of rehearsals and was, says Joe, a hard taskmaster, continually taking the band back to the very beginning every time someone made a mistake. *Sounds*' Steve Peacock was at the session: 'Before Townshend and the others arrived, Mike said, 'It's rather a pathetic little song really – just one verse and a chorus', but they sat round and worked out an arrangement, changing Mike's rhythm to a very Townshendy chugalong chord thing with Keith battering away as is his wont, and it still kept the feel of the original'. Mike says the title is a Chinese euphemism for 'making it, but more emotional'.

No Turning Back rounds off the album with an ungarnished Heron vocal and guitar. Was he making a point? In her memoir, Rose comments: 'The honesty of Mike's songs has threaded them through my subsequent life. When his father died, he went into Edinburgh until evening. He came home, went away into another room overnight and wrote No Turning Back. After all the years and turmoils in between, this was the only song for me to play at my own father's funeral. Hearing it again in a public space, it bridged the years with its expression of love and loss.'

Other songs from the sessions

Steve Winwood was around for the sessions but Mike says: 'we tried a couple of things but it didn't quite take off'. Eleven songs were completed and mixed for potential inclusion, but two weren't included until the Island CD reissue. Lady Wonder (with Jimmy Page on lead guitar) appeared on the B-side to the Call Me Diamond single. Joe says it was left off the album because 'it wasn't good enough'. Steve Peacock may have influenced this – it was 'the one track where Mike lost control', and Mike remembers technical problems: 'By the time Jimmy Page came in, the basic track had been so adulterated he had a really tough time'. Daves Pegg and Mattacks are on bass and drums. Make No Mistake, despite featuring Elton John (used by Joe for recording demos at the time) and Gordon Huntley on steel guitar, was a justifiable reject. This time there were musical problems. Mike: 'The track with Elton John took twenty-five takes and he was perfect and we cocked it up, then we were perfect for the twenty-sixth time and he cocked it up. It was a bad song.'

Updated 2021

Call Me Diamond sleeve. (Island Records)

Stepping Out – how Mike Heron opened the door

Norman Lamont outlines his musical rite of passage

Sometime around 1971 I wrote to Mike Heron and asked him, among other things, about the title and sleeve design of *Smiling Men With Bad Reputations*. The title, he said, came from Timothy Leary's version of *The Tibetan Book Of The Dead*, and the sleeve was 'a Vogue-ish interpretation of the title'. That sleeve has a personal significance for me, as Mike, in presbyterian black, offers a pineapple, that exotic Liberace of the greengrocer's world, to an equally ripe-looking multiracial crew of gatecrashers at a nativity play.

Before this album, my musical world was similarly dour, even allowing for the influence of the String Band. I was approaching music from folk clubs, with a smattering of the cosmic from the Moody Blues, Tyrannosaurus Rex and King Crimson, but I knew nothing of the wider world of music. Despite my friends' promptings I couldn't find anything to get excited about in Cream, The Who, Led Zep or anything 'heavy', as they used to call it. I was deeply suspicious of Marc Bolan's sudden interest in electric guitar, and the short write-up I saw in *Disc* about Mike's forthcoming album with a range of international rock musicians wasn't calculated to make a dent on my worthy world. But when I finally bought it, it opened more doors for me than anything I'd heard before or would hear again. It was my favourite album for years, probably still is, and was definitely one of my most formative musical experiences.

But that was to come. Initially, I'd heard it a few times without even recognising it. In my world there was no place at all for any kind of black music – soul, funk, Motown – all the glorious stuff that was going on in the late Sixties and early Seventies went right past me. Although I might tap a foot to whatever Motown singles were in the charts, and even nod sagely when my bass-playing friends pointed out that the bass playing was brilliant, it just wasn't serious music in the sense that progressive rock or folk-rock (or even Donovan!) were music. How could it be when they did those ridiculous dances on TOTP and wore those daft outfits? Like a cleaner at an orgy, I was blank to the funk. So one afternoon I was listening to John Peel and heard that storm of brass and congas groove into Call Me Diamond; I thought 'jazz' and just mentally tuned out, as I did to much of Peel's playlist. Only this time, I happened to tune back in after the song as he was announcing who it was – surely some mistake here? For a moment I wished for a rewind button, but soon thought better of it and marked this down as an aberration I probably wouldn't buy.

My next exposure to it came months later with a sampler for Island Records called *El Pea* – a beautiful production in the days when album sleeve design was approached with a kind of verve and freedom that few have managed with CD jewel cases. I bought this for the String Band's Waiting For You, but enjoyed a few other things on it. An abridged Feast Of Stephen was on that sampler, and although I found it pleasant in a bland sort of way, I had to listen through it many times when I was listening to other tracks on that side. (It was a lot more effort to lift the needle from a record to skip tracks you didn't immediately like, so the 'growers' usually got a chance in those pre-home taping and pre-CD fast-forward days.) It seemed a funny one – you could never quite figure out what it was as a song – no chorus, no repeated sections, no rhyme, then that odd kind of Hey Jude workout at the end with its strange jerk of timing. I don't know how many weeks or months I listened to it in this non-comprehending way until one day, like Hirem Pawnitof, I suddenly saw the point! That was when it became the album I asked for, and received, for my birthday. Thus began my musical education.

In the year that followed I listened to this album as intensely as only a teenager with about ten albums in his possession can. Every track in turn became my favourite track, and I learned – probably exactly as Mike was learning from John Cale at the time – how a rock song can be arranged. In some people's minds this was the 'rock' intrusion that led eventually to the *Ruinous Feud* and the end of the String Band, but for me each song was an opening to a new world of instrumentation and feel, and to new heroes.

Call Me Diamond was probably the first time any of us had ever heard Mike or Robin sound 'professional' – hence my not even noticing it on the radio. A seamless rhythm section with bubbling congas and the first brass arrangement I'd ever really listened to. Mike sounds like he's having the time of his life singing it, and for my money it's probably his best-ever recorded vocal. As I'll have to note later, I think Mike's voice was always at its best when he was shouting, whether on his own songs or as backing vocal to Robin. He seems to hold the pitch better and have a purity of tone that he loses when trying to be 'intimate' on the quieter songs. This was one of the tracks that attracted most interest from the music writers, many of whom made comparisons with Van Morrison – comparisons which, I imagine, must have given Mike confidence to contemplate a career away from the shadow of Robin's artistic stature, in a field in which Robin couldn't or wouldn't want to compete. As for me, it was years yet before I even heard Van Morrison, and when I did I couldn't relate the barking bullfrog I heard there to the joyous outpouring of Call Me Diamond. My favourite shower song, this!

Flowers Of The Forest, like Feast Of Stephen, was a grower, a song that meandered through structure and mood like a forest stream, although it does have that little chorus to return to as a reference point. I watched Mike play it on stage with Stan Schnier on bass following Mike with the fierce concentration of someone who isn't sure where the song's going either. It wasn't till I got the sheet music that I was able to follow, and to appreciate the novelty of, the chords. As an arrangement on record, though, it's a beaut. The classic Mike Heron guitar scrub (also heard at the start of Worlds They Rise And Fall) is supported by fluid and sensitive bass and drums, and exquisite Richard Thompson guitar. Again, my first hearing of Mr Thompson (I don't know why, but Fairport never really interested me before), and it was the first spoke in my wheel as an up-and-coming guitarist who had always thought that no matter how strange a piece of guitar sounds, if you play along enough times, you'll gradually work out how it's done. Hah! Nearly thirty years later, I'm no nearer than I was the day I first heard it to finding even one of Thompson's phrases on this song. I can't even figure out whether he's playing open chords with a capo. What on earth is the man doing, save creating the nearest thing music has ever produced to a prickly bramble bush?

Eroticism cleaves to music in a uniquely sticky way in a teenager's life, and Audrey, with its wonderfully crafted poetry contrasting the snowy street with the warm and quiet bedroom, was the soundtrack of a million fantasies. Especially as the warm harmonium rises and spreads around the line about 'take your clothes off'. Ooo-er Missus! This was the first track to sound like it could be a String Band track, although Robin would probably have asserted himself more on the backing than John Cale; it even had a little mistake in the guitar arpeggio left in, just like a String Band track! Like tracks for artists as far apart as Nico and Nick Drake, it showed off John Cale's ability to choose exactly the right instruments and in the right quantity to catch the essence of a song. I even love the way it begins to fade out just as it finishes – it somehow adds to the satisfaction at the end of the song.

Brindaban was Mike's first recorded string arrangement, with the rather skimpy thanks to Gerard Dott for his 'technical assistance' (but it was my ideas, right?), and again it drew my attention in a studied way to something I'd often heard but taken for granted – string arrangements. The next to grab my attention was Diamond Meadows on T. Rex's self-titled album! Like so many times before, I feel it's a song where Mike's singing doesn't quite do the song justice. I know many feel his inaccuracy is endearing, or just part of the ISB charm, or whatever; but more and more when I listen to the old stuff, I think what a shame – how good it could have been if he or his producers had taken a bit more care. It's not as if Mike was a bad singer – the live shows I remember and the many live tapes I've heard have hardly any flat or clumsy singing – it's just that he seemed to be willing to accept a take that another producer wouldn't have accepted at all. Sixties spirit or surrounded by yes-men? Who knows? For me, Brindaban points the way to the imaginative and exciting string arrangements Mike would score on later albums. The lyric celebrates Krishna and the Gopi milkmaids by the town of Vrindavan in Hindu legend.

Feast Of Stephen is my favourite Mike song and arguably his finest recorded moment alongside Cellular Song. A perfect match of song, writer and arranger, as Cale subtly builds up a Spectorish wall of resonance and magnificence around Mike's evocative and mysterious story. Every time I listen to this recording I notice something new, whether it's the guitar slashes at 'Don't know her name', the delicious staggered drum roll towards the end, or Cale's screams and roars (or is it Mike?) on the fadeout. For someone who'd never really listened to rock drums (sad, eh?), every repetition of the 'fa la' refrain was introduced by a new, different little fill – what an education! One of the live highlights of seeing the band in 1972 was an everyone-on-stage-now version of Feast with, of all people, Robin savaging the drumkit with all the manic glee of Keith Moon and none of the skill! And for a thoroughly challenging cover of this song, get Adrian Whittaker, Deena Omar and me round a piano with a few bottles – or maybe not! Finally, this was the track that sent me to *Paris 1919* and the discovery of the rest of John Cale's heroic repertoire.

Spirit Beautiful – remember when albums came in decent 20-minute chunks and you had to decide whether or not to listen to the other side? Am I the only one who finds most CDs go on too long? Am I really as decrepit as I feel writing this? [*Yes, yes and yes – Ed.*] Well, the Beatles had started their most famous side two with an Indian drone, so why not Mike? Now for me, Within You Without You was the standout track of *Sgt Pepper*, and likewise this was the first *Smiling Men* track I fell in love with; it was a love I was able to sustain for years because of the complexity and subtlety of the mridangam rhythms, always full of surprise and mischief. Just try finger-rapping a couple of jam jars along to it and you'll see what I mean. I remembered hearing the song first on a String Band radio show and liking its 'community singing' feel, but this arrangement, wisely using 'real' musicians rather than band members and friends, makes much more than the sum of the parts.

Warm Heart Pastry was another part of my musical education – the one that showed me what rock guitar, bass and drums were all about. I'm sure there are proper Who tracks that capture their essence as perfectly as this, but I've not heard many. And I prefer Heron's voice to Daltrey's. I remember someone – I think it was Peel – reading out 'Hey, I'm a hungry man and you know I ain't talking bout grits – Look at you, you got a sour lemon stuck where a smile oughta fit', and saying it's not exactly what you expect from the Incredible String Band, is it? And just at the end, as Keith Moon tries to rein in his mad muse for a finish, Cale comes in with his funereal viola and, no doubt, a funereal twinkle in his eye. Imagine if they had got this on *Top Of The Pops*!

Beautiful Stranger was one where the words were more interesting to me than the music. After all, it mentioned breasts. No, it was another lovely little movie-in-song like Feast Of Stephen, a shipwrecked sailor or lost soldier gradually coming round from his fever to the ministrations of a native beauty. The stop-and-start drum rolls became a distraction after a while, but I loved the tinny guitar, delighted for once to hear a guitar on record that sounded like they did when you just plugged them in in real life.

For me, No Turning Back is frustrating, mainly because of some wobbly singing on the opening line, the most vital part of any song. It's frustrating because he sings the rest of it so well, the guitar playing is innovative and the lyric is intriguing. Rose said in her book it was written immediately after Mike's father's death and that casts light on the touching lyric 'So close and so far is a bad way to leave you.'

So that's *Smiling Men*. Now I'm second to none in my admiration for Robin as a poet, composer, singer and cultural force. But if I could take only one Incredibles item to the proverbial desert island with me it would be this one, which gave me so much pleasure and so much inspiration when I most needed it. Thanks Mike!

Cecilia Fage and *Smiling Men*: 'What would Mike Heron do?'

Adrian Whittaker

Growing up in Muswell Hill round the corner from the 'Fairport' house, surrounded by all the much-cherished Sixties albums in her father's LP collection, it might seem inevitable that Cecilia Fage would eventually investigate the ISB – *Hangman*, maybe, or *5000 Spirits*. But when dad finally deemed her trustworthy enough to lend her his records, it was that one with the bloke holding a pineapple on the cover that intrigued her. She became 'sort of obsessed' with Mike Heron and with *Smiling Men* – what appealed was the sheer range of musical styles on the album, coupled with Mike's directness and 'honest and open' approach to his material. Knowing little about Mike's ISB background at the time, she and her then partner created an imaginary 'Mike Heron' figure for whom they would invent scenarios: 'What would Mike Heron do?' became a regular pastime. Feast Of Stephen and, intriguingly, Audrey, were two favourites from the album.

Fast forward a couple of decades and after two albums with Matt Berry, Cecilia joined keyboard/electronica buff Jarrod Gosling to form Cobalt Chapel, a band which *Shindig!* magazine says 'merges otherworldly electronic music with classical and folk-inspired melodies.' Cecilia says some have compared them to Broadcast, another voice/electronica mix formed by the late Trish Keenan, but they remind me of the way Stereolab combined a hauntological backdrop with Laetitia Sadier's direct and unadorned vocal approach.

A Heron/ISB influence is discernible in the storytelling aspect of Cecilia's lyrics on their 2021 album *Orange Synthetic*. These are predominantly dark and rooted in the Yorkshire landscape (Cecilia lives in Calderdale, Jarrod in Sheffield), covering topics ranging from West Yorkshire's first ever rock festival in Krumlin where, says Cecilia 'an almighty storm descended on it, leaving utter destruction: the devastation of the site, and near-deaths from exposure. The promoter was apparently found wandering the moors, days later.'

A 'warped folk song' titled E.B. is, Cecilia says, 'a semi-fictional tale of the farmer who lived in my home decades ago. I have a copy of an old black and white photo of him and his twin, guns cocked over their arms... He eventually met his end, as legend has it, when he was killed by another farmer in a fight over a flock of sheep.'

Cecilia: 'I suppose my lyrics are quite dark but I do think Mike's lyrics have been more of a direct influence – though he writes with a poetic quality I don't have myself! There's a rural feel and connection to nature in his songwriting, like Beautiful Stranger:

Bright the sky above my head
Streaked with red and yellow wing
Warm the mud between my toes
Darkest green the inland trail...

and that mythic quality to his storytelling – like in Feast Of Stephen:

The ladies danced so well, the ladies danced so light
But it was not mortal step
Drew me from my guests to meet the night
Snow lies deep with friends unseen
I will light my eyes to Venus green...

'There's a feel of inhabiting a role or imagined world in each song which I identify with (and how I write lyrics) and in a way it fits with that fictionalised version of him I had in my mind after first finding *Smiling Men* in my Dad's collection – Mike as a character, if that makes sense? Even though he is clearly very much himself, he became this quite mystical figure in my mind. And I love his ability to turn something which could perhaps be ordinary or trite in someone else's hands, to being magical, lyrically. Like in Audrey...

'Over the years, I have also listened to *The Hangman's Beautiful Daughter* and the ISB's themes and that rural, psychedelic, folkloric quality are a big influence on me generally. I wouldn't say the ISB are a direct influence – but they are a band who permeated and influenced so much of what followed them, aren't they?'

2021

One Man's Myrrh

Raymond Greenoaken

Williamson, Williamson & Williamson

A firm of Edinburgh solicitors? Heart of Midlothian's 1972 halfback line? No: that was Robin's own description of *Myrrh*. Unlike Mike's star-spangled solo outing of the previous year, *Myrrh* was to feature Robin playing just about everything: sixteen instruments in total. Janet Shankman and manager Susie Watson-Taylor pitched in here and there, as did roadie and illegal alien Stan Schnier, with Gerry Conway drumming on one track. [*An American, Stan had no work permit for the UK, hence the range of aliases used in album credits. – Ed.*] But essentially it was Williamson, Williamson and Williamson. Roy Wood and Mike Oldfield were no doubt taking careful notes.

Although *Myrrh* wasn't released until the spring of 1972, it seems that Robin had been toying with the idea of a solo album at least a year earlier. Steve Peacock hints that recording had actually begun as early as 1970. The earliest songs laid down for the album, Dark Eyed Lady and Cold Harbour, were both in the ISB concert set that year, so it's not implausible. This suggests that both Robin's and Mike's solo albums were conceived at around the same time, though the main recording sessions for *Myrrh* took place towards the end of 71.

So what, you may reasonably ask? Well, commentators have been tempted to view the two albums in terms of internal ISB politics, and we could easily infer from this that Robin and Mike were both beginning to feel, in the aftermath of *U*, that they were outgrowing the band. It was notable that the *U* album featured an unprecedented number of solo tracks (interestingly, they were mostly Robin's). From there, the step to solo albums was a short and probably inevitable one, for both men.

It's also worth remembering that in 1970 Robin was still in the early stages of his relationship with Janet. His writing reflects this. Sweetly personal love songs, of a kind not heard since First Girl I Loved, were starting to appear. No surprise, then, that so much of *Myrrh* is in this vein: a solo album would have seemed the ideal vessel for such intimate outpourings.

Chalk and cheese

It is, of course, a very different record to *Smiling Men*. Not merely chalk and cheese, the two albums are frost and fire, moon and sun, yin and yang. *Smiling Men* is built from the ground upward, with a solid foundation of bass and drums underpinning most of the tracks. *Myrrh*, by contrast, is for the most part a thing of air; gravity has little dominion over it. The tone of each album, too, is quite different to that of the other. *Smiling Men* oozes heat and sensuousness. You can feel the summer breeze on your cheek in Flowers Of The Forest, and see the river's sun-dazzle in Richard Thompson's guitar; you can taste the humidity in Spirit Beautiful, Brindaban and Beautiful Stranger; you can almost smell the 'dry earth's smell'. Even the two winter songs, Audrey and Feast Of Stephen, are infused with warmth: the doors are shut, the flame well fed with pine.

Myrrh again offers a notable contrast. It's a winter album, a lunar album, in the same way *Hangman* is. It opens into twilight, and proceeds to turn a deeper blue. It takes us through shadowy dreamscapes, across mist-hung moors under horned stormclouds, into the 'colder west' and a hard haven. The yawning expanse of frosty sky on the cover sets the tone; even the multicoloured motley of the Glen Row mummers (including Likky, Johns Gilston and Schofield, Malcolm, Stan Schnier and Janet) seems washed out in the thin sunlight. And the moon is the presiding luminary, picking out the wracked contours of Weir's castle.

Put like that, it sounds like a work of forbidding bleakness, but in fact it's nothing of the kind. *Myrrh* has a delicate inner glow, like a rose unfolding under the snow. The wintry imagery counterpoints exquisitely with the warm intimacy of love. Robin tended to view the women in his life as muses, in the Gravesian or Yeatsian sense, and *Myrrh* is a muse-haunted album, as is *Hangman*. But there's a crucial difference. On *Hangman* she is an immanent goddess, a sort of force of nature (all that is moving is moved by her hands); on *Myrrh* she is a tender human presence.

There is another major difference between the two solo albums – the record label's attitude to each. *Smiling Men* was the first chunk of new product to come from the ISB camp following the move to Island, and the company accordingly gave it a decent budget and slapped full-page ads in all the music weeklies. And would Sir like a gatefold sleeve? No problem. Contrast this with the catchpenny package that was *Myrrh*. The album was shoved out on Island's low-prestige budget label Help, given desultory advertising, confined to a single sleeve even though the cover design begged for a gatefold, and suffered from a poor-quality pressing that turned the mix to sludge and distorted Robin's voice painfully on at least half the tracks. (The CD reissue finally allows us to hear it as he intended.) The message couldn't have been clearer: only diehard devotees need investigate.

The cover concept of *Myrrh* is evidently a joke – but one with a double edge. Robin stands fronded in autumnal bracken on a Glen Row hillside, one arm across his breast, the other gesturing out of the frame, smiling inscrutably. A cavalcade of fantastically garbed communards, attended by a couple of dogs, approach him with palms raised in a sort of gesture of supplication. At first glance it seems simply a piss-take of the *Smiling Men* tableau; in fact, both Robin and his entourage are effecting the postures characteristic of ancient Egyptian tomb art – a conceit that ties in elegantly with the hieroglyphics decorating the inner sleeve and the accompanying quotation from *The Egyptian Book Of The Dead*. The wide, chilly expanse of the sky recalls the classic Earth/Air symmetry of the *Hangman* cover. The cool, hieratic purple of the title lettering is echoed in the colour scheme of the inner sleeve and chimes aptly with the solemn beauty of the songs, the curly typeface providing a visual analogue for Robin's discursive lyrics and melodic flamboyance.

Realms of fantasy

Critical response was mixed. The ever-loyal Steve Peacock reviewed it enthusiastically – 'beautifully crafted', he declared, but added the caveat that 'there's something about [it] that is very distant – you can reach so far into it, yet there is something that keeps you from knowing it completely.' *Disc*'s Rosalind Russell was less sympathetic. 'Tearfully boring... bleating voice... tedious wailing... flat and heavy,' she hissed. 'Without the earthly talents of Mike Heron, Williamson floats off into realms of fantasy that are impossible for anyone else to reach with any kind of musical sanity.' But she liked the chanter on Lord Of Weir... *Melody Maker*, which had given *Smiling Men* generous coverage, ignored *Myrrh* completely.

Initial sales were brisk, but it was clear that the album lacked the crossover potential of Mike's opus. Much play, indeed, was made of the contrast between Mike's earth(l)y, rooted approach and the ethereal, weightless consistency of Robin's oeuvre. 'Heron's Song of the Earth' was a *Melody Maker* headline; 'Robin – the lone cloud in the sky' surmounted an equivalent feature in *Disc*.

Robin must have been stung by this critical obtuseness. 'I was pleased myself with the album,' he confessed to Russell. 'It wasn't done primarily for self-gratification. Obviously I hoped to please other people, so in that way it was done commercially. I like doing these gentle sort of songs – I'm not a heavy singer.' Was that closing remark a veiled reference to Mike's 'rock 'n' roll holiday'?

However frostily it was greeted by certain pundits, I reckon *Myrrh* has worn pretty well over the years. It musters a handful of gorgeous, poignant songs and some beautiful, painterly instrumental textures, as well as one of Robin's most feral and uncompromising performances on record, The Dancing Of The Lord Of Weir, which still sounds pretty radical half a century down the road. It also contains a couple of clinkers that, paradoxically, pointed the way to future triumphs.

Strings In The Earth And Air is a fragile, contemplative opening track – Call Me Diamond it ain't! This is Ivan Pawle's setting of two related poems from James Joyce's little-remembered Georgian period. A cover version was a surprising move, particularly as an opener; nevertheless, it sets the mood exquisitely. A hauntingly lovely melody borne on a cobweb of violins, changing to flutes after Susie Watson-Taylor's delicate solo, a bit of ghostly mandolin at the end. Short but perfectly formed.

Rends-Moi Demain follows. How come we don't hear Robin playing finger-style guitar no more? Here's a reminder of what a tasteful and inventive stylist he could be. Stan Schnier makes his pedal-steel sigh in the spaces behind Robin's sub-Aznavour vocal on this slight but sorbet-sweet composition.

The Dancing Of The Lord Of Weir is a track carefully confected to perplex and offend every middle-brow music pundit in the kingdom. The ISB previewed this on the 71 concert tour, and even recorded it for Radio One's *Sounds Of The Seventies*. Andy Roberts [q.v.] remarks that it sounded like it was being played by people whose idea of music was different from our own, and so it does: it's a mad babel of howling, buzzing, clattering noise with Robin in fruitless search of a tune. But its sheer strangeness thrilled me to the core when I first heard it, and on *Myrrh* he managed to bring it all into focus. Here was Robin tapping into some dark ancestral weirdness in the way that only he can. Even by his own standards, it's an extraordinary vocal performance. He sounds simultaneously like a Moroccan street-singer, a wizened bodach wailing in a Highland cave, and an operatic diva. And it works! The sheer otherness of it all is a towering triumph of bardic inspiration and brass neck. He still hasn't found a tune, but he's stopped looking. How he does it is the only way it can possibly be done: as a chant. Instrumentally, too, it looks to the Otherworld. Primitive percussion, spooky flutes, and the shamanic voices of shenai and jew's harp. The atmosphere of dark enchantment is conjured up with astonishing vividness. Mind you, it could still be improved upon: the bodhran doesn't have to sound like a strip of wet cardboard, and the climactic dance sequence could be extended. But let's just be grateful that Island let it out into the world at all.

Will We Open The Heavens? is a curiously-structured piece, in which the two verses seem like mere interludes in a classically-inflected instrumental. Guitar arabesques flutter over rumbling cellos, flute and oboe wind elegantly about each other. You can almost imagine Robin playing in dickey-bow and tails. Not an instantly memorable song, but one that generously repays repeated listening.

The warm reverie of Heavens is brusquely dispersed by the opening bars of Through The Horned Clouds, a strange, ambiguous song. Robin double-tracks an open-tuned guitar, over which he unleashes an open-throated vocal. A piano clangs out bass chords like a tolling bell. Through The Horned Clouds is a sort of musical analogue of one of the Victorian painter John Martin's storm-wracked Biblical canvases. Clouds moil ominously above precipitous crags; the arrival of a deity is imminent.

The visitant on this occasion – or one of them, since there are at least two ('I see your faces...') – is evidently the female divinity that haunts *Hangman*. Here she's cast as a redemptive feminine power, moving through fire and foam, restoring sight to the (spiritually) blind to pierce the tenebrae of the world's night. But the tender epithets 'dearest child' and 'sweetest fair', contrasting suggestively with the lofty formality of 'Most High', imply she is also manifest in a loved woman – a very Gravesian, very Williamsonian touch. Hers is not the only presence in the song, however. Who is the 'he' of the third verse ('He comes again, she comes again')? The consort of the goddess? Her son, the divine child of European and Near Eastern myth? This, again, is classic Gravesian territory. If Robin is offering an account of personal redemption, I suppose 'he' could conceivably be L. Ron Hubbard – though such a thought would collapse the song into bathos. Even if we dismiss the notion, Horned Clouds is not entirely successful: the mix is murky, Robin's voice seems somehow uncoupled from the backing track, the vocal curlicues are occasionally overelaborated. But it has undeniable power, a richly enigmatic song.

'Gonna make my living on sandy land,' runs the refrain of the American traditional ditty Sally Ann. Robin uses the image as the kernel for a song that seems to revisit the post-industrial desolation of The Mad Hatter's Song. The sandy land, we can suppose, connotes spiritual desiccation or impoverishment. The tumbling, complex imagery of Sandy Land stands in contrast to the generally chaste language used elsewhere on *Myrrh*. The 'urban nightmare' scenario may explain why, alone on the album, it features a rock rhythm section. It's a scorching performance, with Stan

Schnier's banshee pedal steel, Robin's jabbing piano, blaring oboes and whiplash vocal, and Gerry Conway flaying the drumkit with the demonic energy of Keith Moon on Warm Heart Pastry. It's *Myrrh*'s answer to Warm Heart, except that it's here and gone in just over three minutes.

At seven and a half minutes, Cold Harbour is the album's centrepiece, and easily its starkest track: just voice, guitar and echoing space. Another lyric that seems to celebrate the redemptive nature of a woman's love. It's an intense, inward performance, memorable for the way Robin stretches the syllables of the title phrase to the limits of their elasticity, and for an unnerving 'speaking in tongues' central section.

Dark Eyed Lady – more voice-and-guitar simplicity, this is as warm and sun-dappled as Cold Harbour is wintry and crepuscular. Some commentators have felt that the buzzy open-tuned guitar work is a tad untidy. I can't see the problem. Like Mike's guitar on No Turning Back, it's close-miked and naked of studio amelioration; to me, this conveys the honest intimacy of both songs. Should have been the album's closing track, leaving the listener in a Nightfall-esque swoon of honeyed langour. It's followed by a puzzling, inconclusive piece, Dark Dance, which has the feel more of a technical exercise than of a fully-realised composition. Its chief interest lies in the way it prefigures Robin's soundtrack work of a decade later.

I See Us All Get Home is another oddity, which finds Robin in Robot Johnson mode at the piano. On the surface, a simple, bluesy love song; Edward Pope has hinted that it was addressed to the entire Glen Row community, though only verse three would easily admit such an interpretation. It may be significant, therefore, that when Robin revived the song for a later solo CD, *Ring Dance*, he pruned it of the other two verses. The *Ring Dance* version is a majestic, anthemic piece, whereas the *Myrrh* original is pedestrian and strident. The bass runs between verses have a clunky, over-emphatic feel to them, and Stan Schnier's organ sounds like a vacuum cleaner. For all its excellence, then, *Myrrh* splutters out rather limply.

I began this piece by comparing *Myrrh* with *Smiling Men*. I suppose, therefore, I should address the question: which is the better album? The two albums, within their shared generic context (early Seventies singer-songwriter/folk/soft-rock...) are so strikingly dissimilar that, in the end, it comes down to personal prejudice. For myself, I love them both in equal measure. Each succeeds magnificently, for the most part, within its chosen terms. Whimsically, I prefer to see the two albums as the twin components of an 'unofficial' ISB double album: yoked together thus, they'd knock spots off any post-*U* product.

They may have been built to a different plan, but they were both built to last.

The Lord of Weir – A Fairy Story?

Andy Roberts

The Dancing Of The Lord Of Weir is probably the strangest song Robin Williamson ever wrote, both lyrically and musically. Its first public exposure came in October 1971; Robin introduced it with the following:

'Some people hold that fairies are the life or consciousness from anything, like a plant or a small forest, a wind or a sea – the consciousness of natural things. And some people say that fairies are, in fact, legendary memory of a different and non-human race who lived probably in Britain and Europe and possibly survived in remote places until as late as the 15th-17th centuries.' At another gig, Weir was prefaced by:

'This song is another quite new one. I got the idea from hearing this story that a long time ago in Britain there was different races living here apart from human races. There was this race of people who lived in the outlands and in the moors and in the very high places and they were accredited with supernatural abilities and they lived life in a very crude way, herding deer etc. And they were very wild, and they're supposed to have given rise to legends of fairies, and I wrote this song taking that as a viewpoint...' And again from an interview:

'It's a fantasy story about a remote, imaginary past. It's based on the idea that there were actually fairies who were a race of people who lived in wild parts of Britain and were slightly different from ordinary mortals... They lived there for a long time until they eventually got wiped out by persecution.'

An interesting idea and one widely held by many scholars in one form or another, the idea being that rather than the fairies being a 'different and non-human race', they were Neolithic peoples who retreated before the advent of metal users and fled to remote places where they lived simply, often underground in the 'hollow hills', revering the spirits of nature. The country inhabitants knew of their existence but were wary of their ways and magics and left them to themselves. This legend may be the origin of many a medieval 'wild man' story, and several counties have tales of 'Brownies' and the like who came from the hills to help at harvest time, without whose help the harvest would fail and the milk curdle. Further explorations of this idea can be found in the works of Margaret Murray. The William Golding book *The Inheritors* takes a similar angle too, as does John Buchan's story *The Watcher On The Threshold*. The same theme is covered in a poem from early last century which begins: 'Up the airy mountains, down the rushy glen / We daren't go a-hunting for fear of little men / Wee folk, good folk / Trooping all together / Green jacket, red cap / And white owl's feather.'

Suffice to say that folklore was obviously the source of the song and it demonstrates Robin's deep knowledge of and influences drawn from the period where ancient history and folklore overlap; mythic times when deeds became legends and magic was definitely afoot. Weir was certainly an intimation of what was to come with Robin's later focus on Celtic myths and legends.

The song tells the story of how the local lord ('Weir' is an adaptation of an old Scottish word for 'war') gets above his station and steals one of the fairy tribe's women, 'she of the wild eyes, she of the wild hair'. Using their 'small magics' the tribe enter Weir's hall disguised as minstrels and play the fairy dance, compelling the mortals to dance against their will out into the world to be saved only when they think 'one kind thought'. Their kinswoman is rescued and they return to their home beneath the ground.

Weir is, like its subject matter, otherworldly. The instrumentation actually sounds like it's being played by people who have a different concept of music to the rest of us, while Robin's voice wails and skirls the story over the top. The version on *Myrrh* is an outstanding track; it resonates with an incantatory force which reinforces Robin's reputation as a modern bard.

ISB SOUNDMAN AND LATTER-DAY MEMBER STAN SCHNIER RECALLS WORKING ON *MYRRH*

Robin was highly organized and specific. He had a firm grasp of where he wanted the material to venture. The performances were at times whimsical and free but there was no 'let's roll tape and see what we come up with' silliness going on. No rejected material at the end and we did it within a very tight timeframe. However, we did spend a great deal of time exploring ways to create soundscapes, like on the Lord Of Weir we spent hours creating the sound of a distant cannon. This was a large marching bodhran with loosened head lying over the strings of the piano, with me lying on the floor holding down the sustain pedal while Robin hit the drum with an extra soft mallet. And the orchestral feel in Strings In The Earth and Air was mainly multiple layers of softly strummed mandolin and high strung acoustic. Sandy Land was a blast, getting to play with legendary Gerry Conway!

Overleaf Likky on stage. (Rose Simpson collection)

Chapter Nine

Liquid Acrobat, *Earthspan*, Likky, *No Ruinous Feud* – and Gerard Dott!

At some point between Christmas and New Year 1970/71, Rose made up her mind to leave, as she explained for Fitting Pieces To The Jigsaw:

Rose: 'By the end of what turned out to be my final US tour with the ISB, Mike, Robin and Licorice were absolutely committed to Scientology and, without actually confronting me about it, had made it clear that things couldn't go on as they were. I had to join them wholeheartedly in the Scientological endeavour, share their enthusiasm for it and embrace the lifestyle it demanded. We all went back to Scotland for Christmas together but I was miserable with the whole state of affairs, and tormented by the insecurity of a whole life now hanging on a belief system which I disliked. I couldn't see any way out of it except a whole change of life, so I walked out on all of it before a New Year got going and carried me along with it. I don't think anyone, not even me, knew I was going to leave. In the same way I had drifted into the ISB, it just happened. I didn't discuss it or notify them, just went. If Joe Boyd had been around, I would have talked to him, but he wasn't... I tried to never look back and, in general, I succeeded.'

The ISB slowly realised that Rose wasn't going to come back, either to Glen Row or to the band. Rose: 'I don't quite know how the information got through to them, probably via their personal manager Susie Watson-Taylor who, like Joe, was someone I would talk to a bit.' The ISB had a spring tour lined up and desperately needed a replacement. Richard Thompson had said no, but Ivan Pawle, a friend of theirs for years and a good all-round musician, was the obvious choice. He was then back in Dublin, rehearsing with Tim Booth and Terry and Gay Woods, who'd just joined the Strangelies to replace Tim Goulding. One evening at the Sandymount Orphanage, Ivan was summoned to the phone.

Ivan: 'After we had started rehearsing, I got a call – I think it was from Mike Heron – asking would I be interested in joining the ISB to replace Rose. I was seriously torn, but the fact was that I had already agreed to the Terry and Gay arrangement. So that's what decided me. I don't believe in what-ifs! It was a difficult choice, one of the hardest decisions I have ever had to make. But, there you go. In retrospect it was probably the right choice.'

New boy Malcolm Le Maistre, like Ivan, was already part of the Glen Row family:

> 'Likky and Susie came round and said Mike and Robin would like to see you. And then they asked me to join the band. It was really, really a shock... I didn't believe it. I'd been suggesting they got Krysia Kocjan in to replace Rose. I was not a musician – I'd written a few songs, including a 20-minute epic about the changing seasons! – but I didn't really understand why they wanted me in the band: I didn't play anything!
>
> They said we'll teach you – and that's what they did! For the next three months, I was sweating my guts out learning five or six instruments, so when it came to my first performance I *looked* like a multi-instrumentalist – the audience just didn't realise I could only play one thing on each instrument!'

A real turning-point

Adrian Whittaker

In Spring 1971 a number of things converged for the ISB, marking a real turning-point in their career. Joe, having left for the US, was no longer their manager and producer, leaving the band much more in charge of the artistic decisions. The *U* production problems and the stressful all-night *U* recording sessions had reflected the decline in Joe's power to provide the kind of musical/career guidance and support he had provided to the ISB and his other bands such as Fairport Convention. For better or worse, his departure left the band more in charge of its own destiny and consequently increasingly dependent on the more rigid support structures provided by Scientology. This was reinforced by the fact that new manager Susie Watson-Taylor had rapidly also become a Scientologist. Rose's departure loosened the link with the old *Wee Tam* free-form era, and Malcolm's membership provided a third lead vocalist with a rockier vibe.

As part of Joe's leaving deal with Chris Blackwell, the ISB were assigned to Island Records. This meant a greater responsibility to the label in terms of recording budgets, previously extremely flexible in the Witchseason set-up. The growing pressure to be more 'commercial' in the 70s came from both Susie (and probably Mike) and from the label, who grew increasingly disaffected with their wayward charges, hoping instead for an outfit that was tight, glam, and with a few hit singles. The 'tight' aspect was gradually taken on by Mike; *Smiling Men* had given him a taste for using well-established guests and session players rather than doing it all in-house. No more Rose on bass, of course, and Likky would never play drums again. The 'glam' aspect fell to Malcolm, and eventually his At The Lighthouse Dance was earmarked as a potential hit single. But we're getting ahead of ourselves here...

Liquid Acrobat As Regards The Air

Liquid Acrobat *was released in October 1971. It's generally considered the best of the ISB Island-era albums; it actually made the top 50 at the time on the back of some very positive reviews. Below, Andy Roberts dissects this 'pivotal' album.*

Lying between the faded hippiedom of *Be Glad* and the arrangements of *Earthspan*, *Liquid Acrobat* marked a watershed in the ISB career, following which the 'old' String Band was gone, almost forever. But *Acrobat* holds the balance perfectly between a pure acoustic/folk sound and the electrification which was to be the String Band's lot until their demise. Drums were brought in for three tracks, courtesy of Gerry Conway, and serious electric guitar began to emerge on tracks such as Painted Chariot and Dear Old Battlefield, the two main contenders for the ISB's admission fee to the world of rock music.

The String Band could folk, we knew that, but could they rock? Or was it that they had no choice? Remember, this was 1971, you just couldn't get away any more with sitting around with a bunch of weird instruments on a Persian carpet singing twenty-minute songs about the problematic size of amoebas. Heron's foray into solo-album land with *Smiling Men* had obviously left him with a taste for rock that was to grow, and his early influences and times with bands such as 'Rock Bottom and the Deadbeats' were coming through again to rival Robin's more whimsical notions and looser song structures. The band was moving with the times, and whether they should have entered the rock arena or just played on in the car park outside is one of the hottest debates in String Band-dom.

Acrobat was the first ISB album not to be produced by Joe Boyd; the sleeve credits 'Incredible String Band and Stan Schnier' with the production chores. The sound is crystal clear, with everything placed just-so in the mix.

A note from the co-producer

Stan: I had started doing the ISB live sound in March 1971 and had a fantastic relationship with both Mike and Robin.

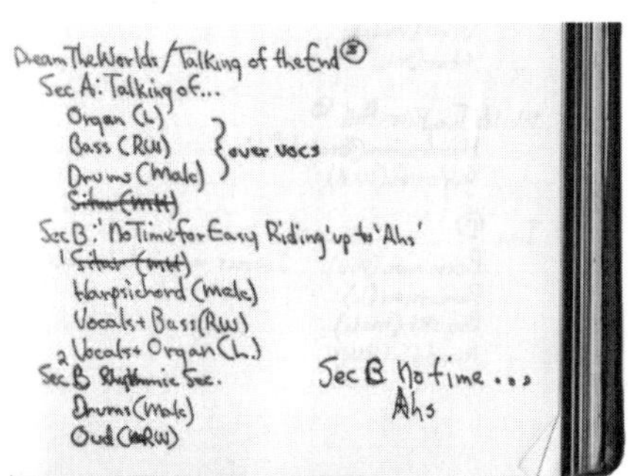

Stan's production notebook, detailing an unused sitar part for Talking Of The End.

They were not too savvy on the use of mics, or electronica in general and I seemed to be a bridge to that world, at least in part, and so when they headed into Sound Techniques without Joe Boyd, they asked if I would help them in the studio. Of course, I was thrilled. I had not worked in a recording studio, so I felt it made sense to keep notes of who played what on which song, which was complex especially since we only had 12 tracks and a rather small mixing console. I used my little sketchbook that I used to carry in my pocket, a leftover from my art school days. With all the changes on a song like Talking Of The End it was quite a job to keep track of everything....and during the mix-downs, there were usually three or four of us, all moving faders and equalizers, rehearsing the moves, remixing, back and forth.

Back to Andy: Some people have complained that it's a trifle clinical sounding, and compared to the live stuff so it is, but overall it's better than most of its time. The album title seems, like many of the other titles, to have been of Robin's devising: 'It was to do with music, flute music I think'.

The album opens with Talking Of The End, a song about getting one's act together, both personal and planetary: 'better start to live before you start to die'. It is virtually split into two parts: the second half is a sitar-backed paean to the earth, with some lovely harmonies from Likky. The String Band concept of the human organism being part of a living, breathing earth (a theory developed well before today's wet new-agers) still lives on here. Amoebas are still very small but they're learning how to think! A contemporary live tape from a New York gig features a beautifully sung coda which unfortunately never made it to the finished album.

Dear Old Battlefield, about re-incarnation, may well have been influenced by Williamson's growing interest in Scientology, with the 'magic man who finally led me out of the wood' a direct reference to L. Ron Hubbard [*see Gil Murray's Scientology article for more on this – Ed.*]. Whatever its origins, Battlefield is an atmospheric piece marched along well by Conway's military precision drumming, underpinned by Heron's lead guitar and led strongly by Williamson's voice. Incidentally, it was the favourite ISB song of Gorky's Zygotic Mynci, who were at one time considering a cover version.

Cosmic Boy, a joint Heron/McKechnie song, however, may have proved too much for some people. Is it just a quaint, high pitched, plinky-plonky love song or a genuine, heartfelt tribute to Likky's beau? I don't know. Some days I can really enjoy it, others it grates appallingly. A song of its times perhaps. This is followed by Worlds They Rise And Fall, one of Heron's strong, well-sung homages. Simple, direct and to the point, Worlds... is moving and reverential – 'sometimes it's all I can do is bow to her'. Evolution Rag evolved from one of Robin's dreams and is a Bonzo-esque ragtime romp through evolution with that added extra Darwin just hadn't thought of. One of the many ISB 'fun' songs, you either like it or loathe it. The uncredited instrumental part here is Dallas Rag, associated with the Dallas String Band, who recorded it in the 1920s.

Side One ends with Painted Chariot. What's it about? You tell me. Organised religion? The acid experience ('look here sonny can't you see it's real as pain?')? Or were Robin and Mike into archaic transportation renovation? Whatever the case it's a fitting side closer, with icy guitar picking leading into this most curious of songs. The idea of the 'coachman' and 'chariot' seems to be a vaguely Eastern idea, Indian perhaps, to do with the apparent nature of reality being just, after all, an illusion – the whole thing being just a 'painted chariot'. Heron's voice throughout sounds distant and slightly world-weary; desperate to get us not to 'trust that coachman', the band chorus that it's 'only' a painted chariot, then comes an odd churchy bit in the middle and the song builds into some serious rocking, which is just beginning to roll when it ends. String Band at their rock and roll best – should've been much longer. A powerful side closer, I always found Painted Chariot an eerie, unsettling, almost frightening song.

The evolution theme continues to Side Two which offers us Adam And Eve – human creation put to a bright reggae beat. You can singalongaRobin to it, it has an ace whistle solo by Malcolm and unlike later ISB 'fun' songs it actually works and has some great guitar work from Robin. Red Hair is another of Heron's powerfully sung, direct love songs. Robin's cello and Mike's harmonium conspire and build with Likky's pipe organ to a resounding but short crescendo in which love is perceived as a physical force ('sometimes it seems the only things real are what we are and what we feel'). Again, perhaps a reference to the illusory nature of the senses, harking back to Maya from *Wee Tam And The Big Huge*. The flaws of perception were always dear to the String Band's heart. Here Till Here Is There features excellent recorder work and vocals split between Robin and Likky, giving it a medieval, courtly feel.

Liquid Acrobat *was generally very well received upon its release. This review, from* Melody Maker, *gives a flavour of what was being said:*

'The Incredibles can take an idea and transform it into song in a way that would be roundly condemned if attempted by anyone else... They turn fragments into foundations with quick-witted appreciation of the worth of some phrase or riff. Their originality...never seems to be forced...The album begins on one high note and ends on another. To begin with there is an imaginative concoction of ideas and sound called Talking Of The End. When the end is reached it reveals Darling Belle, which must be the band's version of Oh What A Lovely War! The tracks starts in a sober romantic style, but some good vocal combinations, Malcolm Le Maistre's glockenspiel and the orchestral arrangement instil bitterness into the superficially simple lyrics... Likki sings solo on Cosmic Boy but her words and Mike Heron's music don't really hold the interest with the power of [its] companion tracks. After the reggae beat of Adam And Eve, Mike Heron gives a rare demonstration of the full extent of his lead vocal capabilities with Red Hair. Also included is a series of jigs...Unfortunately [Robin's] fiddle playing is not all that it could be. His phrasing is awkward. At least it is the only setback on the album.'

Tree is next, revived from the first album, but standard fare, as are the Jigs which follow, with only Williamson's Eyes Like Leaves standing out among the other three 'trad' compositions. The album closes with the magnificent Darling Belle, of which more shortly.

Tapes from the Spring tour of 1971 show the band trying the material out on stage, breaking in new member Malcolm Le Maistre and generally having lots of fun prior to the August recording sessions. Malcolm: 'I remember playing the church organ on Darling Belle in a church over the road from the studio – that was a hell of an experience. Anyone could've played what I played but I got elected to do it – Robin's on his hands and knees under my legs playing the foot pedals with his hands, I'm playing the keyboard, Mike's back in the hall somewhere trying to make sure the sound's all right...' Stan's production notes reveal that it was originally intended to record the Royal Festival Hall (or 'a cathedral') organ for this, but budgets won out.

Several of the soon-to-be *Acrobat* tracks were aired on the BBC in March 71 (now to be found on the *In Concert* CD), and they show the material already polished, with both playing and singing being top notch.

Personal likes and dislikes aside, all the songs are of startling quality, and none more so than the piece de resistance, Williamson's Darling Belle. Robin ranks Darling Belle as one of his major songs (the others being Pictures In A Mirror, Queen Of Love, Creation and Invocation) and explained in an interview:

'I wrote Darling Belle very quickly; or rather, wrote it down very quickly. I was lying in a hotel room in Rotterdam just before I fell asleep, and I began to hear these voices outside my head, and they were telling the story of Belle and James. Two voices, a man and a woman, and of what they said I jotted down fragments and the following morning I wrote parts of the song; about four months later I wrote the rest. It only lasted a few moments.'

Belle and James are childhood friends, would-be sweethearts from an Edwardian childhood who lose touch, only to meet again at a society ball, finding companionship again this time in a sexual encounter and a swift and short marriage brutally ended when James is sent to France to die in the trenches. Belle is left to wander, statusless, 'migrant guest from relative to in-law', with only her memories for company. Shot through with a melancholy not found before or since in the String Band's work,

Darling Belle is a plaintive hymn to lost childhood (a recurrent String Band theme), the futility of war ('sits in her brother's widow's house' speaks volumes of the widespread slaughter of the First World War) and the pain of lost love. To hear Licorice intone 'aura like a daffodil', particularly on the *In Concert* version, is to know true sadness.

As an artefact alone the album sleeve is a delightful period piece. The back cover has a photograph of the band looking wistful. It's reminiscent of a photograph you might find in an old person's house – Belle's perhaps – a fading memorial to an age past; perhaps appropriate in the light of the change in direction future albums were to take.

The String Band took the *Liquid Acrobat* material out on the road in the autumn and the album reached the dizzying chart heights of No. 46 in October (the peak of the tour). It was to be the last time they had an album in the charts. If not the best, then one of the most indispensable String Band albums and a pivotal moment in the ISB's career.

Updated 2021

Onstage at Bardney festival, 1971. (Raymond Greenoaken collection)

THE LIQUID ACROBAT COVER

The cover shots and inner gatefold photographs for *Liquid Acrobat* were taken at Horsburgh Castle, though Robin called it Horsburgh Keep, which is probably a more accurate term. Overlooking the River Tweed, it is situated to the south of the A72 Peebles to Innerleithen road, about two and a half miles from Peebles. Built by the Horsburgh family on the site of an earlier castle in the mid-1550s, it was one of a chain of castles running down the Tweed valley. It was a ruin by the early 19th century; the photo here dates from the 1890s. When living at Glen Row, band members would have driven past it dozens, if not hundreds, of times on their way to Peebles or Edinburgh. The trees shown on the sleeve are no longer there and the surrounding area is now developed; Cardrona, once just a tiny railway station, a farm and a few cottages a little further down the road, now boasts a substantial executive housing estate, a golf course and a hotel. GH

Into The Embers

Bob Nutbein offers a critique of Robin Williamson's Darling Belle.

papa would take me to the park to see the swans
by hansom cab trotting so high
holding his hand to see the swans
hissing louder than rustling dresses of gracious ladies bustling by

see swan ships come sailing in
white as the clouds on a windy day

James I suppose would be in school
James I suppose would be in school
I was I was learning to spell
laughing at loud smells
avoiding the rod of the codfaced master
was it your absence made me quiet at noon
playing British bulldogs on the gravel
was it your presence coloured my dream
I burrowed in cupboards like a mole all Saturday
under old chairs and old ladies knees
I framed your half remembered face
with frail white embroideries
calling to you down the mousey garden
calling to you down the mousey garden

o did you meet him at the ball?
eighteen years on
tall soldier now and you full grown
Belle did you meet him at the ball

o do you remember me
thin girl with cold hands
you in your scarlet and you knew my name
step to the veranda under the wisteria
in mysterious November

dancing as if with death or fate
to the moon black ballroom
of the silk skinned lake
kissing me you lifted my skirt
under the willow trees

keep the home fires burning
though your heart is yearning
though the boys are far away
they dream of home
there's a silver lining
in the dark clouds shining
turn that lining inside out
till the boys come home

o did I see you march to the train
did I cry was my nose red
my two-day bride can you feel me in your memory
I will be the redness in your iron fire
how could I write
my words would seem sad or gay
we regret to inform you
we regret to inform you

meet me by gaslight in dark dawn
on Waterloo Bridge we will walk arm in arm
hearing the leaves fall with a whisper into the foggy dew
when we are dead
when we are dead

now she sits in her brother's widow's house
skin like a lizard aura like a daffodil
migrant guest from relative to in-law
she stares into the embers and remembers

The lyrical structure of this song is essentially dramatic, consisting of a series of internal monologues in the first person, thus conveying a confessional sense of intimacy. Cleverly interleaved with this is the Keep The Home Fires Burning sequence, invoking the wartime milieu, and a final third person narrative stanza, acting as a coda, which neatly rounds off the song.

The song incorporates elements of the poetical format popularised by Robert Browning, known as the 'Dramatic Monologue', wherein imaginary characters reveal their inner thoughts in a first person narrational mode. Darling Belle may be viewed more precisely as a kind of dramatic duologue, as the two primary protagonists, Belle and James, each have 'in-character' speaking parts. The opening section is also reminiscent of *A Portrait Of The Artist As A Young Man* in that it employs the Joyceian device wherein the speaker (or, as here, the singer), in taking the character of the story's heroine, uses an appropriately simplistic vocabulary and childish diction.

The simple choice of the word 'papa' instead of daddy is a hint of social and period colouring reinforced by the song's title. Both 'Belle' and 'papa' are slightly quaint, old-fashioned nomenclature, 'Darling Belle' suggesting also that our heroine is a child of privilege – highborn, well bred and born into a degree of affluence. Belle certainly seems a cherished, if not pampered, little darling. The opening at once creates a charming picture of childish innocence and wonderment.

The detail of the hansom cab establishes the song's period time-setting, and Belle's well-to-do background – she and her father don't have to walk to the park. Belle as a tiny girl feels proud and excited to be so high up from the ground – reinforcing her smallness of stature – and enjoys the trotting of the horse ride.

The reiteration of the phrase 'to see the swans' within the space of three lines reveals to us that, for this little girl, the swans form the real highlight of this memory. 'Would take me' is a phrase implying some degree of paternalistic indulgence (i.e. this was not an isolated visit), as well as, by its past tense, setting the tone of retrospection and reminiscence which characterises the whole song – fragments of memories juxtaposed within a sophisticated yet naturalistic framework.

To a small child who doesn't really understand the adult world, life can seem like a bustling hurly-burly. Belle enjoys the high vantage of the cab, but holding her father's hand emphasises her smallness and vulnerability. Notice the dynamics of this opening verse and the string of onomatopoeic action verbs employed: take – trotting – hissing – rustling – bustling. From Belle's diminutive viewpoint, the world seems to be a noisy, interesting yet formidable place. Might the setting be London's Hyde Park? Do the swans hiss at Belle? She nevertheless finds them interesting and attractive. The ladies bustling by in their long period dresses seem very highborn and aristocratic, and although 'gracious' they are too engaged in their own concerns to pay much attention to the little girl. This small detail is to find a more poignant resonance in the final verse, where Belle is aged and once more finds herself overlooked and neglected by others. It is also mirrored in James – likewise diminutive and (literally) overlooked by the busy adult world, burrowing under old ladies' knees. The alliteration and assonance (Hansom – holding his hand – hissing), together with the internal rhymes, convey a sense of vivacity and energy.

Codfaced master by Steve Small.

The alliterative sibilant sounds in 'See swan ships come sailing in...' confer an impressionistic sense of the elegance of the swans, and their apparently effortless progress. The swans seem proud and majestic as sailing ships. Their whiteness represents the purity and innocence of childhood. Our imaginary camera now pans from the whiteness of the swans upwards to the whiteness of the passing clouds. The wind moves the swans and the clouds as wind would move sailing ships. Now Belle's thoughts drift to her childhood sweetheart: 'James I suppose would be in school...'

This line, sung (slightly inappropriately) by Malcolm, marks a transition in the song. We deduce that James is slightly older than Belle, who still enjoys pre-school leisure for park visits. Now the measured strumming of the acoustic guitar, with an inventive bass-line bubbling beneath, makes the music more muscular and masculine. An organ undercurrent is subsequently added, as James'/Robin's voice now eagerly takes up the story: 'I was, I was learning to spell / Laughing at loud smells' and the last word, being so cheekily stretched, perhaps itself mimics the farting sound. 'Loud smells' is a euphemistic phrase in which Robin adroitly 'devastates our synaesthesia'. Thus James immediately characterises himself as an exuberant, playful and mischievous child in the setting of a prim and fairly authoritarian Victorian school. Blunt internal rhymes ('rod' and 'cod') divulge the games of mutual enmity between schoolboy and pedagogue. The marvellous epithet 'codfaced' conveys unsmiling, mirthless vigilance.

James, in his busy and strictly ordered day, also finds time to think fondly of Belle, missing her companionship – which suggests that they have not long been separated. British Bulldogs – if you didn't know – is an ebullient childhood game in which a wave of boisterous boys make repeated charges from safe base to safe base (usually from wall to wall across a playground), attempting to avoid being tagged by an adversary in the middle ground. With each successive charge the bulldogs' number diminishes as runners caught then join the catcher, the last surviving bulldog being deemed the winner.

A neat verbal antithesis now follows: 'your presence coloured my dream'. Just as Belle's absence makes James sadly quiescent, her presence enriches his imagination. From the slow, fragile delicacy of the opening with wistful glockenspiel and flute, the music now gets into a stridently rhythmical phase.

Belle's little girl status was underlined earlier; James' smallness is illustrated in terms of size and height as he crawls burrowing like a mole 'under old chairs and old ladies' knees'. The repetition of 'old' emphasises childhood's subservience to an established and venerable social order.

The next two lines operate on both a literal and metaphysical level – although the feminine embroideries might more appropriately pertain to Belle rather than James (perhaps they represent a childish gift?). To decorate a photograph of her with lace shows James' fond and romantic nature, or – if the embroideries are mental – means that he fills gaps in his memory imaginatively. Within the song's context, time is moving remorselessly on – already having half-stolen Belle's face from his memory. The whiteness of the embroideries again underlines childhood's purity and innocence. Embroideries are beautiful products of attentiveness and care – but also frail as memories.

The syllables of 'garden' are emotively elongated: this conjures further images of childhood play. 'Mousey' is an unusual yet apt epithet to apply to a garden, effective in showing it as an exciting place for children to play. 'Mousey' has undertones of seclusion and perhaps also of shyness (Belle is a thin girl with cold hands – perhaps lacking in self-confidence). The repetition of 'calling to you' indicates a yearning – a spiritual reaching out which is the true synthesis of the song as a whole. The heartfelt elongation of the syllables meaningfully reinforces this sensibility. It is noteworthy how Robin, Mike and Malcolm, by sharing the vocals, reinforce different time-phases in the skilfully conjoined sectionality of the song. Malcolm's line 'O did you meet him at the ball' reflects a subtle shift in the narrational stance, being addressed to Belle, the third person 'him' referring to James. The childhood sweethearts are evidently separated and lose touch.

We now move into adulthood, and learn that James is a tall soldier now, and Belle full grown, eligible and nubile, meeting James at a ball – a formally structured social engagement. The insistence of the repetition ('Belle did you meet him...') makes the last line of this segment ring as though echoing in Belle's subconscious years later. The music now shifts back

Above 'I burrowed in cupboards...' (Steve Small)

to the slow, wistful delicacy of the opening, with reflective glockenspiel, as the reunited pair reminisce. Belle displays a charming modesty and vulnerability, surprised that he still remembers their sweet bond.

The past tense 'knew my name' takes us further into the future, as Belle is here reflecting upon this reunion from a future vantage. Robin plays cleverly with tenses, and effectively conjures a mood of romantic intimacy. Diction such as 'veranda' and 'wisteria' maintains the grandiose period milieu, as the sweethearts move away from the social swirl of the ball to be alone together. 'Mysterious November' I have always considered to be a marvellously evocative phrase, conferring images of autumn mistiness, and the polysyllabic internal rhyming is impressive.

'Dancing as if with death or fate' carries a sinister echo of the medieval 'danse macabre' – but this is a magical time that reverberates down the years with a vivid intensity. The lovers dance in new-found intimacy, but their future is somehow foreshadowed, as if their destinies are predetermined. This is a potent image, and lends a tragic stature to their love story.

'The moon black ballroom of the silk-skinned lake' is portentous language – but rightly so, as the episode subsequently becomes one of the most treasured of her life. Our impression of the house and gardens, incidentally, is one of elegance and upper-class privilege. To muted guitar accompaniment the lovers slip away to the privacy of the nocturnal gardens.

The lake is a ballroom – its smooth surface is likened in a compact metaphor to a dance floor, its surface, unrippled, seeming like a skin made of silk. Effective alliteration makes this a sententious and memorable line. 'Moon black' sounds strange, but the lake is dark but for the reflection of the moon. Now a breathless, hushed intimacy is evoked in the subtle interplay of oboe and guitar.

The sudden physical passion and new depth of their adult relationship is conveyed with delicacy and economy. The willow trees provide seclusion, but the bell-like shape of the willow's overhang also reflects Belle's voluminous skirts. This stanza moves us from the simplicity of Belle as she was – innocent thin girl with cold hands – into womanhood, through images of romance and opulence – veranda, ballroom, silk-skinned lake – back to the couple themselves, caught in an act of secret intimacy. Robin's poetical sweep is almost cinematographic. (He has attributed his inspiration for the song's composition to a dream he had, and this is reflected in the fluid, episodic structure.) There is a suitable pause at the end of the stanza, and this hiatus marks another transition, from love to the intervention of war.

The wartime song Keep The Home Fires Burning served to maintain morale in much the same way as Vera Lynn's propagandistic anthems during the Second World War. Its interleaving is effective as it places Belle's and James' situation in its wider context: they are one of the many couples separated by the conflict. Robin, Malcolm and Mike sing together in a music hall style, and banjo and clarinet accompany the singalong with a stirring jocularity that is eminently apt. Belle has been left to keep the fire of her love burning whilst James, mobilised, is far away, dreaming of home. The song's insertion is an (ironic) appeal to remain optimistic. Note how the metaphorically threatening 'dark clouds' have now taken the place of the white clouds mentioned earlier in the song. Unfortunately, the hollow optimism of the 'silver lining' is, for Belle and James, to prove illusory. A stridently strummed guitar now prefigures the remorseless march of events, as the next stanza represents an imaginary colloquy between the lovers.

Belle's self-deprecating humility is part of the charm of her characterisation – ashamed of her tears at their parting, as James takes the train that leads him away to 'dance with death or fate'. She fears her red-nosed tearfulness may have vitiated his parting image of her – the last time he was to see her. (They part as man and wife.) 'Can you feel me in your memory?' could be James' ghost speaking to Belle as she keeps the flame of her love alive whilst she stares into the embers.

James' explanation for not writing reveals a dilemma: to express his heartache at their separation would have increased her sadness, but by putting on a show of cheerfulness, he might have deceived her into believing that he was not truly concerned. In a masterstroke of economy, James' death in action is now revealed to us in five simple words – repeated in an eerie interplay of expressionless monotone voices: 'We regret to inform you' – the opening phrase of the standard notification that she, like so many others, has become a war widow.

The next segment ('Meet me by gaslight') features glorious vocal harmonies between Robin and Likky, to a piano accompaniment. (This piece still thrills me to the core after 30-odd years of listening.) 'Gaslight' is part of the skilful layering of period details maintained throughout. 'Dark dawn' is a splendidly alliterative phrase evoking an atmosphere of desolation and gloom – of Belle wandering sorrowfully in reminiscence. James' death does mark a new dawn for his widow – but holding none of the optimism usually associated with the word. The 'Waterloo Bridge' line recalls for me the old film of the same name starring Robert Taylor and Vivienne Leigh, in which it is however the heroine who dies there, believing her husband killed in the war, and

Taylor who sorrowfully retraces their steps over the bridge. The phrase 'arm in arm' I suppose represents the figurative triumph of love over death – Belle's retreat into the past leaving only memories and dreams for comfort. The 'leaves fall' in another 'mysterious November' where the atmosphere is one of silence and reverential intensity. The falling of the leaf is itself symbolic of death and change – the 'whisper', as well as the sound of the leaf, could also be James speaking to Belle in her imagination.

Echoed in the stately solemnity of the churchy organ which follows 'when we are dead' is a hint that this ghostly rendezvous is a prefiguration of the lovers' only hope of a reunion – in the afterlife. The last segment of the song is a spoken postscript – reinforcing the tragedy with its aftermath. Belle has clearly remained a widow for the rest of her life – holding her lover's memory sacred, and remaining faithful to it.

Belle now lodges with her sister-in-law – and what a deliberately offhand description of her circumstances: at twice remove. The song has taken us all the way from Belle's girlhood to her twilight senescence, where she's left dependent and lonely. Belle resides with another widow – not in any truly social sense, but merely 'in her...house'. Her sister-in-law by implication is not a particularly willing hostess – merely tolerating Belle as a matter of familial obligation – and then only on a temporary basis as she is shunted back and forth between people with whom she feels no real bond of friendship.

The way the two final similes are spoken in polyphony creates a hubbub of whispery voices around her, from which Belle remains apart and excluded – echoing her social circumstances – as if she is being spoken about behind her back.

Robin doesn't tell us merely that Belle is now old: the first simile shows her wrinkled and physically atrophied, couched in an image at once slightly unpleasant and uncomplimentary – as if Belle is being viewed with scarcely concealed repugnance by her relatives. Beneath the veneer of social convention which obliges them to provide for her, they probably resent her as a guest. It is a very poignant picture with which to end. The phrase 'aura like a daffodil' I find haunting – disturbingly evocative. Belle may also resemble a lizard by reason of her immobility: 'She sits... She stares...'. Impassive and withdrawn, she yet maintains an aura – her real world being her inner world of memory and retrospection, in which she appears isolated, transfixed, and yet self-contained. Even if there is little dignity in her social dependence, she nevertheless appears to maintain an inner sense of resignation and calmness, which is the only vestige of dignity to which she has recourse. Even the yellowness of the daffodil seems apposite: an image of gentleness and fragile delicacy, the colour possibly also referring to Belle's pallid complexion.

Her thoughts are enclosed, and she has turned inwards, returning to the past, staring immobile into the redness of the iron fire. The song ends on a resonant, lingering organ chord which perfectly summarises the scene. With a cyclic neatness, the song has encapsulated her life – from the vibrant, vivacious images of childhood life (trotting/hissing/rustling/bustling) to a silent immobility of shrunken introspection. Belle, like the daffodil, has had her brief flowering – cut tragically short, yet still immeasurably precious, to be treasured in the silence of her heart.

Revamping the live show

Adrian Whittaker

Following Rose's departure, the planned Spring 1971 UK tour was rescheduled and once Malcolm had settled in, the band spent May touring the States. They returned to play a one-day folk festival at Tupholme Manor Park, Lincoln alongside Pentangle, James Taylor and The Byrds, followed by some European dates. By the time they started the major *Liquid Acrobat* tour in October, they had rethought their set.

Once the tensions caused by the North American collapse of *U* had subsided, and with Malcolm now a permanent band member, Robin was able to reconnect with his theatre and mime enthusiasms. The autumn 1971 tour showcased two such pieces, but with Mike now liberated from any compulsion to dress up, often safely ensconced as 'The Storyteller' at a huge lectern. A November 71 *Melody Maker* review informs us Mike narrated a 'witty sketch of the lives of John Codswallop (Robin) and Henry Borisbrick (Malcolm) watched over by an angel (Licorice).' Another reviewer commented that the 'ineptitude' in the sketch 'was more than compensated for by a genuine humour and good heartedness.'

The mime piece Poetry Play Number One, which, also according to *Melody Maker*, was 'a silent representation of pictures in a poetic form' (eh?) was also debuted on the tour. Mike, supported by Stan Schnier and Susie Watson-Taylor, provided the pre-taped background music. Raymond Greenoaken caught an October 1971 gig at Newcastle City Hall: 'At the end of How We Danced The Lord Of Weir everybody trooped offstage, leaving the audience to work out whether what they'd heard was music in the normal sense of the word. A Revox tape machine was placed near the front of the stage, and after a while a big reel of quarter-inch tape began whirring round and strains of rather impressionistic music filled the auditorium. Out came Malcolm, Robin and Likky clad more or less identically in loose charcoal-grey tops and knee-breeches, and proceeded to unfold a series of dancey-mimes (or mimey-dances) straight out of Lindsay Kemp repertory: waking from sleep, peeling back invisible curtains, firing arrows from a longbow, all knitted together in a very loose narrative. You could tell at a glance that Malcolm was the professional and Robin and Likky the eager novices. Mike, as always with these on-stage divertissements, stayed well out of the action. At the end I asked my companion, who had a background in mime and modern dance, her opinion. "Not bad," she said.'

For the tour, props were made by various Glen Rowers and Stan cooked up some kind of witch's cauldron effect for onstage use. The Revox master-tape has long since disappeared, but for *Tricks Of The Senses* I found the original multi-tracks, recorded at Craighall Studios in Edinburgh, and Ben Wiseman and I used them to create a collage of the more interesting bits, which were labelled Flute Tune/The Archers/Man Swimming/Faery Tune/Looking For A Face In The Crowd. The sections we didn't use were Card Game, Flee and Aggravation, which were all very sketchy. Mike's on piano, guitar and vocalisations, with Susie on flute and Stan on bass and percussion. Neither Robin nor Malcolm can remember much about the content, though Robin remembers that the initial flute piece was used for scene changes. The Archers section is scary; on the original tapes Mike can be heard instructing his musicians to sound 'more voracious.' Faery Tune is actually four overdubbed electric pianos à la Terry Riley. Looking For A Face In The Crowd sounds like something off the *Be Glad* soundtrack and makes for a suitably anthemic closer.

The Electric Cello

Stan Schnier, fast becoming the ISB's version of the Beatles' Magic Alex, was also pressed into service to help Robin construct a home-made electric cello.

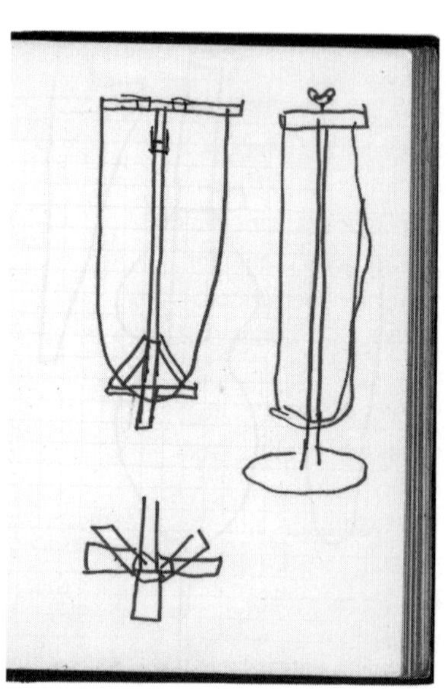

Stan: 'In autumn 1971, I was sitting with Robin in his cottage as he sketched an idea he had for a cello that could be heard against the increasing onstage volume. He based it on a Fender Stratocaster, a slab body with a bolt-on cello neck. We headed down to the local joinery, which had originally been a wheelwright's. It was really something: cobblestone courtyard, wood steamers, jigs and forms for this lost art. Up in the loft were racks of wood that were seasoning. The carpenter pulled out a lovely log of plane. We liked it and he cut a plank; then, using the sketch and off the top of our heads dimensions plus measurements taken from Robin's acoustic cello, he cut the shape on his band-saw and off we went. Robin planed down the body while I ordered cello parts from a supplier in London: an end pin, bridge, saddle, nut, fingerboard, neck and tuners. We did the hand finishing at the Row and I think the local joiner attached the neck for us. Robin decided to give it a paint job, in line with his other decorated instruments. It was light blue... a blue with a touch of red maybe, or very light purple ...not sure. I had an upright bass pickup which we mounted on the bridge and by DOG, it actually worked. A bit scratchy by today's standards, but plenty of volume on stage. When the band hit the road, the cello came in handy – on Red Hair, it really worked – came in like a tidal wave!'

As well as Red Hair, the cello was deployed on Sunday Song, Painted Chariot and Mike's unreleased song Lowlands Away, when Robin used it through a wah-wah pedal to striking effect. It was retired after the autumn tour, however, and never used again.

2021

In summer 72 the band got really good receptions at Bickershaw, Bardney/ Lincoln and other festivals in Holland and Germany, still with Likky. The next album, Earthspan, *which came out in November, was decidedly patchy, though. It was also the last to feature Likky; she sings, but plays almost nothing on the album. She had left for good by the autumn of that year and was 'replaced' by Gerard Dott, who joined them for the* Earthspan *tour in autumn 1972. Before Likky left and Gerard was signed up, however, the band were considering either replacing Likky or maybe trying out a supplement to the existing line-up in fiddle and viola player, Stuart Gordon. On the album, there generally seems to be an emphasis on Mike's string arrangements using Stuart's 'cleaner' playing and not Robin's.*

Earthspan: 'The band was diverging.'

As this was probably the most 'Malcolm' of all the ISB albums, we asked Mr Le Maistre to listen back to it from a 2021 viewpoint:

> 'My overall feeling about the album is that the band was diverging. It was never going go mainstream, the songs spoke strange and wonderful things that nobody else wrote about and I doubt whether Robin or Mike would have changed in that way. To paraphrase Robin, 'Bands They Change' and that was the beginning of that. All the three final albums have some great tracks and ideas (whoever else would have attempted Ithkos?) but the vision was blurring... The Scientology thing didn't impinge on my songs, they came from some other places. For me personally it was an important album because I realised that I could write songs that some people liked. In other words I had stepped out of Mike and Robin's shadows and, whilst I was never going to write their kind of extraordinary songs, I knew I could write my kind.'

Opposite: Bickershaw Pop Festival, 1972 – note obligatory hippy lady dancing backstage. (Philip Newby archive)

‘I loved it from the first play.’

Grahame Hood’s 2021 take on Earthspan,
with interjections from Malcolm.

My introduction to the ISB was through the son of a neighbour, justifiably concerned about my musical taste, loaning me a copy of *5000 Spirits*. Then I bought the *Relics* Elektra compilation, but *Earthspan* was the first proper String Band album I owned. I paid 60p for it in a Dumfries junk shop and loved it from the first play.

With the wisdom of hindsight we can see just how big a change of direction *Earthspan* was for the band. It was the last record on which Licorice would feature, though that was not to become obvious for a while, and also showed Malcolm rising in prominence within the ranks, with three songs on it, one co-written with Robin. A review of the album in *Time Out* said, a little unkindly, though Joe Boyd would certainly have agreed: ‘I can only suggest that for two outstanding musicians to give space to bring on lesser talent is an act of generosity and should perhaps be seen as such.’ Malcolm: ‘There was never a democracy in the ISB that I was aware of. You came up with a song and it was either accepted or rejected. I’m not sure how I ended up with 3 songs. For better or worse my songs seemed a little different to theirs and of course they had a big input into how they were arranged. I was writing quite a lot by then but was not prolific.’

Following their well-received appearance at the Lincoln Festival on 27th May 1972, the ISB had no more gigs booked until The Chichester Festival Theatre on 30th July. Likky was billed to appear but none of her songs from the setlist were performed at the gig, so Lincoln may have been her last appearance with the band. Her departure was mysterious but not dramatic. Malcolm: ‘She just seemed to slip away. One moment there, the next not.’ In *Melody Maker* of 25th November their folk correspondent, Andrew Means, wrote: ‘Licorice has departed on an “extended holiday” which doesn’t mean she has left the group but at the same time no-one knows when she is coming back.’ It was later admitted that she had left the group in Autumn 1972.

'I loved it from the first play.'

The previous December, on the 8th, Mike had played a solo concert (the only one during his time with the ISB) at the Renold Theatre, UMIST, Manchester. He was supported by a group from Liverpool called Sticky George, who joined Mike onstage for Spirit Beautiful. Their violinist, Stuart Gordon, made a particular impression on Mike and Stan Schnier recalls accompanying Mike on the train down to Liverpool to sound Stuart out about the possibility of him joining the ISB to augment the line-up as a multi-instrumentalist. As well as playing on sessions for the new album, Stuart undertook a series of gigs with the band, beginning at Chichester, with three more West Country gigs, at Penzance on the 10th August, Plymouth on the 12th and Torquay on the 13th.

The next day the band recorded a BBC John Peel session at the Playhouse Theatre, which was broadcast on the 29th. Stuart appears to have left the band soon after, unwilling to get involved with Scientology. With an American tour booked to begin on 23rd September, Gerard Dott was rapidly recruited to fill the multi-instrumentalist role, and was rehearsed and ready by the time the band flew across the Atlantic.

Liquid Acrobat had a sometimes harsh and rocky sound, with a strong live feel. Not so *Earthspan*. Each song was simpler in structure than before, and arranged as an individual piece. Apart from the vocals, there is no recognisable ISB sound any more. The styles range from traditional folk through light jazz with only Sunday Song harking back to their earlier style. No clashing electric guitars here, my friend.

Someone obviously thought it was time the band was better presented and the very attractive sleeve demonstrates this with a collage of band member photos. Mike, who had recently taken a course in music arranging, is shown working hard on his music notation, and relaxing with his girlfriend (and ISB manager) Susie Watson-Taylor. Robin is smiling in a corduroy jacket and a rollneck sweater. Likky plays on a swing, holds a bird in her hands and sits at the piano with her hair in braids. Malcolm is seen in a quite extraordinary checked jacket and in a shot that looks as if he is trying on his mother's clothes when she is out at the shops.

The album was recorded in sessions during March, July and August 1972, and released in October. Reviews were generally good; the *Time Out* review concluded: 'If you like moments of celebration to lighten your care-worn days, and relieve you of the desire to fit a cow-catcher to the front of our car and ram every silly bastard who gets stuck across a junction when the lights are in your favour, then you can do worse than step into this album for a spell.' Praise indeed. A few years later the author of *Electric Muse* wrote: 'with *Earthspan* ... the ISB reached its second peak. Here the musicians brought electric instrumentation under their control which, coupled with the superb orchestrations scored by Mike Heron, allowed them a far wider canvas than ever before. And also of significance is the emergence of Malcolm Le Maistre as a songwriter, with his dry surrealism and acute powers of observation. *Earthspan* is a superb album from any point of view, mixing elements of rock with those of jazz, traditional folk and classical music to give a result that is as impressive for its variety as for its originality.'

The album begins with Malcolm's My Father Was a Lighthouse Keeper. One reviewer was confused from the start: 'Why? Why? Why? Asks the seventh line, presumably an expression of solidarity with the listener. So we are left to wonder – is Malcolm Le Maistre's father a lighthouse keeper? Was he ever a lighthouse keeper? He doesn't know and neither do we.' Actually we do know that Malcolm's father was actually a journalist, so the song is not autobiographical. My interpretation of it was inspired by a quote by L. Ron Hubbard about the 'E-Meter' – 'It sees all, it knows all, it is never wrong.' Malcolm adds: 'Lighthouse Keeper was never a Hubbard song per se. None of my songs were. Not sure I how wrote the song – possibly during one of my illicit acid trips! Regarding Scientology, you must remember I was only 21 when I joined the band and I guess in awe of Mike and Robin so whatever they were into had to be good. But I was never a proper believer. I was probably worried I'd be chucked out the band if I questioned things too much.'

Nevertheless the lighthouse keeper is almost certainly Hubbard. He tends a light which is there for all to see, but he cannot help those who fail to see it ('saw the waves getting steeper/saw the ships going down'). He has had many past lives, has seen 'the waves slip by and the stars explode,' and seen them again and again. The beach is life and Malcolm is bored by the things he finds there; his lover (his faith/opinions) has proved false. The people who sit smiling and eating in their big cars have come to the beach but do not venture on to it and do not appreciate its beauty. Malcolm's lover returns, he sees the way ahead, and his father, who sees it all and knows it all, looks down on him with a smile.

Mike's Antoine is one of the songs in which he takes on the personality and experiences of a historical figure and describes them, in this case the composer Hector Berlioz, regarded as the first of the European Romantic composers. In a biography of the composer by Robert Clarson-Leach I found an account of an incident which inspired at least the first verse of

'I loved it from the first play.'

Heron's song. 'As a child Hector attended Mass every day and received Holy Communion on Sundays. He took his first Communion on the same day as his sister Nanci, at the Ursuline convent where she was a boarder. He was called to the altar first, extremely conscious that he was surrounded by young girls dressed in white. When he had received the Sacrament he became aware of the beauty of the music that followed, which turned out to be an adaptation of Quand Le Bien-aimé Reviendra (When My Sweetheart Returns To Me), a somewhat curious choice for Holy Mass. However, this appears to have been the boy Berlioz's first conscious musical experience, though it would be ten years before he learned what the tune was and could put a name to it.' Mike's powerful church organ backing is hugely enhanced by Stuart Gordon's moving viola part. 'Ambitious,' says Malcolm. 'Would anyone else have written such a song? Mike has the capacity for beautiful but fleeting bits of melody.'

Robin's first composition on the album is Restless Night, a moody jazz-tinged piece, with a strong vocal and topped by a charming horn arrangement. Malcolm adds: 'Actually it seems like two tracks, in the great tradition of ISB chopping from one style to another. I like the collaborative nature, Mike's piano and arrangement, Robin's singing.'

Sunday Song features lyrics by Likky and music by Mike. The album's title comes from an unused line in the song: 'We were having an earth-span of silence to contemplate Supreme Being.' I make no attempt to analyse the lyrics, though there are some lovely lines: 'Venus fell for a while in England', 'Air was sweet as milk', 'Kissing petals, swishing tails' (Likky was very fond of horses as a girl). Most enigmatic of all, 'Strange surprise, grass being green, on planet Earth, Galaxy 13'. Musically it is powerful stuff; Mike's vocal, when it comes in following Malcolm's, is exceptionally powerful and passionate. Brian Davidson, late of The Nice, contributes suitably bombastic drums. Malcolm adds: 'What a song. Is it awesome? Sort of, but its ambition is perhaps lost because of its subject. It stands the test of time melodically (lots of hooks and weird imagery) but the arrangement is strange and the strings at the end are way too loud. God is love ....hmmm. But actually I find it rather moving, especially Likky. My primary puzzle is why Mike's is singing is so overwrought. Toning it down would have been a good idea.'

Side two opened with a new version of Black Jack Davy, as featured on *I Looked Up*, now renamed Black Jack David. It's a great song, well performed with Robin and Stuart playing round each other on fiddles and a nice little bit of mandolin from Malcolm. Soundman Stan Schnier adds bass and percussion. Island Records put it out as a single, with Restless Night on the flip, the band's first single since This Moment over two and a half years previously. Perhaps the idea was to get a folk-rock hit out of it, or maybe Mike was short of material. It is based on the many traditional ballads of similar name, themselves all variation of the Raggle Taggle Gypsies theme. Mike: 'I'd heard a few versions of this song – all from the point of view of the aggrieved Lord of the Manor, and always set to a dismal tune, in a minor key, in which forelock-tugging peasants express their disapproval. So I wrote words in the first person and gave him a jaunty tune that I thought might reflect his mood more accurately.' Malcolm's verdict on the new version: 'Pointless. Found myself listening to [*out-take*] Secret Temple and realised just how much Likky brought to the band. Very underused.'

Robin's Banks Of Sweet Italy follows, and continues to show his increasing skill in writing in the traditional idiom. It is a lovely song, the young bride thinking of her sailor husband and dreading his failing to return to her, with another fine vocal from Likky. Malcolm: 'I always loved this song. Stunning in many ways: the melody, the opening, Likky's singing – the whole concept, and I loved singing the Barbary chorus. Made me sad hearing Likky's gentle voice. She should have gone solo. A unique talent. Quite a straightforward song for Robin, a natural follow-on from Darling Belle.'

With Robin's music and Malcolm's lyrics, The Actor certainly shows Malcolm's powers of observation. He depicts the jaded actor, at the peak of his profession but lacking love. He is enchanted by a lady beneath the arches of a church while driving home in the rain after a performance: 'The lady wore no makeup but she stood like a swan. Thin body of a dancer, her dress was quietly torn.' He seeks her out and marries her. There is a world-weary sound to the piano and the words at the beginning of each chorus. Malcolm: 'I wrote this and presented it the others and they liked it – the first song they accepted that I had written. Robin felt it needed a rewrite so he took it on... I think it stands up well with the other tracks on the album but could do with being one verse shorter. Unique but naïve.'

Moon Hang Low shows Robin as a night club crooner, brushed drums, muted horns. Though Mike wrote the score for the session musicians, Robin wrote the trumpet solo. Who could have imagined music like this on an Incredible String Band album in 1967? But it worked, and well. In Malcolm's view: 'Erratic and bit overwrought. Not sure if Robin is a jazz singer. But hey, it was the ISB.'

Malcolm's Sailor And The Dancer is a song that, over the years, has grown in stature for me as a listener. The warm tone of the harmonium is lovely and Likky's high harmony quite exceptional. Malcolm: 'Not about

'I loved it from the first play.'

Scientology per se. Very much of its time; I do think the lyrics reflect a rather overly airy-fairy period of my life. I was probably reading too many fantasy books at the time. I wrote it on an old harmonium in my back room – I love harmoniums. Some might say this a daft song, others find it beautiful. I think the coda is very catchy and on another song would be a hit. I like the melodies and the way it's quite cleverly structured. Likky's harmony pulls it all together. Its brevity is to be admired, something some of the others' songs might have benefitted from.'

The inspiration for Seagull came from a voyage Mike had recently made on the Apollo, the flagship of Scientology's Sea Org. This was a former ferry, the MV Royal Scotsman, which had operated between Glasgow and Belfast before being requisitioned by the Royal Navy in 1940. The Sea Org bought her in 1967. It was notorious for the high standards of discipline on board and Mike may well have been a little nervous; according to some accounts, this was his first meeting with Hubbard. He has his doubts; he needs a sign to show him it will be alright. There is a very odd lyric: 'It's very true, there's nothing to complain of here. You know I've tried, and not found an enemy to fear, here.' We hear a very melodically unusual electric guitar (the only one on the album?) and whistle duet before he decides that it is indeed alright out on the rolling sea, with everyone joining in on the sea shanty-like ending. Malcolm: 'Unclear what this is about but it is quite arresting. I like the seagull chorus, catchy – and so maybe the rolling sea one is superfluous.'

All strength to the Commodore, as the inner bag notes said, also introducing us to new member Gerard Dott, who we could applaud on the next tour...

STUART GORDON

Grahame Hood

Stuart was born in Wallsend, near Newcastle, in 1950. He learned to play the violin and joined the Northumberland Youth Orchestra, with whom he toured extensively. He was also involved with the Northumberland Experimental Youth Theatre. Though academically very gifted, music was always his main interest, and he prided himself on never having had a 'proper' job. Attending university in Liverpool, he formed Sticky George, a four piece band who formed musical bonds with several of the Liverpool Poets. In December 1971 Sticky George supported Mike Heron at a solo concert in Manchester and this led to him being asked to join the ISB as a multi-instrumentalist; though primarily a violinist, he could also play guitar and keyboards. He chose not to stay with the ISB and re-joined Sticky George, going on to provide music for an Adrian Henri TV play, appear on *Coronation Street* in a band booked to play at the Rovers Return, and provide the music for a documentary about the electrification of the railway line from Crewe to Glasgow. With ex-Sticky George member Phil Harrison he formed the Short Wave Band in 1975, who made two albums. Stuart and Phil later joined The Korgis and played on their huge 1980 hit Everybody's Got To Learn Sometime.

Stuart went to play with many famous musicians, including Peter Gabriel, Alison Moyet, Massive Attack, XTC and The Beach Boys! He toured with ex-Van Der Graaf Generator frontman Peter Hammill for many years and latterly in a trio with Steve Tilston and harmonica player Keith Warmington. He also composed a great deal of music for films and TV. Everyone who knew him spoke of his humour and love of music and his incredible enthusiasm and skill as a player. It is a great shame that he chose not to continue with the ISB; he could have been very good for them. He died of cancer in 2014, at the tragically early age of 63.

Above Stuart in Youth Theatre days
Right Stuart, Short Wave Band era

Out-takes from *Earthspan*

Album left-overs, as well as Secret Temple (see below) also included Robin's instrumental Curlew, arranged by Mike for two cellos, a viola, hardanger fiddle and two whistles. Robin's got no memory of the origins of the piece, but comments that it shares a Moorish influence with some of the tracks on his solo album, *Myrrh*, and was probably composed on the Glen Row harmonium. Malcolm's on whistle and Robin plays hardanger fiddle and second whistle. We are fairly sure that Stuart Gordon is the uncredited viola-player and the (double-tracked) cellist. It's a beautiful, keening piece and is included on *Tricks Of The Senses*.

Likky leaves the band

Adrian Whittaker

It's hard to really know exactly why Likky left the band when she did, and probably only she could really tell us. Initially it was announced that she was 'on holiday,' and perhaps, as with Rose's departure, the other band members were thinking she might still return. It's safest to say that, by summer 1972, a number of factors had come together.

Likky seems to have been happy up at Glen Row, often spending late nights with her best friend Mal drinking tea, smoking rollies and swapping tales of Celtic myths and legends, fairies, cosmic happenings and distant galaxies. Stan Schnier, at that point Mal's partner, remembers: 'They were both beautiful and oh so charming. Had great senses of humour, love of cigs and tea with lots of sugars. In her cottage, which had lots of silver paint, she would sit by the fire in her chair and flick the ashes of her cigarettes onto the lovely vintage rug, telling me it was good for the rug as it kept it from getting mildewy in the Scottish mist.'

Her position in the band itself, though, was increasingly ill-defined. Rose's departure had left Likky more isolated, a sort of hangover from the *Hangman* era – and though she and Rose were not close friends, they had been allies when things got tricky, as Rose describes in her memoir. Scientology had engendered a growing professionalism in the band, perhaps a reason why Likky was asked to play so little on *Earthspan*. Mike was studying and writing string arrangements, Robin was experimenting with jazz, and there was a slow move towards an orthodox rhythm section: in concert, roadie Jack Ingram played drums on some songs and, after Likky turned down the chance, Stan Schnier stepped out from behind the mixing desk to play bass live on Adam And Eve. Malcolm had brought a new dynamism and energy to the band; he was also another songwriter submitting possible (and more accessible) album material, maybe a reason there was no room on *Earthspan* for Secret Temple. All this led, quite probably, to Likky feeling disheartened about her role in the ISB. Rose feels she had periods of depression, and this too may have been a reason for her to take a break – from which she never returned. She soon left Glen Row for the Scientology HQ at East Grinstead and then for LA with her boyfriend at the time, David Zimian.

I'm calling to you – the Licorice enigma

Raymond Greenoaken

Of all the protagonists in the ISB story, Christina 'Licorice' McKechnie is probably the most enigmatic. Licorice undeniably had a glamour about her, in the sense of a quality of magical enchantment. Whereas Rose's stage persona was that of the Head Girl letting her hair down, Likky seemed almost otherworldly, a creature of mist and cobweb, a changeling child flitting through our world in a permanent state of puzzled amusement. She'd tiptoe across the stage in some fluttery, weightless garment, strum something here, bang something there, sing the odd chorus in a piping, birdlike voice and giggle girlishly at frequent intervals. And of course she never said anything at all.

The real Christina McKechnie was all of these things – but the opposite is also true. The childlike innocence, though real enough (face it – no-one would write Cosmic Boy unless they really meant it) existed side by side with an uninhibited sexual appetite. As Robin remarks affectionately, 'She had a great number of relationships on the go simultaneously, all of which she entered into with great spirit.'

Similarly, she had an assertive side to her. Joe Boyd recalls that 'Licorice was quite a powerful personality in her quiet way.' [*See Joe Boyd interview*] And if she said little or nothing in performance, it was not because she had nothing to say. She wrote poetry from an early age, with passion and – according to Robin – no little skill. In the Edinburgh days she would read regularly at poetry clubs. 'There was a poetry circuit in those days,' says Robin, 'with people like Brian Patten and the Scaffold, and she used to go and read her poems on those occasions early on.'

Eventually, of course, she began writing songs too, four of which featured at one time or another in the ISB repertoire. At this time she was not a prolific songwriter; according to Robin, her songwriting 'just developed spontaneously; she wasn't pushed into doing it... She wasn't particularly discouraged from doing it either. 'But these seem to have been only her first cautious steps. In 1975, in a letter to a fan, she claimed to have composed seventy new songs with her songwriting partner of the time David Zimian.

There is a certain poignancy in writing about Licorice at this juncture. I like to think that she's still out there, painting her pictures, singing her songs, or just living a happy, normal life somewhere in suburbia. Maybe she's just folded her wings away...

Likky enters the String story in 1963, when Robin, Clive and Bert Jansch were sharing squats around the less salubrious areas of Edinburgh. Robin recounts in *Mirrorman's Sequences* (in which she's referred to as Sleeka) that she left home while still at school to marry Bert (easily recognisable as Bart). In Robin's version of the story, her father administered the future guitar god a 'Christian thump', but was unable to restore his errant daughter either to school or to the family home. When Bert took off for London in the summer he left her behind, whereupon, as Robin tells it, she fell into his arms. He quotes a line from one of her poems: 'Another circle was drawn, freehand and perfect.'

He also touches upon her other creative skills. She 'developed a taste for tapestry, wove wool into trees of birds and dancing foxes, bagpipers and zebra-lions'. And he hints at her dreamy, unworldly Celtic nature. 'I must have forgotten to summon up the "me" who likes cooking,' she apparently said after burning the pea soup one day. But he points out that she could 'nevertheless relate and talk and be in the world quite well... could relate to actors from Liverpool and to young bookstore keepers'.

One of the most moving pieces on Robin's later solo album *Mirrorman's Sequences* concerns a time when Likky had moved to Dublin and was living in the famous 'Orphanage' communal house, later immortalised by Dr Strangely Strange. Not knowing the number of the house, he nevertheless set off for Dublin in search of her and ended up conversing with a nightwatchman next to a hole in the Mount Street tarmac. After a few hours, Likky happened to walk by, 'wearing a black and white op-art beret', and the scene shifts to the Orphanage for a tender reconciliation: 'They made love as though nothing had changed.'

Likky on stage. (Simpson collection)

ORPHAN LIKKY

In *Fitting Pieces To The Jigsaw*, Ivan Pawle remembers Likky's first days in Dublin. Their mutual friend Orphan Annie was actually christened Patricia Mohan, but had been re-baptised by Ivan, and so the large flat she rented at 55 Lower Mount Street soon became known as 'The Orphanage.'

Annie ran away from home and went off to Scotland when she was about sixteen, where she met Ian McCullough, with whom she travelled to Morocco for a few months. She then started studying weaving in Edinburgh, where on the crafts scene she met one Christina McKechnie, who had left school to work as a ceramic artist in the Buchan Potteries, painting some of their best-selling designs involving a thistle with a bluebell and heather.

Ivan: 'Back in Scotland, Annie moved between Glasgow, Edinburgh and Mull with a cohort of Beats. In 1965, the next time she came back, she brought Likky with her.'

In autumn that year, Annie decided to rent a flat for them both and invited Ivan to move in; he assumed the persona of a sort of butler/valet/batman. The three settled into the new place. Ivan: 'We were a happy, harmonious trio.'

Likky was there for a few months. Though she had already met Robin Williamson by that point and they had what Robin has called an 'on-off relationship,' she was on the run after her intended marriage to Bert Jansch had been called off. After seeing the banns posted in the local registry office, Likky's family had warned Bert off, feeling the marriage was 'unsuitable.' Bert, by all accounts fairly philosophical about this, had taken off for London and fame without her. Before they broke up, Bert had taught Likky how to play Anji, a notoriously tricky rite-of-passage finger-picking piece with a descending bass line, written by Davy Graham.

As Likky was now a resident, she and Annie had a conceptual link-up in mind. Ivan: 'She tried to get a job in Bewley's cafe in Grafton Street. Bewley's, a Quaker family, only employed orphans, but she didn't technically qualify as an orphan, so she got a job as a model in the School of Art.'

Relationships in the house were complicated, though. After a brief affair with Likky, Ivan 'foolishly fancied Annie and moved to her room.' Robin Williamson eventually turned up in search of Likky, and she went back to Scotland with him that Christmas.

Bert Jansch spins some Mingus: Likky far right, her friend Ash far left. (Rod Harbinson)

Robin and Likky went off to Morocco together in 1966, and on their return they holed up in Mary Stewart's cottage at Balmore. Likky can be heard on the Balmore Tapes singing and talking. At one point she improvises a song based solely around the words blue, golden yellow and black; at another she reads what sounds like a short self-composed memoir concerning bicycles, drum lessons and a friend called Frank.

When *5000 Spirits* was released the following summer, Likky's voice was featured on a couple of tracks: Painting Box, on which she also clinks some finger-cymbals, and Gently Tender, on which she joins the shamanic chorale near the end of the song. She also appeared on *Hangman* six months later, famously uttering the words 'Amoebas are very small' on A Very Cellular Song and joining the chorus of Bid You Goodnight – as well as turning up on the back cover. After the UK *Hangman* tour in March 1968, she was drawn into band politics for the first time, as Joe Boyd explains in his interview in this book.

By the time of *Wee Tam*, the girls were regarded as members of the band – at least by Robin and Mike. They were called upon (or allowed, depending on your point of view) to do things in the studio that the lads would normally have done – play hand-drums, strum a harp – as well as add their distinctive voices to the choruses. Joe was not best pleased.

Nevertheless, by the point *Changing Horses* hit the shops in November 1969 the process was complete. There sat Rose and Likky on the front cover, leaving no doubts over their status. Notwithstanding Joe's disapproval, the ISB audience unanimously took them to its collective bosom. Men fell for them (there is abundant anecdotal evidence of this) and women may well have regarded them as role models.

For the ISB's 1969 Spring tour, a concert programme was printed that included three whimsical stories about the band by the mysterious Fate and ferret from Pittenweem (we've reprinted two in this book). Also featured was a double-spread photo of all four flashing their teeth wolfishly. It will have come as a shock to many to see that Likky had a shadowy gap where one of her front teeth should have been. Though it gave her something of a witchy aspect, the effect was not altogether displeasing. Indeed, the impression this conveyed was one of airy unconcern for conventional notions of beauty. The String Band, you could see, didn't play to anybody's rules. They were utterly themselves, and none more so than the gap-toothed girl at the front. Likky's lost tooth instantly became a sort of icon, if an absence can be thought of as iconic. A dentist had offered to fill the gap but she had declined the offer, declaring an aversion to anything artificial. By 71, however, a denture had appeared. At this time the band, influenced by Scientology's stress on effective communication, had become more image-conscious, and Likky's falsie might have been a sign of this. Unlike Rose, she was a committed follower of L. Ron's teachings.

But there were limits, it seems. When, less than a year later, Mike took the stage at Bickershaw Festival sporting a shorty haircut and tank-top, it was a bridge too far for Likky, who reportedly ticked him off for slavish obeisance to the whims of fashion. By autumn 1972, she was gone – from the band, and from Glen Row.

Rose had left the year before, of course. It may be significant that, shortly after she and Likky became bona fide band members, they ceased being girlfriends. What seems sure is that they allowed their own views on how the ISB was developing to influence them in a way they might never have done if they'd simply remained appendages of Robin and Mike. Rose's disenchantment with Scientology and the *U* debacle undoubtedly hastened her departure. She's always maintained that she had no real ambitions as a performer, other than to become a decent bassist. Likky, by contrast, developed her role within the band considerably.

For the *U* stage show, she pitched in with Stone Monkey, and contributed her first song, the tremulous I Know You, which she performed entirely solo. By this time, also, she was singing the occasional lead vocal on songs by both Robin and Mike. In the wake of *U*, dance or pantomimic interludes became a feature of String Band concerts, especially after Malcolm joined the band in early 71. Likky took a prominent role in these divertissements, portraying Eve in the Garden of Eden, a Chinese princess (in Willow Pattern Song), a stork, and much more. At the same time, she was bringing the odd song into the repertoire. Cosmic Boy and Sunday Song were co-written with Mike, but the haunting Secret Temple was almost all her own work.

Likky shows off new tooth, 1970. (Rose Simpson collection)

Likky and Mike, Glen Row, early Seventies.
(From Mark Anstey collection)

SECRET TEMPLE

Adrian Whittaker

Likky's ISB swansong was until recently only available as a fairly obscure 1972 BBC session version. However, a trawl through the Island archives for the *Tricks Of The Senses* project revealed unmixed versions of the individual song sections, recorded for the *Earthspan* sessions in April 1972. Interestingly, a final mix version of this song was also listed but the relevant tape had been removed a very long time ago by persons unknown (possibly Likky herself).

Likky left the ISB a little later in 1972. It's tempting to speculate that having her song turned down for the album (whilst new boy Malcolm was granted two and a half tracks) was the last straw. She did get to perform it live on French TV before she left, though the camera remained obdurately trained on Mike and Robin for most of the song. The opaque lyrics have been the subject of some discussion – was it a song to a lover or a spiritual piece? 'Yes I'll believe you're in trouble / Yet I see you as life's lover / How long?' Her nephews Don and Ben, when they heard the track, were convinced she was in dialogue with herself.

4-piece on ice, Glen Row, 1970

Likky, it's fair to say, was not an especially accomplished musician. In accord with ISB philosophy, she coaxed musical sounds out of a variety of instruments with minimal technique. By 1972, however, her instrumental duties were effectively confined to live performance. Her only instrumental contribution to *Earthspan* was a bit of bass on Seagull. Perhaps, then, her departure that autumn was on the cards, particularly since we'd reached the era of the on-stage roadies, when Stan Schnier and Jack Ingram, as well as Janet Shankman and Suzie Watson-Taylor, would appear from the wings whenever an instrumental gap needed plugging.

The circumstances of her leaving remain obscure, however. Her close involvement with Scientology caused her to move down near East Grinstead, where the Church has its UK headquarters. She was pictured in an advertisement for Scientology that appeared in the music papers around this time, skipping through flowery fields and looking as winsomely happy as a 'Clear' should be. The *NME* carried a sniffy little item in March 1974 about a 'bunch of Scientologists who gigged together at the Adeline Genee Theatre, East Grinstead last week'. The accompanying photo shows Mike Garson, Woody Woodmansey, Ray Royer (ex-Procol Harum guitarist) – and Likky, dressed as ever in something wispy with a tambourine at her feet.

By the end of the year she had left for LA, and was soon in contact with Robin and Janet, who had moved to Hollywood after the break-up of the ISB. By November she had assembled the Silver Moon Band, in which she was 'mostly singing and playing some bass.' It's not clear whether the Silver Moon Band ever got off the ground.

However, Likky finally found her way onto vinyl again when she contributed some backing vocals to [Robin's] Merry Band's debut album *Journey's Edge* in 1977. By this time she had met, married and was playing with the guitarist Brian Lambert. She was still moving in Scientology-muso circles, and counted the jazz-rock pianist Chick Corea as a 'dear friend'. By the early Eighties she and Brian had parted, and it looks like her involvement with music ended with the separation. According to a 1991 article in *Dirty Linen*, she had 'reportedly worked as a waitress and cloakroom attendant', and had apparently fallen on hard times. Outstanding royalties for her ISB songwriting were, however, unclaimed.

There is some evidence that her health and perhaps state of mind were in decline at this time. She also appears to have broken her ties with Scientology, an organisation known for harassment of its former members. A *beGLAD* correspondent claimed to have encountered her, looking dishevelled, on the streets of LA. She allegedly recognised him as an old acquaintance and fled in shame. Again, a dateless anecdote. The last verified contact with Likky was a letter from her to sister Frances in 1990.

And there, alas, the story seems to peter out. She is believed by her family to be now living in sheltered accommodation in California. There's undoubtedly a sense of sadness that she has disappeared so completely from view, and in circumstances that suggest she was down on her luck. Some, clearly, remember her as 'carrying the weight of the universe on her shoulders'. Others, who knew her in happier times, still speak of her as 'utterly charming, full of fun, optimism and the joys of living'. And that, obviously, is how we'd prefer to remember her.

"STAR MUSICIANS At Adeline Genee" said the handout that arrived with this unprepossessing picture. It refers to a bunch of Scientologists who gigged together at the AG Theatre, East Grinstead, last week. Included are Mike Garson, from the Spiders from Mars, Woody Woodmansey who used to be a Spider, Licky McKechnie who used to be in the Incredible String Band and Ray Royer, who used to be in Procol Harum. This caption was written by Seth Nettles, who used to play with himself in the bath till he discovered a Better Way Of Life.

Scientology gig at East Grinstead, March 1974. (*NME*)

A still from the *Be Glad* film. (Peter Neal)

The Girl on the Silver Bicycle

Adrian Whittaker talks to Likky's elder sister Frances Harding.

Frances: Likky was born at home. I remember the day she was born (2nd October 1945), we went out to play in the communal gardens at the back of the block of flats where we lived. We came upstairs, Connie and I (my older sister) and there we are, we had this little tiny baby girl. She was always a clever child, she was easily the cleverest in the family and talented in many ways. Musically she was very talented. My mother and my older sister played the piano and she did too. I remember her always dancing whenever there was music. I suppose we all did. There weren't the opportunities then as there are now, of course, for different kinds of dancing. Scottish country dancing, that was the big thing, they played for half an hour on the radio. This was in Edinburgh, in Viewforth.

Adrian: What did your parents do?

My father was a tradesman – he was an electro-plater, so he made things silver, which was very magical; and one thing he did for Licorice was – it must have been her fifth, sixth or seventh birthday – he electroplated or chromium-plated, anyway he made it silver, a little two-wheeler bicycle, so she was the only kid on the street who had this silver bicycle. It was really wonderful. My mother never worked. There was a different attitude then; I think she loved being a housewife. Anyway, I would say that for all of us a great sense of music comes from my mother's background, whereas I would credit my father with a sense of the visual arts. He liked to draw.

I suppose the big thing in Christina's early life was, just before her third birthday in October, she became ill with peritonitis. I remember her in her cot, very unwell, and lighting the three candles on the birthday cake and this little child just barely raised herself up to blow the candles out. Then she was taken off to hospital. She was there for three months with peritonitis. For that time we didn't see her at all, my sister and I. I think my mother probably saw her for a only short time once a week, so it was a dreadful wrench for my mother. Likky must have felt very distanced from all of us.

In fact she survived it and, again, I remember when she came home. We had a new doll for her, a big baby doll and a pram which was really quite an item to buy in those days – I'm talking about the late 1940s. I can just see where the pram was sitting and the baby doll in it, and then Christina coming home, still just three years and three months.

Then she went to St. Peter's school, the same primary school that we all went to. I think she was more or less first in her class all through school. We were all graded in those days all the way through, and certainly she became Dux [leader] of the school when she was eleven. She was a very clever child. I don't know that she ever really enjoyed secondary school to the same extent.

She was starting to write poetry then and took part in poetry readings – I suppose that was by the time she was 16. She wrote that lovely little poem, 'Whatever the seasons, my feet always walk on dead leaves...'

Of course, the main thing was she went to work in the Buchan potteries in Portobello – she was painting designs on cups and plates. She left school to do that. I had got married by then, so I'm kind of fuzzy on that point in her life; we had gone to live in Nigeria in 1963.

The story runs that she left school to marry Bert Jansch...

Yes, I think that's absolutely true. I certainly know exactly where the banns were put up, in what was then a registry office up at Bruntsfield. My husband David can tell you the story much better than I can [*see box – Ed.*]. A friend of ours saw these banns up and said 'I see that your sister's getting married, Frances,' – and we knew nothing about it! There is a whole funny story which I'm sure Bert Jansch could tell you.

Doesn't this involve your father getting cross and giving him a clout?

I don't think he ever laid hands on him, but he certainly went to a well-known bar and told him to back off his little girl! That marriage never took place, anyway.

But what I do know is that, prior to that, if I'm not mistaken, she and Robin had already met up when she was fifteen. There weren't clubs or anything like that in those days, but we did go to a place that the churches ran up at Bruntsfield, at Morningside. It was actually called Holy Corner, because there was a church on each of the four corners. We went to a sort of dance that was held there every Saturday. I've a feeling that's where she first met Robin, and then by chance they met again in later life. It was in the interim she went to marry Bert.

Do you have any of her poetry from the early days, or memorabilia, old photos?

She was bridesmaid at both my wedding and my sister's wedding, so she's there in the photos looking very pretty. She loved horses and horse-riding – she spent a lot of time out at the stable at Spylaw and Redford, to the south of Edinburgh. I've got a photo of her in her jodphurs from that time.

Were you in touch with her in the period she was in the band?

We were just coming back from living in Africa – it was at the time of the Biafra crisis in 1967 – but then we didn't live in Edinburgh either. We had small children, so we were pretty well out of a lot of things. We did manage to get to one concert they had at the Usher Hall, and we all went afterwards for a Chinese meal, Robin, Mike, Licorice, Rose as well. That was nice. But yes, we saw her sometimes. She called round at our flat a few times with her baby fox...

Would you say she was quite ambitious about her musical role?

I wouldn't say ambition was a word I at all associate with her. Is that something that's thought of her?

Joe Boyd said that she was pretty keen... In autumn 72 there was this whole period when it was announced she had left the band and gone on an 'extended holiday', from which she never actually came back.

Yes, I would imagine that whole Scientology thing must have really enveloped her. I think that sort of thing must have happened without my being aware of it. I really wasn't very involved then.

Did you follow what she was up to in the States?

Likky at 13, helping out in the stables at Spylark. (Frances Harding)

No, we lost touch for a long time.

When did you start hearing from her?

I suppose it would have been the mid-Eighties. She would write to my older sister rather than me, never saying very much. I'm not sure that she hadn't become a born-again Christian – I remember a letter from her recommending prayer as the answer... I know that she got married in the late Seventies. David went over to see her in LA in 1976. She and Brian Lambert were rehearsing a new band with a couple of session musicians in the flat at the time, and he was given a copy of L. Ron Hubbard's autobiography to read while they finished. Of course, he put it down and went out for a walk instead.

I think later on she was involved with someone else, who died. She loved him, she really loved him – he was an American Indian, he had been wounded in Vietnam. I think that was a great tragedy in her life, that really was. I wouldn't know when that happened, early Eighties probably. She wrote to my sister, all the time saying life was tough, that she was painting and sometimes working in a health store and sometimes doing gigs around clubs. That seemed to be more jazz music than anything else. She also went back to College at some stage; I'm not sure what she studied.

She always came across as a bit otherworldly...

Oh, I think she was quite fey – and yet I don't know why, we're a very practical family!

The last time you heard from her?

I think the last address we have for her is in Sacramento. I've moved around a lot too, so she probably doesn't have any permanent address for me, but my older sister, my late sister, she always stayed in the same place. So she does have that address, and she knows she can always get in touch, which of course we wish she would, we very much do.

I gather she came back to see your mum in the mid-Eighties?

Yes, my mother was already quite ill then, and she came back to Edinburgh to see her in 1986. She didn't get in touch with me, of course. I've always moved around with my family, so I expect that's part of the reason why.

In fact, she didn't see anyone else at all – and when she left, she must have just rushed off and got the next flight back to the States.

The last letter from her is dated 1990, and that's certainly from Sacramento. She seems to have had some major surgery and is recovering, but is not feeling either strong physically or entirely at ease mentally. She had a tough time, I think. I feel a sense of not belonging must have first asserted itself from her early illness – a near-total separation from the family at three years old for three months.

It's nice, I think, that she was able to sing and compose songs and play music as much as she did; she was certainly a very free spirit. Such a pity she got trapped by Scientology, and maybe she wasn't strong enough to shake it off without it leaving its mark on her.

2000

Likky in the *Be Glad* film. (Peter Neal)

MARRIAGE LINES

David Harding remembers Likky and Bert

A friend told me about the banns – 'Bert Jansch, musician, to marry Christina McKechnie, ceramic artist'. I went round to talk to Bert about it, up a spiral staircase to one of those old top-floor Edinburgh tenements. It was unfurnished, and the fireplace was the rubbish tip. A 6' 2" black guy called Gary the Archer who was a sort of minder figure in the music scene back then, was sitting in a corner whittling – he made bows and arrows. Anyway, we fixed up that Bert, myself and Christina's dad would all meet up in the Crown Bar to talk about the suitability of the marriage – which we did. In fact, the discussions were very reasonable – I don't think there were even any raised voices. And as you know, after that Bert went off to London without her.

But there's a postscript to the story! Years later, towards the end of the Sixties, I was at a big post-show party after a concert by the Dubliners and the Fureys at the Usher Hall, and Owen Hand, who I'd known around the folk scene for some time, came up to me. We started chatting and he asked me if I remembered that time in the Crown Bar when I'd told Bert Jansch to back off. 'You didn't realise,' he said, 'but there were ten of us in that bar watching you, ready to wade in and beat you up if you'd so much as laid a hand on him!!'

Likky's memoir

Transcribed from the Balmore Tapes

Smoking in my bath tonight, the ash fell on the scar that like a crushed white lily sinks in my hairless belly, and I remembered you. I could see you nailed in the lizard bath, your head up like a tortoise in surprise, your eyes saying nothing, coy bubbles and wisps of smoke. Your eyes said nothing, only your hands drumming on the side of the bath, off for your proud hills beckon.

(*Ticking clock*)

I was right in the middle of working out a change step four down the stile step to manage the double curve with the Rothesay train line under the bridge in three steps, when who should arrive in a strange Land Rover there but Frank, who went to my primary. Really there was no need for him around the place. He asked where Robin was. I was alone in the house, father pottering about nearby. And after he knew he was away giving drum lessons, he offered to give drum lessons too.

'Perhaps if your Robin doesn't come back I could go and give drum lessons instead'.

Oh, really, it was just a tiny wee thing he had to teach. Like this... (*Drumming*)

'And if he can play the most superb complicated rhythms for three hours non-stop, I think he'll manage this little job alright, thank you'.

'Well, perhaps I could help with bicycles?'

'I don't think so,' I said, now busying myself cooking inside the cave. Daddy had just gone out to mend the handlebars of his bike, and really as a bicycle mender he seems to be quite adequate.

'What about a chimney sweep, then?'

'Chimney sweep! Hey, what do you think she's been doing all morning but chimney sweeping?' cried Father, neatly flying into the cave room on his bike which was made of palm leaf sculpture, like paper sculpture. And he'd solved the problem with the handlebars very nicely, using split cane in a circle. I looked up proudly, absently too.

'She's a great chimney sweep'.

(*Ticking clock*)

Edward Pope had been part of the ISB extended family ever since his days in the Exploding Galaxy dance group with Malcolm Le Maistre, joining the ISB in Glen Row in 1969. This is his tribute to Likky.

For Likky

if you were a broken beggar winking at me from the pavement
an inmate of an institution with a wicked cackle
or long since dead and born again a beautiful baby
i would not regret life's lottery
but from a mountain cave in arizona
a wise woman watches the world
speaking to us in dreams.
on the night of halloween nineteen ninety two
i stared at the flames for hours after the last guest left
and stumbled home to my boat to sleep
i dreamt i was with the incredibles
licorice was mad but i cured her madness
by having sex with her in the head to toe position
then we went to the mansion of the malevolent magician
and by sliding a chip sideways out of his big toe
the magician and all the fabric of his mansion came undone
and we fell from the balcony landing softly on the lawn
i awoke with this song fully formed in my head
'there is no evil, just the fire of pain
either you face it or you don't
if you don't face it, you'll be comfortably cool and sane
but if you face it you'll be blazing
there is no truth in words, they're just the door to thought
there is no ugliness except where love is short
there is no evil, just the fire of pain
either you face it or you don't
if you don't face it you'll be comfortably cool and sane
but if you face it you'll be blazing.'

Likky I never knew you

Allan Frewin hasn't forgotten

It was the voice. Hand to heart, I had no idea what she even looked like. I didn't know her name or anything else about her. Licorice McKechnie, arch-hippy lady with the angel voice and the amazing gaze of a lysergic Mona Lisa festooned in gypsy finery. What first hooked me was the unearthly cadences of her voice.

When I read that she had decamped to California, I wrote a little lament to mark the occasion. It was called 'Christina'.

Christina, though both land and sea divide us
still we sail the sky on a ship of air and music
your song still sings love's rhythm through my life
oh, and you're here again...

There was more, but you get the gist. Tossed like a new-born seal by the hormonal ocean breakers of my teens, it seemed to me that Likky was the ultimate fantasy woman for the weekend-hippy tie-dyed freaky-straight urban urchin that I was. Like Goldberry stepping out over the threshold of Tom Bombadil's enchanted house, she arrived unannounced one Summer afternoon, slipping somehow through into the 'real' world for my wonder and for my delight.

Hard choices had to be made in those days: was it to be Melanie Safka? Sandy Denny? Licorice? Or would I be feeling strong enough to entertain the phantom presence of Grace Slick? Likky was less of a threat; one wouldn't be dashed to pieces on her rocks, one would sit at her feet and fall into an eternal sorcerous sleep of beatific bliss. Or so it seemed back then.

There is an alchemy that is created for me when male and female voices twine together in harmony. (Maybe this is because most interactions between the sexes have all the harmony of a pram-load of colical infants bouncing down the Odessa steps – or not, as the case may be.) I've always loved bands where the boys and the girls sing together: early Fairport Convention, Jefferson Airplane, Mr Fox, Judy Henske and Jerry Yester, Trader Horne, Steeleye Span, Waterson/Carthy, the String Band – name your own purveyors of the divine cadence.

I first heard Likky and Robin in a record shop in Hastings. Job's Tears. Hello, I thought, here are voices. Here's poetry. Here's a door into heaven. Back at the holiday cottage at Camber Sands my father declared none of them able to sing a note to save their lives. He much preferred Black Sabbath. Trust me. He did. My father didn't like the String Band. The blessing of parental disapproval was invoked. The circle was complete. Nirvana attained!

I can still listen to Likky singing stratospherically of the golden book of the golden game and feel quite convinced that this is not a thing of this earth. This is the stuff that dreams are made of. And then Mike joins in and the three of them call to us from over the high green wall of the magic garden and we pass through the golden gates and never come back. Well, some of us at least. Some of us find the whole thing silly and pretentious and dopey, but we're not here to talk about them, are we?

My first encounter with the visual Likky was on cover of *Hangman*. I sort of assumed she was the beautiful daughter in question. It was the smile. As though all the secrets of the universe swam in her head, but – glorious as they were – she simply wouldn't divulge. No, it was the hair. Wild and free and whipped by winds from unattainable Borealis. No, it was the rainbow-hued cloak-thing. A prophetess glimpsed in the cave mouth at Delphi. No, it was the hands clasped around Leaf the dog. The lucky dog. No, it was the delirious fact of her sitting alfresco on the dried and crinkled leaves of some past Autumn. No, it was the entourage of strangely-garbed attendants that posed in her wake. No, it was the memory of that voice in my head.

Likky waits patiently for Allan to wake up. (Peter Neal)

The wistful Licorice-led dreams of my adolescence were never born of unrequited lustful longings. I didn't fancy her. She was beyond fancying. Unless, of course, the desire of a face and a voice and an aura has animal undertones below the acuity of the human ear to detect. In fact, members of the jury, the very first time I thought of her in ways other than through the refining-glass of the chaste delicacies of Courtly Love was relatively recently, when, in the Penwern article someone commented on the way she would waft around the countryside with no clothes on, much to the dismay of the locals, for whom walking abroad naked consisted of leaving home without a sensible hat and knitted scarf.

Then there was the cover of *Changing Horses*. I had that pinned up on my bedroom wall, you know. Remember those plastic sheaths you could buy to keep your album covers pristine? I'd staple them to the wall beside my bed and slip a constantly-changing gallery of album covers into them. You don't just buy into the music – you buy into the whole package: sights, sounds and sensualities. And there they were, up a tree in a bosky garden. And there they were, curiously blurred on the back cover of *I Looked Up*; Likky smiling that enigmatic smile (yes, I know about the tooth), her face shining like the face of an angel.

And then the songs began to emerge. I Know You, sweet and simple as running water. Blodeuwedd's child finding the perfect balance between being birds and flowers. Cosmic Boy, with a grinning Mr Punch at the piano, lolloping over the ivories like a March hare on speed. Oh, and I nearly forgot the giggle on This Moment. If that doesn't fill a fellow with the melancholy thrill of unattainable sweetness, then I don't know what would. And the whole 'thingummywhojemmyflippery' on The Juggler's Song. We'll never see that kind of elfin brightness again, live we ever so long.

I saw them performing Sunday Song in the Drury Lane Theatre years ago. Someone was banging a huge drum. 'Love is god, is god, oh, sweet joy!' Likky departed shortly thereafter, and the Incredible String Band was never the same again.

Where is she now, Christina Licorice Likky McKechnie, other than in my head and in my record collection and between the pages of this book? They say she wandered off into the desert. Maybe so. I have a theory, you know. Captain Beefheart lives in the same desert. I believe they met. I believe they are out there making strange and oblique music together. I don't care if it's not true. I'd rather believe an enchanting lie than a toothless truth, any day of the week. And if you don't believe me, just open your heart and your ears and your sunset windows and listen at twilight-time to the voices of the West Wind. She's in there sometimes. I'd swear she is. You just have to listen and believe.

Something Strange

Raymond Greenoaken (with Gil Murray)

Around 1971-72 something rather strange happened to the ISB. The clues are to be found in the packaging of the albums *Liquid Acrobat As Regards The Air* and *Earthspan*. *Liquid Acrobat*, released in October 1971 and featuring material played in concert earlier that year, had a satisfyingly Stringish look to it. The colour scheme is untypically muted, but Janet Williamson's intricate, tendrilly ink decorations and lettering evoked the secret forces of nature, and the photos of the band striding together across Minch Moor under a tumbling sky underscored their collective ethos. Electric instrumentation and a rock rhythm section were added to a handful of tracks, but otherwise the message seemed to be: business as usual. The ISB were still dressing like elvish princelings, still turning out songs that seemed to go on forever, and had replaced their departing bassist with a dancer.

Earthspan hit the shops a year later. Its cover had a different tale to tell. For a start, though both sides of the sleeve were plastered with photos of the band personnel, there was not a single group shot. Suddenly the ISB were a collection of somewhat disparate individuals. Mike flourished butterfly lapels, tank tops and a schoolboy haircut. Robin looked like he'd stepped out of a leisurewear catalogue. Malcolm was in a state of acute sartorial crisis, feverishly switching between Ricky Fulton-style tartan blazers and the contents of Isadora Duncan's wardrobe. Only Likky, all coy smiles and muslins, seemed comfortable with her old ISB persona – but by the time of the album's release, she was gone, replaced by a geeky jazzman recruited from an Edinburgh music shop. Something strange was indeed happening, and the omens were not good...

On one level, the cover reflected the album's contents. *Earthspan* was a wildly various selection even by String standards: each track seemed to occupy its own stylistic microclimate. It spoke of a band whose members were each ploughing their own furrow and drawing on the other members essentially as backing musicians. But on another level, the cover seemed to be broadcasting a different message. To the sceptical eye it looked like a rather half-cooked attempt to present the band as less 'otherly' and more amenable to mainstream delectation. There was a 'style magazine' vibe to the whole presentation.

The ISB may have been holed up in a remote community in the Scottish Borders, but they were well aware of the way the currents of popular culture were flowing. The dress codes of Britain's youth in 1972 were leaving the hippie couture of the late Sixties in sere and yellow leaf; the male style gurus of the day were, inter alia, David Cassidy, David Bowie and Noddy Holder. (Those were the days, my friend...) So it was not to be wondered at if members of the band might have felt the need to move with the times a smidgen; after all, they were still in their twenties and not arthritically set in their ways. But there was clearly more going on. It looked, on the face of it, like an artistic failure of nerve: after years of uncompromising oddity, the ISB were, it seems, trying deliberately to be more (dread word) 'accessible'.

Some of the impetus behind this, it seems reasonable to suppose, will have come from their manager of the previous year or so, Susie Watson-Taylor. When Joe Boyd pulled the plug on Witchseason in early 1971 and beat a path to Warners in Los Angeles, Susie, a Witchseason stalwart and soon also a Scientologist, stepped up to the plate as full-time manager of the band. A shrewd and experienced operator, Susie will have seen the way the wind was blowing, and may well have felt that nudging them towards the mainstream was the key to artistic longevity. Nevertheless, that wasn't the full story. Tucked away in the bottom corner of the inner sleeve-cum-lyric sheet were some curious and revealing credits. Photography and sleeve design were attributed to Mitch Walker, who earlier in the year had done a tasteful job on Robin's *Myrrh* solo album. But on both jobs, there's a sense in which he was acting on instructions: an enabler rather than an originator. For *Myrrh*, the guiding hands were those of Robin and Janet; for *Earthspan*, the likelihood is that Susie was standing at his shoulder.

We also learned from the credits section that the band's tonsorial needs were ministered to by a King's Road salon called, yes, Sissors [sic]. Did we veteran Stringheads really need to know that? Probably not, but it wasn't directed at us. Susie was credited as Executive Director, in a sudden and unsettling outgushing of corporate-speak; similarly, Malenie Schofield, who looked after the band's fanmail, was now proclaimed Letter Registrar. And just when you thought this couldn't get any worse, the section concluded with the all-caps salutation ALL STRENGTH TO THE COMMODORE. Y'know...the man whose shadowy visage lurks on the album sleeve if you look very closely – L. Ron Hubbard himself. (Who was not, literally speaking, a Commodore, or a possessor of any other naval rank; but he lived on a yacht, so you get the drift...)

Which, I would surmise, brings us to the heart of that 'something strange' I alluded to at the beginning of this piece. History states that the ISB hitched their wagon to the euphemistically-named Church of Scientology back at the end of 1968. Their involvement with the organisation was occasionally alluded to in press coverage, and prompted the odd speculative discussion wherever Stringfandom assembled; but it was easy enough to ignore – it was the elephant at the bottom of the garden. However, something seemed to change in 1972. Suddenly you couldn't read an ISB press interview without Scientology bulking large. The band were cagey at first ('It's great – next question...!'), but soon began to talk like moonstruck devotees. Concert-goers would find leaflets on their seats advertising L Ron's easy (and expensive) route-map to spiritual liberation. In quick time the ISB became Scientology's poster boys: after all, they had more of a media profile than Chick Corea or Woody Woodmansey.

Unlike many quasi-religious cults, Scientology doesn't prescribe achieving exalted awareness by cutting yourself adrift from the ways of the world in a bubble of contemplative bliss. Its methods, indeed, have much in common with modern corporate culture and come wrapped in graceless Hubbard-minted technobabble. The ISB, somewhat surprisingly, took to this with gusto. 'In order to operate further, I learned the organisational tech from the OEC ('Organisation Executive Course') volumes and we learned how to really run an organisational operation...' babbled Robin a few years later in an interview with the Church's house-journal *Celebrity*.

2021

Robin's new look. Not the sort of thing we expected from the Incredible String Band.

Gil Murray explains Scientology's 'Organisational Tech'

The OEC (Organization Executive Course) that Robin referred to was a long course, centred around eight fat and somewhat intimidating volumes. It would have been sold to the String Band as a way to help them work together in a unified way, cleanly and productively... and in the process, contributing massively to their spiritual wellbeing. However it's hard to find anything very spiritual about the OEC, which is based on L. Ron Hubbard's 'Administrative Technology' and its central concept of the 'Org Board'. It all seems very like 1950s management science, tarted up as follows:

'Transcending anything Man has previously understood on organization, the Org Board embraces the whole of life, delineating purpose, the alignment of purpose for each of its members, a built-in system of self correction to prevent counter-purposes – and all of it paralleling The Bridge with each successive department representing an awareness level directly corresponding to those an individual ascends on the Grade Chart.'

(Blurb from LRH book *Org Board And Livingness*)

In fact, the Org Board was a chart showing the different functions and posts that you would find in any large enterprise, arranged into divisions. Scientologists are taught that this is the ideal (and only) form of successful organisation – for any endeavour, large or small. The seven divisions of the Org Board were (in non-Scientology terms):

Communications, Sales/Marketing, Treasury, Production, Quality Control, Public Relations, Executive. This structure was to be imposed on organisations at every level. Not just on companies, but also on individuals and even planets and galaxies!

With will and imagination, Hubbard's Admin Tech could be shoehorned/twisted to address the needs of the band. Susie Watson-Taylor was 'Executive Director', Mike became 'Musical Director' and Robin was responsible for 'Quality Control'. Statistics were everything. You would monitor an 'Org's' progress by recording the statistics of each department. These would be examined at regular intervals, and if the trend was down, actions would have to be taken. In Robin's case, as 'Quality Control Officer', he would probably have kept statistics for 'number of mistakes corrected'. Mike, as 'Musical Director', might have kept them for hours spent arranging new material, or rehearsing. Mal's 'Letter Registrar' job was a sub-section of the Org Board. According to LRH, this involved writing to 'customers and prospects', 'enlightening' them for Scientology services and turning them into 'Hot Prospects'. I expect the band tried valiantly to make Scientology's

Admin Tech work for them, convinced it would be as valid, effective and liberating as their Scientology auditing and processing had been. But it surely must have been a disappointment and their commitment must have wavered. In fact I would be surprised if any of them managed to complete the OEC – which was a huge course if I remember correctly.

On the positive side, the order and discipline may have helped to some degree (and by 1973, there was even a Glen Row Rule Book!). However, in the long term, the real needs of the band were not to be addressed by the Admin Tech, and the 'slow and unsteady decline' described by Robin Denselow in *The Electric Muse* would continue to its inevitable conclusion.

Gil Murrary

In Mike's role as 'Musical Director', and from *No Ruinous Feud* onwards, producer, he also tended to handle the press interviews; his beaming smile became a feature of the pop papers over this period. Robin's 'Quality Control' role, rather modest by comparison, was to ensure that the band was well-rehearsed for recording and concert performance.

This crisp, very formal approach to String business is confirmed by Gerard Dott. When Gerard was invited to join the ISB in September 1972, his audition took the form of a loose jam with the band at Glen Row. But once he enlisted in their ranks, he found they ran a much tighter ship. 'Rehearsals were planned and punctual,' he recalled. 'Down Before Cathay at 11 o'clock. Explorer at 12. They were almost bureaucratic.' It all seems a far cry from the sometimes shambolic spontaneity of their late Sixties concerts. By this time the ISB were serious artists, with a responsibility to their audience, in concert and on record. Scientology had taught them that; it placed great stress on effective communication, a theme that wound its way constantly through their press interviews from 1972 onwards. The whole internal culture of the ISB was becoming informed by a Hubbardian focus on goals, clarity of purpose and effective working practices. It may even have been that Robin and Mike recognised something here that chimed in with their middle-class Edinburgh backgrounds. 'Edinburgh is a very business-y town,' Mike once reflected in a press interview.

The most obvious evidence of this new Scientology-fuelled seriousness was 1973's *No Ruinous Feud*. Stung by criticisms of *Earthspan*'s 'disjointedness', the band were quickly back in the studio, having – for once – thoroughly rehearsed the basic tracks at The Row. This was Mike's debut as the overall producer (along with engineer Roger Mayer), and he drew upon a lot of frank advice dispensed by John Cale during the *Smiling Men* sessions a couple of years earlier. Build from the bottom up, Cale had urged him: ensure a firm foundation exists as a platform for the florid elaborations and delicate arabesques. And sure enough, *Feud* had a structural solidity never before seen on an ISB album; its contents were hardly less diverse stylistically than *Earthspan*'s, but there was an underlying consistency of tone that made the whole thing more approachable to the typical rock fan of the day. And, in a quiet way, it rocked – something that no ISB album had ever done before.

And that, for many dyed-in-the-satin Stringheads, is precisely what's wrong with *No Ruinous Feud*, which is by some distance the least-loved album the band ever produced. There was a sense that the ISB were diligently discarding everything that made their music unique and cherishable, and loading up with things that just didn't belong. But the band were philosophical about this – or at least Mike was. As the woad-stained flower children wilt away, he opined to Steve Lake of *Melody Maker*, the band would attract new fans less locked in a 1968 time-warp.

That, then, was the calculation: the ISB would inevitably lose fans as they tiptoed towards the mainstream, but there was a new audience out there to be seduced and entranced: one that was currently grooving to Bowie, Led Zeppelin and Genesis (all of whom, incidentally, have confessed to being influenced by the ISB). There was a sense in the String camp that greater commercial success was within reach, and some of the members fancied a piece of it. Mike and Malcolm, in particular, were very keen on making a successful single, and pulled whatever strings they could pull to get the *Feud* single At The Lighthouse Dance onto the Radio One schedules. In vain, as it turned out. Chris Welch reviewed it for *Melody Maker*: 'Not one of their best efforts, and t'would seem a dreary roundelay, despite the addition of fisherfolk drums and tam o'shanter guitar.'

With a shinier, poppier production it might have caught the programmers' attention – even though it has as many structural changes in its three minutes as Bohemian Rhapsody has in six. Nevertheless, its absence from the playlists did not discourage some people from thinking big.

It was around this time that journalist Steve Peacock, hitherto a devoted fan, visited the band at Glen Row. He recalls: 'At this distance I can't remember how it happened that, as a staffer at *Sounds*, I was commissioned to write a piece about the Incredible String Band for the relatively new London edition of *Rolling Stone*. It didn't go well but it could have gone better.

'I'm not even sure of the year but it was early in the 70s and the band, led by their manager Susie Watson-Taylor, were signed up to Scientology. (I was only vaguely aware of this at the time. Later of course, Joe Boyd said one of his greatest regrets was leaving Susie alone in a room with a representative of the 'church').

'As I remember it, the band seemed rather at odds with one another and I struggled to find a coherent story to write. Whatever I wrote it clearly wasn't what was wanted because the London editor of *Rolling Stone* – a former *Daily Express* sub-editor, completely re-wrote it in full 'spaced-out-pixies-in-the-forest' mode. How I blushed.

'The story was actually staring me in the face from a 'goals' chart on the back of a kitchen door in the one of the Glen Row cottages. I can't remember what all the steps were, but the final goal on the chart was: 'Bigger than the Osmonds!' Presumably, Scientology had no interest in their recruits languishing in the folk charts.

'I asked the band about it but they wouldn't discuss it and asked me not to write about it. I didn't. By then, I suppose I couldn't be arsed to argue.' [*In putting this article together, we asked Malcolm if he remembered the chart – he doesn't, but reckons 'it was probably something to do with management.' – Ed.*]

So – was Scientology, that Something Strange in a Commodore's cap, the downfall of the ISB, the dark alchemy that gradually transformed their golden dreamscapes to base metal? Or was it more a matter of just growing up and moving on? Even with the benefit of hindsight, it's hard to tease these two factors apart and analyse them in isolation. For every half-remarkable question there is an infinity of answers. Looking back in 2021, Rose adds: 'Maybe Robin's abilities made ISB at its best, aided by Mike, and as the power-balance and the direction changed, Mike just didn't have the power, creative or personal, to take it forward as the dominant force. And Scientology kept them together for a while.'

All That Jazz: Gerard Dott

Gerard Dott effectively 'replaced' Likky in the band. Norman Lamont did the interview with Gerard in Spring 2003, Raymond Greenoaken wrote the rest.

Gerard Dott is a paradoxical figure in ISB history. He was a member for less than a year; he wrote nothing that became part of the canon; even his very name suggests a vanishing insignificance. And yet he has become symbolic of the ISB's most ill-starred period – 'the Dott Period', we often call it – the lurch into mainstream accessibility that spawned *No Ruinous Feud*.

Of course he was a symptom rather than a virus. It seems clear that he was parachuted in to give the ISB a range of less folky, less esoteric instrumental options, at a time when Robin and (especially) Mike were sniffing the air and sensing a change in the musical zeitgeist. Which he did to considerable effect; he enlarged the band's tonal palette and imparted a technical solidity they'd hitherto managed to do without. Despite this, his recruitment was generally viewed with astonished incomprehension – less, perhaps, because of the sounds he made than because of the way he looked.

The alarums began to ring with the photo squeezed into the bottom right corner of the *Earthspan* inner sleeve. 'This is Gerard Dott. He's a new member of the band,' proclaimed the accompanying caption, adding gratuitously, 'You can applaud him on the next tour.' The photo depicted a geeky, owlish chap who looked like he's just stepped out of a Kingsley Amis novel. Unfashionable specs, sleeveless sweater (beige, at a guess), collar and tie, eyebrows that met in the middle and thinning hair swept across his dome in Bobby Charlton style. His natural habitat, you'd have thought, was a grammar school common room rather than the Fillmore East.

Gerard: I was concerned that I didn't exactly look like the typical String Band member. Mike and Robin reassured me I would fit in fine. I'd have been embarrassed to dress like a hippy, but by that time they were wearing more 'normal' clothes. I also doubted whether I would fit in from a musical point of view. I thought of myself very much as a jazz clarinet player and the ISB music was very different from anything I'd done. But Mike and Robin were certain it was what they wanted. What I wore didn't seem to concern them at all.

Worse, it looked to all the world as though he'd been drafted in to deputise for the elfin, otherworldly Licorice, off on an extended 'holiday'. Apparently not. By the time the ISB hit the road in Autumn 1972, it was plain that Mr Dott was a bona fide member of the band. A velvet blazer was his only attempt to blend in with the peacock finery of his fellow bandsmen. When referred to onstage, he was invariably called 'Gerard', not Gerry, which only added to the fustian quality of his persona.

Gerard Dott, it can fairly be said, rose without trace; his name had never graced the pages of *Melody Maker* or *NME*. Eventually we learned that he'd played alongside Robin in a trad jazz group in early Sixties Edinburgh; despite his retro dress sense and premature baldness, therefore, he was of the same generation as Robin and Mike.

> Gerard: I was at Heriot's school with Mike. His dad was our English teacher. We used to call him 'Kipper'. Robin and Mike Travis went to George Watson's School, the traditional 'enemy' of Heriot's. Mike Travis was in my brother's Scout troop, hence I got to know him and then Robin. At 17 we formed a trad band, the Mound City Jazz Band, where Robin played banjo and I played clarinet. Mike Travis was the drummer; he and Graham Blamire, the bass player, went on to become respected jazz players.
>
> Then we all lost touch and I was surprised they had both drifted into folk. I caught Mike doing a solo set in a folk club, singing Dylan covers. Then Robin came round to my house one day, having heard I possessed a tape recorder. He asked if I could record him to let him hear his singing. He'd never thought of himself as a singer before. He told me that he thought jazz was becoming too intellectual and technique-oriented and he thought folk music could communicate more directly. He sang two songs, one of which was Whisky In The Jar. He and Mike Heron had yet to meet each other.

We'd already seen him credited on *Smiling Men*, where Mike thanked him for his help with the strings and woodwinds arrangement on Brindaban. That figured: he looked the sort of boffin who could toss off a semi-classical score on demand.

Gerard backstage in Homestead, USA. (Christine Santiago)

Gerard: Mike called me up out of the blue, asked me to come down to London for the day, where he was working on a solo album. I wrote the score, from Mike's ideas, and played clarinet on the recording. He was good at arrangements and very serious about it.

Prior to joining the ISB, Gerard had worked in a music shop in Edinburgh: a perfect case study of mild-mannered anonymity. But what could he bring to the Incredible String Band that they needed but hadn't already got?

Gerard: About a year after Brindaban, during which I heard nothing from them, they suddenly asked me to come out to Glen Row for a jam. After an enjoyable couple of sessions, they asked me to join the band. I was quite taken aback, but at the same time excited. What they wanted was to become more musically sophisticated. 'Quality' was the watchword. This was very much Mike's vision, and by the time I joined, he was in charge. Professionalism was the order of the day. There was some tension between Mike and Robin about this – Robin disliked My Blue Tears and Lighthouse Dance, thinking they were too overtly commercial – but all conflict was 'handled' through Scientology techniques, and Robin was clearly still trying to make it work within the band context. He was more interested in incorporating a bit of jazz; he'd already tried it with Evolution Rag, for instance.

Gerard was clearly a capable multi-instrumentalist. The Autumn concerts saw him turning his hand to clarinet, saxophone, organ, piano, banjo and guitar; and on *No Ruinous Feud* he added some dreamy vibes to Mike's Little Girl. Fair enough, but his sensibility was clearly that of a jazzer; jazz had not been an ingredient in the rich soup of the String Band's music heretofore. We know that Robin and Mike had listened to the likes of Mingus and Coleman in their Edinburgh beatnik days; the inclusion of Restless Night and Moon Hang Low in 72 set lists gave notice that Robin at least was now ploughing a jazzier furrow; and Mike's horn arrangements for those two songs on *Earthspan* showed that he too was exploring the idiom with some sensitivity. So, it made sense, sort of...

Another crucial element was Gerard's facility on the sax. In retrospect, we can see Mike's hand in this. Always more interested than the others in the current rock scene, Mike was doubtless paying close attention to the use of the tenor sax in bands like Roxy Music and the *Sticky Fingers/ Exile On Main Street*-period Stones.

> Gerard: Malcolm and Mike in particular were very keen on a Top Twenty hit. Malcolm worked hard to promote Lighthouse Dance to anyone who would listen, trying to get on *Top Of The Pops*. Robin was not at all comfortable with that idea.

Linking Gerard's saxy skills with those of roadie and occasional drummer/saxman/guitarist Jack Ingram, the ISB suddenly had a horn section. It was String, but not as we knew it. Nor, it must be said, did we like it, much. For the dyed-in-the-satin Stringfan, the spirituality at the heart of their music was linked intimately with their range of acoustic and particularly Eastern sounds. We'd muttered uneasily during the ISB's occasional flirtation with rockier forms (The Letter, Lady Wonder, Dear Old Battlefield), but given the lads the benefit of the doubt: after all, Mike even referred to *Smiling Men* as his 'rock 'n' roll holiday'. But with the arrival of Gerard Dott, it looked ominously like the ISB were gearing up for a more 'contemporary' sound.

> Gerard: I think they recognised that times had changed and they had to tighten up their act. While exoticism might let you get away with tuning a zither for half an hour between songs, it's not quite as fascinating with an electric guitar! Fans would come backstage as always to meet the band. They always seemed rather suspicious of me, as if I was the cause of the changes in musical direction and presentation, as if I was leading them astray!

An Island publicity still from 1973 – Gerard on far left. (Philip Newby archive)

Well, distance lends enchantment, and thirty years down the road I'm ready to come out and defend the Dott Period, and the part played by the man himself. When the Incredible String Band first thrust themselves into our lives, they were so multi-faceted, so unlike anything else that we naturally believed their music to be already fully achieved: where else could they go, and why would they want to anyway? Of course, that's not how the artistic temperament works. The true artist is always developing, always questing, always looking to make a leap in the dark. Robin and Mike both claimed (in the 'questionnaires' included in the first ISB songbook) to be innocent of ambition. In musical terms, however, nothing could be further from the truth. The Incredible String Band were distinguished by a vaulting ambition to impress their unique collective vision on as wide a spectrum of musical forms and idioms as possible. They didn't want to be virtuosi within any chosen form; they just wanted to extract its essence and make it work for them. So it was inevitable that they'd move on from the astonishing music that filled *Hangman* and *Wee Tam*, and explore other parts of the ethnomusical map. It wasn't to do with wanting to be Stan Getz or King Crimson: it was their visionary Whitmanesque desire to contain multitudes.

It was perhaps inevitable that this would lead them down paths that their fellow-travellers didn't want to follow. Perhaps Likky jumped ship because the ISB was embracing forms that she was uncomfortable with or unenthusiastic about, though Rose says now: 'I would happily have gone along with ISB diversifying into anything I could join in with. It was never the music that alienated me from the band.' It's probable that Robin's burgeoning interest in jazz and Mike's reconnection with rock 'n' roll dovetailed sometime in 1972 into a shared desire to bring someone in with an affinity for those forms.1972 was, as it turned out, the Year Dott.

Gerard: I didn't want to move in with them, and every house in Glen Row was full anyway, so I drove to Innerleithen every day for rehearsals. But after that initial jam when they asked me to join, there was strictly no jamming. Rehearsals were planned and punctual. Down Before Cathay at 11 o'clock, Explorer at 12. They were almost bureaucratic, which seemed to come from Scientology. I pretty much played what I was told. I would have liked more involvement. I felt like a permanent session musician.

No Ruinous Feud is the most vilified of all ISB vinyl ventures. Certainly it contains at least one outright failure and a few things that go off at half-cock, but also quite a bit of music that has actually stood the test of time rather well. And whenever it works best, there you'll find the bloke in the specs: the smoky, vibe-drenched beauty of Little Girl, the honking bass-clarinet-driven euphoria of Dolly Parton's My Blue Tears (they were her earliest champions outside of the Country scene), the crisp, saxy Weather The Storm, the belting, raspy Explorer with its punchy oboe and clarinet interjections, the swooning Turquoise Blue and its slithery clarinet solo. Purists might sniff at the cod-reggae postures of Second Fiddle, but that track highlights one of the ISB's key strengths over that period: the Dott-Williamson instrumental interplay. Here it's clarinet and whistle; in concert it was clarinet and fiddle. The two had a real rapport, producing the tightest and most organic duet playing since the cunning knotwork of twin guitars on *5000 Spirits*.

> Gerard: There was some nice stuff on that album. But we were stuck for a title. We all sat round one evening thinking of titles but no-one was very inspired. *No Ruinous Feud* was just the least bad!

I think that the recruitment of Gerard Dott was, in a quiet and subtle way, an inspired move. The gaucheness of Gerard's stage persona masked a musical sensibility of considerable panache and wit. And for such a quaintly old-fashioned-looking figure, he was strangely ahead of his time: his party piece at gigs would be a deftly executed Scott Joplin piano rag such as The Entertainer or Swipsey Cakewalk. It wasn't long afterwards that the Newman-Redford film *The Sting* ignited a brief worldwide fad for Joplin's compositions.

The Dott Period was not to last, however. Within a year of his arrival, Gerard was history. His departure, in the Summer of 1973, was attributed to 'musical differences'. In the lexicon of rock, this can mean anything from unpleasant personal habits to attempted homicide; occasionally it can even mean, well, musical differences. In Gerard's case, the problem seems to have been personal rather than professional. There are hints in Malcolm's tour diary for 1973 that he was not temperamentally suited to the rock 'n' roll lifestyle, even in the genteel form practised by the ISB. At the end of the tour, Malcolm says he was 'asked politely to leave'. More to the point, his 'outsider' status left him uncomfortable with the band.

> Gerard: I don't know what Malcolm was thinking of there. I never felt part of the band and never would because I was the only one in the band and entourage that wasn't a Scientologist. I knew little or nothing about Scientology at the start, but as I learned more about it my attitude hardened against it, and this in turn was resented by the rest of the group. I just didn't like what I read, although it seemed to have done

them some good. Robin told me, 'It just gets me where I want to go.' I think they gained a lot in terms of discipline, but perhaps went too far to that extreme. Everything was so tight and organised. There was no overt pressure on me, and no crass attempts to promote it to the audience, at least not at that time. But I knew I couldn't be a real part of it until I joined Scientology, so I told them I was leaving. They gave me time to think about it, and although I confirmed my decision, I sometimes felt later I should have stayed longer. But they found new members pretty quickly.

Gerard Dott returned to the quiet obscurity from which he had briefly emerged – to the same music shop, in fact, where he'd worked before.

Gerard: I hardly ever heard anything from them after I left. It just seemed like a strange, exciting year out! I went back to playing jazz with the Charlie McNair band and many others. I haven't thought about those days for so long. I must put the album on when I go home!

In the wake of his departure, the ISB promoted Jack Ingram and sound-man Stan Schnier (aka Stan Lee, Stanley Buttons) to full band status, on drums and bass (and occasional pedal steel) respectively. The stage was set for the leap, later that year, to full rock band status with the arrival of electric guitarist Graham Forbes. The Dott Period, then, was a short-lived experiment, long regarded by fans as a dead end. Was it simply an aberration, a wrong turning? The ISB themselves seem to have regarded it as such: that cool Latin groove they'd toyed with disappeared completely and the gap was filled with proggy synths, snarling blues-rock solos and Malcolm's visual pyrotechnics. Progress? A year later, the ISB was no more.

So let me doff my hat to Gerard Dott, a man who made a fascinating contribution to the story of String. He may be among the most obscure figures in 20th century popular music, but, half a century on, we're still talking about him.

Updated 2021

Feud *was released in February 73; it only reached #46 in the album charts. It was followed by a UK tour, where the focused rehearsals seem to have paid off. One concert reviewer noted that 'each number was anchored to a really strong rhythm section' and the 'subtle yet firm order in which the potential raggedness of four people's ideas were brought together,' which he felt was down to 'Mike Heron's new role as producer as well as arranger, composer and player.' You can hear what the Dott line-up sounded like live on the* First Girl I Loved *live CD. As well as playing the UK and the States, they were one of the first UK groups to play in Spain, performing a memorable gig in May 1973 at the Palau de la Musica in Barcelona as censorship began to loosen at the tail end of the Franco dictatorship. Gerard's last gig appears to have been in August 1973 at the London Music Festival, Alexandra Palace.*

Throughout most of 1973 and 1974, Malcolm Le Maistre kept a journal, which he recently rediscovered in a dusty attic box. What follows is part of the section which covers the ISB 1973 North American tour...

I'm getting worried about Gerard...

1st April 1973
Today we sailed (flew) gloriously into the USA, full of heat and concrete, curiously patterned tiles, coffee shops exuding varieties of fattening foods, long, lean, mean silvery cars, subtle colours escaping across the hilly landscape of LA, chasing the fumes of the car in front of us. Shining new cement and houses that slither silently amongst the palm trees sheltering coke bottles from a 'still' yellow sun hanging hopefully above an oily sea. It is a large country and this is but a glimpse...

Gerard disappears with his camera.

Tuesday 3rd April
Our first gig at the Troubadour. Impressions – the decor was wood with rather staid candles on the tables and large crumpled Mucha prints all over the walls...

The gig: well, it was full of variable and unfortunate incidents. Our first set, in the smoky atmospherics of the much-maligned folky environment, was, to say the least, somewhat erratic and exciting. But out of jet-lagged chaos things can go right, especially when I notice some attractive ladies in the front (always an uplifting moment). Before we played, there was John Martyn who is a slightly nervous, musical Scot with long curly hair of pale brown hue and a beard of some two years' growth. He plays guitar with extreme fervour, never losing control of his lapses. A sensitive individual. Our second set has considerably more merit.

Wednesday 4th April
Another very hot day chock-a-block full of heat. Breakfast with Stan (Schnier) with whom I shall be sharing a room for the rest of the tour. Swam in the Sunset Marquee pool where the actor Van Heflin died and Bob Dylan wallows. A brief chat to a young lady called Leslie amongst the umbrella stands and plastic woven chairs, some of which rock in a crude metallic manner. As for today's gig, the first set was ace, full of press and friends, even another young woman who held my hand and said she hoped I'd visit her (...foolish person). The second set was tired but we still seemed to play quite well.

I'm getting worried about Gerard...

<u>6th</u>
Another night at the Troubadour club... the new Gilles [*See cartoon*] hit the hearts of some but failed to reach greatness.

<u>8th</u>
Last gig at the Troubadour... phew!

<u>10th</u>
Last day in LA was spent watching the rain, but in the morning I was on television. Met John Cale (Velvet Underground fame) who combines idiocy and talent with inebriate ramblings. We sat in his office and played Monty Python records. He told me about racing cars and laughed horribly... lovely guy.

<u>11th</u>
Inspiration amongst the Mormon groves of Salt Lake City. One is reminded of Conan Doyle's *Study In Scarlet*. Statues of Brigham Young abound. The mountains rise shadowesque, picturesque, stuffed with granite, cascading incandescent light via reeling snow [*this is getting more obscure than Lighthouse Keeper! – Ed.*]. The gig was in a beautiful hall. Very fluid. Gerard disappeared with a woman! God forbid.

<u>13th</u>
Friday the 13th – an ominous day in San Francisco. Our gig was rather sad. Not many people in a large, lovely hall with red seats leaping up at you with great assurance. Even with little response from an audience I enjoy gigs for what they are, for the unexpected.

<u>14th</u>
Another empty desultory affair, challengingly empty; those who were there seemed thick... except for Caroline Plage, a delightful young lady who managed to keep the audience slightly enthusiastic by sitting in the front row and shouting, clapping and being very gracious.

<u>15th</u>
Today's gig was fun and a pleasure to play, to an audience who were enthusiastic, contented, noisy and full of that precious reaction – laughter. Los Gatos is an odd little town, but the countryside is stunning...

Top Malcolm as Gilles' girlfriend Gloria Beaver, 1972/3. (Malcolm's collection). *Right* Malcolm & admirers backstage in Homestead, USA, 1973. (Christine Santiago). *Left* Gilles waxes romantic—onstage, 1973. (Malcolm's collection)

16th
An odd gig at Berkeley in the Keystone Club. Caroline Plage was extremely nice to me today, giving me a rose and some pretty words. I leave some of the petals between these pages. [They are still there now].

17th
Today consisted of flying, during which we lost three hours of our lives. Mike continues to amuse me. His obsession with penguins is turning him into one – his white shoes and stubby legs. A very fine person. So here we are in Rochester N.Y., sitting in a Holiday Inn amongst the concrete highways of America, a food stand on every corner and love being made in every other bedroom. Sometimes I loathe American culture – but a supremely beautiful country.

18th
A lovely gig in Rochester. The New Gilles worked well. Rochester is an extreme example of the horrors of US culture but it is very funny. No love today. Maybe N.Y. will remedy that for me. I enjoy that most dramatic of cities.

19th
A lovely dossing day. Dossing in the air. Dossing in the motel. Dossing in the airport. Dossing in the taxi, the Holiday Inn etc. Just having one of those boring days. Precisely nothing happens.

20th
Down to Philadelphia, the old capital. Fur coated dudes oiling down the street with pearly perception. Drag queens, housewives and crumbling old husbands. A poor man's N.Y. The gig is very nice and takes place in a large round hall with red upholstery and a beautiful chandelier hanging down from a frothing ceiling, adorned with angels and angles painted by a seedy American painter with a head for heights.

21st
And so to the dark city herself. A night out with Stan... Saw Procol Harum. Was impressed. Then on to Max's Kansas City, that meeting place of the mindless and the social. Decadent and attractive. After eating we went upstairs to watch two groups. One was very Randy Newman, the other was Charlie

Rich, a great country singer with an amazing guitarist. Back to the hotel… We watch Judy Garland on a flickering TV.

22nd
A classic gig in N.Y. Something one often dreams of but rarely achieves. A real gem. There is little I can say about such a night. The stage lined with gifts. Smiles, a woman named Jan, another named Jenny whom I really liked.

23rd
Toronto. A disappointing gig, although signing autographs in a record shop had its distractions. The hotel, the Waldorf Astoria, is vast and ugly but has that quality of human lowness that fascinates the artist or the psychologist.

25th
Back to New York. Saw Chick Corea. Very good but really not to my taste. Larry Coryell was incredibly bad. Musical wanking. The Deep Purple of jazz.

26th
Dinner at Hector Mercardo's. Hector dances with the Alvin Ailey dance company. I really like his wife. We ate chili and chatted in a sort of mildly interested/bored N.Y. way. There was a man called David from Putney (my home town) who left the Royal Ballet when 'Rudi joined'. All oddly low key.

27th
A nothing day. N.Y. is a sea of umbrellas and mingling eyes.

29th
Gerard worries me. He's been looking increasingly out of his depth and seems to be sinking into a death-like state, his moustache looking more ponderous each day.
Reached Washington. It is hot and horrible. At such times I long for Scotland and the spaniel. Soon.

30th
Our first gig in Washington at the Cellar Door. Small and pleasant. I feel doubt about my future in the band, it's been bothering me for a while. Met Donna whom I am very fond of (from before). She gave

some bread and smiled. Suzy is leaving us tomorrow for somewhere.

2nd May
Still stuck in Washington – a distilled part of the world with no romance and a dirty river. Met a lovely woman in a flower shop. She has a little girl called Sasha. It was all very City Lights. The gigs are good. Robin amazes me with his Hendrix-like fiddle playing.

5th
Our last gig in Washington which seems to have become an eternal city. Good gigs. Nice folk. Met Donna again. Feel strongly paternal towards her. (Why?)

6th
Tampa, amongst the palm trees and mangroves, crocodiles. Today I love America for its hugeness and its diverse landscape. It is exceptional. The gig was dire. Sound problems. Led Zeppelin played to 65,000 last night, a record for the band. If only.

7th
Back to New York and My Father's Place. I took a walk around Westbury. Horses. Houses with little lawns. Chubby candy-eating children full of fat and foolish games. Lethargic old men locked in the memories of routine that have pervaded their lives. It is sad seeing it. Is it the belt of life that holds us, abducts our individuality and sends it spinning into the abyss of impersonality? The gig was pleasant and redeeming after the fiasco of Tampa.

8th May
High point of our second My Father's Place gigs was meeting Jenny Charm again. Very sharp, very attractive. She is from the local town of Great Neck and has a friend called Polly Sweet. Spent the day in N.Y. Got some nice red shoes. The gig was warm and energetic, full of wit and humour. El Rato seems to have found its legs again which is very good as it is a bit of a classic. Ho hum.

9th
Moved west to Champagne, Illinois which is certainly a place not to be often visited. A place of extreme brutishness, tough football playing youths strolling along mottled streets. Mottled by the oafish pranks of its ugly, twisted and insane community,

the strange fraternities, the sorority girls; an utterly unreal world. But perhaps most bizarre was the promoter who, having told us that the turnout would be small, then announces he is doing a degree in advertising (his thesis will be – bad advertising example – our show). It was bad and we sunk to the occasion.

10th
Second gig had a little more champagne than the first. A good enthusiastic response and a girl called Bianca. Spent some time in the sauna which was definitely very odd.

11th
Today has been strange. A boring but fundamentally fascinating day. A long drive through the hot Midwest then Chicago, that most soporific of cities. No energy, little beauty or sanity. Very much my least favourite American city. But one thing that I like is the buildings of the 1900s, rising majestically above the waterfront – or do I… Christ I wish I wasn't here. Need to sleep.

At this point, there is a break in the journal, but there is one more entry:

14th May
The tour is over… Banal but rewarding. Not sure if I love touring or hate it. Probably love it as it means meeting people.

Back in Scotland. No Holiday Inns, no coffee shops, no beautiful American girls, no noise. Looking forward to sanity but also to going back to America. J.C. may visit me.

I am slightly disturbed, concerning my status in the band. I shall sort this fucking thing out soon.

Gilles Crooked Deal

In the early Seventies, Robin wrote several pieces which were vehicles for Malcolm's performance skills. Gilles Crooked Deal was 'a spoof', as Robin terms it, about a criminal crocodile who misses his own birthday party. You can hear a version on it on the live CD *First Girl I Loved*. Below, Allan Frewin guides you through the characters in the song (who were all played by Malcolm).

No Ruinous Feud – Masterpiece or muddle?

The scene: A courtroom carved from living wood and wound with bright ivies and trumpeting haws. In the public gallery sit a Hedgehog, some Puppies and a Caterpillar among other strange creatures. In the dock stand Robin, Mike, Malcolm and Gerard Dott. Robin looks uneasy as he leafs through a Cosmos Skytours American holiday brochure. Mike grins and looks nervous but confident whilst Malcolm adjusts his cravat and looks into the future for a streetlight to be under. It's 1973, that most portentous of years for the ISB. Had they lost the plot entirely with No Ruinous Feud, *or was it the beginning of another era, if only... Above them the pale ghost of a black haired, gap-toothed girl flits disconsolately, whispering 'I know you'. The judge, a distinguished figure in black robe with scythe accessory, much given to telling people his name, draws himself to his full height and declaims: 'Incredible String Band, you stand before your creations and subjects accused of making an appalling album, of leaving your public behind and of sundry other offences against the taste of those who thought* Wee Tam And The Big Huge *was enough to base a religion on. How do you plead?' Every fan they ever had leans forward expectantly...* Andy Roberts

Norman Lamont mounts a half-hearted defence

No Ruinous Feud appeared in March 73 and was the ISB's attempt to break into the mainstream of 'progressive' rock (itself a dying category). Take the title. Clumsy, the first ISB title not to ring like crystal. We wondered what the feud was: the Williamson and Heron solo albums? The 'me and my backing band' approach of *Earthspan*? The departure of Licorice? The less devoted would just find it an odd mouthful.

If the title was puzzling, the sleeve was a deliberate challenge. Never mind the hippies, here is a sophisticated piece of modern product. The familiar 'The' was dropped from the name. The title was emblazoned on a tacky pop-art flash (later used for Dylan's equally tacky *Shot Of Love* sleeve), stuck onto four clumsily matched David Bailey portraits of the Men. Mike leads the way into the Brave New World by sporting a collar and tie and a corrugated tin blazer. It's sobering to reflect in the light of current fashions that Mike's lapels here seem more dated than their garb on *Wee Tam* or *I Looked Up*! As Raymond says, the sleeve seemed to confirm that the band had lost their vision, their innocence, their bearings, and – not least – their dress sense. If I dwell on the sleeve it is because it was a fair ride home on the Glasgow Underground on that frosty morning. My feelings of anticipation and puzzlement worked on the inner and outer sleeves for a good half-hour before I got it on the turntable.

The opening seconds were another farewell to the misty world of *Wee Tam*. B.J. Wilson on drums kicks us into Mike's Explorer. After *Earthspan* was criticised for lacking in continuity, Mike took the helm for *Feud* and decreed a rhythm section of bass and drums to underpin all the tracks, to give the ISB the authentic rock voice he longed for. What doubts I had gathered over the sleeve were blown away by this confident piece with its biting rhythm; Mike sings strong and true and the wind arrangements provide interest for many subsequent hearings.

The recruitment of Gerard Dott was intended to beef up the musical credentials of the band, replacing serendipity with professionalism. And were those really Janet Williamson and Susie Watson-Taylor on glossy 'backing chick' vocals, or uncredited Island regulars like Sue & Sunny or Lisa Strike? [*Mostly the latter – Ed.*]

Down Before Cathay is the great country and western tune that Marco Polo never wrote. Beautifully produced, all cascading guitars over a happy ambling rhythm; Malcolm's romantic verses promise more than they deliver when you actually read through them ('the admire-able deeds of Kubla Khan we admired...' he declaims without irony) but the promise is enjoyable enough. Sadly it is Robin and Mike who betray the polished veneer of the song with their sheep-like entrance on the chorus. [*Malc disagrees: 'I like the clipped vocals on the refrains' – Ed.*] While fanatics like me gloried in hearing them sing together again, friends hearing them for the first time raised quizzical eyebrows at this moment. Listening again after all these years, it is Cathay out of all the tracks that stays in my head.

Ah, but Saturday Maybe was the business. It convinced the fans that Robin could still work magic, but also that Mike's rock and string experiments could complement it perfectly. In thirteen short lines Robin recreates a sad, furtive relationship in visual, tactile and emotional detail. 'Lead me by the light of your electric fire... Across the sheets your nut-brown curls go tumbling.' A friend said this was an old song, confirming the impression that Robin was losing interest about this time. As a songwriter myself I can only wonder at this perfect little gem.

After these three tracks, however, the cracks begin to show. A round of jigs followed; fine in concert but unnecessary here, lacking the rough edges and sense of fun of the Grumbling Old Men set. Old Buccaneer – OK we've had rock, country, folk and Saturday Maybe, but what is this? Gerard Dott and Robin appear to have cooked up this and Circus Girl between them. Though Robin plays electric guitar with that kind of RW jazz phrasing, on the 1 beat on the last section, this wasn't even jazz, and though we tried to love it, well... Unlike Cathay, however, a close reading of the words rewards the effort handsomely.

At The Lighthouse Dance was the last ISB single, and was probably intended, in one ISB head at least, to rocket Malcolm into the fashionably camp ranks of Bowie, Bolan, Harley and Mercury. Live he mimed the pop star, strutting and fey in turns, but oh dear, it looked like he meant it! A pleasant sequence of pop chord changes with lyrical nonsense of the powder-and-lace space cadet school, it was cited by many as evidence for the prosecution in the ongoing trial by fandom that Malcolm was subject to. [*Whilst on tour, the band had visited Ulverston in Cumbia, where Malcolm went out to a local dance. Towering above the town is the lighthouse-shaped monument to Sir John Barrow, a local and a great promoter of Arctic voyages of discovery. And so a song was born – Ed.*]

Here I probably depart from ISB heterodoxy and declare that I love Second Fiddle, which is a Duke Reid-composed instrumental over a backing track by the reggae band Greyhound, who'd had a chart hit a year or two earlier with the nursery ditty Black and White. Island Records had the idea for a series of collaborations between their reggae artists and their pop/rock roster, of which this is one. It kicks off side two with a short burst of exuberant joy.

Raymond Greenoaken adds: They were barking up the wrong tree with Lighthouse Dance. Second Fiddle is actually a perfect copper-bottom single. Remember those novelty instrumental hits of the early 70s – Mouldy Old Dough, Desperate Dan, Popcorn, Return Of Django etc? Second Fiddle would have fitted that novelty niche like a calfskin glove: funky, catchy, irresistibly smile-inducing (I find) and with a voguish groove. A smash in the making! I somehow can't see Robin and Gerard tootling away on *Top Of The Pops* (imagine Robin's reaction...): rather, it would be a chance for Pan's People to undulate fetchingly in Caribbean garlands, with bright green inflatable violins under their chins. In a parallel universe this all happened...

> Back to Norman: Circus Girl was like Buccaneer, only worse. Rambling and not even funny. Despite the efforts of Mike to forge a singularity of purpose, Robin and Mr Dott seemed to be pulling in another direction, a pull that seems more ruinous than on the happily patchwork *Earthspan*.

Turquoise Blue, along with Little Girl and the first three tracks, is probably the sound of the album Mike wanted to make, with Gerard providing the polish rather than the furniture. He smoothly recreates the mood of some tropical beach holiday, probably with the girl from Ipanema. Nowadays this would be called AOR; in those days it was just very good.

I'd venture that Malcolm instigated the cover of Dolly Parton's My Blue Tears; if so, I rest my case [*It was Mike actually – Ed.*]. Again, the band come together and complement each other, Robin adding jovial fiddling to the deadpan harmonies of Mike and Malcolm. Weather The Storm had featured live for ages, a kazoo and footstomp closer of sets. Here, however, it is held down rather than pushed along by the sax arrangements. The ending is fun, the rest isn't.

The album plays out with Little Girl. Mike's been at his Steely Dan albums again; but they've inspired an intimate little love song, afloat in ringing vibes from Gerard. Mike seeks to close the album as it opened, the work of a modern rock band.

In retrospect it would have taken more than a tight rhythm section and a strong production to pull the diverse strands together. Mike had his vision, Malcolm his ambition, Robin seemed aimless, and Gerard Dott had the uneasy post of everyone's session musician. Out of the album I think you would get a good Mike Heron EP, and a single of Saturday Maybe, backed with the cover versions Second Fiddle and My Blue Tears – but you'd still not have a band.

ROBIN INTRODUCES CIRCUS GIRL AT A 1973 GIG:

'It's about an acrobat in the circus seen by a young boy. I had the idea that it should be played by a very miraculous kind of band playing music for trombones and ice-cream cornets and preferably with those cutest of faces where they have ears coming out of their eyes. We're going to have Malcolm playing percussion and also Gerard's going to do orchestral effects on the organ here. Maestro, please...'

Allan Frewin puts the prosecution case

So. How do you go about analysing *No Ruinous Feud*? Track by track is the usual method, so I won't bother with that. Too technical. It's the general feel that's important.

I vividly remember my first encounter with the ISB. I stroll into this record shop for a quick root through the covers. And I come across this weird album. No pictures, just a white cover with lyrics printed on it, the first letter of each song illuminated with flowers and fairies. Open it up and there's these two men gazing out at you. Hippies. Real hippies. Not like us school kids, our hair creeping cautiously over our ears, dreading to hear at any moment the clack of approaching scissors. My heart went out to them the same way it soon went out to this cracked American musician, posing on his album cover with a fish held to his face and a shuttlecock on top of his hat (but that's a story for a different fanzine). Those were the days my friends. The days of listening booths in record shops. The days when you could say; can I have a listen to a bit of this? I came out of that booth like a boy who had peered through the gates of heaven. Job's Tears. Voices like I had never heard. Music from another world. A world I wanted to be in – head, hands, feet and heart. It was like falling in love.

Well, now. What has all this got to do with *No Ruinous Feud*? Bugger all, possibly – or everything. It's got a lot to do with falling in love with music. Well – more than music, really. It was everything about the ISB. What they looked like. The things they wrote about. The whole swirl of stuff that they carried about with them. It's about gobbling up the new album, whipping it out of the rack almost before it settles. Taking friends home in a bag and listening to them telling you about where they've been. Where they're going to take you. Over the hills and far away. And then, as the Sixties came crashing down, the feeling that your old friends aren't quite what they were. As if they've done something to themselves. As if they've stopped talking about life, the universe and everything and started droning on about mortgages and life insurance. Eeek!

I remember a review of *Earthspan* at the time. A lament, really. The reviewer was positively lachrymose over the fact that she just couldn't summon her old enthusiasms for the band. As if it was a problem with *her*, not with them. As if she'd grown up. As if the ISB was a like a teddy bear or a beloved doll that one day finds itself in the bottom of a wardrobe. And, I've got to admit, it *did* feel a bit like that for me as well.

My friends and I would spend hours wondering about it. What had gone wrong? Was it because Joe Boyd wasn't producing them any more?

Was it because the girls had gone? Was it because it was 1973? Or were we too old? Or were the ISB making crappy albums?

The crunch came with *No Ruinous Feud*. We couldn't like it – and that's as honest as it comes. We played it over and over and over, snatching at straws. Trying to make a curate's egg out of a sow's ear. Trying to pretend it wasn't happening. It was almost a relief when Robin went to America and it was all over. ISB fan club member five-hundred-and-something packed his break-up letter from the band, his collected reviews and photos, and put them, along with his teddy bear, in a quiet grave at the bottom of the wardrobe. That's what it felt like at the time.

But why? What was really going on? They hadn't gone commercial. I'd had to come to terms with that when T lost its yrannosaurus and went electric. It wasn't that. It was something else. As if they were *trying* too hard. Trying very hard to be...what? Relevant to the Seventies?

The album cover. Now then, what can we say about that? All the bands you love come as a complete package. It's not just the sound they make. It's what they look like as well – the paraphernalia they carry with them. *No Ruinous Feud* consisted of four glossy David Bailey photos that seemed they could have been slung together by anyone. This was just... nothing. It didn't draw you in. It didn't promise to take you anywhere.

The feeling of being let down really started with *Liquid Acrobat* – especially for anyone who had heard the band perform much of the stuff on it on the radio.

It was as if Mike's production took the songs and shrink-wrapped them into shiny, disconnected, dead pieces. Butterflies pinned to the mixing desk. Cold and sterile. You could almost see Mike rubbing away at the songs until they shone with an empty, lapidary brilliance. The songs tightened and hardened and became brittle and unlovely; all the magic sucked out of them. For heaven's sake, I *liked* it when the songs sounded like a shambles. I loved that. The days when, for whatever reason, a cock up by the fiddles on Log Cabin Home In The Sky was just left there. It was part of the magic. The way the seeming chaos of Creation still hangs together. The times when, on When You Find Out Who You Are, it sounded like Mike was tinkling away on his piano in a different room. (According to Joe Boyd, he may well have been). The times when the whole rickety, rackety chariot seemed to keep to the road by a single spinning wheel-rim.

But it wasn't just that the craziness and joy had gone out of it. It was the feeling that the balance had shifted. Where Robin had stood like a shaman on the hillside, leading us all on into the strange places of his imagination, it now seemed that we had been taken into an up-to-the-minute recording studio with Mike grinning away at the controls. The technician, it seemed had taken over from the mystic. And it felt like Robin had got bored, utterly bored with the whole thing. As if Mike's reported comment that they wanted to get into shorter, more accessible songs left no room for him to do what he did best. As if someone was trying to cage a phoenix so people could get a better look at it. And the phoenix was just sitting there, staring miserably through the bars and gradually getting greyer and greyer.

Look at Robin's songs on *No Ruinous Feud*. Where's the magic gone? Where is the enchantment? A dreary, back street love affair with someone else's wife. Not even a love affair, by the time the words hit the page. Just a glimpse of grinding unhappiness. A prosaic tale of a dead sailor, and two children looking bleakly back to what once was. And, god help us, the prime candidate for worst song in the ISB pantheon, a pointless little ditty about an acrobat.

'The ringmaster's hat is black as a Wellington boot'? What? Did Robin Williamson, the cunning, crafty word-spinner and dream-catcher *really* write that? Why? Yup, that's the crux. Robin was bored shitless and seemed to be going along for the ride. Listen to his vocal on Dreams Of No Return on the *On Air* CD, if you don't believe me. There's someone who'd rather be doing something else.

And Malcolm? Well, I quite liked his songs on *Earthspan*. He must have liked them as well because he wrote them all over again for *No Ruinous Feud* – only not as well. In fact, the only person who seemed to be in top form and thoroughly enjoying himself was Mike. A Mike Heron solo album would have been infinitely preferable to *No Ruinous Feud.*

I also thought the album title was wrong. There should have been an exclamation mark after No, and an 'Oh' in front. 'Oh No! Ruinous Feud'. That would have made more sense. Take Explorer, Turquoise Blue and Little Girl and you'd have a lovely Mike Heron EP. Take Saturday Maybe, Old Buccaneer and Circus Girl and you've got someone who'd lost the plot and who ought to take himself off somewhere and spend some time on a sunny beach. Someone who should come back to us after a good rest and dazzle us all over again. Just as he was bound to do.

It seems a little pointless to go through the tracks. 'Shall we stick some jigs on somewhere? They always seem to go down well at concerts.'

'Yes, OK, if you like.'

'People are listening to a lot of reggae these days – what about a reggaeified instrumental?'.

'Yes, if you like'.

'And there's this Dolly Parton song...'

'Yes, if you like. Put what you *like* on it, I don't care. I don't even want to be here anymore. Have you seen that American tourist guide about anywhere?'

I've just noticed that I haven't even mentioned Weather The Storm. 'Stormy weather in the world since the day I was born...'. Yes, well, it certainly *sounded* like it Robin. It certainly did. And maybe you should have stopped bailing and swum for it a couple of years earlier. But then we might not have got Cold Days Of February and that would have been a shame.

It won't have gone unnoticed that a couple of hoary old ISB debating points have been left out of this piece. Scientology and Gerard Dott, to be precise. I didn't think Scientology was the problem. As for Mr. Dott, I remain as bemused today as I was at concerts at the time, when the rest of the band would wander off so that he could do his ragtime party piano piece. Very nice, I'm sure, and well-played – but what was the point? Was it that the idea of co-opting untrained musicians had passed its sell-by date? Was it because Mike was now into scoring all the songs, and thought that a 'real' musician would be better able to follow what he had written? Or, in the grand old ISB tradition, was it simply because Gerard Dott was in the vicinity?

Well, that's about it for *No Ruinous Feud* and me – of course, this is an overview and not a review. I'm sitting here listening to it on CD (Yeah! I *bought* it on CD – after everything I've been saying! What does that tell you eh?), and I'm thinking, you know, it's not *that* bad. I mean, Explorer is actually dead good now I come to listen to it again. But that's not the point. The point is about feelings from 1973. The feeling that a love affair was over. Except that it wasn't, not really – and probably never will be. A quick chorus of 'First Band I Loved', anyone?

'In one way *No Ruinous Feud* was the end of a cycle. And at this point now we're far enough ahead from the end of that cycle to be writing in the middle of another one. It's a fruitful time right now. It's going to be really exciting to see what shoots on.'

Mike Heron, 1973

Finally, here is Malcolm's 2021 take on *No Ruinous Feud*:

I like Explorer. It feels like Mike is trying too hard to veer towards rock but remain ISB. A conflicted song... but still one of the better ones. I think Down Before Cathay stands the test of time, and I like the concertina and clipped vocals on the refrains. Saturday Maybe is great because it's

Robin being true to himself. It sounds like a description of Edinburgh in the 50s. Quite cinematic and I think the arrangement is very nice. Uniquely ISB, and it would work fine today. It's my favourite song on the album. Lighthouse Dance was the intended hit single. This was probably a misstep and not really single material. We should have restructured it and lost one of the sections, but I liked the 'Oh do you dance ...' bit. A proper rock band would have made more of it. Turquoise Blue grows on you, although it's not my cup of tea. It veers into MOR smooth music but is actually rather more than that. My Blue Tears is actually a rather good version, although there was no need to do any covers as there were other songs around including my own Did I Love A Dream. A mystery why it was never recorded! Weather The Storm is very confusing, but I like Little Girl, although the vocal is just a bit too laid back.

I enjoyed listening to this again but the tension is there. Despite the title of the album the battle lines were drawn. And there was me stuck in the middle. As for the cover – not one of Davis Bailey's finest moments, Susie's idea I think. Mike looks like a jumped-up gangster in his Tommy Nutter suit, Robin bemused, Gerard loving it and me somewhere else.

My overall view is that this is an album of two halves in three ways: the album itself, side one with several very good songs, side two not so hot. Robin is trying to be modern and failing as he is still essentially old school ISB. (I mean that as a compliment.) Mike is moving more and more towards where he wanted to be although his romantic side still shines through.

Overleaf At a Scientology event, 1970

Mike Heron looks back over the ISB's career, we examine the role of Scientology and Zen in their work and take a walk on the Wyrd side.

COME TO LIFE!

Chapter Ten

Mike Heron

Andy Roberts

Cohen, Dylan, all the other singers of a 'certain age' are still around and I queried how Mike felt to be going into his sixth decade, still playing music.

Andy: When you started off with the String Band did you have any inkling that you might still be doing it as the twentieth century shambled to a close?

Mike: I never thought about doing anything else really.

When did you first pick up a guitar?

Well, it was a ukulele. I did piano lessons but I wasn't a brilliant success at school, I was generally kind of rescued by interesting boys who liked to take care of the waifs. And I wasn't good at sports, so I made these interesting friends and one time I went to a scout camp in Perthshire and there was a boy there playing the ukulele who was absolutely the life and soul of the party, so I immediately bought a ukulele and taught myself how to play and became the life and soul of the party doing Fats Domino songs.

How did the early String Band sound on the first album come about – because it is 'world music' before it existed as such – and there must have been nothing around to influence you at the time... or was there?

No, there definitely wasn't. The first album is really the kind of music that we would have liked to think a jug band – 'cos it was meant to be jug band – would play. In fact an alternative name for the String Band was the Fruit Jar Drinkers, suggested by Clive, and it was that kind of thing, it was a jug band format we were after. But it was not a jug band like any other one. The New Lost City Ramblers would be about the closest, but then you'd have Clive not doing the Earl Scruggs finger picking, he would be doing the old fashioned frailing, and Robin would be doing the fiddle playing without the customary American vibrato, so it was immediately becoming quite bizarre, it was an invented music to accommodate the three of us and to make it something we could sit round and listen to because there wasn't much music then. There was The New Lost City Ramblers, Ravi Shankar, Blind Gary Davies.

Did you listen to John Renbourn and people like that at the time?

Well we employed them! When we moved from the Crown Bar and did Clive's Incredible Folk Club in Sauchiehall Street it was all night and so we had a lot of guests. We had John Martyn on a few occasions. We'd start off with me doing a little set on my own and then Robin would do one on his own, then Clive, interspersed with different acts and the acts were like Archie Fisher, John Martyn, Bert Jansch of course who was living with Robin at the time and that's how we met John Renbourn, through that.

Following the first album Robin went to North Africa, Clive to India and Afghanistan. What did you do?

Yeah, I did Frutch! [*a naff song on* Chelsea Sessions – *Ed.*] I did a complete tour of most of Scotland and few gigs in England too that Archie Fisher set up in the folk clubs. I did it with a harmonica rack and I did Dylan songs, In My Time Of Dying, and it was crowd pleasing, folky stuff, harmonica and vibrant energetic guitar.

Was there any reason why you didn't follow Robin and Clive on what was then the nascent hippy trail?

I wasn't really tempted. I was just enjoying the fact that I liked getting audiences. You see Clive didn't like the first album because it was already going in the direction of what they [Elektra] really wanted, which was writers. Nobody really wanted a British version of the New Lost City Ramblers, particularly in America, and it was an American label. So they wanted songwriting and that's where I came to the fore because before that I'd just been a strummer really, for them to do their violin and banjo and whatever over, so I came into my own when the first album was made and Joe Boyd indicated that we would be very popular with the company if we did a lot of original material, and Clive just had a couple of songs and so did Robin.

> *Your songs seem to be the strongest on the first ISB album. Do you agree?*

Yeah, well, I'd been writing songs for a long time and Robin had been doing more poetry.

> 5000 Spirits *followed, without Clive Palmer. What do you think of it now?*

Robin came back from Morocco and I was doing my solo bit and he'd come back with all these wonderful instruments [*see Appendix – Ed.*] and suggested we got together. So we got in touch with Joe and he got us into a studio, I think it was Sound Techniques, and we'd played the songs briefly to each other before, but not really. So they're really songs that we wrote on our holidays. And that's why there is a liveliness to it.

> *Who were the ISB songs written for – a specific audience or for yourselves?*

Very much to provide a kind of music that wasn't there. Because this is pre-Andy Kershaw, people weren't exposed to that kind of music and just felt a gap. We didn't like pop music much – I did more than Robin, he'd been brought up on folk ballads.

> *Rose and Licorice were to join the band in the late 1960s, but what about the two female dancers who appeared with you before then, the mysterious Mimi and Mouse?*

Yeah, one of the things Robin liked to do was multi-media stuff, involving the audience and so on. It left me completely cold, I didn't really like it, wasn't what I wanted to do. But being as how I was a fan of Robin's I liked to see him expand in that direction, he was fulfilling himself by doing that and it entertained the audience. So all the things with Malcolm and Mimi and Mouse were more condoned by me...

On to Wee Tam And The Big Huge, *to my mind the most naïve – in the correct sense of the word – and unaffected album they ever did, and a peak one. Puppies for instance. As John Peel once said, only the String Band could get away with singing about such things and be 'innocent of deceit'.*

Yeah, it's one of the things not often tackled in the music business. But it's very easy to get into thinking that music is the be all and end all, the most important thing and really Puppies is about that, about how you have to balance things and how it's never that important.

Air – another famous Heron song – was also used as part of the soundtrack for Milos Forman's film Taking Off.

Milos Forman was a big fan and always trying to get us in a film, but he couldn't really think of a way of doing it without taking the piss!

Is Air taken from a Tahitian melody, as rumour has it?

No, it's not a pinched tune – more influenced. Now White Bird is a pinched tune, from a very obscure Pakistani or Indian film. [*The chorus tune is nicked from a 1966 Bollywood number called Aayega Aanwala, performed by Lata Mangeshkar, one of India's most influential singers, known as the 'nightingale of Bollywood', died in 2022 in Mumbai aged 92, with two days of national mourning declared in her honour – Ed.*]

What about the String Band and TV? Besides the three Julie Felix shows you appeared on there doesn't seem to be much else for a band of such stature at the time. Was there anything else?

The most wonderful one we ever did was for a regional station in Norfolk and that was quite fantastic. Just me and Robin. We went in the afternoon and met this guy who'd just got the job as presenter – he usually did the weather or something – and he was really nervous and uptight. Anyway, so Robin laid out all his instruments on the table in preparation for the interview later and then we would do a couple of songs.

Then Robin and I went out by the river and had an enormous joint, and came back in, and the guy presenting was really nervous and he'd made loads of mistakes already, and he got to us and took us over to the table, telling the viewers how he was going to interview us and then we

Performing 'Geordie' with Julie Felix on her TV show, February 1968.

Mike on sitar: Iron Stone session at Sound Techniques, early 1969. (Peter Neal)

would do a song. So he said, 'Robin, tell me, how many instruments do you play?' And Robin said, 'I don't know'.

And we did a couple of kids shows, one for Yorkshire Television, about three I think. I always enjoyed the Julie Felix shows and she was so nice. She was the kind of person that was so nice you wished she could sing! Actually the same thing applied to Sandy Denny, she could clear a pub in five minutes. But she kept at it and became an absolutely beautiful singer.

Away with such scurrilous talk – Was it a conscious decision for you and Robin to write separately, Dust Be Diamonds being the only joint composition?

Yeah, we were both quite private songwriters and we'd tend to roll up with a song and say 'Here's this song, what would you like to do with it?' And be very open about it. That's in fact, that's how I ended up playing sitar because what would happen would be I'd turn up with my songs and Robin would have a whole selection of things he could do with them, whereas all I could do is add guitar or a bit of keyboard. So a sitar seemed like the ideal thing to interpret them, particularly after the one played by Soma on The Mad Hatter's Song. Soma was a sitar teacher who taught me a little bit.

Did you like the sitar as an instrument?

I loved it for that but when the band broke up I never played it since. It's hopeless for writing on. But for the purposes of embellishing things that Robin did it probably reached its peak in things like Nightfall. That song's very satisfying to me, and for the job I was doing it's just right, but it's not really something that I would do in the normal course of events.

Between Liquid Acrobat *and* Earthspan *there seemed to be a major change in both production values and songwriting.* Earthspan's *cover, with its melange of cover photos of the String Band looking like smart young men and women about town, features you in one picture huddled earnestly over a music score. Cover hype or reflection of your interests at the time?*

That was really because at one point I thought it was about time I learned to score music and so I did a crash course in scoring and arranging with a guy in South London. It was such a luxury, there I was, able to do this for a few months and then have the London Symphony Orchestra and what I did was an arrangement for Sandy Denny with the LSO for one of her tracks, I've forgotten the name [*Man Of Iron – Ed.*]. But she commissioned me to do it and another guy who did film scores.

> *You also have two songs credited to yourself and Licorice. Was this at your insistence?*

No, she was very keen. But there just wasn't the time to do more with her ideas.

> *Late period ISB is represented in the James Archibald film,* Rehearsal. *It seems that there was considerable strain in the String Band at that time. Robin looks pissed off and Malcolm distinctly worried by it all. In the rehearsal for Ithkos it almost seems like the Beatles' Let It Be film, people just not getting on, knowing each other too well and being on completely different wavelengths.*

Just a normal rehearsal really, Robin was in a bad temper that day for some reason, but there wasn't a rift at that point at all. It was a documentary and we were pawns, the guy probably used the bits where there was arguments or whatever.

> *Methinks Mike doth protest too much... In the Seventies you almost broke into the big-time American music scene with the Casablanca solo album:*

I did a publishing deal for Chappell and they said toddle off and write all these songs and every time you write a song we'll send you some money to make a demo of it. So we got a collection of them which became *The Glen Row Tapes*. Then we got in touch with Hugh Murphy [*who was behind Gerry Rafferty's Baker Street single and Bowie's* Station To Station *album*]. He found a record company, Casablanca, to work with, so really the Casablanca album was the one that came out of the Glen Row recordings.

> *Has it been fun for the past thirty years?*

Very much so, it's been wonderful and I've been very fortunate.

The interview was conducted in 1993.

'A quiet mind and a way through to tomorrow'

Gil Murray grasps the nettle of Scientology.

Just how far can you take me

One of the more controversial aspects of the Incredible String Band was their long involvement in Scientology. In this article I'm going to take a look at the influence this practice had on the band and their music. For those who don't know, Scientology is a self-improvement system developed by the American writer L. Ron Hubbard. He defined it as 'the study of the human spirit in its relationship to the physical universe and its living forms.' A British High Court judge was later to describe it, or at least the organisation that grew up around it, as 'corrupt, sinister and dangerous' and 'immoral and socially obnoxious.'

Central to Scientology is the concept of a 'Bridge to Total Freedom.' Today's Scientology clients pay increasingly huge fees to traverse the 'Bridge' in search of spiritual enrichment. The total cost has been estimated at up to a quarter of a million pounds per person. At one time or another, just about all of the String Band and entourage were involved to some degree. In the early days they were very open about it, influencing many admirers to try it out. Some were persuaded to work for Scientology, and you can still find the occasional old ISB fan in the organisations today. Other fans sensed a change for the worse and rejected it as an expensive American fraud.

Robin Denselow, summing up the rise and fall of the band, said: '... they peaked after a couple of years, after a period in which I felt they could match even the Beatles in writing ability and sheer inventiveness, and then went into a slow and unsteady decline... Musically... the String Band failed to live up to their early high standards. They continued to give some fine concerts, and some of their album tracks remained impressive. But the spark of enthusiasm, excitement and idealism in their work gradually dimmed. In place of exotic instruments they moved to a more conventional rock line-up of electric guitars, bass and drums. In place of the unspecific romanticism they became Scientologists.' (Robin Denselow, *The Electric Muse*, 1975).

The whole thing developed into a lasting controversy, to such an extent that the band withdrew from making public statements about Scientology altogether. So, what was all the fuss about? Some of the answers may be found in the music itself, and in the interviews of the day. Let's go back in time to November 1968, New York City, just after the band had gigged at the Fillmore East.

They were introduced to Scientology through a friend of Joe Boyd after the gig. First Licorice, then Robin enrolled in the New York Scientology Centre, and Mike and Rose followed suit in London after the band returned home. This puts their first contact with Scientology after the release of *Wee Tam* (November 1968), so we have to look at the next String Band project for the first signs of their involvement. This was the 1968/1969 film *Be Glad For The Song Has No Ending*.

Early Scientology influences are in evidence to those in the know. Robin makes some telling remarks in the interview sections: '...Everyone creates their own Universe you know... Some people think they're bodies... some people think – know – that they're spirits...'

But confirmation comes with the musical collage that accompanies The Pirate And The Crystal Ball sequence, part of which was known to the band as Theta. Theta is the Scientology term for 'thought, life force, élan vital, the spirit, the soul, or any other of the numerous definitions it has had for some thousands of years.' It is further defined as 'reason, serenity, stability, happiness, cheerful emotion, persistence, and the other factors which man ordinarily considers desirable' (both definitions by L. Ron Hubbard). Musically however, when you compare the instrumental soundtrack (Side Two of the original *Be Glad* LP) with the sublime inspiration of the previous albums, it's in the shallows. It's nice enough as far as it goes, but for the first time there is an amateurish feel, and it seems that the various random string twiddlings no longer issue from charmed wizards frequenting the Old Golden Land. I see in Theta the first indications of the decline that was to follow.

Let me go through

Mike, defending Scientology in 1973: '...People always ask whether our music changed because of Scientology – well what changed was the introversion thing... Our communication was down, we couldn't organise ourselves and we were hopeless with chicks and we just couldn't put anything together, from handling money to doing interviews...We were completely saturated in drugs and we realised we were screwing up and going out of our minds... I don't think the albums that came out immediately after *Wee Tam* were necessarily of the same stature, but it was necessary to sit back and reappraise what was going on.'

Icarus himself couldn't have flown any closer to the sun than the String Band did in their heyday. Neither he nor they were immune from the price that was to be paid.

Many people around the world were looking for another path. Personally, the band found solace for a while in Scientology, and who would deny them that? Sadly though, while it may have helped them through the internal pain, it was incapable of sustaining the unique creativity of the band that had gone before. What I see here, with hindsight, is the convergence of three factors:

1. Flight from drugs.
2. Adoption of Scientology.
3. The Muse starting to withdraw.

Whether it was the farewell to drugs, the turning to Scientology, or a combination of both, the fact is clear – the shining peak experience of *5000 Spirits*, *Hangman* and *Wee Tam* was long gone, never to return.

A horse, a horse, my kingdom for a horse...

And so to the next album. *Changing Horses* was just what the title suggested. The weary, saddle-sore chemical horses were being exchanged for cleaner healthier beasts. On the one hand was Mike's White Bird, which appeared to tell of the more painful of drug experiences, and was written before Scientology:

Who among you
who has not laid his head beneath some holy awning
would think that such a night of tortured travelling
could bring such a glory morning

On the other hand was Robin's cheerful Dust Be Diamonds:

Dust be diamonds, water be wine
Happy happy happy all the time time time!

The contentment of Dust be Diamonds is matched by the throw-away good-time irreverence of the 'Amethyst Galleon' section at the end of Creation, complete with extended kazoo finale. In a Seventies *Time Out* interview Robin said of the ending: '...that's what Scientology is all about, getting through one's own sorrow and pain so the world can be funny again'

Changing Horses has its moments. It is an album of personal and musical transition. Vestiges of the old chemical/mystical tradition are mingled with hopeful calls to wakefulness. The cover is 'right' but there's something missing in the music. That sense of magic, once free-flowing and abundant, now seems distant to my jaded ears.

By the time of the next album (*I Looked Up*, April 1970) most of the band had gone 'clear' through their Scientology counselling. A 'clear' is a person 'released from all physical pain and painful emotion.' Judging from the wide, natural and peaceful grins on the cover, they were feeling pretty good.

I Looked Up reveals the better side of Scientology. We used to enjoy guessing which counselling procedures had influenced which songs. For example, did the grim death and glad rebirth of Pictures In A Mirror come to light during 'Dianetics', or the 'Potential Trouble Source Rundown'? Did Mike write This Moment after doing a 'Communication Course'?

There are many positive messages on this album. For the first time there seems to be a specific emphasis on reaching out to help the listener, using Scientology 'group processing' techniques:

Just look around and notice
where you are
Just look around and notice
what you see

The same thing was happening in the concert halls:

'...Robin Williamson sat up front, brushing very long hair off his face. "I'd like you all to look at that wall over there... thank you. Now could you all look at that wall over there... thank you. And now, if you'll turn to the person in front of you, the person behind you, and the person each side of you and say hello... That's very nice. Hello."' (*Rolling Stone*, August 1969 – University of York gig)

The Scientology 'Bridge to Total Freedom' did not stop at the 'state of clear', and so the journey continued. In a contemporary interview by Brian Cullman, Robin looks back on those days: 'I think what I was looking for was largely, well, peace, spiritual insight, and enhanced awareness by natural means. I guess that that's what I'm still looking for, but I've already achieved a lot of it. What I'm looking for now are really spiritual abilities.'

Not long after the release of *I Looked Up*, came the theatrical production *U* and its associated double album. There is of course Bridge Song:

To the South a brightness
And I must go
The bridge opens its arms and bends low

But one song from this production deserves a special mention, as I believe it expresses what many people were hoping for in Scientology at the time, and that is Robin's Cutting The Strings:

When useless walls come tumbling down
Sparrows will sing on the frozen snows...
...Free to make my own tomorrow
...Free to be me, free to be free

In October 1971, *Liquid Acrobat* was released, with some veiled references to L. Ron Hubbard, and to the meeting of friends from lifetime to lifetime through the ages:

Age long, cradle song
almost had me sleeping for good
if not for the plan of the magic man
who finally helped me out of the wood...
...Lovers and friends meet again and again
On the dear old battlefield

But Scientology proved to be a bit of a mixed bag. Along with the 'healing technology' and the 'religious philosophy' came a control element which was evident in Scientology's 'ethics' and 'administrative technology'. This latter provided a huge framework of rules for running businesses, and the same framework was used by the individual to put more order into his or her personal life. By *Earthspan* the band were definitely getting into the 'organisation' thing. It seemed to include a bit of a (cringe) image cleanup, judging by the haircuts, shirts and jackets on the cover!

No Ruinous Feud and *Hard Rope And Silken Twine* followed *Earthspan*, in 1973 and 1974 respectively. I don't want to dwell on them, save to make the obvious statement that the light had surely died a death. *Hard Rope*'s inner sleeve photograph said it all. Who were this serious bunch of 'hard' looking men with their haircuts, straight clothing and polished shoes? Nope, sorry, I don't recognise any of them...

Spot the odd one out...at the Scientology bookshop in Toronto, 1972ish. (Malcolm Le Maistre collection)

A very un-cellular song

It is ironic in the extreme that the last, and worst ever, album the ISB was involved in was a recording of a benefit concert for Scientology, held at the London Rainbow on May 1974. This was an unashamed advertisement from start to finish, with a massive picture of Hubbard and sales pitch for his *Dianetics* book on the gatefold sleeve. Three of the nine tracks were by the String Band – Black Jack David, Circus Girl and the ending of A Very Cellular Song. The wheel had come full circle. A Very Cellular Song was a chilling parody of its original self. If you can imagine this sacred anthem being shouted by a vacant punk band, you'll be on your way to understanding the horror String Band fans must have felt when they heard it. And yet Robin and Mike continued with Scientology for a good while after the band split in November 1974.

Tell me more – what then?

Starting with *Myrrh* (April 1972), all of Robin's solo albums throughout the Seventies bore the inscription 'Thanks to LRH'. As far as I am aware he was eventually near the 'top' of the Scientology 'Bridge to Total Freedom'. On the few occasions when I asked him about it, he spoke in very favourable terms, describing Scientology in a letter of February 1988 as: 'the only way I've yet encountered or believe to exist in the world at this time which provides a workable way forward in the problems of the human condition towards the unknown future of the race and the unknown potential development of the individual.'

But by the mid-Nineties he had left it completely.

Mike has also finished with it, saying in an April 1987 interview:

'Well I'm completely out. Four years I've been completely out...I feel it's just totally a personal thing, and the fact that I'm in or out shouldn't influence anyone. But... I've nothing to do with it anymore. It's just a personal philosophy some people find useful.' This puts his time of departure at 1983, a time of great upheaval in the Scientology world. To understand what happened it is necessary to separate the subject of Scientology from the organisation that 'ran' it – the 'Church of Scientology.'

The Scientology church that the String Band became involved with in the Sixties has changed immensely today. To many ex-members it has not been a change for the better. Following Robin's footsteps these days could set you back up to a cool quarter of a million pounds. With prices like that, you have to ask yourself whether the organisation's intentions really are to reach out and help people as they claim.

The Eternal Variety Show at the Rainbow, May 1974. L. Ron presides over the Long Time Sunshine all-star finale with (L-R): Mike Garson, Woody Woodmansey, Geoff Appleby, Robin, Graham Forbes, Malcolm, Stan Schnier, Mike, John Gilston and Chick Corea. (Philip Newby archive)

Around 1983 there was a large scale exodus from the church, when a whole host of top Scientology members broke away from the main organisation. This was in protest at the draconian measures being introduced by the new management who had taken over when Hubbard lost control. The dissenters felt that the new leaders had sold out on Scientology's original ideals in favour of money and power.

They set up independent Scientology groups, and tried to practice their techniques outside of the church, offering Scientology counselling at a fraction of the now exorbitant church price. Subsequently they fell under heavy pressure from the 'new' church which tried to put them out of business through any and every means, but ultimately failed. (On a side note, if you are tempted to try it, you might just be better off going to one of the independent groups. At least you'll be able to give it a fair trial without bankrupting yourself.) I understand that Mike was sympathetic to their cause. This was more or less exactly the time when he left Scientology himself. What he did Scientology-wise after 1983 is a mystery, but I personally get the impression that he just jacked the whole thing in and got on with the rest of his life.

No turning back

Perhaps Scientology gave something with one hand, and took something away with the other. On a financial level, the Church of Scientology definitely profited in a BIG way. I wouldn't be at all surprised if the String Band connection had generated tens of millions of dollars for them, all told. On a personal level, the ISB probably paid hundreds of thousands (each) into Scientology, and claimed that it helped them. It's fair to assume that it did! On a musical level, it was another story entirely.

Now I'm not saying that Scientology was exclusively responsible for the decline of the music of the String Band, but I do think that it was a contributing factor. In the end there are some objective observations to be made. On one hand we have the written interviews of the time in which Robin, Mike, and Malcolm publicly claim that Scientology was improving their personal lives. At the same time we have the albums which show the music getting steadily worse until the break up of the band in 1974.

Lastly we have all the core String Band members leaving Scientology. One final word. What would the String Band have been like if they had never found out about Scientology? First thoughts – possibly another magic album or two, but they might have split up sooner. Second thoughts – who knows what might have come along in its place? It's just going to have to remain one of those unanswered questions.

I asked the ice it would not say
but only cracked and moved away

Whatever you think it's more than that...
A Zen journey with the ISB

Ian Genzan Finlay

I was a very alienated 15-year-old listening to the John Peel show on Saturday Radio One when Painting Box was played. The following Monday I bought *5000 Spirits* and so began a long association.

It was an association that has lasted to this day, for at that age I was just beginning my spiritual journey, a search for the answer to those half remarkable questions, 'What is it that we are, what is it that we are part of?' It was a journey that would lead me to Christian mysticism, Douglas Harding, Buddhist monasteries in Thailand and Nepal, to train briefly as a Zen monk and to my Japanese Zen teacher, Hogen, who gave me the middle part of my name. And all the time the music of Robin and Mike was an inspiration, reflecting my experiences. At times years must have gone by without my actually hearing the String Band, but it was there, in my head, and at odd times, meditating in a jungle in Thailand or on an intensive retreat, snatches of song would come to me.

Looking back over their songs, very few mention Zen specifically; nevertheless their music is pervaded by Zen ideas, attitudes and experience. How much Robin and Mike knew of traditional Zen I do not know – they would obviously have been very aware of some aspects – they had read Jack Kerouac and met Douglas Harding so would have absorbed much of Zen philosophy. I also feel that a lot of similarities may be coincidental: Robin and Mike happen to see things in a 'Zen' way, as anyone might who has truly looked at themselves. At the same time their spiritual influences are extremely wide-ranging – one can pick out Christian, Hindu, Babylonian and Norse elements in their songs. Nonetheless there does seem to be, throughout much of their work, an awareness of what Aldous Huxley called the Perennial Philosophy – that awareness that is at the root of spirituality and finds one of its clearest expressions in Zen.

So, to start at the beginning of the String Band's work, there are intimations of what was to come on the very first LP. On October Song Robin says 'I've found a door behind my mind and that's the greatest treasure', hinting at a world of experience beyond intellectual concepts. But there is also Mike Heron's The Tree, a remarkably mature song. The tree seems a symbol of life and fulfilment. The song traces a journey, from self knowledge as a child, to a time of loss, when the tree disappears, to rediscovery and integration at the end. It is a theme Mike was to return to many times and has many echoes in Zen. 'At first mountains are mountains and trees are trees, then you find the mountains and trees are no longer mountains and trees, then they are again, but different.' Innocence, loss of innocence, and eventual return to source but with the understanding of experience. The song also reflects much of Douglas Harding's philosophy, though it is perhaps unlikely that Mike knew of Douglas at this time.

...another Zen paradox, stillness in action

5000 Spirits is very different from the first LP, much more complex, innovative, very mystical and experimental but with little of the Zen-like quality that was to come later. I now find The Mad Hatter's Song the most remarkable achievement, with the author setting his vision against the corruption of the world. His eyes yearn after the 'the unsullied sight' and later, like Zen masters, he informs us that he has only 'one eye.' Presumably this is the all seeing eye, awareness itself that cannot be divided, just as all movement comes from the stillness – 'dancing without movement after the clear light' – another Zen paradox, stillness in action.

Hangman is possibly my favourite LP; richly textured, it is far more pagan in feel, with songs like Waltz Of The New Moon, Three Is A Green Crown, Witches Hat and The Water Song. Not that there is anything that contradicts Zen in these songs; on the contrary there is a sense of the great joy and wonder of life in both the music and lyrics, and on Mercy I Cry City Mike expresses the desire to be 'nothing else but what I am'. There is also the most extraordinary jumble of images, as if the floodgates of consciousness have opened and lines come tumbling out – 'The ocean that only begins' is one that springs to mind and certainly the band were truly 'setting (their) foot where the sand is untrodden' with this record.

With *Wee Tam* I feel that the full promise of earlier songs has been fulfilled. The very first song, Job's Tears, sets the theme, with the 'happy man' who has transcended intellectual thought, ('whatever you think it's more than that') wandering in 'the old golden land.' A land of pure experience where, as the Zen mystics would say, there is only the One

Mind. You Get Brighter is one of Mike's seemingly simple songs – a love song, perhaps, but with very mystical overtones. 'You give all your brightness away but it only makes you brighter', and the lines 'You know you belong to everybody but you can't deny that I'm you' indicate the state of oneness, of non-separation referred to so often in both Zen and the String Band. Robin's Half-Remarkable Question – 'What is it that we are part of?... what is it that we are?' asks the essential question for all seekers, the basic Zen koan 'Who am I?' (one that I have worked on for years on Zen retreats.) The answer is perhaps contained in the song, for we are, indeed, all things, everything is contained in our consciousness – 'the flower and its petal, the root and its grasp'. Drop the idea of self, of separation, and look at a flower. That flower is all there is, it is the universe.

Maya (from the Eastern experience of the world as illusion or play) is one of my favourites from the albums. The image of the 'great man' whose 'skin is all patchy / but soon will reach one glowing hue / God is his soul / Infinity his goal...Civilisation he leaves behind / Opinions are his fingernails' is surely that of the enlightened man, and they are the most moving lines I have ever heard. Compare the 17th century Zen master Shosan – 'In your walking, sitting, lying down, your mind will be at rest. Naturally and without effort the Buddha mind will be realised; becoming a person of unobstructed freedom, in the freedom of Nirvana's marvellous joy you will walk alone in the universe, joyous through future ages. What joy can equal this!' This is surely what the String Band are trying to convey in so many of their songs. I find it easy to imagine Robin's great man, totally integrated, striding through the universe, free from the delusions of maya.

The other very Zen track on the album has been discussed earlier in this book – Douglas Traherne Harding. The song is another of Mike's which traces the journey from childhood oneness to alienation to eventual enlightenment, and the experience of the central character, who 'seeing the ferryman and seeing the tollman the light within him leaps to greet them' can be compared to the ox-herding pictures of Zen, where, after a similar journey, the hero returns to the market place with 'bliss bestowing hands'. I was somewhat surprised when speaking to Douglas to discover that Mike only met him after he'd written the song. Douglas himself identified very strongly with the early Zen masters; his experience – of having no head – of seeing with a single eye – was their experience. Thomas Traherne, of course, knew nothing of the Zen masters, but his writings show that he also shared this experience, of being one with, and the 'sole heir' along with 'all men' of the universe.

Changing Horses is rather different – it restates some themes: 'And Buddha declared, it's right where you are', but White Bird, by Mike, is the really powerful track. It returns to a favourite theme of Mike's, enlightenment after suffering, and the experience of all things being contained in one person. 'His head so wide that all life says / has room to live and breathe and have its being.' Similar to the end of Douglas Traherne Harding, where seeing all the people, he 'sees that their faces are none but his own.' One Zen teacher, also a fan, told me that having understood the song, I must now go away and live it. The symbol of the white bird is more Jungian, a symbol of release and the emancipation of the soul.

U I find strangely underrated – it has some classic songs, very much in the mould of those on *Wee Tam*. Queen of Love has some beautiful imagery – 'The snow is on the hills of my heart and to speak is to die'. I remember a friend quoting those lines on a retreat, as we looked out in silence over snow-covered Welsh hills. I simply nodded then, knowing what he meant – as Zen says, 'try to describe it and you lose it.' You can never capture the moment. The song also has the lines 'How can I say where I end and you begin?' and here it is Robin who is speaking of non-separation, where self and other, viewer and object, become one.

Many of the songs are clearly mystical, but it is the humorous Hirem Pawnitof which bears one of the few obvious Zen references – when the hero attains enlightenment when struck on the head with a tray. Zen is full of such stories, of monks attaining enlightenment when struck by the master, or of the nun Chiono's enlightenment when the bottom dropped out of her bucket. Cutting The Strings is more serious: 'I built my prison stone by stone, how many useless knots I tied.' We build our own prison by self and ego; cut through it and we have the clear light of enlightenment. One Zen master I met was fond of saying how we build walls around ourselves to protect us from the pain and suffering. And we are very successful, so successful that the walls become prisons and then we have to get out. And the way to get out? Like the Zen story of the goose in the bottle, the goose was never really in the bottle, it was an illusion all along. Puppet Song is another favourite of mine. Now I know that traditional Zen rarely mentions God, but if it had a god, this is surely what he would tell us – that 'You're one of my kind / You're an infinite mind... And you shall have liberty / It always was yours anyway'. Again, the suffering, the lack of liberty, was an illusion, freedom was there all along, our birthright.

'Mike could not have put the teaching of Zen more simply or beautifully'

I Looked Up was, I feel, the last great attempt to describe the experience directly. 'When you find out who you are – beautiful beyond your dreams' could not be clearer, almost too obvious, I feel. But Mike's This Moment is a classic. My Zen teacher bases his entire teaching on just this moment, the eternal present, the now. 'Be here now, why not now?' And Mike could not have put the teaching of Zen more simply or beautifully. It is very profound and also incredibly joyous. Dropping past and future, dropping all memory, there is just this, this wonderful being alive at this very moment.

Earthspan and *Liquid Acrobat* are also beautiful LPs, but although earlier themes are explored (reincarnation for example), I feel that the music and lyrics begin to lose some of their immediacy; the String Band had said all they could. The journey was not 'a journey to a distant place, it is the journey home' (Zen Master Hogen), or, as T.S. Eliot said, it was 'the journey to the place where you first started' (*Four Quartets*).

There is, however, one final aspect of the String Band which is very Zen-like and must be mentioned, the sense of humour. It comes out in many ways, but the way in which Zen, and Zen painting in particular, treats animals is very similar to the way Robin and Mike see them. Zen picks on the lowest animals, the humblest, imbuing its art with great humour. Thus we find Zen art full of grasshoppers and crickets, of bizarre three-legged toads or meditating frogs, a counterpart surely, of the simple amoeba (happily splitting in two), of Cousin Caterpillar (who nonetheless metamorphosed), or Big Ted, the pig who when he died went like 'snow on the water'. We would indeed be happy in this world of impermanence, 'could we take each change so easily'.

I could never have thought, all those years ago, hearing Painting Box on the radio, that it would be the start of such a long and wonderful relationship with the music of the authors, but rushing out to buy the LP on the strength of that one track, I must have sensed something was happening. Well, well. Whatever you think, it's more than that.

Wyrd

Adrian Whittaker

There is a marked pagan element in many of the ISB's earlier songs and so I thought it would be interesting to look at more recent work by a few 'wyrd' artists who were influenced to varying extents by them.

The Wyrd Folk and electronica bloodline – from Throbbing Gristle to Cyclobe

There's a bloodline of performers who've produced material based round electronica and owing some kind of debt to the darker, more Gothic side of the ISB. Probably the arch-begetter of these was the late Genesis P-Orridge, an early fan of a broad variety of psych-folk. His first work, wrote Alexis Petridis in *The Guardian*, consisted of 'noise, improvisations and tape experiments mixed with songs that sounded a little like a less adept, more chaotic version of psychedelic folkies the Incredible String Band.' Genesis P, at the start of his artistic trajectory, was pretty much a non-musician, and the ISB would have been liberating in terms of his creative approach with his music project, Throbbing Gristle.

Genesis: 'The Incredible String Band... was all acoustic and pretty, fairies and elves and everything, but then they started tripping, as many of us did, and they became something much more: psychedelic troubadours. They took the idea of folk music and turned it into these surrealistic, metaphysical, long, bizarre tracks. Ducks On A Pond is the song that converted me. The lyrics intrigued me – so dense and funny sometimes, real poetry with deeply philosophical questions. We learned that you don't have to have a perfect voice, you don't have to use the structures you've been given and you can play any instrument in any place whatsoever. You have an absolute right to translate poetry in any form with any sound. It's all up for grabs.'

In a 2004 interview he waxed effusive on the ISB influence: 'I had been listening to the Incredible String Band since school. The surrealism and FREEDOM of the lyrics is what continually engages me: the subject matter of absurdity and spirituality combined. I feel the ISB are probably the lyrical geniuses of the Sixties and onwards, far more than the Beatles or Dylan, who become predictable and never really extended the form of the song as an open system in the same way. Once one gets the ISB all the other musics fall into place. These are the true troubadours of the last two centuries. They explore divinity and magick from a lyrical chivalric dimension. Combine this with the interdimensionality and you have works beyond compare. SUBLIME!'

David Tibet, so nicknamed for his obsession with the country and its culture, drifted into the circle around Genesis' later project, Psychic TV, in 1982. That year he set up Current 93 with a shifting cast of other Genesis P associates. It's hard to see direct ISB influences in Current 93, who tended to go for tape loops, drones and Tibet's distorted vocal, though their 1987 album *Earth Covers Earth* had a cover which, featuring various band members and associates under a tree, was effectively a re-creation of the back of the *Hangman* sleeve. In an interview from that era, he says he was 'was getting into a lot of British folk, things like The Incredible String Band's *The Hangman's Beautiful Daughter* and groups like Trees and COB [Clive's Original Band].' Comus' album *First Utterance* was also important. Shirley Collins, though, was Tibet's greatest folk influence. Years later, he was the main instigator of her return to recording and live performance with the *Lodestar* project.

Around the same time, ex Psychic TV member John Balance set up Coil, with, amongst others, Stephen Thrower. Visual artist Ossian Brown joined them later on. Coil, Wikipedia tells us, 'held pagan and alchemical beliefs, as well as a fixation on chaos magic. They worked in such genres as industrial noise, ambient and dark ambient, neo-folk, spoken word, drone, and minimalism, treating their works more as magical rituals than as musical pieces.'

And so we come to Cyclobe, which Stephen Thrower formed with Ossian in the late 90s. In his book *England's Hidden Reverse*, author David Keenan writes that 'they took Coil's experiments in psychedelic electronica into ever more formless realms with austere drones and improvisations that rise like breath in clouds of cumulous F/X.'

By the time I came across Cyclobe, they'd moved on into more structured pieces and they had started to incorporate a wide variety of ethnic and folk instrumentation. In November 2009 Peter Neal and I were invited to The Tate, St Ives to take part in a symposium alongside co-curator Michael Bracewell, writer Philip Hoare, Cyclobe and others, titled 'The Dark Monarch: Magic and Modernity in British Art.' Taking its cue and title from an infamous 1962 book by local artist Sven Berlin, the event set out to explore 'the influence of folklore, mysticism, mythology and the occult on the development of British modernism.' Peter and I showed *Be Glad* and led a short discussion about it, covering aspects of the film such as the 'power residing in the landscape' which Peter discusses in his interview for this book.

Cyclobe's piece for the event, *The Woods Are Alive With The Smell Of His Coming* , a hymn to Pan, fitted well with this theme. Writer Alan Holmes describes it well in a review of the album it came from, *Wounded Galaxies Tap At The Window*: 'A repetitive rhythmic figure played on what might be a marimba continues throughout the piece as all manner of sounds slowly weave their way in and around, taking the listener on a journey through landscapes of another world, at various points scary, soothing, hopeful, sad and even funny. The skilful blending of electronic

Current 93 album cover

and acoustic sounds dislocates the sonic landscape from any trace of the presence of either machines or musicians, giving the music a sense of being a natural phenomenon rather than a man-made construction.'

It reminded me of some of the darker, textural elements of *Hangman*, such as Swift As The Wind or Three Is A Green Crown. There was definitely a distinct whiff of the ISB about them, though back then I didn't really know any of Cyclobe's pre-history. For this new edition of the book I talked to Ossian Brown in 2021 to discover more.

Ossian: I was first introduced to the ISB through Genesis P-Orridge. When I was in my mid teens I left home and moved into his house in Hackney, the old Throbbing Gristle offices. Going through his records I came across Pearls Before Swine, Third Ear Band and Popul Vuh, who also moved me a lot, but it was seeing the cover to *The Hangman's Beautiful Daughter* that really gripped me and sent my imagination swirling. It had me intrigued, this arboreal commune. I wondered who they all were. I found them hard to place, there was a feeling of them existing in many different times. It didn't feel at all contrived, it felt like a true captured moment, and this was how they looked all of the time, it was a magic that was lived. There was something psychedelic about it, but a psychedelia of the earth. It was so autumnal, you could almost smell the woods, the dead leaves, the fungus. I was particularly fascinated with Mike Heron, holding the mask, and Rose who had a slightly feral look about her, right in the centre of the picture, watching you through her hair whilst you explored all the characters of this family. There was a warmth to the group as well, a gentle magical welcoming. It has to be absolutely one of the best record covers. And then listening to the music of course – nothing could've really prepared me for the freedom of sound and emotions I'd experience. A feeling of moving through great networks of passages, like travelling through intricate Celtic knot work, and within all these twisting labyrinthine journeys, surprising chambers would open up to you: some funny, some deeply moving, some enlightening, some confusing. I found it enchanting and completely transportive. It's very beautiful, very playful music, and as organic and mysterious as the cover photograph.'

Adrian: Did the ISB take you into any new directions, musically or otherwise?

Ossian: Clive Palmer's two C.O.B albums are truly remarkable things – *Music Of The Ages* for instance I find absolutely haunting, the ghost of it clings to you long after hearing it. It feels as if it stretches into eternity. You can sense a spirit that connects those C.O.B albums with *Hangman's Beautiful Daughter* and *Wee Tam And The Big Huge*. To my ears there's still a shared voice within it all. Even though Clive's only album with ISB was the very first, there's a similar grain. You know they're rooted to the same tree.

I was always interested in the connection between Shirley and Dolly and the String Band, Dolly's playing is so distinctive, so you know it's her immediately, and when you hear her play on a String Band album, you get this sense of Shirley's presence as well. It wove them all together very beautifully, they seemed to subtly illuminate one another, with Shirley choosing to record Robin's God Dog and also Robin and Mike playing for her on *The Power Of The True Love Knot*. To me it's revealing of how consistently wide and unusual Shirley's approach has always been, always true though, with the song deeply at the heart of her work, of the foremost importance.

> *Adrian: ... and of course you and Stephen later worked on Shirley's* Lodestar, *for which you contributed an original piece, The Split Ash Tree. Were any of the Cyclobe instrumentation and arrangements influenced by the ISB at all? I think I hear them in the track Son Of Sons Of Light – some quite nice Joujouka-style chanter/north African reed pipe on there! And The Woods Are Alive With The Smell Of His Coming, which you did at the Tate Cornwall, reminded me of some of the darker elements of* Hangman...

Ossian: Their openness to working with all kinds of instruments was very inspiring to me, using whatever feels appropriate for the song, with no censorship, either culturally, historically, or in regard to performance, prioritising feeling over ability. Of course they are wonderful

Cyclobe - Stephen Thrower and Ossian Brown

musicians, but to me there's a great urgency in their expression, a need and a race to capture something, there's no desire to hone and perfect a performance. *Hangman* and *Wee Tam* have an exciting rawness and truth to the sound, which I respond to. It all feels untamed, emotionally and musically. It's an alive music. It's certainly something I look for in myself, and aspire to with my own work.

There's a wonderful sense of reaching in Robin's voice, a searching. It's very moving, his feeling of almost losing control emotionally, and the sense of those feelings shifting, becoming tenuous, growing and changing in the holding of a single line, a note. It can be uncomfortable, but you travel though it with him. Through wild and haunted thickets, through the bluebell woods. For me I always gravitated to Robin Williamson's songs. I love his singing most of all, there's no restraint. I find it incredibly soulful. Particularly for me on The Circle Is Unbroken which is beautiful beyond words, or Waltz Of The New Moon which is magical beyond words. You can fly on his voice, sail on it.

Finally, what are your favourite albums and songs?

Ossian: The albums are *The Incredible String Band*, *Hangman* and *Wee Tam*. My favourite songs include A Very Cellular Song, Waltz Of The New Moon, Lordly Nightshade, The Circle Is Unbroken, The Iron Stone, Three Is A Green Crown, Job's Tears, The Half-Remarkable Question, Maya, Greatest Friend and Douglas Traherne Harding.

2021

Alasdair Roberts

Adrian Whittaker

'There is something appealingly fearless about the ramshackle nature of the ISB records which is inspiring.'

I first came across Alasdair Roberts at Joe Boyd's Very Cellular Songs: The Music Of The Incredible String Band, part of Joe's 2009 Witchseason Weekender at The Barbican. Alasdair blew everyone away with an almost a cappella version of My Name Is Death, leavened by a bit of bowed double bass. In Joe's 2017 Edinburgh Festival re-make of the event, he reprised the song but with added guitar. It was still very good – he has a great voice and presence for this sort of song – but the Barbican version was starker and so more powerful. In the Edinburgh second half, he added a wonderful, spine-chilling performance of Maya. Karine Polwart and Barbara Dickson supplied the chorus vocals.

After a few years in his first band, Appendix Out, an indie/Americana outfit which gradually morphed into something more meditative, steeped in the folk tradition, Alasdair has been around since 2001 as a solo artist and, alongside Trembling Bells, has played a leading part in Glasgow's wyrd-folk scene. As Rob Young wrote in a profile for *The Wire*, he 'is on a mission to reconnect the disparate dots of tradition and modernity.' For the past few years he and Ossian Brown (see Cyclobe piece above) have also been playing together as part of David Tibet's Current 93.

I interviewed Alasdair by email during the 2020 lockdown.

Adrian: I think you first come across the ISB via your father, the folk musician Alan Roberts? Which albums grabbed your attention, and why?

Alasdair: Yes, it was my late father Alan who first mentioned ISB to me when I was in my teens. Alan was a musician and lived in Glasgow in the sixties and early seventies. After he died in 2001, I found some old set lists in one of his guitar cases and it turned out that he'd been including October Song in his solo set back then. Oddly enough he didn't actually have any ISB LPs when I knew him, so I didn't inherit any, although perhaps he had owned some back in the day. In any case, I think he noted the way that my musical tastes and interests were developing, and the contemporary artists whose work I was enjoying, and suggested I should look back and check out ISB. I bought a second-hand copy of *Wee Tam* (minus *The Big Huge*) in a Glasgow record shop when I was about 19 – I think it was actually after recording the first Appendix Out record but before recording the second. Later I got into the first album and *5000 Spirits* and, of course, *The Hangman's Beautiful Daughter*. It's probably the latter LP and *The Big Huge* which I listened to the most, simply because they featured most of my favourite songs – Maya, Douglas Traherne Harding, The Circle Is Unbroken, A Very Cellular Song, Waltz Of The New Moon, The Water Song, Swift As The Wind...

Adrian: Did the ISB take you into any new directions, musically or otherwise?

Alasdair: I actually had a bit of an obsession with Robert Graves' *The White Goddess* in my twenties, but I came to it independently of ISB. I think I just saw the old Faber paperback edition for sale in an Oxfam bookshop in Glasgow and thought it looked like something that would align with my interests in mythology, folklore and the natural world, and it did. I knew that both Sylvia Plath and Ted Hughes had been very into it, and reading it I did suspect that it was probably a particular influence on Robin Williamson too! I did come to listen to the Nonesuch Explorer record *The Real Bahamas In Music And Song* thanks to the 'bid you goodnight' part of A Very Cellular Song – and from there to get more heavily into the very great Joseph Spence. I recently finished reading Samuel Charters' book *The Day Is So Long And The Wages So Small* about field recording and meeting Spence and others in Andros, the Bahamas – so the chain of discoveries begun with that ISB song continues to expand. I don't think sartorially or image-wise the ISB has been much of an influence on me personally,

although I definitely know young people in Glasgow nowadays who look as if they might have stepped off the cover of *The Hangman's Beautiful Daughter*!

Adrian: In your early work, were any of your instrumentation and arrangements influenced by the ISB?

Alasdair: I think my early instrumentation choices were largely dictated by the instruments to which I had access. In my case that would have been predominantly acoustic guitar, as that had been my father's main instrument. A defining feature for me of ISB is the dynamic and interplay between Robin and Mike – as I never really had a musical sparring partner in the same kind of way, I don't think the arrangements were consciously influenced specifically by ISB, at least at first, beyond having a shared predilection for acoustic instrumentation. Maybe by the time of the third Appendix Out album *The Night Is Advancing*, I would have absorbed more of their music and the influence can probably be felt more strongly, especially in terms of a greater looseness of approach and an improvisatory edge. There is something appealingly fearless about the ramshackle nature of the ISB records which is inspiring. Perhaps throughout that period of my music there was the general influence of certain productions of that late Sixties/early Seventies era, including Joe Boyd's for the ISB as well as Nick Drake's records and so on.

Adrian: Song structures in the ISB, especially 1968–1970, were fascinatingly episodic. Did you ever try this sort of approach? Maybe with your 2009 song, Unyoked Oxen Turn? Rob Young called your more recent music 'increasingly labyrinthine,' I recall...

Alasdair: I suppose at a certain point as a songwriter, one can either simplify/reduce or complicate/expand. Unyoked Oxen Turn is from the album *Spoils* (2009), which I think is, as Rob Young might say, particularly labyrinthine in places – especially a song like Under No Enchantment (But My Own). I'm certain there would be some ISB influence, just through absorbing their music, in terms of my approach to structuring songs in more episodic ways during that period, or for example on a song like The Wheels Of The World from the album *A Wonder Working Stone* (2013) – but it's also just the result of my having written songs for a few years and so wanting to try new things and explore wider possibilities within the song form. Then again, it's likely that at a certain point of exploring that expanded, progressive type of writing, I'd be subsequently inclined to react against it by contracting and simplifying again!

But returning to Unyoked Oxen Turn – in a way to me that's a relatively simple song lyrically in terms of it following a very linear narrative which is heavily influenced by traditional Scottish folk tales. At the time I had been reading a lot of Traveller tales collected from the late, great storyteller Duncan Williamson, who was also a fine singer of traditional ballads and folk songs. I'm sure that Robin and Mike would have been familiar with those kinds of stories and songs too (particularly Robin, perhaps); our shared interest in that culture is probably also partly to do with our shared Scottishness.

> *Adrian: Some of your more recent work carries a Williamson influence, I think – I was listening to The Book Of Doves (on* Spoils*), and it made me think of Fine Fingered Hands and Maya. Do you agree, and are you more of a Williamson person? You have done brilliant versions of Maya and My Name Is Death at Joe Boyd's events...*

Alasdair: Thank you for the kind words about my interpretations of those songs, first of all! I love many of Robin's songs and many of Mike's songs too and I wouldn't like to choose a favourite ISB songwriter! Having said that, perhaps if I got to know either gentleman particularly well (I've met and communicated with both a few times, fairly briefly), I'd find that I would share more interests and passions with one or the other, or just get on better with one rather than the other – I don't know!

> *Adrian: And finally – favourite albums, favourite songs?*

Alasdair: I think I've probably listened to *Wee Tam And The Big Huge* (the latter particularly) and *The Hangman's Beautiful Daughter* most of all, so pretty much all of the songs on those records are favourites. Outside of those records, some favourite songs are October Song, Can't Keep Me Here, Chinese White, Sleepers, Awake!, Black Jack Davy and Cold February...

Overleaf All 20 issues of the *beGLAD* fanzine

Chapter Eleven

Jeff Rockwell and Deena Omar share some ISB memories, Chris Taylor describes his Room 101, Paul Bryant picks out some key ISB moments, and Neil Tennant recalls his days as a fan.

American poet Jeff Rockwell looks back...

'I bought a pair of very tight-fitting bellbottom pants, a pair of very cool-looking boots, and a loose-fitting flowery shirt that any androgyne would have been proud to wear...'

As I look back on my life from the vantage point of middle-age, I appreciate that there is a deeper life than the one we see with our eyes only; one that is less mundane and more poetic, one that runs like a river underground. Some, if they're fortunate, get pulled into its currents. Others, if they're fortunate, get pushed. Both happened to me.

Growing up in a typically beige American suburb during the Cold War, wondering how miles upon miles of farms and cows and pastures could disappear almost overnight, a few minutes drive from where Walt Whitman lived out his life rewriting *Leaves Of Grass* and entertaining Longfellow and Wilde in Camden, New Jersey, I was born for the second time when I first heard the music of the Beatles, Zombies, Kinks, and Animals. I was twelve years old and, armed with a $15 Sears and Roebuck guitar, I played in my first band, a folk-rock outfit called the Woodsmen. We played cover versions of the latest hits from Britain.

By the time I was in high school, although there were still a lot of bands I enjoyed, rock was not the happy affair it had been a few years earlier. Altamont had happened. The country was in the throes of political and racial unrest. The music got heavier and became more commercial and self-conscious.

A new friend told me about an upcoming music festival, to be held in late August. It was outdoors for three days, featured acoustic music, and he added that I needed to check out this 'new' band that was going to be there – the Incredible String Band. The romance actually began its gestation as I would mull the name of the band over in my head as I prepared to go to the festival by working all summer picking blueberries and tomatoes with a group of migrant farm workers. I didn't save much, though. Just enough for a pair of very tight-fitting bellbottom pants, a pair of very cool-looking boots, a loose-fitting flowery shirt that any androgyne would be proud to wear, and one ticket to the 1969 Philadelphia Folk Festival.

American poet Jeff Rockwell looks back...

Arriving the morning of the first day, I felt I had arrived in Mecca. I set up camp next to a very cordial, older man who spent all day sweating in the sun, working on an instrument he was building – a 24-string psaltery. I was pleasantly surprised that evening when the festival MC welcomed to the stage Bob Beers, and my camping-neighbour walked out and played some absolutely heavenly music on his psalteries as the sun was going down.

Queen Juanita comes in from the cold!

The evening's concluding act was the ISB. They only played for 30 minutes, but when they ripped into Black Jack Davy, I was up and dancing at the front of the stage, in love with a kind of music I had never heard before. The next day was filled with music by Doc and Merle Watson, Mississippi Fred McDowell, Tom Rush, Bill Monroe, Bessie Jones and the Georgia Sea Island Singers, Willie Dixon, and Ola Belle Reed.

The highlight of the festival, for me, was the Sunday afternoon concert – two hours with the String Band. That concert did something (wonderful) to my head and I can scarcely remember the day at all – except that I irreparably split the backside of my bellbottoms swimming in a local farmer's creek trying to get a closer look at the naked woman also swimming there (I was 16 – what can I say?), and that the String Band finished their show with the very happy-sounding Queen Juanita And Her Fisherman Lover [*released on* Tricks Of The Senses – *Ed.*]. Two other images from that day remain vivid were Robin's beautifully enunciated introductions ('Hello, my name's Robin, and this is Mike...') and the exotic image of the band on stage surrounded by flowers and so many unusual instruments.

Amazingly, they played again three days later at the Electric Factory in downtown Philadelphia. While I saw other memorable shows there during that time – the Byrds with Clarence White, The Who performing *Tommy* – the String Band's performance that night was incomparable. The band entered the stage from the rear of the club, singing Sleepers, Awake as they moved toward the stage. I was fascinated, again, by the various instruments, as well as Mike's huge grin; by Rose's and Likky's long dresses, and that look of intense excitement in Robin's eyes. I wrote down the set list, which included This Moment, All Writ Down, Dust Be Diamonds, The Letter, Waiting For You, Won't You Come See Me,

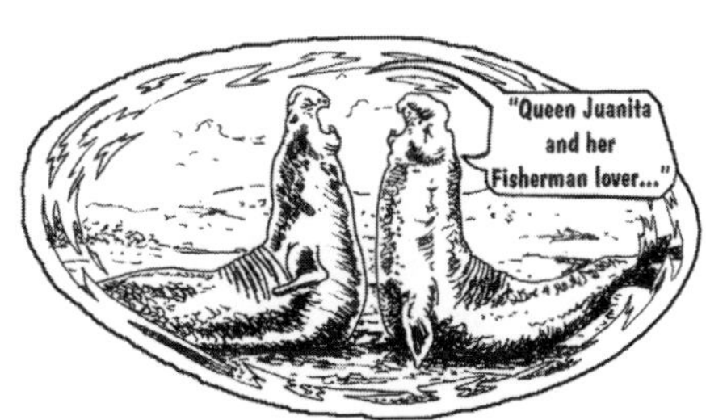

A scene from Allan Frewin's graphic treatment of Queen Juanita.

Pictures In A Mirror, When You Find Out Who You Are, and Queen Juanita (which by now had become my first favourite String Band song). Perhaps the most amazing event that evening was the sight, after the concert, of five hundred people walking down Arch Street (in a bad section of town) holding hands with friends and strangers, singing the chorus from Queen Juanita.

'We formed a band and incorporated sitar, shenai, flute, and kazoos into our line-up'

I had talked two friends I was in a band with into joining me for the concert. On the way home we talked excitedly about finding two female members for our band, which we promptly did. While we were never a String Band covers group, we did come to include Cousin Caterpillar, and Log Cabin Home In The Sky in our repertoire, and we incorporated sitar, shenai, flute, and kazoos into our line-up.

The next three months went by slowly; school assignments, cross-country season, even band rehearsals and gigs became almost a nuisance as I planned my first visit to New York City and the Fillmore East to see the String Band in late November. Meanwhile, I stayed busy wearing out my first copies of *5000 Spirits*, *Hangman's Beautiful Daughter*, *Wee Tam*, *The Big Huge*, and the first album (I wanted to know who this Clive Palmer was and what had happened to him).

In 1969, the Fillmore East was still a fairly new rock venue, although it had seen plenty of entertainment for years as both a Yiddish theatre and a Vaudeville hall. The Lower East Side was a particularly wild place: young kids nodding out on heroin on the sidewalk, others high on amphetamine talking a mile a minute to themselves. I took refuge in the deli next to the Fillmore, ate a meatball sandwich, and kept peering at the marquee: 'Tonight – The Incredible String Band.'

The band got off to a slow, but interesting start, taking a very long time to tune before beginning their first song of the night, Maya. While they were a good five minutes into tuning and fumbling around with various instruments, someone in the back of the hall loudly yelled, 'You suck!' Robin looked up, eyes as wide as saucers, and I felt tension in the audience. Finally, after a long silence, someone else hollered, 'So what's wrong with sucking?!' Robin smiled broadly, the audience laughed and the show began.

The concert was perhaps my all-time favourite. Besides Maya, they performed Waiting For You, Dark Eyed Lady, Cold Harbour (one of the all-time highlights of my concert-going career), Flowers Of The Forest, Beautiful Stranger, The Letter, Long Long Road, Join The Band, Let It

Shine, Pictures In A Mirror, This Moment, When You Find Out Who You Are, and the end of A Very Cellular Song.

I saw the band a couple of more times at the Fillmore East, but, amazingly, skipped the *U* performances (definitely the biggest regret of my concert-going career). I must have confused it with the *Be Glad* film, because I didn't think the String Band was going to be there in the flesh.

'Waiting for the next ISB album to be released was becoming a hobby'

Turning eighteen that autumn, waiting for the next String Band album to be released was becoming a hobby. Fortunately, they were so prolific, I never had long to wait. Additionally, I was carefully searching out other like-spirited music, a journey which still continues. I listened to the Nonesuch Explorer series, Shirley and Dolly Collins, The Third Ear Band, Vashti Bunyan, early Al Stewart, Nick Drake, Fairport Convention, the Pentangle, Uncle Dave Macon, the Carter Family, and various jug bands and country blues artists from the Twenties and Thirties.

Most of my friends couldn't stand the String Band and let me know it. The one person that also loved their music was my high school girlfriend, who was sixteen at the time. With parents that didn't approve of our relationship (was it the drugs they thought we took? the strange clothes?), and madly in love, we ran away from home and lived in a tent during the spring of 71. It was a difficult but romantic time. We had an entire state forest to ourselves, abundant wildlife to enjoy and a lake to swim in, but we had to boat upstream six miles to get to the nearest grocery store, and our only entertainment was a book of poems by e.e. cummings and a small transistor radio. It was on this radio that we first heard songs from Mike's solo album ('What was that rock music?! – Sounded great!') and learned that the String Band were going to be performing in May at the Main Point, a small folk club in a suburb of Philadelphia. Even though the police were looking for us in three states (Pennsylvania included) we took the risk and hitchhiked 120 miles to the concert. We arrived at two in the afternoon and got the best seats in the house.

The concert was my first time to experience (I use this word deliberately) Malcolm, who was a joy to watch. The set included Bright Morning Stars (another concert favourite of mine), Worlds They Rise and Fall, Living In The Shadow, various jigs, Spirit Beautiful, Willow Pattern, Cosmic Boy, Turquoise Blue, Darling Belle (unbelievable), Adam and Eve, and The Circle Is Unbroken.

'I told my friend if he caught up with the ISB's car, I would give him my record collection'

They were playing two nights and as we were leaving the club we bumped into the friend who had urged me to go to the Philadelphia Folk Festival two years earlier. He was with another friend from high school and they offered us a ride and a place to stay in the city. This was great but we had a small problem. We had been hiding out in the woods for a month, no one knew where we were, and if anyone – these friends included – opened their mouths about our whereabouts, we could end up in deep trouble. They were sworn to secrecy.

As we were driving into Philadelphia, a yellow Ryder van (the kind a lot of rock bands use to haul equipment around in) passed us on the interstate. Thinking out loud, I said, 'Wouldn't it be great if that was the String Band's van?' No sooner had I uttered those words then a brown station wagon, carrying the String Band, drove by us. I begged my friend who was driving, to catch up to them. 'No way,' he replied. 'That wouldn't be cool.'

'I don't care if it's cool or not – that's the Incredible String Band in that car ahead of us! We have to catch them and talk to them!'

As we bantered back and forth like this a few more times, I began to see my golden opportunity to meet my musical heroes vanish before my eyes. And then I came up with an idea: I told him if he caught up with their car, I would give him my record collection (which was really good – it had all those String Band and String Band-related LPs in it). We were off!

It's humorous now, but it must have been frightening to be chased (their driver tried valiantly to escape) by a speeding carload of hippies. We caught up with them just as they pulled into a Holiday Inn, tyres screeching. I raced up to them and yelled, 'Don't worry – we love you!' My friends were mortified. The band, with the exception of Robin, looked very alarmed. Robin barely blinked, and said, 'Very well then. Would you care to join us for a late dinner in Chinatown?' How aesthetically romantic that might have been; but Likky protested, saying she was tired. (I felt like saying, 'That's fine. Go back to your room and rest,' but I didn't.)

Robin kindly invited us back to the hotel for lunch the next day. We could barely sleep that night. Early in the morning, we went looking for a gift for the band. We'd been told by two young women who waited in line with us the day before that they liked pomegranates, but we decided on a Chinese tea set instead.

American poet Jeff Rockwell looks back...

'What is it, Mike, that you're most interested in?'
'Enlightenment.'

We arrived back at the hotel at noon, and were met by Robin and Malcolm, who gave us an eloquent and delightful verbal tour of ISB-ology for the next couple of hours. After apologising for the car chase of the night before, my girlfriend and I ordered hamburgers, and I asked Robin, who was sitting to my left, if he wanted a taste. 'No thank you; we're vegetarians,' he told us. And from there we discussed the merits of a meatless diet, reincarnation, karma, communal living, world music, Philadelphia politics (we had a notorious mayor at the time, Frank Rizzo, whom Robin referred to as 'Ratzo'), and the dismal national political scene (Nixon, Vietnam, etc.). Robin and Malcolm, both, were happy to learn that the first Earth Day celebration, during which Allen Ginsberg had led several thousand people (myself included) in a march through the city, had occurred nearby in Philadelphia's Fairmont Park. Surprisingly, the subject of Scientology never came up. At the end of a very nice lunch we were invited to join them backstage after that evening's gig.

The concert, again, was great, although I almost got vertigo trying to integrate Malcolm's stage presence in my mind. Afterward, we met the band backstage and I sat down, a little nervous, on a couch beside Mike. I had a harder time striking up a conversation and ended up asking him about his favourite musicians. He mentioned Joseph Spence, Colin Blunstone, Dolly Parton and Lou Reed. After we finished talking about music there was a pause in the conversation. Finally, I asked, 'What is it, Mike, that you're most interested in?' He grinned that famous grin and replied, 'Enlightenment.'

Ginsberg outed as closet ISB fan

Almost a year went by. We turned ourselves in, moved in with my parents, found jobs, got our own place, played music, changed our diets, studied the *Tao Te Ching* and the *Bhagavad Gita*, learned to meditate and sought enlightenment. I was pleased to learn that Allen Ginsberg would be doing a poetry reading at the Main Point in a few weeks, joined by Happy Traum on guitar.

The reading was entertaining and inspiring, with Ginsberg in his most outrageous gay-in-your face mode one moment, then adroitly switching to tender singing of poems by William Blake, accompanied by his harmonium playing and Happy Traum on guitar. He finished by passionately reading portions of *Howl* and *Kaddish*. I was amazed at how similar in mood his renditions of Blake's material were to some of the music by the String Band.

I had the good opportunity to speak with Allen after the performance. I commented to him about the similarity, at times, between his Blake songs and the Incredible String Band and asked if he was aware of the band's existence. He certainly was – in fact, he considered Robin and Mike to be influences behind his writing the music for those songs. He remarked that he played The *Hangman's Beautiful Daughter* often during this period and described the band's music as 'wonderfully weird,' and felt that on some level they were kindred spirits.

The music for the Blake poems, as simple as it seemed, was actually painstakingly written over a period of several years. Not only was he inspired by the String Band, but also by his friend Bob Dylan (who he said was also fond of the String Band's music), Barry Miles (who was friends with the Beatles), and Lee Crabtree (briefly a member of the East Village band, The Fugs).

I saw the String Band a couple of more times before their break-up, once at the Bijou Theater in Philadelphia (more of a noisy bar than a decent concert venue) and at the University of Pennsylvania, where they shared the bill with Loudon Wainwright and Ellen McIllwaine. This was in the final days, when the girls were gone, and the band consisted of six guys, only three of whom were familiar. The set included a loud, electric Black Jack David and Cousin Caterpillar (nice actually), as well as Dear Old Battlefield, Oh Did I Love A Dream, Restless Night, Down Before Cathay, Cold Days of February, I Know That Man, My Father Was A Lighthouse Keeper, Rends-Moi Demain, Maker Of Islands, Saturday Maybe and Ithkos.

I remember walking home from the concert thinking that the band was going to break up soon. It was a long, sad walk home and when the news was made public that the band did, indeed, go its separate ways I knew it was time for me to explore in earnest the gifts and spiritual values I had gleaned from the String Band over the past five years.

Ginsberg: 'High beings'

Buckminster Fuller used to say, 'Life is not measured by the number of breaths you take, but by the number of breathtaking moments.' Just as the song seems never to end, neither do the breathtaking moments. The last time I spoke with Allen Ginsberg (eight months before he died) we were at a meditation retreat in the woods of upper Michigan.

Going to the men's room late one evening to wash up, I was surprised to find Allen, dressed only in his boxer shorts and Tai Chi slippers, handwashing a shirt in the sink. I said hello and asked him how he was doing. He responded excitedly saying, 'I'm going to be a rock star at 70!'

Allen had recently completed recording Ballad Of The Skeletons with Philip Glass and Paul McCartney.

We talked about musicians he liked: Dylan, Joan Baez, The Band, J.S. Bach, The Beatles, Woody Guthrie, David Amram, Billie Holiday, Gustav Mahler, Philip Glass, Thelonius Monk, Charlie Parker, Dave Van Ronk, Beck (a recent addition), Richie Havens, The Clash, Bessie Smith, The Velvet Underground, Patti Smith, Rambling Jack Elliott... 'and those two Scottish guys, the group that sang that song (at which point Allen starts to sing) "May the long time sun shine upon you!"' Allen's voice had been getting weaker the last year of his life, but he sounded great singing late at night in the bathroom (acoustics are always better in the bathroom anyway). I mentioned to Allen that they had really influenced my life in a large way.

'Yes,' he paused, 'they were high beings.'

From Blake and Whitman to Ginsberg and Kerouac, from Dylan and The Beatles to Williamson and Heron, these are not merely thrilling and enjoyable words and sounds that we have been drawn to but great art – the kind that changes lives. The breathtaking moments are all around us, and, for me, I first began paying attention to those small miracles three decades ago on a farm outside Philadelphia when four magical musicians from Scotland invaded my heart and turned me onto the music of life.

Krishna Colours

beGLAD *magazine ran a series called 'Me & The ISB' in which people described how key points in their lives were defined by the ISB's music. This is one such piece, by Deena Benjamin Omar.*

1976. Council flat, Hackney – Saturday afternoon

Out on the streets, punk is having its explosive way with the kids. Two odd schoolgirls, however, don't know, don't want to know and don't care. They're at Uncle Dave's and are discovering the Sixties.

– What d'you make of Mad Leon then, Shilling? – Brilliant, Dave. He looks mad as well. Can we have that voodoo one on again – what is it? – Dr John, the Night Tripper, interjects Karen in her softly spoken voice. Shilling flicks through a pile of records, marvelling at how many Dylan records there actually are, when all she's heard is *Desire*. This is the beginning of a long tradition of listening to music with no sense of chronology whatsoever. GCEs still a year away, this is a typical carefree Saturday afternoon scene. Shilling contemplates how irrelevant her schoolwork seems compared to what's on offer in Dave's amazing record collection. (This proves later to be true.) The hours roll by, Uncle Dave telling them stories of his hippy exploits in Turkey and Greece, Karen and Shilling giggling helplessly in the way that schoolgirls will. Steely Dan, Joni Mitchell, Dylan and Donovan provide the soundtrack.

At one point, Karen remembers a song Uncle Dave had played her the other week – You've got to hear this Shilling, it's weird and wonderful. This is quite unlike anything Shilling has heard before. It's melodic and sweet, and the lyrics – well, a strange sort of love song, thinks Shilling, but incredibly pretty. Then it changes into something else – a bizarre chant and very strange harmonies. Shilling is mesmerised... She doesn't quite know what to make of this. This music seems to have a completely different set of rules and cannot be categorised. All she can manage when it's over is – well, it's stringy, and they're definitely incredible. What's it called again? – You Get Brighter, replies Karen – don't you think it's wonderful? – Hmm... yes, strange, but sweet. I've never heard of them though. – They split up a few years ago, says Uncle Dave – D'you want to hear some more? – Nah, not right now – let's have some more Leon Russell.

1984. Primrose Hill – Dusk

– I'm surprised you've even heard of them, Pie.

– My friend's uncle played me a bit of them once. Can't remember what it was called now. Dave had a brilliant record collection. That's where I first heard Bob Dylan, you know.

– Well, you can borrow this tape. It's got bits and pieces. The first few tracks are early ones, then there's a few from later albums.

– I remember them sounding rather weird.

– Well, if you like The Third Ear Band, I can see you getting into this.

– I owe a lot to Dave. He was such a character too, had some great stories. He used to call me Shilling.

– Why?

– The approximate value of a Yugoslavian Dinar – get it?

In between shifts at the hospital playing at nurses and working towards the revolution, she would collapse exhausted on her bed while Three Is A Green Crown played at the edge of her consciousness. Her colleagues were into OMD, UB40 and the Smiths. What the fuck is that? they would ask, perplexed. Her comrades were into political music only – Easterhouse, Christy Moore. She was becoming a closet case.

1987. Camden Town – Spring

Short-life housing brought Em and Rune into her life. They were unruly girls. Rune had an unworldly, gypsy spirit, but they were very inner city – products of their time and their environment. The tape was on, one day, playing in the background, when they wandered in, bored. – What are you two up to then? – Nothing. Bored. – How was school today? – Boring. It's crap. – Oh. – Can I light this? – Go on then, just the one. They both took a joss stick each and expertly lit them using her Zippo. They waved them around like sparklers, then soon got bored with that. Black Jack Davy came on, and she sang along with it. – What's this? – Black Jack Davy. – We could do country dancing to this stuff. – Really? Go on then. – Nah, it's stupid. – Go on, show me how it goes. After arguing about who would be the boy, they began their routine. She continued to sing and clap, they skipped and whirled around the room, becoming more animated with each step. She'd never seen them so absorbed or so carefree. It was a sheer delight. At the end they collapsed on her bed, red-cheeked and giggling, out of breath. – That was great! Do you do that at school? – Yeah, we have to.

– Don't you enjoy it though? – 'S'alright. But you have to dance with boys.

1987. Europe – Summer

It was as if she'd spent her whole life waiting to hear this album. Nothing before, or since, had had quite the same impact on her. It reduced (or elevated) her to a crazed obsessive. She listened to it every day, it was her food and her drug. Her life had become complex and unhappy, and she escaped into it. She'd asked McMarker to tape her an ISB album – she was about to spend the summer travelling and wanted something good for her Walkman. – Oh, you haven't actually heard any albums? he'd said. – in that case, hmmm. Well, I'll tape as many as you want. – Just tape one for now, I want to savour it. What do you think I'd like? McMarker duly came up with the goods, the first entire ISB album she'd heard. It travelled with her throughout Greece, Hungary, Austria, Germany and North Wales. It was The *Hangman's Beautiful Daughter*. What was this?

It led me on a journey... through a deep dark wood, through my subconscious mind... a landscape both strange and familiar... evoking childhood dreams inhabited by bizarre characters and scenarios... through the day and the night, the seasons, emerging eventually into the sunshine, and this was just side one... Side two took me further afield, into darker, unknown territory, until the opening cry of Swift As The Wind *gave me a soaring feeling and brought me straight back to my childhood dreams. Having travelled through countryside and city, dark and light, reflecting on worlds and amoebas, stars and cells,* Nightfall *would put the album, and me, to bed.*

1988. Camden Town – Autumn

McMarker came up with the goods again and, with due inattention to chronology, presented her with *5000 Spirits*. On the occasions when they would meet, they would gush enthusiastically about the music. He had an admirable record collection, on a par with Uncle Dave's, and the conversation inevitably returned to the ISB. However, she didn't see him often, and the only other person she knew who was 'in on it' was Daleth. She'd given Daleth a copy of everything she had. Some of her best memories of that period are of the nights they spent totally immersed in this music that seemed to come from another planet. Daleth didn't quite share the obsession – she would actually listen to other music as well, but it was good to have someone to sing and listen with. She still felt that she was the only member of a secret club... until she saw Robin at the White Horse in Hampstead.

She'd gone alone, and whilst sitting in the bar prior to the gig, noticed a group in the corner that looked like travelling minstrels. One of them had the gig poster. She approached him to find out where he'd got it, and was welcomed into the group. Such friendly people... The one who looked like he'd be the lead singer if they were a band told her he played the crumhorn. She was impressed. She was even more impressed when, during the interval, he chatted away easily with Robin and asked him to sing Maya. Robin said he could never remember all the words, so Hirem P recited the entire song to him! During the second set, they sat huddled on the floor at the front, and were transported as Robin sang Maya – albeit the abridged version.

She invited the travelling minstrels back to her place where they spent all night listening to their shared favourite music. She felt like she'd met up with old friends from another time, another place. In the morning Hirem P picked up her guitar and sang Talking Of The End. He sang it beautifully. She was in heaven. It would be six years before she would see him again.

1989. Fitzrovia – February

Another year, another short-life dwelling. Her collection so far consisted of a couple of compilation tapes, *Hangman* and *5000 Spirits*, in that order. One day the co-op gas plumber came round to plumb in a gas fire. After the usual polite chit-chat and awkward silences that often accompany these occasions, he noticed her music collection. A couple of hours later she had two gas fires illegally in place in her basement flat, and the promise of *Wee Tam And The Big Huge* on tape. It was duly delivered the next day – labelled '*The Big Huge and The Wee Tam*' and with a John Prine track stuck on the end to fill the space. It didn't matter.

1992. On the Run

When life got bad, she would run away. This summer saw her escaping once more to the Greek Islands, clutching onto a cassette copy of *Hard Rope And Silken Twine*. The ferry was only a couple of hours late out of Piraeus. Through the night she nursed her pain across the beautiful Aegean, meeting a violet dawn on Lesbos...

Hard Rope goes well with a broken heart. Maker Of Islands, Glancing Love, particularly Dreams Of No Return – they were the soundtrack to a winter of deep unhappiness. Best of all though, to accompany the self-indulgent wallowing and soul-searching were long, candle-lit baths spent listening to Ithkos. To this day, the opening oud tune brings to her mind choppy seas and foamy water splashing against the tub, the smell of salty winds and heather bath oil. She would be back among the islands without even leaving her bathroom. By the end, she would be wrinkly, clean and purged of some of her angst, the bath water cold.

1993. Chelsea – The Discography

93 was a hard one. She had to move to another short-life flat with no bath. By now, though, McMarker had presented her with a photocopy of the *ZigZag* Do It Yourself ISB Discography. It was the only information she had about this band that no-one in the known universe (well, hers, anyway) seemed to have heard of. She'd long since lost touch with Uncle Dave. Karen had, sadly, left the battlefield early that year. Hirem P and his Merry Minstrels had disappeared as magically as they'd arrived. She'd still spend many a happy evening singing with Daleth, but Daleth was trying to introduce some Elvis into their repertoire and it wasn't quite the same. So she held her discography like a tongueless bell, reading and re-reading it, ticking off the albums she had, making notes of those she had yet to hear, and wondering... She played with the idea of writing to the compiler as invited – 'please write to the following address with any additional info'. Fishman lived in Dalston, a stone's throw from Uncle Dave's old council flat and not far from her birthplace. She never did write to him.

1993. Hackney – The Rio

The most fateful thing McMarker ever came up with was the invitation to the Rio. Well, not including the albums, and how can you exclude them? She didn't even know the films existed. [Peter Neal's *Be Glad* film and *Rehearsal*] They were full of anticipation as they drove to Hackney.

This was the first time (since Uncle Dave's) she'd ever heard ISB music being played outside her own home or Walkman. It felt a bit like being naked in a public place. And all those people who had come for the same reason – as much for the sense of occasion as the films themselves. She went to the pub with McMarker afterwards, propelled by the rumour (unfounded) that Mike Heron would be playing, and the general vibe. They had a brief chat with the guy that organised the event who, unknown to her, was Fishman. She went home happily clasping the first ever issue of *beGLAD* magazine, bought from a gruff but amiable Yorkshireman with a pony-tail.

The Rio programme

1965 - 1977 - an occasional series. Compiled by ADRIAN WHITTAKER with thanks to PAUL HUNTER (additional research) and RICHARD BOON (art-work and layout).

ROBIN WILLIAMSON + CLIVE PALMER have one track on an Edinburgh Folk Festival LP. (1965?) produced by Bill Leader on Decca. Nobody I know has heard it, but according to Karl Dallas it features a "funky minstrel-type instrumental." Sounds interesting!

INCREDIBLE STRING BAND ALBUMS.

"*The Incredible String Band*" (June 1966) EUK 254 (mono) - now only available on import EKS 7322.

MAYBE SOMEDAY / OCTOBER SONG (one of Dylan's favourite songs, according to an interview in Sing Out) / WHEN THE MUSIC STARTS TO PLAY / SCHAEFFER'S JIG / WOMANKIND / THE TREE / WHISTLE TUNE / DANDELION BLUES / HOW HAPPY I AM / EMPTY POCKET BLUES / SMOKE SHOVELLING SONG / CAN'T KEEP ME HERE / GOOD AS ME / FOOTSTEPS OF THE HERON / NIGGERTOWN / EVERYTHING'S FINE RIGHT NOW.

The folkiest album of the lot with a 3-piece ISB. (Heron, Williamson and Clive Palmer). They split up after the album came out (Williamson took his share of the loot to Morocco) and Palmer didn't re-join - he never quite learned the song.

"*5000 Spirits or the Layers of the Onion*" (July 1967) K42001 or import EKS 74010.

With its Simon + Marijke cover, the essence of '67 psychedelia. Danny Thompson plays string bass and John Hopkins of U.F.O. and I.T. adds bluesy piano on "Mad Hatter's Song."

CHINESE WHITE / NO SLEEP BLUES / PAINTING BOX / MAD HATTER'S SONG / LITTLE CLOUD / EYES OF FATE / BLUES FOR THE MUSE / HEDGEHOG SONG / FIRST GIRL I LOVED / YOU KNOW WHAT YOU COULD BE / MY NAME IS DEATH / GENTLY TENDER / WAY BACK IN THE 1960's.

Decidedly more esoteric - weird instruments like the gimbri make their first appearance. Both the above albums reached No. 1 in the folk charts but real success came with.....

"*The Hangman's Beautiful Daughter*" (Feb. 1968) K42002.

"The hangman is the past 20 years of our life and the beautiful daughter is now" - Heron. It reached No. 5 in all the national charts and won them accolades from The Times, Guardian, Melody Maker - and Kenneth Tynan. The String Band started gigging more regularly (only 20 major appearances in their first 2 years of existence) and did their first American tour.

KOOEEAADI THERE (the title letters were picked at random by throwing a dice) / THE MINOTAUR'S SONG / WITCH'S HAT / A VERY CELLULAR SONG / MERCY I CRY CITY / WALTZ OF THE NEW MOON (draws heavily on Robert Graves' "White Goddess") / THE WATER SONG / THREE IS A GREEN CROWN / SWIFT AS THE WIND / NIGHTFALL.

Dolly Collins plays flute-organ and piano and Licorice makes her second appearance on disc (the first being finger-cymbals on "5000 Spirits").

Rated by most as the best ISB album ever. In April, June + July '68 they recorded "*Wee Tam and the Big Huge*" originally

The *Zigzag* do-it-yourself discography. (artwork by Richard Boon)

Epilogue

The rest, as they say, is her story. That first magazine led me to the first ISB convention at Hebden Bridge, where, together with Daleth, I met and identified Fishman (setting off a remarkable chain of coincidences, but that's another story...), plus a whole host of other characters who also became friends. Hebden Bridge led to me and Fishman assisting that pony-tailed Yorkshireman (the legendary Mr Roberts) with a Leeds ISB event, where I finally met up with Hirem P again. I eventually completed my collection of ISB albums, with the help of Fishman and many other generous people. Just about everything on the discography has now been ticked off – in no logical order of course.

Postscript

Reader, I did not marry him. However, Fishman and I now live together a pebble's throw from the Rio in Dalston, Hackney. He gets brighter every day...

'There was a fearlessness in ISB's approach which we have in Pet Shop Boys': a 2020 conversation with Neil Tennant

Liking the ISB 'was like joining an exclusive club, with arcane references to half-remarkable questions and natural cards revolving, never changing. Progressive rock fans sneered, which was great: this was our own territory.' *Neil Tennant,* Q *magazine.*

I'd wanted to interview Neil Tennant for *Be Glad* ever since I came across the above quote in Q, years ago. When the first edition of the book was being prepared I didn't manage to get in touch with him, but the 2020 lockdown and the subsequent cancellation of the planned Pet Shop Boys Greatest Hits tour gave him time to take part in this email conversation.

Adrian: Hello, Neil. I've wanted to do this interview ever since I read that your first group, Dust, was named after the first line of Maya, but had no clue about how to get in touch! I'm a couple of years older than you and the first time I came across the ISB in 1968 I was sixteen, and in the fifth form at grammar school. There was a little clique of misfits and would-be creatives which, during Maths class, would discuss the latest musical obsessions – Sixties Dylan, Cream, John Mayall, Bert and John – but it was me who introduced the ISB after finding Hangman *at the local record library and having it out on repeated loan for months. A few of us became major ISB obsessives, poring over the* Hangman *cover (Who were all those people? Whose were all the kids?) and the lyrics for hours. How did you first come across them?*

Neil: I attended a youth theatre on Saturday mornings in Newcastle, the Young People's Theatre, and in 1970 made friends with a boy the same age as me (15), Chris Dowell. He had been introduced to ISB by his elder sister and had become a big fan and was quite evangelical about them. He played me the album *The Big Huge* (he didn't have *Wee Tam* at that point) so the first song I heard by them was Maya. I thought it was awful! It was like nothing I'd ever heard before. Then, as now, I was a pop fan and ISB's music was too 'weird' for me. My friend suggested I borrow the album and I took it home. It didn't take me long to realise that what I had regarded as the weaknesses of the ISB – strange lyrics, obscure instrumentation, whimsicality etc – were in fact their strengths.

As a pop fan, this was a difficult period. The Beatles had broken up and both heavy rock and cheesy bubblegum pop were everywhere. I loathed both. The 'Increds' (as we always referred to them) filled the gap between the Beatles and David Bowie. From 1970 to 1972 I was a dedicated fan. All of our group of youth theatre friends became fans. It was like a badge of honour, a way of manifesting that you were different from 'normal' people. It was almost like being members of a cult.

I even kept an ISB scrapbook for a couple of years, which I hid from most non-believers – How far did you take the fan thing? My parents were seriously concerned when I went to see U *twice at the Roundhouse in 1970.*

Neil: I lived in Newcastle so didn't get to see *U* but I saw ISB at the City Hall a couple of times and would listen out for sessions by them on Radio One. But mainly I sat (on the floor probably) at friends' houses listening to their albums and getting to know their songs intimately and speculate on their relationships. Cloaks and kaftans and communes: it was fascinating.

Chris Dowell and I both played the guitar and we formed a folk group, largely inspired by ISB, called Dust, which like ISB consisted of two boys and two girls. As you have read, the name of the band was inspired by the first word of the first ISB song I ever heard! I had been writing songs at home for a few years and now I had a chance to perform them in a group. We played our first concert in a comprehensive school on Gateshead and then entered a talent competition in Newcastle. We got through to the semi-finals when we were knocked out.

Left: A young Neil practising guitar. (Tennant family); *right* an older Neil, preparing for Dust. (Rosemary Van Miert).

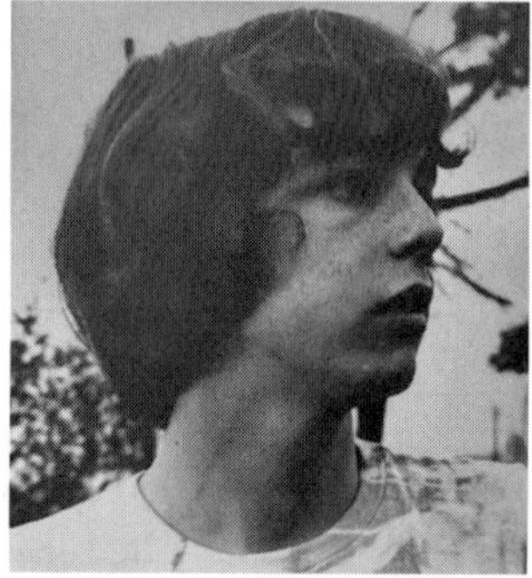

I began to write songs with slightly mystical/whimsical lyrics, again inspired by ISB. Chris Dowell had the ISB songbook which I borrowed and I learned several of their songs, e.g. First Girl I Loved. Our ambition was to write a very long, episodic song, along the lines of A Very Cellular Song but we never quite managed it. Our high point was recording a radio session of five songs for BBC Radio Newcastle which was broadcast at the beginning of 1971.

> *Sadly I missed seeing them when I would have most liked to, the* 5000 Spirits / Hangman / Wee Tam *era. By the time I realised you had to buy* Melody Maker *to find out about gigs in time to get tickets for them, it was 1969 and the four-piece line-up had moved on from hard and sharp laughter to singing about great old pigs. This was a shock. But in time I grew to love the newer stuff too, and Rose and Likky seemed to be having such fun on stage. I was always too self-conscious to try to talk to them after gigs, though. How was it for you?*

Neil: I was fascinated by the looseness of the performances and also the occasional theatricality. The atmosphere was of extraordinary communality and it became clear that we weren't the only ISB obsessives in Newcastle. The second time we saw them we went backstage and chatted to them which worked because you somehow felt that they were friends. They didn't behave like 'stars'.

We loved the Robin/Mike/Rose/Likky line-up but didn't disapprove when Malcolm Le Maistre joined them, introducing a different voice and increasing their theatricality. However, the drift to a more rock sound seem to bring them down to earth and the magic started to evaporate.

In early 1972, I became aware of David Bowie through the album *Hunky Dory*, his appearance on *The Old Grey Whistle Test* and sessions on Radio One and through his interviews in the *NME*. Then in June that year we went to see Bowie at the City Hall which was a life-changing experience. I remember saying to Chris Dowell as we drove away from the concert, 'Well that's it for the Increds! It's all about Bowie now.'

> *Being an ISB fan did a lot to open up my world view – reading Graves'* The White Goddess *– because they had, Thomas Traherne, various introductions to Buddhism,* Music Of The Bahamas, *Shirley and Dolly Collins'* Anthems In Eden *(because there was a Williamson song on it!)... But I could never really accept their line about politics being a whole other thing, man*

(neither could Rose, I later found out!). And later on in the early 70s, Scientology was just plain odd. Did the ISB take you into any new directions?

Neil: Only in song-writing. The mysticism appealed to me as a style but not as something to explore intellectually. I was brought up as a Catholic and went to a Catholic school so that was quite enough mythology for me! The last time I saw ISB was at a Scientology benefit gig at the Rainbow in London in 1973 and we got sent Scientology propaganda through the post for a long while after that. Chris Dowell actually went to a couple of classes at the Scientology Centre in London but was very unimpressed. The Scientology thing was a negative for us and it felt like its influence on ISB was negative as though it was gradually destroying the magic. However, there were some beautiful songs in the later ISB albums: Queen Of Love, Red Hair, and one of my all-time favourite Robin songs in 1973, Saturday Maybe.

I can't claim any great musical influences; I played, badly, but never really wrote songs – but struggling through the first ISB songbook did make me learn more than three guitar chords and even a bit about open tuning. Your 'folk music band' Dust was influenced by the ISB – how did that manifest itself? Instrumentation? Girls in the band? Wearing dressing-gowns onstage (in lieu of kaftans), like Andrew Greig and his mate George?

Neil: In the instrumentation and the style of the music. Chris Dowell was much more into folk music and I was really a pop fan so it was a bit like the musical differences between Robin Williamson and Mike Heron and finding common ground. After a year or so, Dust broke up and Chris formed a folk band while I started a sort of acoustic rock/pop group inspired by Marc Bolan, David Bowie, glam rock. I sang with two girl singers and a friend played bongos (like Mickey Finn in T. Rex). And my song-writing was evolving to include piano ballads – I'd taught myself to play the piano we had at home. I moved to London to study history and tried to interest music publishers in my songs.

I'm afraid my PSB knowledge is restricted to the hits, really (and live at Glastonbury!). I currently really like Burning the Heather. It would be easy to assume there are no ISB influences – but are there any subtle nods to them in any of your PSB work? And was there any kind of transition era from Dust-style stuff to PSB?

Neil: No, you'd struggle to find an ISB musical influence in PSB but there is the occasional acoustic ballad. There was a fearlessness in ISB's approach which we have in PSB – a desire to create our world – and I think ISB helped to educate me in that. And we like to explore a wide range of musical styles within the framework of PSB.

And finally – favourite albums or songs (and why, if you like)?

Neil: My favourite is the double-album *Wee Tam And The Big Huge* because it has the freshness, the magic and the range of song-writing which made them so special. The Incredible String Band were like no other band and this is the perfect statement of their uniqueness.

My Room 101 – a personal depreciation of the ISB

Chris Taylor

The thought has often occurred to me that every *Abbey Road* has its Octopus's Garden, every *Astral Weeks* has its The Way Young Lovers Do: find a pearl and there's usually a great fat swine squatting just behind it somewhere. In all great work there's usually something murky in the corners. Not an a priori truth admittedly but it's the theory which is mine.

Even the most fervent die-hard follower of the String Band knows in his/her heart that among the rich and wonderful garden of song there are one or two, how shall we put it, turds. The odd footslip, the occasional lapse of editorial perspicuity. You know the ones – the cringingly awful tracks that would seem to have been put there for the sole purpose of embarrassing you if your parents walked into your bedroom. Or just when you'd decided to chance *5000 Spirits* on your uninitiated mates.

Because of the sheer output in so short a time, because of their slightly wonky, haphazard experimentalism, because of the rapid trajectory from no-nonsense jug funk to spaced-out world-view all-ethos-encompassing star-gazers and seed contemplators, it would be a harsh judge indeed who would not forgive the odd skipper (oh, the advantages of CD). With this in mind I thought it would be fun to knock out my own personal Room 101, as it were. I don't want to step on anyone's sacred cows here, just an affectionate poke in the ribs – the music of the Incredible String Band has been a constant sound track to my formative and adult life, sometimes playing quietly in the background, sometimes swelling 'til it's a mighty noise. Sometimes on a record player, but more often in a continuous tape loop behind my waking dreams.

So, down to business, and what have we got then? Well, top of my ho-hum list has got to be Little Cloud. Now I can take talking caterpillars, I can even take talking hedgehogs although that's pushing it a bit. But really, a cute little talking baby doll cloud with a golden string – and this really hurts – when it rains it is actually the cloud crying – happy tears! Get a grip man, have you no pride? This song is so soppy you just want to slap its face. When this one appeared in the ISB songbook Happy Traum only gave us the first verse – make up your own minds. The only part of the song I will admit to quite liking is the odd jerky lurchy rhythm – ta ta ta ta tow wow but no thanks. Next please...

Bad Sadie Lee? Nah, that's too easy and it's all been said already. Fair enough, it's a Janet Shankman vocal and you can't blame her – the guilt lies with whoever thought it was worth recording/releasing in the first place (answers on a postcard please). In my warped imagination it suddenly provokes the nightmare vision of a Robin & Janet collaboration a la *Two Virgins*. Passing on quickly...

Adam and Eve! It is certainly true that Teddy Boys don't knit, and I would add that folkies shouldn't play reggae. Toots Hibbert this is not. In fact I find the whole thing rather patronising and distasteful – Lance Percivalesque silly accents (Gossip Calypso, anyone?) with the very dodgy attitude of using a different cultural style merely for novelty value with no apparent appreciation or understanding. Admittedly this was more prevalent at that time but these lads really should have known better. Don't think much of the lyrics either.

Circus Girl. I feel on safer ground here, I don't think anybody likes this one. This is an inherent problem with 'funny' songs in that if they're not actually funny they just become annoying. Waiting For You is funny – Circus Girl isn't.

Minotaur's Song – I've no particular attraction for tar and feathers but I just don't like this. Never have. Just what is it all about? Is it supposed to be an elaborate lampoon on bombast and bigotry or was it a vehicle for dressing up in foolish costumes and singing bad puns in silly voices? I don't know. But it still sounds like a lot of old bullshit to me. Next... Astral Plane Theme. A great man once said 'I could make a better noise with my bottom,' which I think sums this plonker up quite nicely.

It struck me that if El Rato had been put on *U* and Hirem Pawnitof left off then El Rato would get slagged off and Hirem Pawnitof elevated to rare and fascinating collectors' item status. History being the way it is I'll slag off Hirem Pawnitof then. Actually it's not that bad – this is Mike Heron's Norman Collier to Robin Williamson's Dick Emery I suppose. Still, I think you probably had to be there – I'll wager they all wet themselves to this one due to prolonged side holding.

Having waxed lyrical over *Wee Tam*, even that has its less than half remarkable moments, 'When I was born and had no head...' are you boasting or complaining? Douglas Traherne Harding has always been a tricky pancake, 'cos try as I might, try as I may, I always get bored with it. A dull, plodding repetitive dirge which might have sounded like nirvana (not Nirvana) on *No Ruinous Feud*, but this one light isn't bright enough for the company it shares.

So what else is there? Second Fiddle of course, but I've always thought of it as just a so-what filler that's soon out of the way, not something you could get passionate about one way or the other. Evolution Rag and Big Ted? Teetering on the brink, but nah, they can be forgiven. Ithkos? I know this scored highly in a readers' poll of worst songs but I will keep a candle burning for Ithkos for purely sentimental reasons, although I award it bonus dodginess points for 'talkin' 'bout your fluted pillars and your muted life.' Perhaps the result of a heavy night on the ouzo?

Dump those and what does that leave us with? Well, about 150 odd songs of stark grace, sometimes visceral joy, intelligence and unselfconscious wonder, which to this day are still being discovered, pondered over, criticised or simply enjoyed. An A-Z of another world with all the place names muddled up. Not a bad average. No children, that's not bad at all.

These Moments

The lesser is the greater, says Paul Bryant, who picks out a few of his perfect ISB moments.

The 39 seconds which begin at 5.48 in A Very Cellular Song, just a little mandolin shuffle, a fragment, a coloured flake in the kaleidoscope changing to form a new picture and gone as soon as you know it's there, so disproportionately exhilarating for such a small thing, crystallises one of the ISB's principal pleasures: the demonstration of the greater in the lesser, the universal interconnectedness.

Lyrically, in Spirit Beautiful the idea becomes explicitly and conventionally Blakean as the seed becomes the forest, the bubble the ocean, the pebble the mountain. But elsewhere the ISB were able to shape these insights in the form of the song and the curve of the melody. In Waltz Of The New Moon, a transcendent masterpiece, the unwary listener is liable to suffer vertigo as the song swoops ever upwards from the snail beneath the stone beneath the wall, way way up to the eagle and the eyelid of God. From the physical to the metaphysical. As the perspective heightens so Robin's voice (he never sang better) climbs the scales, and climbs, and climbs.

The 39-second mandolin tune, embedded in a song so long you could stroll to the corner shop for bread and milk and still be back for the last chorus, is one of the ways the ISB, in their profligate musicianship and intellectual ebullience, were able to nudge, cajole, charm and surprise the listener into sharing insights, or points of view, which may be classed as religious by some. Like koans, they used non-sense and brevity, small startling aural occurrences located within the largest of canvasses. Their subject was not just *the Big Huge*, but *Wee Tam* too.

One of my favourites of these epiphanies is Robin's sly observation, after Mike's genial anti-20th century diatribe in Mercy, I Cry, City, 'but the opposite is also true'. At the time, I admit, the phrase gave me pause. Is it? Is the opposite also true? It's a great ISB moment.

These moments happen pretty much all the time. Think of the shock of the first guitar/sitar note of Half-Remarkable Question; or the strangulated rough harmonic yelling at the end of the first Black Jack Davy before a sudden silence which has you teetering horribly on the edge before the helter-skelter panic rush of the fiddles and guitar into the brick wall at the end; or the exquisite bass guitar part down there at the end of Light In Time Of Darkness (6.55).

The ISB were always an extremely personal thing for their hardcore fans. Not just a good band. Mike's song The Letter addresses this directly. How they must have been inundated by fans thinking that the ISB had the answer. Not just the General All-Purpose Answer to Life but the answer for Me, here and now. And here's Maria from Chicago, Illinois writing just one of those pleas to Mike, who says, 'She's got a lot of things – ah – she gotta work out'. What eloquence in that 'ah'. Was exasperation ever so kindly or compassion so understated? Another String Band moment. Mike earthed the ISB, as has so often been noted, and it was in songs like The Letter and, of course, This Moment, which contains another Mikeism. It's that spoken phrase 'I just want to tell each one of you that...' – the cheesiest, most hackneyed, ungenuine, abused and threadbare Las Vegas audience-massaging device known to man, redeemed in this song about rescuing the uniqueness of the banal. Again, content is form. Mike pulls the very same stunt in Rainbow – 'I'd hate to go till I see everyone here shine like a rainbow,' – and it works there too.

Their melodic invention was so prolific that both Robin and Mike would throw away in one song tunes which others would have based whole numbers on. It used to bother me. That's so great, I'd think, why is it so short? In The Mad Hatter's Song there is the 'I am the archer' section; in Darling Belle the wrenching 'Meet me by gaslight' part; in Ithkos there is 'The beautiful Aegean Sea'; a lovely whistle tune buried and lost somewhere on Side Two of *Be Glad*. Sometimes you thought to yourself, they know what they're doing, but sometimes you thought, they don't know what they've got.

In instrumental fecundity they came at you from all sides, great aural ideas, some developed, some cast aside. Like the swooping sarangi at 12.08 in White Bird and the rolling bumping drums in that song's final chorus; like the flute break in Painting Box and the bass part of Darling Belle. In each case an idea used once and discarded. Sometimes it went wrong. If ever a song needed a big chord to finish on it was Red Hair, and if ever a song didn't need dodgy feel-over-technique cello passages, it was Red Hair. Heron made up for the first mistake in Antoine. That's got a big chord at the end.

And vocally, no one but Robin could glide out into those uncharted waters with quite as much confidence, and who else tried? His use of melisma to stretch both word and melody at key moments was entrancing – I suspect it is the single aspect of the ISB which some find so alienating. But I listen as Robin sings the words 'all we can' in Cold Harbour, wringing unidentifiable emotions from the strange lyric; I hear him entranced in Waltz Of The New Moon – hear 'victories of' or 'palaces' – how many melodic inflections? My favourite of these is an early one, My Name Is Death. The introduction is almost one note ('I am the question etc') until the final 'Pray what is my name?' is answered by Robin's voice cascading like a fountain through the rest of the verses in a contradiction of the inevitability it describes. Form subverting content.

There are many others and it would be easy to launch into a list (Robin's pronunciation of the word 'iron' would be there, too) of these short moments in such long music. Well, I already did. *Wee Tam* is *the Big Huge*. And the opposite is also true.

Overleaf Backstage in Zurich, 1974.(Felix Reut) Robin, John Gilston, Graham Forbes, Mike, Malcolm, Stan Schnier.

Chapter Twelve

In which we hear from Stan Schnier, Graham Forbes and Steve Blacknell and get the Malcolm Le Maistre story.

Song And Dance Man

Adrian Whittaker talked to Malcolm Le Maistre in 1997.

Malcolm's career was closely entwined with the ISB for six years – as dancer, actor, musician, songwriter and, from 1971, as a full member. These days, Malcolm and his partner Mary live outside Edinburgh in an old farmhouse, with various eco-projects on the go. There are a lot of projects on the go and much purposeful activity. We settled down to talk in the calm of Malcolm's studio, which is festooned with ancient ISB posters and stacked with dusty piles of unlabelled tapes, and started at the beginning...

Adrian: We want the truth – was your father really a lighthouse keeper?

Malcolm: Let's get this straight: my father was not a lighthouse keeper. He was of French origin, brought up in the UK. He travelled around in his early years – he was based in Paris during the war, and then spent two years in India, where he met Gandhi. He was about forty-seven when he arrived back in Britain and met my mother, who was American and was a writer and working as a theatre scout for MGM. Dad was by this point a committed Socialist and working as a journalist, and my childhood was spent in those sort of circles. Anyway, they eventually split up, and by the time I was eight or nine I was pretty disturbed – a total underachiever, always getting into trouble. I ended up seeing a child psychologist, who felt I'd be better off removed from the conflict.

So I went to Frensham Heights, a progressive co-educational boarding school, which is where I first got into theatre and particularly dance. My teacher felt I should really be a dancer, and that was my plan by the time I got to the sixth form.

I left in summer 1966. In retrospect, I should have gone straight to dance school; I realised later they were desperate for male dancers at that time. But I was starting to get into the counter-culture...

Ivan Pawle was in a pink tutu

A major turning point was the *International Times* benefit at the Roundhouse at the end of 66. Lindsay Kemp and Ivan Pawle were hanging out together, both dressed in pink tutus; Soft Machine and Pink Floyd were playing... I remember feeling this was my community.

I'd like to claim in print that I put on the first gig by the Pink Floyd. I was going out with a girl whose sister was Nick Mason's girlfriend. They didn't have a name at this point. I phoned up to offer them a gig at the school dance, which they agreed to, and then I had to hang on while they decided what name to put on the poster. Eventually, Nick came back and said 'Pink Floyd'. I've still got the poster we made – probably a collector's item now! Later on, I did some roadying for Pink Floyd in the Syd Barrett era. I remember one gig with Graham Bond where the dancefloor was packed and emptied completely when Pink Floyd came on!

Anyway, after the Roundhouse I decided this is where it's at, showing a sort of rebellious side, and that was the end of my formal dance career – I decided to dance naturalistically...Which I did... I did go to some dance classes though. Part of the problem was my sexuality: in those days there were very few non-gay male dancers, so I didn't fit into the scene.

Are you and Rakis 'together'?

I'd teamed up with Rakis – John Koumantarakis, who was at school with me – and we got right into the culture. I saw Jimi Hendrix's second gig ever, lots of other bands, and we started going to UFO. That's where I met David Medalla – he walked up to me and asked me if I'd like to join a dance theatre group! I went back with him to Balls Pond Road... I had no idea what I was letting myself in for.

I was going up the stairs and this French guy, Christian, said: 'If you're worried about David you can come and sleep in my room – you'll be quite safe with me!', and everybody collapsed laughing. They all turned out to be extremely nice, and David was a very charismatic person. I was the second or third person to join the Exploding Galaxy, and then Rakis joined too. Through the Galaxy I came into contact with people like Bowie and Lindsay Kemp, usually at parties thrown by gallery owners who were friends of David's. I went to an opening at Lissom Gallery and Derek Jarman asked me and Rakis if we were 'together'. We said, well, yes, we were together and he asked us if we'd like to make up a foursome! We were only eighteen and still a bit naïve – but it was a good laugh, we had a great time.

Someone spiked the orange juice...

Galaxy performances were sometimes chaotic events. At one Warwick University gig, someone spiked the orange juice just before we were due to go on, and so we did our performance on acid to this bunch of bemused students.

Our most famous experience was when we were crossing the Dutch/Belgian border. They suspected us to be 'druggies' so we were taken off the train and all the guys were put in one cell, the women in another. One of the men had some acid, and there was no toilet to dispose of it – so Rakis said let's take it, which we did. It was a completely mad thing to do. The result of all this was when we finally got off the train at Utrecht, there were a few press photographers who'd come to cover the arrival of this notorious group – and all the guys were completely out of it. The women were all helping the men off the train; we looked like a bunch of invalids... I was trying to dive off the platform!

At one gig at the Palais de Sport, Cat Stevens was on the bill, and he spent the whole evening pursuing David Medalla in the belief that he was a girl. I must say, David didn't disabuse him of this notion! We can only speculate what happened when they went off together... I'm sure he'd love to be reminded of that now!

Anyway, the Galaxy was really important to me. David Medalla was a great, a visionary artist, and he started to really draw me out... He was like a really early community arts leader. He was also one of the first people to be into recycling materials, which we called 'scrudging'. We also had more disciplined performances – dance dramas. Rakis and I had been exposed a bit to Indian dance and we used to do Indian dance dramas – Krishna stories – with David and others, in which I would invariably be Arjuna and David or Rakis would be Krishna. And I think some of that rubbed off on my work with the String Band. In fact, the first time I met Robin that's what we did [*at the Fillmore East in June 1968 – Ed.*].

Time for something new

Eventually, in the spring of 68, Rakis and I said OK, we've been doing this for a year, it's time for something new. So we went to New York to see my Mum, who was living in the Chelsea Hotel. She wrote a book about it later on. We got to Customs – I remember Rakis was wearing this kind of long robe, and of course we were strip-searched. They didn't find anything, though. There was only one room going at the Chelsea Hotel – which no-one wanted. It had been Valerie Solanas' room, and she'd shot Andy Warhol a week earlier. We moved in there.

Our stay in New York was fantastic for all kinds of reasons. All kinds of rock stars were passing through the hotel, there were lots of parties, and we met some interesting people there. Every morning Jerry Garcia would be sitting in the lobby, eating roast beef sandwiches and reading the *Christian Science Monitor*, which always struck me as an interesting combination! There was an Australian, Brett Whitely, who later became a famous artist. Lord Harlech's daughter lived there; and there was this guy who wrote Tubby The Tuba, George Kleinsinger, who lived with a menagerie of animals. His room was like a jungle, and in the middle of it was this grand piano on which he'd serenade his guests – mostly young girls! There was a well-known couturier, Charles James, who kept a large basset hound which he'd trained to pin young men to the wall and then slobber all over them. This would give him an excuse to invite them into his boudoir to get cleaned up. Rakis and I allowed this to happen to us so we could visit, and his room was full of these amazing Thirties velvet dresses. We'd put up a notice which mentioned masturbation, and for some reason a lot of very weird people were attracted to us...

I also met Allen Ginsberg and Tim Leary – they were holding a debate on Vietnam, and Wavy Gravy was there too, dressed as a Vietnamese general with a chest full of medals. It was fascinating watching these huge figures argue with each other, but at the end of it, nothing had really been said. I realised at this point that was where their heads were at – they weren't really sure where anything was going or what it meant.

Had you seen the ISB before you met them, with the dancers Mimi and Mouse?

I'd seen them three or four times. Mimi and Mouse did Indian dance with them, kind of ethereal stuff. I went to the Festival Hall gig where Robin had all these taped whistles, and got invited up on stage to join in...

So you'd already performed with them! Along with Salman Rushdie...

Ah, so we have got something in common! After the New York gig, Robin said we should meet up again in Britain and maybe live together. He asked me to try and find something suitable in Wales – which turned out to be Penwern.

A French heiress and deserving causes...

John Schofield and myself discovered Penwern. It was a beautiful farm with a huge farmhouse, a big yard and garden. Around this time we found out the Galaxy had met this woman, Silvina, in Paris who had inherited a vast fortune, some of which she'd given to them. So Rakis and I thought, let's join the club, and we went off to Paris to see her. We waited around in this flat, which was full of a variety of con-men, and Silvina would just appear unexpectedly and write out cheques to people she felt were deserving.

In the end, we asked for £5000, which was a lot of money in 1968 – £2000 for me and £3000 for Rakis! Rakis' story was that he was going off to Nigeria to film drummers, and mine was about setting up Stone Monkey. John and Ishy, who'd been in the Galaxy too, also had some money from her, so we put it all together and went off to Wales. Robin and Licorice joined us, and Ivan Pawle was living there for a time.

[Rakis disagrees: 'The Silvina money came later and was for me to bring Yoruba musicians to an event at the Roundhouse that never happened and for Malcolm to make a movie of The Monkey King. She also gave money for a farmhouse in which to explore our creativity in 1969 – after Penwern.' 2021]

We continued to perform with the String Band from time to time – we did Edinburgh with them – and met Joe Boyd. We were having a curry with him one night when he realised he only had five minutes before his train went, and he grabbed the plate of curry, literally poured it down his throat and ran off for the train. We just sat there gaping at each other for five minutes. He was always a bit strange, Joe... I liked him, though, he was a nice guy. It was a very enjoyable summer in Penwern, and we all collaborated on The Pirate And The Crystal Ball. Mike and Rose lived in Roman Camps – very near where I live now – while Robin was in Wales, but they came down for the film.

Was your bird scene influenced by David Medalla?

Yes, I think it was. I remember we were filming a chase scene when the cord on Rakis' trousers came undone – you can see them falling down – and then he tripped and fell flat on his face. Of course, Peter Neal kept it, and it turned up in the film. The Gods bit with Mike and Robin was filmed in the back garden at Penwern, and the Fates part was down the road at Pentre Ifan.

Then Stone Monkey moved to a new house, Kilmanoyadd, near Llandrindod Wells. It was a beautiful building, a twelfth century farmhouse – I remember we uncovered this wonderful fireplace five or six feet deep which you could actually sit inside. The house was inhabited by members of Exploding Galaxy and Stone Monkey. I think Robin and Licorice used to visit... We stayed there till we were told we were moving to Glen Row – on 19th November 1969. Stone Monkey had done a few things with the ISB since *Be Glad*, an Albert Hall gig... When this new idea came up, *U*, it seemed natural we should all live together. Licorice and I were the first two to move in – she tried to seduce me that night, but it was a bit difficult as I was still with Mal [Schofield] at the time. Licorice

Malcolm and Mal outside the Kilmanoyadd cottage. (Malcolm Le Maistre collection)

'LIKE A FLOCK OF STARLINGS'

Way up in the remote hills of Mid Wales stands the Pales, a historic Quaker Meeting House, where Martin and Lynda Williams lived as wardens. Next door, quarter of a mile away, is the farm Rhonllwyn; next door but one, a mile away, is Kilmanoyadd... Martin reported on how the locals remember the smiling men with strange reputations.

David Ingram of Rhonllwyn, a teenager at the time of Stone Monkey's stay, remembered their van particularly, and the communal trips to the nearest pub, the Severn Arms in Penybont—and the chaotic bicycle rides back afterwards!

David's mother, Mrs Ingram remembered them clearly and very, very, fondly. I showed her some pictures of Malcolm and she immediately exclaimed, 'Oh, I remember him, lovely boy. Oh they was nice people, they'd do anything for you, real neighbours. When they first came out, they was hippies, long hair and all. But they were so kind and honest, we missed them so much when they went, they was like another family. I remember they used to meet at night on that big yard there, and they'd come from all around, like starlings we used to say, they'd come all in a flock and then be gone in a flock. But they'd get together and they'd be strumming away till the sparks flew. There was a drummer too.'

had split up with Robin by then and moved into Number 7 next to Mike. Robin was in 5, John and Ishy were in 6, I was in 4, Rose was in 2, Ivan Pawle lived in no. 8 and Tim Booth was in no. 3. There was a period when 3 was a sort of rehearsal room, and when Licorice left, no. 7 became the sort of roadies' house. Jane Mock was in 8 for a while; that's where she made all the costumes for *U*.

My first introduction to Scientology came from Robin and Licorice. Rakis was never into it... At that time he and Rose were in a lustful relationship. Quite a bit of interchanging of partners went on at that time. I hated it, I have to say. Anyway, we created this bizarre U-shaped story which we rehearsed in the village hall.

I'd describe *U* now as naïve but interesting – within it, there were some good bits, from both Stone Monkey and the ISB – but on the whole, we just weren't good enough for our ideas. I can see why the Americans didn't take to it. It was an ambitious piece. I don't know whose idea it was to do such a big production – probably Robin's, though everyone enjoyed sitting around coming up with crazy ideas – it's just that some didn't work. *U* got some of the most amazing reviews I've ever read in my life!

Did you take reviews like Tony Palmer's to heart?

Tony Palmer always hated me – but anyone who likens the Beatles to Schubert can't be taken seriously anyway... As far as judging the quality of Stone Monkey's work, he's right – it wasn't very good. But it also wasn't very bad and it was also rather imaginative; we were lacking in technique and experience. We were only 19, 20 years old and were never going to be the Royal Shakespeare Company – we were trying to do a slightly wistful, mad production. A lot of people enjoyed it including Billy Connolly and Marc Bolan. It did really well in London, we came close to selling out every performance. The guy who's now one of the most successful entrepreneurs in Scotland, Pete Irvine, came up to me recently and said *U* was one of the best shows he'd seen!

Going to New York was great fun, though I think the audience wasn't really ready for us. After one gig Mike was chatting up this 'girl', who we'd all realised was a transvestite – and he hadn't... He came back an hour later looking rather shocked!

Looking back at the 67, 68 counter-culture period, how do you judge it now?

It's interesting to answer that question with a daughter who's 21 and a son who's 18... I feel there was a fundamental difference then, a sort of consensus, a kind of philosophical base. At the moment it seems to be about Having A Good Time. The peace and love ethic was quite a real thing – yes, it got mixed up with a lot of sex – but underneath that there was an energy which said we can change, things have to be different – as in Times They Are A-Changing. Maybe they weren't, but there was a belief it was true...

What I believe now is that out of that culture came quite a lot of significant people who are now in their forties, fifties and in positions of power – but also retaining some of that idea.

What about the drugs side – acid and so on?

I see all drugs and all belief systems as like an opening of a door. Acid opened a door in my head, but I realised very quickly that was all it would do. It wouldn't make me understand myself. I'd have to live more of my life to understand myself. I got into Scientology as I stopped taking drugs – my last acid trip at the Glen was around 71. We were sitting around outside having gut-ache, laughing our heads off over and over again at this record which is the greatest piece of kitsch, hippie nonsense you'll ever hear. It's a work of genius, by a band called Milkwood Tapestry. Everything is magnificently over the top, all the worst hobbity cliched pseudo-mystical poems you could possibly write sung to this pseudo-Hendrix feedback guitar... it was so funny... There's a lot of hysteria about drugs but I don't regret that period, I think I've stayed totally sane! There are always people who will abuse anything, whether it's drugs or food...

...and that leads into the usual Scientology question. How do you see all that now?

For myself, it was tied up with all kinds of complicated things in my life. It was associated with the ISB – I'd have probably got out a lot quicker if I hadn't joined the ISB. It's an interesting philosophical belief system.

Above Malcolm in 1969. (Malcolm Le Maistre collection)

This stuff about 'Scientology broke the band up' is claptrap...

Did you grow as a result of Scientology?

Only as much as I grew through taking acid – but in a different way. I haven't really got an axe to grind – I think Scientology left me with some useful pieces of knowledge which I always use. I'll defend Hubbard on one level – if he was a charlatan, why did he write so much? He must have spent a great deal of his day writing. One side of him gets forgotten – he was very right about psychiatry and ECT, which have since cleaned up their act. I also like the way he said that pregnant women should be respected and treated well as they hold our future...

Of course he also had a space cadet side, extremely bureaucratic – but you can't get much more bureaucratic than the Christian Church! I never actually met him. All this stuff about 'Scientology broke the band up' is claptrap. People go into Scientology because they've got problems – and bands break up all the time. Almost all belief systems get corrupted and Scientology was no exception – but it did provide some valuable teachings. I left in 1983 – it coincided with my marital split from Annabel. I'd tried to get some help from Scientology, but it didn't work.

Back to Stone Monkey...

In 1970, after *U*, Stone Monkey came back to Edinburgh and did a show, *Dobson D De Bray*, at the Edinburgh Festival. We put the show together and got an empty shoe shop in St Mary's Street. There was no advertising, and at first no-one came; but gradually the word got around, and people kept coming back. We got to know our audience on first name terms. That's where I met John Gorman from The Scaffold, they came regularly, and where I first met Lindsay Kemp.

I'd split up with Mal and moved out of the Row to a cottage down the road, and one day I was asked to join the band. Rose had left by then. That's when I moved back to the Glen.

Did you join as a full member?

Yes, though I was on a smaller percentage than Robin and Mike. At the end of the first tour the money was shared out and I got $3,000 in cash – more than I'd ever earned in my life. It was quite a surprise – so I went off for a holiday in Mexico!

Did Mike and Robin consciously write vehicles for you?

I suppose they recognised my range was limited and I had a lowish voice. Robin and I would figure out a story, then he'd write a song to go with it. I'd say it took me a year to settle in.

By the time of Earthspan?

Yes, especially live. With the ISB there were always these gaps between songs, which I started to fill. As time went on I developed a really strong performance style. I don't know if it's true, but Billy Connolly told me he took some inspiration from my anecdotes. I went to see him backstage with Mike once and he said the thing about my stories was, I could talk about absolute rubbish! I think he got that thing of talking about the hall from me. Anyway, after that, he and Mike went off to a David Essex party and he sent me home in his limo!

With the anecdotes, I'd begun by just talking to the audience. As it went on, when I arrived at a town, I'd spend the first twenty minutes walking as fast as I could, just looking around and noticing things... Like I'd say 'Have you noticed the smell in this town?' and people would start laughing because it smelt of Trebors and Refreshers, but no-one had really thought about it. I suppose it was a sense of timing, coupled with a deadpan manner – like Eddie Izzard now. In America I was really known for it – they'd say get up on stage and tell us a story!

MALCOLM INTRODUCES 'INDIAN TUNE', EARLY 1973:

'We're now going to play another number which takes us to India, which is somewhere I never managed to get to although in the summer of 1966 many people went to India. The thing to do was to go to India and then come back and nod knowingly in a sage-like manner, but I never made it. I only got as far as Paris, although I had great intentions of going to Australia as well.'

What about your memories of recording albums?

Being in the studio was so weird for me, there was so much pressure – playing the bouzouki in this sort of goldfish bowl! *Earthspan* was the first record with my songs on it...

A strange story of desperation

So what was Lighthouse Keeper about?

I don't know! I don't like the second one I wrote [Lighthouse Dance] – it was written purely as a follow-on! The first one is a more organic song. I did have this surreal imagery kind of mind, and it had something to do with that. There's a strange story of desperation in there. It was very much arranged by all of us in the studio. Some of the backing harmonies are a bit out!

Your favourite song?

Down Before Cathay – and Did I Love A Dream. There weren't many unrecorded; I wasn't prolific at that point.

I think Glancing Love is the nearest to what you do now – it's more personal, less mannered...

It's about a real person, a Jewish ballet dancer I'd met in New York – a real case of unrequited love! I met Mike Garson [*co-writer*] at Saint Hill and the music was written on the grand piano in the chapel there. I also met Bowie in 73 – we spent the entire night talking. He'd just come back from Japan on the Trans-Siberian express and he was telling me stories about the journey. I met John Cale around then too. Mike knew him; he was a staff producer at Warner Brothers. He wanted to buy a piano but he was completely zonked and scruffy looking – and we went into this exclusive piano shop in LA where they were reluctant to even serve him. Then he sat down and played this stunning sonata! He was a very charming bloke.

Wasn't there a Robert Plant connection too?

Well, he came to a gig in Dudley and took us off for a pub crawl round Wolverhampton! I wrote a song for him, actually, which I never sent him. I'd read his favourite book was *News From Tartary*, by Ian Fleming's brother Peter. I'd just read it too, so I wrote him a song about it. I've still got the demo!

Back to the ISB. Tell me about the touring.

We did a lot – America, Britain, Holland, Spain. In the States, we did one gig in Atlanta, then back to the hotel before we did a breakfast TV slot. So after half an hour's sleep we were told to get up again and went to 'the largest diner in the world' – this fifty metre counter. We arrived at 7.30 and there was a chirpy host in a bright red blazer, and an audience consisting entirely of kids in summer camp. On the other side from us was Monsieur So-and-so, the chef who was going to demonstrate a meal. The show started, there was a bit of news and then the host said 'And now for the Incredible String Band – this is Robin,' and stuck a microphone in my face. 'So Robin, how do you like Atlanta?'

I said 'That's Robin over there,' and he stuck the microphone in Mike's face... Finally he got it right and we did Black Jack Davy or something and everyone was forced to clap. Then it was over to the chef, who was cooking lobster. He had this big pan of boiling water and this huge pepper pot stuffed with shredded garlic – and the lid came off, so about 20 cloves of garlic fell in the boiling water! Of course they had to clear all the kids out, their eyes were streaming, and so to cover this it was – 'Hey we've got another song from the ISB!', which wasn't scheduled at all. We looked at each other blankly and then did a really bad version of something else from our set... It was complete mayhem on those tours. I loved touring America. We did a lot of TV – it's funny so little has survived on video.

MALCOLM'S AMERICAN REVIEWS:

[We were...] knocked dead by his uninhibited free-form dancing, his dual portrayal of Sherlock Holmes and Watson in a long skit that made up in fun what it lacked in tightness (and) his inspired stint on assorted junk on Evolution Rag... (*LA Free Press*, June 71)

In addition to singing, dancing and imitating the rhythm section of a circus band in Circus Girl Malcolm filled the tuning breaks with anecdotes... (*Stanford Daily* 72)

The constant changing of instruments would have created long dead spots in the performance were it not for Malcolm Le Maistre's little monologues. His portrayal of an Englishman's first experience with the American incredible plastic inevitable that is the nearby K-Mart was hilarious. Le Maistre's point of view was like that of a dubious little kid. He'd make a stand-up comic. Le Maistre's personality was his greatest asset, for his voice is not so hot, though a good deal of the singing was his to perform. (*Great Speckled Bird*, Atlanta, August 74)

A very bizarre choice

How did Likky leave and Gerard Dott come to join?

I can't remember much about Likky leaving: she just disappeared. It was quite a weird episode. Gerard was asked because he was a good musician and both Mike and Robin knew him from the early days. He was thrust into something he didn't fully understand. Gerard lived with his Mum and worked in a music shop – and when he left the band, he went back to the shop. It was as if nothing had happened. Whenever we got to a town, Gerard and I would disappear. I'd be looking at things and talking to people and Gerard would be out taking photographs. It was strange for him – he was thrust into this famous band, on a world tour, girls chatting him up... I think at the end of the tour he was politely asked to leave [*Memories differ – see Gerard Dott article – Ed.*]. It was an aberration I will never understand – a very bizarre choice really.

Back to 1973 – did you have any other songs apart from Glancing Love?

In that period I had a lot of good songs that never saw the light of day – I'd bought a harmonium and they were all based round chord progressions on the harmonium. But they were all rejected.

Was there a time towards the end of the band when you began to feel a bit uncomfortable?

That's a very interesting question... In some ways I passed the buck a bit – but I was aware of this tension. Part of it was Janet's desire to be the manager of the band, a rivalry between her and Susie – this is just my opinion, but I think it was always what she was going for. And there was also this thing about the representation of the two main men in the band. I was aware of all those undercurrents...

Were things exacerbated at the end by pressure from your new label Neighborhood to make a more mainstream, radio-friendly album?

It's not my recollection, no. I don't think I was told about those final studio sessions – at the end of the American tour I went off. I was hanging around with this guy called Barry Smith, who was the original Marvel Comics illustrator of *Conan The Barbarian*. He introduced me to Black

Russians, which is vodka and Tia Maria, which, even though I didn't usually drink, I was enjoying – and meanwhile I was having another go at trying to seduce this ballet dancer (of Glancing Love fame) – you know, 'Look, I've written you this song,' – but it still didn't work out!

I didn't find out about the split till I got back to the Row and Mike rang me to say the band had broken up and would I like to join [*his solo band*] Reputation! I was pissed off – my income took a dive for a start, but I thought why do it *now*? – when we had these big Australian and British tours lined up. It was very brutally done. I knew there was a problem, I knew things were not being talked about... There had been a lot of anger about Ithkos earlier on – in some ways it might have hastened the break-up of the band. And then there were these power struggles for management which went beyond the members of the band itself. I found Janet quite difficult, I had a sort of love/hate relationship with her. She could become quite entrenched... I was sad that the ISB had veered away from being experimental, the stuff Robin used to do. It had been taken over by other people, become more mainstream... But at the end of the day, everyone has a different story to tell!

Finally, is there a particular moment you'd pick as the highlight of your musical career?

After my first British and American tour with the ISB we came back to do some summer festivals, and walking on stage at the Lincoln Festival was the most euphoric moment of my musical career. I had this sense of

'I had a love/hate relationship with Janet...' Janet Shankman in action, 1973. (Christine Santiago)

complete and utter freedom – it was a defining moment in performing terms. The welcome we got from the audience – 40,000 people – and Mike going through this whole routine of 'tell the rain to go away!' For the whole duration of our set it didn't rain – and when Steeleye Span came on it poured. That's the absolute truth.

For dance, it's going right back to the Galaxy days – the whole thing, really... Maybe a gig we did in Paris at the Palais de Sport. Theatre-wise...I think the best moments in theatre are to come!

Stan Lee's Odyssey

When the first edition of this book came out, we had lost touch with Stan Schnier, latter-day ISB bass player. This is Stan's story, starting with when he was house manager at the Fillmore East on the night of the ISB's first New York gig...

One Friday evening in April 1968, Bill Graham sat us down in the front of the house, and went over the upcoming schedule. The Fillmore East, located at ground zero of the 'Summer of Love,' was the epicentre of rock and roll, rhythm and blues and, to a lesser degree, contemporary folk (for the most part, folk artists could not attract large enough crowds to fill the 2,400 seat venue).

In that particular staff meeting, Bill mentioned that one of the upcoming shows was to be 'An Evening With The Incredible String Band'. I believe this was the first time Bill had booked a show without any opening acts. Afterwards, he did the same with Ravi Shankar. All that I knew about the ISB was that they were psychedelic folkies from the UK – visions of brown rice, velvet frocks and maidens playing finger cymbals. Maybe I had heard them on the local rock station once or twice. I was mainly a big Hendrix and Who kinda kid.

There were three of us house managers. When the college students and other part timers showed up to work as ushers, we assigned them places around the theatre and then began our nightly job of policing the venue. On a typical night, we would find kids smoking or passed out in their seats, dealing drugs in the bathrooms or trying to sneak in the fire exit doors. Our job was to keep on the move all night, patrolling, supervising, and acting as the heavies. We always positioned our biggest guys up near the stage and a couple more in front of the theatre.

That night, when the doors opened, our jaws dropped. A continual stream of quiet, smiling and happy people walked into the theatre. There was no smoking, no yelling, no garbage on the floors, and most of all, they were extremely polite.

What made this even more notable was that only a few weeks prior, some Hell's Angels had come up to the front doors and claimed they didn't need tickets. A scuffle had ensued and Bill ended up with some cracked ribs. The front door could be rough.

The ISB crowd were unexpected and a relief.

Above An early self portrait of Stan around the time he started at the Filmore.

Once the show began, no one got up or made any noise. No one tried to 'rush' the stage. Near the end of the show, the entire audience stood up and began dancing, whirling dervish-like. The show ended and the audience walked out. Once more, our jaws dropped because there was no garbage to pick up off the floors, no one was passed out in the balcony and even the bathrooms were still clean!

I nearly felt guilty from lack of the type of work I was used to. My feet didn't hurt and my back wasn't sore. I hadn't had to use my flashlight even once.

The next time the band played there later that year, the same thing happened. Since there was no work to do, as soon as the audience was seated and the band hit the stage, I headed for Bill's office. Within twenty minutes, the entire Fillmore staff was crammed in there. We could not believe how quiet, sweet and passive the Incredible String Band's audience was. For the next few years that the Fillmore was open, an evening with the Incredible String Band was for us, the employees, an evening off!

And in a very funny/not funny bit of irony, the second time the ISB came to the Fillmore, I was in my apartment getting ready to leave for work when a knock came on my door. When I opened it, five New York City Narcotics detectives nearly fell over each other attempting to break in. I lived in a single room apartment where there was not enough room for so many adults at the same time, so they took turns ripping apart my place. Three men would stand in the hallways and every few minutes, they would change shifts, with me standing handcuffed in the bathroom.

Even though it was a case of mistaken identity, I spent that night in the infamous 'Tombs' in lower Manhattan awaiting arraignment the next morning. After that, I considered the Incredible String Band a *bad omen*.

How was I to know that a few years later I would become very good friends with Mike and Robin, move next door to them at Glen Row and eventually co-produce and play their wonderful music on-stage with them?

'Muddy Waters offered me the bass chair in his band'

I came over to the UK with a US group, The Voices of East Harlem, comprised of school kids from Spanish Harlem. Jimi Hendrix passed away during the tour and it broke everyone's heart. It put a sad note onto what should have been the time of my life. At the end of the tour, I decided to stay in London for a few weeks. After Hendrix, the wind was knocked out of my sails and I didn't feel like going back to NY for a while.

Several of my Fillmore associates were on a European Stones tour. They had hired Chip Monck, the brilliant lighting designer, to create a 'produced' show. This was the first time they put on a self-contained show with superb sound and lights, all state of the art. The technical crew came from the Fillmore East. One thing led to another. We were helping each other find work at the end of the tour. Several of us took a large flat at a wonderful place called Digby Mansions off the Hammersmith Roundabout.

Various Fillmore alumni were on the road and for me, the best part was taking Muddy Waters around the UK with his Chicago band, in a Ford Transit. We had a great time. Muddy taught me how to lose at cards – all in fun. His harmonica player, Carey Bell, started to show me bass riffs at the sound checks. At the end of the tour, Muddy offered me the bass chair. I was overwhelmed by his generosity and, although I had the foresight to turn it down (I felt I was too inexperienced), for many years afterwards, I would ask myself, 'What if I had... ?'

Up the hill from the Roundhouse, a few blocks away, was a tiny blues club called, I think, Mother's. We got a call from Ian Stewart. I still remember what he said: 'The lads would like to come down for the late show tonight. Can you hold some tables?'

The Lads!

Before this tour, Muddy had been in a bad car accident in the US. His driver had been killed as I recall. Muddy had broken his hip and suffered life-threatening internal injuries. He had to sit on a stool and was walking with a crutch during our tour. He was on the wagon, too. I think the accident had really shaken him up.

The Stones arrived with their entourage, fur coats and beautiful women everywhere, and sat down at the front tables. In the middle of the set, Muddy said, 'I want to say hello to some very special guests we have in the audience this evening. When I had my accident, their magazine said some very kind things about me... the ROLLING STONES.' It was sweet and unpretentious.

The tour ended a few weeks later in Dublin, where I said goodbye and met up with a wonderful woman named Johanna, who was the girlfriend of one of the members of Dr Strangely Strange. They were on tour and she invited me to use their guest room and for a few nights, she introduced me to the nightlife of 1970 Dublin. There was a pub called Toners that had sawdust on the floor and traditional music. Every night, there was a young kid selling mimeographed copies of his poetry out front. He must have been the only black person in Dublin in those days. His name was Phil Lynott.

I was, and still am, enchanted by Dublin. I returned on the ferry to Liverpool on Christmas Eve. Across from me was an elderly gentleman from Dublin who was going to visit relatives in the UK, and at his feet was a bag containing the Christmas Goose, its feet staring at me the entire night.

I kept crossing paths with various Stones connections. I did some amplifier and guitar work for Ian Stewart and he bartered some instruments with me. I had two of Brian Jones' guitars – a Gibson Firebird and a Buddy Emmons pedal steel (which he used on *Satanic Majesties*). I had one of Keith's first electrics, an Epiphone Casino, and a beautiful little practice amp, a Vox AC 5.

After the Stones moved to France, they were robbed and I got a call from Ian asking if I would be willing to return the instruments, because, as he put it, 'Keith is devastated – he's lost all of his guitars.' I had everything on the next train to London. I can't imagine what the value of those guitars and amp would be today! But I have a clear conscience. I had the guitars just long enough to add a pedal steel guitar part on Robin's solo album, *Myrrh*, on a song called Rends-Moi Demain.

Somewhere along the line John Morris, the original producer for Bill Graham and also Michael Lang's partner at Woodstock, began putting together the Rainbow Theatre in Finsbury Park. I was the stage manager for the first month. It was like a Fillmore East reunion, as the entire technical staff had worked there. I had also taken over at the Roundhouse, filling in for the resident stage manager, who had gone on a tour for a few months. One great show was John Cale and Nico. She was stunning and mysterious, playing a harmonium. Mike Heron was the opener as he and John were finishing up Mike's solo record, *Smiling Men*.

'The ISB sound man was disastrously underqualified...'

The work at as a stage manager at the Roundhouse was coming to an end. Joe Boyd's Witchseason office was on Charlotte Street. Each of his artists had their own office with an accompanying road manager to take care of the daily chores. Shortly before Joe was to relinquish Witchseason, early in 1971, a mutual friend recommended me for a job with one of his groups. The interview went quite well until we started talking about money, at which point the discussion broke down and insults began flying around the room. Red-faced, (they had had just said something to the effect of 'You bloody Yanks think you own the world!') I stood up, bid farewell and began walking down the hallway.

A beautiful woman came out of one of the rooms and introduced herself. She had overheard the conversation and asked if she and I could meet that afternoon. A few hours later, I was sitting in a pub under the Castelnaugh Bridge in Hammersmith with Susie Watson-Taylor, who was about to become the ISB's official manager, working out how I might be able to come up to Sheffield in a few nights to meet the ISB.

It happened to be one of Malcolm's first shows and it was his birthday. A couple of his Stone Monkey pals, Malenie and Rakis, had come to celebrate over a bowl of granola. This was quainter than anything I was used to, having just stage-managed a full week of the Stones. Hadn't seen much granola back stage at the Roundhouse.

I met Mike and Robin during the interval at the Sheffield show. Their sound man was disastrously underqualified and the band were inaudible. Mike was terribly upset.

He asked if I thought I might be able to salvage the second half of the show. Suzy had words with the sound guy and I took over. I went into the hall and did the set cold. It wasn't rocket science, if you knew what all the knobs and switches were supposed to do. In those days, I did.

The second half of the show was audible, but not much more, since I had no idea what they were going to play and the system was limited in scope. Nothing fancy. But it wasn't fuzzy and distorted and so I got hired by Susie right after the show.

A few weeks later, I was living in a small cottage in Glen Row next door to Mike on one side and Malcolm on the other, Robin up a few more doors. Likky, in her diaphanous frocks, chain smoked roll-ups and lived up at the other end of the Row in a cottage painted silver. She frequently arrived at my door at three or four a.m. for a smoke and a cup of tea, with talks about 'wee people' and 'distant galaxies,' all the while flicking her ash onto the floor in front of the fireplace. The experience was enchanting and I will never forget those days and nights in Scotland.

After the ISB I moved back to my native New York City and started working on a crew that was building a state of the art recording studio up near Woodstock. Robin called me from Los Angeles and asked me if I would come out and help him in search of a new band. We found a large community of avid folkies in LA, much to our pleasant surprise, including Sylvia Woods, who was a brilliant harpist (I believe she eventually won the All Ireland medal). She in turn introduced us to her inner circle and thus were the beginnings of Robin's second act, The Merry Band. Man alive were they good – what I would call, ahead of the curve.

I left Los Angeles and settled back in New York a few years later, where I had the good fortune to meet the talented singer-songwriter Janis Ian. She and I became fast friends, bonded, and thus ensued a wonderful working relationship that lasted ten years. I took over her management and publishing responsibilities. After Janis moved to Nashville, I took over the management of Art Garfunkel, but after a few years, decided my days of travel and music had come to an end.

Since 1992, I have been a freelance photographer in New York. I do what is referred to as 'commercial' photography which covers everything from corporate events, photographing notable and not so notable people, capturing works of art for several art galleries and most enjoyable of all are my school clients, where I get to spend endless days on my knees, crawling around photographing stunningly beautiful children engaged in the learning process and extracurricular activities. These photos end up being used for annual reports, web pieces and promo.

I continue to pursue my own photographic pursuits. I became a University Professor of Photography where we still use old-fashioned film, as well as Smartphones. I teach on Mondays, starting the week with a wonderful boat ride across New York Harbour, and have been building a portfolio of images of this bustling port.

Stan 'Lee' Schnier, July 2012

The view from the amps

Latter-day ISB lead guitarist Graham Forbes writes his time with the band.

I had heard about the String Band when I was still at school in Glasgow. A friend used to go watch them at a club in Sauchiehall Street but unfortunately they'd moved off by the time I got round to going to see them. I was more into Blues music at the time; I had started playing guitar at 14 and all I really wanted to do was be a blues guitarist. I heard a B-side of a Spencer Davies Group single called Stevie's Blues and that was it. Glasgow was a wild town at the time – still is – and everyone was into Tamla Motown. Some neds threw me out of the cafe I was in when I put it on the jukebox. All I did after that was try to learn to play blues music.

I loved the second two ISB albums and spent a lot of teenage time sitting in safe havens in Glasgow with those covers on my knees with a few other people who shared the same...well...interests. Glasgow was a hard drinking town and people like us who had hair halfway down our backs were rather looked down upon to say the least. In retrospect we were spiritually arrogant... thought we knew it all and that we alone were interested in other realities... but it was a wonderful time.

By the time I was 22 I was playing full time in a rock band called Powerhouse unless, of course, someone needed a wedding band and we'd change our name accordingly. We didn't play anything different except maybe an instrumental first waltz. We were loud and heavy and played anywhere naive enough to book us. Sometimes we'd just turn up at pubs, unload our gear and play. Or I would go out and talk my way on-stage at some folk club and play blues instrumentals or something. Then I'd get the band up and we'd play some electric blues. I was upsetting the folkies even then, I suppose! Anything to be on-stage in front of an audience. I remember I used to play bottleneck with a plate, God knows why. Anyway, I clearly remember standing in Edinburgh one day and suddenly knowing that one day I was going to play with the String Band. It just came to me out of nowhere as these things usually do. This was a surprise because although I loved a great deal of *Wee Tam* and earlier material I have to say I found things like *Be Glad* rather disappointing.

I bumped into Mike one day in a waiting room about a year later. It was an entirely chance meeting. I liked *Smiling Men* and decided to chance my arm and offered him the services of my band back in Glasgow if he was doing another solo album and wanted backing. I really had no plans to leave Powerhouse – we shared a crazy band flat in Glasgow in the student area in which we did all the things young rock bands do; agents knew which pub to telephone if they needed a band in a hurry and all the other bands in Glasgow hated us. We loved it. I see the other two guys from time to time. Both are still playing – what else can you do? One lives in New Zealand and the other still lives in a bedsit in the University area. Both are alcoholics. I played with them again after Mike Heron's Reputation but I kind of saw the writing on the wall and have been off the 'vino collapso' for many years. I'm wealthier but I think they have better parties!

I had no idea I was being auditioned

So Mike did call me and asked me to go down to Glen Row where he played me some tapes, then asked me to stay over for a week and dub on guitar parts. I had no idea I was being auditioned for the ISB. I got the bus back to Glasgow and carried on doing the chaotic gigs we did, trying to avoid irate parents and lawyers and then I had a call from Mike asking if I'd be interested in joining the band. (Actually I think I got the gig because I suspect Richard Thompson turned it down). I had ten days rehearsal for a three month tour of Europe and the UK... Oh and yes, could I learn the banjo part for Log Cabin and a keyboard part for Everything's Fine? Both instruments I'd never touched before! It was great!

A major change was happening to the band which really started with Mike writing Ithkos. On the first British tour I did with the group we had been supported on about 40 gigs – tours really were tours in these days – by McGuinness Flint who had just had a Number One chart single and been on *Top Of The Pops* and all that stuff. A large proportion of the audience were young kids who never knew anything about the early albums and had come to see McGuinness Flint. While some die-hard ISB fans didn't like Ithkos – actually I wrote a small part of that [*Port of Sybaris, which comes after the Dreams Fade bit – Ed.*] – a lot did and they were augmented by these new audiences. When Robin got going on jigs and reels they went crazy. We were playing Cardiff once and I will never forget the look on Robin's face when there was a stage invasion – suddenly all these kids were up on the stage grabbing everyone. Nothing like it had happened before.

I loved playing with the band and being on the road and shared a great many common viewpoints with the guys. The manager, Susie Watson-Taylor, was fantastic to work with but there were one or two people associated with the group with whom I didn't get on too well. I just felt they took themselves rather too seriously. And to be fair, I was a good bit younger and one or two people probably (rightly) regarded my rock and roll lifestyle as not quite ISB. But I was a bit like a kid at Christmas, it was all very exciting and I felt touring in a band should be fun. All this world is but a play... So when the tour ended at Oxford at Christmas 1973 I really didn't think I'd be invited back.

Oddly enough I was asked back and in January 1974 was introduced to John Gilston. He was one of the finest drummers I have ever heard and a truly beautiful person. It sounds very schoolboyish but very soon John and I were best friends.

The final incarnation of the ISB. From left: Robin, Graham Forbes, Malcolm, Mike, John Gilston, Stan Schnier. (Island Records)

Robin was never really happy about the electric direction

Now as most people know the String Band was by then really two groups. Robin would arrange his material and we would more or less do as he wanted and Mike would do similarly with his songs. Robin was never really happy about the electric direction the band was taking although I must say he is a truly breathtaking musician. He could play anything.

With Gillie and myself pushing hard, Mike felt far more able to develop the rock material which he had been interested in for years. Whereas Robin tended to live quietly with Janet and tankards of hot spiced punch of a winter's evening, Mike was far more likely to be out raving with Steve Marriott or hanging out with Pete Townshend or someone. So Mike's writing really took a far rockier turn and I think some of his best stuff dates from this time. [*Solo songs*] Strong Thing and Draw Back The Veil were ISB songs which we did on the last tour. Stranded In Iowa was another. Without meaning any disrespect to Mike, who I see regularly and like a great deal, I feel these songs lost a lot in later Reputation days when they became over elaborate and elongated.

When John joined, the band immediately became immeasurably tighter and more musically organised and the audiences kept growing and growing. The ISB were not banned from TV in Europe as they were in Britain and I recall one TV show we broadcast over the whole of Europe. Just us, no chat, no twee folk singers – just the band doing an hour-long session. It didn't do us any harm.

We played in Denmark and where Status Quo got 17,000 the night before, we pulled 25,000. We did three shows in the same day in Rome and they had the riot police out with hoses because there were so many people locked out. Steeleye Span, who Mike and Robin seemed to have a considerable dislike for, were booked to support us in Zurich. They pulled out, much to our amusement. (They were even in a rehearsal room upstairs from ours in London once and apparently on hearing we were downstairs immediately vanished to the pub!)

There is no doubt the band's following was building by the week. Of course, in true ISB fashion, we managed to antagonise the press when the person responsible for ensuring they got passes into our gigs apparently wouldn't allow them into a gig in Drury Lane in London. That was a great pity since there must have been a thousand over the hall's capacity inside. A hell of a lot of people had just bribed the doormen or something – it was astonishing – the place was literally packed, the aisles, bodies everywhere. Among others, four busloads of 'new' fans had travelled all the way from Newcastle. Our contract was up for renewal and Island were not showing any great interest in keeping us on the label. A good bit of press at that moment could have changed everything.

Remarkable rock violin and astounding Hammond organ

We peaked in the US Tour in 1974. I have to give Robin credit because, even though I'm sure he disliked a lot of the new material, he wrote Jack Straw's Wishes which was a remarkable piece of musicianship. He played rock violin on that better than anyone I have ever heard before or since. Completely out of nowhere he started playing these astonishing solos. The audiences in America used to give him ovations every gig. Mike too was outstanding on Hammond organ on this piece.

Robin was clearly uncomfortable on this tour. Janet was away in LA the entire time and he definitely was not at his best without her. Robin is an extraordinary person – he is definitely not of our time. He is a visitor here. There is no-one else in this world who could have written Maya or The Iron Stone or My Name Is Death and so on. Not Dylan, nobody. One day scholars will study these works. But he needed someone to look after him in this 20th century world. He couldn't drive, I don't recall ever seeing him with money and wonder if he knew what it was. I could truly sympathise with how ill at ease Robin felt surrounded by all these amplifiers and cables and roadies and effects units but despite this he really excelled on the tour, even though I suspect he hated a great deal of it. And of course, the young American girls just loved this Greek God although I don't think he noticed. I remember persuading him to do some acoustic songs alone in the middle of the set and he started to do First Girl I Loved again at this time.

We did 2 gigs with Bruce Springsteen and I remember thinking that Mike was similar but could write far more intriguing lyrics. That was the entire point of Mike's writing – he was saying things that were really interesting within a rock framework. A great deal of rock is basically groin music and while that is definitely OK it was interesting to hear Mike input rather more challenging concepts. I know there were String Band die-hards who were dead against this sort of thing – although I think playing live the Band catered for everyone. The thing that made the String Band what they were was the fact that Robin and Mike were so innovative. All that Mike was doing by developing in a rockier direction was continuing that tradition, and I was surprised that some people couldn't see that and move along with the Band to see where it would lead.

There was something ominous in the air

The band just got better and better – if, of course, you liked the mixture of rock and esoteric which really was the first sort of World music that people such as Peter Gabriel do now. We were supporting the Elvin Bishop Blues Band in front of about 10,000 people in Cape Cod and playing so well that we heard their roadies were ordered to pull the plug on us. We were going down far too well with the audience and that upset their management. It was all very exciting. But there was something ominous in the air.

It all ended rather unhappily in New York. Neighborhood Records wanted to sign us and to continue touring the US and become a major commercial band. This was probably Robin's worst nightmare and the final meeting between Mike and Robin was not a happy one. Basically they both began acting like human beings and that was it. Even Susie, who was one of the finest managers of people I have ever known, couldn't calm the situation.

Rock Proms, Olympia, 6th July 1974. At the last ever UK gig, a somewhat subdued-looking band wait for Malcolm to come on and start Ithkos. (Philip Newby archive)

When Sooty Met String

Steve Blacknell ('6.9.1952, Virgo, supports West Ham') is a been-there, done-that music biz veteran of many years standing. He's been a TV presenter, A&R man in the UK and the States, associated with the likes of Kate Bush (his first love) and Pamela (I'm With The Band) *Des Barres, worked on Live Aid, hustled for Steely Dan and much more. But in a box of his most treasured possessions, up in the attic, is a silver ballet pump – as worn by Mally Schofield of Stone Monkey in U. Adrian Whittaker interviewed him in 2002 and heard how he came to join the extended ISB entourage in 1973.*

Steve: At school everyone had their favourites...and I actually discovered, living in Dartford, Kent, the delights of *The Hangman's Beautiful Daughter* and instead of revising for my exams, I used to go up there and listen to A Very Cellular Song ad nauseam. My dad had fixed up speakers in my bedroom and I'd put it on downstairs and when it had finished I would go downstairs and put the needle back and play it 6 or 7 times and write theses on what all that meant rather than doing my revision. I was to find out later from Mr. Heron that it didn't mean all that much at all. It kept me busy. A few of us just got into it more and more and more, and it became obsessive.

As the hippy times rolled on, in the early Seventies, myself and a guy called Roger Woods (who later became a String Band roadie) and a few other reprobates were living in a house called Sausage (as you do) in Kent. One day I had had quite a lot of *coffee*, if you know what I mean, and I decided to write a letter to them about starting up the Barnehurst branch of the ISB appreciation society. I dispatched the letter and thought I'd never hear again. About three weeks later I had a call (in this house called Sausage) from a lady called Malenie Schofield. She said hi, is that Steve – I said yes – she said my name's Malenie, I work with the ISB – I said who *is* this? Anyway the phone call went on and on until she eventually convinced me it was her.

They invited me up to Glen Row and I went up there (I went sick, I was a nurse at the time), met them, they offered me a job doing the merchandising – in conjunction with Island Records – I went on the road with them and I think in the first week I earned more from my merchandising than the head roadie (who was McCartney's roadie) did. He was very peeved and I did very well.

I started with them on the Autumn 73 tour – the first date I was on was the Brighton Dome and my dad drove me down there. I didn't have any records with me to sell, Island Records had delivered records to the gig so I drove down with a bag with my glove puppet in it. Dad dropped me off – and I can see this now – I walked into the hall, Susie Wotson-Telly (as we used to call her) walks up and says – there's been an awful mistake – I said – what? – and as far as I can recall, the gig was off. There had been a mistake with Island Records or something. At that point I burst out crying! I was 21 then – hadn't cried for a while – and as far as I recall, she said – but Janet Williamson's coming down in two hours, we might try and resolve it. I walked along the beach and actually contemplated jumping in the sea.

I didn't jump in the sea, and two hours later it was resolved. I wiped the tears away and that night I was selling my ISB stickers for 10p a go, the poster and the songbook. Like I say, I became one of the highest paid people on that tour because I kept all the money from the stickers. I've just found the letter from Susie saying what I could earn on the road – she said you might be able to earn as much as £30-35 a week – but I was earning about £90-100 a week, I was coming back loaded! We had a signing-in book on the road as well, so I struck up all these friendships, I used to travel and see all these girls... Rona in Aberdeen, Ecky in Uxbridge, all these sort of followers who latched on to me as a way in, but at the time, of course, I just thought – well, it wasn't the glove puppet – I was incredibly good looking. But no, I was a fat hippy.

The albums I was selling on the road were the Island ones including *Hard Rope And Silken Twine*, so this was the legendary Ithkos tour, with the Mighty Hammer of Croc. [*This was a red plastic hammer which was one of Malcolm's props – Ed.*]. So I would set up and I always wore my slippers at the gigs and I had my Sooty glove puppet and we sort of became an extension of the group in a funny sort of way. I would stay with them prior to the tour at Glen Row, then after all that I would just go back to Dartford and live with my parents in between tours, it was most bizarre.

Adrian: So Sooty was selling the merchandise?

Sooty was there all the time, yeah. I've only had two Sooties, he at that time was 20 years old. I lost him about 8 years later when I put him on a car top and drove to Cambridge – never saw him again. I should put an ad in the paper – 'Lost, one glove puppet'. But, anyway, it was a kind of bizarre thing, and I couldn't believe really that I was working with them. Although they were by then a different incarnation of the ISB, Robin and Mike were my Lennon and McCartney, I just couldn't believe I was doing it. And all I thought was, one day, perhaps, one day maybe I could MC an ISB gig... I thought that'd be nice, but, ah, that'll never happen... [*Steve was MC at the ISB reformation gig in 2000 – Ed.*]

Did you see the split coming?

You could feel the band falling apart... at least musically. Being on the road with them you weren't really aware of much tension, I think they were just getting on with the job, but when you had the second half of a concert starting off with Cold Days Of February and ending up with Painted Chariot, which owes more to Baba O'Reilly than whatever the Cold Days Of February yearns for, you knew something was up. Robin looked very ill-at-ease and Mike was taking off doing this Townshend stuff, but having said that it was still good and they'd come back and do a jig and everyone would be really happy... it was definitely a weird time, but I know when I heard about the split I was deeply upset, just like everyone else.

So who did you hang out with when you were with the band, who were your mates?

Malcolm and I... my sister was in love with Malcolm... I suppose Jack Ingram and Leda, Jack was then the drummer, I wouldn't have thought of Mike and Robin as being mates, I just couldn't believe I knew them, let alone mates. I sort of shacked up on the road with Jack, the late Johnny Gilston, Stan... Great times, just fantastic. I'm sure Malcolm's told you about his friend Rakis. I don't think I *ever* spoke to Rakis, I was just in awe of his mysticism, I just was totally in a spin.

We had the late Princess Margaret over at the Hall, and that day when Princess Margaret was singing Look On The Bright Side of Life with a fag hanging out of her mouth, with a few drinks...

Didn't they put on a kind of pantomime, and perform it to the 'royals'?

Yes you're right, but I was never with them at Christmas because I was always with my folks, but yes you're right. I remember that... Wonderful times. Robin used to make

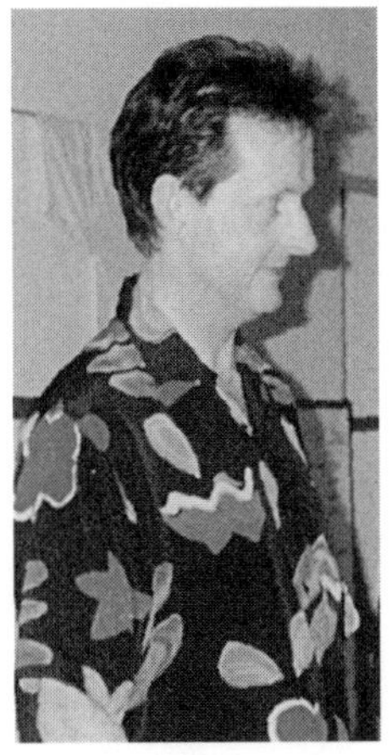

Steve backstage at Andy Roberts' 1994 Leeds ISB event. (Andy Roberts)

this wonderful drink...mulled wine thing...one time he asked me in for a drop of it, and I thought life can't get better than this, I'm happy to drink with him, it'd be like sipping angel juice with God. It's a bit personal, this, but he said:

'*Long may yer lum reek, and yer peat fire drottle, jumping jordies in yer pooch, and whisky in yer bottle*' which is a little thing I still say when we're having a drink.

But of course, the interesting thing is, it's like – Robin Williamson – oh what the comedian? No yer dumbo, that's Robin *Williams*... he's such a cult hero but in mainstream, a lot of people haven't heard of him, so its really odd having a hero that not everyone has heard of. I mean you can say John Lennon, but if you're trying to impress someone – 'and then I went and had a drink with Robin Williamson' – *who*? Later on I was living out in Hollywood for a while, Robin and Janet were living there then, and I saw Janet one time and said do you want to come over for dinner? So she and Robin came over and as they walked through the door I got this complete acid flash of Robin offering me the wine. I said, 'Do you want a glass of wine, Robin?' I thought, that's weird! I was trying to impress my wife then; we'd had Tiny Tim over for tea, she was Miss Catherine, she wasn't in the GTOs but had an affiliation with them, but Tiny Tim knew her as Miss Catherine. She said Tiny Tim's coming over for tea, I went yeah right – of course he came over for tea and played the ukulele for two hours non-stop...one of the most extraordinary beings I've ever met. So I was trying to impress her with Robin Williamson but as she'd only just about heard of the String Band, it didn't quite work! Nevertheless, I had Robin round at *my* house this time – which certainly did it for me!

Overleaf Late 1973 line-up. L-R: Malcolm, Robin, Jack Ingram, Mike, Graham Forbes, Stan Schnier. (Island Records)

Chapter Thirteen

In which we consider the band's Seventies soundtrack work and assess their final year, final album and eventual split.

Documentaries, Docu-Dramas and the Duke of Edinburgh

Adrian Whittaker

The Incredible String Band's film soundtrack work with James Archibald

'We've been taken up by a film director in Britain – a very good documentary director called James Archibald who has featured our music in three movies.'
(Mike Heron, February 1974)

The late James Archibald became known in the early Sixties through his work on one of the original 'teen culture' movies, *Some People*. It featured Ray Brooks, later in *The Knack*, as a working class hero with musical ambitions, and pioneered the 'docu-drama' approach, intermingling professional actors with ordinary people playing themselves. *Some People* signalled Archibald's on-going interest in music and youth culture (the theme song made it to *Top Of The Pops*), compounded by his later position as Chairman of the National Music Council of Great Britain. In July 1968 he went on to shoot some remarkable footage of the Beatles recording Hey Jude in Studio Two, Abbey Road for a short, titled *Music*!

The three films he made with the ISB in the early Seventies involved a creative team of Robert Young (director), David Taylor (editor) and James as producer. The initial link with their music came through James' secretary at the time, an ISB fan.

Time For Thought (1972, 35mm, 40 minutes)
The ISB provide the entire musical sound track for this entertaining polemic about the growing need for creative and stimulating use of leisure time. It includes footage of Adult Education classes, community centres and community theatres, school parties on Outdoor Pursuits trips to Wales and the Blackie Community Arts Centre in Liverpool. There was a scene in a cigarette factory (the film was sponsored by WD & HO Wills) which clearly made an impression on Mike Heron at the time:

'There's a story about a guy who just sits at a factory bench watching a cigarette machine in case it suddenly starts to put out one huge, long cigarette. This happens about once every four days. So there he is, doing nothing, man – by this machine all week long. And then at the weekend he goes out to be a park warden.'

The music for the sequence where the factory worker heads for the hills was Air, which had already been used in Milos Forman's *Taking Off* as the backdrop to a scene where middle class parents attend a seminar on tuning in and turning on...

On the evidence of *Time For Thought*, there must be an ISB song for every occasion. There's some neat intercutting of music and speech – the 'cod-faced master' bit in Darling Belle segues to the head teacher of a secondary school talking about the school trip; You Get Brighter is played over scenes of smiling pensioners at a social club; the 'boys and girls come out to play' part of Ducks On A Pond used for a scene of – just that, and the credits roll over the verse from The Circle Is Unbroken which talks of 'unborn children glad and free'.

Other (largely instrumental) bits of songs used are Beyond The See, Evolution Rag, Lordly Nightshade, Talking Of The End and Job's Tears (the original LP versions).

It seems that the selection of tracks was down to the editorial team mentioned above; James Archibald liked mystical and gentle music, and felt the ISB soundtrack would provide more of a lasting element than other contemporary pop. *Time For Thought* won an award at the Florence Film Festival.

Rehearsal (1974, 35mm, 55minutes)

This is the best known of the three films – it was shown twice on Channel 4, and won prizes at the Cork, Chicago and Melbourne film festivals. It was much more of a collaborative project, and shows the ISB doing Ithkos, both in rehearsal and in performance.

The concept was to 'give an insight into the rehearsals of four very different kinds of musical performances, and their common denominator of practice and hard work.' The National Musical Council sponsored the film, and the other three subjects were the Band of the Scots Guards, the Royal Opera and Wandsworth Boys Choir. James Archibald picked the ISB to represent the pop/folk element in the film because of their keen 'musical intelligence', coupled with their extremely diverse instrumentation and a considerable cult reputation. Again, it was felt the timeless quality of much ISB music meant that their segment would not date so quickly. Robert Young says that the team's relationship with the ISB was much closer than with the other subjects; they lived at Glen Row for four or five days during the summer of 1973 to film the rehearsal bits, and he has strong and pleasant memories of halcyon summer days, and of the elements of spirituality and communality which were part of the Glen Row lifestyle. He found the ISB interesting to work with from a visual angle too – he remembers them as a 'good looking and varied bunch'. Part of the subtext of the film was the differing values and cultures represented by the musicians involved, and in this he says the ISB made by far the greatest contribution, their latter day hippiedom contrasting with the money and sense of hierarchy involved with the Royal Opera, for example.

The team took a straightforward, fly-on-the-wall approach to documenting the rehearsal sessions; they didn't stick rigidly to a script, and the film continued to evolve as shooting progressed. The ISB agreed to be filmed without editorial involvement, and allowed some revealing behind-the-scenes glimpses; some Glen Rowers, though, feel that these were staged for the cameras, as any real conflict would have happened off-screen. We see a somewhat fed-up looking Robin complain at the lack of variety as Mike proudly unveils Ithkos to the group: 'Is this *all* intro?' he asks pointedly, and deems it 'vastly too long'. In the rehearsal, Mike gets irritated with Jack Ingram's below-par drumming and Malcolm is seen rather self-consciously working up his sub-Jagger moves.

According to Robert Young and Sheila Archibald, the topic of Scientology was avoided by both sides; it was a period when the ISB were often down at East Grinstead for weekend courses etc. but, says Sheila: 'they wouldn't have got very far on that with James!'

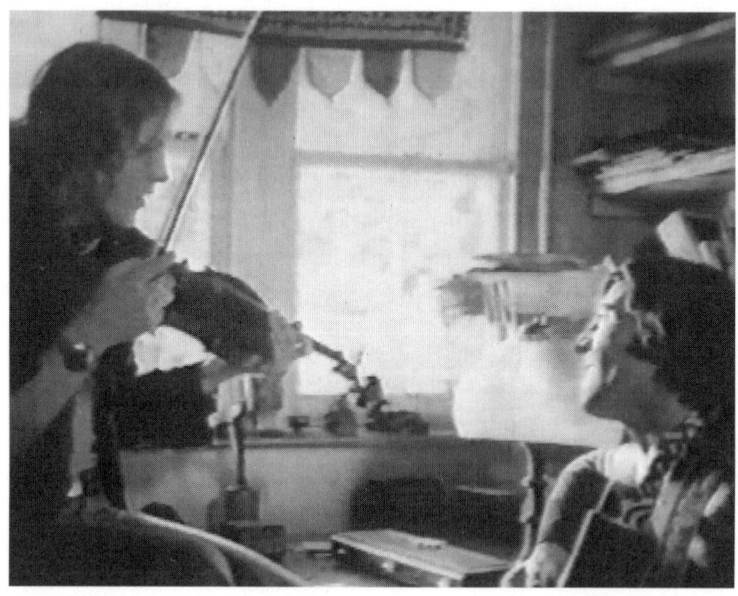

'Is this all intro?' Rehearsing Ithkos at Glen Row, 1973. (Sheila Archibald)

To complete the film, three cameras were taken to the Colston Hall, Bristol, in October 1973 to film the ISB live; the costs involved meant that only Ithkos was filmed. The film ignores the mysterious addition of Graham Forbes on lead guitar, who had joined the band after the Glen Row rehearsals.

Rehearsal has stood the test of time well and, quite apart from the intrinsic interest of the ISB segments, is a revealing and amusing documentation of the processes involved as a piece of music takes shape.

No Turning Back

(**Working title: *White Bird*. 1974, 35mm, 100 minutes**)

The final film in the trilogy, made over a six week period in 1974, has to be the most obscure film the ISB were involved in. It was not formally released and was shown only three times – a world premiere at the Bristol ABC, once in Birmingham and at the 1975 Bulgarian International Festival, where it won a prize. Robert Young had never seen the finished version, which has been lost for a couple of decades. I eventually tracked it down in the recesses of an EMI film vault.

Ironically, it was a major project; an ambitious, full-length film which was to be distributed as a B-feature round Britain by EMI – and for which the ISB again provided the entire soundtrack. The idea was to extend the 'docu-drama' approach by using well-known actors and actresses in the lead roles, but with a reliance on extemporisation then rare in mainstream productions. Budgets were a recurrent problem during the making of the film, and the whole project was very much touch and go. The documentary element of the film was footage of the construction of Concorde leading up to its first flight; most of the filming was carried out on location in Filton, Bristol and in Toulouse. The drama was set around the struggling marriage of an overworked British Aerospace engineer (Alan Dobie) and his wife (Monica Grey, later in *General Hospital*) who has sacrificed her teaching career for him and their children.

There are other subplots involving their teenage daughter Carrie's relationship with Paul (unemployed and heavily into pills and booze) and subsequently with an older man, a colleague of her father's. Paul meanwhile ends up in hospital after an overdose. Son Colin is estranged from his father and it's hinted that he may be in a gay relationship. Carrie is also, through the local youth club, involved in the Duke of Edinburgh's Award Scheme, which she attempts to interest Paul in as a rehabilitation move. Quite a heavy weighting towards 'youth' issues in short, though character development and motivation are rather sketchy; the film tries to cover a lot of ground using an innovative mixture of documentary

BRITISH PREMIERE
SUNDAY OCT 13th

ABC BRISTOL WHITELADIES RD Tel. 33640

FOR THEM THERE WAS...

NO TURNING BACK

AA

ALAN DOBIE · STACEY TENDETER in

NO TURNING BACK

with KIM BRADEN and MONICA GREY

Music and Songs by THE INCREDIBLE STRING BAND

EMI

COMMENCING SUNDAY, OCTOBER 13

Sun: Two separate performances: Mat: doors open 2.30. The Go Between 2.45. No Turning Back 5.05

Advert for the *No Turning Back* premiere. (*Bristol Evening News*)

NO TURNING BACK

A feature film with the title of NO TURNING BACK has been made as a successor to SOME PEOPLE. Once again, the film is set in Bristol but the story is very different. In brief it is as follows:

"The film is about the break-up of what is on the surface an ordinary family. The father, George Batterson, is a senior engineer on the Concorde project; although not unfaithful to his wife, their relationship has become a dead one.

Their son, Colin, is twenty and at Bristol University, he dislikes his father and blames him for his mother's unhappiness. He lives away from home and has formed a homosexual attachment with an older rich student.

The daughter, Caroline, an eighteen year old sixth form student at thellocal co-educational comprehensive school, has an unsatisfactory affair with a boy of her own age, who, although attractive, is on drugs and alcohol caused by the early death of his father and total lack of understanding from his mother. Jill, Caroline's friend, who is also attracted to Paul, tries to help by getting him involved in the activities of the local youth club. A group of young people there do therapeutic work with mentally retarded patients. Paul in unable to face the challenge and is ultimately beaten up by one of his mother's men friends when he is in a dangerously drugged state. He is sacked from his job and goes on the loose.

Jane Patterson, by chance, discovers her son's problem and there is a major row on George's return from a working visit to Toulouse.

Caroline feels an obligation to find Paul and enlists the help of Michael, her father's friend who has known the family for many years. They have always got on well and by this close association find total affinity despite the difference in their ages. George finds the relationship totally unbelievable, but has ultimately to recognise the happiness in this situation. He also makes a great effort to communicate with his son.

Paul nearly dies from the effects of drugs and alcohol and one is left with the impression that there might be some hope in Jill's affection and strength of character, but that the marriage of George and Jane Patterson will never regain the happiness that might have once existed. "

Once again, the film would be distributed free of charge by EMI Film Distributors and any profits that are made would go direct to the Duke of Edinburgh's Award Scheme.

The film stars Alan Dobie, Stacey Tendeter, Kim Braden and Monica Grey. The music is by the Incredible String Band.

The EMI film synopsis for *No Turning Back*. (BFI)

shots, scripted scenes and on-camera improvisation, very much ahead of its time – which was the critical consensus.

It's tempting to speculate that its anti-drug message would have endeared the film to the all-clean Scientology era ISB; it certainly gave their music a very up-front role. Unusually, whole songs were played rather than being faded in and out as background music, and the song lyrics often provided a kind of substitute script. No Turning Back provides the theme song, cropping up three times (including title and credit sequences). As Carrie goes canoeing with Award Scheme mates The Explorer is used, Dumb Kate makes an appearance on the home transistor radio, and part of See All The People turns up again for a romantic scene in a wood between Carrie and Paul. Alan Dobie's encounter with a beautiful French colleague in Toulouse is wordless – Adam and Eve says it all. Old Buccaneer crops up as teen disco fodder in a youth club scene, and Beyond The See makes its third film appearance as Award Scheme participants socialise with mental hospital patients. The introduction to Beautiful Stranger provides an unexpectedly ominous backdrop to a scene where Paul is beaten up by his father, and Worlds They Rise And Fall (later used in a similar way in *Hideous Kinky*) is used to comment on Carrie as she frantically searches for Paul, who has been kicked out of home. There's only one non-ISB selection – a Vivaldi guitar concerto. The credits read 'Music by the Incredible String Band – compositions by Mike Heron and Robin Williamson'.

Like *Some People*, *No Turning Back* was partly financed by the Duke of Edinburgh's Award Scheme through their Filton office – they were trying to broaden their range of participants, and it was felt that the film would be a good publicity vehicle. The Scheme were also to help with distribution costs (and would have received a percentage of any profits), but tragically the key public relations officer at their head office died in a car crash shortly before the premiere; this, coupled with a poor reception at the Bristol ABC, meant that EMI got cold feet on the distribution deal and the film was effectively shelved. Probably even more impetus was lost when the ISB broke up just after the premiere; we can only speculate how successful *No Turning Back* might eventually have been, and whether Mike and Robin would have been offered other film sound track work as a result...

All three films are archived at the British Film Institute.

With a highly topical background and scenes shot around Henbury Comprehensive School and Bristol University, **"No Turning Back,"** at the Whiteladies **(AA)** should have an unusual local appeal.

It has a strong theme of youth running through it and has been taken up by the Duke of Edinburgh's Award scheme.

The story concerns the break-up or a family — father works on Concorde — and the trouble that afflicts the student youngsters — drugs and homosexuality among them.

Starring is Alan Dobie, once a stalwart of Bristol Old Vic.

The Evening News preview

1973 – 4

Adrian Whittaker

In Autumn 1973 Gerard Dott was replaced by Graham Forbes. Scientology was still playing a large part on the band's life, and in May 1974 they played a Scientology 'benefit' at London's Rainbow Theatre which, as Gil Murray has said, resulted in a particularly dire live compilation album (long since deleted). Island Records dropped the band after Hard Rope *and they were at yet another critical point in their career when they broke up (or, as they wrote to fans, 'started a new phase') in Autumn 1974. Ironically, they were then in the middle of a world tour (their biggest ever) which would have taken them to Australia. The writing was well and truly on the wall, though; as Mike said in '1968' (one of the last songs they recorded, for Radio 1 in June 1974): 'Are we lost?'*

Glaswegian electric guitarist Graham Forbes joined in the autumn of 1973. At least one of the *Hard Rope* tracks had been already recorded, but he was in time to be part of recording Ithkos, adding rhythm and lead parts. On the eve of the 73 tour, the band confirmed the full-time employment of their first ever rhythm section, bassist Stan Schnier and Geordie-born Jack Ingram on the drums, both of whom, in ISB tradition, were adept on a variety of musical instruments.

Stan: 'Jack and I had carried on as roadies with the ISB for a good two or three years. But along the way, Mike and Robin asked us to fill in on a song here and there and eventually we were playing on around half of the set each night, while mixing the shows, fixing gear, driving, humping boxes. Finally it got to be too much and we walked backstage after a show one night and cornered Mike and Robin. I told them that I loved working for them and would gladly continue as a roadie, but truth be told, would really enjoy playing full time for them, but I / we could no longer cover both of these gigs. One or the other. I was fairly certain this was to be my final chance at standing on stage, thumping the bass. To our surprise, they both chose the latter and our truck driving days came to an end, except for every now and then when there was an "All Hands On Deck" situation.'

The autumn 1973 tour was the biggest the ISB ever undertook. At an exhausting 32 dates in just 40 days, the tour was, truthfully, far too big. While the big city venues, including London's Rainbow in November, were packed out, many of the provincial dates had barely half-full halls – which played right into the hands of some of the critics.

In late October James Archibald filmed Ithkos for the 'performance' part of his film *Rehearsal* at Colston Hall, Bristol. The entire gig at the New Theatre Oxford on 20 November, the final one of the tour, was professionally recorded by the Island Mobile. Possibly this was an attempt to record the entire *Hard Rope* album live, as all the tracks on it were performed, alongside other material from the back catalogue; in the end only Dumb Kate was used, alongside a live version of Cold February from an earlier gig at the Rainbow. It might be that Robin forgot to change the lyrics for this song at Oxford: the song was actually specific about Northern Ireland, but a line about 'in Belfast and the streets of Derry' was replaced for the recorded version to avoid seeming 'political', in much the same way that Rose's remarks about Vietnam in 1970 had seen that interview nixed. The released version substituted 'cried o'er their bones unburied,' though Robin soon reverted to the original.

Drummer and ex-roadie Jack Ingram left the band at Christmas. He was not into Scientology, which set him apart from Mike and Robin, and there'd been a question mark against his name since the rehearsals filmed by James Archibald in the summer, when Mike is clearly irritated by his overloud and pedestrian percussion ('That was great – apart from you, man'). It's a mystery why Mike used Jack's drumming on the studio recording of his cherished Ithkos, as he would usually get in real studio professionals such as B.J. Wilson or Alan Eden. 'Mike was always quite loyal,' says Malcolm, though 'it was obvious that a "real" drummer would greatly benefit the band.' Graham Forbes: 'I seem to remember Mike was being loyal to Jack for the album. He didn't have a clue about playing drums, but he was a very tasteful guitarist! As I recall, he had roadied for Family and Jimi Hendrix.'

After Christmas, John Gilston replaced Jack Ingram on drums and touring continued in January and February 1974, with concerts in Denmark, Netherlands, Switzerland and Germany and the UK.

'The go-to guy on the West Coast recording scene...'

Raymond Greenoaken

From drumming on Ithkos to working with Michael Jackson – the surprising – and sad – story of the ISB's final recruit, John Gilston.

During the sessions for Mike's solo album *Smiling Men With Bad Reputations*, said Mike, John Cale had told him ISB material 'was being wasted because there's no way to relate to a lot of it. I think if some of the Beatles' tunes had been done in the same way as the early Incredible albums they would have immediately excluded a huge audience.'

So it was perhaps not surprising that the band began to veer in this direction: they wanted that missing part of their audience. On the following three ISB albums, *Liquid Acrobat As Regards The Air*, *Earthspan* and *No Ruinous Feud*, they dragooned a total of eight outside drummers into the studio, and in live performance they drew upon the services of their roadie Jack Ingram, who could find his way around a drumkit at a pinch. But all was not well. Critics at their live shows spoke of 'pedestrian drum thumping'. Graham Forbes agrees, albeit more delicately: 'Jack was a roadie who was way out of his depth. He did the best he could...' Jack also sported a large feral beard and was thus somewhat at odds with the clean-shaven *boulevardier* look the band was cultivating at the time. Hey, these things matter, you know...

After Jack departed, the search therefore resumed for a drummer who would give the band the needed drive and cohesion. And, as so often with the String Band, he turned up (clean-shaven) right on their doorstep. 22-year-old John Gilston was born and brought up in London as one of four siblings (his father was a trad jazz band drummer), took up the drums at 13 and spent some time in Fat Grapple, an outfit featuring future Roxy Music instrumentalist Eddie Jobson. He had first met the ISB at the *U* performances at the Roundhouse and in 1970, he moved to Scotland, sharing time between his London base and a cottage in the village of Traquair.

Malcolm Le Maistre: 'John was a good guy and of course a very good drummer. Musically he was top notch with lots of ideas. He was a good friend. When at the Glen, John lived in a cottage down the valley at the end of a very long track. I had met Lindsay Kemp (of Bowie fame) in 1970 in Edinburgh during Stone Monkey's Fringe show after the New York failure of *U*. I got to know him very well and would in fact cite him as an influence. Several years later I introduced him to John, and Lindsay instantly fell in love. He pursued John (who was flattered but very straight, I think). One night Lindsay turned up determined to find John's cottage and proclaim his love. He was very drunk as he staggered up the track only to find (as I recall) that John was out. In drunken desperation he fell into a ditch wailing. (He was always very dramatic.) We rescued him...'

Graham Forbes takes up the tale: 'When I came down to the Row after Xmas 1973 I was told we would be auditioning drummers and was asked if I wanted to try out anyone I knew. I'd never met John, and recommended a guy I'd played with. But John came to the Row and after one song I knew he was a fantastic musician. I told Mike immediately John had my vote. Right from the start, he made a huge difference to the band. It was much tighter and songs like Ithkos immediately sounded far better. He could also play jigs and reels properly so that was great for Robin too. John brought a fresh enthusiasm to the band. He was totally into the music. His technique was great. I've played with drummers from Rory Gallagher, David Bowie, Sensational Alex Harvey Band, Deacon Blue, Rezillos, Allman Brothers and many more, and John was right up there with them.'

John, ISB era

Right John with the Heron band in a onesie his mum knitted for him. *Below* John, USA in the 80s, photo by Michael Tishler.

John never recorded with the ISB (apart from a single track on *No Ruinous Feud*, and the limited-issue *Concert For Scientology* album), but many years later a version of Ithkos found its way onto the *First Girl I Loved* concert CD. It was part of an hour-long performance for Radio One's *In Concert* series in which John's drum heroics take the ISB into a different place, and in true String tradition he also steps up to the marimbas on the reflective and drum-less Heron composition 1968. Within a few months, however, the String Band were no more, and when Mike gathered his Reputation line-up from the remains of the band he took John with him. The *Mike Heron's Reputation LP*, released the following year, featured John on most of the tracks; when the band rebranded itself as Heron and reshuffled the personnel, John remained on board and it's his drumming you hear on the 1977 *Diamond Of Dreams* LP.

The Heron line-up disbanded later that year – allegedly crowded out of the gig circuit by the emerging warriors of Punk Rock – and John relocated to the US, fetching up in the Los Feliz district of Los Angeles with his new wife Lori. (He was only a few minutes walk from Robin and Janet Williamson's home in downtown LA.) There he began to explore electronic drum programming as well as developing his skills still further on the conventional kit. He became known as 'chief studio programmer' for Simmons Drums (an electronic kit), although it was really about tuning them, as he told *Modern Drummer* in 1984: 'You're not programming it in the sense of sequencing like a Linn. I was getting calls to come and get the sounds for people. I developed a reputation quickly for doing that. Although I wasn't playing on most of these dates, now I'm getting more calls to actually play them.' He quickly became a go-to guy on the West Coast recording scene, and his CV is stuffed with session credits for the likes of Michael Jackson (he's on *Thriller*!), Donna Summer, Sheena Easton, Earth, Wind And Fire, Herb Alpert, Lionel Richie and Mike Nesmith. Graham Forbes points out that he was involved in five of the Top Ten singles in the US in 1983.

Another of John's passions was windsurfing, but this was to result in his tragic early death in 1984. His sister Jane says: 'From what I understand he went out on a day not so good for [surfing]. I don't know if it was bad weather or a strong undercurrent but he did not make it back to the shore. His body was washed up a few days later quite far away. I think he started out surfing at Malibu and his body was found on the beach at Santa Anna. Because he was living alone at the time – he and Lori had separated – there was no one there to think something amiss that he didn't return home. The coroner's report said he actually died of hypothermia, not drowning, although he was wearing a wetsuit – I don't know which is worse...'

Nearly forty years after his sad demise, John's memory is still green. He left behind him a loving family and many devoted friends. Jane Gilston again: 'I'm not just saying this because he was my brother, but he really was a special person, apart from being very talented. Very caring, good sense of humour, even though most of our lives we lived quite far apart, being in different countries, he was always in touch. The short time we were both living in the UK – he was in London, I was in Brighton – I would go up to stay with him in London and we would have a great time.'

Graham Forbes: 'John and I were like brothers and he loved the band. We stayed best pals and to be honest it broke my bloody heart when he drowned.' Gray Levett, photographer and husband of Stone Monkey's Mally Schofield, recalls: 'John was stylish, talented and great company. I remember his great kindness and generosity and was deeply saddened by his death. Following the tragic death of Mally, I spent some time staying with John and Lori.' Malcolm again: 'Not long before his death John wrote to me (I still have the letter) talking about his enthusiasm for starting a band with me, and telling of his Indian summer (after his failed marriage) with "the young ladies" and how his phone bill was bigger than his rent. One other thing about John I recall was his appalling time-keeping. He was always late for everything. Susie would tell him to be in the hotel lobby at least an hour before we needed to be, knowing in that way he would be on time. Undiagnosed ADHD perhaps.'

Stan: 'John would come around and was really sweet, kind of spaced out. He once invited me and my girlfriend Mal for dinner. What was most notable was that it took him around four hours to prepare the dinner, by which time we were absolutely famished, and this became an amusing sidebar: a guy who keeps perfect time is actually superbly slow. And this was born out later on when he joined the band and was compulsively late, seemingly incapable of arriving on time, yet had a superb sense of time behind the drums.'

A drummer who couldn't keep time? There's something very String Band about that... But let Malcolm have the final word: 'When I think of him, I miss him. A gentleman and a gentle man.'

John Gilston: Born 10 May 1951. Found dead 21 April 1984.

2021

Mike was having to carry most of the pressure

Adrian Whittaker

As the final year of the ISB's existence progressed, band life was getting more conflicted for the two principal songwriters. Robin's two songs on *Hard Rope* were both, stylistically, throwbacks to the 'old ISB' – Cold February was from the same Celtic mould as The Circle Is Unbroken (*Wee Tam*), and Dreams Of No Return was almost a throwback to *5000 Spirits*, with Mike on sitar and Danny Thompson on string bass. A move towards more crowd-pleasing material saw these two dropped on the final US tour, as was Robin's one new song, Precious Blues And Greys. Increasingly his songs on the set list were jolly Malcolm vehicles like Evolution Rag, a Gilles Crooked-Deal song or Circus Girl. Robin's other contributions were sets of jigs and reels, or electric violin-led instrumentals.

The band could be relied on to put on an entertaining show, getting audiences up and dancing, but behind the scenes there were definitely tensions. Mike addressed this in his old-style ISB song 1968, featuring Robin on bowed gimbri, the sound at the heart of *5000 Spirits*. The lyrics show a nostalgia for the past with references to older songs, but also suggest that 'warm hearts are getting thin'. Though addressed to the all-inclusive 'you', clearly he is singing to Robin:

Did we step wrong somewhere?
Did we my friend?
Are we lost? Are we lost?
Are we lost, my friend?

On the other hand, Mike was coming up with both softish classic singer-songwriter material like Evie and rock songs like Draw Back The Veil, both released on later solo LPs. His material was much more tailored to the full six-piece ISB, now boasting a crack rhythm section with the addition of John Gilston, and so the band as a whole gravitated more to Mike, who it's fair to say was having to carry most of the pressure. Apart from the push from Island to be more commercial, dwindling record sales meant concert income had to cover the costs of wages, plus being on the road with six musicians, two wives/managers and two roadies, two vehicles, trains, planes and hotels. Income also had to cover the costs of running Glen Row, the home base.

Hard Rope and album covers

Adrian Whittaker/BA

It is easy to forget, in an era of downloads and Spotify, quite how important LP covers were in the 60s and 70s. As you may have read in some of the preceding pieces in this book, on the bus home from the shops ISB album covers would be closely scrutinised for signifiers, even examined for hours before needle was actually put to vinyl. Such was the impact of Robin's photo on the *Earthspan* sleeve that a young Green Gartside (of Scritti Politti) immediately took himself off to have his ears pierced, causing him to be exiled by his parents to his grandparents' home. The *Earthspan* message was: 'Hey! We may be in a band, but we are four very different people!' The *No Ruinous Feud* cover took that a stage further by telling us: 'Hey! We are still four very different people but we all work together, with precision, under a corporate logo!' What are we to make, then, of the anomaly that is *Hard Rope*? It did not augur well for the band's future.

The band weren't even pictured on it – a first. This may well have been a dodge to avoid first-guessing who would actually still be a member by the time the album was released. It also avoided deciding who to feature – just have the key three song-writing members left from *Feud*, or whether to also include the two rhythm section players, or whether to take a gamble on also including the new lead guitarist (who was still in his trial period at the time the album was being assembled). Here was another clue that the ISB was in a state of flux. On release, drummer Jack Ingram had already left, John Gilston had replaced him and Graham Forbes had been confirmed in post after his autumn tryout. The black and white photograph on the inner sleeve revealed six shadowy figures who almost looked interchangeable and confirming, to quote Raymond Greenoaken, that 'satin and cheesecloth were a distant memory'. Malcolm: 'It's obvious from that picture that things were not happy in the ISB garden. Robin looks like he is wondering why he is there.'

The front and back illustrations are early work by Wayne Anderson, now an award-winning illustrator of children's books and fantasy novels, and use a bestiary-like approach, with images easily recognisable in his later work: mice, birds, dragons and nymphs. These are set in a large circle made up of dark colours and swirling patterns, in stark contrast to the bright, vibrant and eye-catching designs of the earlier ISB albums.

Over to Wayne: 'Here is the story re the artwork as best I remember it. Having seen my 1973 Paul Raymond magazine illustration, 'As Long As It's Black', the band (I was told) decided that they wanted a similar feel for their album cover, so that kickstarted the project. [*Raymond published* Men Only *and* Club International; *short erotic stories in those mags were often illustrated to quite a high standard, because Raymond wanted to be the UK Hugh Hefner, whose* Playboy *mag often had articles by quite high-minded characters such as Vladimir Nabokov, Gore Vidal and Margaret Atwood – Ed.*] The record company made contact through my agent and commissioned me to create images for the front and the back of the album. I produced black and white development drawings based on the written lyrics from only one of the songs plus the album title. The LP was still 'work in progress' as the band [*Mike and Susie, in fact*] were on a Greek island and working on the unfinished songs for the album [*Ithkos*]. My ideas were approved by the band and the record company and I then created the finished artwork.' Island's marketing department would by this point have control over cover art, needing to ensure 'rack space' with the aim of recouping costs and turning a profit. Again, a long way from the *Wee Tam And The Big Huge* double, which featured only the lyrics on the front cover!

That song was Dreams Of No Return. Wayne: 'There is a spider and a blackbird mentioned in the lyrics, so I guess that I picked up on these and incorporated them into the image. The spider would have supplied me with the 'Silken Twine' thought, hence the spider's web, and the snake was the '*Hard Rope*.' The pose of the naked nymph to some extent mirrors that in the original 1973 illustration, which was probably down to the demands of Paul Raymond and his readership.

Just six months before the band broke up, there was a postscript for Wayne: 'After the album was released I did go to see the band when they performed in Leicester. They were good.'

2021

Hard Rope LP cover

The knotty issue of Hard Rope And Silken Twine. *The final ISB album was released in March 1974. Sales were poor, and this probably tipped Island Records into not renewing the ISB's recording contract.*

It evoked fairly strong reactions from fans at the time. Mike Swann sets out the background to the album and comes out unequivocally in favour, whilst Shane Pope is decidedly guarded on the matter.

Looking out on an endless view

Mike Swann

Hard Rope highlighted the ISB's stylistic contrasts rather than obscuring them in the way that *No Ruinous Feud* had done. In a profound and mature manner, it covers virtually the full spectrum of their nine years of remarkable music.

The year between *Feud* and *Hard Rope* was one of considerable activity and upheaval, involving a number of personnel changes, as well as two UK tours.

The second, 10-date tour was in February 1974, ending on the 23rd at London's Drury Lane Theatre Royal. The new album had been due to be released on the same day, but various problems held it up for over a month. The workload did not slacken though; as well as taping a Danish TV special, they played a concert at Oxford Polytechnic, the result of winning a poll among the students as to whom they would most like to headline a gig. This proves how enduring their popularity was – especially on the college/Uni circuit – for a band that critic Steve Lake three months earlier had said were 'rapidly disappearing into obscurity'.

Hard Rope was issued with minimal publicity, not even the usual full-page ad in the music press. Reviews were hardly ecstatic, *Music Week* saying: 'Not an outstanding example of the brilliance and versatility of this band...Any fan who looks back more in sorrow than anger to the vitality and invention of early LPs like *5000 Spirits* will wonder if the String Band has grown old and stale.' The writer did, however praise the 'tour-de-force' of Ithkos, saying it showed off 'some of the group's old multi-instrument talents.' *Sounds*' Steve Peacock gave the album a reasonable review, saying of Ithkos: 'Heron has blended it all together with skilful subtlety and the band plays with a kind of controlled intensity of which I didn't think they were capable...'

The work does have one or two noticeable flaws, but these are more than offset by its return to the style, profundity and scope of their pre-*Feud* albums. I will never understand how it managed to amass such a garland of poor reviews.

Side One begins with Mike's Maker Of Islands, an exquisite song which is one of his very best. A lovely, mellow tune and an emotional lyric that Mike handles with sensitivity, with just his piano, unobtrusive bass, and an occasionally slightly overdone scoring for strings. His soaring vocal on the 'in my soul' line near the end is positively spine-tingling. A classic.

Track two, Robin's Cold February, is another popular favourite – like Islands, a slow song but powerful and melodic, an ideal vehicle for his strong, piercing vocals. A very atmospheric piece, heightened here by Mike's solo organ and Robin's shrill whistle passages between verses. The main fault with this track lies in the live recording. A sparse song like this would have been better in the studio; everything here sounds too much in the background, as if recorded from the back of the hall. Much of the song's power and atmosphere thus evaporates. Ostensibly, this concise and lyrical statement decrying war and violence is about Northern Ireland, but I feel the substituted line '...cried o'er their bones unburied...' does lend the song a universality more appropriate to its classic feel.

Malcolm Le Maistre and Mike Garson's Glancing Love is the third track. I'm a Malcolm fan; he added so many dimensions to the band in the Island days, mostly in the dancing/theatrics of their live gigs of course, but also in the songs he contributed (I particularly like his *Earthspan* tracks, The Actor and Sailor And The Dancer). This is a goodie as well; it is another slow song which, in terms of programming, may not have been a good choice at this point, but I feel that Side One does have a very relaxed feel that nicely complements and contrasts with the rockier climes of Side Two's Ithkos (and, certainly, *No Ruinous Feud*!). However, the full potential of the new band line-up is not being realised on this side. This is a splendid track though: Mike's organ, deep in the background, sets a strong base, while Robin's crisp acoustic, Graham's tasteful electric guitar and Stan's bass add to the laid-back feel, leading into excellent flute solos by Robin after verse two, and on the coda.

The fourth track, Robin's Dreams Of No Return, is another quiet beauty. Even most of the generally disapproving reviews liked this one. As with Cold February, it is steeped in Williamsonesque atmosphere, and harks back to *Wee Tam* days in style if not execution. Robin sings the piece with perfect diction and intonation, playing acoustic guitar in counterpoint to Mike's sitar (making its first appearance in quite some time). Danny Thompson's string bass is another highlight. A fine melody: complex in structure and intervals perhaps, but that really is Robin's forte, and he handles the whole thing with precision and strong feeling.

Side One's closer is Mike's Dumb Kate, the only one on this side to feature the full band line-up and an ideal vehicle for Robin's spirited fiddle-playing. It is also a concert recording, but though more suited to a live feel, the production makes the vocals at times sound cluttered and indistinct. It is a splendid track though, giving a perhaps necessary lift after the slow, reflective songs preceding it. An amusing tale of a young lady who moves from San Diego to Nome, Alaska and keeps the local male populace happy through the winters: '...she used to serve tables down in the Last Post Grill Room / where they chewed on the beef with a lean and a hunted jaw'.

The whole of Side Two is given over to Ithkos, which lasts a full 19 minutes, one of the most ambitious ventures the band undertook. One's overall view of this album will be coloured by whether one likes Ithkos or not. I love it, and thus rate *Hard Rope* highly. The band only really stretch themselves and show the true potential of the new line-up on this song. Although critics described the piece as 'episodic', I never found it so – it flows well, and it is difficult at times to distinguish where sections begin and end (there are nine separate 'pieces' listed on the album's inner sleeve). Though a very 'modern'/ prog-rock venture for its time, parts contain much of the old evocativeness and atmosphere, as well as the sheer power and expression it gains from its predominantly rock content. The whole song is by Mike, but the opening instrumental passage, Sardis (Oud Tune) is by Robin. A fast, furious main tune and interplay with the orchestral section is very effective, and sets the Mediterranean / North African atmosphere. In the second part of the passage, acoustic and electric guitars signal the song's forthcoming rock elements; Robin's whistles on top strengthen the 'Greek Islands' feel too.

Graham Forbes' biting lead guitar heralds the second section, Lesbos – Dawn, with Mike on organ and acoustic. The rhythm section gradually builds up to lead into the first vocal from Malcolm, singing of Ithkos, a merchant visiting the isle of Lesbos. Robin's electric violin – perfect here in a rock context – duets well with Graham's guitar, switching quickly to organ/acoustic guitar backing on the massed vocal chorus lines. In the third section, Lesbos – Evening, the bass/drums/guitars elements strengthen and quicken the tempo as the vocal breaks off into a staggering violin solo.

A short pause leads us on to the fourth passage, Aegean Sea, where Mike takes lead vocal for the first time. This is a gentle, flowing section conjuring up the tranquil Aegean; Robin accompanies on mandolin/ backing vocal/acoustic then flute as the track builds before the strings and rhythm section bring in section five, Dreams Fade, with Malcolm on vocal.

Section six, Port Of Sybaris (co-written with Graham Forbes) begins with Robin's pounding congas, with the drums and guitar making for a distinctly rhythmic passage. Malcolm again takes the vocal. A short gap leads to a Mike Heron piano solo, edging into a duet between the string section and the lead/bass/drums element of the band. This passage builds so much in intensity that the sheer force of the music is breathtaking by the end – one of the most distinctive passages of music in the ISB discography, and a pointer to how they had mastered the rock idiom. Another small pause moves us into a stunning straight electric rock track, Go Down Sybaris, with pulsating lead guitar from Graham, Malcolm's strongest ever vocals, and a very lively rhythm section, showing that the new line-up could rock as well as any electric band of the time. Congas and acoustics bring in the final pieces, Huntress and Hold My Gaze, where Mike takes the main vocal, accompanied by his piano, the strings and lead guitar. One of the most beautiful, romantic parts of the whole cut, Mike sings of Ithkos' love for Hippolyta. A superb melody here; this passage is possibly the finest in the whole piece, as the vocal edges away into the stirring coda where woodwinds and strings, backed with the bass and drums, close Ithkos in the most uplifting fashion imaginable.

Hard Rope was the final String Band release and a better, more wide-ranging 'swansong' it would be difficult to imagine.

The Ithkos strip on the next two pages is by Allan Frewin.

ITHKOS
I sailed out from Sardis, just one day past...
Sailed to meet the dawn on Lesbos fair...
My merchant's task on this Isle is done.
I call soft evening forth to ease my care.
Aphrodite's temple is sweet with Sandorac...
Bright torches start the night to praise her.
Ithkos wipes his mouth and drops the wine skin...
Salt wind fresh in my mind.
Bark brown eyes hath Ithkos from Sardis newly come...
the carmine lips of Lesbos fail to please...
And through the noisy night just one plaintive song will match my heart...
I can't stand by. I'm like a thief in the night...
The beautiful Aegean Sea brings out an aching need in me...
...while that aching lovely light shines on... ...on...
Dreams fade now, a new day rings.
Trade pulls the galleon ever on...

To rich Sybaris
port of our call...
... beyond the blue Aegean.
How good the sights of peopled shores
to a wanderer such as I...
Known from here to Lydia far...
Sybaris knows not my tread.
And fear stalks
in my heart
for reasons unknown...
Gotta come right out and say it
pale Sybaris, I bear you great scorn.
You know, I'm talking about
your fluted pillars
and your muted lives...
It's worse to me
than death's own chariot
rolling...
Oh, hold my gaze
oh, light of day...
That my thoughts they will
not stray to Hippolyta.
The vows
that set her free
denied me...
It was right there
in Sybaris famed...
... that I met with her
who's named Hippolyta.
Oh, hold my gaze
bring not the sight...
... of that awful,
wondrous night ...
... Hippolyta...
... and far outside of the city walls
the Huntress Dance does call...
... Hippolyta...
The vows
that set her free
denied me.

A Load Of Old (Hard) Rope?

Shane Pope

A couple of live tracks, nineteen-odd minutes of Ithkos – all a bit of a hotch-potch, thrown together as the band fell apart? At least, that's what I first thought.

The album opens with Mike's Maker Of Islands, a piano-led piece much in the singer-songwriter mode of say James Taylor or Joni Mitchell. It's a pleasant enough song, with echoes of some of the tracks on his 1996 *Where The Mystics Swim* album, though the orchestration spoils it: I find it just a bit too intrusive; a simpler arrangement, maybe just Mike at the piano, would have been preferable.

Robin's Cold February is the stand-out track on the album. It's a beautifully melancholic piece about the futility of war – as such, maybe it could be seen as something of a companion piece to Darling Belle from *Liquid Acrobat*. Instrumentation is suitably sparse; a lovely fluid whistle weaves around a moving solo melody which seems, for a split-second, like it is going to break into the tune of Koeeoaddi There ('and there was a tent you played cards with the soldiers in' – or is it just me?). An uncharacteristically direct song, lyrically, but among his best.

Next up is Malcolm's Glancing Love. Now I'd always loved Malc's songs; he's got a wonderfully distinctive singing and writing style (which is just as good today, as seen on his *Nothing Strange* solo album), and this is a typical example. A gently strummed acoustic guitar and organ that threatens to cross over into Procol Harum territory at times (frightening thought!), plus little fills from a second guitar and interjections from alto flute all add up to a nice little song.

Dreams Of No Return is another fine RW song, which harks back, musically at least, to the glory days of *Hangman* or *Wee Tam*. Certainly it could have sat fairly comfortably within either of those collections, with Mike digging out his sitar again for a welcome final return. The song seems to suggest a comparison between the way a past dream could not be revisited (Robin's later *Dream Journals* CD informs us that he kept a dream diary throughout his ISB days) and a lost love – or it could possibly be seen as an epitaph to the String Band in its final days, as lyrically it is far more world-weary than the child-like wonder of times past? Maybe he had just had enough of it all? [*With hindsight, it's tempting to see the song as a farewell to Likky, perhaps even an apology to her. Intriguingly, a BBC session version from 1973 has an 'I still love you' coda. Ed*]

Well, now we have to deal with Ithkos. It's too overblown, pompous even, and is the only time one of the very long ISB songs outstays its welcome. The over-done middle-eastern sounding orchestration at the start, lyrics about ancient Greece that veer dangerously towards the pretensions of the 'progressive' rock of the time, the distorted rock guitars – 'Well I'm as free as a bird, babe, and this bird is gonna fly...' You can almost hear that ten-minute drum solo beckoning. It's not all bad. Robin throws in some rather tasty rock fiddling, the gentler middle section is actually quite pleasant, the fuzzed-up Stones-style rockin' boogie bit towards the end is fun and the final section is also far from unpleasant. Maybe it should have been trimmed down a little, or split into a couple of shorter sections, but this is what Mike intended, and although, years later, it is easy to criticise and ponder what might have been, perhaps it is best left as is.

So there it is, the end of an era. Is this a fitting epitaph, then? Well, a reserved yes, I think. There's one track which is probably as good as anything Robin has done previously or since, a couple of other great songs, others that are at least fun, and really only a small section of one track that I don't like. Have a listen – you may find that you are pleasantly surprised.

Hard Rope – by Mike, Robin and Malcolm

This is what the songwriters said about the tracks in 1997, with some 2021 additions from Malcolm:

Maker of Islands
Mike: 'It's one of those songs where there were originally a lot of ideas, pared down to the essence of the song (like Worlds They Rise And Fall). The piano arrangement took a long time to get that simple. It's basically a love song.'

Malcolm: 'Very nice song. Typical of Mike's meandering melodies. Actually as a general comment if he'd taken some of those melodies he wrote throughout his career and resisted the temptation to go somewhere else and instead repeated the melody he might have written many very commercial songs (the thing he hankered after). Still a wonderful writer of melody.'

Cold February
Robin: 'This was originally specific about Northern Ireland. The lines about Belfast and Derry were changed at the time not because of the record company, but because some of the people around the band felt we should soft-pedal a bit. I prefer it the way I originally wrote it.'

Malcolm: 'Exceptional. Should be a standard, but because *Hard Rope* was not received so well by fans and the demise of the band it sort of got lost. There is a power and beauty that is equalled by few other so-called songs about war.'

Glancing Love
Malcolm: 'The finest song I ever wrote with Mike Garson. Seriously, a lot of people love this song although I'm not sure why. There is a certain innocence but I don't like the way I say achin' instead of aching. Quite annoying. Nice tune.' See the Malcolm interview for the tale of his unrequited love for a New York ballet dancer!

Dreams Of No Return
We asked Robin if this could be seen as a *Dream Journals*-type song. Not really, sez Robin, '...it's goodbye to an earlier idea of God, looking at the idea that death is not total extinction...'

Malcolm: 'A throwback. Love the sitar. I like it but the ending sounds like it's come from another song. It should have had more conviction to build the coda, riffing on the sitar.'

Dumb Kate

At the time, Mike said it was a case of needing a song of this type – which he wrote to order. 'I was trying to write a song in Log Cabin style, but with a Cajun, Wild West feel – or maybe the Canadian wastes. We nearly got killed playing that in Berkeley: the audience rioted, we had to stop the concert. It went down like a lead balloon. I did my little speech from the stage, explaining that men could be dumb too – as a chair whistled past my head... We dropped it from the set after that. But I'd still defend it a bit – not something I'd go to the wall for, though.'

Malcolm: 'A fitting title for a low point in Mike's career. I could say more but I won't.'

Ithkos

The genesis of this song was a three-week holiday Mike and Susie had on a fairly remote Greek island (possibly Skiathos, says Mike). He'd taken his guitar, and 'we had this little, very private villa and a beach – and that was all. I'd have quite liked a bar, actually. So I wrote loads of material in this Conan The Barbarian, historical vein, making a story out of that time period, and refined it down. Yes, I still quite like it.'

Robin: 'I've been re-listening to old ISB stuff recently, and Mike's written a lot of good songs. But this isn't one of my favourites. We were forced into it by the situation – we'd been forced into playing really big venues.'
Malcolm: 'I felt a bit on the sidelines making *Hard Rope*. For Ithkos we had a drummer who couldn't drum... It didn't feel right – it was supposed to be a vehicle for all of us, but it came out disjointed and uneven. I was never quite sure what it was. I think there's a bit of a Hubbard influence in that song – he wrote a book about using memory to pinpoint old cities around the Mediterranean. I do think there are some really lovely melodies in there we could have made more of.'

Malcolm (2021): 'Ithkos is extraordinary in its ambition! It is a quite bizarre flawed thing. But strangely I like it. There is much to admire and some stunning bits of music. Specifically it seems like different two different visions fighting for ascendancy: Mike's future ISB and Robin's desire for a different future, with me stuck in the middle, literally. The constant switching between rock and pastoral was a mis-step and having Mike sing odd bits seems a bit perverse in view of the first person narrative. His singing on the end section strikes me as particularly strange. The writer-producer pulling rank perhaps. Having said that, I think it's full of unexplored gems and if it was broken down a bit there are least 5 great songs there. The "gotta come right out and say it..." bit is almost New York Dolls and the brief Dreams Fade section is just a beautiful melody. Thinking selfishly Mike should have had the courage to let me sing it all.'

1974

Bill Allison/Adrian Whittaker

The ISB went back into Sound Techniques in April 1974 to start recording a possible new album/single. We came across the details during the preparation for *Tricks Of The Senses*. The three tracks were all Heron-led: a very basic keyboards/bass demo of Easy Street, a completed version of Evie with Susie Watson-Taylor on backing vocals (it was Melanie on Heron's later *Reputation* album) and a completed version of Blue Moon with Mike and Robin sharing the chorus, bottleneck guitar by Forbesy and Malcolm on Moog. They give a few pointers to the possible shape of the next ISB album, as envisaged at that point.

On the 17th May the band recorded their final BBC session, *In Concert* at the Golders Green Hippodrome, London. It was broadcast on the first of June. The unreleased material included Mike's 1968, which Grahame Forbes says 'had all six of us playing acoustic instruments, sounding like the early days'. There was also Robin's Jack Straw's Wishes, along with the set of jigs and reels that closed the show: Good Morrow To Your Nightcap/Crowley's Reel/Small Coals For Nailers/Katy Hill. Jack Straw's Wishes was a ten-minute-long heavy instrumental which some have seen as Robin's revenge for Ithkos. The most interesting thing about it was the title. Jack Straw was one of the leaders of the Peasants' Revolt of 1381, a major event in the history of England; the peasants' plans were to kill the king, 'all landowners, bishops, monks, canons, and rectors of churches', set up their own laws, and set fire to London.

Both Robin and Mike made guest appearances at Melanie Safka's concert at the Theatre Royal, Drury Lane, London on 23rd June. The concert was recorded and the live version of Chart Song on her 1974 studio album *As I See It Now* came from this show. Mike plays Moog, acoustic guitar and contributes background vocals, whilst Robin adds kalimba. Together with Melanie they sang Do It Yourself (Desert Song) which Mike had written specially on the morning of the show and sounded as if it could have been a vintage acoustic ISB song. In 2020 the full show was released as *Melanie Live at Drury Lane 1974*, including Desert Song and nine other tracks.

The band played an attenuated set at the Olympia London Rock Proms on 7 July, but the last ever full ISB gig in the UK was at the Pavilion, Hemel Hempstead the day before. The set included three new Heron songs but, worryingly, few new songs from Robin, apart from possibly the only ISB performance of his Precious Blues And Greys and the 'world premiere' of Poor Little Playboy, a new Gilles Crooked-Deal vehicle for Malcolm. Here's the set list, with thanks to Paul Hunter.

Painted Chariot
Evolution Rag
It's A Strong Thing
Poor Little Playboy
Jack Straw's Wishes
Draw Back The Veil

Sound TechniqueS
46a Old Church Street
London SW3
01-352 2354

CLIENT ISLAND PRODUCER MIKE HERON
ARTIST I.S.B. DATE 24/4/74

EVIE (F/L E/L)

1 BASS	5 GTR O/D	9 Vlns / Intro 12str	13 EL GTR (FX)
2 B.DRM	6 VOX-M	10 Violas / Intro 12str	14 TOP KIT
3 SNARE	7 Acous GTR (Mike)	11 Back Up Vox ([illegible])	15 Intro Acous / Celeste
4 TAMB.	8 Back Up Vox (Robin)	12 PNO	16 Intro Acous / Acous GTR

BLUE MOON (F/L E/L.)

1 BASS	5 TOP KIT	9 Lead Vox Mike	13 Solo GTR
2 B. DRM	6 GTR	10 Conga	14 Maestro - Moog
3 SNARE	7 Chorus Vox Mike	11 Bottle Neck	15 Maestro - Moog
4 TOP KIT	8 Chorus Vox Robin	12 Moog	16 Maestro - Moog

EASY STREET

1 BASS	5 SPEECH	9	13
2 PNO	6	10	14
3 VOX	7	11	15
4 VOX (ECHO)	8	12	16

STATUS 16T ORIG REPLAY 15 NAB DOLBY TAPE 8/16 ENG. [illegible] LOC.

Interval
Ithkos
Born To Be Gone
Precious Blues And Greys
1968
Black Jack David
Dumb Kate
The new set of trad jigs and reels

Encore
May The Longtime Sun medley
Jigs (Grumbling Old Men et al)

US tour, summer 1974

Adrian Whittaker/Bill Allison

The US tour was an odd mixture of three/four-night residencies in small clubs alongside support slots for big name bands like Three Dog Night. Mike was reported as saying they needed to 'break the band again' in the States, as these were the first gigs there for over a year. Perhaps in an attempt at crowd-pleasing, Robin's role was largely instrumental, reduced to being the superstar electric violinist. Neither of his 'old-style' *Hard Rope* songs were now in the set and his new song, Precious Blues And Greys, was absent too. By the final gig in New York Robin's contributions comprised two violin-led electric instrumentals, Evolution Rag (now a percussion showcase for Malcolm) and *three* sets of jigs and reels. Malcolm was allowed one (new) song, I Was Born A Wanderer. Ithkos, though, appears to have been dropped, and surprisingly Mike retained two acoustic songs: 1968 and an encore of This Moment.

Some of the club gigs were poorly attended, notably a three-night residency in a Memphis club. Malcolm: 'The first night only a dozen or so people turned up, including a guy who told us, "I'm all the way from Arkansas" (over the river). A few more came on the second night and we rounded things off with everyone who'd seen us the first two nights coming back with their mates on the third night. At the close of the gig we ended up jamming with the support band (yes, there was one!).' Mike's 1975 song Down On My Knees (After Memphis) sums up his reaction at the time: '...feeling so small, like a faded country star when there's no hope left at all'. Some gigs were fun, though. Malcolm: 'There were good crowds at all the other headlining shows. I recall that Nashville was OK. Julie Christie was filming there at the time and brought her crew along with her. Graham remembers that the bar stayed open after the gig and he and John Gilston had a marathon drinking session with them all! Louisville was memorable – there was a decent audience and a very good party afterward where several of us got quite stoned due to spiking of the stew, a pleasant reminder of the past. The other support gigs were variable, but the Bruce Springsteen gigs were great because they were packed and enthusiastic and Bruce was a very nice guy. [*ISB supported Bruce Springsteen for 2 mid-August gigs at the Carlton Theatre in New Jersey, an early and a late show – Ed.*] Then there was the infamous huge Three Dog Night support gig, to which we arrived late and were blown out! The tour was probably OK for the lesser band members as we had plenty of fun and I have to say I loved touring. New places, food, girls blah blah. I know that Stan, Graham and John were having a good time, looking forward to touring UK, Europe and the sadly lost Australian tour.'

Onstage, the band were loud. They would open with a thumping organ-driven version of Everything's Fine Right Now. Stan: 'John Gilston was now in the band and he played a very contemporary, large rock kit. On several of the songs, Mike asked us to "Dig In!" And dig we did, but I struggled a great deal, standing next to the drums and especially the cymbals. When John hit them, it was so much louder than anything I had ever been subjected to. And certainly louder than anything the ISB had tried in earlier times. I struggled with my hearing as a result and most nights, after the show, I had a terrible ringing in my ears. On one particular night at the Bottom Line club in NY right before the end of the band, when we walked off stage after the first set, Mike got angry with me. I can still remember that look on his face. He wanted me, in particular, to "dig in" as he stated. After that, for the remaining shows, trust me, I dug in! But overall it was seemingly getting to be a wider divide between Mike and Robin in terms of the dynamics of the material, from quiet acoustic to forceful, hell's bells.' Malcolm: 'Mike and Robin were obviously diverging with Mike probably the happier of the two. Robin was growing increasingly irritable.'

Four nights at the 400-seater club My Father's Place on Long Island were followed by some more support slots and finally a four-night residency at The Bottom Line in New York. The last gig was on 29th August 1974, after which the band began discussions with a new record company.

2021

The natural cards revolve...

Bill Allison

The ISB's album deal with Neighborhood Records implodes

Contracts with Island in the UK and Warners in the US had come to an end and were unlikely to be renewed owing to poor sales. Susie Watson-Taylor was therefore looking for a new record deal and at this point, Peter Schekeryk becomes a main player in the story. He was a controversial figure who had started off his music career in a 1966 garage band called The Magic Plants, later becoming a record producer. He was also Melanie Safka's husband, and together they had founded Neighborhood Records in 1971. Schekeryk planned to offer the ISB a contract and had started research by asking the principal songwriters to send him demos of their new songs for consideration before the band arrived in New York and the recording sessions scheduled for the end of the US tour.

Schekeryk wanted to 'break' the ISB in the US rock market, and felt, with the right compositions, this could happen. He told Mike that he could sing as well as Bruce Springsteen, who the band had just supported. Schekeryk was desperate for hit material, as his label was struggling; in fact, Neighborhood ceased operations completely in 1975, soon after Mike's solo *Reputation* LP was released.

On arrival in New York, all the band signed a contract with Neighborhood and were told that Mike's songs Meanwhile The Rain and Evie would be their first single and the album would follow. This would, of course, have been exciting but different and perhaps sum up the direction the music was taking. The hit single that Schekeryk envisaged, though, was with just Mike and Robin on vocals, supported by Melanie on backing vocals plus a group of Atlanta session musicians.

The band found this out the hard way. Stan Schnier: 'We were starting early afternoon to lay down some new tracks in a New York recording studio. When we got there, Schekeryk suggested we go out in the studio and "jam." One thing we never did was jam. Never! We started to play a jig and he ridiculously entered the room and started conducting us. I thought it was a comedy routine, this clueless man acting the fool. But it seemed he was serious. After an hour or so we were released. Next morning, we headed back over to the studio. When we entered the control room, Schekeryk jumped up from the mixing console. Concerned. Embarrassed. Sternly sending us out the door because the studio was full of session musicians! John Gilston and I were devastated. All I remember was the thought that I was unwilling to be humiliated by him or possible bad decisions made by Mike etc.' The band members returned to the UK while recording continued.

In late 1974 Melanie recorded her *As I See It Now* album at Media Sound in NYC, produced by Schekeryk. It includes the one track from the Drury Lane London show that Mike and Robin did with Melanie, and Mike's distinctive vocals are also heard on the studio recordings Eyes Of Man and Don't Think Twice, It's Alright. On these studio tracks, Robin may well have provided some of the musical backing; Susie Watson-Taylor is also credited with providing backing vocals. Topping a long list of session musicians credited on the sleeve were the power trio of Roy Yeager on drums, John Mulkey on bass and Barry Harwood on electric lead guitar, who amongst other things had all backed Joe South on tour.

On the two tracks intended as the ISB single, the same trio backed Mike on lead vocal and Robin on backing vocals and oud, whistle and Jews harp, with additional backing vocals by Melanie. We can assume that these two tracks were recorded at the same time and the same sessions as Melanie's album. Both recordings were eventually used on Mike's solo LP.

Stan says now that there was 'a series of poor decisions between Schekeryk, Mike and Susie' leading up to the final crisis. Schekeryk had reviewed the demos of songs for the album, including several Heron tracks such as Draw Back The Veil and It's A Strong Thing which cropped up on Mike's later LPs. Malcolm appears to have been omitted completely, and devastatingly Schekeryk is reported to have told Robin that, as much as he liked him, he felt that his songs were not as commercial as Mike's and he would only use one or two of his songs at most. This was understandably anathema to Robin, a founder member of the band and someone who up to this point had selected LP tracks on an equal split basis with Mike.

However, to prove a point, Robin turned up the next day with what some considered the most commercial song he had ever written, a 'classy' reggae song called Bad Penny. Unfortunately, however, Bad Penny has never been released and Malcolm has no recollection of it. Seven demos of Robin's unused songs from this era, including Precious Blues And Greys, saw the light of day in 2008 as bonus tracks on a reissue of his *Journey's Edge* solo LP. Recorded with Stan Schnier and an unknown drummer, they are brisk, accessible and slightly poppy.

By this point, already increasingly unhappy with the focus during the tour on electric/rock material, Robin wanted out. Meetings were held in late September to attempt to resolve the differences about musical direction, but things came to a head. Despite the fact the band had a recording contract, despite tours of Britain, Ireland and Europe which had been lined up (and provisionally, a tour of Australia), they could not find a way forward.

Eventually the meetings became very tense. Malcolm: 'Mike and Robin were still trying to work things out, and I gather they had a session in a hotel room in New York where they brought in two Scientologist friends, Paolo Lionni and his girlfriend, as facilitators to try and work out a way forward. But it just turned into an extremely heated argument, and after that I suppose it just became irreparable. It had to come, though. The band broke up because these guys were changing – they were getting older, suddenly they're in their thirties, thinking about their future careers. I'd been around them for four years and I'd watched Mike and Robin develop as people – and they'd started to diverge.'

The band's other members had suggested that the worldwide fan base was owed a little more. There was talk of a farewell tour, which would also have provided some financial security for the musicians to help them move onto other projects, since a great deal of money was tied up in the band. Robin, though, was adamant that they had reached the end.

In October there was an initial, holding, press statement by the ISB's UK agency that all the tours were cancelled while the ISB were 're-evaluating their artistic futures' and that 'when they return from various parts of the world they will then make a further statement.'

A week later came the band's press announcement that they had broken up. Mike said later: 'We dissolved the band in the States. Robin and I decided that we didn't have a lot more music to make together. What we agreed to do was to finish the Incredible String Band and that no one has the rights to the name.' Stan: 'Robin never uttered a bad word about the past but he was then (and now) adamant about leaving the ISB in the rear view mirror.'

Graham Forbes still regrets that the band didn't stay together at least long enough to do a farewell tour: 'The wonderful people that followed the band deserved that.'

Malcolm: 'The breakup was appallingly timed. I think the others were pretty pissed off that it ended so suddenly. I certainly was. I knew something was up and was expecting to be consulted but when the call came, it was to tell me it was all over. As I think about it, it still rankles.'

In late October 1974, the Friends Of The ISB fan club sent out a final 'special news release' to members: 'We realise that we have learnt a lot and achieved much in our years as the Incredible String Band. That stage in our careers is over and now is the time for all of us to start a new phase.'

2021

Epilogue

Adrian Whittaker

The ISB break-up had been anticipated by many people in and around the band, and probably came as a relief to some. 'Actually, I should have done it at least two years earlier,' Robin told *Folk Roots* in 1997. 'Mike was looking for success in a more rock context and I wanted to go back to being acoustic... My main happiness has always been to break new ground. I want to be the first guy over the mountains, not the guy who hangs around to build the city.' Nevertheless, there was a lot of anger and resentment involved; it was eventually agreed the name Incredible String Band could not be used separately by either founder-member, and Mike and Robin had no communications with each other for several years.

The following 25 years should properly be the subject of another book. Briefly, Robin moved to the States and released a remarkable album, *Journey's Edge*, with The Merry Band, a very successful acoustic ensemble which he worked with from 1976-79. When that folded, he worked solo, becoming an excellent harpist and a story-teller of note. After his separation from Janet Shankman he moved back to Wales, embarking on an increasingly diverse and eclectic selection of projects. *Ten Of Songs*, *Mirrorman's Sequences* and *Island Of The Strong Door* are amongst the best of these.

Mike formed the rock band Mike Heron's Reputation (later renamed Heron) out of the remnants of the old ISB and recorded and toured with them until 1977. A solo album for Neil Bogart's Casablanca label disappeared shortly after its release in 1979 when the label went bankrupt (it was later re-released as a CD). He was predominantly a songwriter rather than a performer in the 1980s (releasing material on *The Glen Row Tapes*) apart from one brief tour with an electric band. In the Nineties the resurgence of interest in the ISB prompted him to form Mike Heron's Incredible Acoustic Band, who did several tours and released the CD Billy Connolly rates so highly, *Where The Mystics Swim*.

Malcolm, after a brief experiment with a solo band, moved into theatre and performance, forming The Mandarin Theatre Company with Ishy, John and Rakis and his wife Annabel. After a period doing children's storytelling, and cabaret work with Pete Baynes, in 1991 he started his current work in environmental theatre. He released a solo CD, *Nothing Strange*, in 1994 and remains a prolific songwriter.

As the years passed Mike and Robin got into sporadic telephone contact with each other, and articles in *beGLAD* magazine offered them both a forum to make positive comments about each other's work; editor Andy Roberts even put them on the same bill at a Leeds ISB convention (but on separate days!). The magazine played an important role in the Nineties rehabilitation of the ISB; it was, for example, the source of much of the material in Q and *Mojo* features on the band. But in an odd quirk of fate, it was Joe Boyd who unwittingly brought them together on the same stage. In a 1997 article for *The Guardian*, he'd described the tensions in their relationship in the Elektra period and commented that 'Mike and Robin had no great fondness for each other'. Aggrieved, Robin rang Mike and they both agreed that was not how they remembered it. They decided to show a united front and later that year they shared stages together in Glasgow and London, billed as 'Mike Heron and Robin Williamson'. They even sang (a bit shakily) a few old ISB songs together. It was heart-warming stuff and old fans, Rose, Robert Plant *and* Joe Boyd turned out to celebrate.

The final ISB chapter feels oddly familiar. Towards the end of the Nineties Robin and Clive Palmer combined forces as a duo, but on the eve of the millennium (December 30th 1999) they were joined at an Edinburgh gig – as a 'strummer' – by Mike Heron. Billy Connolly, Archie Fisher and Bert Jansch all did a turn, too. A full-blown 'original' ISB reunion was set in motion, with the nucleus of Mike, Robin and Clive joined by Robin's wife Bina and keyboard player Lawson Dando. The ISB Mark Two started gigging in August 2000 but was an occasional grouping, leaving room for solo projects. They toured once or twice a year, featuring material no-one thought they'd ever hear live again, like Ducks On A Pond, Douglas Traherne Harding and Waltz Of The New Moon.

The band never quite gelled to the point where they could work collaboratively on new material, and Robin grew increasingly ambivalent about the project. After a major ruction in the reformed band, he no longer worked with them and in late 2002 returned to solo and duo work. Robin maintained a dignified silence, though some have seen his solo song Just Like The River as a comment on the split: 'In the end my friend it's just about the trust you stole / you'll have to go stumbling away alone with your tarnished gold'.

ISB Mark 2 continued sporadically with the addition of multi-instrumentalist Fluff, but slowly ground to a halt, playing their last gig in September 2006.

Mike's Incredible Acoustic Band prepare to leave Dalston, 1995.
L-R: Dave Haswell, John Rutherford, Mike. (Adrian Whittaker)

Malcolm with Pete Baynes, Irish Centre, Camden, 1995. (*beGLAD* archive)

Mike and Clive both returned to solo gigs, though the two were briefly reunited at Very Cellular Songs, the 2009 Barbican concert organised by Joe Boyd. Disobeying Joe Boyd and egged on by Dr Strangely Strange, Rose made a brief surprise appearance at the end of the show. She was back officially on the encore for Joe's 2017 Edinburgh event, the Music Of The Incredible String Band, which featured Mike alongside luminaries such as Robyn Hitchcock, Green Gartside, Barbara Dickson and Alasdair Roberts.

Robin had been approached by Joe to be part of both these events, but turned them down. Around the same time, ISB were up for a Lifetime Achievement award at the Radio Two Folk Awards, but this was nixed because Robin refused to perform at the event as any part of a joint line-up with Mike. In November 2019 ISB were awarded the Nordoff Robbins Scottish Music Living Legend Award, but Mike collected this on his own 'on behalf of the band'.

Sadly, it seems unlikely that Mike and Robin will share a stage again. But never say never!

Overleaf Detail from the cover of *Seasons They Change* compilation LP, by James Hutcheson

Appendix

Where are they now?

Joe Boyd After a period in the States with Warner Brothers in the Seventies, Joe returned to found the Hannibal label which was responsible for a vast array of world music and folk releases, later moving back to New York to work with Rykodisc. For some time now he's been based in London again and in 2005 published a much-acclaimed book about his Sixties work, *White Bicycles*. In 2009 he put together Very Cellular Songs, a celebration of the ISB's music, at the Barbican, London. Mike, Clive, the Strangelies, Richard Thompson, Green Gartside and Robyn Hitchcock took part, sadly without Robin Williamson. Joe is working on another book about world music and on his usual eclectic variety of film and recording projects.

Gerard Dott has retired from his work as a guitar amp technician and lives in Eddlestone, Peebles. Having returned to his first love, trad jazz, he now plays clarinet in 'The Maid Of The Forth Stompers' on the eponymous jazz boat; from time to time The Stompers also play a Friday night at Edinburgh's Jazz And Jive club.

Graham Forbes lives in Edinburgh. Having sold his two very successful companies and retired, he's written several books based around his travels and his life in music. He writes: I have two sons I'm very close to and if I'm not doing things with them I'm out hill walking or on my mountain bike or rock climbing. I get a tremendous buzz from it, very similar to the excitement of playing. I love standing on the tops of mountains watching the sunset. A lot of people take delight in pointing out surrounding mountains and naming them and all that stuff but frankly I haven't a clue what most of them are called. I prefer to see them as they were thousands of years ago and of course, they didn't have names then.

Malcolm, Stan Lee and Graham reunited in 2010 to play the Edinburgh Fringe as 'Not The Incredible String Band.' 'That is exactly who we were,' says Stan.

John Gilston See the piece on John in the 1974 section. He died in 1984.

Mike Heron lives mainly in Newcastle with his partner Corrina; daughter Georgia is based in Scotland. After a period in the Nineties with his own

Incredible Acoustic Band and a solo album, *Where The Mystics Swim*, Mike became part of the reformed ISB for a few years. Later, he toured for some time with a small band including his daughter Georgia, Mike Hastings of Trembling Bells and multi-instrumentalists Nick Pym and John Frogpocket Wilson. He's also collaborated with novelist/poet Andrew Greig and with The Album Leaf, and had a joint tour with Trembling Bells in 2013. Website: www.mikeheron.co.uk

Jack Ingram (Stan Schnier writes) After the ISB, Jack continued living at Glen Row for a while, working for on and off Family and Reputation. After a few years, he headed out to California with his wife Lida and daughter Tara and went back to doing professional sound mixing, touring with big acts including Weather Report, Santana, Humble Pie and Nana Mouskouri. He settled in LA and started doing in-house audio at places like the Greek Theatre, Universal Studios and many live TV shows. He retired recently after a very long and successful career. Jack has always been a great and daring birder of the first order. Some 35 years ago, he called me and told me about the plight of nearly extinct California Condor. He was in on the ground floor of the capturing, controlled breeding and rerelease. Today this is an often quoted success story on the saving of an endangered species. The condors are thriving.

Malcolm Le Maistre now lives with his partner Mary Gajenska in North Lanarkshire having spent 20 crazy years in West Lothian restoring a former arts and crafts quarry workers' community. He reached the nadir of his performing career ('I hope') working as Santa Claus at a Sky call centre in Livingston ('Thank God no one could recognise me behind the beard – the money was good though!'). A third solo LP is in the pipeline, and his current ensemble project, The BarrowBand, performs spirited songs about fruit and veg. Otherwise he is the artistic director of the Environmental Arts Theatre Company, specialising in environmental education using performance and music. He writes: 'I guess I'll be happy if, whilst waiting for a bus in some far flung part of the world, someone in the queue begins humming one of my songs.'

Christina McKechnie (Licorice) As of 2021, Likky is believed by her family to be living in sheltered accommodation in California.

Mimi lives in the Bay Area, San Francisco, and Mouse near Fresno, CA. They both (separately) still teach and dance. **Mouse** teaches Bharata Natyam, the classical South Indian equivalent of ballet.

Peter Neal still works as a film-maker, including *The Lion Sleeps Tonight*, a social history of the song Wimoweh. He spent much of the Nineties working on *Room Full Of Mirrors*, a definitive Hendrix documentary, on ice for a decade owing to legal problems with the Hendrix estate, but now scheduled to soon see the light of day as *Starting At Zero*.

Clive Palmer spent some time living in Brittany, but after becoming semi-retired he lived on a modest pension in Penzance with his partner Gina where he occasionally played with local musicians.

He was a member of the reformed ISB and appeared at the Barbican, together with Mike, in the Cellular Songs ISB tribute concert. He died in 2014.

Clive outside his house in Brittany, 1995. (Clive Palmer)

Ivan Pawle lives in Kenmare, Count Kerry. Dr Strangely Strange played a one-off UK gig for *beGLAD* readers in Leeds in the mid-Nineties. After a 25-year break, they released that 'difficult third album', *Alternative Medicine*, on Ace Records in 1997 and since 2007 have headlined in both London and Dublin, most recently at the Camden Jazz Cafe in 2012. They are still active now – for more info, see the book *Fitting Pieces To The Jigsaw*.

Edward Pope (1948) is a retired life model whose interests include history research and forest gardening. He was in the legendary Exploding Galaxy performance group with Malcolm Le Maistre and is the Glen Rower without a hat on the cover of *Myrrh*.

Rakis Former original Stone Monkey member Rakis (aka John Koumantarakis) has changed his name to Oliphant (he hoped to assume the title Lord Oliphant but was beaten to it by a distant cousin). Having spent many years in Italy, he now lives in Japan teaching English at a university. Malcolm and he still have hopes of one day treading the boards together again.

Ishy Schofield writes: Between 1971 and 1982 I enjoyed being at home in the country with John and our three young children. We had a small menagerie, grew vegetables and were part of the craft community. For the past 30 years I have worked helping to promote many local festivals and community projects in the Scottish Borders. I consider myself very lucky to live in such a beautiful place as Traquair.

John Schofield writes: After *U* I started to make a living doing woodwork. Commissions to make kitchens for Robin and Mike started me off. I became a good wood-turner and did this for about 15 years, with a workshop at Traquair House and then in Peebles. I then decided to become a teacher and worked with children with special needs, helping them to learn woodwork, computing and music. I'm retired now but I still do my own woodwork.

Mal Schofield formed a short-lived group called When Stars Collide with her partner Gray Levitt. She died of cervical cancer in 1979. Robin wrote the (solo) song Fare Thee Well Sweet Mally about her.

Stan Schnier (aka Lee) former ISB bass player, sound engineer, tour manager and, according to Malcolm, 'voice of artistic reason', returned to the States after the ISB split, worked briefly with Robin and currently lives in New York. He still plays bass and lap steel guitar.

Janet Shankman does not work for the Scientology Organisation, as we erroneously wrote in the last edition. She runs a booking agency in L.A.

Rose Simpson lives in Devon, in an area 'twinned with Narnia.' She writes: 'I'm pleased to say I still live in the country with a dog, a cat and chickens. I still rejoice in landscapes and sunsets and thoughts of wonders and mysteries but living in a body is less entertaining these days. Imagination is better than ever, now I have the patience to sit still for longer. Looking back to past times is a privilege of age but I aim to enjoy the days now as much as I did those back then. This moment is different but still full of futures.'

Susie Watson-Taylor went on to administer L. Ron Hubbard's publishing rights worldwide as boss of 'Author Services Inc.' She died in 2007. Mike wrote a song about her, Long Shadows.

Robin Williamson lives in Cardiff with his wife Bina and their daughter Vashti. He continues a prolific writing, recording and international solo touring career. He made four recordings for ECM, *The seed-at-zero*, *Skirting The River Road*, *The Iron Stone* and *Trusting In The Rising Light*, the latter three being collaborations with jazz musicians on settings of Whitman, Blake and others. He's also been involved in countless solo projects released on his own label, Pigs Whisker Music, including music for theatre, TV productions and brass bands, and church performances of the Psalms in Latin, released on the *Carmina* CD.

For some years now, Robin and Bina have also been recording and performing together. They continue to perform as a duo in an ongoing series of seasonal concerts in celebration of the Spirit Of Life. These bring together their origins of East and West, drawing newly on the Celtic heritage in the common ground of all faiths.

For further information on Robin, or Robin and Bina projects, see: www.pigswhisker.co.uk

2021

Robin and Bina, 2003. (Robin Williamson)

Incredible String Band Family Tree

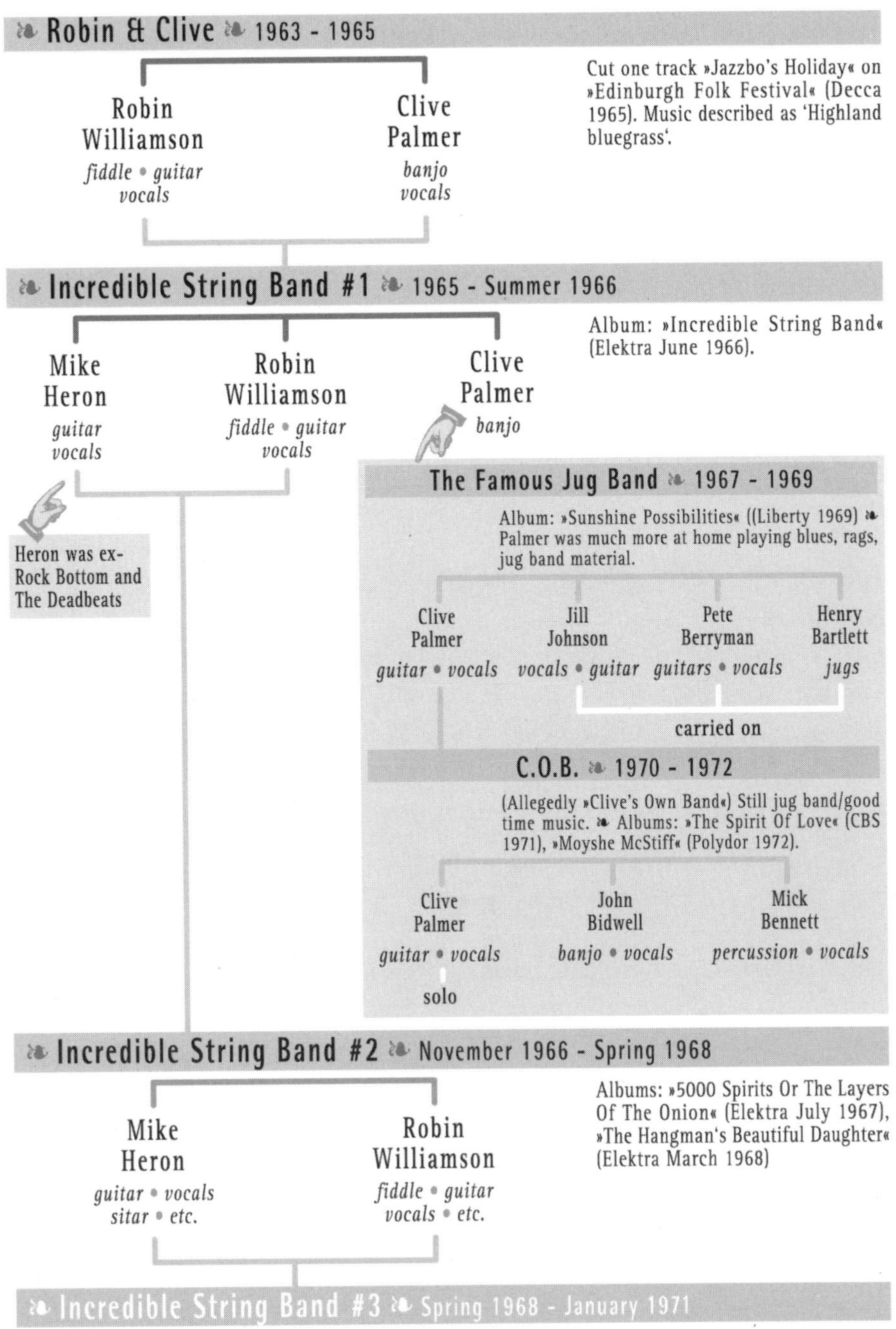

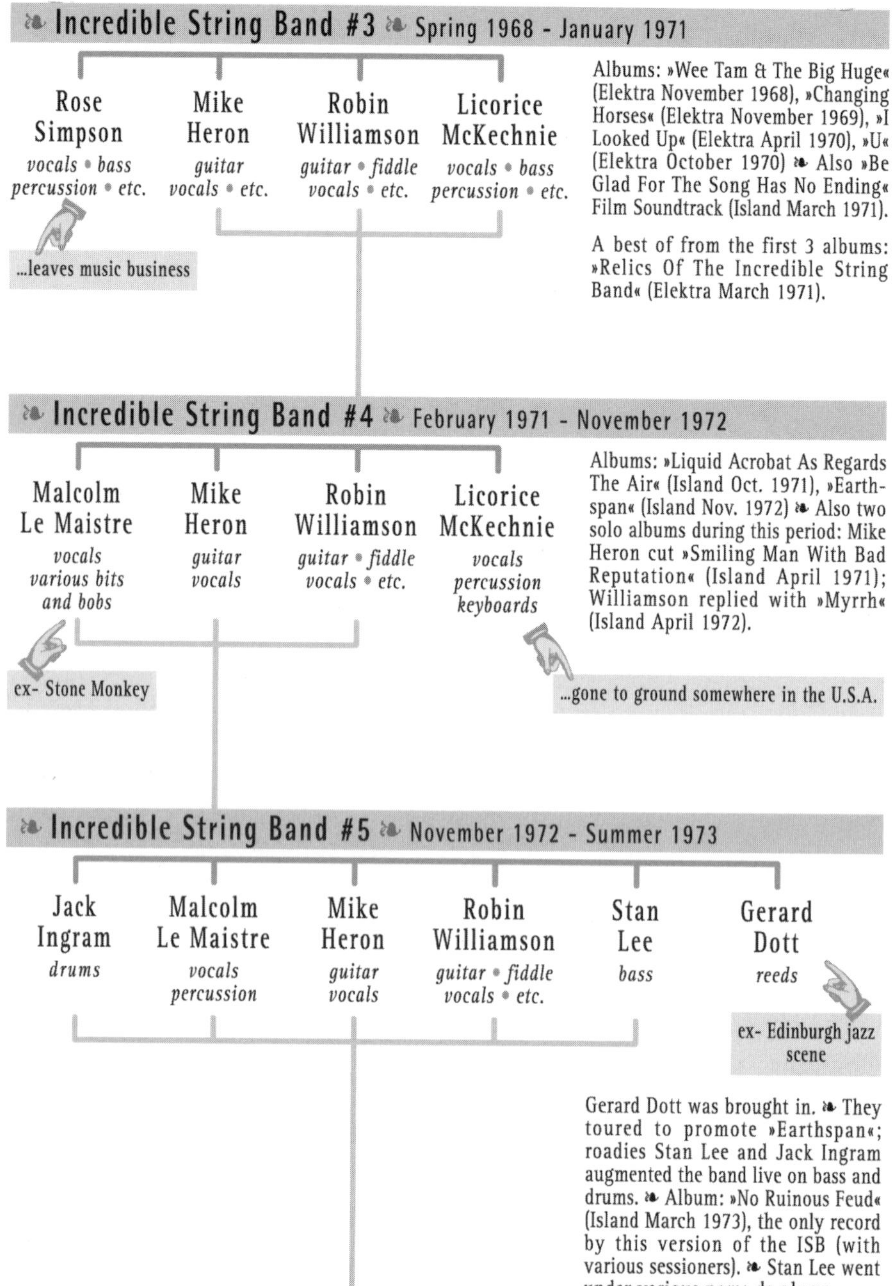
❧ Incredible String Band #3 ❧ Spring 1968 - January 1971
Rose Simpson
vocals • bass percussion • etc.
Mike Heron
guitar vocals • etc.
Robin Williamson
guitar • fiddle vocals • etc.
Licorice McKechnie
vocals • bass percussion • etc.
...leaves music business
Albums: »Wee Tam & The Big Huge« (Elektra November 1968), »Changing Horses« (Elektra November 1969), »I Looked Up« (Elektra April 1970), »U« (Elektra October 1970) ❧ Also »Be Glad For The Song Has No Ending« Film Soundtrack (Island March 1971).
A best of from the first 3 albums: »Relics Of The Incredible String Band« (Elektra March 1971).
❧ Incredible String Band #4 ❧ February 1971 - November 1972
Malcolm Le Maistre
vocals various bits and bobs
Mike Heron
guitar vocals
Robin Williamson
guitar • fiddle vocals • etc.
Licorice McKechnie
vocals percussion keyboards
ex- Stone Monkey
...gone to ground somewhere in the U.S.A.
Albums: »Liquid Acrobat As Regards The Air« (Island Oct. 1971), »Earthspan« (Island Nov. 1972) ❧ Also two solo albums during this period: Mike Heron cut »Smiling Man With Bad Reputation« (Island April 1971); Williamson replied with »Myrrh« (Island April 1972).
❧ Incredible String Band #5 ❧ November 1972 - Summer 1973
Jack Ingram
drums
Malcolm Le Maistre
vocals percussion
Mike Heron
guitar vocals
Robin Williamson
guitar • fiddle vocals • etc.
Stan Lee
bass
Gerard Dott
reeds
ex- Edinburgh jazz scene
Gerard Dott was brought in. ❧ They toured to promote »Earthspan«; roadies Stan Lee and Jack Ingram augmented the band live on bass and drums. ❧ Album: »No Ruinous Feud« (Island March 1973), the only record by this version of the ISB (with various sessioners). ❧ Stan Lee went under various noms de plume.
❧ Incredible String Band #6 ❧ Autumn 1973 - February 1974

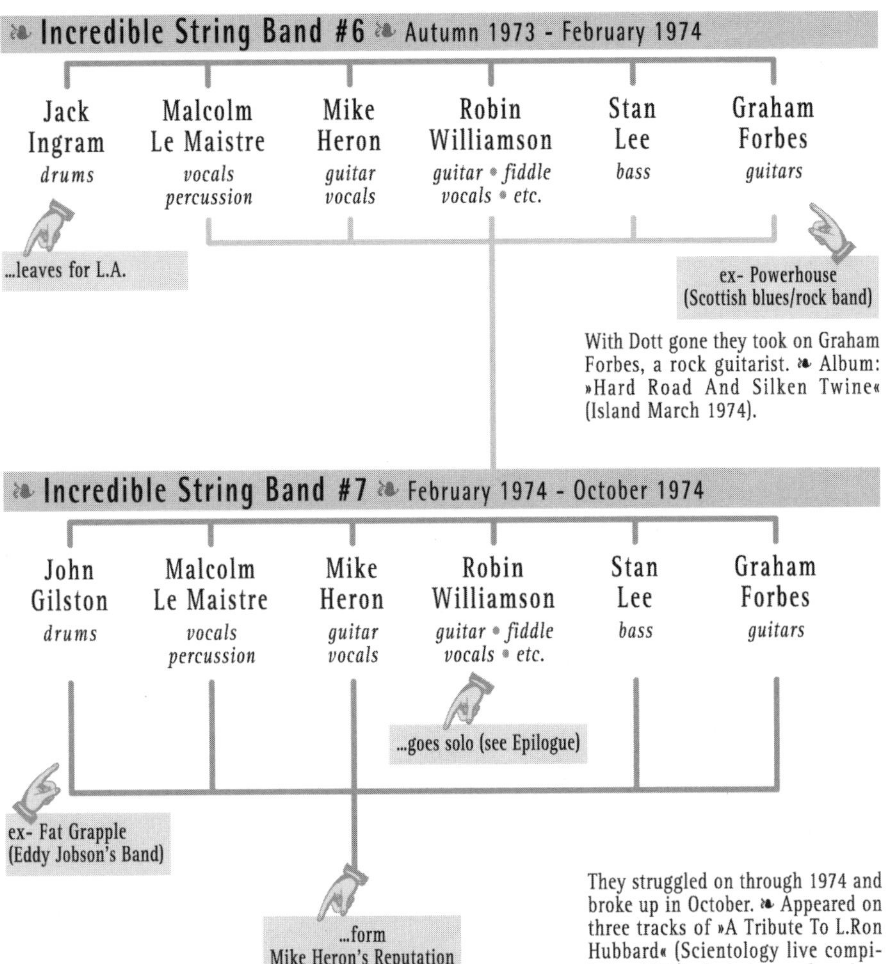

Info: Adrian & Andy ❧ Design: Mychael Gerstenberger

Strings And Things

One of the many charms of the ISB was their ability – or at least willingness – to produce interesting noises on a vast array of musical instruments, many of which originated in distant and uncomfortable parts of the world. We nodded approvingly whenever a shenai, or a sarangi, or even a soondri made an appearance in album credits, even though we could only guess wildly at what it might be or whence it came. Raymond Greenoaken guides you through over eighty ISB instruments.

Instruments are listed alphabetically; most have individual entries, though the majority of percussion instruments are gathered together under a general heading (PERCUSSION, properly enough). The coverage is confined to ISB albums and other performances (including the eight albums released after the band's demise, *Seasons They Change*, *On Air*, *In Concert*, *The Chelsea Sessions*, *First Girl I Loved*, *Across The Airwaves*, *Tricks Of The Senses*, *Live At The Fillmore 1968*, plus *Smiling Men* and *Myrrh*). Albums are designated by the initial letters of their titles, as follows:

ISB – *Incredible String Band* (first album); FTS – *5000 Spirits*; HBD – *Hangman's Beautiful Daughter*; WTATBH – *Wee Tam & The Big Huge*; CH – *Changing Horses*; ILU – *I Looked Up*; U – well, *U*; BGFTSHNE – *Be Glad For The Song Has No Ending*; SMWBR – *Smiling Men With Bad Reputations*; LAARTA – *Liquid Acrobat As Regards The Air*; M – *Myrrh*; E – *Earthspan*; NRF – *No Ruinous Feud*: HRAST – *Hard Rope And Silken Twine*; STC – *Seasons They Change*; OA – *On Air*; IC – *In Concert*; TCS – *The Chelsea Sessions*; FGIL – *First Girl I Loved*; ATA – *Across The Airwaves*; TOTS – *Tricks Of The Senses*; LFTPFF – *Live From The Philadelphia Folk Festival*.

ACCORDION, PIANO Used only once on record – on the chorus of Seagull (E) – though it turned up on Did I Love A Dream on a 1972 Peel session, included on OA, and (possibly) on the *Sounds Of The Seventies* performance of Ring Dance. It was also featured in concert on Robin's Cajun Song. Played on all occasions by Mike. (But see CONCERTINA.)

AUTOHARP A 20th century modification of the zither (see ZITHER). Approximately 30 strings are arranged across a wooden soundboard. Chord bars are attached, which, when depressed, damp all the strings except those needed to form a particular chord. It was popularised in the Thirties by the Carter Family in the USA, where it is strummed with fingerpicks. Appears briefly on the LAARTA dance tunes set, played by Licorice (with a plectrum), and on 1968 (OA), where the player is uncredited (probably Malcolm).

BANJO An American 19th century development of a primitive African lute brought across the Atlantic by slaves. Occurs principally in 4 and 5 string forms; the 5-string variety has an additional treble string tuned to G, with a tuning peg halfway up the neck. 6-string varieties were also produced, usually known as banjo-guitars and tuned accordingly. It's the 5-string banjo Robin's playing in Darling Belle (LAARTA). Also plunked by Graham Forbes on Log Cabin as featured on OA and ATA. Peter Grant played 5-string banjo on Bad Sadie Lee (U). On the first album, banjo was the sole province of Clive Palmer (Schaeffer's Jig, Ni**ertown).

BANJO, CHINESE A vernacular term encompassing various types of Chinese lute; such instruments have no direct relation with the banjo as it was developed in the United States. The instrument so designated, as played by Robin on White Bird (CH), is probably the pi'p'a, a lute – reputedly devised 2000 years ago – with four silk or gut strings and a shallow rounded back.

BODHRAN Irish circular frame drum, usually with a goatskin or – on cheaper models – a calfskin. Popular (excessively so, some might argue) in the playing of Irish dance music. Its origins are obscure. It seems at first to have been struck by the hand; latterly a single- or double-headed beater has been preferred. The name means something like 'thunderer'. In Eire the name is pronounced BOW-RON ('bow' rhyming with 'cow'); in Ulster it's pronounced BORE-AN. The ISB's preferred spelling – 'bironne' – may be an attempt at a phonetic rendering of the former. Played by Licorice on the LAARTA dance tune set, on the Bird That Lives On Rain fiddle medley (recorded for *Top Gear*) and by Robin on The Dancing Of The Lord Of Weir (M).

BASS DRUM See PERCUSSION

BASS GUITAR See GUITAR, BASS

BASS, DOUBLE The Pentangle bass-player Danny Thompson appeared on FTS and years later on HRAST (Dreams Of No Return), despite declaring publicly his unease at Mike's and Robin's sheer oddness. Concert bootlegs confirm that Stan Schnier occasionally played double bass on stage, notably (and perhaps exclusively) on Maker Of Islands.

BELLS, TUBULAR See TUBULAR BELLS

BOUZOUKI The ISB favoured the spelling 'bazooki', inviting confusion with the anti-tank weapon. A long-necked Greek lute, probably quite a recent development of the Turkish saz; it has four courses of paired strings and a rounded back. In the early Seventies it was adopted by Irish musicians and is now usually manufactured with a flat back for ease of playing while standing. It's the round-backed Greek form of the instrument played by Malcolm on Tree (LAARTA) and Robin on The Dancing Of The Lord Of Weir (M); Robin may be playing something similar on Theta, the final tune on the Song Has No Ending medley (BGFTSHNE).

BONGOES See PERCUSSION

BOWED GIMBRI See GIMBRI, BOWED

BOWED PSALTERY See PSALTERY, BOWED

CELLO First album appearance, in Robin's hands, is on LAARTA (Worlds They Rise And Fall, Red Hair) Liberally used on M, and once on E (My Father Was A Lighthouse Keeper). Robin produced a singular-looking solid-bodied electric model, made by himself and Stan Schnier, in concert in late 71 (Sunday Song, Red Hair, Painted Chariot); it was never seen, or heard, again. The *Earthspan* out-take Curlew (included on TOTS) has cello parts probably played by Stuart Gordon.

CHANTER So designated on M (Lord Of Weir). The chanter, properly, is that part of the bagpipes on which the tune is fingered. Scottish pipers tend to practise their fingering on a mouth-blown version. By extension, the term can be used of any single or double-reeded pipe, such as the Breton bombarde or the Indian shenai (see SHENAI); and perhaps it's the shenai Robin is playing on The Dancing Of The Lord Of Weir.

CHIMES See PERCUSSION

CHINESE BANJO See BANJO, CHINESE

CHINESE FLUTE See FLUTE

CHURCH ORGAN See ORGAN

CLARINET Reed instruments come in two basic forms: those with a single-reed (clarinets), and those with a double-reed (oboes or shawms – see OBOE). The Welsh pibgorn and the Scottish stockhorn, both now obsolete, are examples of indigenous folk clarinets. The classical clarinet was developed around 1700 by the German instrument maker Donner. It was occasionally played by Malcolm – on Darling Belle (LAARTA, IC) and Willow Pattern (IC) – but became an integral part of the ISB sound with the recruitment of Gerard Dott, who also laid down a clarinet part on Brindaban (SMWBR).

CLASHERS See PERCUSSION

CLAY DRUMS See PERCUSSION

CONCERTINA It's been suggested that the instrumental break in Down Before Cathay (NRF) is essayed on a concertina; neither the instrument nor its player, however, is mentioned in the credits. To my ears, it sounds like it could be an accordion.

CONCH A large tropical sea-shell used as a horn or trumpet by Pacific islanders, and by Robin on Queen Juanita And Her Fisherman Lover (STC).

CYMBALS See PERCUSSION

CYMBALS, FINGER As the name suggests, small cymbals attached to the thumb and first finger, producing the delicate chiming sound heard on Painting Box (FTS), A Very Cellular Song (HBD), White Bird (CH), and Theta, the final piece in the *Be Glad* medley (BGFTSHNE).

DOUBLE BASS See BASS, DOUBLE

DRUM, BASS See PERCUSSION

DRUM, SYRIAN According to ISB legend, Rose was presented with this drum shortly after meeting the band and invited to whack it at their prestigious Albert Hall concert the following week. She dutifully whacked – the rest is history.

DRUM, TALKING An African hour glass-shaped drum whose skin is held taut by vertical cords. By pressing the cords towards the waist of the drum, the pitch can be raised to varying degrees. Heard on Creation (CH) and Theta (BGFTSHNE).

DRUMKIT The conventional Western drumkit was developed by American jazz musicians in the early years of the century, and now underpins most forms of rhythmic, amplified ensemble music. Prior to the ISB employing a specialist drummer (Jack Ingram, on HRAST and FGIL, John Gilston on FGIL) just about everyone in the band had a shot. Robin can be heard pattering through Lordly Nightshade (WTATBH) and in the rockier sections of White Bird (CH) and Queen Juanita (STC); Licorice, often on the drum stool in concert, spanking the skins through such head banging classics as Lady Wonder and Down Before Cathay, gives her all on Bridge Theme (U). Even Mike was seen to pitch in on occasion. The ISB also lured drummers from other bands onto odd album tracks: Dave Mattacks (Fairport Convention), Gerry Conway (Fotheringay), Alun Eden (Trees), B.J. Wilson (Procol Harum) and Brian Davidson (The Nice); and SMWBR features American sessioneer Mike Kowalski – and Keith Moon! From time to time the ISB assembled less conventional kits of their own, usually consisting of ethnic drums of varying sizes. Examples can be heard on When You Find Out Who You Are (ILU), Bridge Theme and Rainbow (U) and Waiting For You (BGFTSHNE).

DRUMS, CLAY See PERCUSSION

DULCIMER, HAMMER(ED) A broad zither (see ZITHER) struck with hammers or beaters. It was introduced into Europe from the Middle East in the 11th century, and was popular among fashionable European audiences from the 17th to 19th century. It has survived as a folk instrument in many European countries, including England (where, curiously, it is largely confined to East Anglia). The prefix 'hammer(ed)' has been recently attached to distinguish it from the Appalachian dulcimer (which is actually a plucked zither rather than a true dulcimer). Mike used it to good effect on Witches Hat (HBD), and Licorice drew some suitably eerie timbres from it on Pictures In A Mirror (ILU). Last heard on the concert version of The Dancing Of The Lord Of Weir.

ELECTRIC GUITAR See GUITAR, ELECTRIC

ELECTRIC PIANO See PIANO, ELECTRIC

FIDDLE In folk circles the violin is invariably known as the fiddle, though as a taxonomic term 'fiddle' embraces the whole range of bowed instruments. Robin used fiddle throughout the band's existence, particularly in the later phase of their career; during Rose's time with the band, she occasionally 'doubled' with Robin, as on Log Cabin Home In The Sky (WTATBH) and Black Jack Davy (ILU). In 1972 Stuart Gordon recorded with the band on fiddle and viola (see VIOLA), on My Father Was A Lighthouse Keeper, Antoine and Black Jack David (E), and on a radio session that found its way onto OA (Black Jack David again); but he seems never to have been on official member of the band, or of its 'extended family'.

FIDDLE, HARDANGER A modified violin developed in the area around Hardangerfjord in Norway. Usually beautifully carved and decorated, it is fitted with four or five additional resonating strings below the melody strings to give it a keening, droning sound. Used by Robin on Banks Of Sweet Italy (E) and Curlew (TOTS).

FINGER CYMBALS See CYMBALS, FINGER

FLUTE Robin used a variety of flutes with the ISB. His flute playing is first heard on FTS (No Sleep Blues, You Know What You Could Be, Gently Tender), and the models used there are probably of North African origin, made of wood or cane. The Chinese flute (ti-tzu) is used on The Dancing Of The Lord Of Weir (M) and Sailor And The Dancer (E), and an Indian flute (probably the bansri) once, on Through The Horned Clouds (M). By 1971 Robin was also playing the metal concert flute, and on the odd song, both on record and in concert, was joined by Janet Shankman or by Susie Watson-Taylor. Mike also had a stab at the instrument in concert, performing capably on Willow Pattern and perhaps less well on Darling Belle (both IC), and made a solitary appearance on vinyl on Here Till Here Is There (LAARTA). It features in the strings and woodwinds arrangements for Queen Of Love (U) and Brindaban (SMWBR), played by session musicians. On Glancing Love (HRAST) Robin plays the lower alto flute.

FLUTE ORGAN See ORGAN, FLUTE

GIMBRI A small North African lute, more usually spelled Guinbri, commonly played with a plectrum made from a 'hard native reed' (to quote Robin); it is a popular street instrument and is associated with the Berber people. As far as can be discovered, Robin was the first person to take a bow to it (actually a double bass bow) – which is why it is sometimes prefixed 'bowed' in album credits. First heard on Chinese White (FTS), it was little used after U but made a poignant reappearance on the coda to Mike's pensive 1968 (OA) at the very end of the band's career. It's hard to say whether the 'bass gimbri' listed on Gently Tender (FTS) is a different instrument; there's a theory that it's a larger-bodied model owned by Pete Stanley, and fitted with cello strings. Robin's instrument eventually went into storage in Los Angeles, where it was, famously, eaten by rats.

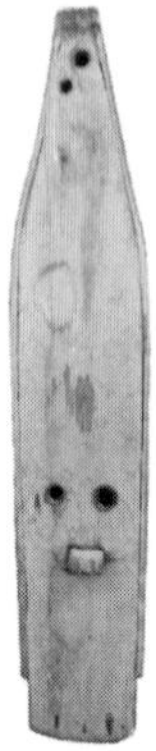

Andrew Greig: Some years ago, Mary Stewart gave me Robin's and Clive's home-made instruments which she had found in the back of a cupboard at Temple Cottage many years later, and this is one of them. She also showed me the giant Witches Hat Likky had made. And I held the odd red dragon/lobster toy her children used to play with, that Robin is holding on the *Hangman* cover! That was a bit special.

Grahame Hood adds: I remember reading about someone making instruments using cheap wooden fruit bowls which were sold in gift shops. They were probably dried African gourds. With a plain carved top glued on you had the basis of an instrument. The two holes at the top would be for violin style tuners, the bottom two sound holes, burnt with a poker? Looks like only one string over the bridge so maybe the other string was a drone. That points to it being a gimbri rather than a rebec which I think has a fingerboard. So maybe Robin made it; Clive was more of a craftsman, I think.

GLOCKENSPIEL Regarded in the West as something of a 'toy' instrument – one model was marketed in the 60s as the Pixiephone (as used by Tyrannosaurus Rex before truncation and teeny acclaim). Its sole appearance on record is on Darling Belle (LAARTA, also IC); it was also heard on the concert versions of The Dancing Of The Lord Of Weir and You Get Brighter.

GONG See PERCUSSION

GUITAR, ACOUSTIC Central, of course, to the ISB sound from their folky beginnings to the rockist posturings of their final days. Though Mike and Robin were the band's 'specialist' acoustic guitarists, almost everyone picked one up at some time or other, from Clive Palmer to Graham Forbes. Even Gerard Dott and Rose contributed modest measures of fret-fondling in live performances; to my knowledge, the only abstainee was drummer John Gilston. As with Jansch and Renbourn in Pentangle, Mike and Robin brought quite contrasting styles as guitarists. At the outset both favoured fairly intricate finger-picking techniques, but as the arrangements grew more spacious less emphasis was placed on this approach. Mike's picking style became greatly simplified around the time of HBD, and he cultivated a vigorous strumming style from WTATBH onwards. By HBD he was playing a handmade guitar by John

Bailey (whom Robin is seen visiting in the *Be Glad* film) with a highly distinctive, almost abrasive tone. His second guitar, a 'very cheap' Japanese Cavalier, was occasionally seen in concert but seems not to have found its way onto record. Pre-Bailey, he played a small-bodied Gibson, which has recently turned up again after being apparently lost for decades. Of Robin's early efforts on guitar, Wizz Jones reports that 'he was much better at the bluesy, Broonzy-style guitar stuff than any of us'. 'Us' then included the likes of Jansch, Renbourn, Archie Fisher and John Martyn, as well as Wizz himself – illustrious company! That blues influence is everywhere apparent on the first album, but by FTS an utterly new element had entered his playing. The scurrying, flat-picked arabesques on Eyes Of Fate, Painting Box and No Sleep Blues seem to draw their inspiration from the North African oud styles Robin had been studying in Morocco the previous summer. On Born In Your Town from TCS, the influence is even more plain. It's clear that at this time Robin was working to liberate guitar accompaniment from the rhythmic constraints of the ubiquitous blues-based styles. The fact is that the Irish and Arab elements in his singing require something more flexible than conventional guitar techniques; years later he was to observe that 'the harp is the instrument I should have been playing all along'. This thought may have entered his mind in the early Seventies, when he was employing a harp-like ripple effect (perhaps derived from flamenco?) on the guitar on Darling Belle (LAARTA) and Will We Open The Heavens (M). The two influences – the harp and the oud – intertwine in his playing throughout the Seventies, and it may be significant that when he took up the harp seriously his guitar playing reverted to the pure, oud-based flat-picking style. Robin's preferred guitar was a Swedish Levin, donated in the early Sixties by a friend intending to become a monk! Robin stripped the varnish from the soundboard and decorated it lovingly with coloured inks. Around the time of FTS he added attachments that imparted buzzy, sitar-like timbres to the upper strings. Robin occasionally used 12-string guitar on record – This Moment (ILU), Time (U), My Blue Tears (NRF) – and in concert; and Licorice played tenor guitar – a 4-string guitar devised in the '20s as an equivalent to the 4-string tenor banjo – on the Peruvian whistle tune featured on IC. Robin also had occasional recourse to Spanish (nylon-strung) guitar – Banks Of Sweet Italy (E) and Did I Love A Dream (OA). He also brings some flamenco stylings to El Rato, from the *U* show (TOS).

GUITAR, BASS First appeared on WTATBH, played mostly by Robin. In concert, however, the mantle fell early on Rose. Joe Boyd has offered a somewhat jaundiced account of the politics surrounding this move, but Rose's own account is more laconic: 'Mike came home one day with an electric bass and a Harvey Brooks record on how to play... and he said here you are, plug it in and get going.' True to the ISB ethos, however, everyone played it at one time or another before Stan Schnier was anointed official bassist in 1973. Dave Pegg (then with Fairport Convention), John Cale, Pat Donaldson (Fotheringay) and Ronnie Lane discharged bass duties on SMWBR.

GUITAR, ELECTRIC Earliest album appearance was on CH (Big Ted, Dust Be Diamonds, Mr And Mrs), though Robin had attached a pick-up to his Levin acoustic to approximate an electric sound on All Writ Down (BGFTSHNE), and this may be the instrument used on CH. Initially used exclusively as a lead instrument. Robin and Mike shared the duties, latterly with Jack Ingram. In their final year they drafted in Graham Forbes 'whose playing style,' *The Melody Maker* pantingly reported, 'is said to resemble Rory Gallagher's'. Simon Nicol, Richard Thompson, Pete Townshend and Jimmy Page all played electric guitar on SMWBR, though not, perhaps sadly, at the same time.

GUITAR, SPANISH See GUITAR

GUITAR, STEEL Solid-bodied electric instrument plucked with fingerpicks or plectrum while sliding a metal bar – or 'steel' – along the strings. It comes in two forms: the Hawaiian or Lap Steel guitar, which, as the name implies, is usually played resting across the knees; and the Pedal Steel guitar, which is mounted on a stand and has floor pedals and knee levers for changing string tunings during play. The Pedal Steel is an elaboration of the Hawaiian. Stan Schnier's Pedal Steel adorns the coda of Talking Of The End (LAARTA), Rends-Moi Demain (M and OA) and Sandy Land (M), and was a prominent feature in the concert arrangement of Down Before Cathay. The late Gordon Huntley played pedal steel on Make No Mistake (SMWBR, CD reissue); he was playing with Matthews' Southern Comfort at that time.

GUITAR, TENOR See GUITAR

GUITAR, 12 STRING See GUITAR

HARMONICA Both Mike and Robin played harmonica intermittently through the ISB's career – Blues For The Muse (FTS, TCS), Mercy I Cry City (HBD), Make No Mistake (SMWBR), Greatest Friend, Ducks On A Pond (WTATBH), Frutch (TCS); there's also an uncredited harmonica on Log Cabin Home In The Sky. Mike's playing is the more blues-inflected. Malcolm is featured on Darling Belle (LAARTA), playing Keep The Home Fires Burning. And of course there's Walter Gundy on Big Ted (CH).

HARMONIUM Like the Harmonica, Concertina and Accordion (see individual entries), a member of the free reed family of instruments, in which the sound is produced by air vibrating arrangements of fixed metal reeds. Resembling a small organ and fitted with a foot-operated bellows to produce the air supply, it was patented by Debain of Paris in 1848. In contrast to the organ, it has a mellow, wheezy sound. Smaller portable models with hand-operated bellows were popularised in India by Christian missionaries. It crops up in the ISB's middle period – side two medley (BGFTSHNE), Worlds They Rise And Fall, Red Hair (LAARTA), Sailor And The Dancer (E and OA). Played by Mike, Malcolm, Licorice, Joe Boyd (on BGFTSHNE – his only instrumental credit, consisting of two two-fingered chords) and John Cale – Audrey, Beautiful Stranger (SMWBR).

HARP In the Eighties the harp became Robin's main solo instrument. 'I bought a harp in the Sixties, went to Dublin on the boat from Wales... a little one, and tootled around with it for a while, but I didn't really take it up seriously till 79.' Used for 'harp effects' on The Circle Is Unbroken and The Iron Stone (WTATBH), in the latter instance by Licorice. Classical harpist David Snell plays an orchestral harp (scored by Dolly Collins) on Waltz Of The New Moon (HBD). An anonymous harpist plays on Queen Of Love (U).

HARP, JEW'S see JEW'S HARP

HARP, WATER A small African harp, its soundbox filled with water, plunked by Robin on Water Song (HBD). This produces a muffled 'rubber-band' sort of sound.

HARPSICHORD A plucked-string keyboard instrument; depressing a key causes a quill to pluck an adjacent string. This produces a brighter, crisper sound than a piano, in which the strings are struck by hammers. The first successful examples were made in Italy in the 16th century. The harpsichord is arguably one of the defining sounds of HBD – played by Mike on Witches Hat, A Very Cellular Song and Waltz Of The New Moon. Only occasionally used thereafter – You Get Brighter (WTATBH), played by Robin, The Letter (ILU), by Mike, Queen Of Love (U), by Janet Shankman, and Talking Of The End (LAARTA), by Malcolm.

HI-HAT Two cymbals on a stand, clashed together by means of a foot pedal. A feature of the Western drumkit. Used by Stan Schnier on Black Jack David (E, OA, FGIL), while simultaneously playing bass.

JEW'S HARP Or Jaw's Harp. Consists of a flexible tongue cut out of, or attached to, a small frame, usually of bamboo or metal. An extremely ancient instrument, found worldwide and not especially associated with Jews. The tongue projects at one end and is plucked by a finger (or occasionally a cord) while the frame is held against the teeth. The basic pitch (or fundamental) can be modified by altering the shape of the mouth, though the fundamental continues to sound, giving a droning effect. Used by Robin on A Very Cellular Song and Koeeoaddi There (HBD), and The Dancing Of The Lord Of Weir (M), and by PJ Money on Spirit Beautiful (SMWBR), where it is given its South Indian name, MOORSING.

KAZOO A novelty instrument consisting of a simple (usually plastic) tube and a thin membrane positioned over a lateral hole. The membrane is vibrated by any vocal sound made by the player, giving a characteristic buzzing effect. Children's kazoo marching bands are a popular and alarming phenomenon in N.E. England. The kazoo was used by American jug bands in the Twenties and Thirties; the ISB have often acknowledged their jug band influences. Used by Robin on A Very Cellular Song (HBD), Ducks On A Pond (WTATBH) and Evolution Rag, by Malcolm and Licorice on Evolution Rag (LAARTA) and by Licorice on Dust Be Diamonds and Creation (CH). Also used on the *Be Glad* medley (BGFTSHNE), where it is uncredited, and on I Know That Man (IC, FGIL) – either Robin or Malcolm, I'd say, in the latter instance, and Licorice in the former. Lastly – or firstly, depending on your point of view – Clive Palmer played it on Everything's Fine Right Now (ISB).

MANDOLIN Celebrated – and occasionally derided – for its delicate tinkling tones, the mandolin has been popular in European folk and popular music from the 18th century onwards. In 20th century America it spawned mandolin bands, featuring larger versions of itself – mandola, mandocello and mandobass. It appears on most ISB albums, usually played by Robin, occasionally by Mike (Creation (CH), Fairies' Hornpipe (U), Witches Hat (OA)), Malcolm (Painted Chariot and dance tune medley (LAARTA), Black Jack David (E, OA, FGIL), Willow Pattern (IC)), and once by Licorice (Waiting For You (BGFTSHNE)). Rose had a shot too, in concert and on radio sessions (Won't You Come See Me). An anonymously played mandolin features in Queen Of Love (U).

MARIMBA A Central American xylophone (see XYLOPHONE). There is an orchestral marimba, essentially a deeper-voiced version of the orchestral xylophone. Its solitary appearance on an ISB album is on 1968 (OA), played by John Gilston.

MOORSING see JEW'S HARP

MOUTH ORGAN see HARMONICA

MRIDANGAM South Indian double-headed cylindrical drum, the equivalent of the North Indian tabla (see TABLA). Played on Spirit Beautiful (SMWBR), by PJ Money.

OBOE A generic term for the family of double-reed instruments – as distinct from the single-reed Clarinets (see CLARINET). Folk oboes or shawms are usually loud and shrill, and thus better suited for outdoor use, though quieter versions evolved during the Renaissance, cf. crumhom, Rauschpfeife. The orchestral oboe was developed in the 17th century, probably by the Hotteterre family in France. Robin used assorted folk oboes with the ISB, notably the shenai and Chinese shawm or sona (see individual entries); eventually he introduced the orchestral version, as on Worlds They Rise And Fall, Painted Chariot and Darling Belle (LAARTA), Sunday Song (E) and Explorer (NRF), Secret Temple (ATA, TOTS) and on much of M. Lower-pitched relations of the orchestral oboe – the Cor Anglais and the bassoon – are a feature of the score for Queen Of Love (U).

ONDES MARTENOT An electronic instrument devised by Maurice Martenot and popular in the Thirties, revived recently by Jonny Greenwood. It produced musical tones by means of oscillating frequencies via a keyboard and a ring moved along a wire. Specially hired by the band for use in Queen Juanita And Her Fisherman Lover (TOS); probably played by Mike.

ORGAN, CHURCH The church organs on Darling Belle (LAARTA) and Antoine (E) were recorded on location, in a church across the street from the studio. Played by Malcolm (with Robin on foot pedals) and Mike respectively.

ORGAN, ELECTRIC Omnipresent both on record and in concert; almost everybody had a stab at it at one time or another. Rose's demure one-fingered technique is preserved for public gaze on a German TV *Beat Club* recording of Everything's Fine Right Now.
ORGAN, PIPE A scaled-down version of the church organ; the air is blown through the pipes by an electric motor. Also known as the flute organ. Played by Licorice on Red Hair (LAARTA), and by Dolly Collins – who pioneered the instrument – on Water Song (HBD) and God Dog (TCS).

OUD A short-necked Middle Eastern lute, the prototype of the European Renaissance lute. The word lute is derived from the Arabic al'ud. Robin studied oud playing while in North Africa in 1966, and brought one back to Britain. As discussed above, his plectrum guitar style is plainly influenced by oud styles. Heard on You Know What You Could Be (FTS), Swift As The Wind (HBD), Talking Of The End (LAARTA), and Ithkos (HRAST, FGIL).

PANPIPES Also known as the Syrinx. An arrangement of graduated pipes joined together in a raft or bunch shape. The sound is produced by blowing obliquely across the tops of the pipes. As the name implies, the instrument is associated with the Greek demigod Pan. The nymph Syrinx, fleeing Pan's amorous advances, disguised herself in the shape of a reed – but to no avail: he made the reed into the first syrinx and played upon it, we're told, for consolation. In fact the instrument was developed independently in most parts of the world. It makes a solitary appearance in Witches Hat (HBD), deftly and hauntingly played by Robin.

PENNY WHISTLE see WHISTLE

PERCUSSION The ISB employed a dauntingly vast and variegated array of percussion devices in the course of its career. Almost everyone, sooner or later, was called upon to shake, rattle, slap or bring objects into violent contact with each other. There are far too many, indeed, to allow each a separate entry here; instead, I shall simply list as many as I can confidently identify. (A few have entries of their own, either because of some particular significance they hold in the history of the band, or because of pure caprice on my part.) On album credits they are invariably referred to simply as 'percussion'. Of all the ISB albums, only the first is entirely innocent of percussion – unless you agree with 19th century musicologists, who classified the banjo as a percussion instrument! Afterwards the following were used, roughly in order of their first appearance:

Finger cymbals, scraper, mallet and tube, clay bongos (naqquara), gourd rattle or shaker, tambourine, thumb piano (sansa – see SANSA), small bells (jingles, pallet bells, clapper bells), sticks (claves), tympani (see TYMPANI), pail of water (see WATER, PAIL OF), washboard (see WASHBOARD), talking drum (see TALKING DRUM), Syrian drum (see SYRIAN DRUM), chimes, drumkit – conventional and customised (see DRUMKIT), tabla (see TABLA), bass drum, tall pottery drum, gongs, cymbals, wooden rattle, spoons (see SPOONS), mridangam (see MRIDANGAM), clashers (quaquaal), bodhran (see BODHRAN), glockenspiel (see GLOCKENSPIEL), hi-hat (see HI-HAT), snare drum, mouth percussion, vibraphone (see VIBRAPHONE), congas, tubular bells (see TUBULAR BELLS), marimba (see MARIMBA) and perhaps xylophone (see XYLOPHONE).

Evidence trawled from radio sessions, concert recordings and memories, and the *Be Glad* film, suggests that this list could be extended to include wooden bongos, temple bells, assorted hand drums, rommelpot (see ROMMELPOT), the Irish lambeg marching drum, domestic utensils, feet. Let's not omit handclaps: their use on Bid You Goodnight in A Very Cellular Song (HBD, OA) to simulate the rapid pattering of drums is novel and effective; Mike and Robin reprised the combination on Shirley Collins' *The Power Of The True Love Knot.*

PIPE ORGAN see ORGAN, PIPE

PIANO In the Sixties the piano was not seen as a 'folky' instrument, and this may in part explain why neither Mike nor Robin resorted to it on the first two albums. John 'Hoppy' Hopkins, of course, contributed a bluesy piano part to The Mad Hatter's Song (FTS). Keyboards were much in evidence on HBD, though Mike stuck to organ and harpsichord until CH (Big Ted). There is debate as to whether it was Robin or Dolly Collins tinkling the ivories on The Minotaur's Song and A Very Cellular Song. My own guess is that Dolly played on the former and Robin the latter. Elsewhere in the discography the credits are clearer. From ILU onwards Mike assumed the bulk of keyboard duties. Gerard Dott played piano on Circus Girl (NRF), and often essayed a ragtime piece in concert. He renders one such piece, Swipesy Cakewalk, on FGIL – but this is on electric piano (see PIANO, ELECTRIC). Licorice played piano on her own Secret Temple (TOTS). Janet Shankman played piano on Will We Open The Heavens (M). Other guest pianists include Ivan Pawle on Creation (CH), Dudu Pukwana on Call Me Diamond (SMWBR), John Cale on Feast Of Stephen and – notoriously – Beautiful Stranger (SMWBR), and Elton John on Make No Mistake (SMWBR, Island CD reissue).

PIANO, ELECTRIC Often used in concert, rarely on record. Mike plays it on Adam And Eve (LAARTA), Audrey (SMWBR), and My Father Was A Lighthouse Keeper and Restless Night (E), Robin on The Actor (E), and Gerard Dott (at a guess) on the radio session version of Little Girl (OA).

PIANO, TACK Tacks or drawing pins were often pressed into the hammers of upright pianos to achieve a tinny, 'bar-room' timbre – the classic Wild West saloon piano sound. Used by Mike on Bad Sadie Lee (U).

PIANO, THUMB Or Sansa. An African plucked instrument consisting of a number of metal or split cane tongues arranged across a wood board or box resonator. The tongues are plucked by the thumbs, hence the name. It may be a sansa that Robin plays on Koeeoaddi There (HBD) – or it may be a sort of xylophone (see XYLOPHONE).

PSALTERY, BOWED The psaltery is a medieval board zither (see ZITHER), descended from the Middle Eastern qanun. Historically it is played with the fingertips or a plectrum; however, in the Sixties the folk musician Barry Dransfield took a bow to it and produced a keening, ethereal sound that has delighted listeners ever since (and offended not a few, it has to be said). Used by Licorice in the concert arrangement of Painted Chariot (1971).

RATTLE: See PERCUSSION

RECORDER: A renaissance fipple flute or whistle flute (see WHISTLE), revived in the early 20th century by Arnold Dolmetsch, chiefly for use in schools. It comes in a variety of sizes, from the sopranino to the great bass. The descant is the most popular and easily playable of the range. Rose and Licorice play some frankly shaky descant and treble lines on Come With Me (BGFTSHNE); Robin plays bass and Malcolm tenor on Here Till Here Is There (LAARTA).

ROMMELPOT A friction drum, with a stick piercing the drum-skin. Pulling the stick up and down, or rubbing it between the hands, causes the skin to vibrate, producing a sound that – to my ears at least – imitates a flatulent bullfrog. If my memory serves me fairly, it was used by Mike in the concert arrangement of The Dancing Of The Lord Of Weir (1971). There is an Indian equivalent, the ektara.

SANSA See PIANO, THUMB

SARANGI A squat, box-like North Indian fiddle (see FIDDLE) with three or four bowed strings and a variable number of sympathetic (freely resonating) strings. It is said in India to be the instrument that most closely approximates the human voice. Its swooping, ululating sound is used to thrilling effect by Robin on Yellow Snake (WTATBH); the *Be Glad* medley (BGFTSHNE), and – especially – White Bird (CH). On the CH instrumental credits it is mistakenly called sarang, which properly speaking is a Kashmiri folk fiddle resembling a scaled down sarangi.

SAXOPHONE The newest member of the single-reed Clarinet family (see CLARINET), invented in about 1840 by the Belgian Adolphe Sax. Comes in various sizes, ranging from the squeaky sopranino to the mighty subcontrabass. It is only the mid-range – soprano, alto, tenor, baritone – that is heard in mainstream rock and jazz. The sax arrived in the ISB with Gerard Dott and Jack Ingram; NRF is the only album on which it is played by band members (Old Buccaneer, Weather The Storm). On SMWBR Dudu Pukwana turns in some ferocious solos on Call Me Diamond, with the Brotherhood Of Breath horn section, augmented by Osibisa's Teddy Osei, joining him for some ripe fills; anonymous session players play on Mike's horn arrangement for Restless Night on E. Late concert arrangements of Mike's unrecorded Ladies/Lowlands featured Gerard and Jack on sax duty.

SEA MACHINE Want to evoke the sounds of surf and breaking waves? Try the Sea Machine! The band hired it from a catalogue, expecting a modestly-sized device. It turned out to be a huge wooden trough, loaded with pebbles to which water was added and the whole thing upended. Crude but effective – and possibly very messy. On Queen Juanita And Her Fisherman Lover (TOS).

SHAKER See PERCUSSION.

SHAWM, CHINESE A succinct descriptive term for the sona, a popular Chinese folk oboe or shawm (see OBOE, CHANTER). Robin plays massed sonas on the *Be Glad* medley (BGFTSHNE).

SHENAI Variously spelt shanai, chahanai on ISB album credits. The word, in one form or another, occurs throughout Asia and North Africa as the name of a folk oboe or shawm (see OBOE); the Chinese sona and the soondri (see SHAWM, CHINESE and SOONDRI) are two such variants. The shenai is a North Indian shawm, only recently (and begrudgingly) admitted into classical music. Robin plays shenai on Three Is A Green Crown (HBD), Partial Belated Overture and Bridge Theme (U), and – possibly – on The Dancing Of The Lord Of Weir (M) (but see CHANTER).

SITAR A North Indian long-necked lute with five to seven melody strings and up to 13 sympathetic strings, played with a plectrum attached to the first finger. Undoubtedly the best known Indian instrument owing to its vogue in the Sixties and its introduction into pop music by George Harrison and Brian Jones. Many fans feel that the guitar/sitar combination is the quintessential ISB sound. Its first appearance was on FTS, in the hands of Nazir Jairazbhoy; thereafter, Mike made it his own and played it on most albums up to and including LAARTA, after which it made a solitary appearance on Dreams of No Return (HRAST). After the ISB's demise in 1974 he reportedly sold it through *Exchange And Mart*. Historically, the sitar is a North Indian development of the vina (see VINA); it has a larger, deeper relative, the surbahar, which unlike the sitar is little played nowadays.

SITAR, VOICE Asked about this mysterious instrument in a November 1970 issue of *The Melody Maker*, the ISB spilled the beans. 'A voice sitar is a flat board about 4ft long fitted with the same number of strings as the drone strings on a sitar and it includes an electric pick-up and a sending device, enabling you to feed any sound into the instrument, which will vibrate the sympathetic strings. The vibration is picked up and fed back out of the instrument. This is what was done with piano and violin on Invocation [U]. Our voice sitar is the only one of its kind in the world and was made by an American named Greg Heet. We happened to hear it while in the States and asked if we could buy it.' All that needs to be added is that Robin's voice was, of course, also put through the instrument, giving it that wonderfully eerie, oracular quality. After Invocation, the voice sitar was never used again by the band. Theirs was the prototype, and Heet reportedly never made another. He did, however, go on to become famous as the inventor of the EBow guitar gizmo.

SONA see SHAWM, CHINESE

SOONDRI The soondri was played by Robin on Bridge Theme and Rainbow (U). He has described it as a small Indian folk oboe (see OBOE). The word is obviously cognate with shenai and sona (see SHENAI; SHAWM, CHINESE); it sounds like it might be a South Indian form.

SPOONS Two spoons can produce a busy, cheerful rhythm when bounced against the other arm, or the thigh – even the head, in the case of some extrovert performers. Originally an accompaniment to American minstrel tunes, now commonly used for jigs, reels, etc. Licorice rattles them winningly on Hirem Pawnitof and Fairies' Hornpipe (U) and the dance tune medley on LAARTA.

STEEL GUITAR see GUITAR, STEEL.

SYNTHESISER Nowadays ubiquitous in popular music, the synthesiser came in two comparatively primitive forms in the late Sixties and early Seventies – the Moog and the VCS. Both were monophonic – that is, only one note could be played at a time. Synth boffin Tony Cox piloted the VCS through Beautiful Stranger (SMWBR) and At The Lighthouse Dance (NRF); Stan Schnier produced a brief blast of Moog at the end of Ithkos (HRAST), though he's credited only with Moog programming – an obscure distinction, which may mean that Mike did the actual playing. He definitely did the playing in concert performances (FGIL), as well as on the unreleased instrumental Jack Straw's Wishes.

SYRIAN DRUM see DRUM,SYRIAN

SYRINX See PANPIPES

SWANEE WHISTLE see WHISTLE, SWANEE

STRINGS String arrangements were an occasional feature of ISB albums from LAARTA onwards. Needless to say these were executed by anonymous classical musicians, aside from Robin's multi-tracking efforts on Worlds They Rise And Fall (LAARTA), My Father Was A Lighthouse Keeper (E – abetted by Stuart Gordon) and Dark Dance (M). The scores were invariably the work of Mike. An aside from Rose: 'When I was in the band, Mike and Robin laughed together at the people who attempted to score their songs. I remember they were looking at Happy Traum's work in the first songbook and they both said it was wrong and impossibly difficult to play, dismissing it.'

TABLA The collective name for the combination of cylindrical drum (tabla) and conical drum (banya), the latter tuned lower than the former, that underpins most North Indian classical music. The mridangam, a double-headed cylindrical drum, is the South Indian equivalent (see MRIDANGAM). Used, it seems, mainly by Rose – The Iron Stone (WT ABH), El Wool Suite (U) and the *Be Glad* medley (BGFTSHNE). Her rudimentary technique – classical tabla technique is astonishingly sophisticated – can be studied in the performance of The Iron Stone on the *Be Glad* film.

TACK PIANO see PIANO,TACK

TAMBOURA Four stringed fretless Indian lute, used exclusively for sounding a continuous tonic chord for an instrumental or vocal recital – in other words, a drone. The first notes on *U* – the opening bars of El Wool Suite – are played upon an uncredited tamboura, possibly by Licorice. Licorice can be seen playing tamboura on The Iron Stone on the *Be Glad* film; she also stroked it on Fine Fingered Hands (ATA). Also played by Nazir Jarazbhoy on The Mad Hatter's Song (FTS) and Vshailendra on Spirit Beautiful (SMWBR).

TAMBOURINE see PERCUSSION

TALKING DRUM see DRUM, TALKING

TIN WHISTLE see WHISTLE

TROMBONE A feature of the brass arrangements on Moon Hang Low (E) and Circus Girl (NRF), played by studio sessioneers.

TRUMPET The trumpet is featured as part of the brass arrangements on Moon Hang Low (E) and Circus Girl (NRF), and on Moon Hang Low there's a lovely, deliquescent trumpet solo, executed anonymously and scored by Robin. The ensemble trumpet parts for Beautiful Stranger (SMWBR) were arranged by John Cale.

TUBA Featured in the brass arrangement for Circus Girl (NRF); player unknown.

TUBULAR BELLS A series of brass or steel tubes of varying lengths suspended from a frame and struck with hammers. Famed, of course, for their use in Mike Oldfield's record of the same name. Each tube is tuned to a standard pitch. Played – we know not by whom – on Queen Juanita And Her Fisherman Lover (TOS) and by Mike on Ducks On A Pond (WTATBH).

TYMPANI Large orchestral kettledrums, tunable to specific pitches. Used by Robin on Waltz Of The New Moon (HBD).

VIBRAPHONE Or, more briefly, vibes. An orchestral xylophone (see XYLOPHONE) equipped with sound-modifying electric fans, which produce a characteristic warm vibrato effect. Played by Mike on Dust Be Diamonds (CH) and Gerard Dott on Little Girl (NRF).

VINA Sometimes spelt veena. A sophisticated Indian form of stick zither (see ZITHER). In India, the stick zither evolved into two main forms: the vichitra vina of North India and the South Indian fretted vina, which resembles a sitar and is played in roughly the same way (see SITAR). The fretted vina has fewer sympathetic strings than the sitar and has therefore a mellower, less buzzy sound. Played by Vemu Mukanda and Mohana Lakshmipathy on Spirit Beautiful (SMWBR).

VIOLIN see FIDDLE

VIOLA Larger – and until Mozart and Haydn, relatively neglected – form of the violin (see FIDDLE). It has an attractive, rich tone, almost cello-like in its lower register. Occasionally used by Robin – The Actor (E), My Blue Tears (NRF) – and by Stuart Gordon on E (My Father Was A Lighthouse Keeper, Antoine).

VOICE SITAR see SITAR, VOICE

WASHBOARD The old-fashioned domestic washboard was a popular percussion instrument in American jug bands and Old Timey outfits. Usually played with thimbles, it was sometimes fitted with horns, cowbells and small cymbals. Played by Mike on Log Cabin Home In The Sky and Ducks On A Pond (WTATBH), by Robin on Big Ted (CH) and Bad Sadie Lee (U) (you can hear the cymbal), and by Malcolm on I Know That Man (IC, FGIL).

WATER HARP see HARP, WATER

WATER, PAIL OF The celebrated pail of water, as flawlessly played by Robin (or was it Rose and Likky?), is of course a crucial part of the arrangement of Water Song (HBD).

WHISTLE As a category, the whistle or whistle flute is an end-blown flute with a sharp-edged hole just below the mouthpiece – the fipple, so-called. This enables a note to be blown with more ease than with a flute, where the air must be directed across a hole or notch at a precise angle. Whistles are found throughout the world, made of bone, clay, wood, cane and latterly metal. The recorder (see RECORDER) is perhaps the most commonly played of modern whistle flutes, though the penny whistle or tin whistle – much used in British and Irish traditional music – now rivals it in popularity. Robin played whistle throughout the band's lifetime, and later wrote an instructional book for the instrument. On Mercy I Cry City (HBD) he memorably plays whistle and harmonica simultaneously. The whistle used on the first album is allegedly Indian, so may be of wood or cane. Malcolm also played whistle (Adam And Eve, Eyes Like Leaves (LAARTA), Banks Of Sweet Italy (E), Sailor And The Dancer, Witches Hat (OA), and, in duet with Robin, on Whistle Tune (IC). Licorice is shown lifting a whistle purposefully to her lips in a couple of publicity shots, but to my knowledge she played it only on a Radio One session performance of Beautiful Stranger (ATA).

WHISTLE, SWANEE A novelty whistle without fingerholes; the pitch is altered by means of a plunger, rather in the way of a trombone. The effect is unavoidably comic. Played by Robin on Queen Juanita And Her Fisherman Lover (TOS) and Lover Man (TOS); it makes an uncredited appearance on Weather The Storm, played either by Robin or (my guess) Malcolm (NRF). It also turned up on late concert versions of Everything's Fine Right Now, probably played by Malcolm.

XYLOPHONE An arrangement of tuned wood bars on a frame that are hit by hammers. There are orchestral versions, including the marimba and vibraphone (see individual entries), but it may he a simple African folk xylophone Robin plays on Koeeoaddi There (HBD) – if indeed it is not a thumb piano (see PIANO, THUMB).

ZITHER A group of instruments with strings that run the entire length of the body and parallel to it. Zithers take a variety of forms, some of which are ancestral to the lute family (see SITAR, VINA). The psaltery, autoharp and hammered dulcimer (see individual entries) are board zithers, as is the toy instrument Mike is seen plucking in concert footage in the *Be Glad* film. The Pirate And The Crystal Ball soundtrack also features a plucked zither, probably played by Robin. It's not included in the *Be Glad* medley (BGFTSHNE).

Bert's blood & the midnight chord

Robin offers some instrumental anecdotes

Here Robin sheds some fascinating light on his practice of playing every instrument devised by human hand. The vast variety of instruments used by the ISB in their heyday was integral to the band's mystique and is undoubtedly part of their enduring legacy. On the folk scene, certainly, mastery of only one instrument is nowadays regarded as something of an oddity, a sign of either obsessive devotion or a singular lack of ambition. Expanding the possibilities of music was what the ISB were always about, and multi-instrumentality was a particularly exciting aspect of that. And although all members of the band, at least up to 1972 or thereabouts, picked up whatever was to hand, it's an area in which Robin was always perceived as the motivating force. Raymond Greenoaken met him in 2000 and wondered how it all came about...

Robin: There were two waves to it. There was the Edinburgh junkshop wave, 'cause you could find all kinds of stuff in junkshops left over from colonial times, in the way of gongs and bells and so on. But the next big wave was finding a shop in New York which stocked instruments from all over the world. The grandson of the original owner still runs it in Greenwich Village to this day. And that was where a lot of my things came from, and also from places round about Central London and elsewhere. The percussion came from London. The Chinese reed stuff came from San Francisco – I used to hunt around Chinatown and see what there was.

Raymond: Were you just hoovering up whatever caught your fancy?

Just hoovering up, yes. That's been my theory all along.

Legend has it that you brought an impressive pile of exotic instruments back from Morocco in 1966.

A very small pile, really. There was just the gimbri and a pair of small hand drums...and a few flutes. Just what you could carry in a knapsack, really. Plus the oud, which you couldn't carry in a knapsack. But basically I only brought back from Morocco what I could carry.

Had you taken a bow to the gimbri while in Morocco, or was that a later innovation?

Later. It was after I began playing the sarangi, which I used a big bow for; though for the gimbri I always used a double bass bow.

Did you use exotic instruments simply to achieve specific effects in performance, or did you actually play them for recreation?

Oh yeah. We used to sit round and play them for sport, right enough. But the fact of the matter is this, that certain instruments you have to be born and raised to. I really believe this. One of them's the sitar, and another's the oud. I don't think that anyone could really play the oud that didn't grow up in an oud-playing culture. That's why the harp is so great for me, because it goes right back into the ancestral corpuscles; whereas the oud, wonderful though it is, will always be a very exotic instrument from the land of the Arabian Nights. The oud goes even further back than that, through ancient Persia and right back to dynastic Egypt, long long ago. But it's somebody else's ancestry, you see.

You need to feel a sense of cultural connection with an instrument?

Well, I feel that now, but in the old days I was quite happy to have a go at anything. But that's why you can't take it to any great depth, because to all intents and purposes you're making noises on something rather than playing it to its full potential.

Did you ever pick up the sitar?

No, never. I didn't see the need, because Mike seemed to have it covered pretty well. He did some pretty nice things on the sitar. I wish he'd pick it up again.

You took to playing what looked like a solid-bodied electric cello on the Autumn 1971 tour. You played it on Sunday Song, but as far as I know you never featured it again. What's the story?

It's one that I made myself, using an old cello neck.

It looked pretty space-age...

Ha! It was! Pretty Trekky... It was painted purple. I made a couple of electric violins out of various odds and ends, too. There was one that was painted red, and another that was painted green. They had various electronic innards, tone controls and the like.

So there was a whole armamentarium that we never saw...

Well, I was always collecting bits and pieces that you could make things out of. There were bags and boxes, drawers full of bits and pieces. I'm a magpie. Some of these things have recently come into play again in such [*later solo*] projects as *Ring Dance* and *Dream Journals*. They get dug out. The oud came out again recently to play on *Dream Journals*. I'd dig out the gimbri except the rats ate it!

That's a sad tale. Pete Stanley [banjo wizard and sidekick of Wizz Jones in the mid Sixties] *said that you stayed at his house – where he maintained his sizeable collection of gimbris, still extant – during the recording of* 5000 Spirits, *and thinks that you may have used one or other of them on the album. True or false?*

Robin gets to grips with yet another weird instrument, 1968. (Peter Neal)

Mmmm...I don't think so. Well, he may be right, but I can't recall it. But I do remember staying at his house, and sleeping in this room with all manner of banjos hanging on the wall, and one night one of them made this extraordinary noise – Plingg! – all by itself. So I got up, and I fingered it, and there was no way that noise could have been made in that tuning – it was a chord. There was no open chord on any of the banjos. It was a fourth or fifth position chord, and it played entirely by itself, and I thought, 'My, that's great!'

The force was with you! But still with gimbris... The so-called bass gimbri on Spirits: Pete surmises it might have been one of his that you fitted out with cello strings.

Jesus, I can't remember anything about that... Maybe that was one of his. It might have been a bigger one than what I had. They do come in various sizes.

The gimbri and the sitar sort of defined the exotic quality of String Band music in the late Sixties, but the legendary Levin guitar, decorated with intricate coloured designs, ran them close. Tell us a bit about it.

A guy called Barney had the guitar originally, and then he decided to give it to me. He was going to become a monk, though later he didn't become a monk, but by that time he'd given the guitar away. So that guitar was used by me and Bert [Jansch] when we were sharing rooms. The inside of it has still got the evidence of a nosebleed that Bert once had, which all went inside the guitar. There are large brown blotches inside the guitar to this day, which are actually Bert Jansch's blood! As for the painting... Well, I stripped the polish from the front, and covered it with various kinds of ink and crayon designs, but they didn't last past the repairs that John Bailey did in the early Seventies. He just took them off! I'd rather he had kept them on, really.

Why the repairs? Just general wear and tear?

General wear and tear, yeah... I glued bits of piano keys on it at one point. There used to be pianos lying around rusting on tips. And of course the ivory all falls off, and you can take it away with you. I had bags of it!

The Levin was retired from active service around 1972. Any particular reason?

It was devilishly hard to tune, always, even with new pegs and so on. I got the Gibson Dove at that time, which was a bit easier to tune. I just figured it was time to get a new guitar. It had its various charms, the Levin, but it was very hard to actually operate because it buzzed and hummed and rattled...

> *I thought that was intentional!*

Well, it did buzz intentionally on the bridge, but it buzzed unintentionally nearly everywhere else...

> *An instrument you used once and never again, and which has engendered a good deal of interest and speculation, was the voice sitar, as featured on Invocation on* U. *What's the story behind that?*

There was an extraordinary guy I bumped into in, I think, San Francisco. Greg Heet was his name. He was an electronics wizard. He thought up a number of things that later were used to greater or lesser success. This was in the days before the microchip got going, of course. He was still doing things with wiring, and one of the things he invented was the EBow, which was a thing you could put on the guitar strings and it

Bert's blood not visible – the Levin, 1968. (Peter Neal)

would give you instant sustain. But you had to hold it in your hand, and pick like this [*demonstrates*], and it would give you instant and unending sustain. So that was a minor success, but rapidly replaced by various boxes which you operate with your feet. He had a couple of other things at the time. He invented a drone that went round and round forever, a kind of wooden box powered by a battery and which had strings, and once you set the strings going they would just continue in endless feedback. And the other thing was the voice sitar, which you plugged inside the centre of a piano... which was quite a nice idea, quite an interesting sound. You wouldn't think of doing it that way now; you'd do it in some other way with algorithms... It could only be used on the piano, and it was used in the studio. I didn't own it and he never developed it, it was a prototype. I did own one of his drone boxes, but God knows what became of it. I've still got an EBow somewhere as well.

The Words and Tune are None of my Own

Robin Bynoe

Some time ago a yoga group started using the chant at the end of A Very Cellular Song. Encouraged, they recorded it and sold the CD. I believe that they had found it on *Hangman* but assumed that it was traditional, in other words that Mike Heron had in his turn found it and incorporated it into the song. There is also, after all, the long 'I bid you goodnight' section in the same piece, which includes material previously used, if no more than that, by Joseph Spence, and which in turn was performed and recorded by the Grateful Dead, who assert that both words and music are traditional. It never occurred to me that the 'Longtime Sun' section might be anything other than ancient. That of course was the way we thought in those days. 'Come let us build the ship of the future / In an ancient pattern that journeys far.' It's the ancient pattern, natch.

Mike Heron's publishers took exception. It's Mike's original composition, they said; it's a breach of his copyright. To the surprise of many, including no doubt the apprentice lawyers sent off to inspect Vedic texts on the office computer, the words did not predate his composition, and the yoga people made financial recompense, apologising, I imagine, through gritted if blissful teeth.

Copyright law cannot be described as anything other than tricky. This is because it is designed to be enforced by any available judge, and the bottom ten percent of the judiciary, reflecting society as a whole, are cloth-eared. These are the basics, though there are many complications and exceptions.

There is separate copyright in the words and music to a song. This starts out belonging to the writers, but for commercial reasons they will have sold it to a publishing company, which exploits the song and shares the money earned with the writers. The publisher will be able to enforce the rights whatever the writer thinks. The individual Beatles were delighted, for example, to have Neil Innes parody their songs for *The Rutles*, but their publishers nevertheless exacted their pound of flesh.

When it comes to tunes, the law concentrates on sequences of notes. The unique timbres of a singer like Mike Heron or Tom Waits can be electronically reproduced these days but are not protected by copyright. Likewise, the law has difficulty getting to grips with harmony, let alone instrumentation. Some of the most bitter rows in the history of rock music have arisen because of how copyright attaches to the simple notes of a tune and not what lies beneath, the essence in most cases of the music. Levon Helm went to his death convinced that Robbie Robertson had stolen from him; the below-the-title Wailers went to law because they said that it was their sound that conquered the world, not just Bob Marley's words and tunes. That does not however concern us directly; with Mike and Robin it all came out in the wash: Mike's sitar on Robin's songs, the fiddle on Mike's.

There is a further copyright in the recorded track. As often as not, the record company owns this. It has come into its own as a money-spinner in this age of sampling. Three other points need to be mentioned. Copyright dies seventy years after the writer's death: so traditional stuff is fair game, but it has to be quite traditional. Secondly, in the mechanics of popular music, publishing income is where the real money is to be found, and it goes on reliably for decades. Robbie Robertson became rich; Garth Hudson, who wrote no songs but without whose unique instrumental contribution The Band would not have sounded as it did, went repeatedly bankrupt. Mick Jagger has real estate in the best part of the Caribbean; Charlie Watts had nice suits. Thirdly, it is worth the cost of a lawyer only if there is money around.

Way back in the 1960s, those were the rules too. However, there were very few copyright lawyers then, and as a result many ambulances went unchased. Things were freer and easier – and more ignorant – and particularly so in the folk world. Harry Smith's momentous *Anthology*, which set the ball rolling, in the Greenwich Village scene at any rate, was a comprehensive copyright steal. Bob Dylan would take anything that wasn't nailed down – and still does: old blues singers, the *Anthology*, Woody Guthrie, ancient folk tunes that came over with the Mayflower, the *Child Ballads* – and The Mississippi Sheiks and The Carter Family, who were still very much in copyright. He would claim copyright for himself and, I understand, then settle up privately with those he had taken material from.

Percy's Song ('Turn, turn to the rain and the wind') is an example. It certainly sounds traditional. When I sing it to myself, on walks with the dog, it invariably segues into Uncle Tom Cobley And All. But Dylan claimed ownership. It was covered by Fairport Convention, who presumably paid a fee to Dylan's publisher. Much later Dylan credited Paul Clayton for the song's 'beautiful melody line' and for introducing him to The Wind And The Rain, a variant of The Twa Sisters, a traditional Child Ballad. Many such songs were a complicated mixture.

The other thing that folksingers would do is to credit a song as traditional but arranged by themselves, enabling them to deny copyright money to any writer but claim it for the arrangement. The Incredible String Band were no different. Apart from A Very Cellular Song, and at random: The Mountain Of God is all unoriginal, nearly all venerably ancient except the bit of A.A. Milne. Ducks On A Pond ends with a nursery rhyme and some Woody Guthrie. The melody for Air comes from a Nonesuch LP titled *Tahiti – The Gaugin Years*. Log Cabin takes a tune from Guthrie, who had also found it, and it's probably out of copyright. Most intriguingly, Mike has said that White Bird 'is a pinched tune, from a very obscure Pakistani or Indian film'. Copyright as regards Indian films is a snake pit, so, although there are other borrowings, I will leave it there.

Does it matter, in an age when everything is cut and pasted and available online? You'd think not, but since musicians are barred from touring for as long as the plague times persist, barred for touring Europe for so long as Brexit persists, and hampered in selling CDs for so long as Spotify persists, they can do with all the help they can possibly get.

Robin Bynoe, a longtime contributor to the fanzine, is also a (retired) copyright lawyer.

2021

Old-Timey Bands, Jugs, Explorers and the ISB

John Quigley examines some ISB musical influences

The striking thing about the String Band was the way they absorbed so many seemingly disparate musical forms... thereby, perhaps, illustrating 1960s concepts of a new openness to diverse cultural influences, like Marshall McLuhan's 'global village' or Andre Malraux's 'museum without walls'; or reflecting Robin's ideas of a secret link between all kinds of world music and of a community not bound by time or space... Be that as it may, one effect of the early ISB records on me was to stimulate an interest in the music which had influenced them; many relatively rare or obscure albums found their way into my record collection in subsequent years. The stuff I discuss here should amply illustrate my point, and also reveal some of the many non-pop sources from which the ISB drew.

1. Old-Timers and Jug Stompers

Early press releases on the ISB usually talk about their origins as a kind of Scots-hillbilly string band playing, among other things, songs by Uncle Dave Macon. Clive Palmer's idea of calling the band the Fruit Jar Drinkers is actually a reference to Uncle Dave's classic old-timey band, which recorded prolifically in the late 1920s under that very name! In fact, I discovered Uncle Dave's music in an unusual way: by listening to AFN. In the late 1960s, American Forces Radio in Europe offered an alternative to the limited and commercialised output of BBC Radio One – especially late at night, when R1 was off the air. One evening in 1968 or 69 AFN played a whole hour of Uncle Dave Macon! Having read of the influence Uncle Dave had exerted on the early ISB I was naturally curious to hear what he was all about, and having been fascinated by the reissues of scratchy old 1920s recordings proliferating in the late 60s blues revival, it wasn't too strange an experience. What was surprising, however, was that the very next day I visited my local (and quite small) record shop and found the album I'd heard just the night before – *Uncle Dave Macon – First Featured*

Star Of The Grand Ole Opry (Decca/Ace Of Hearts). The material is a mixture of songs and banjo features by the larger-than-life Uncle Dave, and exuberant band tracks – banjo, guitar and two fiddles. It's impressive stuff, but there's not much of a direct connection with the ISB's recorded material. Later, however, I got *Uncle Dave Macon – Early Recordings* (County), which is maybe easier to relate to the String Band; the songs on this collection tend to be a bit more subdued, the fiddle and banjo pyrotechnics and breakneck tempi giving way to slightly melancholy, gospel-influenced vocal harmonies and instrumental blends, which sometimes recall the trio tracks on the first ISB album. Listen to songs like Rock About My Sarah Jane, Take Me Home Poor Julia, and Gwine Back To Dixie. The County album also contains a wild string band version of Sail Away Ladies, a song revived in the 1950s by numerous skiffle groups – and in the 1960s by John Fahey, who, accompanied by 'Mysterious' Al Wilson (of Canned Heat) on the South Indian veena, transformed it into a dreamy ISB-like instrumental which became a favourite of John Peel. It's on Fahey's *The Great San Bernardino Birthday Party And Other Excursions* (Takoma).

If you look for a parallel to the ISB of Log Cabin Home In The Sky and Black Jack David in 1920s old-timey music, though, then perhaps Charlie Poole and the North Carolina Ramblers would come to mind. Charlie Poole died young, in 1931, and he wasn't quite such a big star as Uncle Dave Macon, but his band's music is still influential. They were a banjo-fiddle-guitar trio, a little more relaxed, 'laid-back' even (also a little more in tune), than the majority of wild and woolly hillbilly bands, and had an unusually wide repertoire ranging from traditional songs and dances to popular songs – both late 19th-century weepies and 1920s ragtime/pop hokum. If you look I daresay you can find examples of all these genres in the ISB repertoire (for hokum try the ending of Creation, or Waiting For You); anyway, the Poole material has been reissued by County Records – last time I looked (quite a long time ago, admittedly) there were four LPs.

Everything's Fine Right Now, with its kazoo and mandolin accompaniment, bears a certain family resemblance to 1920s jug band music – as do later ISB songs (the 'ain't got no home in this world any more' section of Ducks On A Pond, the live Weather The Storm...) – again, probably a more direct influence on the original ISB concept (even on Empty Pocket Blues?) than the spirit of Robert Johnson. Like the old-timey bands, the jug bands had a mixed, eclectic repertoire – blues, jazz, pop, hokum, traditional songs... The two greatest are Cannon's Jug Stompers and the Memphis Jug Band, both of whom can be heard on numerous reissues. There is a fine Memphis Jug Band collection on Yazoo Records, while Cannon's complete works have been reissued several times – I have a double album on Herwin Records, although I believe this has been superseded by a CD reissue from Japan! Again, it's the poppier material which most recalls the ISB, e.g. the Memphis Jug Band's Stealin', covered in the 1960s by Arlo Guthrie and many others, Gus Cannon's Walk Right In, an early 1960s hit for folkies The Rooftop Singers, and his Prison Wall Blues, the source of the chorus for John Sebastian's Younger Girl, a big US hit and UK pirate radio turntable hit in 1966 for The Critters. Many of the bluesier items in the Cannon's Jug Stompers repertoire were taken up in the 60s by the likes of the Grateful Dead, Canned Heat, and the Jim Kweskin Jug Band. Yazoo Records has a fascinating compilation of classic blues tracks (including Cannon's Walk Right In; Henry Thomas's Bull Doze Blues, the origin of Canned Heat's Goin' Up the Country; Charley Patton's Spoonful, etc. etc.) which were revived by rock bands: Roots of Rock.

Tony Russell's book *Blacks, Whites and Blues* (Studio Vista, possibly out of print, but at least Tony himself is still around...) is a good source of information on the interaction – important for the development of rock and roll – between hillbilly music and blues during the period. Someone somewhere should write a history of 60s music showing how, and maybe even why, material from the 20s was stolen/adapted. For example, how in Everything's Fine and Younger Girl rough and rowdy blues-based material is fashioned into tender pop love songs. My own memories of the 1920s in 60s music range from the UK trad jazz boom, represented by such oddities as the Temperance Seven's Pasadena at the start of the decade, to the country blues revival, which brought forth the Woodstock theme tune Goin' Up the Country just before its end. A fascinating topic.

2. Explorers and Exotica

The String Band did sessions for John Peel's *Night Ride* programmes in 1968-69. This was, as Mike says, very much 'pre-Andy Kershaw', and the kind of 'world music' to be heard on the radio then was mostly inspired by the fashion for things Eastern, and thus quite different from the urbanised, semi-pop stuff Andy tends to favour. Rather, it tended to be very obscure and often quite weird tracks drawn from the BBC Sound Archives – there is a classic compilation album, *John Peel's Archive Things*, issued by BBC Records in 1969. But specialist labels (Folkways, Ocora, Argo) were beginning to issue records of non-Western music, often from countries on the 'hippy trail', ranging from the Balkans to North Africa, Nepal and Tibet. The ISB, as Elektra recording artists, were given many albums on Elektra's subsidiary label Nonesuch and its Explorer album series, which was one of the first catalogues of 'world music' to appear. Mike revealed that 'Jac Holzman [*Elektra boss in New York*] said take what you want, so we walked out with about 100 albums, all we could carry. It took us ages to get through customs.' Many of the key records in the series were issued during the late 60s, and I got my copies in the early 70s when, for a while, the label was imported and distributed by Transatlantic. Scholars, fanatical collectors and seekers-after-truth will have plenty of fun seeking them out.

The ISB's recorded career begins with Maybe Someday – 'Bulgarian, Indian, Scottish and schizoid'. Well, Mike's guitar and Robin's fiddle do provide an approximation of the characteristic sound of Bulgarian folk music, nowadays more familiar to us because of the world-wide success of *Le Mystere Des Voix Bulgares* and its successors. One of the first LPs of Bulgarian folk music to appear in the West was issued on Nonesuch – Music of Bulgaria. The performers here, as on *Le Mystere...* are a professional stage ensemble rather than village folk musicians (Nonesuch also had a couple of fine LPs of Bulgarian village music). The album apparently influenced the likes of David Crosby and Graham Nash; and Albert Grossman, he who managed Bob Dylan, Janis Joplin, etc., was involved in its release.

Probably the best-known Nonesuch Explorer LP as far as the folk and rock audience is concerned is *The Real Bahamas In Music And Song*. This contains the Pindar Family's version of I Bid You Goodnight, together with their version of Great Dream From Heaven, in which they are accompanied by Joseph Spence, the legendary and eccentric guitarist who strongly influenced Ry Cooder and – or so it seems to me and Raymond – might have been a source of the Caribbean-style inflections in Mike's early work (Can't Keep Me Here, The Hedgehog's Song, Little Cloud...). There are also numerous Nonesuch albums for those who, like Robin, were/are inspired by Eastern music – from India (e.g. *Classical Music Of India*; for folkier stuff, *The Bauls Of Bengal*, and *Kashmir: Traditional Songs And Dances*, Japan (*Koto Music Of Japan*; *A Bell Ringing In The Empty Sky* – an ISB-like title for a beautiful meditative album of solo flute music), Bali (*Music From The Morning Of The World*), and Iran before the ayatollahs outlawed music (*A Persian Heritage*); think about Pictures In A Mirror with its hammer dulcimer accompaniment and wailing vocals, only slightly less melodramatic...).

These albums still have plenty to offer to the listener who's willing to 'open up the ears' (sounds painful but isn't, necessarily) – and, uncharacteristically for recordings of exotic music, they were affordable and well-recorded, with good sleevenotes and even pretty album sleeves. And for those who suspect that it might all be too obscure and far out, let me recall the experiment which a group of psychologists carried out in the mid-1970s. They took a piece of modern, 'difficult' classical music and played it to two groups of sixth-form students at a school in Wales, telling one group that it was from a new solo album by the Pink Floyd's Roger Waters and the other that it was a piece by the contemporary Japanese composer Toru Takemitsu... and guess what? The first group's verdict was positive ('great'), the second groups less so ('boring'). Which must prove something...

The things that you're li'ble to read in the Bible...

beGLAD's *scriptural expert Grace Divine DD checks out the quotes on* Wee Tam And The Big Huge.

Several commentators have remarked on the 'Biblical' atmosphere pervading *Wee Tam*. There are certainly a number of Biblical allusions and references, some overt, others merely hinted at. We've examined the Biblical content of Job's Tears; here's a quick guide to the rest of the album.

The 'holy bread of Heaven' in Ducks On A Pond is perhaps the Manna dispensed to the Israelites in the Wilderness: 'I will rain Bread from Heaven.' – Exodus 16:14. The 'open door' from the same song is a common scriptural image, occurring in Psalms 78:23-4 in connection with Manna: 'He commanded the clouds from above, and opened the doors of Heaven/ And had rained down manna upon them.' It also occurs in a potent passage in Revelations 4:1: '...behold, a door was opened in Heaven; and the first voice which I heard was as it were of a trumpet talking with me; which said, Come up hither, and I will shew thee things which must be hereafter.' The Holy Grail, also mentioned in the song, is of course of post-Biblical provenance.

Jesus, Moses and the Three Kings are all fellow-mariners on the world ship in Maya. Jesus also appears in Ducks On A Pond – 'Lovely Jesus nailed to a tree', an image echoing Acts 5:30: 'The God of our fathers raised up Jesus, whom ye slew and hanged on a tree' – and also in Job's Tears. And some scholiasts might take the view that Jesus is Mike's 'greatest friend' in the song of that name: both the musical and lyrical idioms draw on the Appalachian Sacred Harp hymnal tradition. (But Mike has recently hinted that the friend is something to be ingested rather than adored...)

The Son of Noah's Brother – the phrase is riddlingly ambiguous (as with the brain-teaser 'The son of Pharaoh's daughter was the daughter of Pharaoh's son'). If our titular hero is indeed one of Noah's three sons (the son-of-Noah's brother), it may be that the coat referred to in the lyric refers to the coat that Shem and Japheth flung over their drunken father's naked body in the curious story in Genesis 9:23. Robin has indicated, however, that the reference is not primarily Biblical, but an allusion to Irish myth, wherein the first person to settle in the land of Ireland was Partholon, described in one source as brother of Noah. The son of Noah's brother, in this context, could therefore be a son of Partholon himself, or of one of Partholon's brothers. As it happens, one of the few narratives in the corpus of Irish myth that seems to hint at a notion of physical reincarnation ('Many were the lifetimes...') is the story of Tuan Mac Cairill, who led successive lives as various animals, birds and fishes. Tuan was the son of Sera son of Starn, brother of Partholon, and therefore in a loose sense one of the sons of Noah's brother. As pointed out in the Job's Tears article, the concept of reincarnation is largely foreign to Judeo-Christian thought.

The Mountain Of God is the most concentrated assemblage of Biblical quotations on the album. 'Behold the mountain of the Lord in latter days shall rise' is from Hymn 312 of the Church of Scotland Hymnary, based on Isaiah 2: 2-5. 'Hark the herald angels sing' is the opening line of Wesley's popular carol, and 'Hush, hush, whisper who dares / Christopher Robin is saying his prayers' is from the syrup-dripping pen of A. A. Milne. 'Do ye not fly as clouds and as doves to your windows', more or less word for word from Isaiah 60:8, segues neatly into 'Who serve as the shadow and the example of heavenly things', a close paraphrase of Hebrews 8:5. 'As Moses was admonished...' through to '...on the high mountain' is from the same passage in Hebrews. The rest of the song – from 'Glory be to the Father' to the end – is from *The Book Of Common Prayer* (in fact, it's the conclusion to the Latin Mass), though the phrase 'World without end' occurs in Isaiah 45:17.

'His/My eye was single and his/my whole body was filled with light' – this Douglas Traherne Harding line, as Prydwyn Piper argues, is based on Jesus' homily, delivered as part of the Sermon On The Mount. Both Matthew (6:22) and Luke (11:34) record that 'If thy eye be single, thy whole body is also full of light' – though it's pertinent to note that *The New English Bible*'s translation of this line is: 'If your eyes are sound, you will have light for your whole body': prosier, certainly, but perhaps a more faithful rendering.

The sheep and goats in Douglas Traherne Harding seem to have a vaguely scriptural flavour – the Son of Man separates the one from the other in Matthew 25:31-6 – but any connection is tenuous to the point of invisibility. 'Eye...light' apart, therefore, all the unambiguous Biblical references on *Wee Tam* are from Robin's pen. As his settings of the Biblical Psalms in *Carmina* suggest, he has carried his interest in scripture on into later life.

ISB Quiz

If you think you know your ISB, you might like to try this quiz – 50 questions in all. Some of this is quite obscure, though it starts off fairly easy. Not all the answers are in the book.

Half Remarkably Easy Section

1. Sitting here with my arms around _____?
2. B is for _____?
3. Who lived in Chicago, Illinois?
4. Which famous American singer/songwriter thought October Song was 'quite good'?
5. Name a song written by Licorice.
6. What has Mike Heron got in his hand on the cover of the *Smiling Men* album?
7. What has proved that oysters cry?
8. Tree by Mike Heron – what's unusual about it?
9. Guide me with gold of *whose* wing?
10. In what song has Billy stored the map safely underground?

Geographical Section

1. What is the birthplace of Bad Sadie Lee?
2. Where did the old man lose his pearly girl?
3. Which fortifications did Malcolm and his mates gaze on?
4. Which European cities did 'she' toss her hair at?
5. Where did the strangely silent Kate settle?
6. Where does the sun shine yellow?
7. Which two rivers has Robin spoken with?
8. Where were the fluted pillars and muted life?
9. Which northern places did Hirem Pawnitof ride on to?
10. Moving pieces – where?

Connections – what connects the following?

1. Puppies + Yellow Snake + Ducks on a Pond + Big Ted
2. Creation + Seagull
3. No Sleep Blues + Dreams of No Return
4. You Know What You Could Be + When The Music Starts to Play
5. Schaeffer's Jig + Jazzbo's Holiday
6. The Actor + Dust Be Diamonds
7. Flowers of the Forest + The Letter + Minotaur's Song

Verging on the Obscure Section

1. Where was the cover photo for *Wee Tam And The Big Huge* taken?
2. In which song does 'famed oriental bass player', Lady Fenola Bum-Garner feature?
3. Who or what is Osmiroid Overloader?
4. If you could hear the 'Low Dales fiddler' which song would you be in?
5. Which album by Vashti Bunyan did Robin contribute to?
6. What method did Robin use to arrive at the song title Koeeoaddi There?
7. What colour is the 'first little ball'?
8. Which album did Malcolm first appear on?
9. How many legs had Cousin Caterpillar?
10. What was the title of the co-written thriller Robin had a hand in?
11. And what was the 'author's' name?
12. Who was the backing band on Second Fiddle?
13. Which ISB soundman ended up playing bass live?
14. And name any two of his aliases?
15. What was Mike before he became a professional musician?
16. Who is Miss Amanda Albuquerque?
17. Who is Dick Steele?
18. Who was the first ISB member to 'go clear'?
19. Greg Heet – what was his connection with *U*?
20. Where was Queen of Love written?
21. Name the ISB odd one out in the *Rehearsal* film.
22. In what ISB song does Robin sing of the 'festival of fools'?
23. What's 15 Glory Road?

Answers to the ISB Quiz

Half Remarkably Easy Section

1. Sitting here with my arms around my music
2. B is for the beast at the ending of the wood
3. Maria
4. Dylan
5. I Know You/Secret Temple/Cosmic Boy/ Sunday Song
6. A giant octopus in the song Queen Juanita
7. Gallantly concealed forceful nervousness
8. Tree appears on two albums, the *First Album* and *Liquid Acrobat.*
9. Gabriel's wings
10. Evolution Rag

Geographical Section

1. Wild Wyoming
2. Lima (in Old Buccaneer)
3. Towers of Tyre (in Down Before Cathay)
4. Paris & Rome (in Did I Love A Dream)
5. Nome, Alaska (Dumb Kate)
6. High Barbaree (in Banks Of Sweet Italy)
7. Thames & Medway (in Veshengro)
8. Sybaris (in Ithkos)
9. Leeds & Carter Bar
10. Plains of Troy (Ducks On A Pond)

Connections – What connects the following?

1. The rolling sea
2. Creatures
3. Danny Thompson plays on both (or sleep/dreams)
4. Lyrics to first are sleeve notes to second
5. They are performed as Robin & Clive duos
6. Both are co-written songs
7. Fairport Convention members perform on them all

Verging on the Obscure Section

1. Frank Zappa's garden
2. Waiting For You
3. A pineapple
4. Feast Of Stephen
5. Another Diamond Day
6. Throwing a dice
7. Red & green
8. *U*
9. 14 (seven pairs)
10. Glory Trap
11. Sherman Williamson
12. Reggae group Greyhound
13. Stan Schnier
14. Stan Lee, Stan Lee Buttons, Stanley.
15. Trainee accountant
16. Licorice/mandolinist (on Waiting For You)
17. Newsweek reporter in *Be Glad* film
18. Likky
19. Voice sitar man (used on *U*)
20. In a café in Oxford Street
21. Graham Forbes (not in the Glen Row Ithkos rehearsals but in the Bristol performance)
22. Fine Fingered Hands
23. An unreleased Mike Heron song

Gimmel and Daleth's Incredibly Strung Crossword

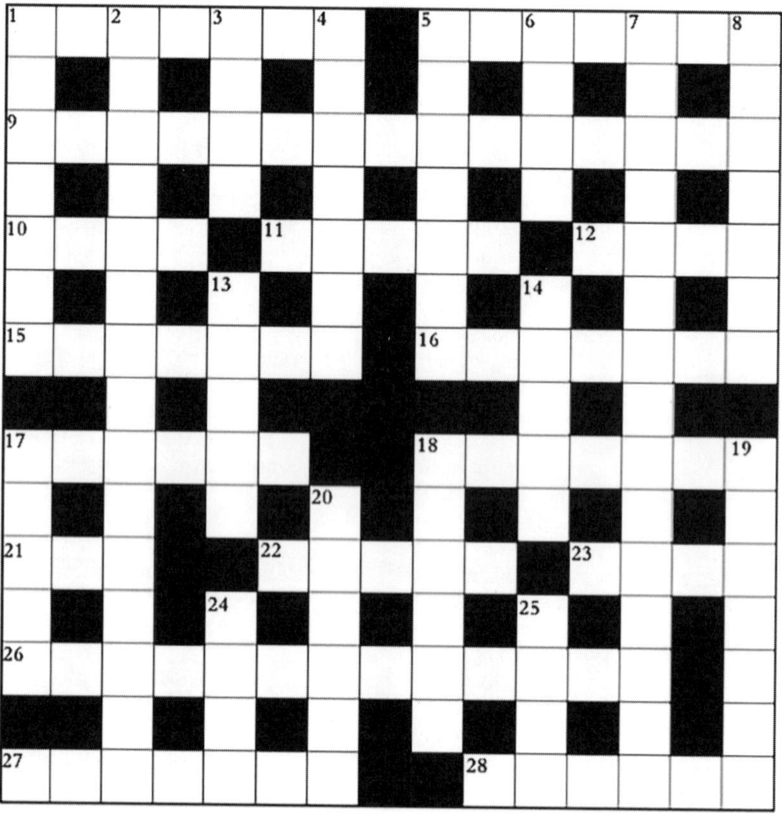

Compiled by ADA and Andy Roberts. Answers on page 683

Across

1. Their hats have considerable warming properties (7)
5. Dealt maternally with withered flowers? (7)
9. Brighter than the brightest star (3,9,3)
10. Falling in our faces? (4)
11. Sea Captain has something to reveal (5)
12. Something that Creation never does? (4)
15. Acrobatic sign off (7)
16. At home in two elements, they indicated veracity (7)
17. It banishes dreams (6)
18. Mixed up chic Tao reviewer described U as such (7)
21. Forms tree trio with oak and may (3)
22. Weather conditions as they drove across the moor (5)
23. Metal footwear ok in this part of the world (4)
26. First four words of alphabetical lyric (3,5,2,3)
27. Spotted in Mike's eyes by a small animal (7)
28. What did Robin want to do with the ringmaster's headgear? (4,2)

Down

1. Survive a feuding storm (7)
2. A finality to the discourse? (7,2,3,3)
3. Not easy to knot in this condition (4)
4. They're mutable (7)
5. Relative larvae (7)
6. Strange maritime variants accompany Fishman
7. I wsa! I wsa! (But failed, apparently) (8,2,5)
8. Noisily worn by gracious ladies (7)
13. Colour of regal headgear (5)
14. Proffered in exchange for dead porker (5)
17. They headed in five directions (5)
18. Where is pussgrass? (6)
19. Real as pain? (7)
20. One of these found on boggy terrain(6)
24. Malcolm loved a French one(4)
25. Home of track 1 *Changing Horses* (4)

A brief UK Discography

The Incredible String Band (June 1966) Elektra
5000 Spirits Or The Layers of the Onion (July 1967) Elektra
The Hangman's Beautiful Daughter (March 1968) Elektra
Wee Tam And The Big Huge (November 1968) Elektra
Changing Horses (November 1969) Elektra
I Looked Up (April 1970) Elektra
U (October 1970) Elektra
Be Glad For The Song Has No Ending (March 1971) Island
Liquid Acrobat As Regards The Air (October 1971) Island
Earthspan (November 1972) Island
No Ruinous Feud (March 1973) Island
Hard Rope And Silken Twine (March 1974) Island
Seasons They Change (November 1976) Island – is long-deleted.

The October 1969 Elektra single of Big Ted/All Writ Down features an alternate, longer take of All Writ Down.

Solo Albums

Smiling Men With Bad Reputations – Mike Heron (April 1971) Island
Myrrh – Robin Williamson (April 1972) Island

CD releases

All the above have been re-released on CD. The first four ISB Elektra albums are now available on Fledg'ling Records as remasters by Joe Boyd and John Wood taken from the original stereo mixes. The current best versions of *Changing Horses* and *I Looked Up* are earlier remasters, also by JB/JW, done for Rykodisc. *U* is only available as a 2002 WEA reissue.

Demon and Island put out the later albums (and the 2 solo albums above); though these are now officially deleted you can still get them in various two-for-one packages.

Later ISB releases:

On Air (1991) on Band Of Joy was a collection of BBC sessions, now deleted.
Live In Concert (1992) on Windsong comprised live BBC recordings from 1971 and 1972 with unreleased tracks Willow Pattern, Whistle Tune, Bright Morning Stars, You've Been a Friend To Me and I Know That Man. Deleted.
First Girl I Loved (1998) on Mooncrest Records is a late 1972 live Dott-era recording from Canada; as well as including Dott vehicles Wild Cat Blues (Bechet) and Swipesy Cakewalk (Joplin), there's a great performance of Robin's Gilles Crooked Deal. Tacked on the end is a live BBC broadcast of Ithkos from 1974 which compares favourably with the album version due to the presence of John Gilston on drums.
The Chelsea Sessions 1967 (1997) on Pigs Whisker is excellent and is discussed in Chapter One.
Mirrorman's Sequences 1961 – 66 by Robin Williamson (1997, Pigs Whisker) was actually written in 1971/2 and contains some fascinating stories about the early Edinburgh days through to his Morocco trip with Likky. Oddly, Robin seems to have now disowned this CD, instructing writer Paul Norbury in 2017 that he should not even mention this CD in his account of Robin's solo work.

There are two CD 'Best Ofs'. The Elektra one, *The Best Of The Incredible String Band*, covers 1966-70 and is an excellent introduction if you own nothing else by the ISB. The Island compilation *Here Till Here Is There*, covering 1971-4, is a more contentious selection – it doesn't include Darling Belle or anything by Malcolm – but gives a reasonable overview of the period.

Across The Airwaves (2007) on Hux Records combines most of the two BBC releases above. It also contains previously unreleased radio tracks All Too Much for Me, Fine Fingered Hand, Won't You Come See Me, Ragupati, Ring Dance, Long Long Road and Living In The Shadows.

Tricks Of The Senses (2008) on Hux Records mostly comprises previously unreleased ISB studio material, including out-takes from *5000 Spirits* and *Wee Tam* as well as a 1968 WBAI radio session, Queen Juanita And Her Fisherman Lover, Likky's Secret Temple, two unreleased live tracks from the U show and more.

Live At The Fillmore, 1968 (2012) on Hux Records is the complete recording of Mike and Robin at the top of their game playing material from *Hangman* and *Wee Tam* to a rapturous New York audience.

Best Buys:
5000 Spirits, *Hangman*, *Wee Tam And The Big Huge* and *Liquid Acrobat*.

Films & Videos

Peter Neal's *Be Glad* film was available as a DVD but is now out of print. It's on YouTube, where you'll also find some Woodstock footage, a 1970 Beat Club appearance with Rose and Likky, and a 1972 French TV appearance featuring songs by Likky and Malcolm.

James Archibald's films are no longer available commercially. *Time For Thought* and *Rehearsal* are archived with the British Film Institute who as yet haven't made a viewing copy. *No Turning Back* is also archived there and can be viewed by arrangement with BFI archives at Stephen Street, London W1.

Unreleased audio stuff

There are quite a few unreleased songs taped from BBC sessions (largely John Peel's) which circulate on tape – try the ISB Discography Facebook page if you're interested in this sort of stuff. There are also innumerable live tapes.

Reading suggestions:

The White Goddess – Robert Graves (Faber & Faber). A 'historical grammar of poetic myth' and a major ISB influence.

On Having No Head – Douglas Harding (Inner Directions Publishing). His take on the 'timeless life'.

Satan Wants Me – Robert Irwin (Bloomsbury/Dedalus). A black comedy about 'amphetamines, weird sex and devil worship' set in 1967 Swinging London, in which First Girl I Loved is crucial to the plot.

Cod-liver Oil & Orange Juice – Hamish Imlach (Mainstream Books). Andy Roberts says it's 'a rumbustious rollercoaster ride through the early Scottish folk scene.'

Dazzling Stranger – Colin Harper (Bloomsbury). A biography of Bert Jansch, who was part of the same close-knit Edinburgh folk scene as the ISB; many early events and characters overlap with the ISB back story in this excellent book.

Fitting Pieces To the Jigsaw: Dr Strangely Strange – Adrian Whittaker (Ozymandias Books). All you'd ever want to know about the Strangelies and more, including many ISB connections.

The Exploding Galaxy: Performance Art, LSD and Bent Coppers in the Sixties Counterculture – Jill Drower (Scrudge Books). Written by a former Exploder, Jill's book is a brilliantly researched and illustrated labour of love.

You Know What You Could Be – Mike Heron and Andrew Greig (Riverrun/Quercus). Essential. A dual autobiography, covering Andrew's experiences as a hardcore fan and Mike's early performing years up to the end of 1966 and Robin's return from Morocco. There was some talk of a Volume Two by Mike, though we gather he now feels the later ISB history is all pretty much in the public domain anyway.

Muse, Odalisque, Handmaiden – Rose Simpson (Strange Attractor). Marco Rossi reviewed it for *Record Collector*: 'It is written without rancour, regret or romanticism, yet her clear-eyed, pragmatic recollections provide an unusually insightful definition of the mutable dynamics which can sustain or erode any close unit's esprit de corps.' A must for all ISB fans.

Malcolm and Rakis are currently entertaining vague thoughts about writing a joint memoir.

Smiling Men With Bad Reputations – Paul Norbury (Grosvenor House). Adds little to ISB history, but the final section of this book is a useful guide to Mike and Robin's post-ISB recordings.

Seasons They Change – Jeanette Leech (Jawbone Press). 'The story of acid and psychedelic folk.' About the ISB, Vashti Bunyan, Pearls Before Swine et al and their contemporary equivalents.

Electric Eden – Rob Young (Faber & Faber). At over 600 pages, an epic which aims to 'unearth Britain's visionary music.' The chapter on the ISB ('Fire') is probably the most insightful piece ever written about the band. The entire book is strongly recommended.

The ISB: Every Album, Every Song – Tim Moon (Sonic Bond). A chronological song-by-song account, the book starts with a musicianly look at the ISB's instrumentation through their career, from ouds and gimbris to the Chinese banjo... Tim runs through the songs in a good-natured but not uncritical manner, and has some useful comments to offer on playing styles. Written with genuine affection and personal insight into how the ISB entered and affected his life, and continues to do so.

ISB online

Robin Williamson is at: www.pigswhiskermusic.co.uk
Mike Heron is at: www.mikeheron.co.uk
Rose Simpson is on Twitter: @IsbRose
Malcolm Le Maistre is at: www.thebarrowband.com

Fan sites

Martin Payne curates an online version of *beGLAD*, with a range of historical stuff, full discography, gigography, links to other ISB sites (e.g. ISB lyrics) and news. It's at: https://www.makingtime.co.uk/beglad

Wolfgang Rostek's ISB site is an invaluable source for gig listings, cuttings etc: http://www.wolfgangrostek.de/5000onions/

Shane Pope's site Relics Of The Incredible String Band has some useful info, especially on unreleased material: http://www.users.waitrose.com/~gimbri/

The ISB Facebook news/discussion group is (misleadingly) titled Incredible String Band Discography.

Grahame Hood also curates a Clive's Original Band Facebook page.

[1]W	I	[2]T	C	[3]H	E	[4]S		[5]C	R	[6]A	D	[7]L	E	[8]D
E		A		A		E		O		P		E		R
[9]A	L	L	C	R	E	A	T	U	R	E	S	A	R	E
T		K		D		S		S		S		R		S
[10]H	A	I	R		[11]M	O	V	I	E		[12]E	N	D	S
E		N		[13]G		N		N		[14]B		I		E
[15]R	E	G	A	R	D	S		[16]S	T	R	I	N	G	S
		O		E						E		G		
[17]C	O	F	F	E	E			[18]C	H	A	O	T	I	[19]C
R		T		N		[20]K		A		D		O		H
[21]A	S	H			[22]M	I	S	T	Y		[23]A	S	I	A
F		E		[24]R		S		H		[25]S		P		R
[26]T	H	E	B	E	A	S	T	A	T	T	H	E		I
		N		V		E		Y		Y		L		O
[27]S	A	D	N	E	S	S			[28]S	E	L	L	I	T

beGLAD *Magazine back issues 1-20: These have been digitised and can be found in the 'Files' section on the ISB Discography Facebook page.*

Contributors to this book

Bill Allison saw the ISB seventeen times and regularly contributed to *Be Glad.* After working for forty years as a teacher he is now regenerated and lives in Lancashire with his beautiful wife Julia and their two grown up daughters, Lucy and Helen.

Dave Barrett (1952) Retired after working many years in IT, now devoting spare time to music, photography, and friends, amongst other things. Favourite song (today's choice): Three Is A Green Crown. The ISB's music inspired him to hit the hippy trail to Kathmandu and beyond in 1973. Plays guitar, mandolin, mandola, fiddle, whistle, keyboards, and harp at home, in sessions, and in a ceilidh band. Owns a gimbri but cannot play it satisfactorily. Ambition – to travel to Northern Norway in winter to photograph the Northern Lights.

Paul Bryant (1951) lives in Nottingham. He first met the ISB in 1970, and in 1971 recalls having a short conversation with Licorice and asking Robin how to spell 'Nenuphar'. He finds this difficult to believe now.

Robin Bynoe is now an ex-lawyer and lives most of the time in the Cognac region of rural France. Many encounters with the ISB over the decades – all with the footlights safely in between, unless playing reggae on a fishtruck in Castletownbere with Ivan Pawle counts.

Peter O'Connor lives with his wife and two children in Tokyo, Japan, where he teaches English and history and researches pre-war newspapers. Meeting and getting to know the ISB made a huge and exciting difference to his early life, but he has now made a full recovery.

Tony Corden (1960) used to live in Machynlleth, Wales, where he organised an annual music circle dance and mental health festival and played in local mystic folk band Cloud Cuckoo. All of the above inspired by the first ISB album. He now lives in Castile and León, north-west Spain. Favourite songs: Empty Pocket Blues and Mountain Of God into Cousin Caterpillar.

Ian Finlay (1952) is a landscape gardener/part-time charity worker with a special interest in tribal people. Just after the Balkan war, was staying in a bombed-out flat in Sarajevo listening to *Liquid Acrobat* with a Bosnian Muslim-turned-Buddhist who was a great fan and had saved his ISB collection from the carnage.

Alistair Fraser is a producer/writer and has made many music and arts programmes for all the main terrestrial channels. He first knew of the Incredible String Band from his big sister whilst at school. A chance meeting with Mike Heron prompted him to put the proposal to the BBC to make a 1997 documentary, 'Retying The Knot' about this most distinctive of bands.

Allan Frewin (1954): Freelance writer of children's books under various names and genders. Sometimes includes subliminal ISB references in them in order to indoctrinate the next generation of String-heads. First encountered ISB in a record shop in Hastings in 1968 – bought the album after hearing 15 seconds of Job's Tears.

Stuart Godfrey (1950) was a designs examiner with the Patents Office, now retired. He once attempted to demonstrate the 'boogaloo dance' during an impromptu performance of Big Ted. These days he lives quietly and has few adventures; he celebrated his half-century with a *U* birthday cake.

Raymond Greenoaken (1952) Fell in to graphic design and DTP by happy happenstance, and learned the ropes on *beGLAD*, co-editing the magazine with Adrian Whittaker from 1996 to 2002. Keeps trying to retire. One day, one day... At other times he's a singer and musician, and the brains behind the ISB covers bands The Half-Remarkable Questionnaires and The Glad Undertakers. At least one of these may rise again. He owns a fiddle made by Robin Williamson, which he can't play.

Grahame Hood (1956) was born in Peebles, a mere six miles from Glen Row. Has lived in the Kent area since the late Seventies and is now retired. He writes for various music magazines, teaches, and plays acoustic guitar, banjo and dulcimer. Favourite song: Maya.

David Kidman (1954) has now retired from proof-reading/editing but still writes about music when time allows, albeit for an ever-dwindling handful of publications. These days he's most known as a singer of "songs worth the singing" (traditional, contemporary and maritime), performing unaccompanied and largely solo (and frequently complementing song with poetry). His repertoire contains a healthy quotient of ISB material including October Song, Sleepers Awake! and Chinese White.

Norman Lamont was an avid fan in the Seventies, and thought he was the only one until *beGLAD* started. He got a kiss from Licorice for his 18th birthday. He is a songwriter at: www.normanlamont.com

Lizzie McDougall is a storyteller and artist in the Highlands. She installed a trail of standing stones in the hills around Dingwall. Each is engraved in Gaelic and English with prophecies of the Brahan Seer; they stand in quiet places where the moss grows green... She travels around the Highlands and Islands gathering, telling and sharing Highland stories. To help keep the story tradition alive she creates projects for communities, museums, feisean, clan gatherings, festivals and schools, moving many projects online during the pandemic – see www.facebook.com/storyquilts

Gil Murray (1960) works as a freelance computer programmer. Robin Williamson sought his advice on preserving Scotland's ancient Caledonian forest. Mike Heron once took him out for lunch at Khushi's Indian restaurant in Edinburgh – during a break in his Scientology training.

Bob Nutbein worked for American Express. His favourite songs were Red Hair and 1968. He died in 2018.

Deena Omar (1962) now teaches Adult Literacy for a living after a gap 'year' that lasted fifteen. Has recorded a cover version of Nightfall as a member of Fishman and the Sea-apes. Both Malcolm Le Maistre and Mike Heron have slept in her bed (not at the same time).

Robert Pendleton: After being rudely forced from Highgate School in 1968, Robert busked in the London Underground for several years; many back royalties (in pre-decimal currency) are probably owed on Painting Box and October Song. He now supports his music habit by teaching writing at two San Francisco Bay Area colleges.

Prydwyn Piper performs solo and has also recorded with 'wyrdfolk' ensembles Stone Breath and Green Crown, and Tom Rapp of Pearls Before Swine. He holds a PhD in Celtic languages from Harvard University, and uses reaction to the ISB as a major gauge of the viability of romantic relationships.

Shane Pope (1970) is a retired software engineer. Favourite String moment was finally seeing Mike and Robin together again at the 1997 Bloomsbury reunion, particularly the encore of the Carter Family's You've Been A Friend To Me.

John Quigley was and remains a man of mystery and should contact Adrian forthwith c/o Strange Attractor where he may learn something to his advantage.

Andy Roberts (1956) works as a hostel manager and author. Once went shopping for a bag with Mike Heron. Author of several books, most recently *Divine Rascal: On the Trail of Michael Hollingshead, LSD's Cosmic Courier.*

Jeff Rockwell is a poet and educator. He lives in Shreveport, LA.

Mike Swann (1949) is a retired radio controller. Author of two published books, one on American singer/songwriters, one on synchronicity. Also wrote an unpublished ISB biography, meeting Robin, Mike and Malcolm several times. Favourite song: Circle Is Unbroken.

Chris Taylor (1956) lives in York and is now retired. Still has a soft spot for the ISB all these years on and a picture of El Wool (bought from Janet!) on the bedroom wall.

Adrian Whittaker (1952) worked in a London FE College teaching Basic Skills until 2020. Was bass-player in a variety of bands in the Eighties and Nineties and has dabbled for years in music journalism. Co-edited *beGLAD* with Raymond from 1996-2002. Mike Heron once sang Feast Of Stephen in his sitting-room.

I'd love to read your reactions to the book – if you want, you can mail me via the Contact page on my website: https://drstrangelystrange.co.uk or post on the book's Facebook page: https://www.facebook.com/begladisb

Thanks a lot:

This book would not have been possible without the help of a great number of people. I'd especially like to thank:

Arlette Alboini; Bill Allison; Sheila Archibald; Lesandre Ayrey; Steve Blacknell; the late Sean Body; Tim Booth; Joe Boyd; the late George Boyter (he died in 2022); Café Oto; Deborah Cole for research and advice; Billy Connolly and Soirai Nicholson at Tickety-Boo; Gerard Dott; Mark Ellen; Norman Ellis for introducing Eyes Of Fate a capella to a bemused staffroom; the late Michael English; Ian Ferguson; Bruce Findlay; Graham Forbes; Allan Frewin for artwork, advice and support; Mychael Gerstenberger for Family Tree and good graphics advice; Peter Golding; Raymond Greenoaken for sourcing text and photo scans, punctilious proofreading and general erudition; Andrew Greig; Rod Harbinson; Colin Harper for support, advice and Edinburgh folk scene info; Frances, Don, Ben and David Harding; Mike Heron; Grahame Hood; the late Hoppy Hopkins; Ishy Schofield; Wizz Jones; Rachael Johnson at Music Sales; Norman Lamont for advice and support; Malcolm Le Maistre; Graeme Milton; London Fields Lido for planning support; Naomi Moran at Warlock Music; Peter Neal; Deena Omar for advice, support, critical reading, research and much more; the late Clive Palmer; Ivan Pawle; Mary Pawle; Federico Permutti; Maia Gaffney-Hyde, Mark Pilkington and Jamie Sutcliffe, SAP; Claus Rasmussen; Steen Møller Rasmussen; Felix Reut; Helmut Rheingans; Rakis; The Rio Cinema; Cathy Richins for reprographics; Stephen Robbins; Andy Roberts for advice; Wolfgang Rostek; Peter Sanders; Johan Schlanbusch; Stan Schnier; Rose Simpson; Matt Smith at Warner-Tamerlane; Caroline Walker for the original book design; Ben Wiseman and Charles White for their work on the *U* video; the late Hilda Whittaker for research; Dr Rowan Williams; Robin Williamson; Molloy Woodcraft; Robert Young; Rob Young.

Special thanks to Maïa Gaffney-Hyde, book design & layout for the new edition!

In preparing this 2021 update I've had grateful memories of my IT guru back in 2003, the late Ikky Johal, who persuaded me it would be a good idea to forget about floppy disks and save the entire finished text on something called a CD-Rom... Thanks, Ikky.

Index - Incredible String Band Albums & Songs

Albums

Songs

Band members

Mike Heron

Albums

Songs

Robin Williamson

Albums

Index

Strange Attractor Press 2023